D1751535

AMONG THE RANKS OF THE CARRION MEN

THE EPIC STORY OF THE THIRTY-SIX-DAY FIGHT IN AND AROUND BELLEAU WOOD

Volume I

The Aisne Defensive
May 27th-June 5th

Seldon, Kevin Christopher
Among the Ranks of the Carrion Men: The Epic Story of
the Thirty-Six-Day Fight in and around Belleau Wood.
Volume I
Includes biographical references, photos, maps, and charts.

ISBN 978-1-387-98197-7

World War, 1914-1918. 2. Belleau Wood, Battle of,
France, 1918. 3. United States Army Division, 2nd —
History. 4. United States Marine Corps. 5. American
Expeditionary Forces, WWI

Seldon, Kevin Christopher 1978 –

Copyright © 1st Edition 2018 by Kevin C. Seldon.
Bedford, Texas, U.S.A.
Printed by Lulu press. www.lulu.com
Lulu Press ID 23183668
1st Edition published 2018

All rights reserved, including those of all foreign, mechanical, or electronic means, both currently and known as well as those to be invented in the future. No portion of this book may be reproduced or used in any form without permission of the copyright holder. For permission, please contact the author.

Every reasonable effort has been made to obtain permissions for the hundreds of sources utilized and quoted in this volume, where it was deemed legally necessary. In some cases, this has been an impossible task. Please contact the author for further information concerning this or with any other questions. Lulu Press assumes no responsibility for the content of this volume.

This body of work is reverently dedicated to the men whose lives were never the same after the battle. The stories and sacrifices of those who remained behind on the battlefield both in body and in spirit must endure for eternity.

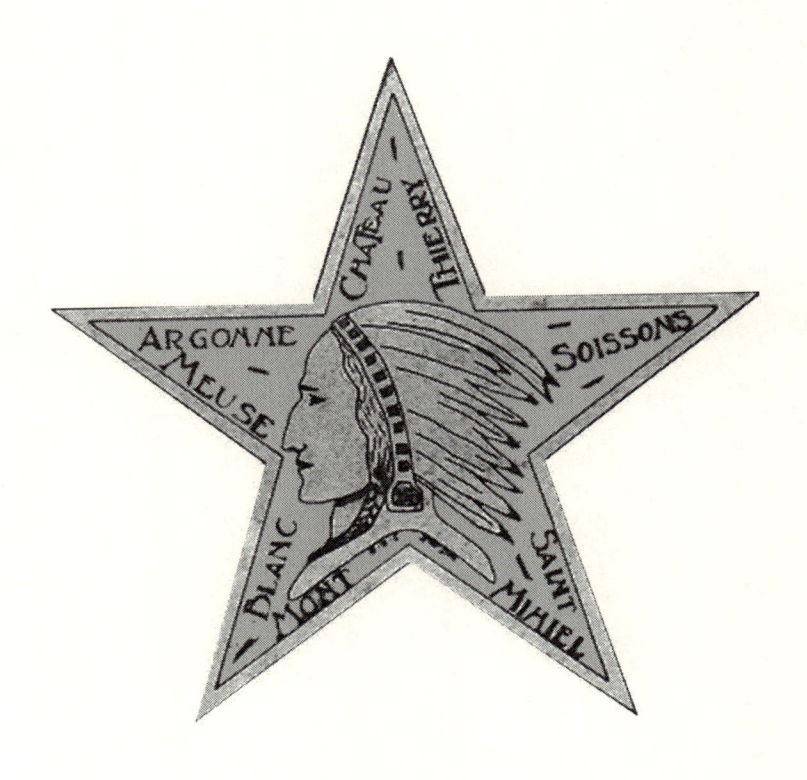

*Blood and destruction shall be so in use
And dreadful objects so familiar
That mothers shall but smile when they behold
Their infants quarter'd with the hands of war;
All pity choked with custom of fell deeds:
And Caesar's spirit, ranging for revenge,
With Ate by his side come hot from hell,
Shall in these confines with a monarch's voice
Cry 'Havoc,' and let slip the dogs of war;
That this foul deed shall smell above the earth
With carrion men, groaning for burial.*
  —William Shakespeare

Table of Contents

Acknowledgements.................................. i
Preface 7
Introduction 12
Background 34
May 30th-31st 44
Chapter I 45
Chapter II 61
Chapter III 72
June 1st 82
Chapter I 83
Chapter II 91
Chapter III 118
Chapter IV 127
Chapter V 135
June 2nd 144
Chapter I 145
Chapter II 156
Chapter III 175
Chapter IV 185
Chapter V 194
Chapter VI 206

June 3rd 211
Chapter I 212
Chapter II 218
Chapter III 227
Chapter IV 242
Chapter V 261
Chapter VI 281
June 4th 290
Chapter I 291
Chapter II 298
Chapter III 308
Chapter IV 329
June 5th 342
Chapter I 343
Chapter II 355
Chapter III 367
Chapter IV 379
Conclusion 390
Bibliography 394
Index 406

The region northwest of Chateau Thierry

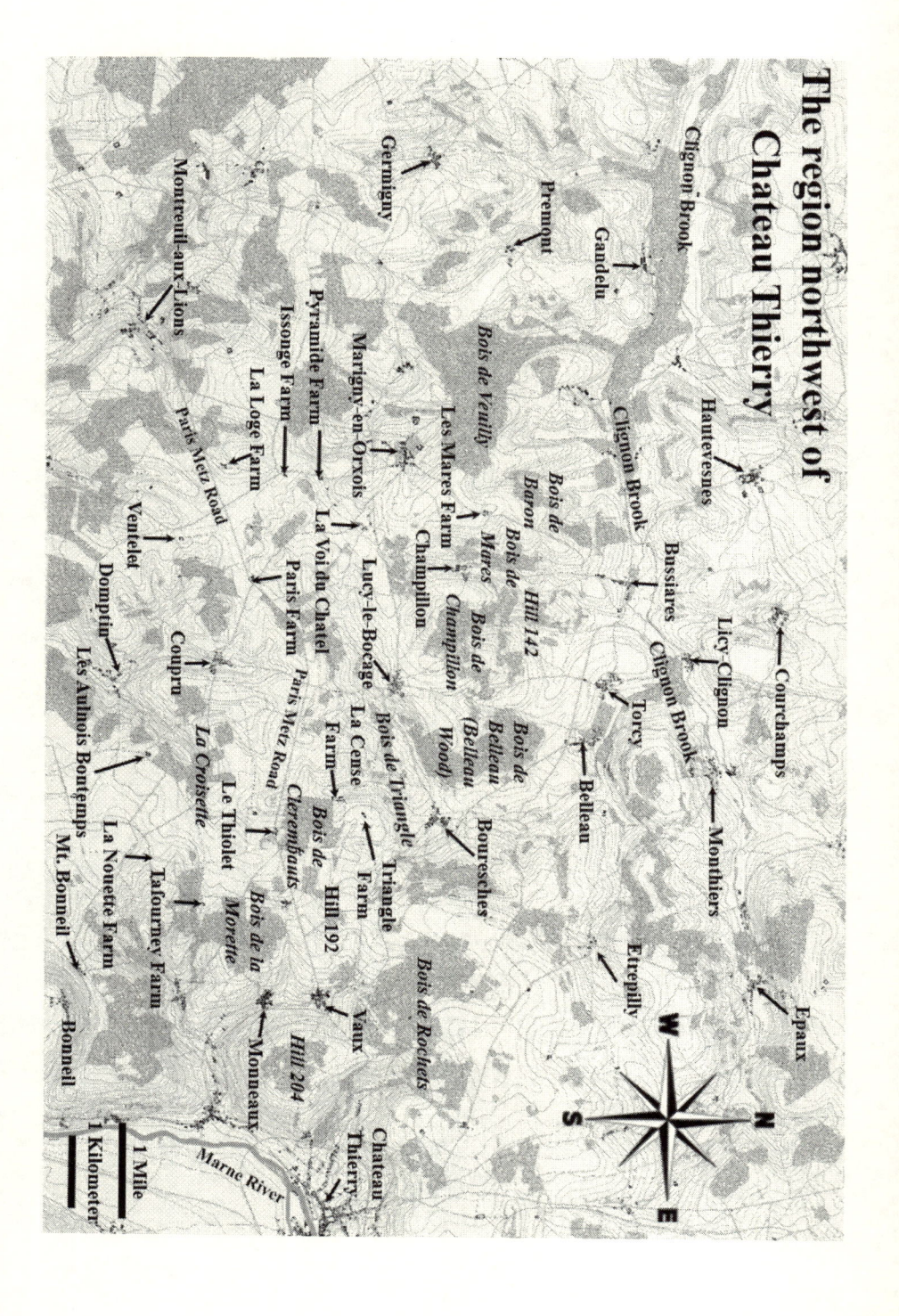

2nd Division American Expeditionary Forces

Major General Omar Bundy
Commanding Division commander

Brigadier General Emory Lewis
3rd Brigade

9th Infantry Regiment
Colonel LaRoy Upton
Headquarters Company
Machine Gun Company
Supply Company

1st Battalion
Company A
Company B
Company C
Company D

2nd Battalion
Company E
Company F
Company G
Company H

3rd Battalion
Company I
Company K
Company L
Company M

23rd Infantry Regiment
Colonel Paul Malone
Headquarters Company
Machine Gun Company
Supply Company

1st Battalion
Company A
Company B
Company C
Company D

2nd Battalion
Company E
Company F
Company G
Company H

3rd Battalion
Company I
Company K
Company L
Company M

5th Machine Gun Battalion
Hdqtrs. Co.
Company A
Company B
Company C
Company D

2nd Engineer Battalion
Col. James F. McIndoe

1st Battalion
Company A
Company B
Company C

2nd Battalion
Company D
Company E
Company F

4th Machine Gun Battalion (motorized)
Hdqtrs. Co.
Company A
Company B
Company C
Company D

Brigadier General James Harbord
4th Brigade (Marines)

5th Marine Regiment
Colonel Wendell Neville
Headquarters Company
8th Machine Gun Company
Supply Company

1st Battalion
17th Company
49th Company
66th Company
67th Company

2nd Battalion
18th Company
43rd Company
51st Company
55th Company

3rd Battalion
16th Company
20th Company
45th Company
47th Company

6th Marine Regiment
Colonel Albertus Catlin
Headquarters Company
73rd Machine Gun Company
Supply Company

1st Battalion
74th Company
75th Company
76th Company
95th Company

2nd Battalion
78th Company
79th Company
80th Company
96th Company

3rd Battalion
82nd Company
83rd Company
84th Company
97th Company

6th Machine Gun Battalion
Hdqtrs. Co.
15th Company
23rd Company
77th Company
81st Company

2nd Division American Expeditionary Forces

Major General Omar Bundy
Commanding Division commander

2nd Headquarters Train and Military Police

Brigadier General William Chamberlaine 2nd Field Artillery Brigade

12th Field Artillery Regiment (75mm)
Colonel Manus McCloskey
Headquarters Battery

1st Battalion
- Battery A
- Battery B
- Battery C

2nd Battalion
- Battery D
- Battery E
- Battery F

17th Field Artillery Regiment (155mm)
Colonel Albert J. Bowley
Headquarters Battery

1st Battalion
- Battery A
- Battery B
- Battery C

2nd Battalion
- Battery D
- Battery E
- Battery F

3rd Battalion

15th Field Artillery Regiment (75mm)
Colonel Joseph Davis
Headquarters Battery

1st Battalion
- Battery A
- Battery B
- Battery C

2nd Battalion
- Battery D
- Battery E
- Battery F

2nd Headquarters Troops

2nd Division Special Units

2nd Supply Train
- A Company
- B Company
- C Company
- D Company
- E Company
- F Company

1st Signal Battalion
- A Company
- B Company
- C Company

2nd Ammunition Train
- A Company
- B Company
- C Company
- D Company
- E Company
- F Company

Foden Disinfecting Squad No. 17
Machine Shop Truck Unit No. 303
Machine Shop Truck Unit No. 363
Military Postal Express Service Detachment
Mobile Surgical Unit No. 3
Railhead Detachment

Sales Commissary Unit No. 1
Salvage Squad No. 2
Veterinary Field Unit No. 1
Veterinary Field Unit No. 2
Veterinary Field Unit No. 3

2nd Sanitary Train

Ambulance section Field Hospital Section
Ambulance Co. 1   Field Hospital 1
Ambulance Co. 23   Field Hospital 15
Ambulance Co. 15   Field Hospital 23

Acknowledgments

A century ago, nearly 27,000 Soldiers, Marines, and Corpsmen of the 2nd Division engaged in an epic battle with the German Army in a verdant sector of rural French countryside located nearly forty-five miles from the heart of Paris. After a thirty-six day fight, the 2nd Division suffered 8,177 casualties of which 1,879 men were killed in action, died of wounds, or were carried as missing.*

The battle centered on a two-hundred-acre patch of forest known as Bois de Belleau (Belleau Wood), which primarily showcased two regiments and a machine gun battalion of United States Marines that made up a brigade of the United States Army's 2nd Division. The Marines assumed some of the most intense fighting—a factor that has generated more than its share of controversy considering that nearly half of the division's casualties were soldiers who also fought and died alongside their Marine brethren in the battle.

This book, however, does not cater to the controversies. It does not thoroughly analyze tactics, nor does it discuss at length the battle's overall strategic or historic significance. This multi-volume work seeks to tell the chronological narrative of the battle in vivid detail through the eyes of the men who were there—told through their testimony, much of which has never been examined. The accounts are woven into a collective sequential narrative to hopefully impress upon the reader what American troops saw, heard, smelled, and felt during the thirty-six day ordeal in and around Belleau Wood.

For the men of the 2nd Division who did the fighting, bleeding, and dying, combat was often confined to a corridor of hell extending twenty-five meters to their front and flank where death loomed constantly and abruptly summoned the ill-fated without theatrics or pity. Those who remained were left to ponder their own fate and phlegmatically deal with the anguish. Survival also came at a costly price—a sum paid with the enduring images, horrific memories, and nightmares that revisited veterans for the rest of their lives. Their individual experiences, often very graphic, provides an invaluable collective understanding of the confusion, chaos, fear, heartache, and heroism experienced during the thirty-six day fight in and around Belleau Wood. This multi-volume series is a tribute to them so that a century later, their stories can endure.

---

* Based on the 2nd Division History, when men who were wounded and returned to duty only to be wounded again are factored in, the casualty figure for the division comes to 9,777 men killed, died of wounds, wounded or missing in action.

Fourteen years ago, William Eugene Lee, the battle's last survivor, left this world at the age of 105. Ten days before his death, I spent the afternoon with him at his assisted living facility in Syracuse, New York. I was amazed at not only how much he remembered about the battle, but how clearly and consciously he expressed those memories. I realized how important my time with Mr. Lee was, not just to be able to express how much I respected and admired him, but because it impressed upon me the dire importance of keeping the memory of Belleau Wood alive as well as resurrecting lost stories that have never been told. The combatants are all gone, but their stories deserve a repository for the world to know. Perhaps that is the most indelible reason for such a lengthy body of work.

Piecing together such a massive narrative was done through a multitude of primary resources, archival material, phone calls, meetings, and emails. I also searched for descendants in an effort to try and piece together this massive puzzle over the past decade. Most importantly, however, there is an endless array of individuals who have instrumentally assisted me in this endeavor.

I could not even begin to name everyone whose words of encouragement have fueled my desire to complete this project. There are, however, several individuals whose material contributions were essential and without them, this multi-volume work would not be possible. I would like to make special acknowledgment of these individuals:

I would first like to thank Gilles Lagin. In 1999 I had the great honor of spending the day in the battle area with Gilles, and we have been good friends since. He is perhaps the greatest asset to the history of the American Expeditionary Forces. Gilles knows the battlefield in and around Belleau Wood better than anyone in the world. Gilles has also done similar work with other American Great War battlefields across France.

For forty years, Gilles has studied the battlefields around his home. He has been a crusader of preserving and honoring the stories of the Americans who fought over this stretch of French soil. He has knowledge that is not available in any book or archives. He has done more than anyone to preserve and perpetuate the memory of the men who fought in the area.

Gilles has given battlefield tours to high ranking officers of all branches, as well as dignitaries from around the world. In 2008, the Marine Corps recognized Gilles as an honorary Marine—the only person in Europe to earn that accolade. Meeting Gilles was a turning point in my pursuit of this project. He opened the door to a vast array of knowledge for me that ignited an already burning fascination with the battle. Gilles has been one of the most significant sources of information and technical assistance in this book. Without him and his friendship, this work would not be possible.

I would also like to thank Steven C. Girard, a retired U.S. Army staff sergeant. Steven his a highly respected historian/archivist of the 4th Brigade (Marine) as well as other units of the 2nd Division. The 4th Brigade is in

Steven's blood. He is the great-grandson of Second Lieutenant Caldwell C. Robinson of the 82nd Company, 3rd Battalion, 6th Marines.

Steven's passion is done in the memory of his great-grandfather who died along the timbered slopes of Belleau Wood. Steven is also related to Corporal John F. Girard, 17th Company, 1st Battalion, 5th Marines. Steven has been an invaluable source for photographs and files of overlooked material at various archives across the nation. Steven had put me in touch with numerous descendants. He has also helped me work through numerous technical questions relating to the battle. Steven has been a rock of inspiration. We have spent countless hours on the phone discussing research since this project got underway and without Steven's guidance, this work would not be possible.

I would also like to thank Michael Miller. Mike worked for the Marine Corps History Division for nearly 30 years and has been instrumental in discovering fantastic resource material from out of the woodwork. Mike was instrumental in coordinating and sharing his vast array of materials with me for the past decade.

Mike is a faithful custodian of the history of the Marines in the Great War. He has been a great friend and one of the most encouraging individuals during this entire process. Mike has provided me with speaking opportunities at the National Museum of the Marine Corps as well as other events in Quantico. He has been a fantastic mentor in pursuit of this project. Without Mike, this book would not be possible.

Robert Laplander who is an excellent historian of the AEF. His book *Finding the Lost Battalion* is the definitive work on that subject. I have aligned myself with his advice, and he has been an absolutely fantastic source of assistance and guidance. Without him, this book would not be possible. He has walked me through the formatting and publishing part of this, and for that, I cannot thank him enough.

I would like to thank my family especially. From the beginning, they encouraged me in this endeavor. My mother even accompanied me on trips to the archives to spend time with me. She has always been a significant source of encouragement in pursuing this project. This book would not have been possible without her support. My father has also been a voice of reassurance and support. His service in Vietnam with the Marine Corps was my inspiration for becoming a Marine and perhaps the root of my passion for history.

My wife Rachel has also been a true warrior in putting up with the countless man hours this project has taken. Since before we were married she has known how important this project was to me and she has never wavered in her support. She has sacrificed immensely by allowing me to pull all night writing, editing, and research sessions. She has always been supportive of me in this project, and no words could sufficiently express my appreciation and how blessed I am to have her on my side.

I would also like to thank the following individuals for their assistance and contributions:

Bob Gill, a retired Marine Corps major and historian, has been fantastic in allowing me access to his vast collection. He has been an excellent friend and a profound mentor in pursuing this project.

Lieutenant Colonel Pete Owen who is a fantastic historian of the 4th Brigade of Marines wrote a terrific book about the 2nd Battalion, 6th Marines. He has been a wonderful friend who mentored me through this process.

The late George Clark who was the definitive historian of the Marines in the Great War. George spoke with me countless times on the phone. He was always an excellent advisor and encouraged me along the way. I am sad George will not see this work because he was an inspiration and willingly fielded my naïve and probably dumb questions without pause. I read nearly everything George wrote on the 4th Brigade, and he is a true icon who will be missed.

The late Robert Asprey pioneered the study of this battle in many ways by keeping Belleau Wood as a relevant topic with his book in 1965. His early work was in many ways the first real published book detailing the battle. I randomly called him years before he passed away and he willingly spoke with me and provided valuable insight on writing this story.

Mark Sanders has been a terrific friend and has helped immensely by pulling files out of NPRC in St. Louis over the years. I made several trips to NPRC, and when I realized that I missed a file, Mark was instrumental in requesting and copying those files.

James Gregory has been an immense help with the editing process. His book *The Story of One Marine*, is an excellent microcosmic look at the war through the eyes of Private Thomas L. Stewart of the 96th Company, 2nd Battalion, 6th Marines.

Marie Silverthorn was fantastic in providing a wealth of information about her grandfather Merwin Silverthorn's service in the war. Marie has become a wonderful friend and a very reliable voice of encouragement.

Joe Fischer provided terrific background and images on his great-uncle, Robert McCaughin Fischer of the 20th Company.

Cathy Lewis was just incredible in providing me information on her grandfather Joyce Lewis of the 20th Company.

Byron Scarbrough whose grandfather was James Scarbrough of the 83rd Company has aided me in this project to no end.

Lenny Moore, whose grandfather Noyes Moore fought with the 96th Company, provided valuable information on the attack on Bouresches that appears in volume II.

Cybele Lane provided me a wealth of information about her grandfather, First Lieutenant Elliott Cooke.

Therry Schwarts provided terrific images and information about the battlefield, most notably the temporary cemeteries.

Amy Canfield Rehbein was an excellent source of information on her great uncle, Roger Irving Canfield.

John R. Canfield III was also instrumental in providing information about his grandfather Roger Irving Canfield.

Eric Voelz who has retired from the National Personnel Records Center was an absolute paramount contact for examining a massive volume of individual service record files over the course of several years.

Mitch Yockelson of the National Archives in College Park was incredibly helpful in streamlining the process of examining a mass array of the burial files before they were moved to NPRC. He also assisted in accessing the divisional records of the AEF.

Trevor Plante provided beneficial assistance in navigating and requesting relevant records at National Archives in Washington D.C.

Stephanie McCollum who has been instrumental in helping me edit which I have found is an endless process.

Bill Anderson, a retired Marine Corps colonel, was also a great voice of encouragement.

Madeleine Johnson was a great voice of reason for me in addition to providing excellent information on her great uncle Captain Lothar Long of the 6th Machine Gun Battalion.

The late George Norstrand was a wonderful man who invited me to California to spend a few days examining his father's papers and getting a plethora of information on Sergeant Major Carl Norstrand of the 1st Battalion, 5th Marines.

Steve Pike, the grandson of Corporal Lloyd Pike, was a fantastic friend and willingly allowed access to his research on his grandfather.

Dennis Jackson, a true custodian of WWI history allowed me access to his fantastic collection.

Frank Anguiano has been a fantastic friend and an outstanding researcher who shared much of his research on the 4th Brigade.

Enrique Chavez contributed significant amounts of resource material on the 2nd Battalion, 6th Marines in addition to other units.

John Schuler was instrumental in helping me with access to some fantastic 3rd Brigade research.

Michael Manifor and his brother Brian Manifor have been fantastic in providing images from their incredible collections.

John Korompilas helped with several resources from his remarkable collection.

Ginger Lee Parker was magnificent about providing information about her great-grandfather Miles Dodge of the 18th Company.

Rob Merriman was invaluable in assisting me in obtaining the very hard to find files on First Lieutenant William Mathews, the intelligence officer of the 2nd Battalion, 5th Marines.

Patricia Blanchard provided me additional information on Charles Boyd Maynard of the 84th Company.

Heather Purvin went above and beyond by providing me with research on her great-grandfather Harley Sanders of the 45th Company.

Pattie Sharky was essential in obtaining information on her grandfather Adam Bernard Kirscht of the 45th Company.

Sheyrl Benitz provided an enormous amount of material on her grandfather Oscar Cooper of the 20th Company.

Scott Dennison was tremendously helpful in providing information on his grandfather Corporal Harry Benton Fletcher.

Sindi McGrath allowed me access to some of her incredible family research on Haskell Waterhouse of the 55th Company.

Frank Nilada was instrumental in providing me with information on Anthony Kowolak.

Melvin Postlewait was generous in his assistance on information regarding his great uncle James Pitts of the 20th Company.

Robert Boyce provided some fantastic research on his grandfather Earle Boyce of the 47th Company.

Andrew Hill was essential in gaining more information on his grandfather Glen Hill as well as Glen's brother Sidney of the 79th Company.

Jeff Tkac also provided excellent information on Glen and Sidney Hill including photographs.

Tim Wilder provided some rare essential information on Frank Welty of the 20th Company.

Jim Austin and Robert Ebberts provided fantastic information on Wayne Austin of the 45th Company.

Carol Houndell was instrumental in helping me with information on William Scanlon of the 97th Company.

Nancy Kizuka provided information about her great-uncle Benjamin Strain of the 45th Company.

Addison Hagan provided invaluable information on his grandfather Joseph A. Hagan.

Joe Palisi relayed information on his uncle, John Tesoro of the 7th Infantry.

Fred H. Whipple provided superb images of his father and uncle who served with the 76th Company.

John Cleveland also provided invaluable information about his relatives as well as putting me in touch with relatives of other descendants.

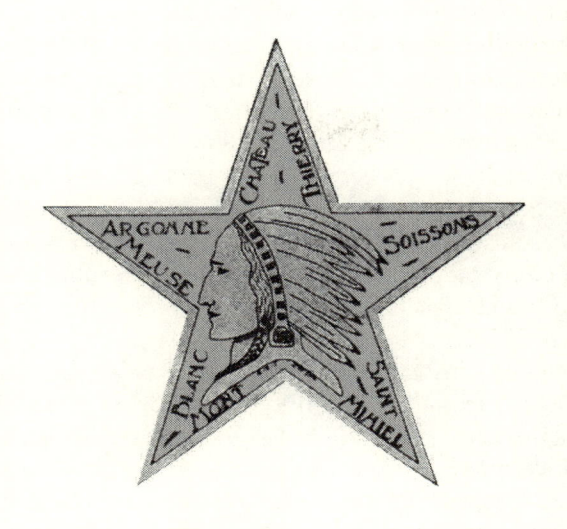

PREFACE

Preface

It was apparent death came almost instantly. The machine gun bullets that passed through his chest and out of his back shredded the tunic which remained stiff from the dried blood that had saturated the wool. He had been dead for some time, perhaps weeks, as the uniform became tightly wrapped around his bloating body. He lay crumpled in a semi-contorted manner over his Springfield rifle still wielding its bayonet.

Grasping what little slack remained in the wool of his shirt, they carefully turned the body over. As the corpse awkwardly rolled with stiff limbs and rigid torso toppling onto its back, the silver marksman pin still fastened above the upper left breast pocket glinted in spots free of the tarnishing dried blood. The medallion was very noticeable against the dirty wool tunic.

His lifeless face, drained of any vestige of persona, appeared so grotesque; it was unyielding in its ability to reveal even the slightest semblance of humanity. They had buried so many of the dead throughout those shattered woods since their arrival at the front a week earlier that it became seemingly impossible to emotionally acquiesce to the tragedy that happened to these unknown men littered about the woods. However, this one man, even in such a grotesque state, caused Private Raymond E. Rice and Sergeant George A. Sweeney to pause and examine this small, devastated corridor of hell which violently ripped the life out of the shattered body before them.[1]

One of the men wedged his hand inside the standing collar to grab the identification tags. Grimace-faced, as his knuckles contacted the cold, bare skin of the dead man's bloated neck; the aluminum discs clattered together as he pulled them up from the tunic's collar. Squinting to make out the name in the fading light of the setting July sun, the aluminum tag read: "Edwin P. Kishler PVT. 134 CO. U.S.M.C."

Kneeling beside the corpse, the two men surveyed the nearby area and noted a discarded Chauchat French automatic rifle on the ground a few paces behind Kishler's body. One of the men picked up the weapon; its bipod swiveled loosely side to side at the end of the receiver. Tilting the rifle to view the left side, he realized that the half-moon-shaped magazine was empty. The nearby discarded shell casings left a trail detailing the last steps of young Kishler's life.

Along this path were a few empty magazines, and not far behind them was the body of another man lying face down and partially submerged in the broken undergrowth covering the gentle rise. His twisted body lay on top of the empty canvas and leather-bottomed bag that held the magazines for the automatic rifle. Every step along this nightmarish landscape, strewn with discarded helmets, weapons, and other gear, conveyed the horrors of battle that unfolded along that sector of woods. More bodies lay along the ground behind Kishler and his assistant automatic rifleman carrying the magazine bag.

This scene of devastation fronted a rocky incline where two large boulders partially concealed an enemy position, which was the focus of the dead men's attack. The two large rocks, between which the water jacket of an abandoned German Maxim machine gun remained visible, were about ten yards in front of Kishler's body.

Hundreds of empty shell casings lay all along the base of the rocky slopes and revealed the horrendous volume of fire that met these men. Kishler expended every round from the Chauchat as well as his Springfield rifle and resorted to charging the enemy position with his bayonet after all of his comrades fell. In this final twenty-yard stretch of broken sloping woodland, he was abruptly cut down.

Against the backdrop of a fading July sun with the distant report of heavy artillery, Sweeney and Rice hastily dug a shallow pit beside each fallen man and marked them with broken tree limbs constructed into makeshift crosses. The burial team collected one of the two identity discs from each corpse before indecorously sliding the dead men into their graves. The loose soil was tossed upon the bodies. Little solace was involved in the process.

After dusk faded into complete darkness, enemy star shells cracked in the distant sky, gradually illuminating the surrounding fields. Against the polychromatic light of these glowing munitions high above the woods, shattered and splintered trees cast an ominous silhouette in the light. The men continued their macabre assignment until before midnight when they committed the last man to the ground. They purposely left Kishler's body unburied where it remained.

Rice and Sweeney crept through the broken undergrowth, breaking branches and crushing vegetation under the hobnails of their boots. Locating the dugout of First Lieutenant Howard I. Potter, the two men explained what they encountered in the northern section of the woods.

According to Potter, commanding G Company, 104th Infantry Regiment, 26th Division, Sweeney, and Rice, "came to my dugout and said they had just had a very unusual experience. They asked permission to speak with Major Lewis, commanding the Second Battalion. Major Lewis' P.C. was located in the ravine at the foot of the woods, and we went together to see him."[2]

Dug into the side of the gorge, Major Evan Lewis clambered out of his hole, and there in the darkness, the two men spoke freely of what they just witnessed. They felt compelled to bring an officer to the scene to see the fate that befell Private Kishler.

Potter followed the two men back over the trampled path through the woods to the spot of the recent burials. Crude wooden crosses now appeared in the faint twinkling glow of a moonlit sky, supplemented by the occasional burst of distant German star shells. Potter gently walked toward Kishler's body, and with Rice and Sweeney, they stood silent for a moment,

Preface

feeling perhaps further away from the serenity of their Massachusetts homes than at any other time since they arrived in France.

In the relative silence of the predawn hours of a dark July morning, the three men committed twenty-four-year-old Private Edwin Porter Kishler to the ground in the same non-baronial manner as his other fallen comrades. His identity disc was cut from his body and handed over to Roual Nordquist, the company 1st Sergeant.[3]

As the night sky grew pale with the early arrival of dawn in the summers of northern France, the story of Private Kishler and his untimely death merged further into the obscured tragedy that befell hundreds of other young men whose random and undignified resting places also dotted the splintered forest. In the coming week, both Private Rice and First Sergeant Nordquist would themselves be among the rudimentary grave markers reverently spanning the battlefield.

The sight of those broken bodies huddled into a small, secluded, and obliterated section of woods stayed with Howard Potter for years to come. The memories of that warm July night remained so vivid; he was compelled six years later to "make some record of this incident, particularly to the relatives of Mr. Kishler."[4]

In the minds of those who buried him, Kishler's identity spanned little beyond a decomposing lifeless mass, personified only by the name crudely stamped into a one-inch diameter aluminum dog tag; however, to Samuel and Jennie Kishler, Edwin's parents, this sector of French forest was where their world began to unravel.

On Mother's day, May 12, 1918, Private Kishler wrote to his parents wondering why he had not received any mail, despite the nearly sixty letters his mother mailed to him since his arrival in France in April 1918. The contents of the last correspondence broke his mother's heart.

According to Samuel Kishler, writing letters to her two sons serving abroad was the one thing that kept Jennie Kishler lived going. Samuel wrote a letter to the Marine Corps on June 14, 1918, urging them to clear up the inefficiency in locating their lost correspondences to their son. "See if you can't trace some of his letters or cable him immediately that mother and all are well and are with him in their thoughts and prayers," pleaded Samuel Kishler.[5] For days, the Kishlers waited helplessly for a reply.

Eight days later, on June 22, 1918, Samuel Kishler received a letter from headquarters Marine Corps stating, "The mail for Expeditionary Forces is extremely heavy, and occasional losses are reported. But there is something radically wrong in the case of your son since you state that all his mail has gone astray. If your son again writes that he is not receiving mail from home, this office suggests that you take the matter up with your local Postal Authorities."[6] However, Edwin's parents received no more letters from their son.

Preface

    Three days after the Marine Corps replied to Samuel's inquiry, twenty-four-year-old Edwin Porter Kishler lay dead in a shattered little corner of woods, seemingly a world removed from his home in south Chicago. It is doubtful Samuel, and Jennie Kishler ever learned the details of their son's final moments. Their distress undeniably grew as weeks and months passed with no definitive word or acknowledgment from their son. The devastating news came October 26, 1918, when a telegram officially informed them of Edwin's death, an agony they undoubtedly carried to their graves.

    Their story embodies the tragic side of an American narrative, which has mostly grown silent with the passing of the generation who lived through the war. The incurable loneliness, devastation, and heartache invaded the lives of numerous families across the United States whose beloved sons, husbands, fathers, and brothers lay in the simple shallow graves of the shattered grounds in and around Belleau Wood.

---

[1] Letter Howard I. Potter to Major Harry C. Miller November 3, 1924, Official Military Personnel File for Private Edwin P. Kishler, Official Military Personnel Files, 1905 – 1998, RG 127, NPRC St. Louis, MO.
[2] Ibid.
[3] Ibid.
[4] Ibid.
[5] Ibid.
[6] Ibid.

INTRODUCTION

Introduction

News of war did little to interrupt the sheltered serenity of life in the small town of Cedar Grove, New Jersey, on that bustling spring Friday in April of 1917. For nineteen-year-old Roger Irving Canfield and his eighteen-year-old brother John, the coming spring meant time to till the land for the upcoming planting season. The acreage of their homestead yielded a healthy-enough corn harvest to keep the boys and their hired help relatively occupied for part of the year.

Besides Roger's job as a clerk as well as the occasional ventures to Philadelphia, Newark, and New York City, life in Cedar Grove remained tranquil for the Canfield boys. So, it may have been no surprise that the allure of the colorful recruiting posters over slogans such as *"First to Fight"* adorning window fronts, intrigued Roger and John during one of their many city journeys.[1]

As the war became an increasing reality to even the most secluded corners of America, the two young men seriously considered enlistment such a likelihood that Roger left his clerical job. On May 2, 1917, the Canfield boys took a train to New York City and walked several blocks to the United States Marine Corps recruiting office on East 23rd Street where a seemingly endless line of applicants stretched from the doorway.

After a long wait, Roger and John applied for an enlistment that would extend through the duration of the war. Five days later, with the monotony of civilian life in Cedar Grove and the innocence and mischief of adolescence left behind, the two men joined the other raw recruits of G Company, Marine Barracks, Philadelphia Navy Yard. Traveling to Philadelphia would be only the first segment of the most defining chapter in their young lives.

William Eugene Lee, an eighteen-year-old from Liverpool, New York, was among the hundreds of other young men arriving at the Marine Barracks in Philadelphia in late April of 1917. Lee left his job at the Syracuse Lighting Company to enlist. "From a kid up I always thought of the Marines. They were my favorite," he recalled. "The war was declared in April, and I became eighteen in March, so I was just old enough to get in."[2]

He left his home on April 16th to be a part of this significant undertaking that had attracted hundreds of thousands of other young men from the tranquility of life on America's farms, in small towns, and bustling cities. Never before had the baby-faced, five-foot-seven-inch, 132-pound Lee ventured beyond the confines of the winter ice rinks and spring ball fields of his small quaint hometown on the northern banks of Onondaga Lake. However, by April 27, Lee's new residence was with Company C of the Marine Barracks, Philadelphia Navy Yard.[3]

Among the ranks of Company C was twenty-year-old Stanley Ashton Ringer from the Allston neighborhood in Boston's west side. Ringer left his job as a clerk with a local exchange and trust company two weeks after America's entry into war so he could enlist. On Friday, April 19th, he

Introduction

waited in line outside the tiny Marine Corps recruiting office in Boston's Scollay Square and applied for enlistment. Days later, after bidding his mother Georgia and Father Clayton a final farewell, he boarded a train for Philadelphia and within days blended into the sea of khaki-clad recruits in Company C.[4]

War euphoria swept through the campus of the University of Minnesota when two of the most school's most famous students joined the Marine Corps. Carleton Wallace, who captained the University's track team, joined the Marine Corps in May. Albert 'Bert' Preston Baston, captain of the football team and a clear choice by Walter Camp as an end for the 1915 and 1916 All-American team also joined the Marine Corps that May.

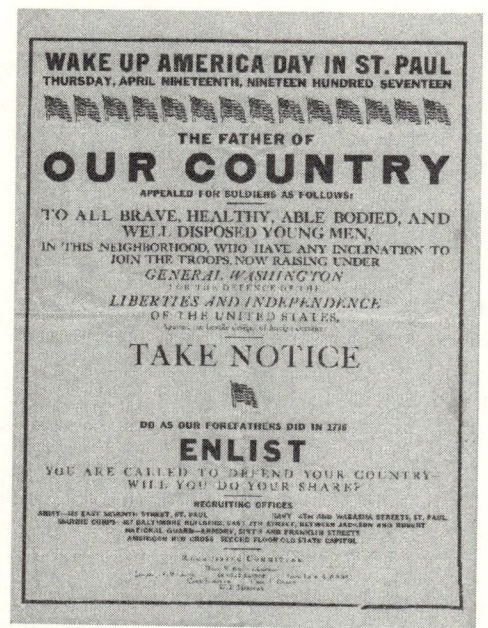

Even before these two campus notables enlisted, several students visited the Marine recruiting office in downtown St. Paul. Merwin Silverthorn, a twenty-year-old chemistry major finishing his junior year, had served with the 1st Minnesota Field Artillery on the Mexican border south of Brownsville, Texas, the previous summer. He found himself torn between rejoining his old National Guard unit as a stable sergeant and enlisting in the Marine Corps.

For eight days, Silverthorn agonized over the decision. "My present wife who I was courting in those days was the agent who directed me to the Marine Corps. She said, 'oh you don't want to be a stable sergeant,' " recalled Silverthorn.[5] His decision came on April 19, 1917, when the city of St. Paul held a "Wake up America Day," and encouraged the young men of St. Paul to answer the nation's call to service.

A pamphlet handed out in observance of St. Paul's 'Wake up American Day.' The pamphlet gave all the administrative information for young men to enlist including the address of all the recruiting offices for each branch of service in the city. Photo credit: Author's collection.

April 19, 1917, Silverthorn and his friend, Stephen George Sherman, a twenty-one-year-old junior in the college's agricultural school, accompanied several other boys from the university on their trip to the Marine Corps recruiting station located on the fourth story of the Baltimore building in downtown St. Paul. When the men arrived outside of the office building, they encountered a swarm of applicants standing in line waiting to set up an

Introduction

appointment for a physical examination. "That line to get your name in the book extended out the office, down the hall, down four flights of steps, down the sidewalk and around the corner just to give you an idea of the enthusiasm," recalled Silverthorn.[6]

Silverthorn admitted he knew very little about the Marine Corps at the time he inquired into the prospect of enlisting. "I knew Marines served aboard ship. If one wanted to fight, one had to get on land so we wouldn't see much fighting," he reasoned.[7] Many of his boyhood friends back on the block of his Minneapolis neighborhood had warned him by relaying some of their preconceived notions about service in the Marine Corps. "If you did get into fighting you were in an unfavorable position because if the ship sank, they only had enough lifeboats or life rafts for the blue jackets. This was something that was truly believed by my neighborhood social group, and so nobody entered the Marine Corps from my neighborhood. I was the only one," remembered Silverthorn.[8] Despite the wild rumors, Silverthorn remained committed to his decision to join the Marines.

Five days after visiting the recruiting office in St. Paul and passing his physical examination, Silverthorn, his good friends Stephen Sherman, and Marshall Branch Williams prepared to depart Minneapolis. Bert Alison Richardson, Frank Jay Tupa, Sigurd Marvin Swensen, Stanley Stearns, Clarence Victor Swanson,

Students from the University of Minnesota await their departure to Mare Island. Several students decorated the Pullman cars at the Minneapolis depot. Photo credit: University of Minnesota.

and several other University of Minnesota students joined Silverthorn, Williams, and Sherman at the train depot in downtown Minneapolis. Silverthorn remembered the scene that afternoon:

> The artists in the group decorated the Pullman cars with lettering saying 'University of Minnesota,' and we were headed for California, and we were going to 'kill the Kaiser.' The Kaiser was the epitome of one's violent feelings about the war, so we weren't going to do anything to the Germans you were going to do

Introduction

something to the Kaiser. So 'the Kaiser was going to be hung' and so forth.[9]

For weeks following the nation's entry into war, patriotism, camaraderie, and probably even peer pressure drove hundreds of University of Minnesota students into the St. Paul and Minneapolis recruiting offices. The euphoric atmosphere on campus was contagious. Leo Moses Hirschfield, the son of a prominent Minneapolis doctor, and nineteen-year-old Harold Thomas Linnell were good friends who often accompanied each other everywhere on campus. It was no surprise that on April 23, 1917, when Harold entered the Marine Corps recruiting office in the Baltimore building, Leo was there to apply with him along with eighteen-year-old Nathaniel 'Nat' Hall Lufkin, a freshman at the university.

Nearly one week later, both Harold and Leo were on board a train headed for their new, temporary residence as recruits of D Company, Marine Barracks, Mare Island, California.

For twenty-year-old Robert McCaughin Fischer, an engineering student and member of the football team at the University of Minnesota, life indeed was not without challenges. He was the second of three children born to German immigrants. His father, Dr. Gustav Fischer, ran a small family practice in New Ulm, Minnesota, a bustling German village of about 4,000 people.

Robert McCaughin Fischer while a student at the University of Minnesota. Photo credit: Joe Fischer.

During the birth of the family's youngest son, Robert's mother died suddenly leaving behind a heart-broken husband too distraught and beside himself to raise three children alone. The boys went to live with their aunt in Minneapolis. Minna Fischer, a schoolteacher, left her career to devote everything she had to her beloved nephews.

When the boys grew older, her desire to put them through college was beyond her financial capacity, so Robert and his brothers worked at Woolworths as supervisors. The Fischer boys took turns working for a year while the other went to school. This method allowed each of the boys to support each other through college.[10]

Introduction

For Robert, America's declaration of war and the decision to enlist must have been relatively painstaking. The patriotic fervor that swept the campus of the university that spring consumed hundreds of young men, many of whom were Robert's friends. Leaving behind his life in school also affected his brothers. As an engineering student, Robert's department even convened to adopt and publish a wartime standard in the university's annual, one that undoubtedly added pressure to his difficult decision. According to the college's creed:

> First-We stand to respond to the call of the country in ready and willing service.
> Second-We undertake to maintain our part of the war, free from hatred, brutality or graft, true to American purpose and ideals.
> Third- Aware of the temptations incident to camp life and of the moral and social wreckage involved, we covenant together as college men to live the clean life and to seek to establish the American uniform as a symbol and guarantee of real manhood.[11]

On April 24th, Robert and his friend Edwin Herbert Winter, a twenty-year-old student in the university's academics school and member of the Beta Theta Pi fraternity, traveled to downtown St. Paul and applied for enlistment at the Baltimore building.

For Edwin Winter, life back in his hometown of Granite Falls, Minnesota, would likely confine him to a steady job at his father's hardware store, far from the adventurous undertaking his classmates had chosen.[12] His application came nearly a week after a fraternity brother and classmate, Marshall Williams, had applied. Thomas Wayman Brown, a nineteen-year-old student at the university, was the son of Danish immigrants and had been a member of the 1916 freshman football team with Fischer.

Robert Fischer (left) and Edwin Winter (right) Photo credit: Joe Fischer.

When word spread of Fischer's enlistment, Brown and another member of the 1916 freshman squad, twenty-one-year-old Gerald Fosten Case, went

17

Introduction

to downtown St. Paul the next day to wait in the seemingly endless line outside the Baltimore Building to apply for enlistment.[13]

Among the applicants waiting in line outside the recruiting office inside the Baltimore Building on the afternoon of April 25, 1917, was eighteen-year-old Joyce Sansen Lewis and his seventeen-year-old brother William Theodore Lewis from the small farming community of Long Prairie, Minnesota. Joyce, a high school senior set to graduate that spring, dropped out with only a few weeks left in the year. William, a high school junior, left school to follow his brother into service.

The boys, with the blessings of their mother Mabel and father Ernest, a judge at the Long Prairie courthouse, were now endeavoring to join the ranks of the service they thought would rapidly bring them to the war front. Their obscurity amidst the long line of fresh young faces outside the St. Paul recruiting office that afternoon contrasted the grand send-off that characterized their departure from their hometown the day before.[14]

The Lewis boys had accompanied eight other men from Long Prairie to the twin cities with the intentions of enlisting in the Navy. This group received a sendoff, unlike anything the town had ever seen. The twelve young men met outside of the village post office so they could walk together to the train depot early that morning.

As the boys gathered, a small band began to assemble across the street along with many of the village's citizens. The procession marched down the road to the cadence of their music, followed by veterans from the local Grand Army post that joined the procession to escort the young men to the train station. Members of the Women's Relief Corps and the village fire department then followed them.

Before long, the parade stretched for blocks. As the assembly passed down the village streets, more than a thousand residents of the town lined the roadways waving flags and cheering the boys. The crowd then followed the procession to the train depot where hundreds had gathered to send the boys off.[15]

At the depot, Charles H. Taylor, the department commander of the Grand Army Post, spoke of the town's admiration for the boys. Taylor's address that brisk April morning before nearly a thousand residents embodied the euphoria of war's declaration throughout the American conscience. According to a local newspaper report:

> He prophesized a glorious victory because he said the cause for which America is fighting is right. America is fighting for liberty and humanity, said Mr. Taylor, addressing the boys and in coming quickly to the defense of your country you have earned the right to take your places in history alongside the boys of '76 and the Boys of '61. Some may think you are too young to enlist, he continued, but you are the age and type of the soldiers who enlisted at Lincoln's first call, and he

said he would rather command a company of volunteers young but willing than a whole brigade of seasoned men who were in the struggle because they had been drafted. He cautioned the boys to take care of themselves, saying that more men died of disease than wounds and said their personal habits would count mightily in determining whether or not they would return safely from the war. He urged them to be obedient to their officers, to take the heroes of American history as their models and he was satisfied they would give good accounts of themselves. Amid the tears and cheers of the assemblage, he wished them God speed.[16]

Speaking for the other nine young men, Joyce Lewis thanked the residents for their show of support and vowed that the men would do their utmost to give a good account of themselves. As the whistles and cheers of the crowd erupted once again, the boys received a collection of money donated by residents of the town to help them with any travel expenses. A representative of the local Presbyterian Church gave each boy a booklet containing Bible passages.

Not even the distant whistle of the train could pierce the commotion of the crowd that eventually swarmed the ten men who shook an endless gamut of well-wishing hands. When the train pulled into the depot, exiting passengers had to disembark on the opposite side of the horde, and the ten men had to nudge their way through the crowd to get onboard the passenger car. The crowd erupted once again into euphoric cheers, and the band broke into song as the train pulled out of the station bound for the Twin Cities.

When the ten men got to the Twin Cities, Joyce and William quickly changed their minds on the navy and left the group, believing that the Marine Corps offered a quicker chance to get into active service. The boys promptly sought the nearest Marine Corps recruiting station and headed for it. Outside the Baltimore building, Joyce and William soon blended with the long line of strangers awaiting entrance into the small fourth-story room, many of whom in a year's time would become close comrades. The boys finally gained entry to the office, passed their examination, and were booked to leave for Mare Island before they could ever bid farewell to their parents.

Only weeks after America's declaration of war, several University of Minnesota men and other applicants from the Twin Cities seemed to fill the trains disembarking the Minneapolis depot headed for Mare Island, California. On the evening of April 25, 1917, William and Joyce Lewis, Edwin Winter, Robert Fischer, and his former teammates Thomas Brown and Gerald Case boarded the passenger cars filled with audacious young Americans headed for Mare Island, eager to do their part in the nation's great undertaking.

In Northfield, Minnesota, the news of war drew Carleton College's star football player, twenty-six-year-old Charles Lloyd Joy, away to service.

Introduction

During the 1915 and 1916 seasons, Charles was instrumental in leading the team in back-to-back undefeated seasons. His success at Carleton College was a resurrection from a personal tragedy that ended his academic career five years earlier.

As a teenager, Charles, a promising young violinist, and vocalist attended the prestigious Benzonia Academy, a college preparatory school dedicated to studying fine arts, music, and culture just a few miles north of his home in Joyfield Township, Michigan. Charles came from humble beginnings. His father, a Union war veteran who suffered wounds during the battle of Shiloh, ran the family farm and scraped enough money together to pay the tuition for Charles to attend the school. While at Benzonia, Charles played for the academy's first football team in 1910 and instantly became a successful athlete and student on campus.

Charles enrolled in Olivet College in the fall of 1911 but left his education behind when he got tragic news of his father's death. He returned to Joyfield Township to help run the farm with his mother and three older sisters. For two years, Charles kept his family afloat, and all the time he longed to resume his education. By 1914, many of his classmates from Benzonia were near college graduation. Charles, still desirous of getting back into school, left Joyfield Township at the urging of a friend who encouraged him to resume his academic career.

Charles began his new life at Carleton College in Northfield, Minnesota, where he studied civil engineering and became a star on the university's football team. On April 6, 1917, the exhilaration of war's declaration did not escape Charles whose education once again went into moratorium. Swept by the excitement of the moment, he enlisted in the U.S. Army. His educational background in engineering made him a prime candidate for the engineers, and he departed Minnesota for Camp Baker near El Paso, Texas.

For Lemuel Cornick Shepherd Jr., America's declaration of war came in an almost meticulously timed coincidence. The twenty-one-year-old was a few weeks shy of graduation from the prestigious Virginia Military Institute.

Lemuel Shepherd. Photo credit: VMI archives.

Shepherd's affluent Virginia lineage was absorbed in military heritage, a tradition instigated by his grandfather and great uncle who served with the Virginia Cavalry during the Civil War. America's inception into the global calamity that spring would have seemingly sent him into a natural state of social exile had he not carried on the family heritage of military service.[17]

The year before, Shepherd became interested in the Marine Corps when the Commandant, Major General George Barnett, visited Virginia Military Institute. His ambitions grew when he discovered that the institute maintained only ten commissioning billets in the Marine Corps for the 1917 graduating class.

His hopes for joining the Marine Corps seemed unlikely because his class ranking suffered a blow during an impishly devised New Year's Eve fireworks display, which stripped him of his cadet corporal's warrant.[18] Other graduates filled the Marine Corps billets, but Shepherd petitioned to the superintendent to be an alternate should one of the applicants fail to pass the physical examination, a gamble that ultimately worked in his favor. "I recall very well it was two days after war was declared that we boarded a train at Lynchburg, stood up all night and reported into the Marine Barracks Washington the next morning for physical examination which we passed without any difficulty."[19] Accompanying Shepherd was his roommate, twenty-one-year-old Fielding Slaughter Robinson of Norfolk, Virginia. The two men took their oath and accepted their pending commissions as Second Lieutenants in the Marine Corps.

On May 3, 1917, Shepherd left Virginia Military Institute, a day that held personal significance to him. "I always recall—this is a sentimental thing—it was the day of the battle of Chancellorsville," remembered Shepherd.[20] Gazing up at a painting of Virginia Military Institute's most famous son, Stonewall Jackson, the general's valiant battle declaration in which he vehemently stated, "VMI will be heard from today," pervasively echoed in Shepherd's conscience.

He noted the significance as he looked at the portrait and realized the day marked the fifty-fourth anniversary of the great Chancellorsville battle where his great uncle died while serving with the Virginia Cavalry.[21] The irony of the moment became a central memory and perhaps, for the first time, enlightened him to the severity of his undertaking.

From a very young age, Alfred Schiani was no stranger to violence. Growing up on DeGraw Street in the heart of Brooklyn's Italian district, Alfred's Italian-born parents hardened him with their rigid discipline. Walking across the street one afternoon as a boy, Alfred witnessed a horse-drawn carriage driver stab another person to death after the two men's carriages collided. The imagery of that horrific scene forever stayed with him and introduced him to the brutal realities of the world. It prompted his protective father, Joseph, to move his wife and six children to a safer neighborhood in Newark, New Jersey.

Alfred was the oldest boy out of six children, and in a community occupied by a diverse mix of first and second generation Germans, Irish and Italians, Alfred grew accustomed to occasional brawls with local hoodlums

Introduction

who would often harass his younger brothers. This environment quickly honed his fiery personality and toughened his demeanor.

Alfred's academic career was rife with turmoil. On one particular occasion, he suffered vicious reprimand when he muttered, "Son of a bitch," in reaction to a teacher's swat across the head with a ruler. The school's principal, grabbing Alfred by the back of his collar, carried out his departure from the building by tossing him down four flights of stairs and out the door. "I was expelled and told that the only way I could be reinstated was to bring my father. This was for me a death sentence. My father, a disciplinarian, would have to lose a day's pay for my misbehavior."[22] Eventually, due to his mother's civility, the school reinstated him and continued attending through the eighth grade.

At thirteen-years-old, Alfred filled out an application for working papers, adding a year to his age to work with his father and received a bountiful wage of $3.60 a week. He continued working as an apprentice machinist for four straight years, eventually working his way towards a wage of sixty cents per hour in a steel factory that produced the nose cones for large caliber naval gun shells. For Alfred, however, life lacked the excitement that often plagued the ambitions of young, thrill-seeking men. He began flirting with the idea of joining the Marine Corps with the hopes of quenching his intense hunger for adventure.

Upon visiting the recruiting office on Market Street in Newark, the recruiters promptly turned Alfred away for being underweight. Persistent in his endeavor, he returned to the same recruiting station sometime later, donning a woolen sweater heavy enough to conceal two five-pound metal weights he covertly placed in the pockets, "but as I got on the scale," remembered Alfred, "the weights rolled out."[23]

The stunned recruiting sergeant, amazed at the young man's tenacity, said he still could not process his application for enlistment, but he advised Alfred to consume a steady diet of milk and bananas to add some quick pounds to his frame. "I did this for days; I was beginning to feel milk and banana logged," recalled Alfred.[24] Upon his third visit to the recruiting office, Alfred apprehensively stepped on the scale to find that he was still underweight. The date was April 13, 1917, and with America's entry into the Great War now a week old, the sympathetic recruiting sergeant administratively added a few pounds to Alfred's chart and accepted his application for enlistment.

For days, Alfred had managed to conceal his recent enlistment from his parents, who from the time he had witnessed that murder as a youngster on DeGraw Street, were protective of their children from the dangers of the world. With only three days left before he was to ship out, he planned to reveal his new plans to his mother whom he hoped would be the one to tell his father. "After convincing my mother, I still had to hear from my father. This was to become one of the worst moments of my life," recalled Alfred.

Introduction

"I had gone to bed on the second night nervously, everything seemed a lost cause. When morning came, my father awoke me up and reminded me I had an appointment with the Marine Corps. I dressed, bewildered, had breakfast, and I marched down to the P.O."[25]

Alfred's father accompanied him down to Market Street. Realizing perhaps he could not keep his son from all the world's dangers, Joseph's mood was quite somber. "I could see tears coming out of his eyes," recalled Alfred. "Suddenly, he turned to face me and said, 'son, I can get you out of this. First, you are under age; second, you do not have my permission. However, I am going to allow you to go.'"[26] With that emotional exchange, Alfred remained steadfast in his pursuit and bid his father farewell as he entered the doorway of the crowded office.

Several other applicants had already gathered, awaiting travel papers for the long journey to Paris Island. The men boarded a train at a nearby depot for the eleven-mile trip to Manhattan where the group proceeded towards the recruiting office on East 23rd Street. More applicants joined the men, and they marched towards the docks where they boarded a coastline vessel that carried them on the first leg of a very memorable journey.[27]

Donald Victor Paradis worked as a high-bill complaint inspector for the City of Detroit Gas Company, a highly prized billet for a twenty-one-year-old man. In recent months, Paradis's new promotion allocated him the luxury of driving a brand-new Model T Ford on the job, a position that made him swell with pride. Upon the nation's entrance into the war, Paradis found himself in the debacle of heeding to a national call to arms even in the midst of his rapidly successful occupational life.

In a verbal debate that nearly escalated into a physical altercation, he lashed out at his father, whose support for Germany utterly disgusted Donald, who defiantly expressed his support for France and her allies. His intentions of enlisting in some branch of service upon America's declaration of war came to greater fruition following the quarrel with his father. Several weeks later, he toured the various recruiting offices in Detroit with a good friend.

When Paradis and his friend encountered a Marine recruiting tent in Grand Circus Park in downtown Detroit, they quickly noticed the recruiting sergeant in his illustrious dress blue uniform. The dark navy-colored tunic and sharp sky-blue trousers caught their eyes. The bright yellow braided sergeant chevrons wrapped around each of the sergeant's arms immediately captivated Paradis. Almost statuesque in appearance, the boys felt envious of the graceful specimen standing before them. Paradis recalled the impression that recruiting sergeant had on him years later:

> They told us a regiment of Marines was being formed at Paris Island, South Carolina for duty in France. If we signed at once, we could be in France in four to six months. This we found later was

Introduction

sheer sales talk as they had no more idea where we would end up than the man on the moon. But, that promise and those clean, snappy uniforms did the trick. I later found that I would never be issued one of those snappy uniforms.

On May 12, 1917, Paradis applied for enlistment with the Marine Corps. Two days later, he and seven other enlistees boarded a train in downtown Detroit headed for the first leg of their long journey to Port Royal, South Carolina.

The Marine Corps recruiting office in downtown St. Louis's North Seventh Avenue bustled with human traffic in the months after the nation's entrance into the war. Thirty-one-year-old Hugh Stanley Miller, a former ballplayer who had tried to pave a career in baseball since 1908, was among the many faces passing through the door on June 4, 1917. Miller broke into the big leagues in 1910, playing first base for the Philadelphia Phillies club, but he only made a single game appearance before going to the minors where he bounced around for a few years.

The creation of the Federal Baseball League in 1913 brought Miller home to St. Louis where he signed with a local club named the Terriers. They finished dead last in an eight-team league during the 1914 season.

Miller was part of a club-level house cleaning that sent him down to the colonial leagues before the 1915 season. J.B. Sheridan, a St. Louis sportswriter, said, "Years of squabbles with his managers and absences from the game handicapped Miller, and he failed as a player even in the Federal League."[28]

Sheridan noted that Miller was "a very good ballplayer," but also apparently had a thrill "for late hours and good times that seriously interfered with his success at his chosen profession."[29] Miller was a very inconspicuous ballplayer, and according to Sheridan, "Indeed, it was held against him that he always kept his head down, never said a word, and while he played good ball, he also played 'dead' ball. His friends are wont to hold that Miller would have been a very successful player had he shown any 'life.'"[30]

Baseball soon became a bygone undertaking for Miller, and he wandered for a year until war awakened the sleeping nation. Twenty days after his application for enlistment, Miller culminated his long journey from St. Louis by boarding a small boat that would steam across the channel from Port Royal, South Carolina, to Paris Island.[31]

Barak Mattingly managed to conceal his real age of sixteen years from the recruiting sergeants the day he entered the same Marine Corps Recruiting Station on North Seventh Avenue in St. Louis, Missouri, in June of 1917. Mattingly, a high school student from nearby Pevely, Missouri, deceitfully added a few years to his life to comply with the age requirements.[32] Even if his youthful appearance created skepticism among the recruiters, so many young men had passed through the door in the nearly ten weeks following America's entrance in the war that names associated with faces vanished from memory as soon as an applicant left the office.

One of the recruiters present that day was thirty-six-year-old Sergeant Fred Stockham, a leather-faced Marine of nearly fourteen years who had seen action in Nicaragua and seemed to embody everything one could expect of a sea-going Marine. Whether Mattingly exchanged dialogue or even made eye contact with Stockham is a detail lost to history, but their mere presence in that busy downtown office that afternoon was the beginning of a tragic twist of fate that would play itself out nearly one year later. Stockham, the old weathered seafaring veteran, and the docile baby-faced Mattingly represented a dichotomy of men who, in due time, would mutually spill their blood half a world away.

Eighteen-year-old James Russell Scarbrough found his job with Procter and Gamble at the Crisco plant in Cincinnati, a dull and non-stimulating method of generating an income. "All I did was watch shortening cans come down the conveyer belt, and throw a little lever to fill them up. It was the easiest job I ever had. That job left me a lot of time where my mind wasn't occupied, a lot of time to think," recalled Scarbrough.[33]

By that spring, the war in Europe had neared its third year, and by now, nineteen-year-old Scarbrough had read a steady dose of propaganda-driven media coverage of the brutality the Germans initiated on the helpless Belgian and French populace.

According to Scarbrough, "The newspapers were full of accounts of horrible things the Germans were doing in France and Belgium, just rolling over Europe, murdering people. I have read all kinds of accounts and reasons why the First World War started since that time, but it was entirely clear back then."[34] Scarbrough reasoned that America's involvement was inevitable.

Faced with the current disillusionment over the monotony that characterized his contemporary life, he shifted his thought toward a pathway of adventure in the military. A few days after his nineteenth birthday, Scarbrough went to the Marine Corps recruiting office located in the Pickering building in Cincinnati's central corridor. "I wanted the best training I could get, so I joined the United States Marine Corps on May 16, 1917."[35] Within days, Scarbrough left home for Paris Island, South Carolina.

For fifteen-year-old John 'Chick' Hubert, war broke out while he was living with former neighbors in Chicago—a temporary arrangement with no prospects of where he might call home next. According to Hubert:

> When I graduated from grammar school, it was necessary for me to work in order to earn enough money to pay my own way. In my youthful years, I loved to read about Buffalo Bill and other

Introduction

> notorious characters of the Wild West. So in the early spring of 1917, I ran away from my monotonous job, from where I boarded in Chicago. I decided to go west and be a cowboy and see the many wonderful places I read about.[36]

This sense of adventure brought Hubert to Denver, Colorado. He remembered:

> Noticing a group of men walking around with their suitcases, I wandered over to the entrance of the establishment that they had come out of, which proved to be a recruiting office. While I was standing there, a sergeant came out and questioned me about my age. He said, 'You know, a couple of days ago, Congress passed a bill saying that you could enlist at 18 without your parents' consent.'[37]

Surprised by the idea and gazing at a giant colorful poster of Uncle Sam pointing his finger, Hubert exclaimed that he was eighteen. "He said, 'Well you look 18 to me,'" recalled Hubert.[38] After completing some of the initial paperwork, Hubert departed for Ft. Logan, Colorado, where the U.S. Army discovered that he was only 5'4" and 112 pounds; just twenty pounds below the weight limit. "However the doctor, in checking my heart and lungs, trapped me into admitting my right age which was 15. He gave me a pat on the backside and said, 'Ok, I'll keep your secret.' So I was sworn in."[39] From there, Hubert headed to Camp Baker near El Paso, Texas, where he would eventually join the 2nd Engineer Regiment.

For twenty-eight-year-old Robert Stauffer Heizer, the complacency of life in Topeka, Kansas, could have easily bypassed participation in the war. He was a tall, slim, handsome young lawyer. A 1911 graduate of Kansas University, Heizer majored in history and excelled as one of the school's top athletes captaining the university's basketball and baseball team during his time as an undergraduate. He was also a beloved member of the Beta Theta Pi fraternity, a member of the Pan-Hellenic council, and a senior member of the university's Sachems society.[40]

After attending the University of Michigan for a year, Heizer returned to the University of Kansas and earned his bachelors of law in 1915. Shortly after completing his law degree, Robert became a partner with the Crane, Hayden, Heizer and Hayden law firm in Topeka, Kansas.[41] Indelibly swept up in the immediate wartime splendor, Heizer decided to leave the law firm, yielding to his feelings of obligation to the nation's call to arms. His application for commission in the U.S. Army was accepted, and he immediately reported to Fort Sheridan, Illinois, to begin training.

Introduction

For twenty-six-year-old Richard Norris Williams, a commission in the U.S. Army was a continuing chapter in an already exceptional young life. Born in Geneva, Switzerland, he was the son of a lawyer from Radnor, Delaware, and the fourth great-grandson of Benjamin Franklin. Young Williams spent much of his youth in Switzerland and became an accomplished tennis player. In his teenage years, he dominated the Junior European circuit.

In 1912, Richard and his father booked a trip back to the U.S. where Richard would get a summer's worth of tournament competition before heading off to Harvard that fall. The two traveled from Switzerland to Paris where they ran into difficulty catching the train to the port at Cherbourg and almost missed their ship, a fateful scenario since their vessel was the R.M.S. Titanic.

Williams survived the fateful sinking of the Titanic on the night of April 14, 1912, by treading water until he was able to get into a collapsible and partially flooded lifeboat. He shed his raccoon fur coat and spent over three hours in the raft up to his knees in twenty-eight-degree water until rescued by the *Carpathia*. His father was never seen again. Severe hypothermia turned his legs so blue that doctors advised amputation to avoid gangrene, but Williams refused and went on to play tennis at Harvard.

He received a number two ranking in the nation after his first year and selected for the 1913 U.S. Davis Cup team. Williams won both the 1914 and 1916 U.S. singles men's championship and quickly became among the world's greatest tennis players. America's entry into the war in 1917 compelled him to place his promising athletic career on hold, and he applied for a commission in the U.S. Army. He reported to Plattsburgh, New York Officer Reserve Corps training.

Ironically, one of the many vessels transporting American troops to France in the summer of 1917 was the *Carpathia*. Years later, William's grandson recalled, "My grandfather wondered if he was going to have to climb the *Carpathia's* decks again."[42] His venture over the waters that nearly claimed his life five years earlier brought the young lieutenant into the threshold of danger once again.

News of America's declaration was a welcome relief for twenty-five-year-old Elliot Duncan Cooke, an adventure-seeking First Sergeant serving with Company H of the 33rd Infantry in the Canal Zone of Panama. His wealthy upbringing in an affluent district of Manhattan made him an unlikely candidate for the life and death struggles that characterized most of his remarkable adolescence. Elliot was the son of Henrietta and Richard Cooke, a successful Wall Street stockbroker.

Following his father into the life of brokering held no appeal to young Elliot, a feeling compounded by the attention Henrietta showed his brother yet denied to Elliot. When he was ten years old, his parents sent him away to Montclair Military School in New Jersey. He returned home in 1905, yet

Introduction

he grew so dissatisfied with his home life that he and a friend ran away from home on August 31, 1905. Cooke was just two weeks past his fourteenth birthday and oblivious to the sensationalism that lay in store over the next few years.[43]

Vagrancy eventually brought the boys to the Gulf Coast where an impromptu voyage on a fruit company transport took them to Honduras. Before long, Elliot found a place among the ranks of hired guns working for Lee Christmas, a notorious mercenary whose secret connections with the United Fruit Company had gained infamy in the violent environment of Honduras.[44]

By the early 1900's, Puerto Cortes, a port city in Northern Honduras had become a haven for runaways, exiles, and vagrants turned mercenary, and Elliot was likely recruited here for his new occupation.[45] By 1905, Lee Christmas was instituting a new brand of justice as the chief of police in the Honduran capital of Tegucigalpa, an appointment made by Manuel Bonilla, the nation's U.S.-supported dictator. Violence in Tegucigalpa was commonplace in the wake of the oligarchic leadership of Bonilla, a man known for his generous concessions to American companies.[46]

By 1906, Elliot participated in suppressing many of the violent uprisings in Tegucigalpa. At the age of fourteen, his occupation familiarized him with operating a machine gun, a trade that catered to his thrill-seeking ambitions. He remained there for a violent and tumultuous six months until he was wounded in the fighting near the capital city and left Honduras.[47]

An invading Nicaraguan force overran Tegucigalpa less than a year later. Bonilla fled into exile, and Nicaraguan troops captured Christmas after he was wounded. Facing execution, Christmas remained defiant to his captors. Christmas, in a show of theatrical mockery, as he awaited execution, requested that his body remain unburied. When asked why he demanded such a request, he is supposed to have said, "Because I want the buzzards to eat me, and fly over you afterward, and scatter white droppings on your god-damned black faces."[48] Miraculously, he escaped death.

Back in the United States, Elliot traveled to Goldfield, Nevada, in June to stay with some relatives. Elliot was just fifteen years old but was able to conceal his age, and he secured a job as a mine guard with the Goldfield Consolidated Mining Company.[49] By late 1906, disharmony between the miners and the monopolizing company exploded into violent demonstrations by the miners.

In 1908, President Roosevelt fulfilled a request to send federal troops on the agreement that Nevada would have to recruit a militia or police force large enough to handle their affairs. The opportunity was appealing to Cooke who, at age sixteen, saw another chance to experience the thrill of conflict. A local sheriff, who assembled a small militia of strikebreaking regulators, hired Cooke who once again lied about his age.[50] Elliot remained in Nevada for a few years until events just south of the border once again drew him into the violent upheaval of Latin America.

In 1910, Revolutionists in Mexico took up arms against Dictator Porfirio Diaz. Within months, fighting erupted into a nation-wide revolution. The conflict quickly attracted hired guns from across the world, and Cooke saw an opportunity to apply his mercenary skills. Enrolled at the Colorado School of Mines, Elliot sought a way to get into the fight.

By the middle of 1911, activities of the Magonistas, a revolutionary wing opposed to Diaz, expanded into Baja California. During this time, several Americans, recruited from southern California, fought on the side of the Magonistas. Elliot quickly joined and by the summer of 1911 was among the hundreds of American mercenaries defending the town of Tijuana from the onslaught of Mexican federal forces. The attack eventually drove the Magonistas out. Wounded again, Elliot escaped with his life.[51]

Danger seemed to follow Elliot wherever he went. His brush with death in Mexico brought him to Porcupine, Ontario, and perhaps provided a period of calm away from peril he had known for the last several years. Porcupine was in the midst of a massive gold rush that hit the region earlier that year, and the settlements in the area drastically expanded. That particular summer had been sweltering and dry.

On July 11, 1911, a series of brush fires ignited most of the desiccated woodland and erupted into a twenty-mile-wide inferno with flames reaching as high as 100 feet.[52] During this inferno, Elliot was instrumental in evacuating several miners before they suffocated in the blaze, an act that earned Elliot a medal of heroism by the company whose workers he rescued. The fire killed over seventy people, destroyed hundreds of thousands of acres of forest, and became one of the worst disasters to hit the region. Elliot remained in Porcupine working in the mines until January of the following year.[53]

Elliot turned up in Nicaragua in late 1911, serving with a mercenary artillery battery.[54] He remained there until 1912 when he temporarily returned to the United States. Elliot solicited his help throughout Nevada, Colorado, and even Canada working as a mining engineer, assayer, and even prospector for various mining companies.[55]

When war broke out in Europe in the summer of 1914, Elliot, believing that the U.S. would soon enter the fray, hurried back to the United States where on November 16, 1914, he enlisted in the U.S. Army at the age of twenty-three.[56] His experiences in combat suited his life in the Army, and he quickly rose through the ranks, but he longed to get back to a life of fighting. In July 1916, Elliot received a promotion to First Sergeant and received orders for the Canal Zone.[57] The war in Europe seemed like a world away to Elliot, but after a two and a half year wait, the United States entered the conflict, much to Cooke's delight.

Introduction

John Joseph Tesoro, the oldest of five children from a working-class Italian family, registered for the draft by that summer. John's parents, Joseph and Antoniette, immigrated to the United States in the 1870's looking for a better life, and like most Italian families in the early part of the century, they endeavored to build their dream from virtually nothing.

For John, military service was just another step into assimilation for his family to blend into the fabric of American society, a characteristic fundamental to the Tesoro family. Both Joseph and Antoniette were insistent upon the family speaking English in their home. Even Joseph, whose birth name was Giusseppi, changed the spelling of their surname from 'Tesoriero' to 'Tesoro' to reflect their new identity as American citizens. Despite his registration for the draft in the summer of 1917, the war did little to disrupt John's life, which consisted of hours of work at the family fruit market. When he the draft notice eventually arrived later that year, John willingly left his home and family for an unknown fate.[58]

The serenity of College Station, Texas, began to yield to the wartime mobilization during the summer of 1917. Like most college towns, the call to service plucked qualified men from the student body in such large numbers that the following fall semester revealed a grossly reduced enrollment at the A&M College of Texas.

By 1918, nearly half of the school's most recent graduating class was in uniform. Among these men was twenty-one-year-old Edmund Laritz Reisner, a 1916 graduate of the college who received assigned that April to Company A of the Texas National Naval Volunteers. Another Aggie who joined the Marine Corps was twenty-two-year-old Thomas Reed Brailsford, a member of the esteemed Corps of Cadets and Aggie baseball star from the class of 1917 from Latexo, Texas.

Carl Andrew Brannen, an eighteen-year-old student at the college, was completing his first year when news of war shattered the university atmosphere. Brannen, also a member of the Corps of Cadets, was caught up in this wave of war euphoria. "Men were going into some branch of service on all sides. I felt that my family should do their bit in uniform, and my age designated me as the most appropriate one."[59]

With his heart set on flying, Brannen sought enlistment with the air service, but failure to qualify as a pilot proved to be too high a risk that would preempt his ability to get into the war, so he chose the Marine Corps, his second choice. "The 'first to fight' Marine Corps recruiting posters were appealing. Accordingly, I joined the exodus from Texas A&M College, as cadets went into different branches of service. My resignation was January 27, 1918, at midterm," recalled Brannen. In February of 1918, Brannen's memorable induction into the Marine Corps began at Paris Island, South Carolina.

They came in droves from every corner of society and every region of the country. They were young, endeavoring boys seeking adventure and able-bodied men coerced by a jubilant nation caught up in the euphoric atmosphere that created societal expectations to serve patriotically. They were promising athletes and intellectuals drawn from the highest of American aristocracy and clutched from the nation's finest educational institutions. They were runaways, orphans, vagrants, farmers, and working-class men drafted or enticed into service from the corners of America's largest cities. They were middle-class citizens from humbled backgrounds in small-town America.

Patriotism, adventure, bravado, and pride all seemed to drive them into the recruiting offices across the country. Their motives were as varied as their ranks were plentiful. They were a cross-section of American society during the first quarter of the twentieth century united by a collective undertaking, one that knew nothing of parentage or social hierarchy.

They all held aspirations that transcended the present crisis. For now, however, those dreams remained on hold and, for too many, never again resumed. For all of these men, this duty thrust them into a world of violence beyond their comprehension and left them with the grizzly images and terrifying recollections that invaded their daily thoughts and revisited them nightly, even into their final years.

---

[1] In Telephone conversations with the author, April 4th, 12th, and 15th, 2010, John R. Canfield III revealed the early life of his grandfather and great uncle. Military Personnel Files of John Canfield and Roger Canfield, National Personnel Records Center (Archival Operations Branch) (NRPAO), 9700 Page Avenue, St. Louis, MO, 63132-5100. From here on cited as Military Personnel File of corresponding individual.
[2] William E. Lee, interviewed by New York State Military Museum, Syracuse, NY, June 19, 2001. William E. Lee, interviewed by author, Syracuse, NY, March 14, 2004.
[3] Military Personnel File William E. Lee.
[4] Military Personnel File Stanley A. Ringer. "Sketches of New England Men in Casualty List," (Boston Daily Globe 26 June 1918, 2). U.S. Marine Corps Muster Rolls, 1893-1940; (National Archives Microfilm Publication T977, 460 rolls); Records of the U.S. Marine Corps, Record Group 127; National Archives, Washington, D.C. From here on cited as U.S. Marine Corps Muster Rolls, 1893-1940.
[5] Lieutenant General Merwin Silverthorn, interview by Benis Frank, Quantico, VA, 1973, Marine Corps Oral History Collection, Gray Research Library, Quantico, VA.
[6] Ibid
[7] Ibid
[8] Ibid
[9] Ibid
[10] Correspondence with Joe M. Fischer, Great Nephew of Robert M. Fischer.
[11] *The Gopher* 1919 Volume XXXII, (Elmer and Engelbert Leo A. Daum 1919), 126.

Introduction

[12] Ibid. Official Service Record file for Edwin Winter and Robert M. Fischer. 1910 Federal Census.
[13] Ibid, Correspondence with Fischer family, service record file of Thomas W. Brown and Gerald Case.
[14] Collection of newspaper clippings from the Lewis Family referred to from here on as Lewis collection. Correspondence with Kathy Lewis, granddaughter of Joyce Lewis.
[15] Ibid.
[16] Ibid.
[17] Robert Chardon, "Lemuel Cornick Shepherd Jr., A Marine's Marine 1896-1990", (N.P., N.D.), 1. This is an unpublished paper written by the great-grandson of Lemuel Shepherd.
[18] Ibid.
[19] Shepherd, Lemuel. 1963. Interview by Robert Asprey June 20. Transcript, Personal Papers collection, Alfred M. Gray Research Library, Quantico, VA. (Hereafter cited as Shepherd Interview)
[20] Ibid.
[21] Ibid and Chardon,"Lemuel Cornick Shepherd Jr.,"1
[22] Schiani, Alfred, A Former Marine Tells it Like it Was, and is, (New York: Carleton Press, 1988), 11.
[23] Ibid, 14.
[24] Ibid.
[25] Ibid.
[26] Ibid,14-15.
[27] Ibid, 15.
[28] Leeke, Jim, "Hughie Miller," Society for American Baseball, 2011. http://sabr.org/bioproj/person/e32e4445
[29] Ibid.
[30] Ibid.
[31] Service Record File Hugh Miller
[32] Military Personnel File of Barak Mattingly. William Mattingly, email message to author, July 18, 2011.
[33] Byron Scarbrough *They Called us Devil Dogs,* (Morrisville: Lulu, 2005), N.P. Note: This was an proof copy of the book furnished to the author by Byron Scarbrough.
[34] Ibid.
[35] Ibid.
[36] John Hubert, Memories of C Company 2nd Engineers (N.P. N.D.), 4. Note: This unpublished memoir was in the personal papers of Merwin Silverthorn, and the booklet contained a foreword by Lieutenant General Silverthorn, as well as correspondence from Mr. Hubert to Lt. Gen. Silverthorn dated 1980.

[37] Hubert, Memories of C Company 2nd Engineers, 5.
[38] Ibid.
[39] Ibid.
[40] *The Jayhawker: University of Kansas* 1911, (Lawrence: University of Kansas, 1911), Page 54.
[41] Myron E. Adams and Fred Girton, *The Fort Sheridan Officers' Training Camps,* (Fort Sheridan: Fort Sheridan Association, 1920), 92.
[42] Wertheim, L. Jon "Unsinkable," *Sports Illustrated*, April 2, 2012.
[43] Compiled group of documents kept by Elliott Cooke put together by his granddaughter Cybele Lane.
[44] Ibid.
[45] Ibid.
[46] Langley, Lester D.; Schoonover, Thomas, *The Banana Men: American Mercenaries and Entrepreneurs in Central America, 1880-1930,* (Lexington: University Press of Kentucky, 1995), 41
[47] Compiled group of documents kept by Elliott Cooke put together by his granddaughter Cybele Lane.
[48] Ibid.
[49] Ibid.
[50] Ibid.
[51] Ibid.
[52] John Gray (2000) [February 1, 1954]. "The Fire That Wiped Out Porcupine." In Michael Benedict. *In the face of disaster: true stories of Canadian heroes from the archives of Maclean's*. New York, N.Y: Viking. pp. 15–31
[53] Compiled group of documents kept by Elliott Cooke put together by his granddaughter Cybele Lane.
[54] Ibid.
[55] Ibid.
[56] Ibid.
[57] Ibid.
[58] Draft Registration of John J. Tesoro, *Kings County, New York*; Roll: *1754224*; Draft Board: *28*. Joseph Palisi, e-mail message to author, July 14, 2011. Note: Joseph Palisi is the nephew of John J. Tesoro.
[59] Carl A. Brannen, *Over There: A Marine in the Great War,* Preface and Annotation by Rolfe L. Hillman Jr. and Pete Owen (College Station, TX: 1996), 5.

BACKGROUND

Background

Men were coughing and vomiting from the effects of gas, and men were blinded. The whole earth around us turned into an inferno-akin to the Three Divisions described in Dante's description of hell.
                              -Unidentified British Soldier of the 5th Army

By 1918, the war on the western front was wearing down already exhausted armies on both sides. The British, who spent much of 1917 locked in extraordinarily costly and ineffective offensives, held their sector in conjunction with very rudimentary coordination with their French counterparts. America's entrance into the war immediately boosted the morale of the British and French, but their euphoria soured when they realized that mobilizing, training, and equipping the U.S. military for sustained combat on the Western Front meant that American troops would not break the stalemate anytime soon.

Added to this disenchantment was General John Joseph Pershing's refusal to place elements of his American Expeditionary Force under French or British command. Acting on strict orders and his vision for America's role in the war, Pershing would carry the United States into the fight as a unified army, not as piecemeal cannon fodder for their weary and decimated allies.[1]

While America's entrance into the war enhanced French and British morale, it placed the German high command in a bit of a strategic vice. Field Marshal Paul Von Hindenburg and Erich Ludendorff, his first deputy, oversaw all military operations for the German army. Together they tried to develop a plan to tip the scales in favor of Germany before the weight of American industrial and manpower potential would break their backs. Russia's departure from the war catered to their plans since millions of German troops were available from the east for a decisive blow on the Western Front.[2]

In the first few weeks of 1918, Ludendorff and Hindenburg hashed out a vague yet decisive plan of action to try and determine the outcome of the war. This preparation relied on sheer manpower to disrupt and ultimately break the weak coordination between the French and British. Because the British spent much of the previous year taking the fight to the Germans and posed the most significant threat, Ludendorff made the British Expedition Force the initial target. He planned a massive offensive in the west in the area of the 5th British Army south of the town of Arras, France.

This plan would launch a strike on a long and lightly fortified stretch of the British lines. By attacking this area, the Germans also sought to dissect any tactical liaison between the French and British, and enable the attacking armies to swarm the British and force them to the coast.[3] Once the offensive materialized, German high command planned to initiate another assault set

Background

to coincide in the north against the British 1st and 2nd Armies in the vicinity of the old Ypres battlefield.[4]

Code-named Operations Michael and Georgette, Ludendorff, and Hindenburg demanded the utmost secrecy in preparation for the assaults. These attacks utilized an overwhelming and sudden volume of pre-registered artillery as well as a new tactic of infiltration carried out by specialized troops known as *strumtruppen*. These soldiers, organized into small units, could penetrate deep into enemy lines while bypassing particular objectives for the main force following close behind.

Once they compromised the enemy's lines, these troops, using weapons such as flamethrowers, light machine guns, and light trench mortars, would immediately disrupt the enemy's rear echelon. As the infiltration bypassed the enemy's main line, the main assault force would deliver a devastating assault.[5]

At 4:40 A.M. March 21, 1918, nearly 6,000 German cannons commenced the largest bombardment of the war.[6] All types of shells from gas to high explosive pounded the trenches of the British 5th and 3rd Armies along a forty-eight kilometer stretch of front. Up and down the sector, British phone lines rang constantly and dispatched the same warning of an overwhelming level of incoming shellfire.

"It sounded as if the world were coming to an end," recalled Lieutenant Herbert Sulzbach, a German artillery officer.[7] "Machine gun posts were blown sky-high along with human limbs," according to one British soldier of the 5th Army.[8] "Men were coughing and vomiting from the effects of gas, and men were blinded. The whole earth around us turned into an inferno- akin to the Three Divisions described in Dante's description of hell."[9]

By 9:35 A.M. three German armies stood lined north to south waiting for the order to attack. *Sturmtruppen* units moved out and immediately placed the British lines under mortar fire. By the early afternoon, German soldiers had overrun the British front.[10]

As the three German armies pressed deeper into British lines, Ludendorff made what would be the first of several strategic errors. While the initial goal of the offensive was to separate the liaison of the British and French sectors, Ludendorff decided the front of the attack should be expanded to exploit weaknesses in the British lines.

The extension of the battlefront placed increasing strain on German supply and artillery support units that were vital resources to sustain the initial momentum. The strategic city of Amiens, a crucial railway junction, and Arras were not taken nor was the liaison between the French and British broken. While the initial overwhelming success of Ludendorff's operation appeared to be a tremendously one-sided victory, it failed to achieve its objectives and cost the Germans over 230,000 casualties. Nearly seventy German divisions had been exhausted. Particularly hard hit were the *Sturmtruppen* formations.[11]

Background

Operation Michael also emphasized the need for better coordination and liaison between command structures of the French, British, and Americans. General Ferdinand Foch, whose official title had been chief of general staff, became Généralissime. Foch's official position gave him command of the operations and coordination of the Entente powers.

From that moment on "General Foch is charged by the British and French Governments to coordinate the action of the Allied Armies on the Western Front. He will work to this end with the Generals-in-Chief who are asked to furnish him with all necessary information."[12]

While each nation maintained command of their armies, no longer were they operating independently of each other. Foch later exclaimed at a conference of allied military leaders in Doullens, France, "I would fight without a break. I would fight in front Amiens. I would fight in Amiens. I would fight behind Amiens. I would fight all the time."[13] The previous statement reflects how strong-willed the French were over even minor objectives. The quote is also reflective of the overwhelming significance of major cities such as Paris, which would soon be in the crosshairs of another of Ludendorff's mastermind plans.

Following the devastating Operation Michael offensive, the Germans launched their second large-scale attack named Operation Georgette. The target was the very northern portion of the British sector held by the British 1st Army. The goal of Georgette was to place essential channel ports at risk. On the morning of April 9, 1918, following a massive artillery barrage, the German 6th Army tore through a sector of the line held by a corps of Portuguese troops of which 6,000 became prisoners, and the remaining 13,000 fled from the front lines into the rear sector.[14]

Terrified that the ports were under threat, Commander-in-Chief of British forces, Field Marshall Sir Douglas Haig, pleaded with Foch to release French reserves to the area. Foch rejected the request. He believed limiting the defenses of Paris was too risky. Commander of the American Expeditionary Forces, General John Pershing, also declined to commit any of the nominal and untested American troops who had arrived in France.

Pershing, adhering to strict orders not to relinquish command and control of U.S. troops unless under American dominion, did not share the panic that overcame the British high command. On April 11, 1918, Haig issued a message of desperation to his engaged armies: "With our backs to the wall and believing in the justice of our cause, each one of us must fight on to the end . . . Every position must be held to the last man. There must be no retirement."[15] While the German drive continued against stiff British resistance, Ludendorff's assault never reached the enemy ports and faltered at another tremendous cost to the German Army.

The British suffered nearly 236,000 casualties and committed fifty-three of the available fifty-nine divisions. As substantial as these numbers appeared, England could replenish the losses. The Germans suffered nearly

Background

300,000 casualties and lost the majority of their best-trained soldiers.[16] Casualties were unusually heavy among the elite shock troops.

For as much psychological advantage as Ludendorff's offensives claimed, they came at a fearful toll of men and material, most of which could not readily be replaced, if at all. Ludendorff was slowly feeding his armies into a grinder with little or no decisive results.

German morale began to wane according to Colonel Albrecht Von Thaer, a member of Ludendorff's staff who visited the front many times. Thaer pointed out that dwindling spirits from such tumultuous losses trickled down the ranks, "The morale influence on the troops has passed to company commanders and junior officers and NCO's."[17] Need for relief came from every unit. Replacements were often lesser quality soldiers. Many of these men were young conscripts or older men who lacked experience.

While Operation Georgette failed to break through to the ports, Ludendorff had not abandoned the target as a possible objective for another offensive. Despite Foch's initial opposition to moving his forces to strengthen the British front, the reinforcement of the British lines by French reserve units created a significant problem for Ludendorff. To successfully launch and sustain another assault in this region, the Germans had to lure French reserves away from the sector.

An attack on Paris was the only scenario that could prompt Foch to relocate his forces. German high command selected a twenty-two-mile stretch of ground along the formidable Chemin des Dames ridge between the towns of Soissons and Rheims, north of the Aisne River Valley, which stood about eighty miles northeast of Paris.

With the selection of this path of advance, Ludendorff hoped to convince Foch that the Germans were aiming to take the French capital. The name given to this attack was Operation Blücher, in honor of the Prussian Field Marshall Von Blücherwho, ironically enough, in 1814 crossed this ridgeline from the south and met Napoleon's army at Craonne.[18]

Operation Blücher was intended to be a limited and diversionary offensive to draw French reserves away from the British sector while appearing to be a committed effort to assault Paris. The region of Chemin des Dames, a quiet area, held only four battle-torn British divisions. The ridges were very rugged and nearly impassable, a factor considered by the French, who drastically underestimated the potential enemy threat in the region.

While French and British units converged on this quiet sector to rest and replenish, Germans forces had spent nearly a month preparing an attack under utmost secrecy. German units mobilized and moved only at night to avoid aerial observation. Routine night raids in enemy lines revealed little indication that the Germans were contriving a significant assault, due to the extra precautions taken by the Germans to avoid capture during periodic night raids.

Whenever French and British forces fired routine artillery barrages on likely enemy crossroads and supply routes, German guns remained silent as not to reveal their presence. German commanders addressed the lessons learned during the previous two offensives. Assault, supply, and transport units carried more machine guns to thwart an air threat posed by British and French aviators. Drills in open warfare maneuvering were carried out in rear sectors.[19]

The German 7th Army, under the command of General Max Von Boehn, consisted of six German corps amassed along the region north of the Chemin des Dames ridge. Few of the twenty-nine German divisions in line, however, were of superior attack order, most were second-rate and sector-holding troops or comprised of units virtually exhausted in the two previous offensives.[20]

The condition of the German soldiers had been significantly weakened compared to the days leading up to the previous offensives. Captain Fritz Wiedemann was tasked with analyzing troop morale among the line units. He found a large number of his regiment desperately needed time to recover before heading back into action; when this fact came to the attention of his division commander, he announced that the attack would commence as scheduled. Wiedemann responded in his memoirs and summed up that the decisions being made by the German high command were playing with the lives of thousands of men not yet ready to go back into action.[21]

Despite the meticulous and covert preparations for the offensive, plenty of signs emerged that gave forewarning of the pending assault. The first bit of evidence came in an alarmingly accurate report issued by a member of General Pershing's intelligence section. Captain Samuel T. Hubbard Jr., a 1907 Harvard graduate, pieced together the daily flow of information arriving from frontline units and envisaged an enemy assault in the vicinity of Laon, France, which sat nearly centered on the sector the Germans planned to attack. Hubbard's report, approved by Pershing, was sent immediately to the French high command.[22]

Hubbard believed the Germans saw the area along the Chemin des Dames as extremely difficult for the French and British to reinforce in response to an assault, the same reason the British and French dismissed his theory. They believed the enemy could never traverse such terrain. This qualm materialized in a reply that, according to Hubbard, stated, ". . . They [the French] had expressed considerable doubt that the American intelligence service could be correct in their summary of what the Germans might do. . ."[23] The second source of evidence came on the eve of the attack. As the sun dipped below the western horizon on the evening of May 25th, two days before the attack, soldiers of the French 22nd Division set out on a routine raid of the German trench line. The raiding party penetrated

Background

into a sector of the the enemy front held by the German 197th Division and captured an officer and a sergeant of the 3rd Battalion, 7th Saxon Regiment.

These two German soldiers revealed everything they knew about the pending assault. This critical intelligence did not reach higher headquarters until the afternoon of May 26th, only hours before the attack was to commence.[24] By that time, the Germans had abandoned the art of concealment, and as French observation balloons surmounted the horizon, enemy formations made their way to the jump-off point. The sector deemed "quiet" weeks before would, in the next few hours, turn into a shell-torn inferno.

Across the ridges of the Chemin des Dames 1,321 batteries of German artillery were ready to unleash hell. At 1:00 A.M., May 27, 1918, firing commenced with unprecedented ferocity. Across the rolling valley southwest of the ridges, a young British staff officer named Sidney Rogerson recalled the terrifying moments when rounds fell upon the lines occupied by the British 8th Division. "The earth shuddered under the avalanche of missiles . . . Ever above the din screamed the fierce crescendo of approaching shells, ear-splitting crashes as they burst . . . The dug-outs rocked, filled with the acrid fumes of cordite, the sickly-sweet tang of gas . . . It was a descent into hell."[25] The purgatory of shellfire unleashed on the British was only the beginning.

After hours of concentrated bombardment, German infantry began their advance. By 5:30 A.M. they drove French resistance off the ridges. Four hours later, German soldiers reached the banks of the Aisne River where pontoon bridges provided a crossing. Hours into the great offensive, alarming details arrived at French headquarters. Civilians inside Paris caught word of the impending threat against their beloved city. The situation eerily resembled the situation of the summer of 1914.[26]

German acquisitions that day far exceeded expectations. In the west, the town of Soissons was threatened; in the east, the city of Rheims was in the path of the German advance. In the center of Ludendorff's lines, the German 4th Reserve Corps made the most significant gains and closed in on a crucial piece of high ground near the River Vesle where the French 6th Army began a fighting retreat.[27] The first day's gains covered more terrain than on any other day of the war. The momentum of the offensive continued into the pre-dawn hours of May 28th and made Ludendorff wonder if such a limited and diversionary attack might still retain enough momentum to develop into a sustained war-ending drive to the Marne River and ultimately into the French capital.

Background

The French government panicked. Prime Minister Georges Clemenceau believed the capital was in peril and pleaded with Foch to act quickly.[28] Foch, the brilliant military mind, did not show alarm. He believed that Ludendorff's latest assault was an effort to divert French forces from the region of Flanders in the west. He also realized that if the main thrust of Ludendorff's drive were to converge on Paris, the Germans would dangerously expose their flank to the French 10th Army. Nonetheless, members of the French government needed reassurance in the form of a proactive move.

Foch decided to stiffen the resistance on the flanks of the enemy's advance. As French units arrived, they were fed into the lines to the east near Rheims and in the west along the densely wooded valley north of Soissons.[29] As that afternoon of May 28th faded into dusk, the advance of the Germans along the flanks had slowed significantly. Ludendorff, displeased with the progress that day, attempted to reignite the pace his troops displayed the day before and fed precious reserves into the fray.[30]

General Ferdinand Foch. Photo credit: Melacy.

As French units arrived, they went into the fight almost as sacrificial lambs to obstruct the German war machine. Thirty-seven French divisions participated in the fighting, and five days into the offensive seventeen were exhausted. Two French divisions suffered such heavy losses they were absorbed into other outfits.[31] French reserve units took positions along the flanks of the German push, stemming the progress made in these regions at a high cost.

In the center, the French 6th Army continued a steady retreat against the onslaught of the German 7th Army. This development created a deep salient along the German axis of advance. The southward depth of the bulge, spearheaded by General Richard Heinrich Karl Von Conta's 4th Reserve Corps, had created a significantly narrow front and made resupply and logistics a dire problem for the advance units of Ludendorff's offensive. This salient also exposed the flanks of Ludendorff's forward units ultimately causing the failure of the assault. Despite this precarious situation, Ludendorff insisted that the Marne River be reached by May 30th, and he continued to feed valuable reserve units into the salient to ensure this would occur.[32]

Background

French units near Rheims made a gallant stand against the eastern portion of the German push. They remained resolute after they bolstered the line with the newly arrived French 5th Army. The French doggedness in this region added to the increasing difficulties German troops faced in advancing towards the Marne River. Foch could concentrate solely on the center and western portion of the threatened area. The French developed plans for an immediate counter-offensive in the west near Soissons that could only succeed if they could stymie the German drive in the center.

While French units continued to plug the elongating salient, General Philippe Petain, commander-in-chief of the French Army, pleaded with Pershing to release any available American divisions to assist in containing the German advance in the center of the battlefront. Pershing quickly realized the critical state of affairs and agreed to release the 2nd and 3rd Divisions—the two most readily available in the American Expeditionary Forces.[33] Pershing's decision bred into the annals of American military history, an engagement that set the tone for America's long-awaited and anticipated role in the Great War.

For thirty-six days, the untested American Army engaged in a costly fight for local control of a nearly twenty-kilometer front and the triumph of morale, which helped define the legacy of the American combat experience in the Great War. When the bloodletting ended, Americans had demonstrated their tenacity and proved the resolve of the American Army's commitment to the war.

---

[1] John Toland, *No Man's Land* (Garden City, NY: Doubleday Inc., 1980), 95.
[2] John Keegan, *The First World War* (London: Hutchinson, 1998), 375-376.
[3] Toland, 10.
[4] Ibid, 137-140.
[5] Randal Gray, *Kaiserschlacht 1918: the final German offensive of World War One* (Westport, CT: Praeger, 2004), 32.
[6] Toland, 15.
[7] Ibid.
[8] Ibid, 18.
[9] Ibid, 18-19.
[10] Ibid, 20.
[11] Cray, 90.
[12] Ferdinand Foch and Thomas Bentley Mott, *The memoirs of Marshal Foch* (Garden City, NY: Doubleday, Doran and Company, Incorporated, 1931), 262.
[13] Robert B. Asprey, *At Belleau Wood* (Denton, TX: University of North Texas Press), 1996.
[14] Toland, 143.
[15] Keegan, 405.
[16] Robert B. Asprey, *The German High Command at War, Hindenburg and Ludendorff Conduct World War I* (New York, NY; William Morrow and Company, Inc., 1991), 397.
[17] Ibid.

Background

[18] Ibid.
[19] Ibid, 412.
[20] John W. Thomason Jr., *The United States Army Second Division Northwest of Chateau Thierry in World War I* ed. George Clark (Jefferson, NC: McFarland and Company, Inc., 2006), 15.
[21] Toland, 234-35
[22] Asprey, *At Belleau Wood, 49-50.*
[23] Samuel T. Hubbard, *Memoirs of a staff officer 1917-1919* (Tuckahoe, NY: Cardinal Associates, Inc., 1959), 36.
[24] Sidney Rogerson, *The Last of the Ebb: the Battle of the Aisne, 1918* (London: Greenhill Books, 1937), 24.
[25] Ibid, 28-29.
[26] Toland, 243. Note: In the summer of 1914, the Germans advanced almost along the same route as they had in the spring of 1918. In what became known as the first battle of the Marne, the French fought what was deemed a battle to save Paris
[27] Ibid, 242.
[28] Ibid.
[29] Ibid, 244.
[30] Rogerson, 140.
[31] Oliver L. Spaulding and John W. Wright, *The Second Division American Expeditionary Force in France 1917-1919*, 38. (New York, NY. The Hillman Press Inc., 1937), 36.
[32] Rogerson, 140-41.
[33] John J. Pershing, *My Experiences in the World War*, Vol. 2 (New York, NY: F.A. Stokes Co, 1931), 189.

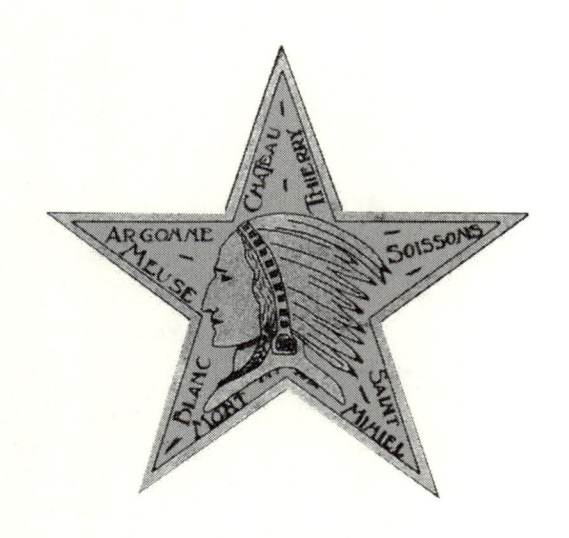

MAY 30ᵀᴴ-MAY 31ˢᵀ

May 30th -31st Chapter I

Suppressed excitement filled the air and was written on every countenance. Dame rumor remained entirely unconfirmed although the air was so charged that one actually felt that a moment of monumental importance was approaching.
-Captain Robert Messersmith 78th Company, 2nd Battalion, 6th Marines

The bugler's rendition of reveille on the morning of May 30, 1918, ushered in a placid Decoration Day for men of the 2nd U.S. Army Division encamped at Chaumont-en-Vexin. The division's camp was dozens of miles behind the active sector of Noyon-Montdidier, but the men were scheduled to move to the front in a few days. Having spent several weeks in the line in the Verdun sector, the troops welcomed a rare respite on Decoration Day. Rumors flowed rampantly among the men that the division planned to move again near Cantigny, where news of the U.S. 1st Division's successful attack had created a wave of excitement among the men.

For fifty-two-year-old Brigadier General James Guthrie Harbord, a twenty-six-year U.S. Army veteran commanding the 4th Brigade, the day remained anything but tranquil. He and his staff prepared for the scheduled movement to the village of Beauvais near the active sector of Noyon-Montdidier. The headlines splashed across Paris newspapers, however, led even the most senior officers in the division to wonder whether the successful German offensive over the Chemin des Dames would affect their scheduled movement to Beauvais near.¹

Brigadier James G. Harbord commanded the 4th Brigade. Photo credit: Library of Congress.

That morning, a religious ceremony began the day for the Marines of the 6th Regiment followed by breakfast and then an array of recreational activities to pass the time. Twenty-nine-year-old Chaplain Harris Anthony Darche conducted the religious services for the entire 6th Marines as the regiment formed a semi-circle around the makeshift pulpit.

Darche, who had been a Catholic priest at Notre Dame church in Chicago, joined the regiment the previous January and soon became the chaplain for the 1st Battalion. Private Martin 'Gus' Gulberg of the 75th

May 30th -31st Chapter I

Company recalled, "Chaplain Darche, in his sermon, told us that pretty soon we were to see real action on a lively front and many of us would not come back."[2] The chaplain's homily forced the men to ponder their fate.

The service held an eerie ambiance for twenty-year-old Corporal Havelock David Nelson, a native of Cincinnati, Ohio, attached to the 97th Company. He remembered, "It all seemed so solemn to me that I could not help wondering just how many of us present would be among those for whom similar services would be held the following year."[3] Several of the men silently pondered over Father Darche's message as they walked back to camp. "In some manner the commemoration address of the regimental chaplain left the members of the platoon gloomy," recalled Private Thomas Alexander Boyd, a handsome nineteen-year-old kid from Chicago.[4] After the religious service, the men headed back to their bivouacs.

Chaplain Harris Darche. Photo credit: NARA.

Along the way, the men of the 75th Company digested the Chaplain's prophetic words. Boyd recalled, "For a long while, as they marched along, there was no sound save for the muffled tramp of feet on the thickly dust-coated road."[5]

Amidst the despondent formation, twenty-three-year-old Corporal William Franklin Kahl exclaimed, "You know, fellows, the regimental chaplain was right. All of us haven't so damned long to live."[6] Immediately, his prophecy triggered sarcastic commentary from of another Marine. Kahl immediately snapped back, "Why do you care? You'll be alive to spit on all of our graves."[7] One man, agreeing with Kahl, claimed that he overheard a conversation between two men at battalion headquarters that the unit would soon be back to the front.

Twenty-one-year-old Private Jack Jolly Pugh of Winston, Mississippi, added his impression when he said, "Pretty damn quick? I guess we are. The battalion runner told me that we was shovin' off for the front tonight."[8] The group remained silent or a few seconds as they processed the accuracy of Pugh's statement but soon resumed their conversation.

They speculated over the pending movement as they walked, and each step seemed to bring increased fervor over the collective anticipation circulating among the men. In a few moments, the mood transformed from somber to enthusiastic as the outlandish, wild hearsay grew more credulous. Pugh continued on his oratory speculation, "You know they say it's hell up at the front now. The square heads have busted through and the frogs are fallin' back as fast as they can. I betcha that we'll be up to the front in less than a week."[9] Another voice, feeding off of the compounding gossip, added, Yeh, an' they say they cut ya where you don' wanna be cut."[10]

Before the conjecture got too far out of hand, an aggravated sergeant at the head of the formation turned his head back halfway towards the bantering men and snapped, "Pipe down, you men back there. Who gave you permission to talk?"[11] In response to the sergeant's burusque demeanor, one embittered Marine resentfully mumbled under his breath, "Who the hell gave you permission to give us permission to talk?"[12]

Down the road from the 1st Battalion's bivouac site, the 2nd Battalion, 6th Marines also enjoyed the day off. Twenty-two-year-old Corporal Lloyd Edward Pike of the 2nd Platoon of the 79th Company joined other members of the regiment in a baseball game played on a makeshift diamond situated in an open cattle pasture. According to Pike in a letter home to Silver Springs, New York, French cows did not quite understand the game of baseball and often stood stationary in the field of play, forcing the men to arrange the bases awkwardly and irregularly. "The troops enjoyed the day off and had little knowledge of the seriousness of the military situation of which they were a part," Pike recalled.[13]

Thirty-two-year-old Captain Robert Eugene Messersmith, of Fleetwood, Pennsylvania, commanding the battalion's 78th Company, did not yet received official word that the situation near the Chemin des Dames would affect them, but scuttlebutt flourished throughout the day. Messersmith remembered, "Suppressed excitement filled the air and was written on every countenance. Dame rumor remained entirely unconfirmed although the air was so charged that one actually felt that a moment of monumental importance was approaching."[14] The men welcomed the potential action at the front with a naïve excitement and false bravado.

Most men of the 2nd Division did not know that the planned movement towards the region of Beauvais, scheduled for the following day, had already been canceled in the wake of the German breakthrough along the Chemin-des-Dames. After 5:00 P.M., foot, vehicle, and motorcycle traffic inundated the 2nd Division's temporary headquarters in the village of Chaumont-en-Vexin.

News of the German breakthrough towards the town of Meaux required General Denis Auguste Duchêne's French 6th Army to summon the assistance of fifty-six-year-old Major General Omar Bundy's 2nd Division.[15] The instructions delivered to Bundy's headquarters only specified that his 2nd Division, transported by vehicles, would concentrate in the area of Meaux. By May 30th, the French 6th Army determined that the German

May 30th -31st Chapter I

advance in the vicinity of Soissons sought to utilize the highway between Soissons and Meaux to press further. Meaux stood seventy kilometers south of Soissons and fifty kilometers east of Paris.

With this latest information, officers of all ranks within the 2nd Division Headquarters staff congregated around large maps sprawled along the table trying to orient themselves with the terrain in question and develop a better understanding of the intensifying crisis south of the Chemin-des-Dames. The division staff knew very little regarding the details, but they certainly understood that the daunting task of preparing the division's 26,815 men for immediate movement, would make for a chaotic night.[16]

Further details and piecemeal directives from the 6th Army reached Bundy's headquarters throughout the evening. Messengers from division headquarters soon relayed the latest available information to the brigade commanders. Soon, orders sent from division headquarters instructed all the regiments of the division to be ready in anticipation of a sudden departure.

Major General Omar Bundy commanded the 2nd Division. Photo credit: Library of Congress.

Lieutenant Colonel James H. Hayes, a Judge Advocate General with the 2nd Division Headquarters staff, spent that day already located near Beauvais ahead of the division's scheduled arrival. Hayes and his team of about thirty billeting officers and 100 enlisted men preceded the division's movement to Beauvais days in advance to secure provisions and supplies as well as arrange transportation to move nearly 27,000 troops to the area. Hayes and his crew nearly completed their exhaustive task when, according to Hayes, "at about 6 o'clock in the evening, Colonel [Preston] Brown called me on the phone and told me that the Germans had broken through at Chateau Thierry."[17]

Immediately, Hayes initiated the process of summoning all of the provisions and logistics they had painstakingly scheduled for the movement to Beauvais and redirected them back south towards the division's current location of Chaumont-en-Vixen in response to this latest news—an arduous task that took the entire evening.[18]

Thirty-seven-year-old Lieutenant Colonel Richard Derby, a surgeon serving as the division's sanitary inspector, felt excitement upon hearing news of the movement in response to the developing crisis near Meaux.

Derby spent most of his time in France enduring hours of training by French instructors who often delivered their medical lectures in French.

For Derby, service abroad made a fitting addition to the American royalty into which he had married. His wife Ethel was the youngest daughter of former President Theodore Roosevelt. All four of the former president's sons, Derby's brothers-in-law, were serving overseas. That afternoon, Derby and several other officers met with the division chief of staff, forty-six-year-old Colonel Preston Brown, about the impending movement. They gathered into the small room and intently listened as Brown read aloud the various embarkation points for the division's units.[19]

Word of the planned movement reached the various battalions of the 4th Brigade throughout the day. Some companies received orders that the division would embark that very night, which hastened preparations. Throughout the rest of the afternoon, information both official and unofficial sent company messengers scrambling to retrieve men who spent their day off scattered throughout the area around Chaumont-en-Vexin engaged in various recreational activities.

Top left: Lieutenant Colonel Richard Derby. Seated next to Derby is his wife Ethel, the youngest daughter of the former President Theodore Roosevelt. Seated with Derby and his wife are the sons of the former President. Photo credit: Library of Congress.

Some units did not receive notification until the last minute, but news of this sudden movement eventually sent everyone frantically preparing. Throughout the day, conflicting orders regarding the specific time of departure added to the already chaotic scene unfolding throughout the division's encampment.

Forty-nine-year-old Colonel Albertus Wright Catlin, the commander of the 6th Marine Regiment, heard news of the crisis developing south of the Chemin-des-Dames days earlier, and he believed that somehow, the division would be involved. "All day long on May 30th we waited for those orders," recalled Catlin.[20] "In the afternoon we received orders to be ready to leave at 6 o'clock on camions which would be provided. Six o'clock approached and no camions appeared. Then orders were changed to 10 o'clock."[21]

Catlin dispatched his adjutant, forty-one-year-old Major Frank Edgar Evans, to deliver a memorandum stating, "Advance information official

May 30th -31st Chapter I

received that this regiment will move at 10:00 p.m. 30 May by bus to new area. All trains shall be loaded at once and arrangements hastened. Orders will follow. Wagons when loaded will move to Serans from train. By order of Colonel Catlin: F.E. Evans, Major U.S.M.C."[22]

At the bivouac sight of the 3rd Battalion, 6th Marines, the 97th Company, under the command of thirty-six-year-old Captain Robert William Voeth, assembled into formation upon news of the division's scheduled departure.

Colonel Albertus Catlin commanded the 6th Marines. Photo credit: Marine Corps History Division.

The men had not received much information except they were expected to relieve the 1st Division who had just conducted an attack Cantigny a few days earlier, but that movement was not scheduled to occur until the next day. Suddenly, however, the men received instructions to prepare to move immediately.

First Lieutenant Edward A. Kennedy, an Army officer attached to the 97th, stood before the formation and called roll just outside of their bivouac site. Corporal Havelock Nelson, assigned to Kennedy's platoon, remained under the impression that this movement would take the division north towards the village of Cantigny.

When formation broke, twenty-four-year-old First Lieutenant Ralph William Marshall of Chicago, Illinois, who was assigned to the battalion intelligence section from the 97th Company two weeks earlier, summoned Nelson. According to Nelson, Marshall gave him orders, "to report with full pack to him immediately at battalion headquarters."[23] Nelson rushed to prepare his gear.

The camp of the 97th Company became a fury of activity as men scrambled to pack up their equipment. Nelson quickly rolled his gear in his blanket, affixed it to his haversack, and flung it on his back. Laden down with the pack, gas masks, and rifle, he trotted down the road to the galley.

Nelson quickly gulped down his meal, scurried down the street towards the battalion headquarters, and found the other Marines casually standing around with their gear. He felt somewhat foolish that his haste had appeared to be for naught as he joined the others who seemed to be patiently waiting. "We waited all afternoon until mess time when we were allowed to return to our galley for another quick bite."[24] The sudden thrill of the situation began to slow as 'hurry up' quickly turned into 'standby.'

Twenty-one-year-old Sergeant Peter Preston Wood, a native of Tonawanda, New York, assigned to the 81st Company, 6th Machine Gun Battalion, was surprised by the sudden orders to move out since he and his comrades had grown somewhat accustomed to the short stretch of free time.

The last few days of relaxation interrupted only by occasional and abbreviated training activities initiated by the battalion's unyielding commander thirty-eight-year-old Major Edward Ball Cole, allowed Marines of the 6th Machine Gun Battalion time to visit the nearby village of Gisors where they eagerly spent their money on beer, wine, and liquor.

The Marines of the battalion who were assigned guard duty found enjoyment heckling the inebriated men returning to camp. One particular intoxicated man who cried uncontrollably in his drunken state became a source of entertainment for Wood and some of the other Marines.[25]

During the afternoon of May 30th, the jovial excursion up the road to Gisors continued as freely as it had the previous few days. Men took full advantage of the time off, knowing perhaps that such luxuries would be far and few between in the coming weeks. Sometime during the afternoon, however, the 81st Company received orders to pack up immediately and be ready to proceed to the Beaugrenier-Diepp-Paris road by 9:45 P.M.

By the time Wood finished packing his gear, he had noticed that many of the company's men still had not reported in, and some strolled into camp unaware of the company's pending departure. "About fifteen absent and about eight or ten so drunk that they had to be held up," recalled Wood.[26]

The Marines of the 81st Company eventually organized and packed gear with a frantic sense of urgency, only to spend hours laying around waiting for further orders to proceed to the pickup point along the roadway. While they spent the night waiting along the thoroughfare, Wood noted an unusual chill that night, and found relief when, at midnight, the company commander, thirty-five-year-old Captain Allen Melancthon Sumner of Boston, Massachusetts, "gave orders to turn in and have reveille at 4:00 a.m."[27] The men quickly went to sleep.

Word of the movement reached thirty-five-year-old Major Benjamin Schofield Berry's 3rd Battalion, 5th Marines late in the afternoon. They had enjoyed a rare, quiet and relaxing afternoon free of the usual training regimen. At 5:30 P.M., the officers of the 3rd Battalion leisurely sat in isolated groups casually conversing with each other in the serene gardens around a chateau in the village of Vaudancourt as they waited for dinner.

Thirty-year-old Second Lieutenant George Vincent Gordon, a U.S. Army reserve officer from Chicago, Illinois, attached to the 16th Company, remembered that news of the sudden departure that night caught everyone by surprise.[28] "Suddenly the battalion's second-in-command, Captain Henry Larsen, came running to us and called out, 'The battalion is leaving, pass the

May 30th -31st Chapter I

word to your platoons to make their packs, as the camions are on the way, and we leave at ten o'clock tonight,'" remembered Gordon.²⁹

This news shattered the tranquility of the late afternoon, and officers soon scrambled to summon company first sergeants and other non-commissioned officers to begin the formidable task of getting hundreds of men packed up and ready to move to a designated pickup point in only a matter of hours.

In the town of Neuilly, just north of Paris, forty-year-old Lieutenant Colonel Frederic May Wise, commanding the 2ⁿᵈ Battalion, 5ᵗʰ Marines, enjoyed a three-day liberty pass to visit his wife Ethel, a nurse stationed at a nearby Red Cross hospital. On the evening of the second day of his leave, Wise and his wife dined at the apartment of a local acquaintance. "We were sitting at [the] table, laughing at a story Mrs. Wise was telling of a happening on shipboard when the telephone rang."³⁰ Wise answered the call and heard the voice of his battalion adjutant, twenty-five-year-old Second Lieutenant James Hennen Legendre of New Orleans, Louisiana, who was with the battalion in the town of Courcelles north of Paris. Legendre exclaimed, "We've been ordered up to the front at once."³¹

Second Lieutenant James H. Legendre. Photo credit: NARA.

The trains of camions were scheduled to depart the division's sector at 5:00 A.M. the next morning. "I was in a hell of a fix," recalled Wise, a Brooklynite with nearly nineteen-years in the Marine Corps.³² "I knew my only bet at this late hour was to get an ambulance from the hospital where Mrs. Wise was working."³³ He immediately summoned his French interpreter, who accompanied him on liberty, from his home in Paris. Wise managed to secure a Studebaker ambulance and sped away towards the division's sector at 1:00 A.M. as air raid searchlights danced off the night sky, and the distant rattle of anti-aircraft fire echoed through the darkness.³⁴

For Wise's men, however, long hours of waiting soon followed the rush to prepare for departure. Twenty-six-year-old First Lieutenant Elliott Duncan Cooke, an Army officer assigned to the 18ᵗʰ Company, 2ⁿᵈ Battalion, 5ᵗʰ Marines, used the prolonged wait as an opportunity to catch some sleep.

Thirty-one-year-old Captain Lester Sherwood Wass, the commander of the 18ᵗʰ Company, allowed his men to lay down and get some rest as long as they wore their shoes and clothing in case the vehicles suddenly arrived.³⁵ Wass, a Dartmouth graduate with service in Vera Cruz and Santo Domingo, was a strict disciplinarian and a no-nonsense officer. Despite his five-feet, five-inch-frame, his cold, steely, grey eyes, his stoic demeanor and deep, hoarse, parade-deck voice all commanded the undying respect of his Marines.[36]

The wait frustrated twenty-two-year-old First Lieutenant Lemuel Cornick Shepherd of the 55th Company, 2nd Battalion, 5th Marines. Orders to move out that afternoon preempted his date with a local French girl he recently met. His numerous encounters with the young woman had so impressed her that she introduced him to her parents. "The next day I had passed inspection and was invited to dinner at their home, a very nice country home. I was thrilled," recalled Shepherd.[37] The current fiasco, however, quickly ended his dinner plans, so he sent his apologies to the family by way of his orderly.

The dire situation, which necessitated the utmost urgency in preparation, was also followed by an afternoon and evening of seemingly endless waiting for the 55th Company.[38] The initial word, according to twenty-four-year-old Sergeant Stephen Brown and eighteen-year-old Private Carl Hugo Geores of the 55th Company, was that the convoy would arrive at 10:00 P.M. and the men sat around waiting for the vehicles.

As hours passed with no sign of the caravan, a subsequent message eventually reached the company stating that the camions would not arrive until the following morning. "Accordingly, every man found himself a place to sleep wherever he could," recalled Shepherd.[39]

Forty-eight-year-old Colonel LaRoy Sunderland Upton, who had days earlier rejoined his 9th Infantry after a stay in a Paris hospital following some dental work, oversaw the timely preparation of his battalions for their scheduled movement. Upton still believed the division was moving to the Noyon-Montdidier sector.

For Upton, a West Point graduate, his namesake resonated throughout the army. His uncle was Brevet Brigadier General Emory Upton, the famous Union officer who led a gallant and decisive Union attack on the Confederate breastworks at the battle of Spotsylvania. Colonel LaRoy Upton's twenty-seven years of service, however, always seemed to keep him from the action, so he saw this scheduled movement to the active front as his long-awaited opportunity.

During the Spanish American War, Upton, a young first lieutenant, remained stateside on recruiting duty. He eventually made it to Cuba after the war and served as the collector of customs, but by this time, America's hot spot was in the Philippines during the insurrection, which lasted from 1899 to 1902. During the mostly uneventful Mexican Border campaign of 1916, he commanded the 30th Infantry.

With the nation's entrance into the Great War, Upton briefly took command of the 16th Infantry until before his transfer to serve as Director of Specialties of the 1st Division. He was then subsequently put in charge of developing and organizing the 1st Army Corps School, remaining in that billet until he took command of the 9th Infantry Regiment just months earlier.

After he left the 1st Division, the 16th Infantry became the first American outfit to engage the enemy on the ground in November 1917 near Bathlémont, France, losing the first casualties of the American Expeditionary Force. The 1st Division also participated in the first American offensive, capturing the town of Cantigny.

Since war seemed to elude him, Upton now savored the notion that he was finally going to get his opportunity within the next few days and worked tirelessly to prepare his regiment for this movement.[40] "We had orders to move up towards the lines on a certain day," remembered Upton, "and had made all our preparations for the march when an order came changing things, saying we would probably embark on motor trucks at 10:00 p.m."[41]

Colonel LaRoy Upton commanded the 9th Infantry. Photo credit: Virginia Richardson Kulpit.

Twenty-two-year-old First Lieutenant Wendell Westover, a Cornell graduate from Schenectady, New York, assigned to Company A, 5th Machine Gun Battalion, knew nothing about the cause of such a fast-paced and lengthy hike which began at 4:00 P.M. His thoughts, as well as the rest of the men's, were preoccupied with the exhaustion and soreness they all felt as they silently questioned how much longer they would march.

When the column finally halted in an open field adjacent to a small village, the men welcomed the relief from the burden of full marching packs. Twenty-three-year-old Captain Andrew Davis Bruce, commanding Company A, barked out in a booming voice, "Form for shelter tents."[42] Bruce, a native of St. Louis, Missouri, recently graduated with his doctorate of law from The Agricultural and Mechanical College of Texas in 1916 and received his commission in June 1917.

Moments later, the loud buzz of a motorcycle engine interrupted the conversation among Bruce's men as they set up their tents. The motorcycle courier, evidently coming from division headquarters, approached forty-five-year-old Major Harry Tait Lewis, who took command of the 5th Machine Gun Battalion just the day before, and handed him a message. As soon as Lewis read the dispatch, the officer excitedly summoning Bruce who darted towards the major.

Westover watched from a distance as the dialogue occurred between Lewis and Bruce. Suddenly, Bruce turned towards the company and shouted with hands cupped around his mouth, "As you were. Roll packs. Mules in harness. We move in ten minutes."[43] As fast as Bruce's troops began unloading their gear, these new orders to move instigated disgust and grumbling among the men.

The disarray and frenzied back and forth kept the men of the 5th Machine Gun Battalion indignantly guessing amongst each other as to the reason for such chaos. The constant and contradictive change in instructions not only tapped into the inherent pessimism of the troops who felt they had been needlessly shuffled around but also hinted that something abnormal was in the works with this movement. "Troops from all directions were being assembled somewhere in the area. Messengers tore along the columns. Something big was afoot," recalled Westover.[44]

Convoys of vehicles whizzed by and produced dust clouds in the path of marching troops. Westover vividly remembered, "Beside the road, hospital trains passed by on their way to Paris. Car after car, with open windows disclosing the forms wrapped in white-save where the white had turned to red. Bandaged heads, covered faces, stumps of arms, crimson torsos, missing legs."[45] The Americans gazed at the shocking scene with naïve curiosity.

By midnight, the exhausted column of soldiers in Captain Bruce's Company A, 5th Machine Gun Battalion halted after another long monotonous hike in the darkness to a nameless little village to billet for the night. They kept their equipment packed in carts, a sign they would once again move upon short notice. Situated in the room of a small house, Westover and Bruce sat with the other officers of the company and took advantage of the long-awaited opportunity to roll and smoke a cigarette. "Rumors of this new offensive had reached us and its possibilities were discussed as we waited for the expected orders," remembered Westover.[46] The mood soured when the major summoned Bruce and relayed orders for a 3:30 A.M. reveille, a directive that meant any prolonged period of sleep would again elude them.

The same duration of waiting plagued members of the 1st Battalion, 5th Marines. Earlier that evening, the company planned to hold an observance in honor of Decoration Day. According to twenty-three-year-old Corporal Frank Saxon Matheny of Blue Earth, Minnesota, "Just about a half hour before the time set for the service to begin, orders came to pack up and be ready to shove off within five minutes' notice. We did not know exactly where we were going but knew what was ahead of us."[47]

Twenty-three-year-old Private Onnie John Cordes, a printer from St. Louis, Missouri, attached to the 17th Company, hurried to pack his gear after he received word of the sudden movement. "We were ready in a very short time," Cordes remembered, "but we had to standby. Some of us laid down in a hay pile and went to sleep."[48] As the delay dragged on for a few hours, the galley served a midnight meal to the waiting troops.

Cordes awakened to the chill of the nighttime air and the mixed aroma of coffee and warm food. Realizing that the mess crew had served chow nearly a half hour earlier, he scampered from his makeshift bed of hay. "I immediately rushed over to find that they had dumped the beans, applesauce, and coffee into one large container. I jammed my mess pan far down and filled it up and ate because I was nearly starved and at the same time I thought it might be the last chow we would get for some time."[49] Cordes relished the meal as if it might be his last.

Within less than twenty-four hours, every member of the 2nd Division knew of a pending movement and prepared accordingly. Despite the hurried efforts, however, an influx of changing directives and departure times kept units on standby. As usual, the troops remained mostly ignorant of the overall situation, but the scenario playing out south of the Chemin des Dames grew increasingly perilous for the French 6th Army, and the Americans would soon play a vital role.

By the evening of May 30th, the ferocity of the Blücher offensive brought the center of the German 7th Army to the Marne River. The French 6th Army had retreated more than thirty miles since the attack commenced on May 27th.[50] The enemy's unprecedented gains placed several German divisions of the 4th Reserve Corps along the northern outskirts of Chateau Thierry situated on the Marne just seventy-nine kilometers northeast of the center of Paris. General Von Conta, a dynamic leader whose battle experience included Tannenberg in 1914 and Verdun in 1916, commanded the 4th Reserve Corps. His men stood perhaps a day's advance from capturing Chateau Thierry and securing a bridgehead over the Marne River.

General Richard Heinrich Karl Von Conta commanded the 4th Reserve Corps of the German 7th Army. Photo credit Christophe Deruelle

For the German high command, however, no strategic objectives lay across the Marne and the Crown Prince, Kaiser Wilhelm, even conceded that the Marne was to be the southern limit for the liaison between the 7th Army in the center of the Blücher offensive and the 1st Army on the left. From this point, they could support the delayed advance of the flanks on either end of the Blücher front. Despite this strategic development, Wilhelm and the rest of the German high command acknowledged the necessity of securing a bridgehead over the Marne, but the river was not to be crossed in force.[51]

The 231st Division of Von Conta's Corps was tasked with securing this bridgehead over the Marne in Chateau Thierry. The two supporting artillery regiments, the 17th Foot Artillery and the 501st Field Artillery, labored to keep up with the advancing infantry. They arrived too late to reconnoiter and occupy battery positions as well as observation posts.[52] They also lacked the necessary ammunition. In fact, the 17th Foot Artillery did not have a single round on hand.[53] The 231st Infantry war diary noted, "Further, the fact that the two artillery units mentioned had no maps on hand was found to be disturbing, as was the fact that the other units of the division also were insufficiently supplied with maps since none were furnished by Division in spite of repeated requisitions."[54]

By May 30, 1918, the German 4th Reserve Corps was aware of a renewed spirit among the French holding the front in the vicinity of Chateau Thierry. The translation of a captured French order issued by General Pétain sent from General Headquarters to the demoralized soldiers of the French 6th Army read, "Soldiers! The enemy has carried out a new blow. Because of superiority in numbers, he was able to penetrate our front lines. But our reserves are hurrying up! You will break his momentum and advance to the counter-attack. Hurrah for the heroes of the Marne! For your home, for FRANCE, forward!"[55] For the gallant French warriors in the path of the German war machine, reinforcements could not arrive fast enough.

In addition to the 2nd Division, General John Pershing promised General Philippe Petain use of sixty-year-old Brigadier General Joseph Theodore Dickman's 3rd Division to address the crisis developing south of the Chemin-des-Dames. The 3rd Division's 7th Mobile Machine Gun Battalion received orders at 10:00 A.M. on May 30th to depart the area of Chaumont, France immediately.

The news caught the 375 soldiers of the battalion off guard. According to twenty-four-year-old Captain John Ross Mendenhall, a 1915 West Point graduate, "It came as a complete surprise for although rumors were circulating that the French were hard pressed, this newly arrived unit hardly hoped to be called upon."[56] Regardless of their inexperience, the American machine gunners would be a saving grace.

May 30th -31st Chapter I

As the 2nd Division in Chaumont-en-Vexin scrambled to prepare for movement during the afternoon, the 7th Mobile Machine Gun Battalion had long departed Chaumont, France, and was in route to the embattled front. Their destination lay nearly 200 kilometers distance at Conde-en-Brie, France, which stood just fifteen kilometers southeast of Chateau Thierry.[57] The battalion traveled all day in exhaustive and cramped conditions.

Their overloaded trucks, with a 1,000-pound weight capacity, now labored to haul 1,500 pounds, which caused springs to rest on axles as they crept along narrow roads. Steep sections of inclining highway often forced the soldiers to dismount the trucks to reduce the weight and ensure successful passage.[58] Despite the hardships, companies of the 7th Mobile Machine Gun Battalion, by the evening of May 30th, stood another day's journey from Chateau Thierry where they would assist in obstructing the German crossing of the Marne River. The battalion had only been training with the M1914 8mm Lebel Hotchkiss French Machine Gun for less than a month and was now about to put their abbreviated training to use in combat.[59]

---

[1] James G. Harbord, *American Army in France 1917-1919* (Boston: Little, Brown, and Company, 1936), 270.
[2] Gus Gulberg, *A War Diary,* (Chicago: Drake Press, 1927), 22.
[3] Havelock D. Nelson, "Paris-Metz Road," *Leatherneck*, January 1940, 10.
[4] Thomas Boyd, *Through the Wheat,* (New York: Scribner's Sons, 1923), 55. Note: Boyd's work in this book is categorized as fiction. Research, however, reveals that the names, places, and events are true and parallel other memoirs and non-fictional accounts of the battle.
[5] Ibid.
[6] Ibid.
[7] Ibid.
[8] Ibid, 56.
[9] Ibid.
[10] Ibid.
[11] Ibid.
[12] Ibid.
[13] Colonel Lloyd E. Pike, *The Battle For Belleau Woods, As I Remember It About 60 Years Later*, 1977, Cantigny Museum Library, Wheaton, IL, 8.
[14] Major Robert E. Messersmith, *Operations of 78th Company Sixth Regiment Marines at Belleau Wood, June 1 to June 13, 1918. Personal Experience,* (Advanced Infantry Course 1928-1929 Fort Benning Georgia), Maneuver Center of Excellence Donovan Research Library.
[15] *Records of the Second Division (Regular)* Volume 6, (Washington: The Army War College, 1927.) N.P.
[16] Ibid.
[17] Lieutenant Colonel James H. Hayes Headquarters 2nd Division, interview by Joel D. Thacker Muster Roll Section Headquarters U.S.M.C. December 12, 1918, Transcript, Box 17, RG 127, NARA Washington, D.C.

[18] Ibid.
[19] Richard Derby, *Wade in Sanitary, The Story of a Division Surgeon in France*, (New York: G.P. Putnam and Sons, 1919), 49. Note: Quentin Roosevelt, the youngest son of Theodore and Edith Roosevelt, was a member of the 95th Aero Squadron and was killed when his plane, a Nieuport 28 was shot down over the village of Chamery, France on July 14, 1918.
[20] Albertus W. Catlin, *With the Help of God and a Few Marines*, (Garden City: Doubleday, Page and Co., 1919), 80.
[21] Ibid.
[22] *Records of the Second Division (Regular)* Volume 5, N.P.
[23] Nelson, "Paris-Metz Road," *Leatherneck*, 10.
[24] Ibid.
[25] *Diary of Peter Preston Wood 81st Company 6th Machine Gun Battalion*, N.P. Entry for May 25th-30th, Author's collection.
[26] Ibid.
[27] Ibid. (Note: Wood eliminated the name of Captain Sumner but simply wrote "Captain_____." Sumner was the only captain on duty with the 81st Company on May 30-31, 1918.
[28] George V. Gordon, *Leathernecks and Doughboys*, (Chicago: N.P., 1927), 52, and United States, Selective Service System. World War I Selective Service System Draft Registration Cards, 1917-1918, M1509, 4,582 rolls, NARA, Washington, D.C.
[29] Ibid.
[30] Frederick M. Wise and Meigs O. Frost, *A Marine Tells it to You* (New York: J.H. Sears and Company, Inc.,1929), 191.
[31] Ibid.
[32] Ibid.
[33] Ibid.
[34] Ibid, 191-92.
[35] Elliot Cooke, "We Can Take It, We Attack," *Infantry Journal*, July-August (1937), 2.
[36] Official Military Personnel File for Captain Lester S. Wass, Official Military Personnel Files, 1905 – 1998, RG 127, NPRC St. Louis, MO.
[37] General Lemuel Shepherd, interview by Robert Asprey June 20, 1963, Transcript, Personal Papers collection, Alfred M. Gray Research Library, Quantico, VA.
[38] Ibid.
[39] Stephen Brown and Carl H. Geores, *55th Co. Marines in World War I*, Box 55, RG 127, NARA, Washington, D.C.
[40] Biographical sketch, LaRoy S. Upton papers, 1887-1927, Minnesota Historical Society Library (MHS), St. Paul, MN.

May 30th -31st Chapter I

[41] Correspondence LaRoy S. Upton to his wife Agnes 10 June 1918, LaRoy S. Upton papers, MHS, St. Paul, MN.
[42] Wendell Westover, *Suicide Battalions,* (New York: G.P. Putnam's sons, 1929), 95.
[43] Ibid.
[44] Ibid.
[45] Ibid, 96.
[46] Westover, *Suicide Battalions,* 96.
[47] Scrapbook of Merwin Silverthorn, Newspaper clipping entitled, "Minneapolis Man Tells of His days in Belleau Woods," Provided to the author by Marie Silverthorn.
[48] Onnie Cordes, *The Immortal Division* (Palm Beach: Merriman Press, 1990), 5-6. Note: Despite the press information printed in the manuscript, this memoir was never published and made available.
[49] Ibid.
[50] Robert B. Asprey, *The German High Command at War, Hindenburg and Ludendorff Conduct World War I (*New York, NY; William Morrow and Company, Inc., 1991), 422.
[51] Kaiser Wilhelm, Crown prince of Germany, *My War Experiences* (London: Hurst and Blackett, 1922), 322.
[52] War Diary and Annexes 231st Division 31 May 1918, *Translations of War Diaries of German Units Opposed to the Second Division (Regular), 1918. Chateau Thierry,* Vol. 4, (Washington: The Army War College, 1930-32.) N.P.
[53] Ibid.
[54] Ibid.
[55] War Diary 4th Reserve Corps 4 June 1918, *Translation of War Diaries of German Units,* Vol. 1.
[56] Major John R. Mendenhall, *Operations of the 7th Machine Gun Battalion (Third Division) in the Vicinity of Chateau Thierry, France, May 31-June 4, 1918. Personal Experience,* (Advanced Infantry Course 1929-1930 Fort Benning, Georgia,), Maneuver Center of Excellence Donovan Research Library.
[57] *History of the Third Division United States Army in the World War for the Period December 1, 1917, to January 1, 1919.* (Andernach, N.P., 1919), 3.
[58] Mendenhall, *Operations of the 7th Machine Gun Battalion,* MCoE, Donovan Research Library.
[59] Ibid.

May 30th -31st Chapter II

Even after being loaded on to the French trucks, the men seemed more like a bunch of kids going on a picnic than a company of battle destined Marines. It was impossible for us to imagine that within a few days fifty percent of the men would be lying in hospitals or in the poppy fields around Belleau Wood.
   -Sergeant Don V. Paradis 80th Company, 2nd Battalion 6th Marines

On the morning of May 31st, the troops of the 2nd Division were picked up at various times along specific entraining points, which meant the convoys departed the area around Chaumont-en-Vexin at different times throughout the morning. They caravans were spread out over the nearly 107-kilometer journey to Meaux.

Delays and confusion seemed to be more of the rule than the exception, and some units waited for hours before their departure. The torturous cramped conditions inside French trucks, where men sat on hard wooden plank seats lining each side of the vehicle beds under the warm sun for nearly thirty-six hours, became perhaps the most unforgettable ride of their lives.

For the next forty-eight hours, the men withstood sleep and food deprivation. They encountered endless streams of refugee and military traffic that bottlenecked the convoys' progress and added hours to the duration of their trip. Many would endure enemy aerial bombardment as well as a last minute change by the French 6th Army that re-routed the entire division from their original destination of Meaux to address a new threat along the battlefront. These sudden changes prolonged the miserable excursion into the hell that awaited them.

For the soldiers of the 9th Infantry, the expected arrival of troop transports the evening of May 30th changed when they received new orders calling for the regiment to stay in place in preparation for departure from a new embarkation point the following morning.[1]

Before dawn, the men shrugged off the stupor of the restless night and stood ready to march from Liancourt-Saint-Pierre two kilometers northeast towards the pickup point in the village of Loconville, France—the eastern-most loading point for the division.[2] The hike to Loconville became a welcome escape from the idleness of waiting.

A night-long slumber in the grass of northern France that time of year soaked the men's wool uniforms with dew, and the cold air only compounded the chilly discomfort. "We got over to the entraining point and found the motor trucks there," recalled Colonel LaRoy Upton, "but waited three hours before starting. Finally, at 8:00 a.m. when all were on board we started east and ran 75 miles, pausing close to Paris on our way."[3]

May 30th -31st Chapter II

Reveille at 3:00 A.M. jostled the slumbering ranks of twenty-four-year-old Captain James Oscar Green Jr.'s Company M, 3rd Battalion, 23rd Infantry into sudden consciousness. Corporal Frank W. Anderson recalled, "We were called out of our bunks by the bugler blowing his old bugle. Didn't we love the bugler?"[4] Before the battalion could even shake off the pre-dawn fatigue, sergeants impatiently ordered the men to roll their packs and be ready to move immediately. According to Anderson, "a hurried breakfast, policed up the town, fell in line and marched to the next town about two miles away."[5]

By 4:00 A.M., most of the 3rd Battalion were in route down the dark winding road towards the designated pickup point. Cumbersome gear added further misery to the men's exhaustion following a sleepless night. By the time Anderson and the rest of Company M arrived, the vehicles were waiting, but still, the company was not ready to depart. Finally, after a half-hour delay, the men loaded their equipment ready to leave.[6]

The cool breeze also greeted the groggy soldiers of Company A, 5th Machine Gun Battalion as they rolled their packs and bedding in preparation for departure. Crews quickly pulled their gun carts toward the road to await the arrival of the convoy. Once they staged their equipment ready to move, soldiers armed with mess kits headed toward the rolling kitchens and eagerly ate a quick breakfast before policing the camp.

After serving chow, the galley crews extinguished campfires with buckets of water. The dancing flames hissed as they vanished into thick billows of smoke silhouetted against the faint morning light. By 5:30 A.M., vehicles still had not arrived, and after another stint of waiting, only a few trucks appeared which confused the men who expected a more substantial convoy. First Lieutenant Westover remembered:

> Soon after, word arrived from Division that the number of available trucks was only sufficient to hold the infantry regiments, and the machine gun battalions would move by train. The 5th was to march to Chars to entrain at 9 A.M. The change meant reloading some tons of ammunition on our own transportation, but the company was on the road to Chars within the hour.[7]

The piercing rendition of reveille sounded by company buglers abruptly jolted members of the 1st Battalion, 5th Marines awake well before the light of dawn. By 4:00 A.M., the 17th Company departed the village of Boury towards the battalion's designated embarkation point to rendezvous with the rest of the battalion. The other companies soon followed.

Nineteen-year-old Private Albert Powis, of the 66th Company, hiked to the entraining point with a heavy heart after receiving devastating news in a letter from his family back in Witt, Illinois, explaining that his older sister

Grace, a schoolteacher, died of influenza. With no time to grieve, he climbed aboard the camion loaded with his gear and an overpowering sense of homesickness.[8]

Reveille at 4:00 A.M. ended a short sleep for Sergeant Peter Wood and the rest of the Marines of the 81st Company, 6th Machine Gun Battalion. With sleep-heavy eyes, the company, adorned with heavy packs, quickly shuffled through a makeshift chow line. Unsympathetic non-commissioned officers urged them to hurry with their meal to begin the long hike toward their pickup point at the Beaugrenier-Diepp-Paris road.[9]

Marines of the 81st Company arrived at the roadway where they met the men of the 77th Company who spent the night at a farm just across from the entraining point. Their mules and carts stood harnessed along the road as the men eagerly awaited the convoy, but dawn soon grew into mid-morning, and the sun now burned brightly over the French countryside with no sign of the trucks. The delay lasted for hours, and company formations long dissolved as the men sat on the ground leaning back to rest against their heavy packs.

Finally, at 7:00 A.M., the clouds of dust stirred up along the roadway from the approaching convoy brought the companies to their feet.[10] Orders demanded that Marines of the 77th Company travel in the bed of the already-crowded trucks with their boxes of ammunition, heavy Omnibus tripods, and fifty-three pound Hotchkiss guns.[11] Mule-drawn carts usually hauled the weapons and gear, but since the animals and tumbrils would move by railhead, some unfortunate souls had to carry the heavy guns while others shouldered the equally cumbersome tripods until their mules and carts caught up with them. The colorful language of non-commissioned officers ushered men into action and urged expediency in putting machine guns and gear into the vehicles.

Captain Bailey Coffenberg commanded the 80th Company, 2nd Battalion, 6th Marines. Photo credit: Bob Gill.

The men of the 2nd Battalion, 6th Marines lined the roadside awaiting their convoy which was also several hours behind schedule, but at 6:00 A.M., they watched the seemingly endless line of vehicles approach through a distant haze.[12]

May 30th -31st Chapter II

    Men of the twenty-three-year-old Captain Bailey Metcalf Coffenberg's 80th Company cheered the arrival of the vehicles. Corporals and sergeants hoisted men weighed down by their equipment up into the beds of the camions before climbing aboard themselves. Private Levi Hemrick remembered, "The rank and file of the enlisted men who boarded those trucks had not been reading any newspapers, seen any official war reports or contacted anyone who had. We had no reason to suspect that a large number of us were making our last move."[13]

    They knew nothing of their destination yet remained euphoric over the idea of moving to the front. Sergeant Don Paradis recalled "Even after being loaded on to the French trucks, the men seemed more like a bunch of kids going on a picnic than a company of battle destined Marines. It was impossible for us to imagine that within a few days fifty percent of the men would be lying in hospitals or in the poppy fields around Belleau Wood."[14] Once aboard the trucks, additional delays pushed the departure time back to 8:00 A.M., and with the postponement, the jubilation faded.[15]

    After an hour-long drive in a borrowed hospital Studebaker ambulance, Lieutenant Colonel Frederic Wise and his French interpreter finally arrived at the 2nd Battalion, 5th Marines' bivouac site in the predawn hours of May 31st. As he exited the vehicle, Wise noticed the camions already lined up, but none of his companies, from his view, had even formed up to board the trucks. He scurried to his quarters only to find that his adjutant, Second Lieutenant James Legendre, already took care of everything during the previous twelve hours. Twenty-two-year-old Private John William McKeown, an orderly with the battalion, even packed Wise's personal belongings during the battalion commander's absence the night before.[16]

    Long before Wise returned to the battalion, his Marines spent the previous night urgently preparing for the movement only to receive news that they would not depart until morning. By dawn, First Lieutenant Elliott Cooke of the 18th Company awoke to the prodding boot of his friend Second Lieutenant Fred H. Becker, another Army officer attached to the battalion. Becker was a native of Waterloo, Iowa, and attended the University of Iowa where he played tackle on the football team. He earned all-American accolades as a sophomore in 1916—the second University of Iowa player to reach that milestone. "They're blowing reveille. Let's eat before these trucks come along," Becker said to Cooke.[17]

    By 4:00 A.M., the morning sunlight was barely visible along the horizon. Cooke, serving as mess officer, shook off his fatigue as he stood up to stretch. "I got up and had the galley crew cook all the chow on hand. We packed what was left for breakfast to take with us in case we actually moved."[18] Marines of the 18th Company believed the vehicles would arrive any moment and they stood by the road donning all their gear ready to depart. Four more hours would pass, however, before the first camions appeared to take them to an unknown destination.[19]

Thirty-seven-year-old Captain John Blanchfield, an Irish-born Marine of nearly fifteen years, commanding the 55th Company, marched his men to the roadway near the 18th Company to await the convoy, but discovered no sign of the camions. The absence of the vehicles compelled the men to drop their packs and rest on the ground. A few hours later the unwelcome, yet all-too-familiar bugle call of 'assembly,' interrupted the respite as the dust trail of the approaching vehicles appeared by 6:45 A.M.[20] The men languorously arose from the ground, slung their rifles and fell into formation.[21]

Blanchfield moved along the ranks of his company organizing and delegating them into groups of twenty to begin boarding the trucks. Men tossed their equipment into the back of the camion before they climbed aboard. "Many of the civilians who had risen early to see the battalion depart now waved their hands in adieu and wished everyone good luck. Waving cheerfully in return, the men smiling watched them as their trucks pulled out. It was a cool, clear morning and despite the fact that the men had no breakfast, everyone was in the best of spirits."[22]

Marines of the 18th Company sprung to life as the caravan arrived. Cooke remembered, "We got aboard with lots of enthusiasm, twelve officers or twenty men to a bus and the whole divided into company and battalion sections. The last man had hardly cleared the tail board when the slant-eyed little Annamese drivers impatiently ground their gears and the column began to roll."[23] The men were relieved to depart the area. Their enthusiasm, however, would not endure in such crowded and uncomfortable traveling accommodations.

Returning to the battalion just after the arrival of the convoy, Lieutenant Colonel Wise discovered that his men had duly prepared for departure in his absence. Wise boarded his vehicle and watched as his men torpidly climbed into the trucks. After what seemed an unnecessary delay, Wise was relieved to hear the trucks revving their engines in preparation for departure:

> The long line started to roll. In a little touring car belonging to the French transport officer, Legendre and I waited until the last camion was on its way, and then sped up to the head of the line. The men were all joking and laughing. As we passed along the road at the head of the column, I learned from the French transport officer that we were not going up to relieve the First Division on the Somme. He didn't know what our final destination was. All he knew was that we were to report at Meaux for orders.[24]

By 9:00 A.M., the arrival of trucks scheduled to move the men of the 3rd Battalion, 5th Marines appeared hours after the battalion's scheduled

May 30th -31st Chapter II

departure time. The incredulous and sarcastic comments uttered by the Marines when the trucks first appeared revealed the frustration they felt.

The drivers were quite a spectacle for Second Lieutenant George Gordon of the 16th Company. He described them as "dusty, sleepy Annamites, the Indo-Chinese, who showed every evidence of having driven a considerable distance. Two of them sat on the driver's seat of each camion, and they took turns at driving for one drove while the other slept."[25]

A few hours into the journey, the convoys of the various battalions bunched up on the roadways. Men, who had endured the torturous conditions in the back of vehicles for hours, desperately longed to stop if only for a minute to stretch their legs. For Wise's battalion, a brief stop in the town of Pontoise just northwest of Paris gave the men a chance to stand up and move around.[26]

Nineteen-year-old Private Alfred Schiani welcomed the brief pause. Shortly after the journey began earlier that morning, he had to answer nature's call. By the time the convoy stopped hours later, Schiani's need to urinate turned into a crisis. He recalled, "I told the sergeant my situation and he advised me to leave all equipment on the truck and if I was lucky I could catch the last truck. But the last truck unfortunately went by."[27] Schiani, now panicked, missed the departing convoy and had no idea as to their destination.

Twenty-year-old Private James Russell Scarbrough of the 83rd Company, 3rd Battalion, 6th Marines, remembered that the trip became tolerable because of the sarcasm and humor of his comrades. "Mostly we just sat in musty hay on the back of those bumpy little trucks and smoked. I remember the talk on the way there was that the 2nd Division was moving into place for some kind of big offensive, but they had said something like that before every one of our moves."[28] Twenty-five-year-old Private Eugene Owen Clark, a sheet metal worker from Rahway, New Jersey, known as 'E.O' by his comrades, and his brother Walter added their opinions to the conversation.

With false bravado, the men complained about the lack of fighting they experienced since being in France. They cynically assumed this current movement was towards another training sector. Scarborough recalled the feeling of resent, "It was like they wanted the Marines to keep away from the fighting and keep all the glory for France! E.O. was talking in this funny French accent and pretending to be a French general to get us to laugh. He said he was 'Generale' Pierre Coon-Ass from Pair-ee!"[29]

The 2nd Battalion, 6th Marines were among the last of the brigade to depart the regions around Chaumont-en-Vexin. Passing through the small villages west of Paris turned into a euphoric experience for the men of the thirty-year-old Captain Randolph Talcott Zane's 79th Company. The young French women, who were waving, blowing kisses, and whistling at the passing vehicles, added to the already heightened enthusiasm of the young Marines who sang, laughed, and joked with each other.[30]

Sergeant Paradis of the 80th Company remembered that the scenery of the French countryside heightened the speculation and theories as to their destination. Peering out of gaps in the tarp-covered vehicle and through the clouds of dust, the tall structures of Paris came into view. "We could see the Eiffel Tower in the distance as we passed the deadly serious long range gun emplacements and watched French engineers building hasty sand bag protections around the guns."[31]

The morning and afternoon journey over bumpy roads created sore backs, and aching tail ends for the men of the 80th Company, and the vehicles' solid rubber tires compounded these conditions. Paradis, seeking relief from the rough seat, removed his helmet from his head and situated underneath his buttocks to provide, if only for a moment, a buffer to escape the bruising effects of the hard planked seats.[32]

The trucks ferrying the 95th Company, 1st Battalion, 6th Marines stopped shortly to allow the men to stretch. Some Marines ate the little bit of hardtack or corned beef they still had and drank the now-cold coffee they kept in their canteens. The respite was brief. "We were soon off again," remembered twenty-one-year-old Corporal Warren Richard Jackson, a former student at the Texas State Teachers College, from Runge, Texas, "and those ahead of us whipped a cloud of dust into our faces."[33]

The afternoon sun warmed the back of the tarp-covered compartment as men sought relief from the heat, and their thick wool tunics compounded their discomfort. French batteries of heavy artillery that were zeroing their guns with muzzles pointed in the direction northeast occupied the roadways to the east along the outskirts of Paris. "That seemed strange, placing guns fifty or more miles behind the front," Jackson thought.[34]

Since the vehicles assigned to the 2nd Engineers arrived especially late that morning, the regiment did not depart until 11:00 A.M., and by that time, the warm afternoon sun displaced the morning chill, adding to the misery of the journey. The precious water in canteens was the only relief from not only the heat but also the dust churned up by the vehicles, which stuck to sweaty faces like paste. This suffocating powder invaded the men's eyes, nostrils, and mouths, which turned saliva to grimy-gray spit.

Company A, 5th Machine Gun Battalion, forced to move by foot overland towards the railyard due to a shortage of trucks, stretched their ranks into two columns on each side of the road with the rest of the battalion. The sun, peaking in the mid-morning sky, bore down on the men. Sweat ran down their foreheads and caught every speck of dust kicked up by the endless stream of passing vehicles. The companies of the battalion finally reached the railhead by the early afternoon but waited several more hours for the first trains.

May 30th -31st Chapter II

Once the locomotive arrived, troops herded mules strapped with gear up ramps into the boxcars followed by carts, wagons, caissons, and rolling kitchens. Within eighteen minutes, the company managed to load all their equipment. First Lieutenant Wendell Westover remembered, "Travel rations had been issued and canteens filled. The men filed into the cars. Signals gave clearance, and the train was off, gathering speed until it became evident that this was no ordinary movement of troops."[35] As the convoys raced east towards the outskirts of Paris, the view of rural French countryside disappeared in the sheet of dust stirred up by the endless train of camions.

Battalion convoys eventually bunched up on the roadways. Men, who by mid-morning and early afternoon, endured near torturous cramped conditions for several hours, were dying for the vehicles to stop if only for a minute to stretch their legs. By mid-morning, the column of trucks carrying the members of the 1st Battalion, 6th Marines was near the outskirts of Paris. Riding in the front seat of the camion occupied by members of his platoon, twenty-three-year-old Sergeant Gerald Carthrae Thomas of the 75th Company took notice of the suburban landscape.

French-speaking natives of Indochina drove these vehicles from the French colonial holding of Southeast Asia and communication between them, and their American passengers proved difficult. Thomas, shouting over the hum of the engine, asked the driver about the battalion's destination, but "he didn't know any more French than I did," remembered Thomas.[36] After some improvised communication methods, he finally learned that the convoy was currently passing through the northeastern suburbs of Paris.

While the 2nd Division motored towards the battlefront, The French 6th Army monitored the latest news and developments coming from crumbling French units along the front. The day before, senior French officers concluded that the German breakthrough along the Chemin des Dames seemed particularly successful in the regions of Soissons, which is what compelled them to direct Major General Bundy's 2nd Division to concentrate near the city of Meaux. Colonel Brown and members of Bundy's staff preceded the rest of the 2nd Division convoys to the destination.

Once in the heart of Paris, Brown visited the U.S. Provost Marshal's office and telephoned the U.S. 1st Corps headquartered in Neufchâteau, France, to inform them of the division's departure and requested the delivery of necessary ammunition and supplies to Meaux—a massive logistical undertaking.[37]

From Paris, Brown and the division staff continued east of Paris towards the French 6th Army headquarters in Trilport, France located adjacent to Meaux. Once there, Brown met with General Denis Duchêne, in hopes of receiving better clarity on instructions regarding the general's desired disposition of the approaching 2nd Division. The situation, however, remained so chaotic for the French that Duchêne had nothing further beyond the orders already issued that directed the Americans to concentrate at Meaux where they would fall under the command of the French 7th Corps. Furthermore, Brown, having just passed through Meaux, saw the immense traffic congestion of escaping refugees and realized the severe obstacle this posed to the division's convoys.

After studying the maps sprawled on a table in Duchêne's office, Brown suggested the convoys should travel the numerous roads that veered around the city so they could instead concentrate at May-en-Multien just eighteen kilometers northeast of Meaux. Unflinchingly, Duchêne concurred with Brown's suggestion and the meeting concluded. Brown traveled back east to Meaux to intercept the eventual arrival of the division and direct them further to May-en-Multien. He perhaps felt less assured than ever following his meeting with the commander of the 6th Army.

Colonel Preston Brown was the chief of staff for the 2nd Division. Photo credit: Chuck Thomas.

Regardless of the uncertainty and the vagueness of Duchêne's plans, the massive convoys of the 2nd Division were in route with more than 26,000 troops who would be seeking further orders.

---

[1] History of the 9th Infantry, Box 48, RG 120.9.3, Records of the American Expeditionary Forces, NARA College Park, MD.
[2] The unpublished diary of Leo Joseph Bailey *The War as I Saw It* as found in the Leo Joseph Bailey Collection, AFC/2001/001/76979, Veterans History Project, American Folklife Center, Library of Congress, Washington, D.C.
[3] Correspondence Upton to his wife 10 June 1918, Upton papers, MHS, St. Paul, MN.
[4] Oliver Spauling and John Wright, *The Second Division American Expeditionary Force in France 1917-1919*, (New York: Hillman Press, 1937), 250.
[5] Ibid.
[6] Ibid.
[7] Westover, *Suicide Battalions*, 99.
[8] Albert Powis, "A Leatherneck in France 1917-1919," *Military Images Magazine*, September-October, 1981, 12.
[9] *Diary of Peter Wood*, N.P., Entry for May 31, 1918, Author's collection.

[10] T. J. Curtis Jr., Captain USMC, *History of the Sixth Machine Gun Battalion, Fourth Brigade, U.S. Marines, Second Division and Its Participation in the Great War.* (Neuweid on the Rhine: N.P.), 13.

[11] Diary of William W. Fullington, Pvt. USMC June 12, 1917- August 13, 1919, Personal Papers collection, Alfred M. Gray Research Library, Quantico, VA.

[12] Messersmith, *Operations of 78th Company Sixth Regiment Marines at Belleau Wood,* MCoE, Donovan Research Library.

[13] Levi E. Hemrick, *Once a Marine,* (New York: Carlton Press, Inc., 1968), 90.

[14] Donald V. Paradis, *The World War I Memoirs of Don V. Paradis, Gunnery Sergeant USMC*, ed. Lt. Col. Peter Owen (Lulu, 2010), 37.

[15] Messersmith, *Operations of 78th Company Sixth Regiment Marines at Belleau Wood,* MCoE, Donovan Research Library.

[16] Wise and Frost, *A Marine Tells it to You,* 192.

[17] Cooke, "We Can Take It, We Attack," *Infantry Journal,* 2.

[18] Ibid.

[19] Ibid..

[20] Brown and Geores, *55th Co. Marines in World War I*, Box 55, RG 127, NARA, Washington, D.C.

[21] Ibid.

[22] Ibid.

[23] Cooke, "We Can Take It, We Attack," *Infantry Journal,* 2.

[24] Wise and Frost, *A Marine Tells it to You,* 192.

[25] Gordon, *Leathernecks and Doughboys,* 52.

[26] Brown and Geores, *55th Co. Marines in World War I*, Box 55, RG 127, NARA, Washington, D.C.

[27] Alfred Schiani, *A Former Marine tells it like it was and is,* (New York: Carlton Press Inc., 1988), 22.

[28] Scarbrough *They Called us Devil Dogs,* N.P.

[29] Ibid.

[30] Captain John West, *Belleau Wood*, n.d., Personal Papers collection, Alfred M. Gray Research Library, Quantico, VA.

[31] Paradis, *The World War I Memoirs of Don V. Paradis, 37.*

[32] Ibid.

[33] Warren R. Jackson, *His Time in Hell, A Texas Marine in France: The World War I Memoir of Warren R. Jackson*, ed. by George Clark, (Novato, CA: 2001), 87, and Official Military Personnel File for Corporal Warren R. Jackson, Official Military Personnel Files, 1905 – 1998, RG 127, NPRC St. Louis, MO.

[34] Ibid.
[35] Westover, *Suicide Battalions,* 100.
[36] General Gerald B. Thomas, interview by Robert Asprey, June 11, 1963, Transcript, Personal Papers collection, Alfred M. Gray Research Library, Quantico, VA.
[37] John W. Thomason, *Second Division Northwest of Chateau Thierry, 1 June-10 July 1918,* (Washington: National War College, 1928), Unpublished manuscript, Alfred M. Gray Research Library, Quantico, VA.

May 30th -31st Chapter III

The procession was noiseless for the marchers were too miserable to more than glance at us as we passed and probably thought 'a few more for the boche to devour.'
-Corporal Leo Joseph Bailey Company M, 3rd Battalion, 9th Infantry

Far ahead of the convoys carrying the men of the 4th Brigade, their commander, Brigadier General James Harbord arrived in the town of Meaux with his staff, Major Harry Lay, First Lieutenant Richard Norris Williams, the Harvard tennis star and Titanic survivor, as well as the French interpreter Martin Legasse.[1] Hoping to connect with officers from the French 6th Army to gain some clarity on the brigade's disposition, the staff found the city in complete disorder.

The vehicle carrying Harbord slowed in the wave of human traffic traveling over the town's cobblestone streets. Harbord and his staff found no sign of any French high command in the city, and this led to a two-hour delay before they could secure definitive information. Harbord's group also arrived before Colonel Brown and elements of the division staff could inform them of the decision to concentrate at May-en-Multien rather than Meaux.

Major Harry Lay served as the adjutant for the 4th Brigade. Photo credit: U.S. Army Heritage and Education Center.

When the brigade staff finally connected with their French liaisons, they received the latest developments. According to Major Harry R. Lay, "We learned the Germans had penetrated the French lines and were advancing on Paris by way of Meaux. We accordingly were ordered to take position and guard the railroad about eight kilometers north of May-en-Multien."[2] Harbord recalled, "The Germans were said to be not far away and we might expect to be attacked before morning."[3]

The designated positions placed the regiments of the brigade west of the Ourcq River, which ran northeast out of the town of Meaux. With this information, Harbord's brigade staff swiftly departed, and as they proceeded north out of the city of Meaux, they encountered the initial flood of civilian and military traffic fleeing the area.

On the outskirts of Meaux, many Marines experienced, for the first time, this byproduct of war. The massive line of trucks nearing the edge of the town ran into the bottlenecked roadway as streams of refugees passed. Camions stammered bumper to bumper along the edge of the road to yield to the mass of refugees passing on the other side. The congestion grew worse as the vehicles moved further east.

Around noon, the camions carrying the officers of the 18th Company, 2nd Battalion, 5th Marines ran into the first wave of fleeing civilians. "Peasants mostly, people of the soil," recalled First Lieutenant Cooke.[4] "Driven from the land, they carried their remaining possessions with them."[5] Livestock labored to haul rickety carts weighed down with as many material necessities as could be loaded in the final moments before these civilians evacuated their homes.

Some carried in their arms the last material vestiges of lives left behind. Men of the 2nd Division ignored their discomfort when the tired and haggard faces of these unfortunate victims of war greeted the convoys with a half-hearted cheer.

Most of the refugees, however, passed in a macabre silence. The convoy carrying the 1st Battalion, 5th Marines also encountered the depressing spectacle west of Meaux. "The heartbreaking sights in and near Meaux were enough to set anyone's blood boiling," remembered Private Onnie Cordes of the 17th Company.[6]

Corporal Frank Matheny, of the 17th Company, recalled how badly the traffic debilitated their pace. "It was a tangle. When we unloaded, we could hardly turn around because of the congestion of traffic. The French were retreating while the Americans were trying to get up there. Everything seemed balled up."[7] In the refugee crowds, platoons tried desperately to assemble and account for their men.

By 2:00 P.M. Lieutenant Colonel Frederic Wise's 2nd Battalion, 5th Marines entered Meaux only to find that the refugee situation had worsened. Wise's staff car stopped, and the French driver immediately exited the vehicle—disappearing out of sight. The battalion convoy remained at a standstill off to the side of the road as Wise impatiently waited nearly half an hour before his French driver returned with definitive information stating that the battalion should proceed out of Meaux and head northeast about twenty-two kilometers to the town of May-en-Multien.[8]

As they departed Meaux, they found the streets north of the town packed with the vanquished residents of the surrounding countryside. Wise noticed that "All looked terror-stricken."[9] Twenty-five-year-old Private Jerry Martin Davin, an automatic rifleman with the 55th Company, vividly recalled the scene:

> I shall never forget the many things I saw on the hike and ride up there, yes I thought and wondered at that time if I would live to tell it all, well there were auto trucks three abreast two going up with

soldiers, and one coming down, cavalry, artillery, and everything. Refugees were coming back by the hundreds. Old women pushing carts, girls driving cattle and sheep and here and there a cow or a horse belonging to some poor old man or women would get struck by a truck, the people wouldn't know what to do, and someone would come along and drag them to one side of the road.[10]

As Wise's battalion traveled beyond Meaux, the sea of civilians seemed to dissipate enough that the convoy maintained a steady pace. Second Lieutenant Fred H. Becker of the 18th Company could not ignore the gnawing hunger cramping his stomach and reached into the box full of sandwiches that some forward-thinking soul loaded into the back of the vehicle earlier that morning.

Becker quickly dispelled the gloomy silence as he passed the sandwiches out to everyone. About that time, an officer in the front seat looked back over his shoulder and, shouting over the noisy engine, summoned the attention of thirty-four-year-old Joseph Daniel Murray, a Captain with the 43rd Company from Concord, Massachusetts. With an outstretched arm, the officer handed Murray a stack of papers and shouted, "If I don't come out of this, will you send these papers home to my wife?"[11] The sullenness of such a request quickly sent everyone else's mind back to the thought of home.

Becker paused with a sandwich suspended halfway to his mouth as the disconsolate idea of death set in. With his appetite suddenly suppressed, Becker proclaimed silently, "I'm not as hungry as I thought I was."[12] He sat back in his seat deep in the thought of his own mortality.

Behind the rest of the 5th Marines, the convoy of Major Benjamin Berry's 3rd Battalion approached Meaux from the west. After the rapture of the movement wore off, twenty-one-year old Private Frank Maurice Jacob of the 47th Company realized the severity of the situation upon his first encounter with the flood of escaping refugees. "Of all the pathetic scenes I ever witnessed, the scenes I saw on this trip to the front were the most pitiful."[13]

Soon these refugees intermixed with French soldiers who had long shed uniforms upon fleeing the battlefront. Jacob and his comrades, enraged and heartbroken by the scene of these subjugated souls, vowed that the enemy would feel the wrath of justice. "Hatred for the Hun increased with every mile, till we could hardly wait for a chance to strike our blow at him," Jacob recalled.[14] Most Americans who witnessed this tragic exodus along that stretch of narrow French highway just outside of Meaux reciprocated the anger felt by Jacob as they stared into the gaunt eyes of France's displaced populace.

May 30th -31st Chapter III

The 6th Machine Gun Battalion, traveling with twenty-two men per truck along with their machine guns and tripods, made the journey along the traffic-congested roads toward Meaux particularly uncomfortable. Twenty-two-year-old Sergeant Arthur Clifford of the 23rd Company recalled, "After about three hours of riding, the outfit looked as though it had come out of a flour barrel, as there had been no rain for over a month and you may have some idea of the dust. Hour after hour we rode that way with but a stop of ten minutes every four hours."[15] Near Meaux, the battalion also encountered the stream of refugees. Twenty-four-year-old Corporal Daniel Edward Morgan, a member of the 77th Company from Edwardsville, Pennsylvania, recalled:

> As we neared the battle area, we witnessed the most horrible sights that up to that time had ever greeted our eyes. We saw hundreds of old men, old women and little children carrying in their hands loaves of bread, chickens, rabbits and pieces of bed clothing, or pushing barrows with all of their life's possessions in them. We were crowded upon trucks, and without any possibility of rest, traveled for thirty hours, seventy-two miles, to the scene of battle.[16]

During the arduous journey of the 9th Infantry, the vehicles of 3rd Battalion got separated from the convoy, and the increasing civilian traffic hindered their efforts to reunite with the regiment until nightfall.[17] "The last ten or fifteen miles of our run on motor trucks took us past refugees in groups, all headed south and a more pathetic spectacle I have never seen," recalled Colonel LaRoy Upton.[18] "I saw one poor woman in the last big town we passed through who was nursing a baby and sitting on a sidewalk with her back against the building; her sole belongings were in the baby carriage, by which stood another child about six years old."[19] The civilian consequences of war suddenly became all too real for the rest of the 9th Infantry who were shocked at the spectacle.

Twenty-three-year-old Corporal Leo Joseph Bailey, a native of Mansfield, Pennsylvania, with Company M, 3rd Battalion, 9th Infantry, remembered the silent despair of the passing refugees. "The procession was noiseless for the marchers were too miserable to more than glance at us as we passed and probably thought 'a few more for the boche to devour.'"[20] The disheartening retreat of the combat-seasoned French compelled some young Americans to question their ability to stop the onslaught.

By 4:30 P.M., the 9th Infantry stopped in the town of Meaux. The men quickly dismounted the vehicles and fell into formation along the side of the road. After a quick roll call, the long columns of the regiment marched north beyond the town. Along the way, they encountered the defeated French army. "We had nothing except what we had on our backs," recalled

May 30th -31st Chapter III

Upton, "and we soon began to pass French troops and trains. It soon became evident that too much wine had been looted from the villages."[21] The rapidly changing situation along the front thoroughly confused the commanders of the French 6th Army as evidenced by the chaos that ensued upon the arrival of the 9th Infantry. From the time Upton's men entered Meaux until 11:30 P.M., the 9th Infantry received six different sets of conflicting orders.[22]

North of Meaux, the 2nd Battalion, 5th Marines rolled into a ransacked village of May-en-Multien by about 6:00 P.M., The officer in the front seat of First Lieutenant Elliott Cooke's camion, turned his head back toward the rear of the truck and announced the name of the town as May-en-Multien. The convoy ambled over the cobblestone street in a jerky stop-and-go motion as the groggy and tired men sitting in the back jostled side-to-side into each other's shoulders until the long file of camions ground to a halt.

Twenty-four-year-old First Lieutenant Gilder Davis Jackson of Dover, Delaware, peered over the side of the truck bed to catch a glimpse of what other vehicles were doing. "They're unloading," he muttered.[23] Officers walking up and down the row of trucks slapped the sides of the vehicle beds and barked out orders for the men to dismount. Stiff joints slowed their efforts and drew the impatient attention of sergeants who hurried everyone along in the curt fashion unique to Marine noncommissioned officers. Platoon sergeants, competing with the roar of the passing convoy, shouted off names on their rosters to account for their men.

As the last Marines left the beds of the camions, drivers wasted no time getting the long procession of trucks turned around to move back west. The bypassing vehicles spewed one last cloud of dust into the battalion as they struggled to hear the names summoned during the roll call over the rumbling procession of trucks racing out of the village.

Lieutenant Colonel Wise's staff car had not come to a full stop before he jumped out into the town's center where an officer from division headquarters greeted him with verbal orders for the battalion to hike fifteen kilometers east towards the village of Gandelu.[24] The Marines, thankful to escape the confinement of the camions, looked inquisitively at platoon commanders for the next bit of information.[25]

The order to move out prompted the abrupt action of platoon commanders to get their men on the road without even a moment to rest. Against the background of a lowering evening sun, the battalion divided into columns and marched indolently under the weight of gear bearing down on legs fatigued from hours of travel in crowded vehicles. The battalion had been without food for hours, and hunger gnawed at their innards every step of the hike.

The horizon echoed with the distant sounds of war as men recognized the hollow cannonade of artillery and the faint rattle of machine gun fire, audible far off to the northwest.[26] They knew nothing of their destination but carried on in the uninformed state of existence that belongs to the enlisted man.

The column marched with as much vigor as they could muster after their long, exhaustive day. About an hour into the hike, the distant buzz of a motorcycle approaching from behind attracted their attention. The bike raced passed the rear of the column and showered the men with dust as it rushed toward the battalion staff. Eventually catching up to Wise at the ahead of the battalion, the motorcycle courier brought word that their destination of Gandelu had already fallen into German hands and that they should return at once back to May-en-Multien.[27] The news crossed the threshold of Wise's frustration, and he fervently protested the order. Cooke watched just within earshot as Wise engaged in a heated dialogue with the motorcycle messenger.

Evidentially frustrated by what he perceived as running from the fight, Wise vehemently disputed his case with the hapless officer in his signature abrasive manner. While Wise escalated the impassioned exchange, the hum of another engine drew the men's attention. "Just then an automobile, a long, low, horizon-blue affair, came skittering up, its wheels showering us with gravel," remembered Cooke.[28] "The occupants were Frenchmen, but Wise and all the rest of us could see that they were neither lieutenants nor noncoms. They were too heavily covered with stars, gold braid, medals and mean looks. Besides, they did all the talking."[29]

The exchange with these senior commanders convinced Wise to go back to May-en-Multien. He indignantly ordered the long battalion column to about-face and moved them back south. The men, mostly oblivious to the reasons behind such conflicting orders, languorously turned around and trudged back the other direction as the last sliver of sunlight fell away behind the western skyline. Cooke recalled, "Behind us the velvet blackness of the horizon flowered into flames, marking the advance of oncoming Germans. The glow of burning houses, haystacks, and ammunition dumps cast grotesque night shadows which mingled with the column and dogged our steps."[30]

Men cursed under their breath and plodded along in a demoralized stupor. The troops grew frustrated and now questioned the reason for the urgency which brought them to the battle front to face the enemy, but directives sent down from the top seemed to do everything to keep them from the fight. With the distant sounds of war at their backs, the men marched with renewed perseverance under the abrasive and unsympathetic urging of sergeants and officers who shared the same frustration.

While Wise's men headed back to May-en-Multien, Private Alfred Schiani, separated from the 18th Company earlier that morning when the convoy left him as he took advantage of a brief stop to answer nature's call, continued his panicked efforts to return to the company. "I had no idea where my outfit was going, nor the means to get there, but after hiking, stealing rides, and asking questions as to where the outfit was headed, I learned where Headquarters was located," recalled Schiani.[31]

After a morning and afternoon of wandering towards the front and perhaps fearful of the retribution awaiting him, he walked into the facilities that he believed served as a headquarters. Inside he found a sea of officers clustered around a large map. When one of them looked up and noticed the baby-faced Marine, he mistook Schiani to be a runner with a message and immediately inquired about his presence.

Seeking any helpful insight in getting back to his unit, Schiani delicately described his situation, but before he could complete his explanation, the impatient officer incredulously screamed, "Get the hell out of here, and get back to your outfit, immediately."[32] Schiani quickly vacated the room and soon located some men more sympathetic to his plight. They gave him what scant information they had regarding the disposition of units, but Schiani's journey to reunite with the 18th went on for the remainder of the late afternoon and into the evening.

By the time Colonel Paul Bernard Malone's 23rd Infantry passed through Meaux, a French cavalry unit, fleeing the battlefront, joined the civilian traffic in their mass exodus to the west.[33] The same tragic scene encountered by the rest of the division entering Meaux also greeted Malone's troops as they passed. "Opposite the road an old woman of 80 years perhaps was seen with a child of five and all that was left of her belongings were in a small basket, while the tears streamed down her face. The horrors of war were never more pathetically represented."[34]

Colonel Paul Malone commanded the 23rd Infantry. Photo credit: NARA.

By dusk, soldiers of the 3rd Battalion, 23rd Infantry disembarked their vehicles and marched toward their allotted sector. The front lines were not far since "the sound of hostile cannon could be plainly heard to the north and the sky was lurid with the pyrotechnics employed by the enemy either as signal lights or to illuminate the avenues of advance. The wildest rumors were current."³⁵ The distant cannonade fueled the conjecture among those going into combat for the first time.

According to Corporal Frank W. Anderson of Company M, 3ʳᵈ Battalion, 23ʳᵈ Infantry, "There was much confusion; thirty thousand men were here."³⁶ The battalion, marching in columns along the congested roadway, soon intermixed with elements of the 5ᵗʰ Marines disembarking vehicles along the roadside outside May-en-Multien. The soldiers of the 3ʳᵈ Battalion pushed and waded through the civilian traffic and managed to move clear of the 5ᵗʰ Marines crowding the roads as they debussed. Frustrated officers tried desperately to get some definitive information regarding the desired disposition of their men—a dilemma further complicated by the darkness of night.

Captain James Green Jr., a 1917 West Point graduate commanding Company M, somehow managed to summon his troops in the midst of the traffic. They hastily formed up along the roadway and hiked north to get away from the vast crowd. "My company was marched to a field," remembered Anderson, "and we stacked arms and waited for a couple of hours for further orders."³⁷ The men eagerly used the inactivity to rest not knowing if the next few days would offer a respite.

So far, every order the 2ⁿᵈ Division received from the French, which ultimately filtered down to the brigades and regiments, emanated from the latest intelligence regarding the most dangerous enemy concentration. Earlier that afternoon, the German advance toward Meaux began diminishing compared to a new and determined push in the region of Chateau Thierry.

This new threat developed in an area significantly southeast of the 2ⁿᵈ Division's destination. This region also fell within the operational control of the French 21ˢᵗ Corps. This situation forced the French 6ᵗʰ Army to redirect the approaching 2ⁿᵈ Division, who were well on their way to their original destination at Meaux, and move them to the most-threatened area by concentrating at the town of Montreuil-aux-Lions. Consequently, this meant the Americans went from the command of the French 7ᵗʰ Corps to the French 21ˢᵗ Corps operating in the vicinity of Montreuil-aux-Lions.³⁸

This development, detailed in Field Order 5, was relayed to the 2ⁿᵈ Division at 5:00 P.M. but did not arrive until 7:40 P.M. leaving only enough time to intercept and re-direct troop trains still in route to Meaux.³⁹ Several of the battalion convoys, however, were already north of Meaux and converging on May-en-Multien either by vehicle or on foot; notably, elements of the 5ᵗʰ Marines. Locating and informing the scattered battalions of the 5ᵗʰ Marines took much of the night. Since most of the 6ᵗʰ Marines departed Chaumont-en-Vexin well behind the rest of the division earlier that morning, they approached Meaux after the division had received Field Order Number 5, and were re-routed to Montreuil-aux-Lions without delay.

May 30th -31st Chapter III

For the men of Colonel Catlin's regiment, however, re-directing the convoys kept the men in the back of cramped camions for several more hours.

The town hall in the village of Montreuil-aux-Lions seen on the right served as the Headquarters for the 2nd Division. Photo credit: Author's collection.

---

[1] Harbord, *The American Army in France*, 275-76.
[2] Major Harry Lay Interview by Joel D. Thacker Muster Roll Section Headquarters U.S.M.C., Dec. 11, 1918, Box 42, RG 127 Records of the Marine Corps, NARA Washington D.C.
[3] James G. Harbord, *Leaves from a War Diary*, (New York: Dodd, Mead & Company), 287.
[4] Cooke, "We Can Take It, We Attack," *Infantry Journal*, 2.
[5] Ibid.
[6] Cordes, *The Immortal Division*, 6.
[7] Scrapbook of Silverthorn, Newspaper clipping, "Minneapolis Man Tells of His days in Belleau Woods," Marie Silverthorn.
[8] Wise and Frost, *A Marine Tells it to You*, 192.
[9] Ibid.
[10] *Diary of Jerry Davin 55th Company, 5th Marines*, N.P. Entry date, Author's collection.
[11] Cooke, "We Can Take It, We Attack," *Infantry Journal*, 3.
[12] Ibid.
[13] Craig Hamilton and Louise Corbin, *Echoes From Over There, Stories Written by Soldiers Who Fought Over There*, (New York: The Soldiers' Publishing Company, 1919), 46.
[14] Ibid.
[15] Correspondence Arthur Clifford to Mabel 20 June 1918, Personal Papers collection, Alfred M. Gray Research Library, Quantico, VA.

[16] Daniel E. Morgan, *When the World Went Mad, A Thrilling Story of the Late War, Told in the Language of the Trenches,* (Boston: Christopher Publishing House, 1931), 27.
[17] Thomason, *Second Division Northwest of Chateau Thierry,* Unpublished manuscript, Alfred M. Gray Research Library, Quantico, VA.
[18] Correspondence LaRoy S. Upton to his wife Agnes 10 June 1918, LaRoy S. Upton papers, MHS, St. Paul, MN.
[19] Ibid.
[20] Diary of Leo Joseph Bailey *The War as I Saw It,* Bailey Collection, AFC/2001/001/76979, Library of Congress, Washington, D.C.
[21] Correspondence LaRoy S. Upton to his wife Agnes 10 June 1918, LaRoy S. Upton papers, MHS, St. Paul, MN.
[22] Ibid.
[23] Cooke, "We Can Take It, We Attack," *Infantry Journal,* 3.
[24] Wise and Frost, *A Marine Tells it to You,* 194.
[25] Cooke, "We Can Take It, We Attack," *Infantry Journal,* 3.
[26] Ibid.
[27] Wise and Frost, *A Marine Tells it to You,* 194.
[28] Cooke, "We Can Take It, We Attack," *Infantry Journal,* 3.
[29] Ibid.
[30] Ibid.
[31] Schiani, *A Former Marine tells it like it was and is,* 22.
[32] Ibid.
[33] Spaulding and Wright, *The Second Division American Expeditionary Force in France 1917-1919,* 250.
[34] *Headquarters, Twenty Third Infantry A.E.F, France, July 14, 1918, Operations of the 2nd Division (Regular),* Box 54, RG 120.9.3, Records of the American Expeditionary Forces, NARA College Park, MD.
[35] Ibid.
[36] Spaulding and Wright, *The Second Division American Expeditionary Force in France 1917-1919,* 250.
[37] Ibid, 250-51.
[38] Spauling and Wright, *The Second Division American Expeditionary Force in France 1917-1919,* 40.
[39] *Records of the Second Division (Regular)* Volume 1, N.P.

JUNE 1ST

June 1st Chapter I

Needless to say, we were all fully aware of the fact that a great battle was being fought or else a lot of unnecessary noise was being made up there a few miles ahead.
 -Private James Hatcher 84th Company, 3rd Battalion, 6th Marines

The abbreviated nights of northern France once again meshed into a blur of dust clouds and exhaustion for Company A, 5th Machine Gun Battalion who marched throughout the night. The sun, visible through the haze-covered eastern sky on the morning of June 1, 1918, went virtually unnoticed by the columns of worn out soldiers hiking in a catatonic-like state of mind. To them, the days and nights seemed to blend after hours without much sleep. First Lieutenant William Westover recalled:

And with the coming of the light, we met a sad procession. Mile after mile, they passed as the column moved forward. Refugees from the invaded territory. Tired, hopeless, haggard-their faces mask-like in their graven sorrow. Old men, old women; mothers with babes at their breasts; children; cattle, pigs, horses, donkeys, sheep, chickens, dogs; a heterogeneous assembly that traveled by such means as was at hand.[1]

There was silent empathy for those displaced civilians. Men, too physically exhausted to vocalize their pity, looked upon those tragic masses as they filed passed. "Few tears were shed, few lips quivered; no laments rose above the tramp of feet. But all eyes of both columns were soft with understanding," recalled Westover.[2] The severity of the situation became even more evident to many of the young Americans who, for the first time, laid eyes upon war's innocent and desperate masses driven from their ancestral homesteads.[3]

The troops of the 5th Machine Gun battalion faced a long day of marching ahead of them. They needed to cover nearly thirty kilometers on foot. The cresting sun added to their misery and hinted to the impending afternoon heat. Westover remembered, "Dust parched the mouths of men and horses. Still we moved along, the men leaning forward the better to balance the weight of the packs on their shoulders, the animals straining at the traces, feet dragging, wheels crunching as they rolled over the hard stone roads. Officers were walking now, alternating their horses among those most weary."[4] Despite the pending battle, the exhaustion and fatigue obscured the minds of the men of Company B, 5th Machine Gun Battalion.

By 4:30 A.M., Brigadier General Harbord, after a few hours' rest, departed May-en-Multien with his staff. The lead elements of his brigade were on the twenty-three kilometer stretch of road between May-en-Multien

June 1st Chapter I

Major General Harbord (seated) seen with his staff. Standing left to right: Major Harry Lay, Brigade Adjutant; Holland McTyeire Smith, Administrative Officer; First Lieutenant Fielding Slaughter Robinson, Aide-de-Camp; First Lieutenant Richard Norris Williams; Martin Legasse, French Interpreter. Photo credit: NARA.

and Montreuil-aux-Lions. Just west of Montreuil-aux-Lions, he found elements of the 6th Marines resting on the side of the road trying to start cooking fires. Harbord's vehicle passed through Montreuil-aux-Lions and continued nearly six kilometers toward the headquarters of the French 21st Corps in the village of Coupru. Just west of the road junction that led south to Coupru, Harbord approached the rear of the long column of 9th Infantry soldiers closing in on the threatened area. The city of Coupru stood just twelve kilometers west of the threatened city of Chateau Thierry.

Winding through the narrow streets of Coupru, Harbord's vehicle stopped outside the building serving as the headquarters of the French 21st Corps. According to Harbord, "At Coupru, a little after six o'clock, I found General Degoutte. He seemed very glad to see us and—[Lieutenant Richard Norris] Williams doing all the interpreting—quickly inquired: 'Where are your troops, General?'"[5] Assuredly, Harbord told his French counterpart that elements of the division were on the Paris-Metz road heading this direction, and in fact, the 9th Infantry was not far. "Have you any instructions for me," inquired Harbord.[6] The General's solemn gaze preceded his dismal and sincere assessment of the situation, and he explained to Harbord:

> Things have been going badly with us. They have been pressing us since the morning of the 27th and have advanced over fifty kilometers in seventy-two hours. I know that your men need rest. Let them get something to eat. If it can be avoided, I shall not call on you today. But it may become necessary. Your troops must be ready to go into the line any time after 11:00 if called on.[7]

Behind Harbord, elements of his brigade were slowly approaching. As Major Thomas Holcomb's 2nd Battalion, 6th Marines neared Montreuil-aux-Lions, the 3rd Platoon, 79th Company commanded by twenty-one-year-old Second Lieutenant John Albert West, a graduate of the University of Michigan, rolled along at a sluggish pace against the mass waves of fleeing civilians continuing their evacuation throughout the night.

Broken down vehicles further funneled the caravan on already congested roads. "Everyone was tired but there was no sleep in a jostling, rabbling, crowded truck," recalled West.[8] By dawn, the long convoy of the 2nd Battalion pulled into the town of Montreuil-aux-Lions. Men wearily escaped the confines of crowded vehicles, handing down rifles to comrades and tossing their packs to the ground before leaping from the truck beds. They found relief standing on stiff and seemingly hollow legs.

The faint thud of distant artillery fire reverberating through the village and echoed off town's abandoned buildings, but it could not arouse Holcomb's men from their sleep-deprived listlessness. The fighting was only a few kilometers to the east, but it may as well have been on another planet, for all they thought of was food and sleep, and the serenity of the desolate town was conducive to such desires.

Colonel Albertus Catlin remembered the feeble state of his exhausted regiment:

> Our Marines rode on those camions from nineteen to thirty hours, according to their luck in reaching their destination. Some got lost and had to hike with their sixty-pound packs. When they arrived they were grey with dust and hollow-eyed with fatigue. They looked more like miners emerging from an all-night shift than like fresh troops ready to plunge into battle.[9]

Holcomb's 2nd Battalion enjoyed the rest but knew they could move out at any moment. According to Sergeant Don Paradis, a battalion runner for Holcomb, "We runners were sent from Major Holcomb to each company commander with orders to billet his men in the vacant houses of that town,

June 1st Chapter I

keeping them under cover and standing by for further orders."¹⁰ Paradis and his battalion runners, too tired to forage for food, took up refuge in an empty house near Holcomb's temporary billet and soon went to sleep. Throughout the town, residents left behind uneaten meals on tables. Linens still hung in yards. Livestock roamed throughout abandoned properties where unsecured stable gates revealed the urgency with which the populace fled.

The men immediately entered the village's uninhabited homes, barns, and storefronts to forage for a decent meal. "The town was deserted and food, not sleep, was the objective," remembered West.¹¹ "Never have I been offered more chicken, rabbit, different vegetables than I was in the next few hours. In every house, men were helping themselves to a feast. Everyone seemed to know how to cook and the food was good."¹²

Sergeant Donald Paradis served with the 80th Company, 2nd Battalion, 6th Marines. Photo credit: Marine Corps History Division.

Twenty-three-year-old Corporal Glen Hill, a former schoolteacher from Rock Harbor, Washington, and his twenty-year-old brother Sidney, both attached to the 2nd Platoon, 79th Company, took full advantage of the available food stock. "We were told to use anything we could find for food. My brother and I who had camped out in the summer all our boyhood days found some rabbits which we cleaned and fried, also some vegetables which we cooked up. Here we struck up an acquaintance with a Lieutenant Osborne who was in a dental unit."¹³ Lieutenant Junior Grade Weedon Edward Osborne, a twenty-five-year-old dental officer from Chicago, Illinois, joined the battalion only two weeks earlier.

A delay in the arrival of Osborne's dental equipment overseas complicated his job as a dental officer, so he offered his services as a frontline medical officer. He was still serving in this capacity when the brigade pushed out for the front. Corporal Hill recalled, "He was quite lost at foraging so we took him and helped him get a hot meal and also filled up his mess kit so he would have something the next day."¹⁴ The sleep-deprived men of the 79th Company, with full stomachs, gave in to their exhaustion and fell asleep.

June 1st Chapter I

Members of the 78th Company also foraged for meals throughout the town. "Orders were given to get into the houses and to keep out of sight and sleep," recalled Captain Robert Messersmith commanding the 78th Company.[15] "However, the men soon found rabbits, potatoes, etc. and great was my surprise when my orderly brought me a meal fit for a king. The meal having been eaten, a vain effort to sleep was made."[16] Twenty-one year old Private Chester Frank Lancaster of Fredericksburg, Texas, and other members of the 78th Company immediately targeted the wine cellars in each house. They soon discovered most of the intoxicating spirits already gone, and only cider remained.[17]

By 6:00 A.M., the vehicles carrying the companies of the 1st Battalion, 6th Marines unloaded on the outskirts of Montreuil-aux-Lions. Several Marines, hallow-eyed from sleep deprivation, sought a decent place to nap, and others raided farmhouses for anything to eat. The 75th Company bivouacked near a patch of woods just off the road, but the men quickly headed for the empty houses and storefronts in search of food.

According to Private Gus Gulberg of the 75th Company, "The inhabitants had left a few hours before we came and we fell heir to everything they could not carry with them. The French officers told us to help ourselves to anything we wanted, because the Germans would get everything eventually. I heard one of the boys remark, 'Gee, that Frog officer ain't got much confidence in us, has he?'"[18]

The conversation among the men revealed no shortage of outlandish theories regarding the developing situation along the front. "Rumors were too numerous to recount," remembered Sergeant Gerald Thomas.[19] "All bore on the magnitude of the allied debacle and German success."[20] The disposition of the dejected French fed into the rumor mill.

The 95th Company held formation in the courtyard of an abandoned farmhouse inside Montreuil-aux-Lions. Tô the men's relief, officers gave them permission to unroll bedding and go to sleep. "The exhausted men were not too tired to eat," recalled Jackson.[21] "The place was alive with everything one could expect to find at the home of a wealthy farmer. French wine that had probably been in the cellar for a quarter century. The farm was alive with chickens, pigs, rabbits, and even young calves were soon slaughtered."[22] With their kill hung up for a later meal, most of the men in the company used the time to grab some sleep.

Forty-one-year-old Major Berton William Sibley's 3rd Battalion, 6th Marines arrived in Montreuil-aux-Lions following their twenty-four-hour venture in the back of crowded trucks. They too partook in the mass foraging of edibles throughout the village. Members of twenty-year-old Private James Ethelbert Hatcher's platoon of the 84th Company broke away from formation to seek out a dwelling for their momentary respite. "In the house which my platoon entered, a canary sang cheerfully in its cage, while Belgian hares, in their coops behind the house, had been forced to forgo

June 1st Chapter I

their morning breakfast."[23] The members of the platoon eagerly dropped their gear as if to stake their claim upon a choice spot to nap. Adjusting their packs for makeshift pillows, most of the men fell asleep and momentarily ignore the reality that they would be moving soon.

After an hour of welcomed sleep, Hatcher and some of the other men left the house. They felt temporarily liberated from the burden of gear that usually accompanied their every move. They came upon the village washhouse and immediately squatted down at the edge of the tarn. They reached wrist-deep into the cold water and brought their dripping hands to their face and necks to wash the dust from their skin.

The men encountered First Lieutenant Mark A. Smith at the edge of the washhouse basin. "He informed us that a great battle was being fought just ahead and that we were to stay near our quarter to be ready to move upon a moment's notice," recalled Hatcher.[24] Hatcher felt somewhat demeaned by Smith's obvious observation. "Needless to say, we were all fully aware of the fact that a great battle was being fought or else a lot of unnecessary noise was being made up there a few miles ahead."[25]

Behind the rest of Sibley's battalion, Corporal Havelock Nelson, who had been detached from the 97th Company to serve with battalion intelligence section, arrived in Montreuil-aux-Lions. As Nelson walked down one of the village streets, he spotted twenty-five-year-old Gunnery Sergeant Morris Calvin Richardson, a familiar face from the 97th Company. Richardson directed Nelson to his platoon located in a courtyard. Nelson recalled:

> I finally located an unoccupied room with a big feather bed in it and threw off my pack. Being hungry, my first thought was to find something to eat. However, if there had been any edibles left behind by the inhabitants of the houses searched by me, earlier arrivals had cleaned out everything. The only thing that even remotely resembled food were a couple cupsful of dried peas. These I carried back to where I had left my pack, with some vague idea that I might later find some means of cooking them.[26]

Behind the 6th Marine Regiment, the 6th Machine Gun Battalion closed in on Montreuil-aux-Lions. The battalion left May-en-Multien at 5:00 A.M. and encountered refugee traffic. Sergeant Peter Wood of the 81st Company remembered:

> Went up the road and one side was literally filled with soldiers of all kinds and military equipment while the other side was pretty full. People evacuating the town carrying all their earthly belongings in their arms on wagons, in wheelbarrows, in baby carriages and in

bags on their backs. Large flocks of sheep and cattle. Many aged men and women unable to stand it completely exhausted on the roadside. A sight I hope to never see again.[27]

The Caravan hauling members of the 77th Company also encountered the tragic civilian masses fleeing their homes. The Marines felt complete disdain for the enemy responsible for the displacement of these innocent souls of France. Twenty-year-old Corporal William Bridges Jackson, a former University of Denver student, recalled one scene that remained vividly embedded in his mind:

The people were exhausted and looked completely broken. This was the only time I saw refugees fleeing before an advancing enemy. It was a pitiful sight. Practically no young or middle-aged men. One very old lady gave up and sat down in the road on her bag. About that time, a 2-seat French staff car came down the road towards Meaux. The passenger was a French officer with a bloody bandage around his head. They reached the old lady—the car stopped—the officer got out, loaded the old lady and her bag in the seat. The officer sat down on the car hood and away they went. Gallantry was still alive.[28]

By 11:00 A.M., the 6th Machine Gun Battalion entered Montreuil-aux-Lions and found it occupied by members of the 6th Marines. "The villages were now vacated, with all their possessions, exactly as one would leave home on Saturday afternoon, to go shopping. The chickens were in the yard, the cattle in the field, the horses in the barn, and everything else that goes to make up life in a country village was in its usual place," remembered Corporal Daniel Morgan of the 77th Company.[29] "As we disembarked from the trucks we began to kill chickens and prepare food in the houses of the people that were journeying back to safety in the rear. Excitement was high."[30] Sergeant Wood recalled finding the real treasures of the abandoned village in the cellars of the vacated homes. Here wine, champagne, and cognac were the desired acquisitions of many foragers.

Brigadier General James Harbord and his staff left Coupru to head back to Montreuil-aux-Lions following his meeting with the commander of the French 21st Corps, fifty-two-year-old General Jean Marie Joseph Degoutte earlier that morning. Harbord's staff care drove slowly between the two seemingly endless columns of 9th Infantry soldiers on both sides of the road moving toward the front. Once he returned to Montreuil-aux-Lions, Harbord learned that the 5th Marines were far behind the rest of the brigade, which had arrived in Montreuil-aux-Lions hours earlier. Harbord could do nothing more but wait for further orders and the arrival of his 5th Marine

June 1st Chapter I

Regiment. He managed to secure some sought after hot coffee and a few slices of bread before retreating to an abandoned house to get a quick nap.

---

[1] Westover, *Suicide Battalions,* 101-102.
[2] Ibid, 102.
[3] Ibid.
[4] Ibid, 103.
[5] Harbord, *The American Army in France,,* 278.
[6] Ibid.
[7] Ibid.
[8] West, *Belleau Wood,* Alfred M. Gray Research Library, Quantico, VA.
[9] Catlin, *With the Help of God and a Few Marines,* 83.
[10] Paradis, *The World War I Memoirs of Don V. Paradis, 38.*
[11] West, *Belleau Wood,* Alfred M. Gray Research Library, Quantico, VA.
[12] Ibid.
[13] Correspondence from Glen Hill to G.M. Neufeld, 17 January 1979, Personal Papers collection, Alfred M. Gray Research Library, Quantico, VA.
[14] Ibid.
[15] Messersmith, *Operations of 78th Company Sixth Regiment Marines at Belleau Wood,* MCoE, Donovan Research Library.
[16] Ibid.
[17] Correspondence Chester Lancaster to Bob Queen 4 June 1976, Personal Papers collection, Alfred M. Gray Research Library, Quantico, VA.
[18] Gus Gulberg, *A War Diary,* (Chicago: Drake Press, 1927), 23.
[19] General Gerald B. Thomas memoir, Personal Papers collection, Alfred M. Gray Research Library, Quantico, VA.
[20] Ibid.
[21] Jackson, *His Time in Hell, A Texas Marine in France,* 87.
[22] Ibid.
[23] James E. Hatcher, *Citizen Soldier I: World War I Recollections of Pvt. James E. Hatcher, USMC,* ed. by Gilbert Hart published Kindle Edition only, Dec. 13, 2013. N.P.
[24] Ibid.
[25] Ibid.
[26] Nelson, "Paris-Metz Road," *Leatherneck,* 11.
[27] *Diary of Peter Wood,* N.P, Entry for June 1, 1918, Author's collection.
[28] Memoirs of 2nd Lieutenant William B. Jackson, 77th Company, 6th Machine Gun Battalion, http://www.monongahelabooks.com/jackmem10.html.
[29] Morgan, *When the World Went Mad,* 28.
[30] Ibid.

June 1st Chapter II

Accordingly Bundy, when Brown was unable to locate the 23rd, turned to me and said: 'General Harbord, you will have to put in one of your regiments.'
-Brigadier General James Harbord

Just ahead of the 6th Marines, the long column of soldiers of the 9th Infantry regiment's 1st and 2nd Battalions continued their long hike. They rested along the side of the road for one hour but resumed their movement east towards the threatened area. Road obstructions were plentiful, and the oncoming hordes of escaping civilians and French military traffic forced the men off the highway. "The French soldiery, which this regiment passed, assured us that the 'Guerre est finit' and that no Americans need try to stop the angry Boche who had a running start for Paris and could not be stopped."[1]

The doggedly resolute, yet utterly exhausted soldiers of the 9th Infantry continued east in a sort of impassive state toward the horizon now well lit by the cresting sun. Colonel Upton led the regimental procession as they reached the intersection of the Paris-Metz road and the road leading south to the village of Ventelet. Twenty-five-year-old Major Clyburn Otto Mattfeldt of Baltimore, Maryland, preceded the rest of the regiment by several hours to obtain more information from the French 21st Corps at Coupru. As he waited for the regiment's arrival, he took a few moments to sleep.

Mattfeldt awoke to the commotion of the approaching Americans and hustled down the road to head off the front of the oncoming columns.[2] When the regiment stopped, the troops took a welcomed few minutes to get off their feet. While Upton spoke with Mattfeldt, officers of the French 21st Army Corps hastily made their way to the intersection where the American officers massed for this impromptu conference. "French officers had come running at us, shooing us off the road," recalled First Lieutenant Hanford MacNider.[3] The agitated Frenchmen urged Upton to get his men off the road since the area was under German observation.[4]

Division Chief of Staff, Colonel Preston Brown, also arrived to greet the lead elements of the 9th Infantry and promptly briefed Upton regarding the situation, as he knew it. According to Upton, the regiment arrived at the outskirts of Coupru around 7:30 A.M. and received instructions to move into a nearby forest under cover. He later explained in a letter home:

> I had just assigned the battalions to woods to bivouac in when the order came to rest under the trees until noon and wait for orders. We ate some war bread for breakfast, and I had just lain down to catch some sleep when at 8:30 A.M. orders from a French Corps Commander directed us to move about five miles further east to take up a sector in line. I issued my orders from the map and started my

June 1st Chapter II

two battalions off. Then I got in the car and went to see the Corps Commander, and he sent me on to see the French Division commander under whose orders I was to be. I arrived there at breakfast time and certainly enjoyed that meal.[5]

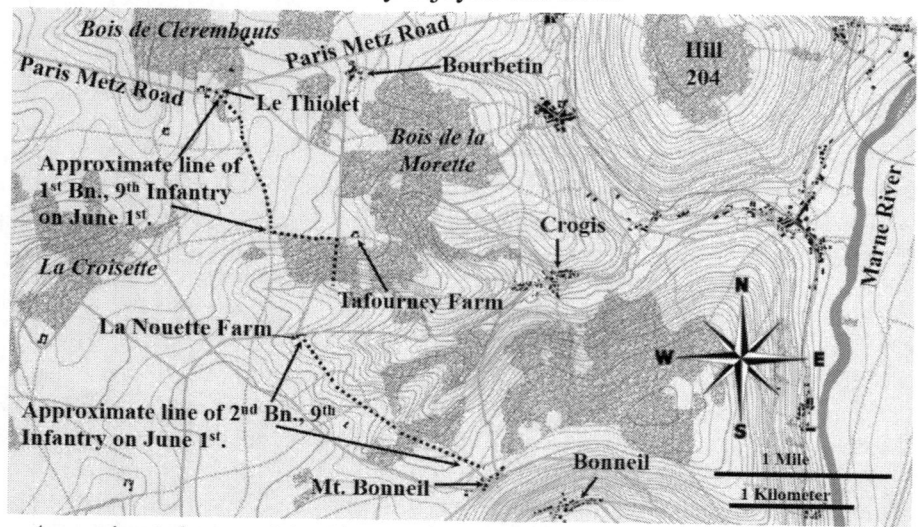

Approximate layout of the 1st and 2nd Battalions of the 9th Infantry on June 1st.

    The 1st Battalion, 9th Infantry under the command of thirty-three-year-old Major Franklin Langley Whitley, a 1908 graduate of West Point graduate, received instructions to move towards the village of Le Thiolet. Orders directed the extension of his battalion across the Paris-Metz Road. The line continued south along the western fringe of the Bois de la Morette and passed through another clump of forest near Tafournay Farm.[6] The battalion immediately began the overland journey through the fields that would take the men three kilometers east of Coupru.

    The 2nd Battalion, under the command of thirty-two-year-old Major Arthur Edward Bouton of Trumansburg, New York, extended off 1st Battalion's flank further south as ordered. The left wing of his battalion took up positions in the buildings at La Nouette Farm. His battalion extended the regiment's line for a kilometer and a half towards the town of Bonneil. Examining the basic hachured maps and pointing out terrain features, battalion and company commanders tried to make sense of the ground before them.[7]

    First Lieutenant MacNider recalled, "Battalions had plodded off in different directions with their orders to block the road to Paris. All that was left was one runner and myself, sitting on either side of the crossroads."[8] MacNider's runner promptly fell asleep and shortly after that MacNider, unable to fight the fatigue much longer, also dozed off.[9] Moving along the low ground south of the Paris-Metz road, the battalion and company commanders of the 9th Infantry took their troops to their designated positions. Officers quickly ushered their men up from their momentary rest. Weighed down with heavy packs, the men rose to their feet for another torturous hike of unknown distance.

Moving parallel to the Paris-Metz Road, they veered south and trekked through the pastures as the heat of the peaking sun supplanted the gentle morning chill. Wool trousers and leg wrappings became increasingly soaked from morning dew with every step through the farm fields. The men knew nothing of their location or destination but likely did not care due to the fatigue and hunger that gripped their spirits. The echo of distant gunfire resonated across the field and intensified as the procession marched closer to their designated positions.

Along the way, they encountered occasional dismounted French Cavalry soldiers evacuating their positions in the north and eastern face of Bois de la Morette. They were elements of a dismounted battalion of the 2nd and 4th Hussars of the French 192nd Division. They acknowledged the fresh-faced Americans with grim, hollow-eyed comradery as they filed past them.[10] The Americans of the 9th Infantry now fell under the command of the French 164th Division.[11]

Upon seeing the column of Americans approaching, many of these cavalrymen promptly returned to their positions in the woods, perhaps reinvigorated by the reinforced line developing behind them. Company commanders assigned platoons to various sectors along the front. There was no sympathy for the soldiers' lassitude following the seemingly endless movement. Their hopes for a quick rest vanished when they received orders to dig and organize fighting positions.

With his battalions directed to their assigned sectors, Upton left the French division headquarters. He took his staff to the small farm at Les Aulnois Bontemps to establish a regimental command post. He was surprised to discover the elements of one of his battalions, "two miles from the place it ought to have been. I sent them up to the line and soon had a strong line established in rear of the French."[12]

By noon, both battalions had moved into positions extending south of the Paris-Metz highway. They became the first elements of the 2nd Division to arrive on the front of what would be a bitterly fought engagement for the next month.

Earlier that morning, near May-en-Multien, the light of dawn on June 1st illuminated the lumps of sleeping men lying in the fields. Colonel Paul Malone, commanding the 23rd Infantry Regiment, gently high stepped through the dew-soaked pasture to roust his unconscious soldiers from their slumber. "In the morning, I was awakened by a loud voice calling, 'wake up, men, we have important work to do today,'" recalled Corporal Frank W. Anderson of Company M, 3rd Battalion, 23rd Infantry. Anderson rubbed his tired eyes to see the regimental commander standing before him.[13]

June 1st Chapter II

The men labored to exit warm bedrolls and shivered upon exposure to the chilly morning air. They rolled up packs, shook the moisture from their wool tunics, and in a half-conscious stupor formed up in two columns to begin a march of an unknown distance. "I had not had anything to eat for many hours but had the foresight to stick a box of hardtack between my ammunition belt, and I munched on these as we marched along," remembered Anderson.[14]

The procession of 23rd Infantry soldiers stretched for hundreds of yards south of May-en-Multien, passing over a railroad junction and continuing for about one mile. They hiked just a short distance before they received orders to fall out to the side of the road, a command that puzzled everyone. "Captain Green told us we would be here for about an hour," remembered Anderson, "so I had three men from the squad go back to the railroad and fill the canteens with water."[15]

Many members of Company M took the opportunity to start fires and cook whatever strips of bacon they managed to salvage from their meat cans. They soaked their hardtack bread in the sizzling grease. For many, it was the first meal in almost twenty-four hours. As the soldiers gathered around the crackling fires, the long columns of several battalions of 4th Brigade Marines filed past M Company. The 23rd formed up just as the tail of the Marine brigade and continued the march. The sun was high and the damp, chilly morning gave way to the muggy afternoon heat. Dirt clouds kicked up by the column of trampling feet once again dusted the sweaty faces of the men with each passing mile.[16]

By 5:00 A.M., members of the 55th Company, 2nd Battalion, 5th Marines, still camped just outside May-en-Multien, awoke to heated demands by impatient sergeants ordering them to roll their packs. With no time for chow or filling canteens, the company departed with the rest of the battalion. Most of the men tried to escape the morning chill by donning overcoats. "We buttoned them back like the French," recalled First Lieutenant Lemuel Shepherd.[17] The sun burned brightly by mid-morning, making the day rather hot. The men had no chance to halt and remove the now burdensome heavy wool overcoats.[18]

Ahead of the 2nd Battalion, forty-one-year-old Major Julius Spear Turrill's 1st Battalion, 5th Marines left before 5:00 A.M. "Well it was a hot day, and we were marching at top speed, 55 minutes hiking—5 minutes rest," remembered Private Onnie Cordes of the 17th Company.[19] Twenty-nine-year-old Captain Keller Emrick Rockey, Turrill's battalion adjutant, recalled, "This was a long hard dusty march especially after a ride of 15 to 16 hours in motor trucks the day before, and with mighty little to eat."[20]

The lack of sleep and food, combined with the heat, began to show its effect on the men. Private Albert Powis, marching with the 17th Company, recalled, "On this march was the first time I ever went to sleep while hiking.

I would wander off the road and start on the slant for the ditch, and that would wake me up, and I would get back in ranks."[21]

Throughout the strenuous hike, the rumor mill began to spin. According to Corporal Frank Matheny of the 17th Company, "Stories about the Germans wearing steel breastplates which broke the American and French bayonets were spreading fast. Everybody was grouchy and 'hard-boiled,' all of which helped to relieve the tension."[22] The battalion made the six and a half-mile stretch of road connecting May-en-Multien and the village of Lizy-sur-Ourcq by mid-morning. To the disappointment of many, they merely passed through the town with no rest and continued another six and a half-kilometer-push east toward the village of Cocherel.[23]

At Montreuil-aux-Lions, Brigadier General James Harbord arrived at the Hotel de Ville, which served as division headquarters, and met with Colonel Preston Brown, Brigadier General Emory Lewis of the 3rd Brigade, and Major General Omar Bundy, the division commander.[24] Their meeting to discuss the current situation had only begun when a motorcycle stopped just out outside the building. A French officer dismounted the bike and ran inside the Hotel de Ville. The Frenchman saluted as he interrupted the impromptu assembly of the American officers, and replied in a thick French accent, "General Degoutte sends his compliments."[25] The officer explained the precariousness of the situation and passed on a request that another of the division's regiments move forward immediately. Major General Bundy turned to Colonel Brown and demanded, "Send in the 23rd Infantry."[26] For several minutes, Brown tried to determine the location of Malone's regiment and figure out when they might arrive to fulfill Bundy's orders.

Brigadier General Edward Lewis commanded the 3rd Brigade. Photo credit: Kevin Kling.

As the staff worked out a plan of disposition and tried to ascertain the arrival time of the 23rd Infantry, more courier motorcycles arrived at with subsequent messages from Degoutte, re-emphasizing the need for urgency. "Accordingly Bundy, when Brown was unable to locate the 23rd, turned to me and said: 'General Harbord, you will have to put in one of your regiments,'" recalled Harbord.[27]

June 1st Chapter II

Despite the exhaustive previous few days and Degoutte's earlier intentions to let Harbord's Marines rest, the situation required the brigade commander to get his men moving. He immediately summoned the 6th Marines. Colonel Albertus Catlin, commanding the 6th Marines, remembered, "Orders came from General Harbord to move two battalions into the line at once."[28] Catlin passed down orders to get men ready to move immediately.

Corporal Havelock Nelson of the 97th Company arrived at Montreuil-aux-Lions with the battalion intelligence section behind the rest of the 3rd Battalion, 6th Marines. Nelson unsuccessfully scrounged for food when he learned they were to shove off immediately:

Being convinced that food was out of the question, I next decided to catch up on my sleep. The weather was hot and sultry, so I pulled the feather mattress off onto the floor before an open window, broke open my pack so as to spread my blanket over the mattress, placed a big soft pillow on the end of the mattress under the window and took off my shoes. For a moment I stood there admiring my handiwork, and imagining how good that mattress was going to feel after so many months without sleeping on one. But unfortunately, the gods of war had other ideas, for at least that very moment there arose in the courtyard a tumult of whistles and shouts of, 'All out, 97th Company, fall in! Combat Packs! Snap into it, we shove off in ten minutes.' Sorrowfully, but hurriedly, I put on my blouse and shoes and made up my combat pack, slung it on my back, carried my blanket roll to the designated storage place, and took my place in ranks in the courtyard.[29]

Corporal Warren Jackson and the rest of the 95th Company slept after skinning and dressing some of the livestock left in the town of Montreuil-aux-Lions, which they intended to cook later. "But the opportunity for sleep was snatched from us, and we had to leave the uncooked rabbits, chickens, and calves hanging there," remembered Jackson.[30] The company quickly formed up along the outskirts of the city and began to march.

The 75th Company spent much of the late morning shaded in a patch of woods off the highway near Montreuil-aux-Lions. They gazed at the endless stream of foot and vehicle traffic passing along the road. "Various orders were being issued," remembered Sergeant Gerald Thomas, "officers being called to regimental and brigade headquarters. Finally, early in the afternoon, our outfit came back, and we got orders to move. [Second Lieutenant David] Redford's sole information was that we were to go forward. After getting clear of the other units about noon, we took our share of the highway and moved east for several miles."[31]

The Marines salvaged whatever food they could carry. "In the line of march that day," recalled Private Gus Gulberg of the 75th Company, "one could see dressed rabbits and chickens slung over many knapsacks. But it was excess baggage, for a lot of them never got the chance to eat their prizes."[32]

By noon the Marines of the 2nd Battalion, 6th Regiment situated in the town awoke from their late morning nap and assembled their gear in preparation to move. Members of the 80th Company grumbled among themselves about their early reveille as well as the endless cavalcade that appeared to take them from one destination to another unnecessarily. "As was often the case when we were preparing to move," recalled Private Levi Hemrick, "someone in the line near me raised the question, 'Where do we go from here?' Our sergeant answered in these words, 'For all we know we are on our way to hell.'"[33]

The men of the 79th Company awoke in the afternoon to a company bugler playing assembly. Platoon commanders, with only scant information, summoned their men and tersely delivered instructions while their Marines, semi-conscious, tried to process the barrage of orders.

Harbord oversaw his men's hastily executed exodus from Montreuil-aux-Lions and remembered:

> The leading battalion of the Sixth Marines had passed through Montreuil and was a few hundred yards east of the town. Some seventeen trucks had come up and were unloading rations to that battalion. Hurrying out there, I started all three battalions and the Sixth Machine Gun Battalion marching along the highway toward the front. The trucks were ordered to throw off their loads at the side of the road, and to pick up the men of the rearmost battalion and hurry them toward the front.[34]

The rearmost battalion was Major Thomas Holcomb's 2nd Battalion, 6th Marines who eagerly boarded the vehicles. Holcomb and the battalion intelligence section departed in the first truck followed by the battalion runners and headquarters staff.[35] The long convoy stretched hundreds of yards east of Montreuil-aux-Lions and quickly passed the other battalions of the regiment.

As the vehicles of the 79th Company followed in the column, a convoy of supply trucks approached from the rear. Corporal Lloyd Pike recalled the dangers of having canned vegetables tossed into the bed of the vehicles. ". . . As they passed us, their crews tossed food cans from their truck to ours. The cans were large, about 2 gallons each, I would guess; and catching one thrown from the other vehicle was a lot like getting hit with a truck. Our truck ended up with a good supply of canned fruit."[36] Second Lieutenant John West, who commanded the 3rd Platoon, recalled, "As we passed the

June 1st Chapter II

outskirts of the town, cans of tomatoes and large round loaves of French bread were thrown into the trucks. If you went by slowly, you got quite a lot—fast, you were out of luck."[37] The men eagerly grabbed whatever food they could.

The battalion found the roads still relatively congested with vehicle and foot traffic. Twenty-four-year-old Second Lieutenant Clifton Bledsoe Cates of Tiptonville, Tennessee, and a graduate of the University of Tennessee, commanded the 96th Company's 4th Platoon. He recalled, "No traffic in N.Y. City can compare with the few miles that we covered that afternoon— truck after truck, automobiles, motorcycles—thousands of troops and lots of airplanes overhead; also lots of artillery and machine guns moving into new positions."[38]

According to Paradis, "A continuous stream of French soldiers trudged against our tide of trucks. We could hear the rifle and machine gun fire and see cannon shells bursting in fields in the air ahead of us as we passed the battery of French 75mm cannon. They were shooting in the open staying close to the road in case they had to move back quickly."[39]

Colonel Catlin traveled with the lead elements of the 2nd Battalion's convoy well past the battery of French field guns. The distant plumes of smoke from artillery shells became visible as the convoy continued forward. "The Germans had some field guns—77's— trained on the road, but luckily they did not shell our trucks," recalled Catlin.[40]

When a German shell hit well in front of the lead truck carrying Major Holcomb, he quickly decided the vehicles have traveled close enough to the front. The long convoy stopped near Paris Farm, and Holcomb promptly signaled for the men in the truck behind him to dismount.

In a chain reaction, one by one, they vacated the camions. "At this point I received orders from the regimental commander, Colonel Albertus Catlin, to take up position from Le Thiolet on the Paris-Metz Road connecting with the 9th Infantry at that point through Triangle Farm to the town of Lucy-le-Bocage exclusive. This point was in support, French troops being still on our front," remembered Holcomb.[41]

Near Paris Farm, Catlin, with Holcomb present, issued the orders directly to the company commanders. According to Captain Robert Messersmith of the 78th Company, "There had been no reconnaissance made by the regimental or battalion commanders, and no time was given company commanders to reconnoiter before placing their men into the line. No maps were at hand except the one in possession of the regimental commander."[42]

According to twenty-two-year-old Second Lieutenant James McBrayer Sellers of Lexington, Missouri, who commanded the 78th Company's 1st Platoon, "The only map our battalion had was a little hachured map about six inches square and very inaccurate. Our company commander did not even have a map."[43]

Catlin stood at the side of the Paris-Metz road near Paris Farm. With his battalion and company officers peering over his shoulder, he pointed out distant terrain features and villages on a small section of a hachured French map. "Triangle Farm, on the right, and Lucy-le-Bocage, on the left, were visible from where the order was issued but no idea of the intervening ground could be gained," recalled Messersmith.[44] The 78th Company left the road to the north, stretched out across the pasture of wheat, and hiked toward their designated position.

According to Messersmith, "The company, as we left the road, hesitated to cut the wire fences, and the idea of moving through the fields, beautiful with ripe grain, was all contrary to previous training."[45] Messersmith's Marines moved into the unknown ready for anything.

Twenty-one-year-old Private Thaddeus Stephenson Allen noted the beautiful pasture upon which the 78th Company hiked. "The country was broken. There were wheat fields tucked in among patches of brush and tall trees.

Private Thaddeus Allen. Photo credit: "Echoes From Over There."

An occasional village half seen, half-hidden among trees and foliage. Ravines, little knolls and hills and, just where we entrenched, a great rough stretch of forest, rolling up and spreading out to either side."[46] The distant reports of gunfire quickly dispelled the verdant beauty of the area and reminded everyone of the perdition unfolding several kilometers ahead.

The 79th Company, situated at the back of the 2nd Battalion's convoy, stopped adjacent to the French artillery battery. The Marines, loaded with gear, disembarked the trucks as the tremendous concussion of muzzles drowned out the curtly verbalized orders of Gunnery Sergeants, Sergeants, and Corporals. For Corporal Glen Hill, the extremely audible presence of that French battery brought the reality of the situation home. ". . . So we realized we were soon to do battle face to face with the Germans."[47] Corporal Pike remembered the beautiful countryside that had yet to see the full destructive capabilities of war, "and I can still remember my surprise when our platoon leader lined us up and gave the order 'load and lock.'"[48] The company moved north of the Paris-Metz highway in a line of skirmishers.

June 1st Chapter II

The Marines of the 96th Company, who also disembarked the convoy along the highway, adjusted equipment while standing in a hasty formation along the side of the dust-choked road near Paris Farm. According to twenty-four-year-old Corporal Peter Christian Ward of Portage County, Wisconsin, "the hoarse command 'fix bayonets' echoed in the nearby woods. With mixed emotions, many of my squad had difficulty in finding the slot where the bayonet fit the rifle slot."[49] The sound of hundreds of individual 'clicks' as the company collectively attached the sixteen-inch blades to the lugs of their Springfield rifles provided no theatrics to this seemingly symbolic arrival to the front.

The men spread out as they moved across the green and brown fields towards their designated position.[50] The realization that he may not survive compelled Second Lieutenant Cates to express his sense of mortality in a letter to his mother, "'Do or die is our motto'—and the mother that can furnish a boy should say—'America'—here's my boy, God grant that he may come back, if not, I am glad he died for a noble cause, and I am willing to give him to you.'"[51]

The line of Major Holcomb's Marines spread out in skirmish formation. They moved towards their designated objective unaware of what they might encounter carrying rifles at port with bayonets fixed. The formation of the 96th Company walked several kilometers, and by 6:00 P.M., they entered the tangle of woods known as Bois de Clerembauts, just north of the Paris-Metz road. Slowly, the back of the company's gear-laden procession disappeared into the tree line.

The Marines pushed aside branches and shrubs that caught bayonets, rifles, and equipment as they walked through the dense woods towards the southern tree line. The right flank of the 96th Company tied in with Major Frank Whitley's 1st Battalion, 9th Infantry at Le Thiolet. The four platoons, assigned to various sectors within Bois de Clerembauts, extended their position from Le Thiolet north along the eastern edge of the woods. "We immediately started digging in—each man would dig a small hole big enough to get down in, so as to protect him from shrapnel and machine gun bullets. Our position was about a kilometer behind the French line—who were out in front," remembered Cates.[52]

Captain Randolph Zane's 79th Company hiked into position and tied in with the left platoon of the 96th Company. The 79th Company's 2nd Platoon centered on the structure of Triangle Farm just north of Bois de Clerembauts. Corporal Glen Hill remembered:

> As evening came, we took up our positions at Triangle Farm, which overlooked a small valley and along which ran a railroad track. We were on the brow of the hill, and the woods were some three hundred yards in front of our lines. My squad and my brother's squad, as was the case in each company, was held in reserve should

the Hun attack, and in the case of a break in our lines, we were to reinforce the line at that point.[53]

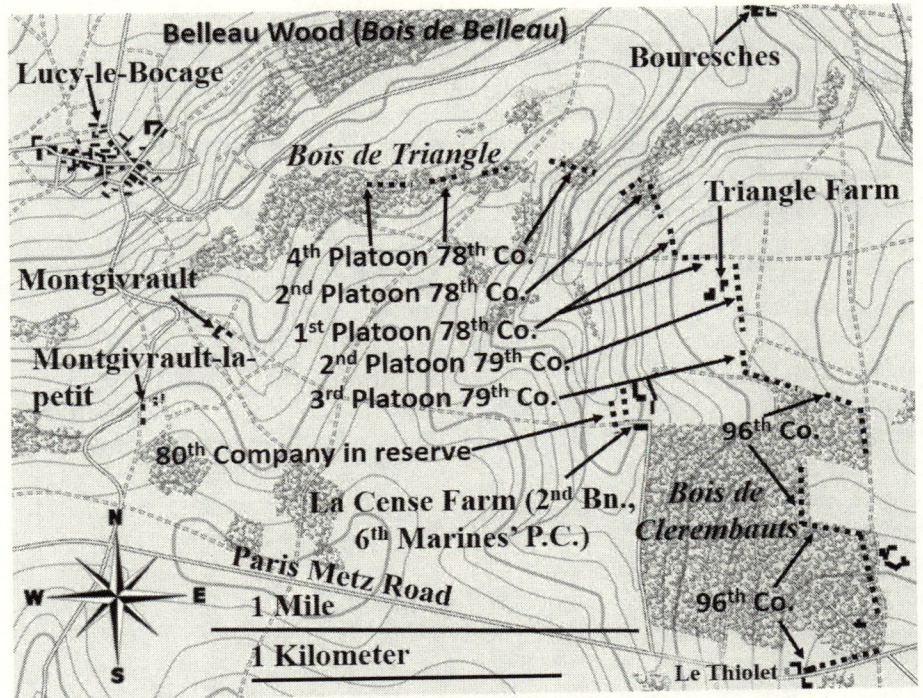

Position of the 2nd Battalion, 6th Marines on June 1st.

    Second Lieutenant West's 3rd Platoon occupied the woods on the company's right flank. With the rumble of artillery nearby, they dug individual fighting holes.[54]

    Captain Messersmith ascertained that the company's sector of the line remained precarious since he extended the battalion's left line two kilometers from Triangle Farm northwest to the town of Lucy-le-Bocage. The village of Bouresches stood about a thousand meters north of Triangle Farm. Lying between Bouresches and Triangle Farm was a rather steep ravine, and just behind the line to the northwest, the red rooftops of the buildings in Lucy-le-Bocage were visible from this position.

    Messersmith placed the 1st Platoon, under Second Lieutenant Sellers, just north of Triangle Farm to tie in with the 79th Company about 150 yards in front of the farm.[55] According to Sellers, "We met two or three stray French soldiers, sampling their canteens of wine, eating cheese and crackers. They told us they were the last of their bloodied units. Although the French were glad to see us, they said on many occasions, 'It's too late.' We could see that no front line was left."[56] Despite the sounds of rifle and machine gun fire echoing through the valley, the field upon which the 1st Platoon was to dig in remained quiet according to Sellers.

June 1st Chapter II

The 2nd Platoon extended the 78th Company's line north. Twenty-three-year-old Second Lieutenant Henry Leslie Eddy, an Army officer from New Britain, Connecticut, who had been with the company for only twelve days, commanded the platoon. They extended the front into the woods several hundred yards north of Triangle Farm and on the south slope of the ravine.

Private Thaddeus Allen recalled, "Our line ran along the crest of ground rising above a small ravine. There were a few rods of open ground and then the woods. My company dug its foxholes along the line of the ravine. The Huns left us pretty much alone while we were at it; I guess because a drove of French 'seventy-fives' somewhere in back of us were worrying them about up to capacity."[57] The French batteries seemed to maintain a constant rate of fire on the distant enemy.

The 4th Platoon commanded by twenty-one-year-old Second Lieutenant James Pickens Adams of North August, South Carolina, carried the left flank of the line due west through the woods. His left flank remained over a kilometer southeast of Lucy-le-Bocage, which created a highly precarious gap in the already thin line. Twenty-one-year-old Second Lieutenant Cecil Raleigh's 3rd Platoon remained in reserve.[58] The 80th Company remained in battalion reserve at La Cense Farm located in the northwest corner of Bois de Clerembauts.

Major Holcomb put members of the 80th Company to work bringing ammunition up. "My memory of the first night is very hazy, but I do remember being on ammunition detail and making one trip to the fighting line," recalled Private Levi Hemrick.[59] "We had established what might be called a fluid line, and until we had time to coordinate our different units, work out a system of communication, and become familiar with the territory over which we were operating, most of us would have a rather hazed, confused understanding of what was going on."[60] When Hemrick arrived in Lucy-le-Bocage, he encountered an incredulous French soldier. The exhausted veteran expressed his displeasure in broken English at the concentrated supply of ammunition by the presence of the American ammunition dump so close to the German lines. His statement implied the town would soon be in the enemy's possession.[61]

Just behind Major Holcomb's men, the 1st Battalion, 6th Marines, commanded by thirty-eight-year-old Major Maurice Edwin Shearer, approached Paris Farm on foot, approximately six kilometers from Montreuil-aux-Lions. Corporal Warren Jackson of the 95th Company vividly remembered:

> Then there met us on the road that day French soldiers, worn-out, haggard, and dejected, retreating in disorder from the oncoming Germans. They reminded one more of hunted beasts than human beings. We had regarded an experienced French soldier as worth several Americans, and now they were retreating. It would not have

been unnatural for the Americans to despair at this turn of affairs, but I do not recall one word of fear or other evidence of a desire to turn back. As we continued along that tree-lined Paris-Metz Road, more and more of the French passed us. Their emaciated faces and eyes that reflected despair told unmistakably of the thousand perils they had witnessed.[62]

The shell-damaged farmhouse at Triangle Farm. Photo credit: Gilles Lagin.

The Column of Shearer's Marines veered off to the side of the road grimacing and squinting with the passing of every truck which stirred up clouds dust that permeated the eyes, mouths, and nostrils of those unfortunate men forced to travel on foot. In the distance, the terrain rose sharply, and according to Sergeant Gerald Thomas of the 75th Company, the battalion, "came to a rise and I judge that rise had been forecast as the place we might come under arty fire. So we got off the road and deployed to the left of the road."[63] Marines scampered into skirmish formation. "The whole line moved slowly forward," recalled Thomas.[64] "It took us three hours to reach our objective, the village of Lucy-le-Bocage, four miles away."[65] Second Lieutenant David Redford, muttered to Thomas, "I believe this is where we're supposed to be."[66] According to Thomas, "We never knew much of what we were supposed to do."[67] The lack of maps and general unfamiliarity of the terrain became a profound source of confusion for those assigned specific positions without the benefit of reconnaissance.

Once inside the village, the Marines of the 75th Company filed past ammunition crates piled along the side of the road. Each man grabbed a bandoleer of extra rifle ammunition and slung it across their already gear-

June 1st Chapter II

laden bodies. The company saw several wounded French soldiers coming back from the front.

Members of the 1st Battalion, 6th Marines arrive in Lucy-le-Bocage where they encounter French troops. Photo credit: Marius Eugene Vasse collection.

Major Maurice Shearer, seen in the center left, is in discussion with a French officer inside Lucy-le-Bocage. These photos were taken on June 1st, just at the arrival of the 1st Battalion, 6th Marines. Photo credit: Marius Eugene Vasse collection.

The sun grew hotter as the day progressed and some men of the 75th dug in with no specific understanding of their position in the line. According to Private Gus Gulberg, "There was no distinct line nor prepared defenses; just open country. We were to take up a definite position in support of the French who were struggling in front with the advancing Germans."[68] For Thomas, "The situation was so obscure that we posted only two squads, reinforced with the platoon's two automatic rifles, on the forward side of the village and bivouacked the remainder in a dry stream bed just in the rear of it."[69]

Members of the 74th Company spent the afternoon hunting for food. Twenty-four-year-old Private Asa Jessup Smith of Wabash, Indiana, was fortunate enough to stumble upon a chicken roaming an abandoned coop as well as a basket of potatoes. Without hesitation, he killed the bird and fried it along with the potatoes. Smith then sat with a few comrades and consumed the best meal any of them ate in days.[70]

The 95th Company followed behind the 75th Company into the mostly abandoned town of Lucy-le-Bocage. "When we went into the village on that bright June day, an air of calm serenity seemed to pervade its sunlit walls and green gardens," remembered Jackson, but the distant sound of fighting in the east suggested otherwise.[71]

A handful of French medics appeared to be the sole inhabitants of the town. The hollow eyes of these French troops, gazing from under the rims of their helmets, placidly acknowledged the arrival of the fresh-faced, young Americans. These French soldiers, who had suffered constant misery in the previous days, exhibited grim sentiments and an attitude of futility at the Marines' willingness to establish a line in the town.

As the men filed past the ammunition dump, they grabbed cloth bandoleers of 30.06 rounds. A few Marines tried to communicate with these gallant yet despondent Frenchmen who summarized the situation with, "Paris, huit jours," meaning it would likely take only eight days for Paris to fall.[72] These cynical veterans reasoned it would take just three days before the Germans will occupy the village streets upon which they stood.[73]

By late afternoon, incoming shells occasionally landed in town. The crescendo of rifle and machine gun fire sounded closer every hour, reinforcing the austere reception Major Shearer's men received from the French medics. Shearer was doubtful of the French willingness to stay and fight. The French infantry colonel personally handed Shearer all his rounds for his flare pistol and briefed him on the protocol for calling artillery. Shearer inquired to the regimental adjutant Major Frank Evans as to the accuracy of this process of fire support. In his message, Shearer states, "Infantry Col. Commanding sector sends me word that in this sector red lights call for barrage. White light calls for lengthening. No difference as to number of stars. Any light will do. This does not seem O.K. but is his dope."[74]

Major Berton Sibley's 3rd Battalion, 6th Marines moved east of Montreuil-aux-Lions along both sides of the Paris-Metz road that afternoon and encountered a convoy which spewed powdery dirt in their faces. The

June 1st Chapter II

97th Company "shouted derisively at them while swallowing their dust," recalled Corporal Havelock Nelson.[75] When they discovered the trucks carried the other battalions of the regiment, they grumbled about moving on foot while their comrades rolled along. According to Corporal William Timothy Scanlon, a twenty-nine-year-old Chicago native with the company's 1st Platoon, "We were so mad that when they hollered at us, 'What outfit?' we yelled back, 'Salvation Army!' The camions were kicking up a lot of dust for us to swallow, which didn't make it any pleasanter."[76] The men resentfully cursed the passing convoy.

The company occasionally passed the dejected hordes of unarmed French soldiers; some were walking wounded, and others, based on their expressions, appeared only to suffer wounded spirits. "Hey, Frog, you're going the wrong way, come along with us," jeered one 97th Company Marine, to which the old French veteran briskly stared back at the column and muttered, "Fine la guerre, fini la guerre!"[77]

According to Scanlon, "Some were on horses, and we tried to wise crack them, but they did not pay any attention to us. Another French soldier came along on foot, slowly. His coat sleeve was cut off and his arm was bandaged. The bandage was red. 'Wonder what happened to that guy . . .' 'He must have been cleaning his rifle and didn't know it was loaded,'" joked another Marine.[78] Private James Hatcher of the 84th Company also recalled the forlorn expression of the French soldiers passing by the battalion's column:

> Their faces were haggard and drawn, and as they staggered along the road, their eyes seemed to stare blankly into the distance ahead. They acted as though they were in a trance, and when an order was passed along for them to halt, they sank to the ground in their tracks. It seemed to me that they suffered as much from nervous exhaustion as they did from physical weariness. Words from us usually met no response, only an occasional weary shake of the head. The French were completely all in.[79]

From the head of the battalion's column, the men cleared the road to make way for two emaciated looking horses hauling a pair of French 75mm cannons. The columns eventually walked past the remainder of the French battery headed out of the woods toward the road. The speed of their departure suggested they had no intentions to stay and fight.

Twenty-three-year-old First Lieutenant Alfred Houston Noble, a former track star at St. John's College in Annapolis, Maryland, who had commanded the 83rd Company since late March, tried in vain to get information from the retreating French soldiers. "Nobody knew where the Germans were. The French would just say, 'En bas' [bottom or downwards likely implying the enemy was down in the valley] . . . you couldn't get any of them to talk."⁸⁰ Despite their general ignorance regarding the situation, Noble's men knew they were very near the front lines.

Some of the French batteries further ahead remained in place. Elements of the 84th Company, making up the rear of the battalion's column, veered off the road into the fields, and deployed in two columns. They hike past the remaining 75mm guns as a French plane flew at a low altitude over the battery and fired short bursts of its machine gun. "I assumed that the aviator was giving some signal for correcting the range," recalled Private Hatcher.⁸¹ The thunderous chorus of the French guns made for a dramatic arrival to the front for Marines of the 3rd Battalion, 6th Marines.

Captain Alfred Noble commanded the 3rd Battalion, 6th Marines. Photo credit: St. John's College library.

The battalion's column reached Paris Farm in the late afternoon. Colonel Catlin greeted Major Sibley with verbal orders to proceed north along the road off to the left (north) of Paris Farm toward the village of La Voie du Chatel. At that point, the battalion would constitute the regimental reserve behind the line.⁸² Sibley and his staff quickly made their way towards the back of the column looking for the company commanders to brief them on the situation. Sibley rushed to catch up to Captain Voeth, prompting the long column of his 97th Company to halt. The men welcomed the relief, regardless of how brief, to get off their feet.⁸³ Voeth and Sibley engaged in a hurried conversation as they walked side by side up the road. Out of earshot of the discussion between the two officers, the men of the 97th Company watched with indifference as Sibley spoke intently with Voeth, directing his attention to a patch of woods in the distance. Nelson recalled:

> The delay enabled us to look around a bit. Aside from the confusion along the main highway, the landscape was one of the most peaceful I've ever seen. Scattered about, far and near, were groups of white-walled, red-tile-roofed buildings gleaming in the brilliant sunshine against the darker setting of rolling hills whose gentle slopes were

covered with waving grain and whose tops were crowned with innumerable patches of green woods.[84]

The 97th Company enjoyed the pause, but it was short-lived as platoon commanders abruptly urged men to get on their feet. Moving down the side of the road, Gunnery Sergeants formed the company into columns of four and drove them north along the path intersecting the Paris-Metz road. According to Nelson:

Captain Robert Voeth commanded the 97th Company, 3rd Battalion, 6th Marine Regiment. Photo credit: NPRC.

As we gazed about, the ever-present reality of war was forced upon us by the sudden appearance of two puffs of bursting shrapnel over a large wood about a mile to the north, and we started to move down the side road directly toward that wood. Moving away from the traffic noises of the main road, the distant rumble of artillery in action became very noticeable, and as we proceeded along our way not only could the reports of individual guns be distinguished, but the hammering of machine guns was added to the slowly increasing volume of sound.[85]

The Company continued north along the road to La Voie du Chatel, a village concealed for the time being from a distant enemy by a cluster of woods. The battalion moved quickly through the town. According to Nelson, "The first house we passed was being used by the French as an aid-station, for there we saw a few wounded Frenchmen with heads, arms or legs wrapped with bloody bandages. We stared at them, frankly interested, as we hurried by. They, in turn, stared back, but indifferently and apparently uninterested."[86]

The town was alive with the sound of a French battery nestled among the trees. One particular 155mm gun fired shells unceasingly as the columns of Sibley's battalion moved beyond the town.

Nearly a kilometer away, the rooftops of the distant village of Marigny-en-Orxois, which was under German artillery fire, came into view. "Only the church-steeple and a few housetops were visible through agitated clouds of dust and smoke," remembered Nelson.[87] Voeth, aware that the company might be under German observation at that point, gave the command for the men to double time to the distant woods. Inside the forest, the 97th Company scattered throughout the groves.

The 83rd Company also hiked into the forest with the sharp pulsating sound of a few distant machine guns as a backdrop. The sight of retreating French suggested the proximity of the German advance. "The French troops we were passing were in what you might call a full retreat," recalled Private James Scarborough of the 83rd Company.[88] "Some of them didn't even have rifles. They were muddy and unshaven and hurrying saying, 'Finis le Guerre!' It was unbelievable; the French were quitting, and we had barely been allowed to fight!"[89] The defeatism of the seasoned French did not sway Scarbrough at all.

Despite the excitement of their arrival into the woods, men of the 97th Company quickly turned their focus to their gnawing stomachs. "I wonder if [Private Clarence] Nagel is in sight with galley," recalled Corporal Scanlon.[90] "He's always pulling that old stuff that an army fights on its belly. He'd better furnish something to make a belly with or there won't be no fighting."[91] The men were accustomed to Nagle always pursuing them with his rolling kitchen, "but we hadn't seen the cook or his grease-balls since we left Chaumont-en-Vexin."[92]

As the afternoon shadows grew longer, Scanlon spotted First Lieutenant Thomas Treston McEvoy, who commanded the company's 1st Platoon, walking through the woods. McEvoy, a University of Illinois graduate, left the Illinois National Guard where he earned a Brevet promotion to Captain, for a commission in the Marine Corps a year earlier. When Scanlon asked him about rations, McEvoy replied, "The men will have to eat from their reserve rations. Let them start a small fire to cook their bacon, but be sure that they use dry sticks, corporal, as there must not be any smoke."[93]

The word passed among the platoons permitting a fire for each squad for a short time. Instructions from company command allowed the consumption of two cans of corned beef and three boxes of hardtack from their reserve rations. Some of the unfortunate men went back to La Voie du Chatel loaded down with the company's canteens to retrieve water.[94]

Before the 3rd Battalion, 6th Marines occupied positions in the woods north of the town of La Voie du Chatel; Brigadier General Harbord arrived at Paris Farm in his staff car with the lead elements of his brigade. He watched as the battalions of his 6th Marines fanned out across the field and disappeared over the distant rise and into the tree lines.

According to Colonel Albertus Catlin, "As our men went into line, there was a very light artillery fire from the German guns, which seemed to indicate a lack of information on the part of the enemy as to the significance of the movement. It did not bother us too much."[95] Harbord hastily ducked back into his staff vehicle and ordered the driver to speed toward Lucy-le-

June 1st Chapter II

Bocage to locate the French division commander reported to be inside the town.[96]

The sporadic artillery landing near Lucy-le-Bocage caught Harbord's attention. "Lucy was a fairly noisy village that afternoon with the windows shaking every few seconds from artillery fire, 'going' or 'arriving.'"[97] By 4:10 P.M., Harbord sent a message from Lucy-le-Bocage to Major General Omar Bundy confirming that he had established liaison with the commanding officer of French 43rd Division—the eastern most division of the French 21st Corps. He further confirmed his Marines were moving into place between Le Thiolet and Lucy-le-Bocage. "Important that available engineers with plenty of tools come as soon as infantry finish with camions. Should de-buss at Ferme Paris [Paris Farm] and march in small columns about evenly distributed from Thiolet to Lucy. Hurry them."[98] The engineers, having spent hours in the back of trucks, now had to hike for several more kilometers to reach their designated position.

The nearest element of the 2nd Engineers departed Montreuil-aux-Lions on foot. The 1st Battalion, 2nd Engineers, commanded by thirty-year-old Major Milo Pitcher Fox, a 1912 West Point Graduate from Mankato, Minnesota, braved the burning sun and hiked the twenty-four kilometers to Montreuil-aux-Lions.

Major Milo P. Fox seen here as a West Point Cadet. Fox commanded the 1st Battalion, 2nd Engineers. Photo credit: The 1912 Howitzer, West Point Library.

Their march followed a twenty-hour ride in crowded trucks the previous day. Their brief pause in Montreuil-aux-Lions allowed the battalion a moment to prepare a long-awaited meal and even fraternize with a few of the French soldiers willing to share what small amount of food they could forage. The brief lull ended, and the battalion formed to continue moving east.[99] The engineers established a supply dump at Paris Farm, and the companies gathered their necessary tools once they arrived. The 2nd Battalion, 2nd Engineers, under the command of twenty-four-year-old Major William Arthur Snow, also departed Montreuil-aux-Lions that afternoon. They too traveled along the Paris-Metz in platoon columns toward Paris Farm.[100]

110

June 1st Chapter II

While his brigade formed some semblance of an organized line, Harbord strategically selected his headquarters at Issonge Farm. This position, situated behind the developing line, stood two and a half miles southwest of Lucy-le-Bocage and about one mile north of the Paris-Metz road. According to Harbord:

> I took the home of an evidently prosperous farmer and stock-raiser who had left it suddenly the day before. It stood on a sloping hill, with a high stone pyramid on the road not far from it. Its roof was red. It was perhaps the most conspicuous place available. There was a French battery of G.P.F.'s about thirty yards from the house in the edge of a small grove. Every time that battery sent out anything it nearly shook the house on its foundations, but it was a comfortable sound to hear them 'going' instead of 'arriving.'[101]

Members of the 1st Battalion, 6th Marines sitting along the stone wall of a building in Lucy-le-Bocage shortly after arriving on June 1st. Photo credit: Marius Eugene Vasse collection.

On the backside of Lucy-le-Bocage, men of the 75th Company lay about the area until further orders arrived. There was sporadic artillery landing on the outskirts of the town, but the heat appeared to be more of a concern for some of the men.

With two squads, including the platoon's automatic rifles on the eastern edge of the village, Sergeant Gerald Thomas and the remainder of the 3rd Platoon, 75th Company took refuge from the heat by bedding down in a dry streambed. "Word was passed down to us from above that we might eat our emergency ration, bacon, and hardtack. Someone found potatoes in a deserted house in the village, which we fried in bacon grease. We pooled the coffee from our condiment cans. Not a very robust meal but appreciated just the same," recalled Thomas.[102] As the afternoon grew late, more retreating French soldiers passed through Lucy-le-Bocage and changed the complacent posture of the exhausted 75th Company. Private Gus Gulberg recalled:

Towards evening, stragglers started to sift through, and bloody men in blue passed through our lines, some walking some on stretchers and some on small carts wheeled by two hospital men. Now we knew the Hun was not far away. I pitied these brave men as I watched them stagger back to the rear, bruised and broken remnants with despair written on their war-weary faces. To them, perhaps the war was lost. One fellow came up to me and showed me his rifle. The butt had been shot away, and he had been hit in the shoulder. He said, 'Beaucoup d'allemands,' [Many Germans] and hurried away.[103]

Members of the 1st Battalion, 6th Marines dig in along the outskirts of Lucy-le-Bocage. Photo credit: Marius Eugene Vasse.

As the afternoon turned into evening, the 95th Company moved to the left (north) out of the village of Lucy-le-Bocage. Corporal Warren Jackson remembered passing the ranks of the 75th Company as they dug individual fighting holes. He spotted twenty-one-year-old Private Albert Mongure Ball of Huntsville, Texas, an old Company D comrade from Paris Island. Jackson looked at Ball and recalled that he "shall never forget the picture of him as he sat upon the ground with the despairing has-it-come-to-this expression upon his face."[104]

The 95th Company hiked northwest out of the village and entered a heavily wooded valley where they moved through Bois de Champillon and halted at the edge of the forest.[105] "We had not been there long when [Corporal] Peter Timmer began digging a hole between two saplings a few feet from me. I felt that Timmer must have a yellow streak. I was to learn," remembered Jackson.[106]

The 1st Battalion, 6th Marines' movement extended the brigade's dangerously thin line from Bois de Clerembauts to the town of Lucy-le-Bocage, and northwest through Bois de Champillon to the northwest portion of the forest. By 7:30 P.M., word reached Major Shearer at his command post in Lucy-le-Bocage that the battalion was in position and an attempt to establish liaison with the unit to the west was underway. The information reached Colonel Catlin by 8:15 P.M.[107]

---

[1] History of the 9th Infantry, Box 48, RG 120.9.3, NARA College Park, MD.
[2] Thomason, *Second Division Northwest of Chateau Thierry,* Unpublished manuscript, Alfred M. Gray Research Library, Quantico, VA.
[3] *The AEF of a Conscientious Subaltern,* Box 1, Hanford MacNider Papers 1902-1967, Manuscript Collections, Herbert Hoover Presidential Library and Museum.
[4] History of the 9th Infantry, Box 48, RG 120.9.3, NARA College Park, MD.
[5] Correspondence LaRoy S. Upton to his wife Agnes 10 June 1918, LaRoy S. Upton papers, MHS, St. Paul, MN.
[6] Thomason, *Second Division Northwest of Chateau Thierry,* Unpublished manuscript, Alfred M. Gray Research Library, Quantico, VA.
[7] Ibid, and History of the 9th Infantry, Box 48, RG 120.9.3, NARA College Park, MD.
[8] *The AEF of a Conscientious Subaltern,* Box 1, Hanford MacNider Papers, Hoover Presidential Library and Museum.
[9] Ibid.
[10] *Records of the Second Division (Regular)* Volume 4, N.P.
[11] American Battle Monuments Commission, *2nd Division Summary of Operations in the World War,* (Washington: U.S. Government Printing office 1944), 8.
[12] Correspondence LaRoy S. Upton to his wife Agnes 10 June 1918, LaRoy S. Upton papers, MHS, St. Paul, MN.
[13] Spauling, Oliver and Wright, John, *The Second Division American Expeditionary Force in France 1917-1919,* (New York: Hillman Press, 1937), 251.
[14] Spaulding and Wright, *The Second Division American Expeditionary Force in France 1917-1919,* 251.
[15] Ibid.
[16] Ibid.
[17] General Lemuel Shepherd, interview by Robert Asprey June 20, 1963, Transcript, Personal Papers collection, Alfred M. Gray Research Library, Quantico, VA.
[18] Ibid.
[19] Cordes, *The Immortal Division,* 7.
[20] Correspondence Keller Rockey to Charles H. Ashley 2 November 1919, Folder 8, Box 6, Ashley Family Papers, Pocumtuck Valley Memorial Association Library, Deerfield, MA.
[21] Powis, "A Leatherneck in France 1917-1919"*Military Images Magazine,* 12.
[22] Scrapbook of Silverthorn, Newspaper clipping, "Minneapolis Man Tells of His days in Belleau Woods," Marie Silverthorn.

23. *The Aisne Defensive,* Whitehead to ABMC, Box 190, RG 117.4.2, NARA College Park, MD.
24. Note: Hotel de Ville is a French phrase that means City Hall. The structure used as division headquarters was the city hall facility for the town of Montreuil-aux-Lion.
25. Harbord, *The American Army in France*, 281.
26. Ibid.
27. Ibid, 281-82.
28. Catlin, *With the Help of God and a Few Marines,* 85.
29. Nelson, "Paris-Metz Road," *Leatherneck,* 11.
30. Jackson, *His Time in Hell, A Texas Marine in France,* 87.
31. General Gerald B. Thomas memoir, Personal Papers collection, Alfred M. Gray Research Library, Quantico, VA, and General Gerald B. Thomas, interview by Robert Asprey, Alfred M. Gray Research Library, Quantico, VA.
32. Gulberg, *A War Diary,* 23.
33. Hemrick, *Once a Marine,* 99.
34. Harbord, *The American Army in France,* 282.
35. Correspondence Lieutenant Colonel Thomas Holcomb to Joel D. Thacker headquarters Marine Corps, 12 December 1918, Box 70, Records of the American Expeditionary Forces, NARA College Park, MD.
36. Pike, *The Battle For Belleau Woods, As I Remember It About 60 Years Later,* 7.
37. West, *Belleau Wood,* Alfred M. Gray Research Library, Quantico, VA.
38. Correspondence Clifton B. Cates letter to his mother and sister 10 June 1918, Personal Papers collection, Alfred M. Gray Research Library, Quantico, VA.
39. Paradis, *The World War I Memoirs of Don V. Paradis,* 38.
40. Catlin, *With the Help of God and a Few Marines,* 85.
41. Correspondence Holcomb to Thacker, 12 December 1918, Box 70, Records of the AEF, NARA College Park, MD.
42. Messersmith, *Operations of 78th Company Sixth Regiment Marines at Belleau Wood,* MCoE, Donovan Research Library.
43. James McBrayer Sellers, *World War I Memoirs,* ed. by William W. Sellers and George Clark, (Pike: Brass Hat, 1997) 54.
44. Messersmith, *Operations of 78th Company Sixth Regiment Marines at Belleau Wood,* MCoE, Donovan Research Library.
45. Ibid.
46. Hamilton and Corbin, *Echoes From Over There,* 13.
47. Correspondence from Hill to Neufeld, 17 January 1979, Alfred M. Gray Research Library, Quantico, VA.

[48] Pike, *The Battle For Belleau Woods, As I Remember It About 60 Years Later*, 7.
[49] Peter Ward, *"Join The Marines," the sign said By Peter Christian Ward* written verbatim by his daughter Marjorie May Ward in 1965. Copy furnished to Lenny Moore by Peter Ward's granddaughter Mary Kathryn Sagedal. A Copy furnished in email to author by Lenny Moore May 6, 2012.
[50] *History of the 96th Company 6th Regiment in World War I* (Washington D.C., N.P., 1967), 50.
[51] Correspondence Cates letter to his mother and sister 10 June 1918, Alfred M. Gray Research Library, Quantico, VA.
[52] Ibid.
[53] Correspondence from Hill to Neufeld, 17 January 1979, Alfred M. Gray Research Library, Quantico, VA.
[54] West, *Belleau Wood*, Alfred M. Gray Research Library, Quantico, VA.
[55] Messersmith, *Operations of 78th Company Sixth Regiment Marines at Belleau Wood*, MCoE, Donovan Research Library.
[56] Sellers, *World War I Memoirs*, 54.
[57] Hamilton and Corbin, *Echoes From Over There*, 13.
[58] Messersmith, *Operations of 78th Company Sixth Regiment Marines at Belleau Wood*, MCoE, Donovan Research Library.
[59] Hemrick, *Once a Marine*, 100.
[60] Ibid.
[61] Ibid, 101.
[62] Jackson, *His Time in Hell, A Texas Marine in France*, 87.
[63] General Gerald B. Thomas, interview by Robert Asprey, Alfred M. Gray Research Library, Quantico, VA.
[64] General Gerald B. Thomas memoir, Alfred M. Gray Research Library, Quantico, VA.
[65] Ibid.
[66] General Gerald B. Thomas, interview by Robert Asprey, Alfred M. Gray Research Library, Quantico, VA.
[67] Ibid.
[68] Gulberg, *A War Diary*, 23.
[69] General Gerald B. Thomas memoir, Alfred M. Gray Research Library, Quantico, VA.
[70] Diary of Asa J. Smith 74th Company 6th Regiment U.S. Marines, American Expeditionary Force Second Division, Personal Papers Collection, Alfred M. Gray Research Library, Quantico, VA.
[71] Jackson, *His Time in Hell, A Texas Marine in France*, 88.
[72] Ibid.

June 1st Chapter II

[73] Ibid, 88-89.
[74] *Records of the Second Division (Regular)* Volume 5, N.P.
[75] Nelson, "Paris-Metz Road," *Leatherneck*, 11-12.
[76] William T. Scanlon, *God Have Mercy On Us* (New York: Houghton Mifflin Company, 1929), 6. Note: Scanlon's book is considered a novel but is based on real events from his experience with the 97th Company. He slightly altered the names in the book. His work in God Have Mercy on Us, won a prize from the Houghton-Mifflin company and the American Legion Monthly magazine for the best novel about World War One. Scanlon has slightly altered the spelling of names likely to protect his comrades who were involved in the story, but events depicted in the book mirror very much the recorded history of what took place.
[77] Nelson, "Paris-Metz Road," *Leatherneck*, 12.
[78] Scanlon, *God Have Mercy On Us*, 6-7.
[79] Hatcher, *Citizen Soldier,* N.P.
[80] General Alfred H. Noble Interview, 1968, Transcript, Personal Papers Collection, Gray Research Library, Quantico, VA.
[81] Hatcher, *Citizen Soldier,* N.P.itizen Soldier I: World War I Recollections of Pvt. James E. Hatcher, USMC edited by Gilbert Hart published Dec. 13, 2013. N.P.
[82] *History of the Third battalion, Sixth regiment, U.S. Marines* (Hillsdale: Akers, Macritchie & Hurlbut), 12.
[83] Nelson, "Paris-Metz Road," *Leatherneck*, 12.
[84] Ibid.
[85] Ibid.
[86] Ibid.
[87] Ibid.
[88] Scarbrough *They Called us Devil Dogs,* N.P.
[89] Ibid.
[90] Ibid.
[91] Scanlon, *God Have Mercy On Us*, 7.
[92] Ibid. Note: Twenty-six-year-old Private Clarence Pierce Nagle is listed as on extra duty as a cook 1st Class in the 97th Company muster rolls for June 1918. Scanlon misspelled Nagle 'Nagel.'
[93] Ibid, 8. Note: Scanlon refers to First Lieutenant Thomas McEvoy as 'McElroy.'
[94] Nelson, "Paris-Metz Road," *Leatherneck*, 12.
[95] Catlin, *With the Help of God and a Few Marines,* 89.
[96] Harbord, *The American Army in France*, 281-82.
[97] Harbord, *Leaves from a War Diary*, 291.
[98] *Records of the Second Division (Regular)* Volume 4, N.P.

[99] Allan Burton, *History of the Second Engineers 1916-1919*, (N.P, N.D), 31.
[100] Ibid, 30-31.
[101] Harbord, *The American Army in France*, 283-84.
[102] General Gerald B. Thomas memoir, Alfred M. Gray Research Library, Quantico, VA.
[103] Gulberg, *A War Diary*, 24.
[104] Jackson, *His Time in Hell, A Texas Marine in France,* 89.
[105] Note: Bois de Champillon is now known as St. Martins Woods.
[106] Jackson, *His Time in Hell, A Texas Marine in France,* 89.
[107] *Records of the Second Division (Regular)* Volume 4, N.P.

June 1st Chapter III

As we got nearer to the front, the French wounded appeared on the scene. The poor Frenchmen, streaming through our lines, cried to us to go back, that we could not possibly stop the oncoming Germans.
-Corporal Daniel E. Morgan, 77th Company, 6th Machine Gun Battalion

    The 6th Machine Gun Battalion had traveled at a sluggish pace for six hours after departing May-en-Multien at 5:00 A.M. The companies of the battalion had hauled their heavy Hotchkiss guns, tripods, and gear in the back of already crowded vehicles for the past thirty-six hours. The battalion's machine gun ammunition carts, as well as other supplies, moved to the front by railhead.
    By 11:00 A.M., the camions pulled into Montreuil-aux-Lions, and following a brief stop, they were herded further east along with the elements of the 6th Marine Regiment.[1] Many of the men did not even have time to eat their foraged trophies. "We had killed a few chickens and prepared to roast them when the order came, 'Into the lines,'" recalled Corporal Daniel Morgan of the 77th Company.[2] Annoyed at having to abandon their meals, the irritated machine gunners grabbed their gear and continued.
    The long procession of trucks carrying the Marines of the 6th Machine Gun Battalion stretched for hundreds of meters east of Montreuil-aux-Lions. The convoy slowly ground forward past a battery of French artillery firing slightly west of Paris Farm where the vehicles stopped.
    Company commanders exited the trucks, and after a quick briefing, the trucks carrying the 77th and 81st Companies continued east toward Le Thiolet. The battalion split into groups of two companies each. The 77th and 81st Companies were under the command of twenty-five-year-old Captain Louis Remsen DeRoode of the 77th Company, a Naval Academy graduate and president of the 1915 graduating class.[3] "As we got nearer to the front, the French wounded appeared on the scene," remembered Morgan.[4] "The poor Frenchmen, streaming through our lines, cried to us to go back, that we could not possibly stop the oncoming Germans."[5]
    Marines of the 77th Company dismounted the vehicles on the outskirts of Bois de Clerembauts. From the back of the beds of the trucks, men worked to pass the fifty-three-pound guns and equally heavy tripods down to the unfortunate ones tasked with hauling them the remaining distance to the line. Quickly, officers led the gun crews across the fields to the edge north of the Paris-Metz road and into Bois de Clerembauts.[6]
    Twenty-three-year-old Private William Wallace Fullington of Westerlo, New York, recalled, "Left our blanket rolls and went forward with combat packs, carrying the guns, tripods, and ammunition. I was a runner so did not have to carry anything."[7] Men walked awkwardly with the heavy weapons or tripods balanced on their shoulder. Others slung rifles to carry multiple

boxes of ammunition. "We took up our position along the Paris Metz road, running out of Triangle Farm," remembered Corporal Morgan.[8] Captain DeRoode's right group established their command post at La Cense Farm on the northwest corner of Bois de Clerembauts.[9]

The 77th Company hiked into positions where elements of the 96th and 79th Companies were digging in along the eastern edge of Bois de Clerembauts. Officers strategically chose gun emplacements along the woods facing the open valley to the east. While they tromped through the woods, they found several French troops who were eager to leave upon the immediate arrival of the Americans.

Corporal William Jackson of the 77th Company noticed one particular French soldier; his graying hair and aged appearance stood in contrast to his younger comrades. Jackson acknowledged the seasoned veteran only to discover he was able to speak English. Jackson learned that the man was part of a French reserve component of the army and became entangled in the extraordinary circumstances of the previous days. "He told me that we were to hold that line through the night and then fall back on them in the new line they would establish during the night. I laughed and told him that would not be necessary now. 'Why not,' he asked. 'Because you have an American Division in here now,' I answered. He roared. 'Ah the optimism of youth,' he snorted and took off."[10]

First Sergeant John McNulty was the First Sergeant of the 77th Company, 6th Machine Gun Battalion. Photo credit: Chris Carroll.

Members of the 77th Company unfolded the heavy tripods and affixed the cumbersome guns to the mounts. They calculated ranges and established fields of fire. Jackson's crew designated someone to be the first one on 'gun watch' while the others unrolled their packs and lay down to relax. In a short time, forty-one-year-old First Sergeant John McNulty, a seven-year veteran of the corps with eleven years prior service in the U.S. Army, tromped along the company's line. When McNulty discovered Jackson's gun crew sitting idly, he admonished the young Marines with a torrent of profanity. Jackson remembered the first sergeant, "bawling us out for not having dug the guns in somewhat and not having made shallow slip trenches for our own protection. This we proceeded to do throughout that day."[11] They dug out of concern of what the German's might throw at them but also out of fear of McNulty.

The 81st Company extended the area covered by the right group of the 6th Machine Gun Battalion. Entering Bois de Clerembauts, the company hauled their guns and equipment through the woods throughout the remainder of the evening. "My section (also all the rest) moved by hand from one end of the day to the other," recalled Sergeant Peter Wood.[12]

The company spent the late evening and night stretching its position north of La Cense Farm through Triangle Farm where men of the 79th Company's 2nd Platoon dug in. The line remained fluid throughout the night as the brigade's front continuously stretched further to the northwest.

The guns of the 6th Machine Gun Battalion's right group tried to cover the entire front southeast of Lucy-le-Bocage. Elements of the 78th Company's 2nd Platoon occupied the elongated finger of woods south of and parallel to the Lucy-le-Bocage–Bouresches road that evening. This area also became the left flank of the 6th Machine Gun Battalion's right group. However, it took most of the night and into the pre-dawn hours for all the gun crews of the right group to select emplacements.[13]

As the 77th and 81st Companies moved east beyond Paris Farm to form the battalion's right group, the 15th, and 23rd Companies, 6th Machine Gun Battalion comprised the left group. Twenty-eight-year-old Captain Matthew Henry Kingman, a Virginia Military Institute graduate from Humeston, Iowa, commanding the 15th Company, assumed command of the battalion's left group.

Kingman spotted Major Edward Ball Cole, the battalion commander, along the road near Paris Farm as the convoy arrived. Cole flagged down the lead vehicle carrying Kingman who recalled his exchange with Cole:

> He gave me verbal orders to take my company and the 23rd Company which was in column just behind us to the vicinity of Champillon and to place both companies in a defensive position along the line Lucy-le-Bocage-Hill 142, that this arrangement of machine guns was called a 'group' and that I was group commander. He handed me one hachured map of the sector, and the two companies proceeded in camions along the road towards Champillon.[14]

Traveling north of the Paris-Metz highway along the road towards the village of La Voie du Chatel, the left group passed several retiring French troops. They also encountered a battery of French guns, which, according to Kingman, "limbered long enough to fire a few rounds and then pulled out."¹⁵ The distant sound of enemy artillery to the north was noticeably clear.

The convoy passed La Voie du Chatel along a road flanked on both sides by a patch of woods where Major Berton Sibley's battalion moved into position. "We had no information as to what line the French were holding ahead if any," recalled Kingman, "and the camion drivers objected to proceeding any further. However, it was considered necessary to get into positions as quickly as possible and not to do anymore carrying by hand than necessary."¹⁶ About 200 yards south of the village of Champillon, the convoy crept to a stop, and the men dismounted.

Twenty-two-year-old Second Lieutenant Victor France Bleasdale, a former sergeant and three-year veteran of the Marine Corps who received a commission three days earlier, recalled, ". . . Jesus Christ, between the time we stopped our truck and we de-trucked—got out of our goddamn trucks—the Germans had advanced from artillery sound to machine gun sound. They were coming, boy, they were moving toward Paris."¹⁷ From the high ground around Champillon, Bleasdale saw a group of French troops down in the valley. The distant rattle of machine gun fire was much closer than they expected. According to Kingman:

Captain Matthew Kingman commanded the 15ᵗʰ Company, 6ᵗʰ Machine Gun Battalion. Photo credit: NARA.

> All the officers and the non-com section leaders were assembled, and after hurried directions, all gun crews moved to a position along the line Lucy-le-Bocage- Hill 142. The line of machine guns ran to the south of the woods because we had no connection with our own front line troops and no information as to the French position. It was my intention to move forward as soon as we established the American lines.¹⁸

Kingman, standing in the field next to Champillon, directed men to their position. He looked at Bleasdale and instructed the young officer to position his gun crew to the left part of the group's line. Kingman quickly briefed his senior Marines while men of the 15ᵗʰ and 23ʳᵈ Companies promptly unloaded, guns, tripods, and ammunition boxes from the back trucks. As his men handled the gear, Bleasdale spotted a set of sturdy wooden shutters covering a nearby farmhouse window. He quickly walked over to the building and had several men tear down the shutters with the intention of using them as a roof to cover his gun emplacement.[19]

Bleasdale moved with his gun crews a few hundred meters north of Champillon up the knoll of the sloping ground along the east side of the road connecting Champillon and Bussiares. This emplacement commanded the lane formed by the narrow path and steep embankment on the left. Bleasdale believed the French held the line further north. When his men reached their designated position, he realized the same group of French troops he spotted earlier had now retreated towards the American position.

One of the French soldiers carried a large container of wine. "I tried to buy a canteen of red wine off of them, and I wanted to give my diggers a couple swallows per man of good old Dago Red, as they call it," recalled Bleasdale, whose time in Haiti in 1915 made him relatively fluent in conversational French.[20] Bleasdale offered the Frenchman a gold piece for the canteen, but he refused the offer.

Second Lieutenant Victor Bleasdale commanded several sections of the 15th Company, 6th Machine Gun Battalion. Photo credit: NARA.

Bleasdale turned his focus back to his section's gun emplacements. "So I put my men, two guns now, to work digging the emplacements, generally speaking about a four by four hole sunk down to ground level and of course, you have to have the barrel above ground."[21] Once the guns crews dug in, they used the window shutters to cover the position and quickly piled dirt on top.[22]

While his crews were improving their gun emplacements, Bleasdale noted the overall lack of French troops other than the small group refusing to give up their wine. "There was still some firing going on up there toward the front, but it had died off a bit, and that had me a little bothered," recalled Bleasdale.[23] He also noticed the lack of traffic along the road from Champillon-Bussiares road, "and I knew of the moving of the wounded and stragglers and all that sort of stuff from my experiences with the French, there is traffic wherever your line—but there was none on that road. It was just a matter of minutes, you know, and things move fast on the battlefield, and I thought there's some goddamn thing funny about this deal," recalled Bleasdale.[24] The situation prompted him to investigate further.

Bleasdale rushed back to find the captain. He recalled, "And I went to Major [Captain] Kingman, and I said, 'Major, can I have permission to go forward to the front line, the French line, and I can order the front line and see who is in front of us, and see what the French Army is doing?'"[25] Kingman permitted him to investigate. Bleasdale took two getaway men with him. Their job, according to Bleasdale, is to "run like hell for the rear and get word to the commanding officers in the rear what has happened to the front, that the patrol, the reconnaissance party or whatever it is, is all dead."[26]

Bleasdale led the assigned men beyond the line and ordered each of them to maintain a distance of one hundred yards between each other whenever terrain dictated. "So I followed the land, the terrain, looking for Frenchmen, the French front line, and Christ, there were no Frenchmen, and in the line, there were no Frenchmen period. I thought what the hell, has everybody gone home—called the war off, or what is going on?'"[27]

With his getaway men following at the necessary intervals, Bleasdale continued to walk north and located a cluster of French troops rapidly digging fighting positions along the side of the road running north to south out of Champillon. He approached a group of noncommissioned officers conversing among themselves and realized they were the same group he encountered earlier while selecting gun emplacements.

Bleasdale, using his best French language skills, inquired as to the location of the front line. One man pointed at the group of French soldiers digging fighting holes. Somewhat stunned, Bleasdale then asked, "où est le Boche" (Where are the Boche). "He rattled on nonchalantly and said, 'Regardez vous! Le Boche.' [Looking at you! The Boche.]"[28]

Gazing out at an estimated 1,500-yard distance, Bleasdale watched German troops slowly moving in pairs through the fields south of Bussiares. Probing further, he asked about the location of any French officers. The exhausted soldier directed him to a clump of woods where a brief and uninformative conversation with a French officer yielded little additional insight and only reinforced the grim outlook.[29]

Before nightfall, Bleasdale returned to his gun emplacements and managed to find Kingman's position in a clump of woods southeast of Champillon. "There's nothing between us and the German Army," he told Kingman.[30] While explaining the situation to the captain, Bleasdale pointed to the north and exclaimed, "The German Army is advancing right over there through those woods over there—they're advancing on the double using infiltration. They'll be down here in an hour."[31] He explained the strategic location of his section covering the road, which ran north out of Champillon. "I said, 'I've got that road covered, and the high land on the

June 1st Chapter III

other side, but there is no rifle troops, and there is nothing—the French have nothing in the front line.'"[32]

That evening, Kingman, using the newly established telephone communication to the 6th Machine Gun Battalion command post near Montgrivault-la-Petit Farm, relayed the precariousness of the situation on the right.[33] The report concluded that, except for those few gun emplacements of the 15th and 23rd Companies, "there were no American troops from Hill 142 to over 1,000 yards east. . ."[34]

Earlier in the afternoon Major Edward Cole left his command post in the field between Bois de Clerembauts and Montgrivault-la-Petit Farm to inspect the lines along the eastern face of Bois de Clerembauts. Here, the machine guns of the 77th Company reinforced the line north of the Paris-Metz road.[35]

At 7:59 P.M., First Lieutenant Lothar Reymond Long, the battalion intelligence officer, relayed the disposition of guns to Brigadier General Harbord at brigade headquarters. Long explained that two Hotchkiss guns held positions along the Paris-Metz Road to cover the right flank of the brigade. The lack of telephone communication between the brigade and the Cole's 6th Machine Gun Battalion command post, a distance of nearly five and a half kilometers, required a runner to deliver the message.[36]

By dusk, the guns of the right half of the 6th Machine Gun Battalion continued working to extend the line between Triangle Farm and Lucy-le-Bocage. The descending sun reduced visibility as Marines of the 81st Company moved single-file through the woods south of the Lucy-Bouresches road. The men of First Lieutenant Shaler Ladd's gun section struggled to keep contact with each other in the dense woods. Hauling heavy guns and tripods further complicated their efforts to extend the line of the battalion's right group as far as possible.

Eventually, it became, "so dark that we could run into trees and the rear of the section would get lost," remembered Sergeant Peter Wood.[37] "The Lt. [Ladd] at last gave the order to lie down where we were."[38] The men dropped packs and quickly gave in to the fatigue that overtook their bodies after two days of nonstop, sleepless movement.

---

[1] Curtis Jr., *History of the Sixth Machine Gun Battalion*, 8.
[2] Morgan, *When the World Went Mad*, 28.
[3] Curtis Jr., *History of the Sixth Machine Gun Battalion*, 8-9, and Official Military Personnel File for Captain Louis R. DeRoode, RG 127, NPRC St. Louis, MO.
[4] Morgan, *When the World Went Mad*, 28.
[5] Ibid.
[6] Curtis Jr., *History of the Sixth Machine Gun Battalion*, 9.
[7] Diary of William W. Fullington, Pvt. USMC, Alfred M. Gray Research Library, Quantico, VA.
[8] Morgan, *When the World Went Mad*, 28.

[9] Diary of William W. Fullington, Pvt. USMC, Alfred M. Gray Research Library, Quantico, VA. Note: Fullington erroneously identifies the P.C. as Triangle farm but implies in his memoirs that it is the same P.C. as that used by the 80th Company which was La Cense Farm.
[10] Memoirs of 2nd Lieutenant William B. Jackson, 77th Company.
[11] Ibid.
[12] *Diary of Peter Wood,* N.P., Entry for June 1, 1918, Author's collection.
[13] Ibid, and Curtis Jr., *History of the Sixth Machine Gun Battalion,* 9.
[14] Correspondence Captain Mathew H. Kingman to American Battle Monuments Commission 30 October 1926, Box 189, RG 117.4.2, NARA College Park, MD.
[15] Ibid.
[16] Ibid.
[17] Brigadier General Victor F. Bleasdale interview by Benis Frank, Transcript, Oral History Section Marine Corps Historical Division Quantico, VA.
[18] Correspondence Kingman to ABMC 30 October 1926, Box 189, RG 117.4.2, NARA College Park, MD.
[19] Brigadier General Bleasdale interview by Benis Frank, Transcript, Marine Corps Historical Division Quantico, VA.
[20] Ibid.
[21] Ibid.
[22] Ibid.
[23] Ibid.
[24] Ibid.
[25] Ibid.
[26] Ibid.
[27] Ibid.
[28] Ibid.
[29] Ibid.
[30] Ibid.
[31] Ibid.
[32] Ibid.
[33] *History of the Sixth Machine Gun Battalion,* 9.
[34] Correspondence Kingman to ABMC 30 October 1926, Box 189, RG 117.4.2, NARA College Park, MD.
[35] Correspondence Captain T.J. Curtis to the American Battle Monuments Commission, 12 November 1926, Box 190, RG 117.4.2, NARA College Park, MD.
[36] *Records of the Second Division (Regular)* Volume 5, N.P.

June 1st Chapter III

---

[37] *Diary of Peter Wood,* N.P., entry for June 1, 1918, Author's collection.
[38] Ibid.

June 1st Chapter IV

We passed French soldiers going to the rear, on the roads and in the fields, the backwash of an army in retreat. Some turned their heads away; others saluted us disparagingly, while a few even shouted, 'Fini la guerre,' and waved for us to go back. They had small faith in our ability to stop the Germans. Well, we had plenty of doubts about theirs, too.

-First Lieutenant Elliott Cooke 18th Company, 2nd Battalion, 5th Marines

Earlier that afternoon, the 3rd Battalion, 23rd Infantry under Major Charles Elliott arrived in the town of Montreuil-aux-Lions. They were the tail end of the regiment's long column and had marched all day. As the exhausted troops hiked down the road, Colonel Preston Brown issued verbal orders for the men to proceed to a designated position south of the Paris-Metz road.[1]

According to Corporal Frank W. Anderson of Company M, 3rd Battalion, 23rd Infantry, "At the top of the hill we passed a huge pile of U.S. Quartermaster supplies, all food, and it looked as though we were going to have plenty of eats."[2] By the time 3rd Battalion's column cleared the town of Montreuil-aux-Lions, the regiment assumed a more tactical approach toward their positions since they were under enemy observation. Anderson remembered, "As we marched through the fields towards a road beyond, we took up combat formation. It looked as though we were really close to the enemy. We were ordered to bring gas masks to the alert position and fix bayonets. I took up my position at the head of the squad which was in single file and we entered the woods."[3]

Colonel Paul Malone, commanding the 23rd Infantry, worked feverishly to direct his battalions into the correct spot. "Our colonel seemed to be everywhere; he bawled out several of the boys for not having their gas masks at the alert and their bayonets on their rifles," remembered Anderson.[4] The 3rd Battalion reached their place in a patch of woods between Coupru and Ventelet Farm that evening.[5] According to Anderson:

> It was dark when we halted in a field at the edge of a woods; the battalion reformed, and each company marched into the woods in a column of twos at intervals of sixty feet to keep down the danger of bursting shell. We were told we would probably be there until daylight and small fires were lighted, one for each squad, and we cooked more bacon, hard bread, and made coffee. We carried the whole coffee bean in our condiment can, which we usually crushed with two stones. This was our first real rest in over sixty hours. We

June 1st Chapter IV

had been ordered to dig holes to lie in, but I was too tired to obey. I unrolled my blanket, laid it out, and went to sleep.[6]

During the early afternoon, elements of forty-year-old Lieutenant Colonel Frederic May Wise's 2nd Battalion, 5th Marines were still moving toward Montreuil-aux-Lions, an exhausting endeavor for troops already fatigued by little food and even less sleep. The 55th Company passed through the town of Lizy-sur-Ourcq, located on the northern bank of the Marne River. The village remained deserted except for a few French soldiers "gazing disinterestedly on the marines, as they filed through the narrow streets."[7]

The company walked along the north bank of the river eventually stopping at an adjacent boathouse. To the relief of the men, they received orders to stack arms and fall out for a quick rest. Most of the Marines used the reprieve to wash off the dust that stuck to their perspiring faces. Some scarfed whatever hardtack they had salvaged, but in short order, the company was back on the move. The men slung their packs and continued down the road.

The company, moving silently through the desolate town, filed passed a group of engineers who ate chow and stared, seemingly without emotion, upon the already exhausted Marines. The sun was high, and the day grew quite hot. The Marines' silently acknowledge civilian bystanders through squinted eyes that gazed up from under the brim of their helmets.

The already sore backs of the men, burdened with pack straps digging into their shoulders, made hiking more physically strenuous. Their sweaty faces, dusted with the fine powdery dirt from the road, revealed the arduous nature of their long journey to the front.[8] After another seemingly endless stretch of marching, the 55th Company arrived at the outskirts of Montreuil-aux-Lions during the afternoon. They eagerly fell out as a supply truck distributed rations.

By about 1:00 P.M., the 18th Company halted along the side of the road for a break just west of Montreuil-aux-Lions. The men lined up behind a quartermaster truck loaded with iron rations. One by one, the men took their chow, placing it in their packs and quickly sought a cool shady place in an adjacent patch of woods to rest their aching feet.[9]

The respite, however, was characteristically brief, and soon the company filed back on the highway. "We passed French soldiers going to the rear, on the roads and in the fields, the backwash of an army in retreat," remembered First Lieutenant Elliott Cooke of the 18th Company.[10] "Some turned their heads away; others saluted us disparagingly, while a few even shouted, 'Fini la guerre,' and waved for us to go back. They had small faith in our ability to stop the Germans. Well, we had plenty of doubts about theirs, too."[11] Against the distant rumble of battle, the column continued.

June 1st Chapter IV

The long exhausted column of the 18th Company eventually reached Montreuil-aux-Lions during the afternoon. They arrived in time to see the last vestiges of abandoned property ransacked by fleeing French soldiers.[12] The looters left homes open, kitchen drawers pulled out, and contents dumped on the floor. They raided nearly every room and turned everything inside out in search of anything of value. Some men were shocked, but most remained too exhausted to care. They merely longed for their painful day of marching to end.[13]

The company stopped on the outskirts of town, near the 55th Company. They received a welcomed lunch of corned beef, canned beans, tomatoes, and hardtack. The men, eager to get off their feet, tore into the first meal in twenty-four hours. The cans of Madagascar 'boeuf boulli,' usually instigated expressions of disgust once the smell hit the unfortunate soul opening the can. However, given the circumstances of the previous days, the men greatly welcomed the chance to eat.[14]

While the 18th Company ate, the noncommissioned officers of the 55th Company just down the road quickly summoned their men to their feet. Discontent with this game of stop and go, Marines disgustedly flung half-smoked cigarettes with the flick of a finger as they loathingly stood up to resume the hike. They threw packs on their back and grabbed their rifles from the stacks.

The men of the 18th Company hardly took a bite of their meal when they too, received the same order to depart—much to their discontent.[15] The battalion, in columns of two, pushed out into the hot afternoon sun once again.

On the way out of the village, several of the men in the 55th Company bucked up at the sight of General Omar Bundy and his staff watching intently as the Marines passed through the town.[16] French military traffic, moving toward Montreuil-aux-Lions from the battlefront, remained steady as Lieutenant Colonel Wise's men moved toward the sound of the guns. The order to clear the road parted the elongated column of men as they cleared a path for ambulances carrying casualties back from the battlefront.

They soon realized how close they were to the front. "On the plateau beyond Montreuil, we were within range of Heine's guns so our battalion broke into small columns," remembered First Lieutenant Cooke.[17] The battalion proceeded east down the sloping ground beyond Montreuil-aux-Lions nearly a mile and a half distance to the intersection between Ventelet and Marigny-en-Orxois. From there, they headed north toward Pyramide Farm situated a mile from the Paris-Metz Road where they passed a battery of French artillery.

The companies veered off the road into the fields. "I recall going down this dusty road and picking up three horseshoes and thinking luck was with me," recalled First Lieutenant Lemuel Shepherd of the 55th Company.[18] The French battery withdrew from the field past the arriving Americans but

June 1st Chapter IV

quickly reestablished a firing position further back and resumed their bombardment. Wise called his four company commanders forward and explained that the battalion would bivouac in the adjacent fields around Pyramide Farm that night.[19] He curtly reminded his company commanders that they must be ready to move at a moment's notice before sending them back to their men.[20]

The men established a bivouac site in the fields surrounding the farm as soon as officers gave the command to unroll packs. No sooner had they shed equipment and stacked rifles than they began to deplete the abandoned farm of any spirits or livestock. The doors to homes remained open, and animals wandered around the farm, revealing the haste with which the civilian inhabitants fled. Wise recalled, "The second echelons—horses, limbers, caissons—of several battalions of French artillery were in the neighborhood of the farm when we arrived. The guns were somewhere up ahead. Except for those French artillerymen, we were alone in the world."[21] Wise and his battalion staff took temporary residence in a stone building on the farm's property.

Captain Lester Wass, high stepping through the knee-high fields, returned to the officers of his 18th Company following the meeting with Wise. In his no-nonsense manner, Wass informed his platoon commanders that the company would bivouac at their present location. He then had the men form up. "We did it all ship-shape, and by the numbers: fall in—right dress—stack arms—fall out," recalled Cooke, who continuously pondered over the possibility of being under German observation during this show of pageantry.[22]

The men were well aware of the enemy's proximity, and the occasional hum and thud of a stray bullet flying sluggishly at the end of its long journey or the distant noise of artillery served as a constant reminder.[23] When Wass dismissed the company, they joined the rest of the battalion scavenging for food.

While Marines of the 18th Company prepared and ate whatever food they could rummage, Second Lieutenants Fred H. Becker, William Wallace Ashurst, Chester H. Fraser, and First Lieutenant Gilder Jackson sat down together to eat. First Lieutenant Cooke's mind turned to the inevitable battle looming on the horizon, which quickly supplanted his hunger with raw anxiety. "My stomach knew I was scared, whether I admitted it or not."[24]

After chow, the officers moved among the tents dotting the field checking on their men before retreating to a grassy area near the farm to roll cigarettes, and they sprawled themselves on their backs.

Gazing up at the sky, the officers engaged in prophetic conversation. As convoys of ammunition trucks cluttered the adjacent roadway, Jackson exclaimed, "Plenty of bullets being brought up."[25] At the end of a smoky exhale, Second Lieutenant Fraser sincerely inquired, "I wonder if a fellow hears the shell coming that hits him?"[26] Becker balked at the statement as he pulled his overcoat around him saying, "I bet if I heard a shell coming it wouldn't have a chance to hit me."[27]

Following the morbid tone of the conversation, the men were suddenly silent in thought while drawing out the final drag of their cigarettes and mulling over their pending fate. "The night was getting chilly, or perhaps it was nervousness that made us all shiver a little," recalled Cooke.[28] With cigarettes extinguished, they got up and walked to their quarters.

The night sky flickered from muzzle flashes as the French batteries nearby unleashed a torrent of fire on the distant German positions. "Cannons rumbled in the distance and a nearby '75' gave an occasional bark like an irritable watchdog," remembered Cooke.[29] "We were on the fringe of battle, but not yet a part of it."[30] The men were hours from facing the enemy.

Members of the 55th Company pitched tents in a field adjacent to one of the farm's houses. They quickly stacked their rifles and began to distribute jugs of cider discovered in the farmhouse. Several men removed their boots to find that the sting felt on their heels, soles, and toes during the day's march were now puss-filled, bright, red blisters. A nearby pool of stagnant water offered the only relief to their throbbing feet and the sole means to wash the sweat-caked dust off their hands and faces.[31]

For many, the fatigue generated by the previous few days won out against the thunder of distant artillery fire, and they managed to sleep undisturbed. Against the backdrop of the French barrage, First Lieutenant Lemuel Shepherd used what light remained in the western sky to write a letter to his mother in Virginia. With his canteen cup full of liberated cider within reach and perhaps a homesick spirit, he sorrowfully wrote:

> Dearest Mother: Am going to write you a few lines tonight. I don't know when I can send it, but it may reach you some time. We are up in the big scrap at last. "Fritz" has been advancing a week now and at present, he is only four kilometers away. We expect to go into action tomorrow morning and try and stop him. If anything should happen—here's my best love and wishes to you all. You will know I passed out like a true Virginia soldier and gentleman. We have been standing by for this show for a couple of weeks. It was indeed pitiful to see the refugees leaving this country. Old men, women, and children with what little stuff they could put on a wagon and their cows and chickens going in one direction, and infantry, artillery, cavalry, etc. going in the other. The place we are staying tonight has just been vacated. Everything in sight is ours. I am at present drinking some of an old farmer's cider and ate some of his rabbits for supper. It's the first meal in two days, so it went good. Well, will sign off now, as I have marched all day and am very tired. Best love to each and all of you. As ever,

June 1st Chapter IV

Lem.[32]

By evening Major Benjamin Berry's 3rd Battalion, 5th Marines entered Montreuil-aux-Lions after their all-day exhausting march. The column stopped briefly in town, long enough for the men to seek shade and rest their feet. Second Lieutenant George Gordon of the 16th Company encountered a haggard and subjugated looking French second lieutenant. The brief conversation between Gordon and the French officer revealed the demoralized state of Degoutte's troops. "The Boche was then only about ten kilometers away, he said, and everything was lost, and to try and stop them was useless. He believed with the speed they were advancing, this town would be taken the next day, and two days after Meaux would be in their hands, and in a week anyway they would be in Paris."[33]

Gordon, somewhat stunned by the severity of the situation, parted company with this man as the columns continued to march up the road. "If his comrades felt the same, then their morale was gone," reasoned Gordon.[34]

Colonel Wendell Cushing Neville (seen here as a Major General) commanded the 5th Marine Regiment. Photo credit: Michael Manifor.

At 4:10 P.M., forty-eight-year-old Colonel Wendell Cushing Neville, commanding the 5th Marines, ordered Major Benjamin Berry to "Proceed at once with your battalion to Pyramide, ready for action. Place your Battalion in rear of 2nd Bn. In column of route on left of road and await orders."[35] Berry, a sixteen-year veteran of the Corps who saw action in Vera Cruz and Santo Domingo, continued his battalion's route east. The column stretched for hundreds of meters through the barren town's narrow causeway lined with centuries-old stone buildings. Along the way, the battalion passed the occasional 'Poilus,' perhaps the last vestiges of a decimated unit. They exhibited the pitiful disheveled appearance of a routed army.[36] One by one, the long procession of men filed past an ammunition dump in the field outside of town, grabbing extra bandoliers of 30.06 rounds. They eventually turned north and arrived at Pyramide farm where both the 1st and 2nd Battalions already bivouacked.[37]

[1] *Operations of 3rd Battalion, 23rd Infantry from 30 May to 12 July 1918,* (paper presented at the Command and General Staff College Ft. Leavenworth, Kansas: 1931), Box 57, RG 120.9.3, Records of the American Expeditionary Forces, NARA College Park, MD.
[2] Spaulding and Wright, *The Second Division American Expeditionary Force in France 1917-1919,* 251.
[3] Ibid.
[4] Ibid.
[5] *Operations of 3rd Battalion, 23rd Infantry,* Box 57, RG 120.9.3, Records of the AEF, NARA College Park, MD.
[6] Spaulding and Wright, *The Second Division American Expeditionary Force in France 1917-1919,* 251.
[7] Brown and Geores, *55th Co. Marines in World War I,* Box 55, RG 127, NARA, Washington, D.C.
[8] Ibid.
[9] Harry B. Field and Henry G. James, *Over the Top with the 18th Company 5th Regiment U.S. Marines, A History,* (Rodenbach: N.P, 1919), 18.
[10] Cooke, "We Can Take It, We Attack," *Infantry Journal,* 4.
[11] Ibid.
[12] Ibid.
[13] Ibid, and Field and James, *Over the Top with the 18th Company 5th Regiment U.S. Marines,* 18.
[14] Field and James, *Over the Top with the 18th Company 5th Regiment U.S. Marines,* 18. Note: boeuf boulli was a type of beef canned as an "iron ration" by the French. Many of these were produced by a company called Madagascar, a name which was printed on the can. The British called this 'Bully Beef' due to the pronunciation. Because of the Madagascar label, many Americans jokingly assumed it must contain monkey meat, and so the name stuck.
[15] Ibid.
[16] Brown and Geores, *55th Co. Marines in World War I,* Box 55, RG 127, NARA, Washington, D.C.
[17] Cooke, "We Can Take It, We Attack," *Infantry Journal,* 4.
[18] General Lemuel Shepherd, interview by Robert Asprey, Alfred M. Gray Research Library, Quantico, VA.
[19] Cooke, "We Can Take It, We Attack," *Infantry Journal,* 4.
[20] Wise and Frost, *A Marine Tells it to You,* 195.
[21] Ibid.
[22] Cooke, "We Can Take It, We Attack," *Infantry Journal,* 4.

June 1st Chapter IV

[23] Ibid.
[24] Ibid, 5.
[25] Ibid.
[26] Ibid.
[27] Ibid.
[28] Ibid.
[29] Ibid.
[30] Ibid.
[31] Brown and Geores, *55th Co. Marines in World War I*, Box 55, RG 127, NARA, Washington, D.C.
[32] Correspondence Lemuel C. Shepherd to his mother 1 June 1918, Folder 29-30, Box 67, Virginia Military Institute Archives Preston Library, Lexington, VA.
[33] Gordon, *Leathernecks and Doughboys*, 53-54.
[34] Ibid.
[35] *Records of the Second Division (Regular)* Volume 5, N.P.
[36] Gordon, *Leathernecks and Doughboys*, 54. Note: The Term Poilus was a term of endearment used to describe the French. The term means hairy. It was used to describe the seasoned and grizzled appearance of bearded or mustached French soldiers.
[37] Ibid.

June 1st Chapter V

They are mad, they come in waves too thick to mow down, they are inspired with the prospect of Paris. Paris is lost. Nothing can save it. Deploy here, and hinder them as you drop back.

-An Unidentified French Artilleryman

In the woods north of La Voie du Chatel, officers of the 97th Company permitted their men to start cooking fires during the late afternoon. They prepared some bacon for the grease which made hardtack bread more palatable. They tried to cook it all before the fading sun made fires too dangerous in the face of German observation. "It was the first time we had ever used our reserve rations," remembered Corporal William Scanlon.[1] "Several of us used the same pan, and when we got through there was quite a lot of hot grease. The hardtack was dry and tasteless, so I took a couple chunks and put them into the grease and let them stew up a bit. Then I fished them out and bit off a piece."[2]

The other men followed suit and made their seemingly rock-hard bread edible—"something like pie crust when it is cooked by itself without any filling."[3] As the order passed throughout the woods to extinguish fires, Scanlon's squad doused the blaze that hissed into a plume of smoke rising through the trees.

First Lieutenant Thomas McEvoy stopped and briefly spoke with Scanlon's squad before moving about the rest of the platoon to ensure that the men extinguished all fires. "When he was leaving he said, 'If you fellows are cooking any bacon save the grease and heat your hardtack in it. It makes the hardtack taste better.'"[4] The other men looked at each other incredulously. "Leave it to the officers to steal the credit," one man remarked upon the departure of the first lieutenant [5]

Some members of the 97th Company discovered a large heifer idly roaming away from the herd in the field at the edge of the woods. One by one, members of Scanlon's squad filled their canteen cups with the cow's milk. Other squads caught wind of the cow's presence and quickly lined up. "The cows didn't seem to mind," recalled Scanlon.[6] "They wanted to stay near us. They looked lonely and forlorn and they mooed very softly, their big mournful eyes fixed on us as if they wanted to tell us something."[7] The men savored the milk as a way of filling their empty stomachs with some sustenance.

When the last sliver of sunlight vanished over the horizon, things became unusually quiet for Major Berton Sibley's 3rd Battalion, 6th Marines. Despite occasional explosions and echoing gunfire in the distance, the men enjoyed the lull in what had been a chaotic previous two days. According to Scanlon, "This was the nicest place we had been in for some time. Everything seemed pleasant, and now that we had our own cows, we were

June 1st Chapter V

contented to stay. Some of the fellows had unrolled their packs and were stretched out in blankets for the night."[8]

Despite the serenity in that immediate area, the battalion vacated the woods in case the enemy had observed their movement, which would inevitably attract incoming shells. The 97th Company filed out of the woods and moved into the ditch along the road connecting the village of Champillon and La Voie du Chatel. Despite the precaution, the night passed quietly.[9]

Major Maurice Shearer's 1st Battalion, 6th Marines spent the night somewhat on edge as the crack of rifle and machine gun fire, seemingly closer than it had been hours before, announced the impending battle. The 95th Company became the battalion reserve. They occupied positions behind the front in Bois de Champillon situated several hundred meters over the rising ground northwest of Lucy-le-Bocage.

The company dug in for the night following a frustrating evening as they constantly shifted positions. The night, however, passed quietly. Corporal Warren Jackson and twenty-year-old Corporal William Caswell Ferris worked together to excavating a dugout.[10] "We took a turn at watch during the night," remembered Jackson, "and I was on for an hour."[11] Peering into the darkness, Jackson listened to the distance rumble of battle.

In the village of Lucy-le-Bocage, Private Asa Smith of the 74th Company observed the forlorn demeanor of a few isolated French withdrawing from the line. Several even gestured to the newly arrived Marines to follow their path.[12]

Except for occasional French soldiers, the town remained deserted. Marines of the 74th Company, however, encountered a feeble elderly couple who stayed behind. The old woman's tears penetrated any language gap that existed, and clearly, they did not want to abandon their home. Officers, however, convinced the pleading old woman that it was not safe and to evacuate the town immediately. The couple reluctantly left Lucy-le-Bocage.[13]

During the evening, French troops continued passing through elements of the 75th Company holding a line along the edge of the town. One particular French platoon strayed into the town looking disheveled and defeated, and Private Gus Gulberg recalled, "They were to make a new stand with us. Upon reaching our line, they immediately threw themselves on the ground in front of us and went to sleep. They certainly were all in."[14] By nightfall, a few light artillery shells landed near the 75th Company's position, compelling elements of Private Gulberg's platoon to dig in.

As soon as they finished excavating dugouts, the 1st Battalion, 6th Marines received orders to extend their line further to the northwest, which forced several platoons to relocate. "We changed positions several times during the night, digging new holes every time we moved," recalled Gulberg.[15] "I was getting damn tired of digging. No one slept that night."[16]

June 1st Chapter V

Despite the misery experienced in Gulberg's platoon, Second Lieutenant David Redford's 3rd Platoon spent a quiet and relatively restful night in a dry streambed on the outskirts of the village.[17]

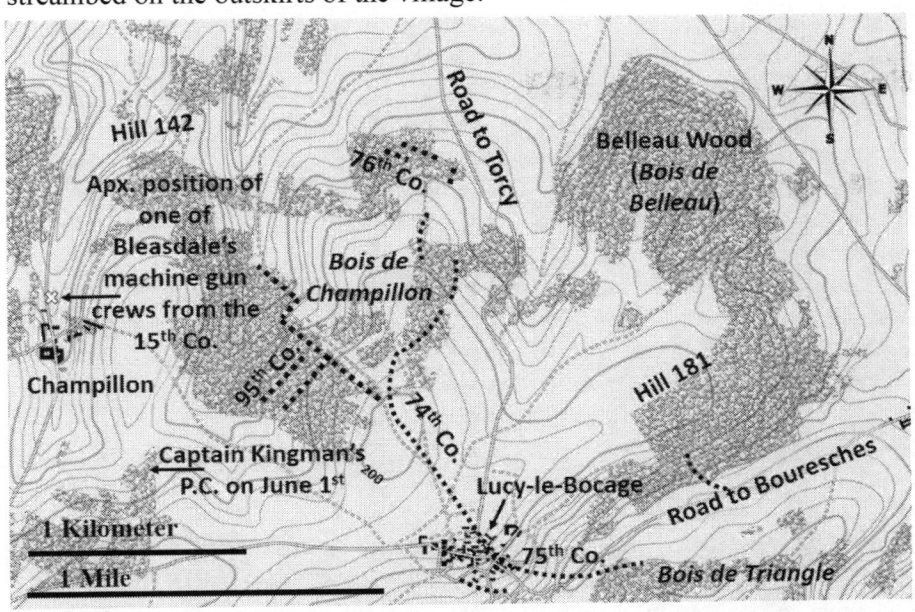

The position of Major Shearer's 1st Battalion, 6th Marines on June 1st.

During the night, the forward lines of the 74th Company occupied the eastern outskirts of Lucy-le-Bocage with no machine guns positioned along their front. The darkness made men flinch at virtually every noise and any lurking shadow. Sometime during the night, Private Asa Smith and other members of the forward line heard movement distinguishable enough that the men were convinced it was an advance enemy patrol. The men collectively opened fire into the murky blackness—the muzzle flashes flickered in the darkness. Men frantically reworked the bolt of their Springfield rifles and repeatedly fired at the unseen yet suspected Germans.

The crescendo lasted only seconds before dwindling into single, discernable single shots along the line and then faded into a distant echo resonating across the field. In just a few moments, the peaceful sounds of night supplanted the thunder of rifle fire without any return shots received. Smith, unable to see anything in front of him, maintained a heightened state of alert as he lay on the ground with his rifle at the ready. Following the thunderous volley, sleep was impossible, and Smith maintained a nervous watch throughout the night.[18]

Private Louis Linn and other support personnel of the 77th Company, 6th Machine Gun Battalion were inside the town of Marigny-en-Orxois that night. On the northeast corner of the village stood a magnificent chateau,

June 1st Chapter V

and it was here that Private Linn and other members of the company bivouacked behind the developing line for the night.

Linn and a comrade approached the outer gates of the estate. "There were French sentries here and he was uncertain if they would let us proceed. However, they did, without any remark. The village was unlighted and abandoned, only occasional French soldiers hurried through. A threatening quiet brooded in its empty streets," Linn remembered.[19]

Despite the feeble line established north and south of the Paris-Metz road, several elements of the 2nd Division continued to struggle against traffic as they marched toward Montreuil-aux-Lions. The 5th Machine Gun Battalion hiked well into the night.

They traveled all day, stopping in the city of Acy-en-Multien for a few hours before resuming their arduous hike. "Up and down hill, in and out of woods, we wound, with the firing always drawing nearer," recalled First Lieutenant William Westover of Company A.[20] "The horizon on our left resembled a vast electric storm—light and sound in continual vibration."[21]

Shortly before midnight, the battalion turned onto the Paris-Metz road for the final stretch into Montreuil-aux-Lions. They found military traffic of all kinds crowding the highway from both directions. One particular French artilleryman grabbed Captain Andrew Bruce by the arm, rhetorically inquiring why they were heading east because there was no way the Germans were stopping. "They are mad, they come in waves too thick to mow down, they are inspired with the prospect of Paris. Paris is lost. Nothing can save it. Deploy here, and hinder them as you drop back," declared the demoralized soldier.[22]

In a dignified manner and with as much diplomacy as his exhausted spirits could muster, Bruce explained to the man that orders specified that they move forward to hold the line. The artilleryman shuddered at the prospect and disgustedly walked away.[23]

The forty-man dismounted detachment of the 2nd Military Police Company arrived earlier that evening. They immediately tried to control the flow of vehicles, animals, and people along the Paris-Metz Road from Montreuil-aux-Lions to the Paris Farm.[24] The traffic became almost too heavy along the road. The lack of light complicated things immensely, so the 5th Machine Gun Battalion pulled the long column off into the fields to let the congestion subside, but the tide was endless. Everything west of Montreuil-aux-Lions, however, remained in complete chaos. The battalion, with its animal-drawn wagon trains and gun carts, could not move any further east under such conditions.

Captain Bruce quickly summoned First Lieutenant Westover and ordered him down the road to proceed to Montreuil-aux-Lions. "Division headquarters should be there. Report the position of the company and ask for orders. Explain the need of rest, and request permission to bivouac until daylight, Hurry," Bruce demanded.[25]

Darkness blotted out the landscape, and the view of distant villages blended into the blackness of night; fires on the horizon were the only illumination in addition to the moonlight. The town was down the sloping road a short distance. Westover soon arrived in Montreuil-aux-Lions.

Traveling down the narrow winding streets now guarded by military police, Westover headed towards the clock-domed Hotel de Ville on the south side of the Paris-Metz road. He recalled, "Ten minutes later I found the Assistant Chief of Staff and the Adjutant in a room wherein maps, messages, orders, and telephones were coordinating the disposition of the units. It took but a moment to state our location and condition." [26]

The senior officer looked at Westover somewhat puzzled as if there were some confusion and rhetorically restated the young lieutenant's questioned, "Company A, 5th Machine Gun, a half-mile south of town? I thought you were to get here by marching. Where did you find trucks?"[27] Tactfully but assuredly, Westover replied, "We did march."[28] The senior officer looked even more mystified and pleasingly replied, "Good god—great work! Tell Bruce to get some sleep. Report here for orders at five-thirty. Have the men ready to move at that time. That's the best we can do. It will help. Tell your men they made a great march. We didn't expect you for another fifteen hours. Now that you're here, you're needed."[29]

Westover quickly returned to the company and relayed the information to Bruce, much to the captain's relief. The battalion was collectively on the brink of collapse. Orders to bivouac hardly reached the men before they unrolled packs and fell soundly asleep. The stream of traffic rolling down the adjacent road and the distant rumble of artillery hardly jostled them from their slumber.[30]

The day before, thirty-six-year-old Major Benjamin Mart Bailey's 1st Battalion, 15th Field Artillery Regiment detrained north of Meaux and had marched from morning until that evening.[31] The entire way remained congested with traffic. According to First Lieutenant Elmer Hess, "The left side of the road was filled with trucks, ammunition, retreating French soldiers, field hospitals—all in great confusion."[32] During the day, the regiment marched toward the town of Lizy, sixteen-kilometers from Montreuil-aux-Lions, where they stopped for the evening.

The men, according to Hess, were "tired, dusty and dirty."[33] The town of Lizy was in an uproar. "Stragglers and infantryman in great confusion, wearing the horizon-blue of the French, dragged themselves to the rear. An entire regiment of French field artillery galloped through the town towards the rear carrying their wounded," recalled Hess.[34] The passage through Lizy, though slowed by refugee traffic, did not stop. "We marched until midnight with practically no rest and on into the morning. We could hear the songs sung by the American artillery marching ahead."[35]

June 1st Chapter V

Along the 2nd Division's front, inside the abandoned village of Marigny-en-Orxois, Private Louis Linn and a comrade took full advantage of the vacated spoils of the empty town. Linn recalled:

> At the public fountain, we were seized upon by two French soldiers, who, with much whispering and drinking of their thumbs, led us to an open cellar door and departed. We went down the stone steps to a large vaulted cellar, whose walls were lined with barrels and kegs and cases of liquor. It must have been the cellar of the village café, for most of the barrels and kegs had stop corks. We went from one to another, mess cup in hand, sampling each in turn. Twice we filled our canteens only to pour them empty again because we found something we liked better. In a final decision between cherry brandy and Malaga wine, we all chose the latter, and after filling our canteens for the last time departed.[36]

After passing once again by the sentry-guarded gates of the chateau, Linn and his more intoxicated comrade ensured their safe passage by sharing some of the liberated spirits with the French sentry. The chateau served as a dressing station, as evidenced by the rows of ambulances parked outside.

As Linn and his comrade walked by, an English-speaking voice devoid of any French accent greeted them. "He was an American himself," recalled Linn, "and had been two years in the French ambulance corps, hence the good English. We stood talking by his ambulance. He showed us several places where shell fragments had torn into the car."[37] The two Marines looked at the shrapnel-riddled vehicle nearly speechless as the man told his harrowing tale. "'Too bad,' he remarked. 'I had two men killed in my ambulance the trip before last.'"[38]

The men inquired about the current situation at the front slightly north of the village in which they stood. "'Ah, the French are coming back as fast as they can, they evacuate towns before we can get the wounded out,' he olds us. 'Last trip we ran into a town that the Germans had; we thought the French still had it. There were only two of us, but we turned our cars around and got out under fire. On the road, we picked up a lot of exhausted Poilus that would have been taken.'"[39]

Linn and his comrade were stunned at the rapidity which their newfound comrade described the German advance. Linn recalled:

> We whistled softly at the direness of these tiding and the thunder roll in the distance became more menacing. 'The line,' he presently continued, 'is only about five miles away now. I would not be surprised if the Germans take this place by morning.' Again, we

fell quiet. We had been talking in whispers, I don't know why, and that oppressive, threatening silence gathered about us. To break it we gave our new friend, and the rest of the drivers, a drink of wine and in return they gave us cigarettes. At the end of this exchange an order was called to them, and with a hasty goodbye, our acquaintance ran with the rest of the drivers to start his engine. 'Day and night now,' he called to us as the cars moved off. 'Good luck,' and he was gone in the night.[40]

At the 6th Machine Gun Battalion Headquarters near Montgrivault-la-Petit Farm, thirty-eight-year-old Captain Thomas Joseph Curtis, the battalion's adjutant, wandered over to the farm where he encountered soldiers of the 2nd Engineers. According to Curtis, "The sole civilian occupant of the town was an old French woman. She seemed to be very distracted; wandering through the territory occupied by the houses of the farm. I did not pay much attention to her that day."[41]

During the next morning, one of the engineers informed Curtis of a terrible scene discovered in the barn. "I went over and looking in, saw the old lady hanging from the rafters," remembered Curtis.[42] "Evidently she had hanged herself during the night. It was a very gruesome sight. No doubt the movements of the war into her home had unbalanced her mind, with the consequent results."[43] The shocking sight remained with him forever.

As the fading sun signaled an end to June 1st, the 2nd Division had placed several regiments along a materializing front behind the shattered remnants of the broken French who gallantly held the badly mangled line. This brave effort by Degoutte's soldiers enabled American troops to continue arriving at the developing front for the next several days.

From the artery of Montreuil-aux-Lions, they fanned out east to extend and strengthen a thinly-held battlefront. For the next several days, the American line would expand and eventually contract to cover a shorter front. Getting the various regiments, battalions, and companies connected and in place, however, remained problematic for the next several days. Gradually, the French front would fade beyond the emerging American line and put Major General Bundy's men face-to-face with a corps of German troops that had been attacking the French vigorously since May 27th.

---

[1] Scanlon, *God Have Mercy On Us*, 8.
[2] Ibid.
[3] Ibid.
[4] Ibid, 9.
[5] Ibid.
[6] Ibid.
[7] Ibid, 9-10.

June 1st Chapter V

[8] Ibid, 10.
[9] Nelson, "Paris-Metz Road," *Leatherneck*, 13.
[10] Jackson, *His Time in Hell, A Texas Marine in France,* 91. Note: Corporal William C. Ferris was awaiting a General Court Martial for mutinous conduct since April 10, 1918, and according to Jackson remained under guard without a rifle. When the 2nd division entered the line, Ferris accompanied the Company but was without a rifle due to his being under guard.
[11] Ibid, 89.
[12] Diary of Asa J. Smith 74th Company 6th Regiment U.S. Marines, Alfred M. Gray Research Library, Quantico, VA.
[13] Ibid, and History of the 74th Company 6th Regiment U.S. Marines, compiled by Sergeant Carl W. Smith, Box 35, RG 127, NARA College Park, M.D.
[14] Gulberg, *A War Diary*, 24.
[15] Ibid.
[16] Ibid.
[17] General Gerald B. Thomas memoir, Alfred M. Gray Research Library, Quantico, VA.
[18] Diary of Asa J. Smith 74th Company 6th Regiment U.S. Marines, Alfred M. Gray Research Library, Quantico, VA..
[19] Louis C. Linn, *At Belleau Wood with a Rifle and a Sketchpad: Memoir of a United States Marine in World War I*, ed. By Laura Jane Linn Wright and B.J. Omanson, (Jefferson: McFarland and Company, Inc.,2012), 88.
[20] Westover, *Suicide Battalions*, 106.
[21] Ibid.
[22] Ibid.
[23] Ibid.
[24] *History of the 2nd M.Ps,* Box 89, RG 120.9.3 Records of the American Expeditionary Forces, NARA College Park, MD.
[25] Westover, *Suicide Battalions*, 107.
[26] Ibid.
[27] Ibid.
[28] Ibid.
[29] Ibid.
[30] Ibid, 108.
[31] *Notes on the 15th Field Artillery prepared by Colonel J.R. Davis May 1919*, Box 82, RG 120.9.3, Records of the American Expeditionary Forces, NARA College Park, MD.
[32] Spaulding and Wright, *The Second Division American Expeditionary Force in France 1917-1919*, 249.
[33] Ibid.

[34] Ibid.
[35] Ibid.
[36] Linn, *At Belleau Wood with a Rifle and a Sketchpad,* 88.
[37] Ibid, 89.
[38] Ibid.
[39] Ibid.
[40] Ibid, 89-90.
[41] Correspondence Curtis to the ABMC, 12 November 1926, Box 190, RG 117.4.2, NARA College Park, MD.
[42] Ibid.
[43] Ibid.

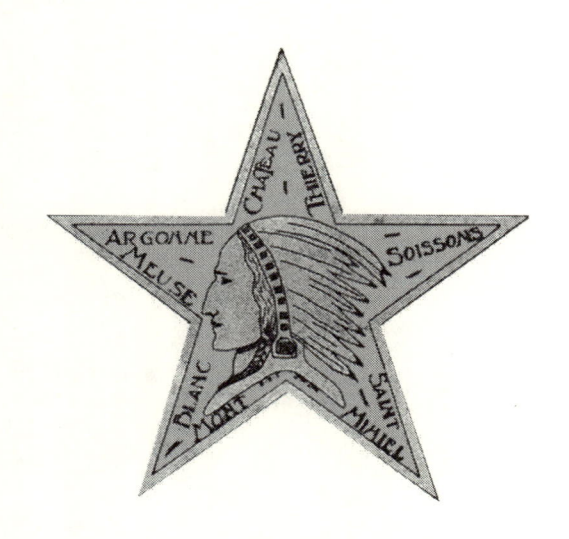

JUNE 2ND

June 2nd Chapter I

The Germans kept up their steady push and the French continued to fall back. It became more and more clearly evident that we had not come a moment too soon and that we had been cast for a role at the center of a seething stage.
-Colonel Albertus Catlin 6th Marine Regiment

After Major Julius Turrill's 1st Battalion, 5th Marines bivouacked for the night of June 1st; a messenger summoned Turrill to report to division headquarters in the middle of the night. According to Turrill, "Late that night I was ordered down to Division Headquarters at Montreuil-aux-Lions, where I found Colonel Malone, of the 23rd Infantry, and the Divisional Chief of Staff, Colonel Brown."[1] The Commander of the French 43rd Division was also present in the dimly-lit headquarters.

During the meeting, Turrill learned that a four-kilometer gap existed on the left of the French 43rd Division now holding the western portion of the line. According to Turrill, "As I remember it, we were told that there were no French troops between the Bois de Veuilly and the town of Gandelu."[2] This problematic situation required immediate action, and Turrill's Marines along with Malone's soldiers went to fill the gap since they were closest to this precarious sector of the front.

Turrill's battalion, rousted from their sleep in the middle of the night, made another forced march toward this portion of the line. "Before daylight the next morning we had to rise and pack up," recalled Private Onnie Cordes of the 17th Company.[3] By 2:00 A.M., the exhausted men rolled their bedding in the darkness. They piled their bedrolls and formed up wearing only combat packs.[4]

The battalion moved fast to reach the southern tree line of Bois de Veuilly before dawn so that this patch of woods would mask their movement from enemy observation. Well before the sun appeared, the battalion took to the road as the advance guard headed to the threatened area. Fatigue overcame the men who marched listlessly down the dark, dusty street. Each man tried to keep the pack of the Marine in front of them at an arm's length so as not to cause the column to separate in the dark.

The entire 23rd Infantry had a thirteen-kilometer hike in the dark to get to the vulnerable gap. "At three o'clock in the morning we were up again," remembered Corporal Frank W. Anderson of Company M, 3rd Battalion, 23rd Infantry. "We assembled in the yard of a farmhouse, lined up, and roll call was taken. Our rolls were dropped and piled up. Later we would come back and get them if we lived that long."[5] By 4:30 A.M., the long column of Major Charles Elliott's 3rd Battalion, 23rd Infantry left the region around Ventelet Farm.[6] The sun crested in the east, and officers pressed their men to move with the utmost urgency before the dawn's light put the battalion in peril.

June 2nd Chapter I

Company C, 1st Battalion, 2nd Engineers followed the columns of the 23rd Infantry. First Lieutenant Arthur G. Spencer, commanding Company C, led the men out of the woods near Ventelet Farm in a single file procession at dawn.[7] Under the peaking sun, the formation broke into columns to begin the daylong hike.

The march, with long shovels, picks, and a multitude of engineering gear in addition to their packs, ammo, and weapons, suggested they would endure more of the same misery and fatigue that characterized the previous few days. Private John 'Chick' Hubert recalled, "The 1st and 4th platoons were assigned to the 1st Battalion of the 23rd Regiment, while the 2nd and 3rd platoons were assigned to the 3rd Battalion of the infantry regiment."[8]

Company B, 1st Battalion, 2nd Engineers established a command post along a sunken road approximately one kilometer south of the Paris-Metz highway and southeast of Le Thiolet. The company's 1st Platoon quickly took shelter along the depression as the men eagerly unrolled packs, and they did not hesitate taking time to sleep.[9] The 2nd, 3rd, and 4th Platoons occupied positions along the woods south of Le Thiolet and the Paris-Metz road. The men, exhausted from the hours of constant movement, hardly budged from their slumber even when enemy shells screeched overhead later that morning.[10]

The predawn reveille also greeted Company A, 5th Machine Gun Battalion. By 3:30 A.M., soldiers on guard duty, one by one, subtly prodded the numerous blanket-shrouded men scattered throughout the field. "The guards who had fought to keep awake during the hours when exhaustion threatened to overpower them took delight in rolling the men out of warm blankets onto the dew-covered ground," remembered First Lieutenant William Westover.[11]

The mess crew for Company A had morning chow prepared much to the delight of the tired soldiers. With only a few minutes to eat, the company loaded gun carts and moved down the road toward Montreuil-aux-Lions. Inside the town, Captain Bruce dismounted his horse and walked with his staff into the 2nd Division headquarters where he received information on the latest developments. He received instructions to take his company about ten kilometers northwest to the town of Coulombs in support of the 23rd Infantry. By the time Company A filed out of town, the sun had appeared and hinted at another bright and warm day. Westover recalled:

> Moving out toward the northwest, the Company was soon under observation from low-flying enemy planes. Ahead the guns rolled and pounded. From the hillcrests, the smoke of batteries in action to the east dotted the country. The Boche planes were not given much freedom. French squadrons were constantly appearing to give

June 2nd Chapter I

chase or battle. The air held continual skirmishes between opposing planes.[12]

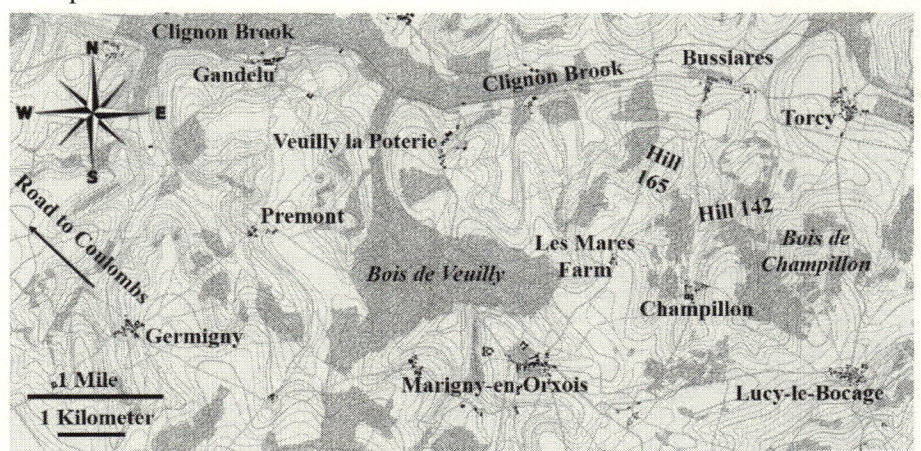

The line from Coulombs to Gandelu and tying into the western-most flank of the 2nd Division in Bois de Veuilly was tentatively held but required the 1st Battalion, 5th Marines as well as the 23rd Infantry to fill the gap.

In the early morning hours, Brigadier General Harbord traveled a few hundred meters from his command post at Issonge Farm to Pyramide Farm as the distant rumble of artillery fire to the north and east signaled another day of heavy fighting.

Before departing his headquarters, Harbord dispatched a messenger to Montreuil-aux-Lions to urge them to get his telephone line reestablished believing the French cut it mistakenly.[13] He remained cognizant that the next twenty-four hours might prematurely transition his brigade from occupying a support position to holding the front line.

The artillery fire and increased presence of French troops retreating from the battlefront prompted Harbord to dispatch a message to Colonel Catlin at 6:10 A.M. Harbord's instructions stated, "Please report every fifteen minutes during day whether anything is happening or not, and no matter whether you are in support or in front line. Your liaison officer has not reported here as ordered. Please give these matters your attention at once."[14] Catlin noted, "On June 2nd, after a night that could not have been entirely restful, our men awoke to the realization that the French were filtering through. The Germans kept up their steady push and the French continued to fall back. It became more and more clearly evident that we had not come a moment too soon and that we had been cast for a role at the center of a seething stage."[15]

Two companies of the 2nd Battalion, 2nd Engineers, were sent to reinforce Catlin's tenuously held line. The engineers eventually located Catlin in the corner of a patch of woods at approximately 3:00 A.M.[16] Due to the darkness of night, the unfamiliar terrain, and a general lack of

June 2nd Chapter I

accurate maps, Company F, 2nd Battalion, 2nd Engineers became separated and went into Lucy-le-Bocage.[17]

Catlin directed Captain Edward N. Chisholm's Company D, 2nd Battalion, 2nd Engineers to move east through Bois de Clerembauts, and reinforce Major Thomas Holcomb's 2nd Battalion, 6th Marines. Chisholm divided his platoons and assigned one to each of the four companies of Holcomb's battalion.

Company E, 2nd Battalion, 2nd Engineers, also sent to support Holcomb's line, remained back while advanced elements of the company conducted a reconnaissance before the platoons moved toward Triangle Farm.[18] From there, Company E spread out to reinforce the line, dug fighting positions, and fortified machine gun emplacements for Holcomb's Marines.[19]

As elements of the 2nd Division arrived along the battlefront throughout the day, Colonel Richard Derby, the division's sanitary inspector, worked to establish field hospitals along the line. Derby left Vincy-Manœuvre early in the morning and traveled nearly thirty kilometers to Montreuil-aux-Lions. When he arrived, Derby promptly reported to the division chief of staff, Colonel Preston Brown.

After a short meeting, Derby left the Hotel de Ville and proceeded by motorcycle sidecar towards the town of Bezu-le-Guery where he planned to establish one of several field hospitals. Bezu-le-Guery consisted of fewer than fifty buildings, centered on a small church and adjoining two-story schoolhouse on the north end of the village's winding street. Derby recalled his arrival in the town and noticed signs of the population's sudden evacuation. Walking into the town's abandoned schoolhouse, Derby noted:

> The schoolroom was high ceilinged, with one wall a black-board. It was a room of ghosts. Under date of May twenty-ninth, still stood the composition lesson of that day. *Un jour de grand vent* [A windy day]. It must have been much more than a day of great wind to the children attending that last class; truly a day of much alarm, borne on the wings of a great Hun advance. Under the caption *La Pensee* [The thought], the lesson went on: *L'homme libre obeit a sa conscience et aux lois de son pays*. [The free man obeys his conscience and the laws of his country]. Almost in the presence of the enemy, the children of France were being taught the righteousness of their fathers' cause. Then came a column of words, that last word unfinished. The lesson had been interrupted.[20]

Derby selected the schoolroom and adjoining church as Field Hospital number 1. The floor of the church, with the pews removed, was to serve as a room for the litters of wounded that would inevitably arrive in the next few days. In the courtyard, division medical personnel erected a tent to serve as a decontamination area for gassed victims. In the schoolroom, blankets draped from the ceilings quartered off a section as a resuscitation ward—undoubtedly a place where many men would draw their final breath.[21]

From the window of a house at Pyramide Farm just before 5:00 A.M., Lieutenant Colonel Wise watched his officers and sentries awaken the 2nd Battalion, 5th Marines. Simultaneously, platoon commanders bellowed their unsympathetic demand for haste as they walked among the still groggy men, and abruptly shouted orders to pack their gear in anticipation of a sudden departure from Pyramide Farm. The men exited their blankets and found the chilly breeze especially uncomfortable against their dew-soaked, wool shirts. They rolled packs and secured loose gear to allow some time to eat whatever scant rations they had. Upon finishing their meager meal, they spent the next several hours waiting.[22]

By 7:00 A.M., officers of the 55th Company shuffled the platoons into the nearby tree line to avoid enemy observation.[23] French artillery batteries from the 37th and 232nd Field Artillery Regiment, positioned just south of Wise's men, unleashed a torrent of heavy fire in support of the French infantry desperately trying to stem the German onslaught. The concussion of the rounds leaving the tube reverberated from their concealed wooded position with such force that the ground beneath seemed to shutter. Members of the 55th Company sat and listened to the dull, distant crunch of the shells landing on the high ground several kilometers to the north.[24]

While awaiting orders, Wise met with his four company commanders and remembered:

> I explained to them there was no doubt the line was broken and the French were on the run. That soon we would be up there trying to stiffen them and that there was no doubt they would start filtering back through us. That on no account were they to let our men get demoralized when the French start coming through us. That when we got there, we were there to stay, and the men were to know it. I told them to explain it to the men, so that there wouldn't be any doubt anywhere about sticking. All that morning we waited in suspense.[25]

Along the high ground in the southeastern corner of Bois de Champillon, Corporal Warren Jackson and his comrades of the 95th Company had a view for several miles to the north over the trees. French artillery fire, targeting a distant village down in the valley far to the north, became a spectacle for the men who watched with great curiosity. Jackson could barely see the distant plumes of smoke as shells fell near a house outside of the town.[26]

June 2nd Chapter I

As small plumes of smoke blossomed on the horizon from shells exploding far to the north, Jackson asked to borrow twenty-four-year-old First Lieutenant Frederick Collins Wheelers field glasses and peered over the treetops of Bois de Champillon as the terrain declined to the north. Every few seconds a shell was dropped in the vicinity of the house, throwing clods and dust into the air, leaving where the round struck, an irregular mass of black smoke. Such was the distance between us and the falling shells that we did not hear the explosion until some seconds after the black puff appeared over the place where the projectile had dropped.

Several men of the company assembled to watch the display with jovial curiosity. The time lapse between the report of French guns to the south and the impact of the shell gave the men time to speculate where along the distant pasture the shell might land. Jackson recalled:

> The shells had been dropping but a short time when, following the fall of a shell close to the house, half-crouching, hatless figures began to scamper in abandoned haste across the open space to the plot of wood-running for their lives. The sight was novel; strange to say, even amusing! Why I was affected by this tragic scene in the way I was I do not understand . . . Yet it was sport now to see these fellows, much like we were and with similar hopes and ambitions, running a race with death.[27]

The gun crews of the 81st Company, 6th Machine Gun Battalion spent the previous night continually moving to locate a more advantageous position along the right half of the brigade's front. One section, commanded by First Lieutenant Shaler Ladd, spent much of the night and predawn hours moving through thick woods and unfamiliar terrain to consolidate that stretch of the line.

Early that morning, Ladd finally settled on a position that he believed offered advantageous fields of fire for his gun sections. His men dug their emplacements, much to the relief of Sergeant Peter Wood, whose gun crew was utterly exhausted.[28] The machine gunners spent the morning under cover of the dense woods and balanced their time between resting and improving their gun emplacements.

By early morning, the distant sounds of gunfire crackled much louder than before as elements of the 2nd Battalion, 398th German Infantry closed in from the east towards the town Bouresches.[29] The 3rd Battalion advanced on the regiment's right flank. German soldiers advanced on a two-company front, the 10th and 12th Companies in the first wave followed by the 9th and 11th Companies.[30] French soldiers, desperately trying to hold the line, broke in the face of the enemy's renewed onslaught and continued to pass piecemeal through the positions of the 2nd Battalion, 6th Marines. Several

French soldiers continued their retreat beyond the developing American line, but several dug in with the Marines.[31]

By 8:30 A.M., from the wooded crest south of the Lucy-le-Bocage –Bouresches road, Marines observed small groups of enemy troops in the distance moving through the fields in three waves. They were too far for the Americans to engage them with their Springfield rifles effectively, but they were within range of heavy machine guns. Section leaders of the 77th and 81st Companies watched through binoculars as dispersed formations of Germans meandered through the fields just east of Bouresches.[32]

Once alerted to the enemy's movements, machine gun section leaders ran along company positions to reestablish liaison between their crews. Gunners of the 77th and 81st Companies sat back on the seats of their tripods as crewmembers broke open boxes and

Eastern flank of the 4th Brigade's front on the morning of June 2nd.

removed strips of ammunition—placing them within arm's reach.

Gunners turned the elevation wheels of the tripods and traversed gun carriages so that their muzzles were fixated on designated points down into the valley within their fields of fire.[33] Everyone watched intently waiting for the command to open fire. Officers cautioned the gunners, tightly grasping the weapon's brass pistol grip with white-knuckled anticipation, to remain patient. With binoculars suspended to their eyes, section leaders watched the rapidly approaching enemy and called out estimated ranges.

Everyone watched the small distinguishable figures in the distance with amazement. For many, it was the first time they had seen the Germans first hand, which they so intensely loathed. These enemy combatants, now visible in the distance, were no longer imagined propaganda-driven entities but rather living breathing, armed, and very determined soldiers advancing toward their lines.

Members of the 77th Company, 6th Machine Gun Battalion seen here on June 2nd dug in along the edge of Bois de Clerembauts near Triangle Farm with their M1914 Hotchkiss Machine Gun. From left to right the members of this gun crew are: Corporal John Henry Sanks, Private Warren Seagrave Norman, Private Nathan Solomon, First Sergeant John McNulty, Gunnery Sergeant Fitzhugh Lee Buchanan. Also present are unidentified members of the 96th Company and several French soldiers of the 356th Infantry. Photo credit: Center for Military History.

From positions along the eastern outskirts of Boureches, French machine gunners of the 214th and 356th Infantry Regiments watched the German infantry approach. Elements of the French 152nd Infantry Regiment dug in along the east edge of Bois de Belleau (Belleau Wood) also spotted the waves of approaching enemy soldiers.[34] Once the Germans were between 1200 and 1600 meters away, officers signaled for the gunners to commence firing.[35] The valley erupted with the pulsating crack of Hotchkiss guns as French and American crews assailed the advancing enemy from three sides. Along the edge of Bois de Clerembauts and Bois de Triangle, gunners of the 77th and 81st Companies maintained an unmerciful barrage of fire in short but accurate bursts. The Germans ranks faltered and quickly went prone. Suddenly, they resumed the advance in small rushes.³⁶

Crewmen working as loaders knelt to the left of the Hotchkiss guns and jammed strips of ammunition into the weapons as soon as the empty ones ejected from the other side of the machine guns. Section leaders directed the fire of their men by observing, through binoculars, the plumes of dust as impacting slugs struck the distant ground. By yelling directions and distances to adjust the fire of their crews, they walked machine gun rounds in on the advancing enemy as well as those laying prone trying to conceal themselves in the tall wheat.

Looking west toward Triangle Farm from the German lines. Photo credit: NARA.

The effects on the German advance were telling as enemy soldiers disappeared in the grain, some for cover—others fell dead or wounded. As the enemy rose up from their prone position to flee, the unrelenting American and French fire inflicted even more casualties. According to the German war diary, "The line was not reached since the enemy resisted vigorously in the patches of woods."³⁷ After a brief but thunderous deluge, the echo of machine gun fire tapered off across the valley, and the adrenaline surge among the crews of the 77th and 81st Companies turned to exhilaration over their brief victory. The Germans, however, would soon return.

Runners quickly delivered news of the attack to La Cense Farm, the command post for the right group of the 6th Machine Gun Battalion. Major Cole's battalion headquarters near Montgivrault-la-Petit Farm received news of the encounter in a telephone message stating, "Enemy attacking along our whole front at 8:30 A.M. They were about 1200 yards from our position."³⁸ A runner was dispatched to inform Colonel Catlin located near Lucy-le-

June 2nd Chapter I

Bocage of the update, and by 9:57 A.M., Brigadier General Harbord carried news of the attack.[39]

---

[1] Lieutenant Colonel Julius H. Turrill interview with by Joel D. Thacker Muster Roll Section Headquarters U.S.M.C. December 11, 1918, Box 17, RG 127, NARA, Washington, D.C.
[2] Ibid.
[3] Cordes, *The Immortal Division*, 7.
[4] Ibid, and Scrapbook of Silverthorn, Newspaper clipping, "Minneapolis Man Tells of His days in Belleau Woods," Marie Silverthorn.
[5] Spaulding and Wright, *The Second Division American Expeditionary Force in France 1917-1919,* 252.
[6] *Operations of 3rd Battalion, 23rd Infantry*, Box 57, RG 120, Records of the AEF, NARA College Park, MD.
[7] *History of the Second Engineers 1916-1919*, 36.
[8] John "Chick" Hubert, Memories of C Company 2nd Engineers, as found with Scrapbook of Merwin Silverthorn, which accompanied a 6 February 1980 letter from John Hulbert to Merwin Silverthorn, Provided to the author by Marie Silverthorn.
[9] *History of Company B Second Engineers,* Box 87, RG 120.9.3, Second Division File, Records of the AEF, NARA College Park, MD.
[10] Ibid.
[11] Westover, *Suicide Battalions*, 108-109.
[12] Ibid, 109-110.
[13] *Records of the Second Division (Regular)* Volume 4, N.P.
[14] *Records of the Second Division (Regular)* Volume 5, N.P.
[15] Catlin, *With the Help of God and a Few Marines*, 91-92.
[16] Ibid, 89-90.
[17] W.A. Mitchell, *The Official History of the Second Regiment of Engineers and Second Engineer Train United States Army in the World War*, (San Antonio: San Antonio Printing Co, 1938), 23.
[18] Burton, *History of the Second Engineers 1916-1919,* 43.
[19] Ibid.
[20] Derby, *Wade in Sanitary*, 57-58.
[21] Ibid, 59.
[22] Brown and Geores, *55th Co. Marines in World War I*, Box 55, RG 127, NARA, Washington, D.C., and Wise and Frost, *A Marine Tells it to You,* 195.
[23] Brown and Geores, *55th Co. Marines in World War I*, Box 55, RG 127, NARA, Washington, D.C
[24] Ibid.
[25] Wise and Frost, *A Marine Tells it to You*, 195.
[26] Note: The village Jackson is referring to is likely the town of Hautevesnes. From the area around Hill 200 the village of Hautevesnes is visible to the north over the trees of Bois de Champion.
[27] Jackson, *His Time in Hell, A Texas Marine in France,* 89.
[28] *Diary of Peter Wood,* N.P. Entry for June 2, 1918, Author's collection.
[29] Thomason, *Second Division Northwest of Chateau Thierry,* Unpublished manuscript, Alfred M. Gray Research Library, Quantico, VA.

June 2nd Chapter I

[30] War Diary and Annexes 1st 2nd and 3rd Battalion, 398th Infantry 2 June 1918, *Translation of War Diaries of German Units,* Vol. 1.
[31] *Records of the Second Division (Regular)* Volume 9, N.P.
[32] Diary of William W. Fullington, Pvt. USMC, Alfred M. Gray Research Library, Quantico, VA., and History of the 6th Machine Gun Battalion, NP, 9.
[33] Curtis Jr., *History of the Sixth Machine Gun Battalion,* 9.
[34] *Records of the Second Division (Regular)* Volume 9, N.P., and Thomason, *Second Division Northwest of Chateau Thierry,* Unpublished manuscript, Alfred M. Gray Research Library, Quantico, VA.
[35] Curtis Jr., *History of the Sixth Machine Gun Battalion,* 9.
[36] Ibid.
[37] War Diary and Annexes 1st 2nd and 3rd Battalion, 398th Infantry 2 June 1918, *Translation of War Diaries of German Units,* Vol. 1.
[38] *Records of the Second Division (Regular)* Volume 5, N.P.
[39] Ibid.

June 2nd Chapter II

If you don't hurry up, the Germans will get there before you do. When you get there, you stick. Never mind how many French come through you.
                              -Colonel Wendell Neville, 5th Marines

By mid-morning, the final elements of the 5,000-man detachment from the 23rd Infantry and 1st Battalion, 5th Marines arrived to fill a four-kilometer gap in the line between the abandoned town of Coulombs and a span of woods five kilometers north of Montreuil-aux-Lions.[1] The 23rd Infantry's thirteen-kilometer march west towards Coulombs took most of the morning and within full view of the enemy. Major Charles Elliott's exhausted 3rd Battalion, 23rd Infantry arrived in position east of Coulombs, and by 9:50 A.M., I Company had established liaison by patrol with Major Julius Turrill's 1st Battalion, 5th Marines on the right. The area remained relatively quiet until late morning.[2]

The other two battalions of Colonel Paul Malone's 23rd Infantry rushed their sleep-deprived troops towards Coulombs later that morning—an incredibly daring move. In many points along the route, the procession marched parallel to the frontlines on the forward slopes of the high ground. Most of the regiment reached Coulombs without incident since they remained out of range of German artillery until late morning. By the time thirty-four-year-old Major Edmund Clivious Waddill, the son of a former U.S. Congressman and federal judge from Richmond, Virginia, led his 1st Battalion forward into the town; enemy artillery was within range and commenced firing. Waddill's battalion, the last to reach their designated position, held the westernmost portion of the line, therefore catching the brunt of the enemy bombardment. The first volley of shells crashed without warning among the ranks of Company A. The violent concussion instantly killed Private Charles Maggoine and mortally wounded Private Paoset Zaico.[3] The exploding shells severely injured two other

Major Edmund Waddill. Photo credit: NARA.

soldiers from Company A. Medics rushed to assist the casualties as the platoons cleared the road upon realizing that they were under observation.

By approximately 10:30 A.M., Captain Andrew Bruce's Company A, 5th Machine Gun Battalion entered the desolate town of Coulombs. The ransacked homes and storefronts illustrated the haste with which the populace evacuated. The abandoned structures provided ideal cover for the men to conceal themselves and the company's animals from enemy observation.[4]

According to First Lieutenant William Westover, "No orders were forthcoming; Bruce took the initiative."[5] Bruce gathered his officers and explained that the company's role was to serve as a secondary line through which the French could fall back. He ordered men to establish machine gun positions on the crests north of the town.

Soldiers of Company A also initiated reconnaissance to establish liaison with the 23rd Infantry and to select individual locations for the gun crews along the northern outskirts of the village as directed. He explained to his officers, "Send runners to learn the routes forward to the positions selected. If the Boche get through the gap ahead, we will hold them on the line selected. There will be no retreat. These guns are to be used to break up an attack; Fire as long as you are able."[6] The company spent the rest of the morning in nervous anticipation.

The 5th Machine Gun Battalion remained the only available machine guns of the 3rd Brigade. The other battalion assigned to the brigade, the 4th Machine Gun Battalion, remained stalled at Compans-la-Ville located northeast of Paris. Their convoy had been in a collision with a civilian caravan the day before, which created not only a ten-hour delay but injured several soldiers.[7] The battalion's movement could not resume until the early morning of June 2nd, and by late morning, they arrived at Ormoy-Villiers to await embarkation at the rail yard.[8]

Forty-year-old Major Edmund Loughborough Zane, commanding the battalion, grew frustrated that the division's motorized machine gun battalion, a designation based on rapid mobility, experienced significant delays. Zane's battalion had yet to receive word that the entire division was redirected from Meaux to Montreuil-aux-Lions the day before. At 11:40 A.M., he dispatched an urgent plea to division headquarters stating, "I report that the 4th Machine Gun Battalion (less Fords) the 1st Field Signal Battalion and Hdqtrs. Troop arrived here at 11:30 A.M. and are now unloading. I request that you send me 14 three-ton trucks to move the 4th Machine Gun Battalion to May-en-Multien as ordered. We have no transportation and cannot even march afoot."[9] Hours passed before the battalion resumed their movement.

Just before noon, a vehicle pulled up to the farmhouse at Pyramide Farm where Lieutenant Colonel Wise's 2nd Battalion, 5th Marines awaited instructions. Colonel Wendell Neville, the commanding officer of the 5th

Marines, stepped out from the back seat and immediately scurried toward the farmhouse as Wise stepped out to greet him, but Neville wasted no time with polite greetings. Wise recalled Neville's prompt instructions. "'You've got to get out of here right away,' he told me. He handed me a map and an order. I saw that we were to establish a line from Hill 142 to the northeast corner of the Bois de Veuilly, as support for the French, who were out in front of us."[10] According to Neville, the French line grew increasingly weak and exhausted, and no hope remained that it would be able to hold. "If you don't hurry up, the Germans will get there before you do. When you get there, you stick. Never mind how many French come through you," urged Neville.[11] With those vague instructions, the regimental commander climbed back into his vehicle and sped off.

Wise immediately summoned his battalion intelligence officer, twenty-four-year-old First Lieutenant William Rankin Mathews of Lexington, Kentucky. After briefing Mathews on the situation, Wise directed him to scout the battalion's designated line. "Colonel Wise sent me ahead to Marigny to see if the coast was clear," remembered Mathews.[12]

Mathews, a graduate of the University of Illinois, was perhaps among the first officers of the brigade to have seen action in France. He attended the British Physical and Bayonet school at Pol, France, the previous January. While attending this school, he spent time at the active front with a West Yorkshire Regiment of the 62nd Division of the British Expeditionary Force. While attached to the English, Mathews participated in the engagement against the Germans at Oppy Woods.

Upon returning to the 4th Brigade, he rejoined the 55th Company in February but then became the battalion intelligence officer by April.[13] As the companies assembled, Mathews departed for the battalion's designated position armed with a set of semaphore or wigwag flags to signal to the companies that the village was, in fact, safe to approach.[14] "I then continued out the road to Les Mares Farm and found a French regimental headquarters."[15]

Back at Pyramide Farm, buglers sounded assembly within moments of Neville's departure. Platoon commanders from Wise's companies massed their Marines into a formation. Since about 9:00 A.M., groups of French soldiers steadily trickled back through the battalion's present position, evidence that the Germans steadily pressed the line. The companies assembled and moved through the fields towards the road that stretched north to Marigny-en-Orxois. Men grabbed bandoliers of ammunition from crates that had been stacked nearby as they gathered on the road.[16]

Inside Marigny-en-Orxois, Mathews and his scouts ensured the village remained clear before bringing the battalion forward. "I entered Marigny with a group of my men and wig wagged back to Wise that it was clear."[17] The village, situated along a flat road across an open plain, stood less than two kilometers from Pyramide Farm. Wise's companies moved forward separately to avoid drawing the attention of German artillery.[18]

As the columns moved closer to the front, members of the 55th Company noticed several French soldiers coming down the road from the opposite direction. The exhausted Poilu, as the American referred to the French Infantry, dropped their gear and nearly collapsed; the utter stress and exhaustion of combat visible through their expressions. The long procession of 55th Company Marines also passed American signalmen who were at work running telephone lines forward.[19]

The frenzied activity seemed to increase as the columns moved further north. The fields on the outskirts of town were alive with French batteries of 75mm guns hammering away. Soon, a single spotter plane circling in the skies above helped adjust the fire of the French batteries.[20] On the outskirts of town, the battalion halted, and Wise summoned his company commanders forward.

One-by-one, company commanders, and battalion staff hurried forward through the winding streets towards the northern edge of the village. They conversed and coordinated with each other as they trotted through the town trying to address last-minute details before bringing their men forward to occupy the line. Wise located an old cemetery on the northeastern edge of town. The stone walls enclosing the graveyard provided excellent protection. The position offered a good a view of the valley below, so Wise promptly made the spot his battalion headquarters.

As he organized his command post, signalmen hauling their massive spools of wire worked to establish telephone communications to connect Wise's 2nd Battalion with Neville's 5th Regimental headquarters near a rock quarry outside of Marigny-en-Orxois.[21] While his companies deployed to their designated positions, Wise informed Neville, "Part of our line is in front of a battery and I may have to change the line a trifle. The men are all out and it will take me several hours to check everything up. At present headquarters cemetery north of Marigny."[22] With that information, Neville informed brigade headquarters as to the disposition of the 2nd Battalion, 5th Marines.

On the edge of town, a cluster of the 2nd Battalion's officers examined the open terrain before them. Standing abreast, they peered over each other's shoulder to get a glance at the few available maps. They tried to match the terrain features on the map with the landscape before them to gain familiarity with the area. After a brief assessment of the ground they were to occupy, officers sent runners back with orders for companies to come forward.

Just north of Marigny-en-Orxois, First Lieutenant Mathews, while scouting the designated line ahead of the battalion, encountered a small detachment of French near Les Mares Farm. "A Frenchman gave me accurate details of the positions of the French and enemy troops in the valley

June 2nd Chapter II

below."[23] Mathews learned that the Germans maintained steady and consistent pressure upon the gradually eroding French line and that the enemy artillery spotters had a complete view of the road from Marigny-en-Orxois to Les Mares Farm.

Realizing that elements of the 55th Company were about to occupy the farm and would likely utilize the road from Marigny-en-Orxois, Mathews had to caution them. "I immediately dispatched a note to Wise and told him that Les Mares Farm was under enemy observation and that no troops should be allowed out to that road."[24] Mathews then headed back to Marigny-en-Orxois and was relieved to discover that his warning arrived in time for Wise to advise Captain Wass and thirty-three-year-old Captain Charley Dunbeck, commanding the 43rd Company, to utilize a protected approach that stretched a few hundred meters northwest to Bois de Veuilly.

The center of the town of Marigny-en-Orxois looking west. The structure on the right is the Mairie building (town hall). Photo credit: Gilles Lagin.

The four platoons of Wass's 18th Company encountered several French Chasseurs vacating Marigny-en-Orxois. First Lieutenant Elliott Cooke noticed the exhausted expression of one French officer and offered the man a cigarette. "He regarded me from a pair of eyes sunk into an unbelievable depth far into his head. Fatigue, hardship, agony and worst of all-despair were pictured there," recalled Cooke.

As the officer grabbed the cigarette and clinched it in his mouth, Cooke inquired hesitantly as to how things were going. The weary man, shielding the cigarette as he lit it, relished the first drag and paused. "'My frien,'" he said with a heavy French accent as he stared intently at the young American officer, "'lose the gun and the bullet, yes, but save the shovel. Neyer lose the shovel—never.'"[25] The man kindly regarded Cooke and continued his exodus south, "his coat tails flapping and smoke from my cigarette trailing behind him," remembered Cooke, who felt somewhat shaken by the apparent anguish of such a seemingly experienced soldier.[26]

The 18th Company pushed through the town of Marigny-en-Orxois just as the piercing hiss of incoming shells ripped through the air overhead. The explosions echoed through the streets of the village. The Marines moved quickly, and to their surprise, the shells landed in and around the center of the town. The smoke and dust from shattered masonry loomed over the village rooftops—close enough to hasten the men's pace as they scurried through Marigny-en-Orxois.

They moved through the town unscathed, and "Out in front strutted Captain Wass, with me three paces right rear, and the battalion following in column of squads," recalled Cooke.[27] German gunners, however, evidently saw the company's movement just as Wass halted the platoons. Before he directed them single-file into the thick Bois de Veuilly, the scream of more arriving shells roared overhead. The split-second whine of incoming rounds preceded the explosion by only a split second and left the men no time to react. The first volley of rounds landed in calculated succession through the treetops. Each explosion sent fragments of jagged steel into the 18th Company's 4th Platoon and sent the rest of the company flat on their stomachs.[28]

The men looked up through the clearing smoke, dust, and drifting leaves from their prone position only to see a ghastly sight. Some men stood frozen with fear, and according to Cooke, "Faces turned white and the company showed a tendency to huddle and mill about."[29] The inactivity and lack of reaction in the seconds after the initial volley of fire drew the ire of Captain Wass who screamed, "Get going! What do you think this is a kid's game? Move out!"[30] As the terrified men raced through the woods, nineteen-year-old Private Joseph McKinley Brock, a mill hand from Eliga, Georgia, lay motionless with a ghastly mortal wound to the head.[31]

No one could do anything to save Brock. His comrades were ordered to keep moving and could do little more than take one final glance at his broken, lifeless remains as well as those of the wounded strewn about the area. Twenty-five-year-old Private Daniel Burt Carter was among the severely injured. A shell fragment smashed into the left side of his jaw and left his face a bloody mass of torn and mangled flesh. Additional shards of steel ripped through his left thigh. Private John Oscar Degenhardt lay on his back in agony as the intense pain set in from jagged fragments that penetrated the twenty-three-year-old's abdomen.[32] The cries for first aid intermixed with angry shouts of officers urging their men to keep moving toward their designated position.

Brazened by the sudden shock of the enemy's barrage, the Marines of the 18th Company continued their adrenaline-induced sprint through the thickets of Bois de Veuilly. Desirous of going back to help the wounded, the men had to leave their comrades for the hospital corpsmen. As the rest

June 2nd Chapter II

of the company moved north through the woods, litter bearers quickly carried the company's wounded men to cover, but Private Brock's lifeless body lay where it fell until soldiers from the 15th Ambulance Company could arrive later that day to bring him back to a nearby dressing station for burial.[33]

During the entire jaunt through hundreds of meters of thick forest, the report of distant guns announced the momentary arrival of more incoming shells. First Lieutenant Cooke remembered, "We scuttled through the woods, ducked and dodged as more shells pounded a shallow trench to our right, and then threw ourselves face down in the northern edge of the Bois de Veuilly. To our front was a wheat field falling away gently to a narrow little valley and rising again to a forward slope some eight hundred yards ahead."[34] Only a handful of French troops remained in position, and one particular officer summoned Captain Lester Wass and, "advised him that it was utterly useless to prepare for a stand here."[35] Wass, the ever-rigid and abstemious commander, just explained to the French officer that the company had orders to hold this line.[36]

Those few remaining French troops seemed eager to yield their position to the recently arrived Americans, and they wasted no time pulling back from the northern fringe of Bois de Veuilly. As French soldiers withdrew from the woods to Marigny-en-Orxois, German artillery shells fell among them, "and those who were retreating through Bois de Veuilly complained of gas and many of them were coughing and choking as they pass," remembered Captain Frank Whitehead of Headquarters Company, 5th Marines located in the town.[37]

Along the northern outskirts of the village, First Lieutenant Mathews arrived at Wise's battalion command post along the village's cemetery wall where he encountered thirty-year-old Captain Lloyd William Williams of Berryville, Virginia, who preceded his 51st Company into the Marigny-en-Orxois to scout his company's designated position. According to Mathews, "After I gave him my information he ducked off the road and skirted through the various ravines and shrubbery to his position on Hill 142."[38]

Mathews still worried about the 55th Company's movement toward Les Mares since the enemy had a clear view of the entire southern approach to the farm. Mathews guided First Lieutenant Lemuel Shepherd, Captain John Blanchfield, and the other officers of the 55th Company on an indirect, but safe route to the farm. Mathews led the company down the road southeast of Marigny-en-Orxois, a kilometer toward the town of La Voie due Chatel.

Once in the village, he directed them north toward the woods just south of Champillon. "I stopped them under cover of the woods behind Champillon and went ahead in company with Blanchfield to see if the town was clear. We found things clear save for some Frenchmen who were pillaging and went on up to the woods in front of the town to the left. I left Blanchfield and told him he should take up a position that took in the head of these woods."[39] After trying to orient Blanchfield as to the best position for the various platoons of the company, Mathews parted ways with the 55th Company to head north beyond Champillon toward Hill 142.

Blanchfield and Shepherd left the platoons in the woods near Champillon and moved forward to reconnoiter the terrain they were about to occupy. Shepherd tried to direct Blanchfield's attention to the features as they appeared on the map. "I don't think he could read a map and he was very vague about where we were going," recalled Shepherd.[40] The roadway running south out of the town of Bussiares grew crowded with retreating French soldiers who proclaimed that the Germans were just behind them.[41] On the way out of town, enemy shells fell nearby as if the enemy were tracking the French withdrawal.

Moving single file, gas masks at the alert position on their chests, the platoons of Blanchfield's 55th Company scurried one by one into the woods west of Champillon—a place designated as Bois de Mares. A small culvert in the coppices provided a concealed avenue of approach. The men moved single file through the forest and noted the body of a dead French medic lying contorted in the undergrowth—a macabre welcoming for many experiencing their first stint along the frontlines.[42] Each platoon moved forward one at a time from the cover of the woods toward the designated position. "I remember going up with the company to a very commanding position overlooking the valley on the nose of a hill," remembered Shepherd. "We just sat up there and could see the battlefront in the distance on the next ridge."[43] When Blanchfield discovered the extremely exposed position of his company, he immediately sent a runner forward with orders to bring the men back. Shepherd recalled:

> My company was completely in a salient. We hadn't been up there half an hour—I remember writing a letter. Then we got word that we should come back—Blanchfield sent me an order to come on back, that I was in the wrong spot and should be about a half mile back so as to tie in with the companies on my right and left. In other words I had gone out—we didn't have any real orders—and taken this good commanding position, but on the other hand, I was out on the salient, so I withdrew my people back a couple of hundred yards down the road and took up another position.[44]

The word quickly passed for the company to move back by platoons. Slowly and quietly, the company filed back toward Les Mares Farm one platoon at a time to avoid enemy observation. According to Shepherd, "It just happened at this particular time the Germans began their attack. This French colonel came rushing up. By this time, his Chasseurs were melting away. He saw us withdrawing and figured we were running away."[45]

June 2nd Chapter II

Shepherd tried to explain to the senior French officer that they had merely pushed out too far and were not retreating, but just rejoining their company.[46]

In the chaos, the 3rd Platoon commanded by thirty-one-year-old Second Lieutenant Arthur Tilghman, an Army officer from Chicago, Illinois, did not receive the word to pull back closer to Les Mares Farm.[47] A misunderstanding in the command left his men behind until Tilghman dispatched a runner for clarification regarding the instructions. "He returned with the order to join the company with the greatest possible speed."[48] Tilghman, despite the continued pleas of the French officer, led his platoon back to Les Mares Farm on the run.

Shortly after the various platoons of the 55th Company reached their position, they immediately carried out their orders to dig individual fighting holes. The 2nd Platoon of the 55th Company, commanded by twenty-five-year-old Second Lieutenant Lucius Quintus Cincinnatus Lamar Lyle from Lauderdale, Mississippi, occupied the buildings of Les Mares Farm. They dug individual fighting positions along the fence fronting the farm with a backdrop of hay lining the yard behind them.

The property seemed relatively insignificant, and Shepherd remembered, "It was a farmhouse with a wall extending around it and the barns—a big hay shed, wheat fields to the front."[49] The farm sat along a narrow, dusty road that gently declined north toward the village of Bussiares. The other platoons of the 55th company dug their shallow pits in the field on the other side of the narrow road leading from the farm to Bussiares.

The grounds, spanning about 500 meters to the east, which bore a farmer's plentiful harvest, was now lined with Marines digging shallow fighting holes. The men, separated from each other by only six or seven feet across the field, individually hacked, chopped, and scraped out their furrows piling the loose dirt at the head of their rifle pits as a makeshift parapet.[50] Throughout the afternoon, French stragglers passed through the farm grounds, many proclaiming that the Germans were on the north side of Hill 165 situated just south of Bussiares.[51]

Further east, irregular patches of woods dotted the steeply sloping ground where the other platoons of the 55th Company dug in along the edge of the trees and extended the company's right flank to the Champillon-Bussiares road. Machine guns of the 15th Company, 6th Machine Gun Battalion covering this path established fields of fire down the narrowing lane, created by the steep sides of the roadway. The ground east of the road lay open for a few hundred meters where it terminated at the tree line of thick woods along the northern slope of high ground just east of Champillon. This open region remained sparsely occupied except for the few Hotchkiss machine gun emplacements covering the approaches from the north.

June 2nd Chapter II

Anchored northeast of the Champillon-Bussiares road, the left flank of Captain Lloyd Williams's 51st Company stretched across the edge of the woods along the apex of Hill 142. Eighteen-year-old Private Roland Henry Fisher, an auto mechanic from Swea City, Iowa, assigned to the 51st Company, recalled how the company arrived and quickly "placed a man about every ten feet and dug ourselves in."[52] Each of Williams's men maneuvered for the most advantageous spot to excavate a dugout within his span of terrain. Through these woods, the 51st Company comprised the battalion's right flank.

First Lieutenant Mathews, who led Captain Blanchfield's 55th Company into the woods south of Champillon, moved to the north and encountered a platoon of Williams's 51st Company protecting the flank of the 55th Company as they maneuvered into position.[53] Twenty-two-year-old Second Lieutenant Robert Henry Rose Loughborough, an Army Officer from Manhattan, New York, commanded this platoon of the 51st Company. According to Mathews, "I told the army lieutenant, who commanded the platoon, that the 55th was on its way up, and he could rejoin his company on Hill 142."[54]

Upon returning to Marigny-en-Orxois, Mathews realized that the battalion's front stretched exceedingly far, and with the establishment of only one forward observation post for the entire battalion, spotting enemy movement would be difficult. Mathews remedied this dilemma and established observation posts along each of the battalion's flanks. "I then divided my groups in two parts and stationed one observation group in Veuilly woods and the other on Hill 142."[55] These forward observation positions were effective.

Mathews recalled, "From the post on Hill 142, the movements of the enemy were plain. They were moving at will down the Courchamps-Licy-Clignon road without molestation."[56] Departing his command post along the cemetery wall in Marigny-en-Orxois, Lieutenant Colonel Wise headed out to inspect his battalion front. "From one end to the other, that line of foxholes stretched a Marine in every hole; platoon leaders and company commanders behind them. It looked damned thin to me. No machine guns. No supports," remembered Wise.[57]

Tromping through the woods on the extreme left flank of his battalion, Wise located Captain Wass dug in with his 18th Company in Bois de Veuilly. Described as forceful, bold, energetic and even-tempered, Wass now held a precarious flank in the line.[58] As Wass's men chipped and hacked the earth away to excavate dugouts, Wass and the battalion commander discussed the situation. Wass claimed that he could not locate the 23rd Infantry's right flank reportedly to the west. "This didn't look very prosperous," recalled Wise, who was powerless to remedy the situation.[59]

Continuing east in his inspection of the front, Wise encountered Marines of the 43rd Company digging in along the northeastern face of Bois

June 2nd Chapter II

Veuilly on the right of the 18th Company. The open gap between Les Mares Farm and the northeastern edge of Bois de Veuilly contained a narrow tree-lined path that remained unoccupied along the already-thin line. When Wise arrived at Captain Blanchfield's 55th Company command post, located approximately 650 meters east of Les Mares Farm in the apex of the woods just west of the Champillon-Bussiares road, he found things relatively quiet. Wise walked along the 55th Company front, passing through Les Mares Farm where Second Lieutenant Lyle's 2nd Platoon dug in. Wise noted a few marauding French Chasseurs from what remained of a battalion. As his Marines scooped out small piles of earth to make some semblance of a fighting position, the distant cannonade propelled them to dig a bit faster.

When First Lieutenant Mathews returned to the 55th Company hours after having guided them to their designated line, he surveyed the immediate area. "I then went over to Blanchfield's position and found that he had taken up a position that did not include one big wood that pointed to the very heart of his position. I urged him to at least place outposts at the head of this wood, but he would not do it."[60] Along the right flank of the 55th Company's position, the proximity of the Bois de Mares created a vulnerability to the American lines should the enemy launched from those woods. Recognizing this dilemma, Shepherd recalled, "I sent out a patrol to reconnoiter a small wooded area in front of our lines along the Champillon-Torcy road, but they returned without contacting the enemy."[61]

The 55th Company's front lacked any heavy machine gun support, so First Lieutenant Lemuel Shepherd regularly walked along the company line which fronted the fence stretching east down the wooded draw to ensure that his automatic rifle crews were adequately covering as much of the line as possible.[62] "My job was more or less a roving one," remembered Shepherd, "which necessitated my sending [Private Oscar Eugene] Martin back to the company command post many times each day and night."[63] Martin moved between Blanchfield and the company front without end and became a vital asset for Shepherd.

Wise ventured further east along the battalion's developing front and located Captain Lloyd Williams and his 51st Company holding the battalion's right flank near Champion. In addition to his signature walking stick bearing an ornately carved 'W' for his last name, Williams was a striking and imposing figure at over six-feet in height.[64] Always a professional and stoic gentleman, he courteously notified Wise that the battalion's right flank was dangerously open. Despite his scouting efforts through the rolling wooded terrain, Williams found no evidence of Major Maurice Shearer's 1st Battalion, 6th Marines reportedly on the battalion's immediate right. With this perplexing development, Wise immediately returned to his command post nearly two and a half kilometers away.

June 2nd Chapter II

As he headed to Marigny-en-Orxois, French 75mm guns fired from positions south of the 2nd Battalion's front. The deafening roar of the guns reverberated across the open field and reminded Wise that his battalion was ever closer to a face-to-face showdown with the enemy. Frustrated and feeling perhaps helpless about the lack of liaison to the east, Wise telephoned regimental headquarters to inform them of the non-appearance of Major Shearer's men expected to be on his right. The voice on the other end of the telephone receiver curtly stated, "They'll show up."[65] Helpless to do much more, Wise could only wait.

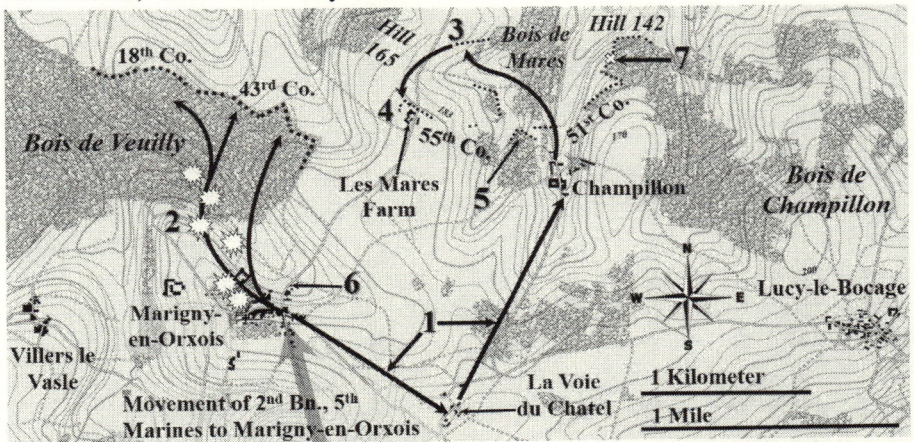

The position of 2nd Battalion, 5th Marines on June 2nd. [1] As the battalion moved up from Pyramide Farm to Marigny-en-Orxois, First Lieutenant Mathews took the 55th Company into position along a less exposed route. [2] The 18th Company was shelled as they moved beyond Marigny-en-Orxois and into Bois de Veuilly. [3] The 55th Company moved too far beyond their designated position and gradually moved back toward Les Mares Farm. [4] Les Mares Farm was defended by the 2nd Platoon of the 55th Company commanded by Second Lieutenant Lucius Q.C.L. Lyle. [5] Captain Blanchfield established his 55th Co. post of command in the apex of these woods. [6] Lieutenant Colonel Wise established his battalion command post along the southern stone wall of the cemetery just outside of Marigny-en-Orxois. [7] First Lieutenant Mathew establsished a battalion observation post in the tree line here.

The Marines of 2nd Battalion, 5th Marines labored to finish digging foxholes along the crest of the farm's property. The lack of machine gun support along most of the battalion's line meant rifles, and Chauchats remained their primary defense.[66] The various regimental machine gun companies were still desperately trying to cover the distance to the front over refugee and traffic-covered roads. The guns of the 6th Machine Gun Battalion were already stretched incredibly thin as they tried to support the entire 4th Brigade's front.

As soon as Wise's battalion went into position, Major Edward Cole, commanding the 6th Machine Gun Battalion, received instructions to provide

167

June 2nd Chapter II

a company of machine guns to support Wise's portion of the line. Cole contacted Captain Matthew Kingman who commanded the left group of the 6th Machine Gun Battalion and directed him to use the available Hotchkiss crews of the 15th Company to augment Wise's battalion. The gun crews of the 15th Company adjusted their positions and created a network of gun emplacements in echelon until additional gun crews arrived.[67] In a 12:05 P.M. message to Brigadier General Harbord, Cole also mentioned that he was "withdrawing six guns from a quiet sector of line and sending them to Wise's support which will complete the order to support Wise with one Company."[68] These six guns came from Captain Allen Sumner's 81st Company southwest of Bouresches. Sumner's crews were directed to support the right portion of Wise's line near Champillon.[69]

Several of Sumner's section leaders uprooted their crews from recently excavated gun pits and, much to their chagrin, once again forced them to haul the heavy weapons and gear to a new position several kilometers away.[70] Sergeant Peter Wood's gun crew was among those of the 81st Company sent to Wise. Wood's men worked all morning digging fighting positions, establishing fields of fire, and estimating ranges when the sudden order to pack up and prepare to move caught them by surprise. "Went by hand today from one place to another where we at last found a place," recalled Wood.[71]

The constant consolidation and extension of the line had a ripple effect on already weak liaisons between companies, battalions, and regiments. When one section of the thinly stretched front was relocated, it forced other units to move and dig new positions along the line so they could maintain liaison. The continual adjusting of the line, often in the open, also attracted enemy artillery fire, which made life at the front increasingly perilous.

Contact with the enemy seemed likely to occur at any moment along the 5th Marines' front, and nearly five kilometers to the east, Colonel Catlin's 6th Marines had endured sporadic shellfire throughout the day. During the morning, Private Asa Smith of the 74th Company ventured east of Lucy-le-Bocage with a corporal to investigate the source of the previous night's ruckus that instigated them to open fire. The rest of the company in town underwent an impromptu rifle inspection. The formation quickly dissipated, however, when the distinct sound of incoming artillery shells screamed over the rooftops. Men scrambled for the cover of the town's buildings.[72]

A platoon of engineers from Company F, 2nd Battalion, 2nd Engineers was digging fighting positions when the barrage began. "We had not been at work more than a half hour when the Germans started shelling us," recalled twenty-three-year-old Private First Class Melvin Hugh Hurlburt of Germantown, California.[73] Before anyone could react, a shell landed about twelve feet away from twenty-three-year-old Private Shelton Brown Beaty of Goldwaite, Texas. The explosion instantly killed him.[74] Corporal Oscar

E. Olson of Decorah, Iowa, noticed Corporal Mart Gentry wilt to the ground nearby when the first few rounds exploded, a sliver of shrapnel hit him in the kidney. "He fell, and I immediately went to his aid," recalled Olson, who tried desperately to get a response from his lifeless comrade. "I questioned him but found he was unable to answer. While I was giving him first aid, he died."[75]

A barrage also landed in the center of the 1st Battalion, 6th Marines, which stretched from Bois de Champillon to Lucy-le-Bocage. Members of the 76th Company who were caught out in the open when the barrage started quickly rushed to their dugouts. A cluster of incoming shells landed among several men before they could reach their holes.

One projectile exploded behind twenty-two-year-old Private William Alexander Bass, riddling him with shrapnel in the lower right back, arm, thigh, and foot.[76] Another shell mortally wounded twenty-two-year-old Private Edward Lewis Heinz. The steady torrent of incoming-rounds stirred up dense clouds of dust and smoke. Before the melee abated, thirty-one-year-old Private William Henry Boyle and eighteen-year-old Private Leon Wesley Hunt were both dead.[77]

Corporal Mart Gentry. Photo credit: Mary Ann Larson.

The barrage stretched along the battalion's front and targeted Sergeant Gerald Thomas's 3rd Platoon of the 75th Company as they prepared coffee while hunkered down in a dry culvert on the western edge of Lucy-le-Bocage. The salvo landed on the high ground behind the platoon.[78] Thomas's men had been in reserve, but according to him, "the enemy effectively dispelled any doubts as to his presence and, at the same time, notified us that it was time to do some digging."[79]

Thomas's platoon dug shallow fighting holes wherever they could. The increasing heat of the day made the work more arduous, and then suddenly orders came for the line to extend even further to the west—forcing them to abandon their newly excavated dugouts, don their packs and shoved off. According to Thomas, "We moved over to the left of Lucy during the day into a little garden plot that was sheltered by some shrubs."[80] Once in place, the men quickly resumed their rest.

The shifting and subsequent thinning of Major Maurice Shearer's 1st Battalion, 6th Marine sector continued as they tried to establish liaison with

June 2nd Chapter II

the 5th Regiment reportedly positioned south of Hill 142 near the Champillon-Bussiares road. For the Marines holding the front, the extension of the battalion line kept them continually moving and digging new fighting holes. They knew nothing of the layout of the battlefield.

The hike to a new position was very often through thick woods with a dense tangle of undergrowth or even into an open field. Moving into a new area guaranteed more digging, which was always accompanied by an equal amount of cursing by the indignant men who saw no end to their miseries.

In their reserve position along the southeastern portion of Bois de Champillon, the 95th Company stretched their front as far as possible. The steady incoming fire along the entire line forced them to spread their fighting positions out, "averaging a half-dozen steps apart," according to Corporal Warren Jackson. "Within hours a few of the men began digging holes in a desultory sort of fashion.

Gradually, all the men took this up, often two or three men digging a hole together."[81] Their dugouts remained rather shallow, and many ingenious members of the company attempted to cover the pit with branches and leaves. According to Jackson, "What good we thought this roof would do, I don't know. It was not to keep out the sun, as the treetops above did that."[82] Once Jackson and the others completed the excavation of their new positions, they went to retrieve their emergency rations from their packs.

Some men, desperate for a warm meal, filtered deep into the woods and dared to build a small cooking fire to brown some bacon and hardtack, an innocent mistake. As the white smoke billowed up through the trees, German observers quickly spotted the haze and immediately relayed data back to the few German guns that had been causing misery for other companies of the battalion. "In the midst of our cooking and eating a shell fell on the extreme left of the 95th Company lines, followed by more shells in quick succession."[83] The men suddenly realized what they had done, as frantic voices echoed through the woods demanding the men extinguish the fires.

---

[1] Note: The easternmost point of Turrill's battalion was a woods known as Bois de Vaurichart.
[2] *Records of the Second Division (Regular)* Volume 5, N.P.
[3] Burial File of Privates Charles Maggoine, Box 3043, RG 92.9, Records of Graves Registration Services, NARA College Park, MD, and Burial File of Privates Paoset Zaico, Box 5386, RG 92.9, Records of Graves Registration Services, NARA College Park, MD.
[4] Westover, *Suicide Battalions*, 110.
[5] Ibid.
[6] Ibid.
[7] *Records of the Second Division (Regular)* Volume 8, N.P.
[8] Ibid.
[9] Ibid, Volume 4

10 Wise and Frost, *A Marine Tells it to You*, 196.
11 Ibid.
12 Correspondence William R. Mathews to Major Ralph S. Keyser 28 September 1928, Box 8, Mathews, W.R. file 1962-1966, Robert Asprey Collection, Howard Gotlieb Archival Research Center, Boston University, Boston, MA.
13 Official Military Personnel File for Captain William R. Mathews, RG 127, NPRC St. Louis, MO.
14 Correspondence Mathews to Keyser 28 September 1928, Box 8, Robert Asprey Collection, Howard Gotlieb Archival Research Center, Boston University, Boston, MA.
15 Ibid.
16 Field and James, *Over the Top with the 18th Company 5th Regiment U.S. Marines,* 19.
17 Correspondence Mathews to Keyser 28 September 1928, Box 8, Robert Asprey Collection, Howard Gotlieb Archival Research Center, Boston University, Boston, MA. Note: Wig wag refers to flag semaphore or signaling flags.
18 Correspondence Lemuel Shepherd to Major Edwin N. McClellan 24 March 1919, *Operations of the 55th Company from June 2, 1918 to June 5,* 1918, Box 29, RG 127 NARA Washington D.C.
19 Note: These signalmen were likely Marines from 5th Marine Regimental Headquarters since the 1st Signal battalion spent much of the day stranded at Ormoy-Villiers awaiting movement to May-en-Multien with the 4th Machine Gun Battalion.
20 Brown and Geores, *55th Co. Marines in World War I*, Box 55, RG 127, NARA, Washington, D.C.
21 Wise and Frost, *A Marine Tells it to You*, 196.
22 *Records of the Second Division (Regular)* Volume 5, N.P.
23 Correspondence Mathews to Keyser 28 September 1928, Box 8, Robert Asprey Collection, Howard Gotlieb Archival Research Center, Boston University, Boston, MA.
24 Ibid.
25 Cooke, "We Can Take It, We Attack," *Infantry Journal,* 5.
26 Ibid.
27 Ibid, 4.
28 Field and James, *Over the Top with the 18th Company 5th Regiment U.S. Marines,* 19.
29 Cooke, "We Can Take It, We Attack," *Infantry Journal,* 5.
30 Ibid.
31 Burial File of Private Joe M. Brock, Box 588, RG 92.9, Records of Graves Registration Services, NARA College Park, MD. Note:

June 2nd Chapter II

The Muster rolls state that Private Brock was killed in action June 8, 1918. The noted burial near Les Mares Farm and the multiple references in Private Brock's official service record file, as well as his Burial file, indicate that he was in fact killed in action June 2, 1918.

[32] U.S. Marine Corps Muster Rolls, 1893-1940; (NARA Microfilm Publication T977, 460 rolls); Records of the U.S. Marine Corps, Record Group 127; NARA, Washington, D.C.

[33] Burial File of Private Joe M. Brock, Box 588, RG 92.9, Records of Graves Registration Services, NARA College Park, MD.

[34] Cooke, "We Can Take It, We Attack," *Infantry Journal,* 5.

[35] Field and James, *Over the Top with the 18th Company 5th Regiment U.S. Marines,* 19.

[36] Ibid.

[37] *The Aisne Defensive,* Whitehead to ABMC, Box 190, RG 117.4.2, NARA College Park, MD.

[38] Correspondence Mathews to Keyser 28 September 1928, Box 8, Robert Asprey Collection, Howard Gotlieb Archival Research Center, Boston University, Boston, MA.

[39] Ibid.

[40] General Lemuel Shepherd, interview by Robert Asprey, Alfred M. Gray Research Library, Quantico, VA.

[41] Correspondence Shepherd to McClellan 24 March 1919, *Operations of the 55th Company,* Box 29, RG 127 NARA Washington D.C.

[42] Brown and Geores, *55th Co. Marines in World War I,* Box 55, RG 127, NARA, Washington, D.C.

[43] General Lemuel Shepherd, interview by Robert Asprey, Alfred M. Gray Research Library, Quantico, VA.

[44] Ibid.

[45] Ibid.

[46] Ibid.

[47] Brown and Geores, *55th Co. Marines in World War I,* Box 55, RG 127, NARA, Washington, D.C.

[48] Ibid.

[49] General Lemuel Shepherd, interview by Robert Asprey, Alfred M. Gray Research Library, Quantico, VA.

[50] Wise and Frost, *A Marine Tells it to You,* 197.

[51] Correspondence Shepherd to McClellan 24 March 1919, *Operations of the 55th Company,* Box 29, RG 127 NARA Washington D.C. Note: The Germans were able to capture Bussiares later that day.

June 2nd Chapter II

⁵² Correspondence Roland Fisher to Aunt Pearl, 28 June 1918, Provided to author by Roland Fisher's nephew, Howard George Fisher.
⁵³ Correspondence Mathews to Keyser 28 September 1928, Box 8, Robert Asprey Collection, Howard Gotlieb Archival Research Center, Boston University, Boston, MA.
⁵⁴ Ibid.
⁵⁵ Ibid.
⁵⁶ Ibid.
⁵⁷ Wise and Frost, *A Marine Tells it to You*, 197. Note: There were a few machine guns of the 15th Company situated along the approaches to Champillon.
⁵⁸ Fitness Reports of Captain Lester Wass found in Official Military Personnel File for Captain Lester Wass, RG 127, NPRC St. Louis, MO.
⁵⁹ Wise and Frost, *A Marine Tells it to You*, 196.
⁶⁰ Correspondence Mathews to Keyser 28 September 1928, Box 8, Robert Asprey Collection, Howard Gotlieb Archival Research Center, Boston University, Boston, MA.
⁶¹ General Lemuel C. Shepherd, Jr. Memoirs, boyhood-1920, Folder 29-30, Box 67, Virginia Military Institute Archives Preston Library, Lexington, VA.
⁶² General Lemuel Shepherd, interview by Robert Asprey, Alfred M. Gray Research Library, Quantico, VA.
⁶³ Official Military Personnel File for Private Oscar E. Martin, RG 127, NPRC St. Louis, MO.
⁶⁴ Wise and Frost, *A Marine Tells it to You*, 246-47.
⁶⁵ Ibid, 198.
⁶⁶ Note: Chauchats refer to the Model 1915 CSRG automatic rifle of the French. The American Expeditionary Forces used these as their primary automatic rifle through most of the war.
⁶⁷ *Records of the Second Division AEF* Volume 5. And Curtis, T. J., Capt, USMC, *History of the Sixth Machine Gun Battalion, Fourth Brigade, U.S. Marines, Second Division and Its Participation in the Great War*. (Neuweid on the Rhine: N.P.), 9.
⁶⁸ *Records of the Second Division (Regular)* Volume 5, N.P.
⁶⁹ Ibid, and *Records of the Second Division (Regular)* Volume 9, N.P.
⁷⁰ Ibid, Volume 5, and Curtis Jr., *History of the Sixth Machine Gun Battalion*, 9. Note: By the next day, two additional guns of the 81st Company will join the six in line supporting Wise's battalion.

June 2nd Chapter II

[71] *Diary of Peter Wood,* N.P. Entry for June 2, 1918, Author's collection.
[72] Diary of Asa J. Smith 74th Company 6th Regiment U.S. Marines, Alfred M. Gray Research Library, Quantico, VA., and History of the 74th Company, compiled by Sergeant Carl W. Smith, Box 35, RG 127, NARA College Park, M.D.
[73] Burial File of Private Shelton B. Beaty, Eye-witness statement Private First Class Melvin Hugh Hurlburt, Box 307, RG 92.9, Records of Graves Registration Services, NARA College Park, MD.
[74] Ibid.
[75] Burial File of Corporal Mart Gentry Eye-witness statement by Corporal Oscar E. Olson, Box 1837, RG 92.9, Records of Graves Registration Services, NARA College Park, MD.
[76] U.S. Marine Corps Muster Rolls, 1893-1940, Record Group 127, NARA, Washington, D.C.
[77] Ibid. Note: The 76th Company suffered three wounded, one mortally and two killed in action.
[78] General Gerald B. Thomas, interview by Robert Asprey, Alfred M. Gray Research Library, Quantico, VA.
[79] General Gerald B. Thomas memoir, Alfred M. Gray Research Library, Quantico, VA.
[80] General Gerald B. Thomas, interview by Robert Asprey, Alfred M. Gray Research Library, Quantico, VA.
[81] Jackson, *His Time in Hell, A Texas Marine in France*, 90.
[82] Ibid.
[83] Ibid.

June 2nd Chapter III

The boys did not simply raise their rifles and shoot in the general direction of Germany. They adjusted their sights, coolly took aim and shot to kill. I cannot believe that one shot in ten missed a mark. The Prussians dropped as if death were wielding his scythe in their midst, rank after rank. It was uncanny.
   -Private Orley Milo Dunton, 96th Company, 2nd Battalion, 6th Marines

    The brief, but intense fire encountered by the Germans earlier in the day just north of the Paris-Metz road near Bouresches, which stopped their advance, suggested that a renewed and determined line of resistance between Bouresches and Triangle Farm had developed. Because of this reinvigorated effort, German artillery registered these positions during the day. Throughout the late morning and afternoon, Companies E and F, 2nd Battalion, 2nd Engineers worked to improve the line near Triangle Farm held by the 2nd Battalion, 6th Marines.

    Members of twenty-three-year-old First Lieutenant Wallace Leonard's 2nd Platoon, 79th Company, situated on the company's left-most flank near Triangle Farm noted an increased number of enemy soldiers visible in the distant woods earlier that morning.

    Corporal Glen Hill and several other members of the platoon scurried back to the rear of the line going from pack-to-pack gathering as many entrenching tools as possible to help the engineers deepen and improve their rudimentary fighting holes.[1] Their presence on that open ground just behind the line quickly attracted enemy artillery fire, and soon the distant thud of German batteries echoed across the valley.

    Incoming shells announced their arrival with a split second piercing screech before they slammed into the woods and fields behind the line. Enemy gunners adjusted their fire, and each subsequent shell landed ever closer to the 79th Company's front. Eventually, rounds fell close enough that the exposed engineers would release their shovels and drop to their stomachs at the sudden screech of incoming shells.

    Enemy artillery gradually enveloped the section of the line held by the 3rd Platoon, 79th Company as well as elements of the French 1st Battalion, 356th Regiment in Bois de Clerembauts.[2] Once enemy artillerymen found the range, shells, arrived in steady succession. The thunderous explosions smashed into the earth and created a downpour of leaves, dirt, and rocks.

    Cursing their helpless situation, the men tried desperately to shield their faces and bodies from the detonating rounds. The piercing whine of more incoming fire drown out the screams of wounded and panicked men. One high explosive shell struck the edge of Private William Dingle's dugout.

June 2nd Chapter III

The explosion instantly killed the twenty-three-year-old, breaking his Springfield rifle in half.[3]

In front of Triangle Farm, First Lieutenant Leonard's 2nd Platoon, also inundated by the barrage, tried to establish contact with the 78th Company's 1st Platoon across the open field over a rise along the ground. The liaison was essential since an enemy assault would likely follow the shelling, and the gap between the two companies posed a severe problem. Corporal Glen Hill and his brother Sidney took their squads to cover this void. "My brother and I were ordered to cross some fifty yards of plowed land and take positions in the clover which was about a foot high," recalled Corporal Glen Hill.[4]

As the men snaked their way through the fields, the lack of fire they attracted along that open stretch encouraged one of the men, twenty-two-year-old Private Charles Jonas Vanek, to cover the rest of the distance on foot rather than crawling. The rest of the men followed Vanek's bold approach. They all rose to their feet and briskly trotted the remaining distance over the plowed rise.

Captain Messersmith of the 78th Company watched with horror as these naïve young men moved upright in the open, and certainly within clear view of the distant enemy. "Captain Messersmith jumped up and yelled at us in unprintable words to get down, or we'd all be killed, but we kept going and reached the edge of the clover."[5]

A rolling barrage quickly swept over the 78th Company's position along the sloping fields and tree line just in front of the ravine north of Triangle Farm. The thunderous bombardment soon subsided, and the only sound was the descent of dust and rock blown skyward by the shellfire. The men remained hunkered low in their fighting holes.

Unmercifully, German machine gunners followed the artillery barrage with a sweeping volley of fire from distant, hidden emplacements. Rounds snapped over the top of men already cringing low to the ground. Bullets hissed and whined at the end of their long flight, clipping foliage and branches from overhanging trees on the 78th company's left flank. "We were being punished without being able to reply, for the woods hid the enemy from us," recalled Private Thaddeus Allen.[6] "The men about me were cursing and swearing in that choice collection of profanity that belongs to the Marines."[7]

In the open field between the 78th Company and the 2nd platoon, 79th Company, the Hill twins leading their squads into the field, lay prone in the dirt amidst the machine gun fire. The men turned their heads to the side, cheek down in the soil to buy themselves a few extra centimeters of safety from the slugs snapping overhead. "Lying on my side, I never worked so hard at digging a hole to get myself under cover," recalled Corporal Glen Hill.[8]

Crawling ahead of Hill, twenty-two-year-old Private John Sens moved about in the open on his belly in a manner that his legs, bent at the knees, caused his feet to dangle in the air. According to Glen Hill, "I called to him to lie on his side, or he would get shot in the legs."[9] In the mayhem of everyone crawling on their stomachs, one of the Marine's rifles accidentally discharged, striking Sens in the left foot.[10] A corpsman braved the fire and bellied towards him to treat his wound. The gunfire subsided enough for stretcher-bearers to carry Sens away "writhing in pain and sweating," according to Hill.[11]

While squads of the 2nd Platoon, 79th Company extended the line under fire, enemy artillery continued plastering the rest of the platoon. Intervals between shells seemed to grow shorter as the bombardment progressed. The men hugged the earth, and in no time the shrill of incoming rounds subsided enough that the men cautiously raised their faces from the dirt to see the approaching enemy in the distance.

Around 5:00 P.M., German troops advanced in short individual rushes then dropped out of view into the high fields of wheat. The advancing waves spanned most of the battalion's front.[12] According to Corporal Lloyd Pike, "The rushes were of such short duration that a defending rifleman had not enough time to get an enemy in his sights before he disappeared into the ground cover."[13]

Unknown to the Americans at the time, the enemy's advance was an attempt to feel out the lines, "but in 1918 when it was happening to a group of young men being attacked for the first time, it surely seemed like class 'A,' all-out war," recalled Pike.[14] Countless French troops had already passed through the line which left nothing but open fields and patches of woods between Major Holcomb's front and the assaulting German waves.[15]

For Pike, the encroaching enemy rendered a helpless feeling. Before arriving at the front, a decree stated that all non-automatic riflemen would carry a rifle and bayonet, and Pike remembered:

> So I, being armed with only with a Colt caliber .45 automatic pistol, was issued a rifle and bayonet. There being no serviceable rifles in the company supply room at the time, I was issued a rifle with a damaged front sight, which would dangle from side to side, however, the rifle was tilted and was completely useless as a sight. But it was an adequate stick on which to mount a bayonet. As far as bayonets were concerned, at no time have I ever looked with favor on them as a method of adjusting differences between people.[16]

All Pike could do at that defining moment was watch as the distant figures approached the 2nd Platoon's line. The Marines and isolated French troops still present along the front deliberately let the advancing waves approach without discharging a premature shot—a facet of restraint and patience of fire discipline brazened into each Marine.

As the 78th Company recovered from the sweeping machine gun barrage, they gazed out to the sloping green fields at distant figures quickly approaching. "'Here they come!' a shrill, boyish voice piped up. 'Hold your fire!' the injunction ran from officer to officer and man to man," remembered Private Thaddeus Allen.[17]

Up and down the line, men steadied their weapons, shaken but focused; they watched the emboldened Germans approach through the sight leaf of their Springfield rifles. The Marines remained calculated and resolute to the methods in which they planned to dispose of the approaching enemy and methodically waited until they were within range. According to Allen:

> The Germans were clear of the woods. On they came with closed ranks in four lines. One looked at them with almost friendly interest. No particular hate or fear. And yet there was a queer sensation along the spine, and the scalp seemed to itch from the tug of the hair at the roots. The fingers bit into the rifle. 'Hold your fire!' As the command rang out on my ears with a sharpness that enforced obedience, I seemed to be standing on Bunker Hill and hear the command: 'Wait till you see the whites of their eyes!'[18]

Allen watched the distant helmet-shaped silhouettes visible just over the wheat as if he were back on the firing line at Mare Island. "The next thing I recall is firing. Firing. Firing. My fingers were tearing greedily at more ammunition, then the instinct of the hunter restrained me. I began to fire slower, looking for my mark, making sure of a hit."[19] Rifle fire erupted into a crescendo. Through the rear sights of their Springfields, members of the 78th Company watched as individual enemy soldiers shuttered from the bullet impacts and slumped out of view.

To assist in repelling the enemy, Sergeant Harold H. Dunn and other soldiers of Company E, 2nd Battalion, 2nd Engineers crept out toward the forward sloping fields fronting Triangle Farm amidst the deafening rifle fire. Methodically, Dunn engaged targets as they appeared in the distance. He noticed Corporal Charles Lloyd Joy, the football star from Carleton College in Northfield, Minnesota, crawling through the fields on his hands and knees about fifty feet away when suddenly he slumped out of sight into the tall grass.

Noticing that Joy had fallen, Navy corpsmen, braving enemy fire, reached the mortally wounded corporal to find that an enemy round had hit him in the neck. They dragged his limp, unconscious body through the grass past Dunn who glanced at the lifeless man long enough to notice the ghastly wound in his throat.[20] Corpsmen ran half-crouched across the field and carried the wounded corporal by stretcher to the nearest aid station. Despite these brave efforts, Joy lost vast quantities of blood and died while they loaded him into an ambulance.[21]

Unable to use his defective rifle, Corporal Pike noticed one Marine on his left firing his weapon so intermittently that his shots were ineffective:

> I crawled over to him and exercising my, up until then, dormant office of corporal, cautioned him (the way new corporals do) about wild firing and urged him to pick a target and continue to follow it until he dropped it. Keep a bead on where the enemy dropped out of sight and when he comes up again be ready for him. His wild firing stopped; and after several attempts, he knocked over one of the attackers. I remember we both shouted, and I am sure we both felt as if we had just won a war.[22]

Corporal Charles Joy. Photo Credit: Carol Rice.

Pike moved up and down the line coordinating and coaching his Marines, steadying their fire and directing it where it would have the most effect.

Twenty-six-year-old Private Orley Milo Dunton, a former carpenter form Allegan, Michigan, who enlisted with his younger brother Harold nearly a year earlier, helped repulse the enemy advance against the 96th Company positions near Bois de Clerembauts. He recalled the incredible fire discipline exhibited by the Marines from their fighting pits that afternoon. "The boys did not simply raise their rifles and shoot in the general direction of Germany. They adjusted their sights, coolly took aim and shot to kill. I cannot believe that one shot in ten missed a mark. The Prussians dropped as if death were wielding his scythe in their midst, rank after rank. It was uncanny."[23]

In front of the 78th Company, concentrated rifle fire from Captain Messersmith's men continued to devastate the enemy ranks. Corporal Glen Hill's squad from the 2nd Platoon, 79th Company in liaison with the 78th Company's left flank, maintained their assigned fields of fire, and "at three hundred yards, it was like being on the rifle range. Any German that came out was almost surely a dead one before he could get back to the woods," remembered Hill.[24] Eventually, the attack faded away. According to Private Allen, "The Huns now appeared to me almost on top of us and then, all of the sudden, there was nothing more to aim at."[25] The roar of rifle fire died out, and tranquility returned to the fields hundreds of meters east of the American front where several Germans now lay dead and wounded.

For the remainder of the day, the Marines and engineers along the line near Triangle Farm maintained a constant vigil. Enemy soldiers remained out of view following their costly efforts that day. "This marksmanship made the Germans realize they were up against a different foe than they had been pursuing, and they became very cautious," recalled Hill.[26]

Sporadic enemy shelling, however, continued to inundate the line throughout the day. The enemy's increased artillery fire enveloped the entire division front. German gunners also acquired targets south of the Paris-Metz road and shelled the woods near Les Aulnois Bontemps and Hill 201 throughout the day where soldiers of the 3rd Battalion, 9th Infantry established a reserve position. Rounds crashed through the treetops at regular intervals, sending troops scampering for cover. One large shell detonated in Company M's location near Hill 201, which mortally wounded Corporal Charles B. Hackney. Medics braving the high explosive rounds rushed to his aid, and litter bearers carried him to a nearby makeshift aid station where he died.[27]

The barrage continued with increasing intensity and soon swamped the entire 3rd Battalion line. One large shell slammed into the northeast corner of Aulnois wood occupied by Company L, and a fragment of the projectiles struck Private Homer G. Harris in the hip.[28] The cascade of incoming fire kept everyone at bay and unable to tend to the wounded. Private Benjamin Grice saw the mortally wounded Harris on the ground, and recalled, "He died shortly after from loss of blood."[29]

The piercing scream of incoming shells did not abate, and the helpless soldiers of Company L braced themselves for the impact of each shell by curling up in their shallow fighting holes. The concussion of each explosion blasted chunks of earth skyward and rained it down on the back of their necks of the cowering men. As the smoke and dust cleared, Private Frank Zebrowski looked up and noticed that Private Wesley J. Stubbs was instantly killed—searing razor-sharp fragments of the shell had riddled his abdomen and nearly disemboweled him.[30]

In the woods near Company K, 3rd Battalion, 9th Infantry's sector, a few incoming rounds sent the men diving for unfinished dugouts. The explosions kept everyone flat, but an angst-ridden and haunting groan immediately followed the explosions of the first incoming projectiles. Private Albert Weston realized that a shell had detonated near Private Victor Kolinsky, a coal miner from Shenandoah, Pennsylvania, who emigrated to the U.S. from Russia. When the bombardment subsided, Weston noticed that large jagged and irregular shell fragments blasted a ghastly hole through Kolinsky's chest and left arm. He was dead before he could make another sound, his blue eyes appeared half-open and lifeless. Blood soaked his olive drab uniform and gas mask bag.[31] Shells landed along the line occupied by the 9th Infantry throughout the afternoon and caused them twenty-six casualties.[32]

Left: First Lieutenant Charles I. Murray seen here as a senior at Culver Academy commanded the 4th Platoon of the 79th Company. Photo credit: Culver Academy. Right: Sergeant George Stine was a member of Murray's 4th Platoon and served as the gas officer. Photo credit: Don Roylance.

In response to the increased enemy artillery fire, the French continued firing in support of the line fronting Triangle Farm since the 2nd Division's artillery regiments had not yet arrived. The French, however, evidently did not know the exact location of the newly developed American line.

Twenty-two-year-old Sergeant George Clarence Stine, the gas NCO for twenty-two-year-old First Lieutenant Charles Ira Murray's 4th Platoon, 79th Company, remained ever alert to the danger of incoming gas shells and stood watch, ready to order the men to don masks. Sometime during the afternoon, a volley of rounds, believed by twenty-year-old Corporal Harry Benton Fletcher to have originated from friendly lines, crashed into 4th

June 2nd Chapter III

Platoon's position. Men scurried for cover as the ground appeared to heave under the force of the blasts. Shell fragments struck Stine in the abdomen, leg, and hip while he stood next to Murray who miraculously escaped unharmed. Corpsman quickly treated the mortally wounded sergeant, evacuating him to a field hospital.[33]

Besides the threat of friendly rounds landing short of their intended target, the presence of the French guns drew even more enemy artillery fire which menaced the division throughout the day. Members of D Company, 1st Battalion, 9th Infantry, occupied a forward outpost in the open south of the Paris-Metz road and just east of Bois de Clerembauts. These men ran across the open terrain for cover when German shells started landing in the open.

The sudden ear-splitting scream of an incoming round forced Corporal Charles A. Parker to duck before he reached the protection of the tree line. He crouched low in anticipation of the explosion which scattered dirt everywhere. A subsequent round immediately followed the detonation of the first shell. The second round landed just before Parker could recover to resume his race toward the woods. The projectile exploded next to Parker who caught the brunt of the blast that wounded eight other soldiers. Corporal Arthur K. Group, who miraculously escaped the momentary barrage, looked with horror through the clearing smoke at the ghoulish results. The explosion reduced Parker to a bloody mass scattered across the ground—blowing off most of his head, neck, and shoulder.[34]

---

[1] Correspondence from Hill to Neufeld, 17 January 1979, Alfred M. Gray Research Library, Quantico, VA.
[2] West, *Belleau Wood*, Alfred M. Gray Research Library, Quantico, VA., and *Records of the Second Division (Regular)* Volume 4, N.P.
[3] West, *Belleau Wood*, Alfred M. Gray Research Library, Quantico, VA.
[4] Correspondence from Hill to Neufeld, 17 January 1979, Alfred M. Gray Research Library, Quantico, VA.
[5] Ibid.
[6] Hamilton and Corbin, *Echoes From Over There, page,* 13-14.
[7] Ibid.
[8] Correspondence from Hill to Neufeld, 17 January 1979, Alfred M. Gray Research Library, Quantico, VA.
[9] Ibid.
[10] Note: Glen Hill indicates that he suffered wounds to both heels by enemy fire. The Muster roll for June 1918, in fact, demonstrates that Sens was wounded by the accidental discharge of a rifle.
[11] Correspondence from Hill to Neufeld, 17 January 1979, Alfred M. Gray Research Library, Quantico, VA.
[12] *Records of the Second Division (Regular)* Volume 9, N.P.
[13] Pike, *The Battle For Belleau Woods, As I Remember It About 60 Years Later*, 8.
[14] Ibid.

[15] *Records of the Second Division (Regular)* Volume 9, N.P.
[16] Pike, *The Battle For Belleau Woods, As I Remember It About 60 Years Later*, 8.
[17] Hamilton and Corbin, *Echoes From Over There*, 14.
[18] Ibid.
[19] Ibid.
[20] Burial File of Corporal Charles L. Joy, Eye-witness statement by Sergeant Harold H. Dunn, Box 2577, RG 92.9, Records of Graves Registration Services, NARA College Park, MD.
[21] Ibid.
[22] Pike, *The Battle For Belleau Woods, As I Remember It About 60 Years Later*, 8.
[23] Orley Dunton, "Mussing Up the Prussian Guard, The Idea that Reversed the German War Machine," *Hearst's*, December 1918, 488.
[24] Correspondence from Hill to Neufeld, 17 January 1979, Alfred M. Gray Research Library, Quantico, VA.
[25] Hamilton and Corbin, *Echoes From Over There*, 14.
[26] Glen Hill indicates that he suffered gunshot wounds in both heels by enemy fire. The Muster roll for June 1918, in fact, demonstrates that Sens was wounded by the accidental discharge of a rifle.
[27] Burial File of Corporal Charles B. Hackney, Box 2034, RG 92.9, Records of Graves Registration Services, NARA College Park, MD.
[28] Burial File of Private Homer G. Harris, Box 2126, RG 92.9, Records of Graves Registration Services, NARA College Park, MD.
[29] Ibid.
[30] Burial File of Private Wesley J. Stubbs, Eye-witness statement by Private Frank Zebrowski, Box 4747, RG 92.9, Records of Graves Registration Services, NARA College Park, MD.
[31] Burial File of Private Victor Kolinsky, Eye-witness statement by Private Albert Weston, Box 2732, RG 92.9, Records of Graves Registration Services, NARA College Park, MD.
[32] *2nd Division Journal of Operations, entry for June 2, 1918*, Box 50, RG 120.9.3, Second Division File, Records of the AEF, NARA College Park, MD.
[33] Burial File of Sergeant George C. Stine, Eye-witness statements by First Lieutenant Charles Ira Murray and Corporal Harry Benton Fletcher, Box 4708, RG 92.9, Records of Graves Registration Services, NARA College Park, MD. Note: Sergeant Stine died at Field Hospital #16 in Juilly France on June 4th.

June 2nd Chapter III

Records of the Second Division AEF Volume 5 also notes that at 2:45 P.M., a message from 2nd Battalion 6th Marines to Major Frank Evans, 6th Marine Regiment Adjutant states "One killed and two wounded by our Artillery firing into Triangle Farm." The other Marine of the 2nd Battalion 6th Marines was Private William H. Brown of the 79th Company.

[34] Burial File of Corporal Charles A. Parker, Eye-witness statement by Corporal Arthur K. Group, Box 3737, RG 92.9, Records of Graves Registration Services, NARA College Park, MD.

June 2nd Chapter IV

The scream of each incoming shell caused our 'insides' to momentarily draw up into an agonized knot until our ears informed us it would not be too close. Gone was the holiday spirit of the previous day.
 -*Corporal Havelock Nelson 97th Company, 3rd Battalion, 6th Marines*

The unreliability of telephone lines continued to plague Brigadier General James Harbord's timely communications with his forward units who were now under constant artillery fire. During the afternoon, 4th Brigade headquarters at Issonge Farm erupted with a fury of activity. The small quaint room of the farmhouse that, only days earlier, was occupied by a family now flourished with frenzied activity as messengers arrived and departed at seemingly every moment.

Adjutants answered the few operational telephones which buzzed constantly. Struggling to brace the telephone receiver between their shoulder and ear, these adjutants frantically wrote down information amidst a deluge of similar conversations.

Officers doubled over tables covered by maps and tentatively discussed the situation with grimaced concentration. Others moved about the crowded room with hurried persistence to meet requests from companies in line and dispatch messages via runner and telephone. All these happenings dictated the hectic nature of brigade headquarters during the early part of the developing battle.

During the afternoon, the German attack against the eastern edge of the line created quite a spell of chaos and confusion. The activity along Major Thomas Holcomb's battalion sector and the subsequent movement of several 79th Company Marines just behind the front as they salvaged entrenching tools from their packs led the French to erroneously believe and report that the American line had wavered and pulled back from Triangle Farm.

When Harbord received this information, he drafted a message at 2:40 P.M. and sent it by truck to Colonel Albertus Catlin at his new headquarters in a stone house at La Voie du Chatel. In the dispatch, Harbord urged Catlin to reply immediately regarding the accuracy of the report about Holcomb's men retreating from Triangle Farm. The prolonged telephone outage at Catlin's new headquarters compounded the confusion since a timely response was not possible.[1]

Ten minutes after Harbord sent his initial message to Catlin, he dispatched a separate dispatch to Holcomb himself stating, "Reported that you are giving away near Triangle. You are supposed to hold your line there at all cost. Keep Colonel Catlin informed of conditions, and Cole, and send me report now."[2] At 3:00 P.M., Harbord notified division headquarters in Montreuil-aux-Lions about the potential breaking of the line on the brigade's right. He also expressed his frustration with the lack of timely updates due to faulty phone lines. He communicated his frustration in a message proclaiming, "Failure [of] your signal officer to give us wireless connection here is great handicap."[3]

Just as Harbord conveyed this message, the telephone lines connecting him to the 6th Marines ironically started ringing at his headquarters, and he continued his dispatch, "Telephone to 6th Marines just in. Both regimental headquarters report have wireless up and trying to communicate with us but cannot. Telephone to your headquarters very unreliable and out of order much of time."[4] The lack of consistent updates greatly frustrated Harbord who waited with aggravated anticipation.

Harbord's demand that Catlin relay information every fifteen minutes was an impossible request due to the telephone outage. Nonetheless, Harbord dispatched a runner with a firm reminder to Catlin at 3:00 P.M. demanding word be sent even if delivered by runners every fifteen minutes.[5]

The inability to steadily communicate with Catlin also complicated Harbord's efforts to establish the crucial liaison near Hill 142 between Major Maurice Shearer's 1st Battalion, 6th Marines, and Lieutenant Colonel Wise's 2nd Battalion, 5th Marines—a dilemma that remained problematic for the rest of the day and into the night.[6]

The predicament of establishing and maintaining telephone lines to forward elements of the 6th Marine Regiment fell upon the signal detachment of the regimental headquarters company, a risky job significantly complicated by the enemy's increasingly active artillery fire. Twenty-eight-year-old Sergeant Thomas James Kelly, attached to Headquarters Company, 6th Marines, led his small group of signalers across open terrain towards the regiment's forward positions to establish and repair telephone lines.

The men carried not only their rifle, ammunition, and heavy packs, but also hauled big spools of wire, entrenching tools, and other signal equipment that slowed their movement across the open fields—a dangerous endeavor in the face of increased artillery fire.[7]

Kelly maintained wide gaps between his men as they moved across the open pasture. Shells detonated along the field leaving a whirling cloud of dust. The men ran as fast as their overloaded bodies would move, but one German round landed adjacent to Kelly, bursting into a plume of smoke just behind him. Kelly's men looked back through the clearing haze to see that the explosion blew Kelly off his feet. Shrapnel tore a massive gash through the bicep of his right arm, and another piece ripped a small hole through the triceps of the same arm. A shell fragment also lacerated the lower portion of his left leg.

As he struggled to his feet, Kelly, with his tunic bloodied and torn, stubbornly shrugged off the assistance of his comrades who attempted to carry his pack for him. Every second they remained in that open field put them at risk. Staggering from his painful injuries, he mustered the strength to keep pace with the others the entire way, but when the detachment arrived at their designated post, his weakened condition and the tremendous loss of blood necessitated Kelly's evacuation.[8]

The efforts to maintain these telephone lines eventually prevailed, enabling Harbord to establish communications with the 6th Regiment. Major Holcomb, furious over earlier reports by the French that his battalion had wavered from the line near Triangle Farm, now called Harbord personally from his headquarters in a little house at La Cense Farm and refuted the false report.

Harbord then relayed the information to Colonel Catlin as well as 2nd Division headquarters, recalling that Holcomb had said, "When his outfit runs it will be in the other direction. Nothing doing in the fall-back business."[9] By 6:25 P.M., Harbord noted that the day's communication was much improved compared to the previous day, and he noted:

Major Thomas Holcomb. Photo credit: Marine Corps History Division.

> The liaison by runners is working regularly and efficiently. I have telephone communication now with both regimental headquarters and with the headquarters of my machine gun battalion and through the latter, with the battalion nearest it [Major Thomas Holcomb's 2nd Battalion, 6th Marines], which is the battalion at the critical point on the line. The regimental wireless stations are up and signal officer sent to establish wireless stations at these headquarters reports will soon be in.[10]

The German barrage intensified during the afternoon, striking further into the 2nd Division's front and inundating the areas around La Voie du Chatel. The distant sound of incoming rounds caught the attention of the Marines from the 3rd Battalion, 6th Marine Regiment. With shells landing nearby, a Gunnery Sergeant temporarily in charge of the 83rd Company's 3rd platoon quickly split his Marines into squads and scattered them throughout the woods approximately fifty yards apart. Despite the precaution, German

June 2nd Chapter IV

shells inflicted several casualties.[11] Private James Scarbrough vividly recalled the horror visited upon 3rd Platoon that afternoon:

> We were concealed in the woods and not making much commotion, so I don't know if somebody saw us or they were just shelling everywhere. That's what it looked like to me, not a deliberate attack by artillery but just pot, shots, harassment with German 77's, three-inch guns. Still, it found its mark and three of our men died. One of the men was John W. Collins of Clarksburg, West Virginia who'd left his studies hoping one day to be a lawyer . . . The second was Frank Snow of Anniston, Alabama, a friend of mine who could have joined the Army and stayed right in his hometown at Camp McClellan. He wanted to be a Marine and was so proud just to be a part of the unit. Frank wasn't twenty yards away from me when the shell hit. He just came apart. There wasn't enough left of Frank Snow to fill a grease can. There's a little white cross at Belleau Wood with his name on it, but I don't know who or what they buried there. [12]

The bombardment wounded several other Marines.[13] Among the casualties was one of Scarbrough's friends, Private Joseph Martin Flanagan from Bellwood, Illinois. According to Scarbrough, he was "slight of build, a wiry kid, but he could run like a bird could fly."[14] A shell fragment virtually disemboweled the seventeen-year-old company runner. "The shrapnel had torn him straight through in the abdomen. Part of his intestines was outside, and the smell was terrible."[15] Comrades carried Flanagan away to a field hospital where he succumbed to his wounds two days later. The third Marine whose death Scarbrough witnessed during the barrage was twenty-four-year-old Gunnery Sergeant James Clair Wertz of Lewiston, Pennsylvania, a sea-going veteran of the fleet Marine Corps and rigid disciplinarian whose incessant demands of a clean and professional appearance won the admiration of his men. "Seeing his dead, broken body shook our confidence," recalled Scarbrough[16]

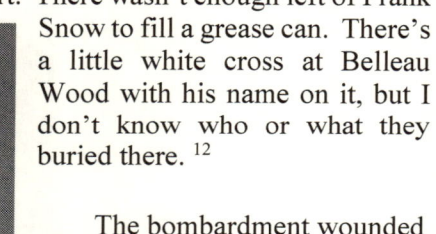

Private Frank Snow. Photo credit: Author's collection.

One shell exploded near Private David Wheaton Hall, a twenty-two-year-old clerk from Chicago, Illinois. Fragments from the high explosive shell lacerated the back of the young Marine's left thigh, tearing the flesh open in several places along the muscle. A few large fragments of steel also ripped through the inner part of his right thigh, punching gaping holes as they passed completely through the leg. The back of his left thigh was a mass of blood and tattered flesh as his hamstring muscle was virtually shredded.[17]

The bombardment also dropped a cluster of shells on the 84th Company. Private James Hatcher remembered the aftermath. "One man was shell-shocked and lay screaming upon the ground for half an hour before he was carried away."[18] Twenty-three-year-old Corporal John David Peoples from Aurora, Illinois, was the unfortunate victim, suffering from such severe psychoneurosis he would never return to duty with the company.[19]

Shells also targeted the wooded position of the 97th Company. Rounds fell with enough frequency that, according to Corporal Havelock Nelson, "faces became set and nerves tightened up. The scream of each incoming shell caused our 'insides' to momentarily draw up into an agonized knot until our ears informed us it would not be too close. Gone was the holiday spirit of the previous day."[20] The 1st Platoon, 97th Company, was in the middle of roll call when the barrage crept toward the edge of the wood.

The men, believing the rounds fell too far away to concern themselves, shouted over the explosions in response to having their name called. "A shell hits a pile of cordwood in front of us, scattering us in all directions," recalled Corporal William Scanlon of the 97th Company.[21] Captain Robert Voeth screamed at everyone to fall back deeper into the woods for cover. Scanlon vividly recalled, "In the woods all around us the shells are crashing heavily."[22]

Twenty-one-year-old Trumpeter Foster Brancalasso was only a short distance from Scanlon when fragments from an exploding shell hit Brancalasso in the left foot.[23] "There is a look of strange surprise on his face as he falls to the ground," remembered Scanlon. "Everybody starts yelling: 'wounded man on the right! . . . Hospital Corpsmen! . . . Hospital Corpsman!. . .'"[24] Brancalasso writhed in pain but still grasped the trumpet he used to signal formation and roll call moments earlier.

While German guns sporadically shelled the positions near La Voie du Chatel, the eastern half of the 2nd Division front endured a steady bombardment from German batteries ever since repulsing the enemy's advance east of Bouresches earlier that morning. Near Le Thiolet Farm, located on the north side of the Paris-Metz Road, a volley of enemy shells fell upon two machine gun positions of the 77th Company, 6th Machine Gun Battalion, at approximately 6:30 P.M. The thunderous explosion rippled through the woods, whipping up a whirl of dust and hazing smoke.

June 2nd Chapter IV

Left: Private William Brown was killed in action along the Paris Metz Road near Le Thiolet Farm. Photo credit: Minnesota Historical Society. Right: First Lieutenant William Croka who was wounded in the same barrage that killed Brown. Photo credit: NPRC.

Another shell careening through the air exploded adjacent to one of the gun positions and tossed the fifty-three-pound Hotchkiss through the air like a toy, shattering the weapon and its sixty-pound omnibus tripod.[25] Several men, caught in the open, dashed for the cover of holes including twenty-year-old Private Charles Francis Brown of St. Paul, Minnesota. Twenty-six-year-old First Lieutenant William Burris Croka, of Hennessy, Oklahoma, who was slightly wounded by one incoming shell, watched as Brown "was killed getting into a dugout 100 feet from the Paris-Metz road."[26]

Twenty-two-year-old Private William Joseph McCarthy suffered shrapnel wounds to the shoulder and was evacuated along with Croka. Three other Marines, including twenty-two-year-old Second Lieutenant Lucius Lisk Moore Jr., of Denver, Colorado, who exhibited the signs of severe shell shock, were treated and evacuated once the barrage lifted.[27]

The enemy's increasingly frequent artillery fire necessitated an amplified reply from the French batteries supporting the line, but in a twist of irony, the ammunition dumps supplying the heavy French 155mm cannons ran dangerously short of shells during the afternoon.[28] The 2nd Division's artillery regiments were still traveling to the front on foot with their horse-drawn guns and caissons in tow.

The 2nd Field Artillery Brigade's headquarters detachment, which arrived ahead of the batteries, busily set up their command post in a schoolhouse and cellar in Montreuil-aux-Lions.[29] After establishing regimental and battery positions, the 2nd Field Artillery Brigade consulted with the French chief of artillery regarding the projected takeover of the front by the 2nd Division scheduled for 9:00 A.M. the next morning.[30]

By 5:00 P.M., the commanders of each regiment of the 2nd Field Artillery Brigade had a general understanding of the designated positions their batteries were supposed to occupy upon arrival. Division instructions called for the 12th Field Artillery to support the 4th Brigade while the 15th Field Artillery supported the 3rd Brigade.

The heavy 155mm guns of the 17th Field Artillery received instructions to move into position on either side of the Paris-Metz road east and northeast of Montreuil-aux-Lions.[31] Their batteries, traveling by rail, remained bogged down in heavy traffic and were still hours away from arrival.

Once the battalions of the 17th Field Artillery reached each of their three different disembarkation points located west of Montreuil-aux-Lions, they began the nearly forty-kilometer journey towards the front. Along the way, they encountered the delays caused by refugee traffic.[32]

Until the division artillery arrived and the French replenished their supply of 155mm shells, the only artillery available to support the Americans and the French units in front of them was the French batteries of 75mm guns spread throughout the area. Delays also kept the 12th Field Artillery Regiment at Chaton, France, eleven kilometers west of 2nd Division headquarters at Montreuil-aux-Lions.[33]

Battery D, 2nd Battalion, 12th Field Artillery spent the previous night in endless march. According to twenty-four-year-old Sergeant Joseph J. Gleeson, "Men and horses about exhausted, but we have to get up there quick."[34] The battery stopped to rest as well as feed and water horses. The men, according to Gleeson, endured "No real sleep for four days."[35]

---

[1] *Records of the Second Division (Regular)* Volume 5, N.P.
[2] Ibid.
[3] *Records of the Second Division (Regular)* Volume 4, N.P.
[4] Ibid. Note: Telephone lines were often cut by artillery fire.
[5] *Records of the Second Division (Regular)* Volume 5, N.P.
[6] Ibid.
[7] Official Military Personnel File for Sergeant Thomas J. Kelly, RG 127, NPRC St. Louis, MO. Note: Kelly had been a signalman assigned to the U.S. Consulate in Vera Cruz during the assault on that city in April 1914. He was a member of the 13th Company Artillery Battalion of the 1st Brigade. He also saw combat at Santo Domingo in June 1916 with the 13th Company of the 1st Brigade.
[8] Ibid. Note: Kelly returned to his unit in October.
[9] *Records of the Second Division (Regular)* Volume 4, N.P.
[10] *Records of the Second Division (Regular)* Volume 6, N.P.
[11] Burial File of Private Frank Snow, Box 4592, RG 92.9, Records of Graves Registration Services, NARA College Park, MD.

June 2nd Chapter IV

[12] Scarbrough, *They Called us Devil Dogs,* 63.
[13] Burial File of Private Frank Snow, Eye-witness statement Sergeant Darel J. McKinney, Box 4592, RG 92.9, Records of Graves Registration Services, NARA College Park, MD.
[14] Scarbrough, *They Called us Devil Dogs*, 64
[15] Scarbrough, *They Called us Devil Dogs*, 64
[16] Ibid.
[17] Official Military Personnel File for Private David Wheaton Hall, RG 127, NPRC St. Louis, MO. Note: Hall's wounds were extensive enough that he never returned to duty with the company.
[18] Hatcher, *Citizen Soldier,* N.P.
[19] U.S. Marine Corps Muster Rolls, 1893-1940, Record Group 127, NARA, Washington, D.C.
[20] Nelson, "Paris-Metz Road," *Leatherneck*, 13.
[21] Scanlon, *God Have Mercy On Us*, 11.
[22] Ibid.
[23] Scanlon refers to Brancalasso as "Benvenuto," but there was only one trumpeter in the company. Havelock Nelson also references Brancalasso in his recollections as having been the first man wounded in the company that day. The incomplete muster rolls were common with the 3rd Battalion, 6th Marines, but Brancalasso's service file verifies his wounds that day.
[24] Scanlon, *God Have Mercy On Us*, 11.
[25] Diary of William W. Fullington, Pvt. USMC, Alfred M. Gray Research Library, Quantico, VA.
[26] Burial File of Private Charles F. Brown, Eye-witness statement by Captain William B. Corka, Box 612, RG 92.9, Records of Graves Registration Services, NARA College Park, MD.
[27] U.S. Marine Corps Muster Rolls, 1893-1940, Record Group 127, NARA, Washington, D.C. Note: The other wounded man for the 77th Company was twenty-four-year-old Private George Francis Oransky.
[28] *Records of the Second Division (Regular)* Volume 6, N.P.
[29] Operations of 2nd Field Artillery Brigade in the Chateau Thierry Sector 30 May to 25 June 1918, Box 81, RG 120.9.3 Second Division File, Records of the AEF, NARA College Park, MD.
[30] Ibid.
[31] Ibid.
[32] History of the 17th Field Artillery, Box 85, RG 120.9.3, Second Division File, Records of the AEF, NARA College Park, MD., and History of the 3rd Battalion 17th Field Artillery, Box 85, RG 120.9.3, Second Division File, Records of the AEF, NARA

College Park, MD. Note: The three disembarkation points for the regiment were the towns of Ormoy-Villers, Dammartin-en-Goële, and Nanteuil-lès-Meaux.

[33] Wahl, George D., Diary of a Battery Commander, Box 79, RG 120.9.3, Second Division File, Records of the AEF, NARA College Park, MD.

[34] Spaulding and Wright, *The Second Division American Expeditionary Force in France 1917-1919,* 253.

[35] Ibid.

June 2nd Chapter V

The fast-traveling roar of the shells as they sped towards German concentration points and routes of advance was the sweetest music. As we advanced, more and more batteries spoke out from right and left.
-First Lieutenant Wendell Westover Company A, 5th Machine Gun Battalion

Near the village of Coulombs, Company A, 5th Machine Gun Battalion waited throughout the day in the town's abandoned buildings until word arrived for them to move into the line. The men got whatever rest they could acquire since it was doubtful there would be time to sleep in the next few days. "But at five o'clock," recalled First Lieutenant William Westover, "the 23rd Infantry notified us that the French ahead had been reinforced and were holding and that we were to return to the division at once."[1]

At 5:45 P.M. that evening Colonel Paul Malone, commanding the 23rd Infantry, dispatched a bicycle messenger to Major Julius Turrill commanding the 1st Battalion, 5th Marines, instructing him that his battalion was scheduled to vacate their current position, which stretched them out along a two-kilometer front. They would then proceed by foot south towards the village of Les Glandons where they would await further orders.[2]

Turrill immediately dispatched a runner with a message to Colonel Wendell Neville to verify, with his commander, the order he just received from Malone. Turrill's message inquired, "Received orders from Col. Malone to go back to Les Glandons, there to get other orders. Understand some other battalion comes here to relieve this battalion. Shall I do so, or await further orders from you."[3] Within an hour, the long columns of soldiers of thirty-six-year-old Major Deshler Whiting's 2nd Battalion, 23rd Infantry arrived from their position in reserve to relieve Turrill's Marines.[4]

The reason for the withdrawal of Turrill's battalion resulted from an intelligence development earlier that afternoon relayed by a German prisoner of the German 398th Infantry, 10th Division, suggesting the possibility of another attack on the eastern sector of the division line where the 6th Marines repulsed two German assaults and remained under frequent artillery fire.[5]

Placing Turrill's men in a reserve position at Pyramide Farm would allow them to meet the threat where best needed.[6] After a day of digging, improving fighting positions, establishing observation posts, eating and laying around without seeing a single sign of the enemy, Turrill's Marines quickly packed gear, formed up, and once again took to the road. Turrill led the march of his battalion towards Les Glandons, and when they arrived in

June 2nd Chapter V

the deserted village, they boarded the awaiting vehicles to move back toward Pyramide Farm.

The dust clouds of the trucks obscured the road from enemy observation, but when the battalion disembarked the lorries and marched the remaining distance, enemy artillery spotters noticed the movement. The distant thud of artillery quickly manifested into the vacuous shrill of a single incoming shell which landed right among a group of Marines from the 2nd Platoon, 49th Company.[7]

When the smoke and dust cleared, eight men lay scattered along the roadway in horrible pain after suffering wounds from razor-sharp, dense shell fragments.[8] Twenty-one-year-old Private Erving Happy Cogne was so among those severely injured in the blast. The explosion tore open the front of his left thigh and the outer part of the upper left arm.[9] Fragments of the round also wounded several others and sent corpsmen scampering to the aid of the most severe casualties while others tried to get the men who were slightly injured to a place of cover.

When Cogne regained his senses, his leg and arm were covered in blood covered, and small fragmentation wounds dotted his entire body. The screams of horribly wounded men added to the chaos as platoons tried to assemble their men and move to a place of safety before more shells could inflict further damage. Riddled with shrapnel, twenty-six-year-old Private Marvin Watson lay dead in a macabre contorted manner. Those who noticed his motionless body could tell that he died instantly, the only fatality in the barrage.[10] After evacuating the wounded and recovering their composure, the battalion moved towards Pyramide Farm and became the brigade's reserve unit.

The potential threat to the sector held by the 6th Marines also prompted Colonel Albertus Catlin at 5:00 P.M. to call upon Major Berton Sibley to dispatch a company to reinforce the line. "Be prepared [to] send fresh Company to La Cense Farm to report [to] Holcomb as reserve. German fresh division expected to attack American right with two regiments north of Paris road and one south."[11]

The companies of Sibley's 3rd Battalion, 6th Marines prepared to move out of the woods near La Voie du Chatel and spend the night in the open following the heavy shelling of the forest earlier that day. Before they could move, one of Sibley's runners from battalion headquarters located the 97th Company and relayed instructions for Captain Voeth's Marines to move out immediately as the designated company sent to reinforce Holcomb's line near La Cense Farm.

The men of the 97th Company assembled in formation and stepped off in their long hike. "We swung out of the woods onto the road and headed in the direction of the firing," remembered Corporal Scanlon. "The rapid pace made our heavy packs bounce up and down on our backs and knocked the wind out of us."[12] The exhausted column, having run most of the four kilometers toward La Cense Farm, had no time to rest. Immediately, they went into the line. Corporal Havelock Nelson's platoon filed through Bois de Clerembauts just as a distant German machine gunner swept the woods with a volley of fire. "I remember the instinctive slowing down of the column as each one in it neared the point where the crackling bullets were, or had been, knocking sparks off some barbed wire on our left and how those who safely crossed the spot crowded on the heels of the man ahead."[13]

Enemy artillery fire also greeted First Lieutenant Thomas McEvoy's 1st Platoon as they moved into an orchard near La Cense Farm. According to Scanlon, "The shells have been passing overhead, but now they are crashing into the farm buildings."[14] McEvoy guided the column, "down a little valley and up a hill. The firing is close up now," recalled Scanlon.

Each squad crept forward one at a time, starting with twenty-three-year-old Corporal Willard Edgar Hensley's 1st Squad. Corporal Warren Freund, a twenty-six-year-old insurance agent from New Orleans, Louisiana, looked back to ensure his men were with him before he led his 2nd Squad forward, followed by the 3rd Squad, and eventually Scanlon's 4th Squad.[15] "Follow the runner," shouted McEvoy. "Have your men take up positions between the men on the line."[16] Scanlon recalled, "The runner goes forward on his hands and knees. I follow. Behind me, one after the other, come the other seven men of the squad. We creep closer to the crest of the hill. The runner stops and points ahead. 'There are the men . . . just up ahead . . . lying down.'"[17]

Scanlon directed four of his men forward crawling toward the line. Laying prone, one of the Marines from Major Thomas Holcomb's 2nd Battalion, 6th Marines along the line turned back, gazing over his shoulder to notice the arriving reinforcements but said nothing and immediately shifted his attention back towards the ground in front.

Scanlon rushed to avoid observation by the enemy and placed his men in the gaps of the very thinly-held line of Holcomb's battalion front. "I passed on the lieutenant's order for each man to take off his pack and place it before him, also to put his gas mask at the alert position."[18]

With firing up on the left, Scanlon was surprised at the relative serenity to his immediate front. He took up position in line and asked one of the 2nd Battalion Marines if the French were in front of them to which he lambasted, "The French! Hell, the French must be in Paris by this time at the rate they were going. . ."[19] Focusing his view beyond the open fields fronting the gentle rise, Scanlon peered at the dimly-lit eastern horizon and spotted the movement of figures in the distance. He inquired to the Marine from Holcomb's battalion, "Then what is that outfit up ahead?" Nonchalantly, the young man simply said, "The Germans."[20]

June 2nd Chapter V

A few kilometers east of Les Mares Farm, the sector of the line held by Major Maurice Shearer's 1st Battalion, 6th Marines stretched from Lucy-le-Bocage through the Bois de Champillon and continued to fumble over the liaison with the 5th Marines on their left. Shearer learned that most of the French 152nd Infantry holding the Belleau-Torcy road had already fallen back. Therefore, the French colonel in command requested reinforcement of the gap just north of Hill 142. With this information in hand, Shearer, at 10:30 P.M., sent a runner to Colonel Catlin at La Voie du Chatel to inform him that two platoons from his 95th Company in reserve were being dispatched.[21]

The most updated information received earlier in the afternoon proclaimed that the left of Shearer's battalion remained one kilometer southeast of Hill 142, but the general lack of specific details prompted Brigadier General Harbord to intervene.

Earlier that afternoon, Harbord demanded that Catlin, "Send [a] reliable officer to [Hill] 142 to find out if Shearer's left rests there and report facts to me as soon as possible."[22] The pressure for Shearer to establish liaison with the 5th Marines to the west stretched his battalion front even thinner. For two platoons of the 95th Company, the task of finding and filling this gap meant another exhausting night of constantly moving and digging while the rest of the company remained in reserve.[23]

Earlier that evening, Corporal Warren Jackson and his comrades of the 95th Company entrenched in the Bois de Champillon. Across the valley, the distant crack of machine gun fire drew their attention. Jackson flinched when stray rounds buzzed overhead and toppled through the treetops at the end of their long journey. According to Jackson, "I was standing a step or two from our dugout when the bullets sang by and one zipped through the twigged roof of our dugout."[24]

As the men neared the completion of their fighting positions, orders to pack up and move pulled them from their laborious exertion. The sudden shift of the company front, a result of the continuous effort to connect with Lieutenant Colonel Wise's men on the right, took elements of the 95th Company across unfamiliar terrain with no idea whom they might encounter, so the two platoons paused to affix bayonets to their rifles before they proceeded further through the forest.[25]

Visibility faded as the sunlight dwindled in the early evening. "We crossed a road," recalled Jackson "and soon came to the edge of the wood. Here we paused, apparently awaiting further orders."[26] The crackle of machine gun and rifle fire, which sounded much closer than before, revealed that a rapidly escalating battle was developing beyond the view from the thick woods.

Subtle sheets of smoke hovered over the valley and now masked the dusky sky obscuring the view of fighting. The men could only sit and listen to the gunfire reverberating across the fields with naïve curiosity. "We were surprised no bullet came our way. In the meantime, several of the men loosened their pack straps, allowing their blanket rolls to drop to the ground. These fellows did not know what lay ahead, and they disliked the idea of being encumbered with a heavy blanket roll," remembered Jackson.[27]

After a very brief respite, the two platoons of the 95th Company moved along a wire fence stretching through the woods. They encountered a few isolated and demoralized French soldiers who, after days of heavy fighting, made their departure from the front line. "These men were bent on getting out of the fray," remembered Jackson.[28] Slowly, the two platoons, hugging the fence line, continued through the woods, trying to cover the gap created by the battalion.

The 95th Company's movement stretched the line excessively thin to develop liaison with the right flank of the 2nd Battalion, 5th Marines reportedly at Hill 142. Jackson noticed two masses along the ground that were hardly distinguishable in the faint sunlight along the fence.

Upon closer inspection, a horrified Jackson discovered two dead French soldiers. Still adorned in their horizon-blue coat and packs, the corpses showed no apparent signs of the trauma, but according to Jackson, "The sight of those two dead soldiers was a thousand times more impressive. Appalling!"[29]

The men continued moving along the fence and eventually reached a road. Jackson and elements of the dispatched platoons continued hiking well after darkness fell. The men passed by the amber glow of cigarettes smoked by men resting along the roadway and, they soon arrived in an open space where they once again dug fighting positions.

The battalion now stretched out along a front of nearly three kilometers between Hill 142 and Lucy-le-Bocage, but the sought-after and vital liaison with Lieutenant Colonel Wise's men remained elusive and would eventually require putting all of the 95th Company in position along the battalion's over-stretched battlefront before dawn.[30]

Throughout the night, French troops, pulling back from Bois de Belleau, passed through the 75th Company dug in along the northwestern outskirts of Lucy-le-Bocage on the 1st Battalion, 6th Marines' position.[31] The company tried to keep liaison with elements of the 74th Company on the battalion's right flank and the 76th Company on their left, which stretched the line ever thinner.

The 76th Company, commanded by twenty-eight-year-old Captain George Andrew Stowell, also extended his company front unusually far and comprised most of the battalion's broad front. The 74th Company remained on the north and southern edge of Lucy-le-Bocage with two platoons on each side respectively.[32] During the night, the 1st and 2nd Platoons were sent to the battalion's left flank to help extend west toward the 5th Marines.[33]

June 2nd Chapter V

Elements of the 76th Company held the battalion's left flank, which supposedly extended all the way to Hill 142. Major Maurice Shearer reported before midnight that his 1st Battalion, 6th Marines occupied positions on the right flank of Lieutenant Colonel Frederic Wise's 2nd Battalion, 5th Marines on the Champillon-Bussiares road about a kilometer south of Bussiares.[34] Liaison with Wise would have to remain a floating one since all the platoons of twenty-five-year-old Captain Oscar Ray Cauldwell's 95th Company held positions in line with none kept in reserve. If Stowell's report was accurate, a gap of just under a kilometer dotted with wooded gullies and broken terrain separated Shearer's battalion and Wise's right flank.

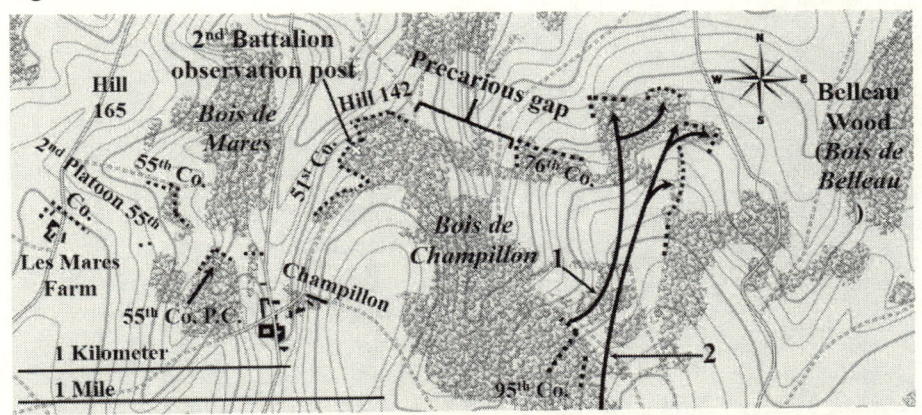

The situation by late June 2nd. [1] The 95th Company initially sent two platoons to help fill the gap. Eventually all of the 95th Company moves north along the edge of Bois de Champillon. [2] During the night, the 1st and 2nd Platoons, 74th Company move from the region around Lucy-le-Bocage to help fill the gap.

Liaison over this ground would be difficult, a factor only complicated by the darkness of night. The front held by the 2nd Battalion, 5th Marines was reinforcement by a few machine guns from Captain Kingman's 15th Company and some Hotchkiss crews of Captain Allen Sumner's 81st Company. These gun crews had the task of covering the line from the edge of Bois du Veuilly to Hill 142. The only reserves for Major Shearer's battalion were elements of Company F, 2nd Engineers, who already suffered five casualties from shelling that day.[35] Throughout the night twenty-three-year-old Private Jefferson Lonzo Holt of Kent, Texas, and twenty-one-year-old Private Charles Steed Raffington of Hutchinson, Kansas made countless trips through woods and open areas to bring in numerous casualties. Concentrated German artillery fire seemed made each trip an incredibly dangerous gamble, but the two men worked tirelessly.[36]

In Lucy-le-Bocage, the bodies of Company F Engineers killed earlier that day were carried on stretchers by members of the regimental medical

June 2nd Chapter V

corps through the debris-riddled streets about eighty meters northwest of the church in the center of the village for burial. Private Harry M. Sundberg recalled the grizzly sight of his friend, Private Shelton Brown Beaty's body. "I saw him before he was carried from the battlefield and his chest and lower limbs were badly shattered."[37] The burial detail unceremoniously wrapped the bodies in blankets.

Father John A. Randolph, the regimental chaplain, was present as they dug the graves at the foot of a short brick wall just off the street. The company started to gather and witness the somber undertaking as the sunlight faded.[38] Corporal Michael Frederickson of Company F watched in silence as the burial detail set Beaty's body into the shallow, freshly-excavated grave. As he watched the internment of his friend Beaty, Frederickson recalled, "He didn't have a real military funeral, but the whole company was at it."[39]

Private Jefferson Lonzo Holt. Photo Credit: Leslie Harrison.

With Beaty's remains interred on the right and Corporal Mart Gentry on the left, Father Randolph marked the somber moment with a brief prayer, and the company dispersed to go about excavating fighting holes.[40]

The darkness of night, although abbreviated in the summers of northern France, made the loose liaison between Wise and Shearer more problematic in the wake of German patrols. First Lieutenant Frederick Wheeler led one of the two platoons of the 95th Company across an open space in the woods where he directed them to deploy.

Ordering his men to prepare fighting positions, Wheeler assured them that the Germans were just ahead and that they had, "Thirty minutes to dig for your lives."[41] Corporal Warren Jackson, sneering at his earlier decision to shed his entrenching tool to reduce the weight of the gear he carried, joined forces with twenty-two-year-old Private Raymond Pigott who had a shovel and dug frantically.

Chipping and scraping at the seemingly solid earth, Pigott sunk the spade of the shovel into the ground where it wedged against a rock and snapped in his efforts to pry it loose. Discarding the broken tool, Jackson and Pigott piled stones and dirt in front of their shallow dwelling before they felt reasonably assured their work would provide some semblance of cover

June 2nd Chapter V

from what they believed would hit them at any moment. Before he could settle into his rudimentary furrow, Jackson was summoned to crawl out well in front of the line and man an outpost.[42]

Throughout the night, French troops pulled back from the region around the town of Torcy and approached the portion of the 95th Company line held by twenty-six-year-old Gunnery Sergeant Peter Morgan's platoon. Morgan, a native of Fairfield, Connecticut, quickly warned his anxious men about the approaching French.

Darkness covered the French withdrawal, but during the night, one of Morgan's attentive men spotted additional figures that were visible in the faint moonlight. The Marines, undoubtedly aware the commotion was not part of the French retreat, realized it was an enemy patrol approaching within 200 yards of the line. The relative silence of the predawn quickly vanished in a crescendo of rifle fire from the 95th Company's lines.

Morgan accurately directed the small arms barrage of his men so they would not endanger the retreating French troops that continued to pass through the American front. Morgan moved along the platoon and crouched behind his men as they shot into the darkness from the prone position. He calmly and efficiently directed their fire. His reassuring presence, a comfort to those men under fire for the first time, allowed them to drive off that enemy patrol.

The rifle fire along the line died out, but the excitement of the engagement remained high. Morgan did not sleep that night, so he could maintain vigilance over his men—even after fatigue supplanted the adrenaline surge. German patrols frequented the

Gunnery Sergeant Peter Morgan. Photo credit: Steve Girard.

platoon's vicinity on several occasions throughout the night, and each time the observant Marines under Morgan's direction responded convincingly.[43]

The elements of the French who pulled back along the line between Major Shearer's battalion and Lieutenant Colonel Wise's position were the exhausted soldiers of the fearsome 152nd Infantry, known as 'Les Diables Rouges' (Red Devils), a unit with roots going back to the French

Revolution. They made a valiant stand during the previous few days. Their fortitude along the fractured front allowed the American line to materialize. Without them, the American predicament would quickly become catastrophic.

When information about the French withdrawal reached Colonel Neville at his command post situated at a quarry just northwest of Marigny-en-Orxois, he dispatched a courier at 3:20 A.M. to inform Colonel Catlin that the French withdrawal created a gap between the two units.[44] Neville was evidently unaware that these French soldiers were only regrouping for a planned counterattack to dislodge the Germans scheduled for the next morning.

With the remnants of the French 43rd and 164th Divisions scheduled to turn over command of the front to the American 2nd Division at 9:00 A.M., the next morning, pressure mounted on the Americans to establish a liaison between their units in a line. At 1:35 A.M., however, a telephone call to the 2nd Division headquarters at Montreuil-aux-Lions stated the Germans had taken the towns of Bussiares, Torcy, as well as the Bois de Belleau the previous evening. Furthermore, a planned counterattack to extricate the Germans from these objectives would occur the following day by the French 43rd Division. By direction of the French 21st Corps, this delayed the transfer of command of the front to the Americans until a time yet to be determined.[45] Harbord took the opportunity to relay the message to his regiments and emphasize that, "the necessary steps be taken to hold our positions at <u>all</u> <u>costs</u>."[46]

French 75mm batteries remained active throughout the night. While Company A, 5th Machine Gun battalion returned to the division sector following their relief from the line near the shattered village of Coulombs; they snaked their way through the fields outside of Montreuil-aux-Lions parallel to the Paris-Metz road.

French illumination shells flickered along the northern sky against the backdrop of distant artillery reports. First Lieutenant Wendell Westover remembered, "As the road led up the hill from the town to the rolling plateau ahead, it seemed that the ding at the top must come from 'arrivals' directed at the traffic; yet when we cleared the crest we found the road lined with heavy howitzers which were sending their missiles toward the enemy lines with a frequency which bade ill for any Boche attempt to continue the advance down the Paris road that night."[47] The ground shook each time one of the cannons fired.

The animal caravan of the machine gun battalion, according to Westover, was surprisingly undisturbed by the concussion of the guns as teams of pack mules trotted past the batteries in the midst of a salvo they were firing towards German positions in the north. According to Westover, "The fast-traveling roar of the shells as they sped towards German concentration points and routes of advance was the sweetest music. As we advanced, more and more batteries spoke out from right and left. Every woods patch concealed at least four guns. And they were all firing. Our own artillery brigade was getting into position with those of the French and the night reverberated with the firing."[48]

Just behind Company A, 5th Machine Gun Battalion, Company B, under the command of twenty-eight-year-old West Point graduate Captain D'Alary Fechet, followed the route out of Coulombs. With their departure from the village, at least one of the 3rd Brigade's machine gun battalions returned to the division sector.

At various intervals, the companies of the battalion spent most of the night hiking the thirteen kilometers towards the 3rd Brigade sector. Westover, exhausted from what seemed like the endless changing of positions, noted that that column passed Brigade headquarters at Ventelet Farm just about 700 meters south of the Paris-Metz road. The company continued toward Larget Farm to the south of brigade headquarters another 900 meters.[49]

"No lights could be shown," recalled Westover, "but this night it was no handicap in locating the animals, carts, and hay lofts for the men; the artillery firing furnished ample illumination."[50] The company learned at Larget farm that they would move out immediately after their 6:00 A.M. reveille and join Companies C and D of the 5th Machine Gun Battalion already in line with the 9th Infantry. For now, however, Company A was to enjoy five hours of the first real prolonged sleep they experienced in days.

The men had endured a ninety-hour window of misery that carried them nearly seventy miles on foot, interspersed with brief periods of rest totaling about six hours. "They were young and hardened. Some of the older regulars felt the strain, but years of outdoor life would make their sleep tonic," Westover reflected.[51] Even against the thunderous backdrop of the night-long artillery barrage in preparation for the morning's scheduled French counterattack, Westover's men slept soundly.

---

[1] Westover, *Suicide Battalions,* 110-111.
[2] *Records of the Second Division (Regular)* Volume 5, N.P.
[3] Ibid.
[4] Ibid.
[5] *Records of the Second Division (Regular)* Volume 4, N.P.
[6] *Records of the Second Division (Regular)* Volume 5, N.P.
[7] _____ "Heroes of Belleau Wood Come Back Smiling," *Recruiters Bulletin,* September 1918, 8. Note: Sergeant David Bates of the 49th Company was wounded by the shell which was claimed to have wounded eleven and killed one. Letter George Hamilton June 25, 1918, to 'V' RG 127 Box 300.
[8] U.S. Marine Corps Muster Rolls, 1893-1940, Record Group 127, NARA, Washington, D.C.
[9] Ibid.

[10] Burial File of Private Marvin Watson, Eye-witness statement by Private Clarence Jenni, Box 5114, RG 92.9, Records of Graves Registration Services, NARA College Park, MD.
[11] *History of the Third battalion, Sixth regiment,* 13.
[12] Scanlon, *God Have Mercy On Us*, 12.
[13] Nelson, "Paris-Metz Road," *Leatherneck*, 13.
[14] Scanlon, *God Have Mercy On Us*, 12.
[15] Ibid, and Official Military Personnel File for Corporal Warren Stone Freund, RG 127, NPRC St. Louis, MO. U.S. Marine Corps Muster Rolls, 1893-1940, Record Group 127, NARA, Washington, D.C.
[16] Scanlon, *God Have Mercy On Us*, 12. Note: Scanlon erroneously refers to the company supporting the 1st Battalion 6th Marines, but the 97th went into support of Major Holcomb's 2nd Battalion from La Cense toward Le Thiolet.
[17] Scanlon, *God Have Mercy On Us*, 13.
[18] Ibid.
[19] Ibid.
[20] Ibid.
[21] *Records of the Second Division (Regular)* Volume 5, N.P.
[22] Ibid.
[23] Ibid.
[24] Jackson, *His Time in Hell, A Texas Marine in France,* 90.
[25] Ibid.
[26] Ibid.
[27] Ibid.
[28] Ibid, 91.
[29] Ibid.
[30] *Records of the Second Division (Regular)* Volume 5, N.P.
[31] General Gerald B. Thomas memoir, Alfred M. Gray Research Library, Quantico, VA.
[32] Diary of Asa J. Smith 74th Company 6th Regiment U.S. Marines, Alfred M. Gray Research Library, Quantico, VA.
[33] History of the 74th Company, compiled by Sergeant Carl W. Smith, Box 35, RG 127, NARA College Park, M.D.
[34] *Records of the Second Division (Regular)* Volume 5, N.P. Note: First Lieutenant William Mathew's own assessment of the situation sketched out on a post-war resurvey map does in fact show the 51st Company's right flank extending all the way to Hill 142.
[35] *Records of the Second Division (Regular)* Volume 9, N.P.
[36] Mitchell, *The Official History of the Second Regiment of Engineers,* 122.

[37] Burial File of Private Shelton B. Beaty, Eye-witness statement by Private Harry M. Sundberg, Box 310, RG 92.9, Records of Graves Registration Services, NARA College Park, MD.
[38] Ibid.
[39] Burial File of Private Shelton B. Beaty, Eye-witness statement by Corporal Michael Frederickson, Box 310, RG 92.9, Records of Graves Registration Services, NARA College Park, MD.
[40] Ibid.
[41] Jackson, *His Time in Hell, A Texas Marine in France*, 92.
[42] Ibid.
[43] Official Military Personnel File for Gunnery Sergeant Peter Morgan, RG 127, NPRC St. Louis, MO.
[44] *Records of the Second Division (Regular)* Volume 5, N.P.
[45] *Records of the Second Division (Regular)* Volume 4, N.P.
[46] *Records of the Second Division (Regular)* Volume 5, N.P.
[47] Westover, *Suicide Battalions,* 112.
[48] Ibid.
[49] Ibid.
[50] Ibid.
[51] Ibid.

June 2nd Chapter VI

The Marne front suddenly became quiet, and our attention and energies were transferred to the threatened right flank. Here the decision would be fought out. Though we told ourselves and our men, 'On to Paris,' we knew this was not to be.

-Major General Walter Von Unruh, German 4th Reserve Corps

As the final hours of June 2 dwindled away, the Germans stood in possession of the town of Bouresches. Elements of the 2nd Battalion, 398th German Infantry finally drove soldiers of the 5th Battalion, 356th French Infantry out of the village by 6:00 P.M. During the attack, the Germans suffered heavy casualties from enfilading machine gun fire emanating from the southeast edge of Belleau Wood.[1]

German soldiers of the 461st Infantry of sixty-three-year-old Lieutenant General Albano von Jacobi's 237th Division, by nightfall, pushed through Belleau Wood.[2] Soldiers of the 462nd Regiment of Jacobi's division also consolidated their captured terrain along Hill 126 on the southwestern outskirts of the village of Torcy.[3] The German 197th Division managed to take the town of Bussiares, which stood less than four kilometers up the road from Lieutenant Colonel Wise's command post of the 2nd Battalion, 5th Marines.[4]

The bigger picture for the German Blücher offensive was a much more austere situation. Of the three armies involved, sixty-seven-year-old General Max Von Boehn's 7th Army in the center had advanced further than other German units on their flanks. This situation put elements of the 7th Army, including General Richard Von Conta's Corps, into an increasingly narrow salient with gradually elongated and exposed flanks.

To the east, General Bruno Von Mudra's 1st German Army ran into considerable trouble in the regions near Rheims. Nearly sixty kilometers west of Rheims, German General Oskar von Hutier's 18th Army encountered stiff resistance in the areas of a Forêt de Retz, a massive 33,000-acre stretch of woodlands surrounding the village of Villers-Cotterêts. The Forêt de Retz served as a strategic mecca for launching further offensives.

The operation between Soissons and Rheims, centered on the regions now occupied by the 2nd American Division, was designed by General Ludendorff to be a limited diversionary drive and was therefore logistically planned accordingly. When the attack in this sector commenced May 27th, the unanticipated success it gained filled Ludendorff and oberste heeresleitung (German General Headquarters) with optimism. "A tactical distraction had become a great strategic victory," said Lieutenant General Robert Lee Bullard in describing the initial phase of the German offensive.[5]

General Ludendorff now faced a critical decision. One consideration was to continue the assault in this area, and given the unanticipated success, this appealed to German high command. Continuation of the advance would sustain the current attack as the primary drive beyond merely its intended diversionary nature, which sought to draw French reserves away from the British front in Flanders to launch Plan Hagen, a massive assault along the British front.

Given the success of the current drive and the fact that it consistently pulled in French reinforcements, Ludendorff's other option was to initiate Plan Hagen as planned. Ludendorff, however, decided to continue the advance of his three armies and to press the center of the offensive. This decision pushed General Von Boehn's 7th Army, and principally Von Conta's 4th Reserve Corps, toward the Marne River near Chateau Thierry. He hoped to advance the eastern elements of General Von Boehn's 7th Army across the Marne River and take the critical city of Epernay to free up the 1st Army stalled near Rheims.

The gains made by the end of May, however, further narrowed Boehn's front, creating perilous supply issues. With time a critical factor, the weakened nature of troops on the eastern flanks of the 7th and 1st Armies, as well as the French Army's ability to feed reinforcements into the area, the German Crown Prince and his Chief of Staff, Colonel Count von der Schulenburg, persuaded Ludendorff to abandon this plan. According to the Crown Prince:

> An advance beyond the Marne was not intended as it would only have lengthened the flanks of the break-through to a dangerous degree. There was also no strategic objective south of the Marne. The still unbroken impetus of the offensive must, therefore, be used in some other direction . . . The left wing of the 7th Army and the right wing of the 1st had to pivot on Rheims. The Marne was to be the southern limit for both attacks and also serve as support for the outer wings. It was not to be crossed in force, but the crossings were to be secured.[6]

Ludendorff instead decided to broaden his front by pressing the attack in the west, which called upon General Von Hutier's 18th Army to push the advance in a westward direction along a roughly thirty-two kilometer front between the towns of Noyon and Montdidier.

Ludendorff's decision forced the Germans to reallocate resources and supplies that would be desperately needed by General Von Boehn's 7th Army and thus guaranteed that any continuation of the drive between Rheims and Soissons, notably the front held by the American 2nd Division, would inevitably slow down. According to Ludendorff:

June 2nd Chapter VI

In early June, we stopped our advance. G.H.Q. did not intend to attack further except between the Aisne and the Forest of Villers-Cotterets [Forêt de Retz], south-west of Soissons. We wanted to gain more ground to the westward, on account of the railway, which leads from the Aisne valley east of Soissons into that of the Vesle and be in a position to give tactical support to the attack of the 18th Army on the line of Montdidier-Noyon.[7]

According to forty-year-old Major General Walter Von Unruh, Von Conta's Corps Chief of Staff, the logistics of supplying the 4th Corps' advance became critical as early as May 30th. Von Unruh explained:

> The question of supply had indeed become acute. We had not mechanized columns, and our railhead was far away in the rear. Besides, there remained the barrier of the Chemin des Dames to overcome. Our four-legged friends, therefore, went through a very rough time, but it was some consolation to be able to feed them well on captured oats! Yet the excellent liaison between the General Staff and the Quartermaster-General's branch resulted in our resources being handled so well that our troops never went short, although we had to exercise the strictest economy in our expenditure of ammunition, an economy which must inevitably militate against the success of any action.[8]

Despite the speed with which Von Conta's 4th Reserve Corps reached the Marne by late May, the limited nature of the offensive as a diversion, which was the initial intention despite General Ludendorff's last minute decision to press it vigorously, was planned and supplied accordingly. German efforts to cross and sustain a bridgehead over the Marne River would suffer as a result. According to Von Unruh:

> In spite of all the precautions we might take, we were bound to lose men, as it would be a costly business to bring the detachments back across the river under fire. We quickly abandoned the project, deciding that now it would have to be all or nothing. We, at any rate, were ready to make a crossing in force, but neither orders nor permission to do so were received. The Marne front suddenly became quiet, and our attention and energies were transferred to the threatened right flank. Here the decision would be fought out. Though we told ourselves and our men, 'On to Paris,' we knew this was not to be.[9]

The drive along the 7th Army front not only sputtered to a leapfrog approach that took away momentum, but the troops felt the limits of the offensive's logistics more with each passing day. Ludendorff's shifting emphasis on the 18th Army's westward drive between Noyon and Montdidier only compounded the logistical limitations felt by Von Conta's men.

By the end of June 1st, with supply a critical issue, casualties mounted in Von Conta's divisions. According to Von Unruh, "But our casualties were increasingly alarming; ammunition was running short and the problem of supply, in view of the large demands, became more and more difficult. It became all too clear that actions so stubbornly contested and involving us in such formidable losses would never enable us to capture Paris."[10]

The general disposition of Von Conta's 4th Reserve Corps at the end of June 2nd lay along the ground just south and parallel to the Clingon brook from the village of Gandelu through the town of Eloup. This position situated the Germans two and a half kilometers northwest of Les Mares Farm and continued all the way to Belleau Wood. Von Conta's front then extended sharply to the southeast, encompassing Bouresches and stretched roughly along the road connecting Bouresches to the town of Vaux.

From there, elements of the 231st Division, commanded by fifty-three-year-old Lieutenant General Bernhard von Hülsen, held the line from the high ground east of Vaux all the way to the northern half of Chateau Thierry, which lay north of the Marne River. Elements of the 231st Division were unable to cross the last remaining bridge in that city due to the determined efforts of the French Army as well as U.S. troops from the 3rd Division's 7th Mobile Machine Gun Battalion.

The following day, June 3rd, Von Conta's corps' objectives were to push south and southwest towards Les Mares Farm, Marigny-en-Orxois, La Voie du Chatel, Lucy-le-Bocage, and Triangle Farm. These were objectives much more modest in comparison to the unprecedented gains obtained at the outset of the offensive. "From June 2 onwards," noted Kaiser Wilhelm, "the resistance stiffened in both directions of our attack, after our outer wings had already had to be content with a step by step advance."[11]

Unbeknownst to Von Conta's troops, the scheduled extension of the line was to seize a more suitable defensive position, but they would first have to contend with a counterattack that the French 43rd Division intended to deliver the following day.

Even though the German offensive in the region vacillated, the regiments of General Omar Bundy's 2nd Division frantically tried to consolidate their front and establish liaison with adjacent units in anticipation for the pending American takeover of the front. For all they knew, the Germans planned to continue the advance as energetically as ever, a fact evidenced by the increased volume of artillery fire pounding the 2nd Division's front. The following day, June 3rd, the German push to obtain

June 2nd Chapter VI

those modest objectives would thrust them immediately opposite the American line.

---

[1] War Diary and Annexes 398th Infantry 2 June 1918, *Translation of War Diaries of German Units,* Vol. 1.
[2] War Diary and Annexes 1st, 2nd, 3rd Battalions, 461st Infantry 2 June 1918, *Translation of War Diaries of German Units,* Vol. 4.
[3] War Diary and Annexes 462nd Infantry 2 June 1918, *Translation of War Diaries of German Units,* Vol. 4.
[4] War Diary and Annexes 197th Division 2 June 1918, *Translation of War Diaries of German Units,* Vol. 4.
[5] General Robert Lee Bullard and Earl Reeves, *American Soldiers Also Fought*, (New York: Longmans, Green and Co., 1936), 36.
[6] Wilhelm, Crown prince of Germany, *My War Experiences*, 321-22.
[7] Eric Ludendorff, *My War Memories,* (Hutchinson and Co., London: 1919) Volume 2, 630.
[8] Sidney Rogerson, *The Last of the Ebb,* (London: Greenhill Books 1937), 143-44.
[9] Ibid, 145-46.
[10] Ibid, 146.
[11] Wilhelm, Crown prince of Germany, *My War Experiences*, 323.

JUNE 3ᴿᴰ

June 3rd Chapter I

The French colonel then informed us that outside of the detachment of French cavalry, there was no infantry in front of the 1st Battalion; the Germans at any moment might sweep through this sector. He begged us to cross the river immediately as he expected to blow up the bridge, which he said was our only avenue of escape.
-First Lieutenant Elmer Hess 1st Battalion, 15th Field Artillery

Just after midnight, the 9th Infantry's regimental machine gun company passed through Montreuil-aux-Lions following their all-day march. The morale and energy of the men diminished with their grueling journey. To their dismay, orders to proceed east for several more kilometers generated grumbling. They headed towards Les Aulnois Bontemps where the 9th Infantry established regimental headquarters. Despite the role the 2nd Division's machine gun units played the day before, the majority were still hiking to the front.

By 2:40 A.M., the 8th and 73rd Companies, the two regimental machine gun companies of the 4th Brigade, passed through Montreuil-aux-Lions.[1] The 23rd Infantry's regimental machine guns departed the town of Bregy, France, at 9:00 P.M. June 2nd, and spent most the night hiking the twenty-five kilometers toward the regiment's command post at Coulombs.[2]

Lieutenant Colonel Frederic Wise's battalion received welcomed reinforcement during the night when the disheveled and exhausted Marines of the 8th Machine Gun Company arrived at the front in the thickets of Bois de Veuilly. Hauling their heavy guns and tripods, they marched in columns through the forest. The tired Marines struggled to maintain physical contact with the man in front of them through the dense woods where lack of visibility in the darkness slowed their progress.

They moved hundreds of meters into the forest before reaching the battalion's position. Gun crews emplaced their weapons along the line in the northern part of the forest to cover as much of the front as possible. With no time for rest, they quickly dug in before the 3:00 A.M. sun appeared over the eastern horizon.[3]

When the morning sunlight glistened over the skyline, camions carrying the 73rd Machine Gun Company of the 6th Marines pulled into La Voie du Chatel. They spent the entire night in the back of trucks; a means of travel they preferred over hiking. The vehicles, which picked them up in the middle of their exasperating march earlier in the evening, were salvation for the tired Marines. They spent thirty-nine hours of the previous two days hiking to the front. According to twenty-four-year-old Private Einar Arnold Wahl, the refugee-clogged roads bottlenecked traffic and impeded the company's progress while they were still far from the front, but then the convoy miraculously appeared to carry them the remaining distance. "Did those trucks look good to us!" exclaimed Wahl. "We learned from the weary, dust-covered drivers (many of whom hadn't slept for several days) that the situation was serious and that we were badly needed. We bumped along all night at a tremendous speed, passing the long lines of dim-shaped wagon trains, truck trains, cannon, troops, and the poor refugees, who, of course, were bound in the opposite direction."[4]

Members of the 8th Machine Gun Company stopping along the roadside for 'canned bill' the afternoon of June 2nd. Photo credit: Part of the photo album of Private Walter Hamm. Author's collection.

The arrival of the 73rd Company gave the 4th Brigade all of its machine gun assets. The somnolent status of the men from their long journey earned them a few hours of rest before moving into the line later in the day. According to Wahl, however, "Excitement began to drive away our weariness then."[5]

Tediously, the Marines unloaded the Hotchkiss guns and equipment from the bed of the vehicles. They took a quick inventory of gear in the darkness before hiking into the cover of nearby woods to catch some much needed, albeit abbreviated sleep.

Ahead of the Marine line, the French 43rd Division prepared to launch their gallant counterattack against positions the Germans had captured the day before. The French artillery, active throughout the night, increased their volume of fire on Bussiares and the surrounding area. They also bombarded the southern region of the Clignon Heights. Only fragments of the French 43rd Division remained intact compared to those who held the front a few days earlier.

June 3rd Chapter I

The steadfast French determination gave the troops occupying the left half of the 2nd Division's line valuable time to reinforce their position with additional firepower from newly arrived machine gun units. French persistence also allowed the 2nd Division to establish liaison along the battlefront—an invaluable benefit for battalions still sorting out the disorganized and chaotic nature of their developing line.

Dawn's light shimmered low along the green-sloped horizon as the sound of close-quarters fighting signaled the beginning of the French counterattack. By the end of the day, the 2nd Division line would stand mostly free of the French buffer before it. The Americans soon found themselves directly opposed to the German 197th and 237th Divisions.

The observations of a 6th Marine officer, following his reconnaissance north of Lucy-le-Bocage, believed the division would soon face the enemy directly. His 4:00 A.M. message reported enemy soldiers spotted approximately a kilometer north of Lucy-le-Bocage. These German were soldiers of the 237th Division closing on the French withdrawal from Belleau Wood.[6]

Private James Hatcher of the 84th Company, 3rd Battalion, 6th Marines awoke in an open field during the predawn darkness soaked with morning dew. Following the bombardment, which hammered the battalion the previous afternoon, the 84th Company moved into the ground on the right of the woods after dark. They spent the night there to avoid the anticipated bombardment of the woods. Hatcher said, ". . . after deploying in a firing line, we lay down along a ridge and waited throughout the night."[7]

As a sliver of sunlight illuminated the morning sky to the east, a lone truck traveling at high speed careened passed the 84th Company. The vehicle, delivering ammunition to the front, caught Hatcher's attention. He could not understand why a truck would dare to venture so close to the front following the bombardment the battalion received the previous day. Hatcher envisaged, "I never expected to see that truck or men again in this world but a short time later it came speeding back still intact; and, as it passed by us and into the cover of the woods the two men gave a shout of relief."[8]

Along the 3rd Brigade's front, First Lieutenant William Westover and elements of Company A, 5th Machine Gun Battalion spent much of the predawn hiking to rejoin the battalion in line with the 9th Infantry. Orders issued the day before withdrew them away from the western-most sector of the division front at Coulombs and returned them to the 3rd Brigade holding the division's right. By first light, the Company traveled parallel to the Paris-Metz road towards the town of Domptin located just a kilometer and a half south of Coupru. According to Westover:

June 3rd Chapter I

It might have been called 'the valley of seventy-fives. Every orchard, every patch of brush, every wood held its batteries protected from observation by enemy planes. Guns spoke from behind buildings in the villages; they burst forth from the farmyards. Here and there, scattered groups of buildings on the more wealthy farms furnished headquarters for the various units. The guns were firing continuously. Sometimes slowly with a regularity that signified the searching of enemy woods or roads. Often with rapid concentration, which denoted information received of assembled troops or an attack in progress. They covered the roads, traversed the slopes, and pounded the enemy's batteries and villages to prevent the continuance of the drive in force.[9]

In the town of Chamigny, located along the Marne River just under ten kilometers southwest of Montreuil-aux-Lions, soldiers of Major Benjamin Bailey's 1st Battalion, 15th Field Artillery, bivouacked in the village that morning. They had traveled endlessly during the previous forty-eight hours and were nearing the front. "The roads around these positions were patrolled by French cavalry," claimed First Lieutenant Elmer Hess.[10] That morning, Hess walked toward Bailey's battalion headquarters and found him conversing with a French colonel and his adjutant. According to Hess:

> Through the interpreter, Major Bailey was begged to remove his battalion across the River Marne to the hills overlooking the river on the south bank. This Major Bailey refused to do, stating that his orders were to take these positions, and until his colonel countermanded his orders, he would stay here. The French colonel then informed us that outside of the detachment of French cavalry, there was no infantry in front of the 1st Battalion; the Germans at any moment might sweep through this sector. He begged us to cross the river immediately as he expected to blow up the bridge, which he said was our only avenue of escape. Again, Major Bailey refused to withdraw. An hour later, we heard a terrific detonation, which we knew meant the destruction of the bridge over the Marne and our supposed last avenue of escape. Lieutenant Peabody, who was in the kitchen of the farmhouse, raised a bottle of wine and drank a health to the bridge in which we all joined before the reverberations of the explosion had passed away.[11]

Several kilometers northeast of Chamigny, the developing division front braced for the French counterattack. From his command post along the cemetery wall outside of Marigny-en-Orxois, Lieutenant Colonel

June 3rd Chapter I

Frederic Wise spent the night in a half-conscious state of mind. He was concerned over the unestablished liaison of his battalion's flanks with adjacent units. French batteries continued their steady and thunderous barrage of the enemy lines far to the north. The distant sounds of rifle and machine gun fire emanating from the front signaled the beginning of French 43rd Division's counterattack. The cacophony of battle heightened the anxiety Wise felt over his battalion's dilemma. He could not stand to remain at his command post, and informed Colonel Neville he was departing to inspect on the battalion's front.[12]

Wise took the most direct route and walked northeast along the road between Marigny-en-Orxois and Champillon despite the likelihood of enemy observation. He ventured toward Captain Lloyd Williams' 51st Company holding the battalion's right flank.[13] Just shy of the village of Champillon, he encountered several French Chasseurs who withdrew through the American lines, which suggested a failure in the initial push against the German line. The sun, clear of the eastern horizon, burned brightly in a sky now alive with the searing whine of incoming artillery fire. "Heavy German shells began to explode here and there in and around Marigny," according to Wise.[14]

Southeast of Hill 142, Corporal Warren Jackson and the 95th Company continued shifting their position west, which further stretched the left flank of Major Maurice Shearer's 1st Battalion, 6th Marines. This constant adjustment of the front resulted from Shearer's tireless efforts to establish liaison with the right flank of 2nd Battalion, 5th Marines, near Hill 142. Throughout the night, Jackson's platoon regularly changed locations.

By daybreak, they moved further to the left once again, this time down a wooded gradient. Along the way, they encountered survivors of the ill-fated French counterattack as they retreated south. "We met a party of French whose dejection disconcerted us," remembered Jackson.[15]

As the platoon plodded along, a morbid spectacle greeted them. Jackson noticed an elongated, freshly excavated trench. He followed the pit at full length and saw a thick crimson puddle of freshly spilled blood in the loose soil. Continuing along the line, they encountered abandoned fighting holes, and several men occupied them. The rest of the company continued west. According to Jackson's recollection:

> When we went a little further, there was no trench and no holes. Here the last of us stopped. I was the last man, on the extreme right of the company. What or who was to my right I could not even guess. I looked with envy to my left at the men who had been lucky enough to have a dugout to get into. However, no shells had fallen in our vicinity since we had taken up our new position, so I don't think we were particularly concerned as to getting below the

surface. Nevertheless, I felt lonesome with the next man to my left some distance away and no one on my right.[16]

On the right portion of the 1st Battalion, 6th Marine Regiment's three-kilometer front, the 3rd Platoon of the 75th Company awoke to the distant sound of small arms fire. Sergeant Gerald Thomas and others noted obscure but visible movement coupled with the crack of rifle fire emanating from the edge of Belleau Wood just under a kilometer across the open pasture.

The gradual stretching of the line between Lucy-le-Bocage and Hill 142 by Shearer's Marines further extended an already-thin battalion front. Once again, the pressure to established liaison resulted in the displacement of Thomas's men. "My platoon received orders to shift to the left and dig a line in the grain field there."[17]

As the Shearer's men continued their frustrated efforts to establish liaison, French units counterattacked to the north, but met heavy German fire and scattered. Throughout the morning, shattered units reassembled and repeatedly launched gallant but futile attacks against the German line only to crumble against withering fire. The gradual withdrawal of surviving French soldiers throughout the day caused the German batteries to increase the range of their artillery. This adjustment placed a renewed and concentrated barrage on the still-developing American front.

---

[1] *Records of the Second Division (Regular)* Volume 4, N.P.
[2] Ibid.
[3] Durant S. Buchanan, History of the Regimental Machine Gun Company 5th Marines, January 20, 1919, Box 67, RG 120.9.3, Second Division File, Records of the AEF, NARA College Park, MD.
[4] Kemper F. Cowing and Courtney Ryley Cooper, *Dear Folks At Home* (Boston: Houghton Mifflin Company, 1919), 140-41.
[5] Ibid.
[6] *Records of the Second Division (Regular)* Volume 4, N.P.
[7] Hatcher, *Citizen Soldier*, N.P.
[8] Ibid.
[9] Westover, *Suicide Battalions*, 113.
[10] Spaulding and Wright, *The Second Division American Expeditionary Force in France 1917-1919*, 249-50.
[11] Ibid, 250.
[12] *Records of the Second Division (Regular)* Volume 5, N.P.
[13] Wise and Frost, *A Marine Tells it to You*, 198.
[14] Ibid.
[15] Jackson, *His Time in Hell, A Texas Marine in France*, 93.
[16] Ibid.
[17] General Gerald B. Thomas, interview by Robert Asprey, Alfred M. Gray Research Library, Quantico, VA.

June 3rd Chapter II

... I was made a little sick at the sight of seeing a bunch of hogs with their snouts pushing through minute pieces of human flesh and blood.
   -Private Levi Hemrick 80th Company, 2nd Battalion, 6th Marines

At La Cense Farm, the headquarters for Major Thomas Holcomb's 2nd Battalion, 6th Marines, members of Captain Bailey Coffenberg's 80th Company wandered about in relative comfort. By late morning, the temperature grew warm as the overcast sky cleared.[1] The company, serving as battalion reserve, spent the previous night turning the farm into their temporary billets. Private Levi Hemrick said, "A small group of fellows and I were idling away the time standing outside the temporary quarters of a doctor and dressing station."[2]

Sergeant Donald Paradis, assigned to battalion headquarters as a runner, returned to the farm after delivering a message to the 96th Company. According to Paradis, "I had just returned to battalion headquarters and was about to have breakfast from my reserve rations when the shelling started."[3] Hemrick and other 80th Company Marines standing outside the doorway of a structure darted for cover. "It was close, and naturally when we heard it coming and realized that it was going to land in the barnyard, we dived for the entrance to the building."[4]

A navy doctor, not accustomed to the art of avoiding shells, obstructed the entrance by standing in the doorway. The doctor's lack of immediate reaction generated a volley of colorful profanity from one impatient Marine trying to gain quick entrance to the building for cover.[5]

Paradis remembered, "One of the first shells came through the roof of the barn where my company was billeted wounding several men in the barn."[6] According to twenty-one-year-old trumpeter Hugo Albert Meyer from Sheboygan, Wisconsin, "A five-inch shell struck the apex of the barn I was in and how I escaped the falling debris I couldn't understand then, but can now—God was with me."[7]

Meyer saw twenty-three-year-old First Lieutenant Thomas Spady Whiting lying nearby with lacerations all over his body from the razor-sharp shell fragments. Another Marine, twenty-five-year-old Sergeant Leo Louis Liptac, suffered a ghastly wound to the foot as others raced outside the building.

Running along the cobblestone street stretching all the way south to the Paris-Metz road, the men sprinted for the nearby woods, "like a pack of sheep seeking questionable safety," according to Paradis.[8] "Well everyone ran about," recalled Meyer, "and an order was given to take to the woods about 100 yards away."[9]

More rounds slammed into the property while several men remained out in the open sprinting for cover. Exploding shells threw broken masonry and rock everywhere. A large chunk of stone hit twenty-eight-year-old Private Albert Henry Berg in the left back side with nearly the same velocity as a bullet, severely injuring him and several others.[10]

When the barrage started, a detail of men hauling ammunition was about 300 meters from the farm out in the open with no cover. According to Hemrick, "While we were watching them, shells began to drop among them and as we watched we saw several of them go down and it looked as if the most of them would be killed if they were not quickly removed and put under cover.

All this happened much quicker than it takes to write it."[11] Realizing the extreme peril faced by the ammunition detail, Hemrick and several others sprang into action. Believing others would follow, he raced down the cobblestone road toward the farm's gated entrance. According to Hemrick:

Levi Hemrick 80th Company. Photo Credit: Jennie Allen.

> As I went through the gate along the rock surfaced road, the warning came that another shell was falling fast and my reflexes took me over and when the shell hit the spot where I had been a few seconds previous, I was in a squatted position in the bottom of a four foot ditch that ran along the side of the road. When the rock and spent pieces of metal blown up by the exploding shell ceased falling on and around me, I eased up and peeped out over the top of the ditch. I saw coming toward me running madly and blindly another soldier. I instantly realized that all that runner could see was the ditch and if I didn't move quickly that a hundred and sixty-pound chunk of human weight following tough hob-nailed brogans would land on top of my head. My trained reflexes again took over and I was able to dodge and escape the threatened injury.[12]

The enemy shellfire was concentrated and intense but quickly subsided. "Where I sat, near headquarters, I knew little about this except the main barn had been hit," said Paradis. "I lay down against the wall, of the horse barn as they put over ten or twelve shells then all was quiet."[13] The cries for help

June 3rd Chapter II

summoned Paradis out of the building. He ordered the other runners to remain in place.

He rushed across the barnyard towards Major Holcomb's command post and found thirty-one-year-old Captain Peregrine 'Pere' Wilmer, the battalion adjutant, nervously wandering across the room. "He said the major had gone to the woods and left word for all runners to evacuate the building and meet him at the woods near the Paris-Metz Highway. Why he didn't quit pacing and come across the courtyard to tell us, I'll never know," thought Paradis.[14] Outside farm's property, he saw for the first time the extent of the devastation caused by the barrage. Both Paradis and Hemrick rushed to the aid of wounded comrades. Twenty-four-year-old First Sergeant Frank Lewis Glick of Marshalltown, Iowa, lay contorted along the road. He was face down in a pool of blood and brain matter that spilled from a large jagged hole in the left side of his head.[15]

First Sergeant Frank Lewis Glick was killed instantly in the barrage of La Cense Farm on the morning of June 3rd. Photo Credit Steve

As soon as Paradis arrived at the entrance of the farm, where several wounded men writhed in agony, more incoming shells suddenly drown out their cries of pain. Paradis continued running for the tree line where Holcomb and several Marines sought cover. Throwing off his pack and dropping his rifle, Paradis pleaded for assistance to pull the wounded out of harm's way.

Noticing wounded comrades sprawled helplessly along the ground and exposed in the open, twenty-four-year-old Sergeant Major Charles Ashley Ingram, twenty-year-old Corporal Archelaus 'Archie' Smith and twenty-one-year-old First Lieutenant John Garth Schneider immediately raced from the cover of the woods to help.[16]

Hemrick, who also assisted, came face to face with Schneider, who had just rejoined the company six days earlier after becoming ill before the regiment shipped overseas.[17] Hemrick, who had not seen his friend Schneider in months, noticed the familiar face. "Our greetings were limited to the exchange of smiles," recalled Hemrick who focused his attention on the wounded, and more importantly on the enemy's resumption of shelling the farm.[18] "I picked up a shelter half and we ran back to the men," recalled Paradis.[19] Nearby, twenty-three-year-old Private Fred Erymn Lomax, a

June 3rd Chapter II

farmer from Hohenwald, Tennessee, lay mortally wounded screaming for help. Paradis vividly relived the horrific scene:

I went to him at once while the other men were examining the wounded, but all were dead. Lomax's leg was broken near the hip and lay at right angles to his side. He kept trying to raise up. I could see from the gray look on his face that he was in shock. I spread the shelter half alongside of him and called 'Let's get Lomax out, he's alive.' I straightened his leg then with the two on each side of him we managed to get him moved over into the shelter half.[20]

Private Fred Lomax was killed during the shelling of the 80th Company's position at La Cense Farm. Photo credit: New York Times Mid-week pictorial.

First Lieutenant John Schneider, seen here as a cadet at Culver Academy, helped carry some of the wounded during the bombardment of La Cense Farm during the morning of June 3rd. Photo credit: Culver Academy.

As Paradis and the other men carried the mortally Lomax a short distance, two more enemy shells landed nearby. "We flattened out. My head lay beside Lieutenant Schneider; he cried, 'My god, my god help us.' We picked up Lomax on the shelter half and managed to get him to the edge of the woods and laid him beside the road with the other wounded."[21]

Holcomb quickly sent Paradis back towards the farm building to fetch Captain Wilmer. Rushing up the cobblestone road, Paradis spotted a pitcher of milk someone nursed from one of several cows roaming the compound and left sitting in the courtyard. According to Paradis, "I grabbed this with

221

June 3rd Chapter II

the idea of giving Lomax a drink, but when I returned he was dead. He must have been wounded in the back also for when I helped lift him my hands were covered with blood."[22]

Near the lifeless body of Lomax, twenty-three-year-old Corporal Walter Smith Duncan had suffered multiple fragmentation wounds to the left leg.[23] Paradis gingerly helped Duncan get a drink of the milk as he shuddered in complete agony. Twenty-four-year-old Private Ralph Oscar Sampson suffered traumatic wounds to his head, both legs, and right hand, which made him too weak to sit up for a drink from the liberated pitcher.[24] As Paradis tried to pour some milk into the wounded Marine's mouth, he spilled it on his neck. Feebly, Sampson managed to muster the energy to cuss Paradis for dumping the cold liquid down his front instead of in his mouth.[25]

When the barrage subsided, ambulances arrived to evacuate the casualties including twenty-six-year-old Gunnery Sergeant Max Krause of Berlin, Wisconsin. Shell fragments mutilated Krause's left arm, which claimed his life the following day.

Comrades loaded Krause into the same ambulance as well as First Lieutenant Thomas Whiting, who suffered multiple fragmentation wounds to the left knee, right arm, and chest.[26] Holcomb came up to Whiting and shook his hand—remorseful for the young first lieutenant's misfortune. "I'll hurry right back as soon as possible, major," replied Whiting.[27]

Gunnery Sergeant Max Krause was mortally wounded in the shelling of La Cense Farm the morning of June 3rd. Photo credit: Author's collection.

After the tragic scene at La Cense Farm ended, men of the 80th Company immediately unearthed dugouts for shelter. According to Paradis, "We wasted no time digging fox holes now, our first of many in Belleau Woods. Battalion headquarters dug in with us."[28] Blood from the company's casualties splotched the cobblestone roads of the farm, and their equipment lay scattered across the property following the barrage.

Shock over the sudden loss of comrades weighed heavily on everyone's mind. Debris and toppled masonry from the farm's damaged buildings littered the courtyard. The bodies of the dead remained at the farm until the following evening when comrades could safely take them into the northwest corner of Bois de Clerembauts for burial.

June 3rd Chapter II

The devastation laying all around reminded the men to excavate their holes as deep as possible in case of subsequent shelling. "Those of us who reached the woods started digging in and, believe me since then we have all had more than our share of that," said Trumpeter Meyer.[29]

Hemrick, who was sent out on duty after the shelling, arrived back at the company's position and noticed the farm's pigs roaming along the cobblestone street. When he reached the gate along the entrance to the property, he realized what the animals were doing and immediately became nauseated. ". . . I was made a little sick at the sight of seeing a bunch of hogs with their snouts pushing through minute pieces of human flesh and blood."[30]

The incessant shelling also convinced members of the 96th Company to get subterranean as fast as possible. According to twenty-four-year-old Corporal Joseph Grant Stites of Hopkinsville, Kentucky:

"The first thing we did was to dig in and believe me it does make a fellow dig in when a big shell is hitting within about twenty feet of him at intervals of about two minutes. There were two of us working on an emplacement for an automatic rifle, and we had gotten about two feet down when we heard a big one coming. We both fell down in the hole, and after the shell had exploded and the shrapnel had stopped falling, we got up, and there was a hole about six feet deep not three feet from us, and you can rest assured we did some digging after that."[31]

When shells fell upon the 96th Company Marines, they scrambled for cover. One incoming shell landed nearly on top of twenty-seven-year-old Private John Percy Street Thompson of Houston, Texas, and the explosion instantly killed him.[32] Thirty-three-year-old Corporal Ollie Henry Johanningmeier, an iron maker with the Chicago Lumber and Coal Company in St. Louis, Missouri, died instantly when an incoming round exploded next to him.[33]

Private John Thompson of the 96th Company, seen here as a member of the Corps of Cadets at Texas A&M, was killed instantly during the German shelling of Bois de Clerembauts. Photo credit: Texas A&M.

Dug in among members of Holcomb's 2nd Battalion, 6th Marines, members of the 97th Company, sent from the 3rd Battalion's position the night before, reinforced the line along the eastern edge of Bois de Clerembauts. The heavy bombardment of La Cense Farm prompted the 4th Platoon, 97th Company to move further south in the woods. Corporal Havelock Nelson, delighted to hike away from the area that was evidently the target of the enemy's shellfire, cheerfully marched through the woods until they reached the regiment's right flank at Le Thiolet. Once there, officers instructed the platoon to dig in.

According to Nelson, "Roberts and I picked out what we thought was a suitable spot in a garden alongside a low stone wall for our fox hole."[34] The loose dirt was conducive to excavating a somewhat cavernous dugout. The distant report of enemy guns paralyzed the two men with fear for a brief moment as they listened for the scream of incoming rounds before flattening out along the ground. "A shell was headed directly for us and it was a big one," Nelson said. "The ground heaved under us, and a deep silence seemed to envelop me. Then I gradually became conscious of falling dirt, a burning acrid sensation in my eyes and nose, and last, of someone chuckling. Suddenly, fully realizing that I was still on this earth and unhurt, I turned over and sat up."[35]

Nelson's comrade exhaled in relief. "'Whew,' he whistled, that was sure close!' 'Look!' he added, pointing to the still smoldering crater so close that we could have spit in it!"[36] Amazed by their miraculous escape, Nelson reasoned, ". . . unless I'm shell-shocked we're on the wrong side of that wall."[37] The two men quickly selected a more concealed and protected patch of ground to dig fighting holes.

Enemy artillery fire also bombarded the Bois de Clerembauts starting at about 1:30 P.M., and prevented soldiers of Company D, 2nd Battalion, 2nd Engineers from digging emplacements to reinforce this portion of the line. The men of the 77th Company, 6th Machine Gun Battalion as well as elements of the 79th and 96th Companies also occupied this sector of the front. They provided the only defense against any potential German advance.

Colonel Catlin made repeated trips to the front along this eastern flank of the brigade. The presence of the indomitable regimental commander substantially boosted the spirits of the 79th Company. According to Corporal Glen Hill of the 2nd Platoon, "Each night Colonel Catlin would walk our front lines admonishing us that we were not to back up a step but we may go as far as we wanted toward Berlin. He was a fine soldier and inspired confidence in him and ourselves."[38]

Soldiers of the Company D, 2nd Battalion, 2nd Engineers arrived along the 79th Company front the previous morning. They went days without much sleep, and now the steady inundation of German shellfire added to their misery. Enemy observation balloons noted the activity at Triangle Farm as well as Hill 182, and soon registered artillery fire on these points.[39] The previous day, machine gunners of the 77th Company aided in stopping a probing German advance. This determined American resistance alerted the Germans whose artillery seemed to take particular interest in that portion of the line.

During the day, Corporal Joseph D. Sanders, a soldier with Company D, 2nd Engineers from Hoisington, Kansas, manned an observation post near Triangle farm. Enemy machine gun and rifle fire continuously snapped and screeched through the tree line forcing Sanders to stay low in this isolated position. The shelling of the woods did not deter him either, as he stoically occupied his post amidst the piercing split-second scream of incoming shells.

During the afternoon, following several close-calls, a round tore through the tree line and exploded nearly on top of Sanders's position knocking him unconscious, but he miraculously avoided injury from shell fragments. Upon regaining consciousness, the steadfast corporal shrugged off any efforts by comrades to treat and evacuate him and insisted on remaining at his post.[40] The artillery fire continued steadily throughout the afternoon as the Germans prepared to seize upon their objectives once the French counterattack fell apart.

---

[1] Operations of 2nd Field Artillery Brigade, Box 81, RG 120.9.3, NARA College Park, MD. Note: the entry for that day mentions an overcast morning which began to clear up.
[2] Hemrick, *Once a Marine,* 113.
[3] Paradis, *The World War I Memoirs of Don V. Paradis,* 39.
[4] Hemrick, *Once a Marine,* 113.
[5] Ibid.
[6] Paradis, *The World War I Memoirs of Don V. Paradis,* 39.
[7] "Tales told by Overseas Marines," *Recruiters Bulletin,* August 1918, 30.
[8] Paradis, *The World War I Memoirs of Don V. Paradis,* 39. Note: The woods mentioned were the northwest corner of Bois de Clerembauts.
[9] "Tales told by Overseas Marines," *Recruiters Bulletin,* August 1918, 30.
[10] U.S. Marine Corps Muster Rolls, 1893-1940, Record Group 127, NARA, Washington, D.C.
[11] Hemrick, *Once a Marine,* 113.
[12] Hemrick, *Once a Marine,* 113-114.
[13] Paradis, *The World War I Memoirs of Don V. Paradis,* 40.
[14] Ibid.
[15] Burial File of First Sergeant Frank L. Glick, Box 1887, RG 92.9, Records of Graves Registration Services, NARA College Park, MD., and Official Military Personnel File for First Sergeant Frank L. Glick, RG 127, NPRC St. Louis, MO. Note: Sergeant Paradis claims to have seen "Top Sergeant Frank L. Glick laying on his stomach, facing me, both legs off just above the knees. He raised his head and smiled as I went by." The burial file for First Sergeant Glick mentions the remains intact, and no apparent injuries to the legs are noted only a hole in the left side of his head.

June 3rd Chapter II

[16] Paradis, *The World War I Memoirs of Don V. Paradis,* 40., and U.S. Marine Corps Muster Rolls, 1893-1940
[17] Hemrick, *Once a Marine,* 114, and U.S. Marine Corps Muster Rolls, 1893-1940, Record Group 127, NARA, Washington, D.C.
[18] Hemrick, *Once a Marine,* 114.
[19] Paradis, *The World War I Memoirs of Don V. Paradis,* 40.
[20] Ibid.
[21] Ibid, 40-41.
[22] Paradis, *The World War I Memoirs of Don V. Paradis,* 41.
[23] U.S. Marine Corps Muster Rolls, 1893-1940, Record Group 127, NARA, Washington, D.C.
[24] Ibid, and Paradis, *The World War I Memoirs of Don V. Paradis,* 41.
[25] Paradis, *The World War I Memoirs of Don V. Paradis,* 41.
[26] Ibid, and Burial File of Gunnery Sergeant Fred E. Lomax, Box 2957, RG 92.9, Records of Graves Registration Services, NARA College Park, MD., and U.S. Marine Corps Muster Rolls, 1893-1940, Record Group 127, NARA, Washington, D.C.
[27] Paradis, *The World War I Memoirs of Don V. Paradis,* 41.
[28] Ibid.
[29] _____ "Tales told by Overseas Marines," *Recruiters Bulletin,* August 1918, 30.
[30] Hemrick, *Once a Marine,* 114.
[31] Newspaper clippings sent to headquarters Marine Corps by F.M. Stites, mother of Joseph G. Stites, Box 300, RG 127 NARA, Washington D.C.
[32] Burial File of Private John Percy Street Thompson, Box 4873, RG 92.9, Records of Graves Registration Services, NARA College Park, MD
[33] Burial File of Corporal Ollie Henry Johanningmeier, Box 2497, RG 92.9, Records of Graves Registration Services, NARA College Park, MD.
[34] Nelson, "Paris-Metz Road," *Leatherneck,* 13.
[35] Ibid.
[36] Ibid.
[37] Ibid.
[38] Correspondence from Hill to Neufeld, 17 January 1979, Alfred M. Gray Research Library, Quantico, VA.
[39] War Diary and Annexes 10th Division 3 June 1918, *Translation of War Diaries of German Units,* Vol. 1.
[40] Mitchell, *The Official History of the Second Regiment of Engineers,* 147.

June 3rd Chapter III

I can't begin to describe my state of mind—you will just have to imagine it. We were getting our first real taste of the horrors of war.
  -Private Einar Wahl 73rd Machine Gun Company, 6th Marines

Against the backdrop of gunfire from the French counterattack several kilometers to the north, Marines of the 55th Company spent the morning unearthing dugouts in open the field around Les Mares Farm. They rushed to dig in before the sunlight revealed their exposed position to the distant German artillery observers. Les Mare Farm, according to First Lieutenant Lemuel Shepherd, "seemed to be the critical point of the line. It was a commanding position from where we could see in all directions. In other words, it was the one spot that must be held in that sector. This would be the objective of any German attack."[1]

During the morning, while the French counterattack escalated to a crescendo of gunfire in the distance, Shepherd cautiously reconnoitered the terrain north of the 55th Company's position. He found a small knoll hundreds of meters north of the company front, and about 300 meters west of the road running between Bussiares and Marigny-en-Orxois.[2] It was a remote spot, "but it was an excellent position for an outpost because it offered good observation to the front with excellent fields of fire," recalled Shepherd.[3]

Upon returning to the company, Shepherd located Captain Blanchfield at his command post. "I asked Captain Blanchfield if I could establish an outpost there. He agreed, and I took out about twelve men—perhaps two squads—and we established an outpost in the apex of a little group of trees. I left them there and went back to the line."[4] Shepherd had left one squad and an automatic rifle with explicit instructions to withdraw if an enemy attack came too close.[5]

The extreme right portion of Lieutenant Colonel Wise's battalion still had no contact with the left flank of Major Maurice Shearer's 1st Battalion, 6th Marines. At 6:15 A.M., Colonel Wendell Neville, from his regimental headquarters at a rock quarry on the western outskirts of Marigny-en-Orxois, dispatched a message to Colonel Catlin in La Voie du Chatel stating:

> Wise and Shearer are in touch but Wise reports his right company (Capt. Williams) has not been able to get in touch with Shearer's left company. Wise has gone this morning to his right to establish this liaison. He thinks there is a gap of some extent between Hill 142 and your left. Have directed him to find where your left is and to extend to the right if he finds that any gap exists. Wise will send a guide with this who can indicate our right.[6]

June 3rd Chapter III

While searching for Shearer's left flank, Wise noticed that several French artillery batteries firing from positions behind his battalion began attracting counterbattery fire from enemy guns. "Heavy German shells began to explode here and there in and around Marigny," Wise recalled.[7] The French counterattack, unbeknownst to the Americans, further crumbled with each renewed push.

French airplanes circling the battlefront tried to identify German strong points holding up the infantry's advance and relayed the information to any available artillery batteries. At 7:11 A.M., a lone French plane dropped a tube containing a message and map near 2nd Division headquarters:

> The message stated that the French Infantry were unable to pass the road about one kilometer north of Lucy-le-Bocage because the Germans had this road spotted on their maps. The question was asked, "CAN YOU FIRE" (pouvez-vous tirer) and the place marked on the maps was on the road southeast of Torcy and north of Lucy-le-Bocage. Major Potter stated that the 2nd Division has no artillery, which could fire on this point, so this message was telephoned at once to Hdqtrs. 43rd Division at La Lodge, and was then sent by motorcycle with the map to the same place.[8]

The 2nd Division soon remedied the inability to respond to the French plea for artillery assistance during the morning. For the better part of the past twenty-four hours, several of the division's batteries remained at Cocherel, France nearly seven kilometers west of the 2nd Division headquarters in Montreuil-aux-Lions.

From the Mairie building in town, Major General Omar Bundy sat with his chief of staff and forty-seven-year-old Brigadier General William Chamberlaine, his artillery brigade commander, finishing a cup of coffee.[9] Bundy turned to Chamberlaine, and in a matter-of-fact demeanor instructed him to put his artillery into position at once.[10]

The chain reaction was immediate. Orders sent from Chamberlaine called for the placement a battalion of the 17th Field Artillery north of their current location. One battalion of the 12th Field Artillery was sent to the vicinity of La Loge to begin fire support of the 4th Brigade. Another battalion of the 15th Field Artillery would occupy battery positions near the village of Domptin to support the 3rd Brigade.[11]

Establishing the liaison between the 5th and 6th Marine Regiments near Hill 142 became increasingly imperative in the face of the faltering French counterattack. Forty-eight-year-old Lieutenant Colonel Logan Feland, the executive commanding officer of the 5th Marines, reconnoitered the problematic area himself. He discovered Wise's right flank on the road in the edge of the woods at Hill 142, as it appeared on the map.[12] Shortly after identifying the exact position of Wise's right flank, a scout dispatched from

June 3rd Chapter III

2nd Battalion, 5th Marines discovered Shearer's left approximately 1,000 meters southeast of Hill 142. Feland immediately informed regimental headquarters of this development. Neville notified Catlin of this discovery at 6:15 A.M.[13]

Reinforcing this gap between the 5th and 6th Marines became critical. Major Berton Sibley's men, situated in the woods along the La Voie du Chatel to Lucy-le-Bocage road, was the nearest unit to fill the void. "During the morning of that day," wrote Sibley, "it was discovered that a wide gap in the line existed between Hill 142 and Major Shearer's battalion of the 6th Marines on the right. In consequence of this, I was ordered to send the 82nd Company under the command of thirty-two-year-old Captain Dwight Frank Smith of Stowe, Vermont and civil engineering graduate from Norwich University, into the line immediately to fill the gap (northeast of Champillon)."[14] Movement of the company during the day in the face of German artillery was hazardous and took hours.

Just before dawn, Sibley's entire 3rd Battalion, 6th Marines, minus the 97th Company which remained attached to Major Holcomb's 2nd Battalion, left the open field where they had spent the previous night to avoid enemy shellfire. By morning, they filed back into the woods to evade enemy observation. Private James Hatcher of the 84th Company moved along the tree line and, "While following along its edge, a German plane flew low over our heads. We drew back into the woods but the airman circled about and flew slowly back over us, then, apparently satisfied, he speeded straight back over his own lines. It was only a short time after the aviator had seen us that the enemy artillery began their pounding again."[15]

Throughout the entire day, enemy guns inundated these woods. According to Hatcher, "Strange as it may seem we had never been instructed in 'digging in' and, although every one of us had a hearty desire to dig a deep hole and get into it, no one wanted to be the first man to start digging."[16] The company remained in place throughout the day and endured the sporadic shelling.

By 9:00 A.M. Captain Joseph Daniel Murray, second in command of the 2nd Battalion, 5th Marines, reported all companies along the battalion front had dug in.[17] "51st Company reports enemy advanced considerable distance late P.M. of June 2nd and that the French retired to a line just in front of the 51st Co. (right of the battalion). 55th Co. reported that the enemy advanced about two kilometers in southeasterly direction."[18]

The battalion's casualty figures submitted to regimental headquarters for the previous day, according to Murray, showed one Marine from the 18th Company died, and ten were wounded.[19] Murray also reported that eight machine guns from the 81st Company reinforced the sector of the line held by the Captain Lloyd Williams 51st Company.[20]

Departing his command post along the cemetery wall of Marigny-en-Orxois, Wise approached the outskirts of Champillon in route to the 51st

June 3rd Chapter III

Company's front. He noted the presence of French Chasseurs in and around the small village. "French artillery just behind our lines was firing again," said Wise. "And now the Germans were beginning to answer it. Heavy shells began to explode here and there in and around Marigny."[21]

The naivety of American troops congregating along roads in plain sight of enemy artillery spotters only facilitated the increased shelling. According to Brigadier General Harbord:

> The French call attention to the practice of people moving on the roads and stopping near important places. This is a practice that I have found great difficulty in repressing in the vicinity of my headquarters. The bombardment on the north portion of my line continues, but there does not seem to be any reason to apprehend any further important activity for the day.[22]

German batteries also targeted the rear echelon of the French counterattack, which continued through the late morning. By 9:00 A.M., German guns dropped an increasing number of shells in and around the village of Lucy-le-Bocage.[23] The 74th and 75th Company, as well as the soldiers of Company E, 2nd Battalion, 2nd Engineers occupied the town. The deafening explosions of incoming shells echoed through the village and sent plumes of smoke above the red roofs.[24]

Up in a tree just behind the 6th Marines' line, a regimental observation post manned by six men watched and estimated, based on the detonation of the projectiles, that these were 150mm shells.[25] Rounds fell at a rate of about one a minute. They shook the ground and fractured large chunks of stone and mason from the city's vast structures.[26]

Twenty-five-year-old Corporal Simon James Madden of Chassell, Michigan, spent the morning occupying the 6th Regimental observation post. He dispatched a message to Second Lieutenant William Eddy, the regimental intelligence officer stating, "Approximately 35/150's dropped on Lucy between 9-10:30 A.M. High explosives and shrapnel."[27]

The German spotters made a note of what appeared to be the reinforcement of the enemy front southwest of Belleau Wood. From an observation post in Belleau Wood, a German Lieutenant named Sievers sent an 11:30 A.M. message to the 237th German Infantry Division headquarters, which they not received until 12:15 P.M. explaining, "They are drawing their reinforcements from Lucy-le-Bocage. This is giving the impression that an attack is in preparation."[28]

The shelling was steady enough to keep the men around Lucy-le-Bocage secluded in their dugouts. For Corporal Miles Neusse of Company E, 2nd Battalion, 2nd Engineers, seeking shelter was not an option. As a runner, he spent the morning and previous night carrying messages nearly two kilometers between battalion headquarters in Lucy-le-Bocage and the company front at Triangle Farm. Every time Neusse arrived at either location, he showed the physical signs of his dangerous assignment.

At one point along his route, a German shell landed close enough to blow his haversack clear off his back. Neusse amazingly escaped unharmed and continued to traverse the woods, gullies, and fields between E Company's position and battalion headquarters. On another occasion, a snipers bullet pierced the excess wool of his uniform but somehow left his flesh completely unscathed.[29]

Several engineers from Company E reinforced the 79th Company's position as infantry. Corporal Lloyd Pike of the 79th Company's 2nd Platoon, received instructions the day before to support these engineers with four of the 79th Company's Chauchat crews. According to Pike, "I spread the guns along the line of the engineers and had my first real combat command. I think I felt more important right then than at any time before or since."[30]

By about 11:30 A.M. the ground erupted and shook when enemy shells slammed into Company E's position. The engineers pressed their bodies against the walls of their shallow dugouts for cover. Corporal William J. Hebner from Seattle, Washington, felt the violent impact of each high explosive round as they shook the ground beneath him. Next to Hebner, a shell instantly killed Corporal John O. Jenkins. Within seconds, another projectile exploded near Private Albert Debacker who died moments later.[31] "I was near him when he was killed," said Hebner.[32]

When the bombardment abated, Hebner noticed the mutilated right leg of Private Earl Mortorff of San Diego, California, who died six agonizing days later.[33] All of this devastation occurred in a matter of seconds within the immediate proximity of Hebner, who inexplicably escaped the hellish barrage shaken but without a scratch. The company suffered twenty-one casualties before the day ended.[34]

After 12:00 P.M., thirty-two-year-old Captain Dwight Smith's 82nd Company, 3rd Battalion, 6th Marines moved forward into the kilometer-wide gap between Wise and Shearer. The long column of Smith's company hurried as they cleared the woods northwest of La Voie du Chatel and into the open. They moved toward the forest where they expected to locate the right flank of Captain Lloyd Williams's 51st Company just northeast of Champillon.

Before the last member of the 82nd Company cleared their wooded concealment, incoming German artillery fire enveloped the exposed Marines. In the company's 2nd Platoon, according to twenty-three-year-old Private Harry Francis Collins, "shells burst all around us."[35] Self-preservation drove the men to sprint the remaining distance towards the cover of the woods.

June 3rd Chapter III

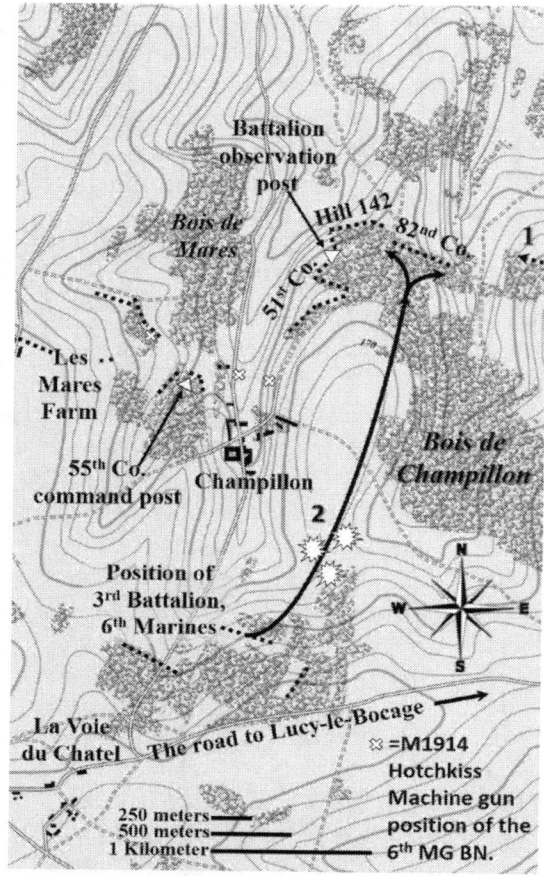

[1] Elements of the 1st Battalion, 6th Marines extend west to try and connect with the 5th Marines. [2] As the 82nd Co. departed the woods northeast of La Voie du Chatel, they were shelled. Four men from 2nd Platoon were killed.

When the tail end of the 2nd Platoon cleared the woods just northeast of La Voie du Chatel, a single shell exploded in the middle of one squad. The projectile landed seemingly on top of twenty-six-year-old Private David Gilbert Wisted, a bookkeeper from Duluth, Minnesota.

According to twenty-one-year-old Private Paul Walker Gordon, the projectile landed "so near to him that he was injured by concussion as well as by fragments of the shell. He had a severe head wound—was killed instantly. I was standing about ten feet behind him when it happened."[36] The scene was horrific.

In addition to Wisted, the same shell killed Privates Harry King Cochran, David Alfred Taggart, and Michael Zippay; their bodies sprawled across the tree line in a grisly display. Shell fragments from the same round hit six other men, including twenty-one-year-old Private Keneston Parker Landers whose wounds later proved fatal three days later.[37]

Nineteen-year-old Corporal Lawrence William Esckilsen, who suffered a shrapnel wound to the leg, saw Winsted's mutilated body. The bloody, pinkish brain matter littering the ground by his broken corpse demonstrated the terrifying effects of artillery fire. "I stayed by him about thirty minutes and walked back to the dressing station. I was only slightly wounded," Esckilsen said.[38]

The rest of the company pushed forward across nearly 300 meters of an open field into the woods south of Hill 142. They had no choice but to leave their fallen comrades. According to Private Harry Collins, "We immediately dig in to protect ourselves from shell fire."[39] Captain Smith

232

wasted no time getting his men into the gap and locating the flanks of the units on his left and right.

Despite the arrival of Smith's 82nd Company, the void in the line remained burdensome for both Wise and Shearer. Poor maps, unfamiliar wooded terrain, and thin battalion fronts exasperated the problem. At 12:45 P.M., Shearer dispatched a message to Wise's headquarters along the cemetery wall at Marigny-en-Orxois explaining:

> Have been trying to connect with your right flank. My left flank is on 142. Liaison man states your right rests on the Champillon-Bussiares [road] about 1 kilometer North of Champillon, My line runs from 142 southeast to Lucy, so if the above is true the vacancy is yours. I am trying to extend to reach your right. Please advise me exactly where your right is, as I cannot spare men to run line past 142, as I understand your battalion line runs from 142 to Veuilly.[40]

After the survivors of the 82nd Company escaped the bombardment of the woods, German gunners increased their range and shelled the village of La Voie du Chatel. Having arrived in the seemingly quiet town before sunrise, members of the 73rd Machine Gun Company soon received their baptism of fire along the developing battlefront. According to Private Einar Wahl, "We realized we were at last in the thick of things.

About noon, a couple of high explosive shells dropped near us. Then another and another. We were caught in an enemy artillery barrage that lasted about two hours."[41] One shell exploded near twenty-one-year-old Corporal Louis Wint Johnson of the 73rd Machine Gun Company before he could reach a place of protection. A large shell fragment pierced his back and passed entirely through his body leaving a gaping hole. Pinned down by the barrage, no one could help Johnson who died within minutes.[42] According to Wahl:

> We sought shelter everywhere, falling flat on our faces as we heard shells come screeching down. That was our only protection. We just had to lie flat wondering if the next was going to get us. One shell landed about fifteen feet from me and exploded. I heard a scream at the same time and looked up. It had landed in a hole where two chaps from another company were lying. Several of us rushed over to the spot and pulled them out. They were horribly cut up, but not dead. A horse tied to a tree about five feet away was killed instantly. I think it was the poor animal that screamed. I can't begin to describe my state of mind—you will just have to imagine it. We were getting our first real taste of the horrors of war.[43]

June 3rd Chapter III

Twenty-three-year-old Corporal Fred William Hill and twenty-five-year-old Sergeant Major Herbert Harris Akers of the 6th Regimental Headquarters Company stood along the open streets of La Voie du Chatel when the barrage began. According to Hill, "We came in for a great 'panning' from Boche artillery fire for several hours and some were too close for comfort."[44] Masonry, wood and twisted metal spilled into the streets as exploding projectiles smashed huge holes through the tops and sides of buildings. The sheer concussion of the bursting shells shattered windows.

One round exploded near Private Roy Amos Judd of the 6th Regimental Headquarters Company and ruptured the twenty-four-year-old's eardrum.[45] According to Hill, "Akers and I had several come so close over us that we could feel the ground 'bounce' when they hit. A few very close ones were 'duds' and did not explode. One ripped up the road about twenty feet from us and about six feet from Major Sibley, and then failed to burst. If there ever was a miracle this was it."[46]

The French batteries positioned throughout the line was the only way the Americans could respond to the enemy's barrage. That afternoon, however, these French guns concentrated their fire in support of the 43rd Division's futile counterattack. One battalion of French troops from the 43rd Division initiated yet another assault on the German lines at 12:39 P.M. supported by their artillery positioned south of Marigny-en-Orxois.

In the chaos of the hastily orchestrated attack, the French infantry battalion advanced under their own barrage, and the assault turned into chaos. Some survivors retreated, others dug in along Hill 165 to hold ground.[47] The French efforts throughout the day to recapture lost terrain were ineffectual, but invaluable in frustrating German efforts to push south toward a more favorable position. The French counterattack also provided the Americans valuable time to stabilize their lines.

German batteries, in an effort to soften up their objectives, resumed their barrage of La Voie du Chatel in addition to other targets throughout the day. The increased enemy bombardment significantly complicated American troop movement. According to Wise, "The German shelling that had started shortly after daybreak grew steadily heavier. That afternoon they concentrated on Marigny."[48] German batteries, at 1:10 P.M., began a rather intense barrage of Marigny-en-Orxois. For fifteen minutes, heavy shells, landing in rapid succession, reduced several structures to rubble.[49]

Captain Frank Whitehead and the 5th Regiment Headquarters Company on the northern outskirts of the town watched as German rounds crashed into the village. According to Whitehead, "The town was under heavy shell fire, and the enemy seemed to be very anxious to bring down the steeple of the church. After several direct hits, the steeple burst into flames."[50]

June 3rd Chapter III

From the cover of his command post on the northeastern outskirts of Marigny-en-Orxois, Wise watched as the enemy bombardment crept closer to his position. "Shells began to fall within fifty yards of my P.C., but they didn't cut the telephone lines. Standing up, I could see roofs flying and walls tottering in the town. The church seemed to be the principal target. Presently the steeple toppled and then the whole building burst into flames."[51]

The town of Marigny-en-Orxois looking south. The cemetery wall in the center of the picture served as Lieutenant Colonel Wise's battalion command post. The church of Marigny-en-Orxois can be seen in the background. Photo credit: Gilles Lagin.

The Americans could not respond to the enemy artillery batteries with their own cannons until later in the afternoon when the American guns began arriving in mass. The regiments of the 2nd Field Artillery Brigade, except those batteries already emplaced, pulled into their designated positions during the afternoon.

During the late morning, the wagon trains hauling the heavy 155mm guns of Batteries A and B, 1st Battalion, 17th Field Artillery, pulled into position off the road north of Montreuil-aux-Lion.[52] Gun crews unhooked the 7,000-pound cannons from their animal-drawn limbers, and shifted the trails of these heavy guns into place and started digging in the spades.

Despite the rush to get the guns up and operational, the lack of ammunition and powder supply remained a critical issue. French batteries had exhausted the stock of 155mm shells the day before.[53] The colossal task of resupply was underway by an ammunition caravan of thirty-two trucks from General Headquarters working continuously for fourteen hours to bring ammunition to the front.

By morning, the artillery dump in the town of Lizy-sur-Ourcq, twenty-three kilometers to the southwest, received a resupply of a million and a half artillery shells of all caliber. The tireless efforts of logistics officers from division and General Headquarters established entraining points at the most advantageous locations. They made supplies available despite the chaos of traveling over the previous forty-eight hours. Because of their daunting efforts to procure ammunition, the American artillery batteries, most of which were still in route, would be able to provide fire support immediately upon arrival.[54]

By 2:42 P.M., the long procession of horse-drawn caissons of the 12th Field Artillery traveled nearly seven kilometers toward Montreuil-aux-Lions after a well-deserved rest the previous day in the town of Cocherel. Due to the lack of telephones, messengers delivered all orders and information about the emplacement of batteries. Since the 12th, 15th and 17th Field Artillery regiments would have to use the same roads to move into position; Brigadier General William Chamberlaine coordinated the emplacements of his brigade. He decided to put one battalion of each regiment in place at a time to avoid congesting the roads, which could offer German observers a delightful target.[55]

The guns of batteries D, E, and F, 2nd Battalion, 15th Field Artillery were still in route from the town of Chamigny along the north bank of the Marne River.[56] The soldiers of the 1st Battalion, 15th Field Artillery were delayed during the afternoon by a lone German plane lurking at a low altitude. Twenty-four-year-old First Lieutenant Robert Winthrop Kean, a liaison officer with the battalion, watched the aircraft swoop toward the ground. "The iron crosses painted on it were very plain as it was only a short distance in the air. It was raking our column with its machine gun, but its aim was poor. No one was hit. Our men rushed to get out their machine guns to reply but in a moment the plane disappeared again over the hill."[57] According to Private John A. Hughes of Battery C:

> We stopped, expecting every moment to hear something drop. He kept flying around and I suppose he had seen the column coming up the hill. Finally, he flew away but in about twenty minutes was back again. By this time, the battery was pulling into a courtyard where there was a big chateau. The aviator kept flying around. There were several French soldiers in the village, and I guess most everyone was firing his rifle at the plane and he was flying very low; in fact, we could see the Iron Cross painted on his plane. I kind of admired his nerve with all the bullets whizzing around him. Someone made a lucky shot as he flew over the chateau. We could see the observer

looking over the side of the plane. I thought that he was going to take a 'Brodie' but they managed to land in a field close by.⁵⁸

Thirty-four-year-old Major Edwin Martin Watson, a West Point Graduate from Eufaula, Alabama, commanding the 1ˢᵗ Battalion, 12ᵗʰ Field Artillery, reconnoitered the terrain along the Paris-Metz. He spent most of the day locating suitable positions for his batteries. Watson sought emplacements offering sufficient defilade and concealment from enemy observation.

Twenty-one-year-old First Lieutenant Thurston Elmer Wood, a West Point graduate from Cape May Courthouse, New Jersey, and Second Lieutenant William L. Monro, a Harvard graduate, assisted Watson's reconnaissance. The men moved across the open near La Loge Farm just over two kilometers east of Montreuil-aux-lions, and a few hundred meters off the Paris Metz road to the north. From this point, the terrain was flat which allowed unobstructed visibility to the north and northeast for several kilometers. Watson and his men seemed virtually oblivious to the sporadic enemy shellfire they attracted along that open pasture and conducted their reconnaissance without casualties.⁵⁹

Major Edwin Martin Watson commanded the 1ˢᵗ Battalion, 12ᵗʰ Artillery. Photo credit: NARA.

Twenty-five-year-old Captain George Douglas Wahl, a West Point graduate, commanded Battery B, 1ˢᵗ Battalion, 12ᵗʰ Field Artillery.⁶⁰ His battery moved down the Paris-Metz road to the chorus of dozens of hooves tapping their hollow-sounding cadence against the path. The distant rumble of enemy artillery fire grew louder as the day progressed. The long procession of caissons and supply carts pulled off the road near the junction of Paris Farm. They turned into

First Lieutenant Thurston Elmer Wood Photo credit: Library of Congress.

the wavy, green, silky fields stretching north nearly to the horizon. One at a time, the gun crews of Battery B filed into the woods northwest of Paris Farm along the road leading to La Voie du Chatel.[61]

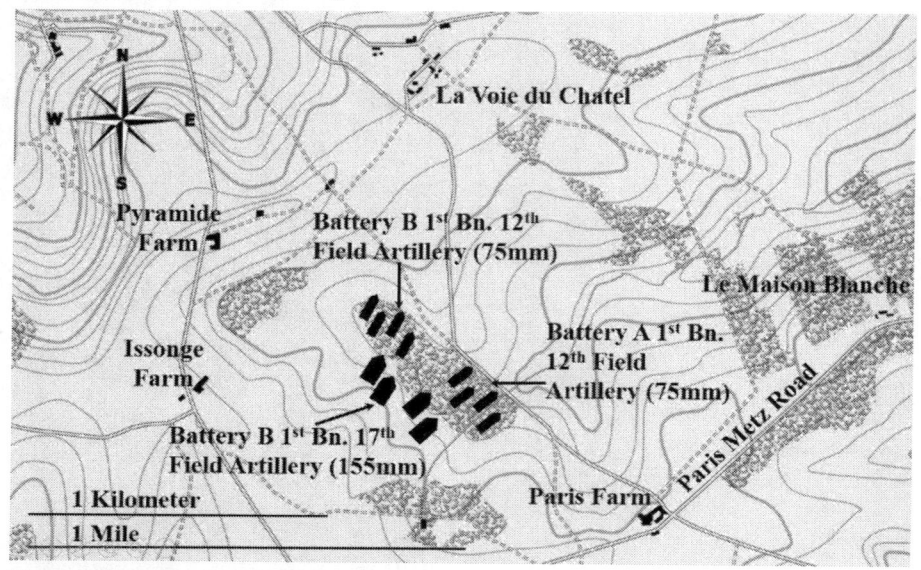

The initial positions of Batteries A & B, 1st Battalion, 12th Field Artillery (75mm) as well as Battery B, 1st Battalion, 17th Field Artillery (155mm) on June 3rd.

    Captain Wahl's men occupied positions just in front of the large 155mm guns of Battery B, 1st Battalion, 17th Field Artillery, which went into the woods a few hours earlier.[62] Wahl's gun crews unhooked the pieces from the caissons. Each team pulled and pushed the 3,400-pound cannons into position.

    The ammunition caisson for each gun remained within reach and loaded with projectiles. In the woods to the right of Wahl's artillerymen, Battery A, 1st Battalion, 12th Field Artillery emplaced their guns. Throughout the afternoon, the artillerymen worked tirelessly to establish telephone lines, set up battery observation points, stockpile ammunition, and improve gun positions. Twenty-two-year-old First Lieutenant Frederick E. Tibbetts Jr. immediately went beyond the battery positions of the 12th Field Artillery to locate the most advantageous location for setting battery observation posts. Tibbetts also frequented the line occupied by the Marines to gain some idea of the general situation and secure information for firing data.[63]

---

[1] General Lemuel Shepherd, interview by Robert Asprey, Alfred M. Gray Research Library, Quantico, VA.

[2] This location is based on research and consultation with battlefield expert Gilles Lagin who has thoroughly explored the layout of the area.

June 3rd Chapter III

[3] General Lemuel Shepherd, interview by Robert Asprey, Alfred M. Gray Research Library, Quantico, VA.
[4] Ibid.
[5] General Lemuel C. Shepherd, Jr. Memoirs, boyhood-1920, Folder 29-30, Box 67, Virginia Military Institute Archives Preston Library, Lexington, VA.
[6] *Records of the Second Division (Regular)* Volume 5, N.P.
[7] Wise and Frost, *A Marine Tells it to You*, 198.
[8] *Records of the Second Division (Regular)* Volume 4, N.P.
[9] Operations of 2nd Field Artillery Brigade, Box 81, RG 120.9.3, NARA College Park, MD.
[10] Ibid.
[11] Ibid.
[12] *Records of the Second Division (Regular)* Volume 5, N.P.
[13] Ibid.
[14] Correspondence Lieutenant Colonel Berton Sibley to the American Battle Monuments Commission, 20 December 1926, Box 190, RG 117.4.2, NARA College Park, MD.
[15] Hatcher, *Citizen Soldier,* N.P.
[16] Ibid.
[17] *Records of the Second Division (Regular)* Volume 5, N.P.
[18] Ibid.
[19] Note: The muster rolls for the 18th Company for June 1918 reveal only five men wounded. The one mentioned in the report as killed is undoubtedly Private Joe M. Brock.
[20] *Records of the Second Division (Regular)* Volume 5, N.P.
[21] Wise and Frost, *A Marine Tells it to You*, 198., and *Records of the Second Division (Regular)* Volume 5, N.P. Note: Murray sent a 6:35 P.M. message regarding Wise's location saying he left the command post about an hour ago.
[22] *Records of the Second Division (Regular)* Volume 6, N.P.
[23] *Records of the Second Division (Regular)* Volume 5, N.P.
[24] Ibid.
[25] These rounds were fired by the German 15 cm (150mm) field howitzer
[26] *Records of the Second Division (Regular)* Volume 5, N.P.
[27] Ibid. Note the six Marines operating the 6th Regimental observation post were Sergeant Joseph D. Broderick, Corporals Simon J. Madden, Albert O. Tester, Privates Joseph P. Elwood, Eugene H. Long, and Merl C. Rockwell. Official Military Personnel Files for six men listed above, RG 127, NPRC St. Louis, MO.

June 3rd Chapter III

---

[28] War Diary and Annexes 237th Division 3 June 1918, *Translation of War Diaries of German Units,* Vol. 4.
[29] Mitchell, *The Official History of the Second Regiment of Engineers*, 140.
[30] Pike, *The Battle For Belleau Woods, As I Remember It About 60 Years Later*, 9.
[31] Burial File of Private John O. Jenkins, Eye-witness statement by Corporal William J. Hebner, Box 2483, RG 92.9, Records of Graves Registration Services, NARA College Park, MD.
[32] Burial File of Private Albert Debacker, Eye-witness statement by Corporal William J. Hebner, Box 1239, RG 92.9, Records of Graves Registration Services, NARA College Park, MD.
[33] Burial File of Private Earl M. Mortorff, Eye-witness statement by Corporal William J. Hebner, Box 3471, RG 92.9, Records of Graves Registration Services, NARA College Park, MD.
[34] *Records of the Second Division (Regular)* Volume 9, N.P.
[35] Harry Collins, *The War Diary of Corporal Harry Collins,* Entry for June 3, 1918, ed. by David Fisher and George Clark (Pike: Brass Hat, 1996), N.P.
[36] Burial File of Private David Wisted, Eye-witness statement by Private Paul W. Gordon, Box 5299, RG 92.9, Records of Graves Registration Services, NARA College Park, MD.
[37] U.S. Marine Corps Muster Rolls, 1893-1940, Record Group 127, NARA, Washington, D.C.
Burial File of Private David Wisted, Eye-witness statement by First Lieutenant Lawrence W. Esckilsen, Box 5299, RG 92.9, Records of Graves Registration Services, NARA College Park, MD.
[38] Ibid.
[39] Collins, *The War Diary of Corporal Harry Collins.*
[40] *Records of the Second Division (Regular)* Volume 5, N.P.
Note: According to the map of First Lieutenant William Mathews, Wise's battalion intelligence officer, the 51st Company's position stretched east of the road between Champillon and Bussiaeres. The 51st Company's right flank, according to his map, rested to the edge of the woods just northeast of the point 142 indicated on the map.
[41] Kemper F. Cowing and Courtney Ryley Cooper, *Dear Folks At Home* (Boston: Houghton Mifflin Company, 1919), 142.
[42] Ibid.
[43] Ibid.
[44] Ibid, 154.

[45] U.S. Marine Corps Muster Rolls, 1893-1940, Record Group 127, NARA, Washington, D.C.
[46] Cowing and Cooper, *Dear Folks At Home,* 154.
[47] War Diary and Annexes 237th Division 3 June 1918, *Translation of War Diaries of German Units,* Vol. 4. Note: Earlier reports erroneously placed elements of the 237th Division in the depression about 460 meters south of Hill 165, a memo by reconnoitering detachments and the artillery, later refuted by an amended report that placed elements of the 237th Division on an unimproved road just south of the village Bussiares.
[48] Wise and Frost, *A Marine Tells it to You,* 199.
[49] *Records of the Second Division (Regular)* Volume 4, N.P.
[50] *The Aisne Defensive,* Whitehead to ABMC, Box 190, RG 117.4.2, NARA College Park, MD.
[51] Wise and Frost, *A Marine Tells it to You,* 199-200.
[52] *Records of the Second Division (Regular)* Volume 4, N.P.
[53] *Records of the Second Division (Regular)* Volume 6, N.P.
[54] Ibid., and Harbord, *The American Army in France,* 285.
[55] *Records of the Second Division (Regular)* Volume 9, N.P.
[56] *Records of the Second Division (Regular)* Volume 8, N.P.
[57] Robert Winthrop Kean, *Dear Marraine 1917-1919,* (Washington D.C.: Library of Congress, 1969), 93-94.
[58] Spaulding and Wright, *The Second Division American Expeditionary Force in France 1917-1919,* 252.
[59] Headquarters Second Division American Expeditionary Forces General Orders No. 40 July 5, 1918, Box 17, RG 120.9.3, Second Division File, Records of the AEF, NARA College Park, MD.
[60] Note: Wahl was the son of West Point alumni Brigadier General Lutz Wahl who was in charge of operations of the General Staff in Washington D.C.
[61] George D. Wahl, Sector North-east of Chateau Thierry (June 1-July 9, 1918), Box 79, RG 120.9.3, Second Division File, Records of the AEF, NARA College Park, MD.
[62] Ibid.
[63] Headquarters Second Division AEF G.O. No. 40 July 5, 1918, Box 17, RG 120.9.3, Records of the AEF, NARA College Park, MD.

June 3rd Chapter IV

Retreat, hell we have orders to stay and hold at any cost, and that's what we'll do.
-Captain Lloyd Williams 51st Company, 2nd Battalion, 5th Marines

Along the right flank of Wise's battalion, Captain Lloyd Williams's 51st Company remained in position from the Champillon-Bussiares road to the woods along Hill 142. Sporadic artillery fire harassed the company's position throughout the morning and afternoon as survivors of the broken French counterattack retreated through the 51st Company's line. Williams believed the French units reportedly positioned on the company's right had all pulled back, and he was not satisfied that reinforcing a kilometer-wide gap with just two platoons of the 95th Company, as was done the day before, would suffice.[1]

Williams already stretched his company thin and could not spare any of his men to extend the front. He was likely unaware that the 82nd Company was sent earlier that day to augment the line. German artillery already took some of his men out of the fight.[2]

The barrage heightened the vigilance of the machine gunners from the 81st Company, who reinforced the 51st Company's position. They were convinced the steady retreat of the French and the increase in enemy artillery hinted at a German attack. Several gun crews fired on what they believed to be enemy soldiers filtering through the woods ahead. "We fired many shots," said Sergeant Peter Wood, "but don't know the results."[3]

Private Roland Fisher scored hits on German soldiers at 1,000-1,200 yards. Photo credit: Howard Fisher.

Private Roland Fisher, a sniper with the 51st Company, crawled well out beyond the company's front to an advantageous and concealed position hours earlier. Throughout the day, he patiently waited for the perfect opportunity to shoot distant Germans who foolishly moved about in the open.

After several hours, he could not believe the carelessness with which the enemy moved. "They had been used to the French and so was as bold as could be, walking across open spaces like no one was alive but them. I crawled out in the open where I could get a good shot at them and put on my telescope."⁴

Stalking one helpless figure hundreds of meters away, Fisher steadied his crosshairs on the human mass barely distinguishable in the distance and gently squeezing the trigger. The recoil jolted the butt of the rifle tucked into his shoulder. The plume of dust, visible through his telescopic sight, marked the bullet's impact. The shot barely missed the distant German but perhaps stunned him once he realized he avoided death by a matter of inches. "The first time I missed—after that, it kept their Red Cross busy carrying them in. I managed to hit several at 1,000 and 1,200 yards," remembered Fisher.⁵ Patiently waiting for other enemy soldiers to show themselves, He stayed in the field far beyond the 51ˢᵗ Company's front throughout the day.

Behind Fisher's advanced position, French soldiers wilted back from the firing line and through the American front. Enemy batteries extended their range to catch the French in their retreat. Shells landed steadily among the 51ˢᵗ and 81ˢᵗ Companies. One round sent a fragment skidding across the left wrist of eighteen-year-old Private Ed B. Donnelly of the 81ˢᵗ Company. The wound was mostly superficial, but it bled excessively. Sergeant Peter Wood saw the severity of Donnelly's injury and pulled open a metal field-dressing container, and tightly wrapped his bloody wrist. Wood sent Donnelly to the rear and then scampered along the line to check on his gun crews.⁶

Captain Lloyd Williams. Photo credit: Marine Corps History Division.

Amidst the chaos of retreating French and the consistent incoming artillery, Captain Williams dispatched a message at 2:15 P.M. explaining to Lieutenant Colonel Wise that the kilometer-wide gap was now minus the French who were in retreat. He also informed Wise of the company's casualties, which resulted from shellfire, and he, "Request that additional men be ordered to fill the gap at once."⁷ The platoons of the 95ᵗʰ Company put in the day before nor Captain Dwight Smith's recently arrived 82ⁿᵈ Company were enough to fill the void adequately.

June 3rd Chapter IV

Survivors of the French 43rd Division's failed counterattack trickled back through the American lines in isolated groups throughout the afternoon. Just behind the 51st Company's front, twenty-two-year-old First Lieutenant Joseph Addison Hagan casually approached Williams who was in the midst of a discussion with thirty-six-year-old Captain William Oscar Corbin, a former Marine gunner. While the two men engaged in their conversation, a group of retreating French Chasseurs walked passed them. One of these distressed Frenchmen, a major, beckoned Corbin's attention and muttered something the American officer evidently could not understand. "Apparently he could not speak English, but he could write it because he took out a memorandum pad and a fountain pen," remembered Hagan, "and wrote, 'retreat, the Germans are coming.'"[8] After reading the scribbled message, Corbin handed it to Williams who silently read the note.

First Lieutenant Joseph Hagan seen here as a cadet at VMI. Photo credit: Addision Hagan.

According to Hagan, "Captain Williams turned then, apparently addressing his remark to us, and said, 'Retreat, hell we have orders to stay and hold at any cost, and that's what we'll do.'"[9] The captain's dismissive reply was instinctive, honest, and devoid of any theatrics.

Williams worried that the French artillery batteries might reduce their range in the wake of their retreating infantry. He dispatched a message to Lieutenant Colonel Wise explaining, "The French Major gave Captain Corbin written orders to fall back—I have countermanded the order—kindly see that the French do not shorten their artillery range—82nd and 84th companies are on their way to fill the gap on right of this Company."[10]

The German shelling, though sporadic, was effective. The 2nd Battalion, 5th Marines' intelligence section established an observation post just east of the Champillon-Bussiares road near the 51st Company's sector of the line. Several members of the battalion intelligence section, under the command of First Lieutenant William Mathews, watched intently from this

June 3rd **Chapter IV**

This photograph, taken at Damblain Training Area November 1917, shows Captain Williams and his company staff. Front Row L to R: First Lieutenant John T. Walker, Captain Lloyd Williams, Captain William Corbin. Back Row: First Lieutenant Nathanial Massie, First Lieutenant Joseph Hagan. Photo credit: Addison Hagan.

forward position for any signs of distant enemy movement. They had no telephone connection, so communication involved runners traversing the open fields blanketed by shellfire to deliver information to the various companies.

The frequent activity around the observation post attracted enemy attention, and soon shells ripped through the treetops of this position. One round wounded twenty-one-year-old Private William Theodore Hayden. A shell fragment struck him in the left groin, but he managed to hobble to a place of protection and treat his own injuries. Shells continued landing in and around the woods. Hayden, in terrible pain, noticed the bombardment intensifying and the desperate screams for help pressed him into action as the area became suffused by the smoke and dust. He quickly applied a

June 3rd Chapter IV

dressing to his wounds and ran as fast as his weak leg could carry him towards the assistance of wounded comrades.[11] At the battalion observation post, twenty-six-year-old Private James Simpson Hodges died instantly when a shell ripped through the tree cover and exploded nearly on top of him. The blast also wounded several others.[12]

The bombardment also fell upon other elements of the 51st Company and the machine gun sections of the 81st Company supporting them. The thunderous explosion of one shell killed twenty-two-year-old Corporal Karl Wilson Locke of Cleveland, Ohio, and wounded twenty-two-year-old Private Robert Roy Pearce of Rochester, New York.

Corporal Karl Locke was killed instantly during the shelling of the battalion observation post along the 51st Company's front. Photo credit: Carol Locke-Folk.

Believing an infantry assault would follow the barrage, Sergeant Peter Wood of the 81st Company ran from one machine gun crew to the next frantically alerting his men of the potential enemy probe. As he braved the incoming fire, a string of shells exploded near one of his gun positions. Within seconds, Wood heard the panicked screams summoning help for twenty-three-year-old Private Floyd Harris Deckro who was knocked down by the explosion, and Wood scrambling to assist. He noticed a body sprawled in the undergrowth adjacent to a smoldering shell hole.

Wood darted towards the motionless figure and realized it was Deckro. According to Wood, "I went to him, and rolled him over and found he was about dead, but in the meanwhile, I was being gassed as he was hit by a gas shell and the fumes were rising from the small hole in the ground left by the shell."[13] The acrid fumes quickly overwhelmed Wood as he tried to save Deckro who died within seconds.[14]

Slightly shell-shocked and suffering from gas inhalation, Wood and other members of the 81st Company pulled back from their forward position. He tried to shake off the irritant effects of the fumes as he walked back from the line, but the effects quickly overwhelmed him. Wood then encountered First Lieutenant Shaler Ladd, who also suffered terribly from gas inhalation and shell-shock.[15] Captain Allen Sumner, commanding the 81st Company, noticed symptoms of shell shock exhibited by Wood. He then ordered twenty-three-year-old Corporal Floyd George Williams to escort Wood back to the battalion aid station at Montgrivault-la-Petit Farm.¹⁶

The bombardment along the 51ˢᵗ Company's line also alerted the machine guns of the 15ᵗʰ Company dug in along that front. One machine gun section commanded by Second Lieutenant Victor Bleasdale held a critical position adjacent to the Champillon-Bussiares road. The other guns of the 15ᵗʰ Company also occupied the line perpendicular to the road leading north to Champillon. The ground inclined steeply along the western roadside stretching out of the village and gave the American gun crew a channeled lane of fire against anything crossing the road.

Sergeant Peter Wood seen here as a first lieutenant after the war. Photo credit: Author's collection.

Throughout the day, they noticed obscured commotion in the distant woods along the road. Suddenly, they spotted several Germans scamper across the lane several hundred meters ahead. Immediately, Bleasdale ordered his section to engage, and one of his gun crews initiated a short burst of fire. Their bullets kicked up the dirt as they skimmed off the road surface and tore through the trees lining the sides of the thoroughfare, but the results were inconclusive.¹⁷

Shortly after that, enemy shellfire smashed into the ground next to the road near several 15ᵗʰ Company Hotchkiss emplacements. Soon, incoming rounds plastered this area, and gun crewmen flattened out in their dugouts as dirt from exploding shells rained down upon them. The artillery knocked out the telephone lines preventing the left group of guns from communicating with 6ᵗʰ Machine Gun Battalion headquarters.¹⁸ The ground shook, and shrapnel blanketed the area as rounds burst upon impact with the treetops. A shell fragment tore into the shoulder and scalp of twenty-one-year-old Private Harvey Bixler.¹⁹ Another exploded near Private Gabe Mansfield of Bertrand, Missouri and mortally wounded the twenty-nine-year-old. Shell fragments perforated the side of his body and hand.²⁰ Gas shells, interspersed with the high explosive rounds, hit the ground with their signature crunch and filled the air with nauseating fumes. Before the incoming fire subsided, three men of the 15ᵗʰ Company suffered severely from gas. Flushed and lachrymose faces teared up as mucus ran uncontrollably down their chin as they kept their eyes tightly shut and affix their gas masks.

Private Gabe Mansfield. Photo credit: New York Times Mid-week pictorial.

Private Charles Herbert Carey. Photo credit: Photo credit: New York Times Mid-week pictorial.

During a momentary lull in the barrage, men scrambled to evacuate the wounded before the shelling resumed. Twenty-year-old Private Charles Herbert Carey from Salem, Ohio, ignored his wounds so he could assist in carrying a nearly incapacitated comrade who was severely gassed toward the dressing station. Blood dripped off the side of Carey's face—the result of a shell fragment which passed through the brim his helmet and tore away a shallow swath of flesh underneath his eye. The smear of blood covering the side of his face concealed Carey's youthful appearance, a feature that affectionately earned him the nickname 'Kid Carey' among his comrades. Despite his injuries, he refused evacuation and returned to the company after his lacerated face was bandaged.[21] In all nine Marines of the 15th Company were gassed or wounded in the bombardment of the company's position north of Champillon. One Marine's wounds proved mortal.[22]

Passing back to the rear, one of the wounded men from the 15th Company informed elements of the 3rd Battalion, 6th Marines of his company's location.[23] This information was vital, and Colonel Catlin immediately relayed it to Brigadier General Harbord to aid in identifying the specific layout of the brigade's line. Catlin also conveyed information, which located elements of the 5th Marines just northeast of Champillon and that, "The French troops [are] ahead with Germans advancing south. This latest verified by the French surgeon of the 133rd. Please caution Wise to keep touch with elements on his right."[24]

June 3rd Chapter IV

On Lieutenant Colonel Wise's right, elements of the 82nd Company completed their move into the woods south of Hill 142 during the afternoon to help fill the problematic gap. They dug in and even occupied abandoned foxholes left by the French. According to Private Harry Collins, the "Germans are in woods and field directly to our front. Also hold village directly opposite us."[25] The town Collins referred to was Torcy, and by 3:20 P.M., reports indicated the enemy advanced 200 meters south of the village.[26]

Soldiers of the French 152nd Infantry Regiment continued retreating through Bois Champillon northwest of Lucy-le-Bocage. Their attempted counterattack against the 3rd Battalion, 461st German Infantry a few hours earlier had failed.[27] These French troops passed through elements of Major Shearers 1st Battalion, 6th Marines and indicated the Germans were not far behind.

Along the road leading to a small farm south of Torcy hundreds of meters north of the American line, German troops carelessly moved around in the open. Marines of the 1st and 2nd Platoons, 74th Company, who had occupied the northern edge of Bois de Champillon the night before, spotted the enemy in the distance. 74th Company snipers soon made the enemy pay for their negligence and killed several of them.[28]

Corporal Willard Nelligan. Photo credit: NARA.

Twenty-one-year-old Corporal Willard Christopher Nelligan of the 95th Company also fired at several enemy soldiers from the northern treeline in Bois de Champillon. Nelligan and a handful of Marines took full advantage of the company's advanced position to harass the enemy visible in the distance. According to Nelligan, "I had charge of the right flank of our platoon on the line as acting Sergeant. The Sergeant over me was put in charge of a 'liaison post.'"[29] The company had been in position along the front since early in the morning. Nelligan already killed several German soldiers with his scoped rifle, and now spotted movement nearby in the fronting field.[30]

June 3rd Chapter IV

He watched intently and patiently until he realized the wind along the tops of the grain was not causing the movement he spotted; instead, it was a group of infiltrating enemy soldiers. According to Nelligan, "When they were coming opposite me the Boches tried to assemble a machine gun, but as soon as we saw what they were up to five of my men's rifles cracked and there was one Boche left out of four."[31] The sole surviving enemy machine gunner abandoned the weapon and "ran for all he was worth, but he didn't get away."[32] According to Nelligan, "Altogether I got thirteen Boches, but I'll have to get over that unlucky number."[33]

During the afternoon, most of the two platoons of the 95th Company were still trying to extend the battalion's left to reach Wise's battalion. After nearly twenty-four hours of digging and moving, Corporal Warren Jackson once again carved out a dwelling in the earth. "A large tree was to the right and some steps ahead. I thought what a good bullet turner this would be and adjusted my position accordingly." While he was digging, the familiar thud of artillery fire echoed in the distance. According to Jackson:

> Then the quiet was broken by the unexpected fall of shells to the left. And following this unwelcome surprise two of the men, who had decided the position they were occupying was undesirable, came with transcending speed down the rear of the line in my direction. It was as though one of the shells had released a spring in the fellows. They shot by. One of those on the flight was a dried-up, red-haired, boasting fellow; but on this occasion, his characteristic chesty, flaunting stride was rather impaired, if vastly accelerated.[34]

Before the two men could flee, the thunderous voice of twenty-four-year-old Gunnery Sergeant Forest James "Buck" Ashwood permeated the air. Immediately, his invective shout coaxed the two terrified Marines back into their dugouts.[35] Suddenly, the scream of more incoming rounds pierced the air and landed behind Jackson's hole.

Before the dust could settle from one explosion, another shell detonated nearby. The concussion of each blast was beyond anything most of them had ever experienced. "Never in my days had I been possessed of such an overwhelming desire to get down into the earth," remembered Jackson. "Our feverish digging of the night before was almost unsurpassable, but the human voice could not in a thousand years give the inspiration to dig that those shells afforded. With frenzied movements we used mess kits, along with the remaining accouterments of chow warfare, and bayonets and helmets were drafted into the all-important approach to the heart of mother earth."[36]

When the bombardment subsided, several wounded 95th Company men shouted for help as the tapering echo of the explosions reverberated through the woods. Among the casualties, Private Nelligan suffered a severe wound from a large fragment that tore in the right side of his chest, leaving him in horrible agony.[37] "It seems the shell went in my side and out my back," remembered Nelligan.[38]

First Lieutenant Frederic Wheeler, commanding Jackson's platoon, was also wounded, but adamantly refused evacuation. He remained with the company until he was struck a second time the following day.[39] Despite the devastation of the barrage, most men were tired of digging and vowed never again to excavate a dugout, regardless of the risk. "They would just as soon be killed then as later anyway," reasoned Jackson. "Furthermore, if a fellow was bumped off right there and then, he would not have to undergo the hell of shellings ahead. No, they would not dig another lick. In the midst of this kind of talk, a shell would fall somewhere. With it, declarations were immediately forgotten, and the onslaughts of the digging brigade were renewed with unsurpassed vigor."[40]

Captain George Stowell's 76th Company in the Bois de Champillon also endured the wrath of the German barrage, which kept everyone pinned into their holes for much of the day. Since noon, the enemy maintained a steady seven-hour artillery bombardment of the line stretching from Bois de Champillon to Lucy-le-Bocage—the intensity of which varied.[41]

Most of the barrage consisted of 77mm high explosive shells filled with diphenylchlorarsine, an odorless and tasteless vomiting agent. Gas rounds were interspersed with the diphenylchlorarsine shells. Once the gas was detected, and troops donned their masks, they unknowingly trapped the toxic diphenylchlorarsine fumes inside the respirator. As the poisonous agent took effect, men instinctively tore off the respirator to vomit, and removal of the mask further exposed them to other toxic gasses.[42]

Since noon, incoming rounds steadily crashed through the treetops along the line occupied by the 76th Company. Identifying gas by the characteristically weak blast was difficult since some of these rounds contained bottles filled with the diphenylchlorarsine packed inside the TNT-lined shells, which resulted in a high explosive detonation. Other rounds burst along the ground with the typical crunch of a gas round spilling out a sulfur-mustard agent.

The cries of gas sent men fumbling to unsnap their respirator bags hung around their necks. Tearing off their helmets, the men stretched the elastic bands of their respirators over their heads as unsteady, terrified hands tried to tighten the masks and create an airtight seal. Several men struggled with their respirators as the fumes nauseated them.

More shells exploded in the treetops and blasted dirt into the air which fell back on top of the cowering men. Even when they were able to don respirators, everyone suffered from the mustard gas which penetrated the wool fabric of their uniforms, and settled into the folds of the body like the armpits, behind the knees, and in the crotch, causing intense blistering.[43]

June 3rd Chapter IV

The barrage saturated the woods with pockets of mustard gas and diphenylchlorarsine fumes. High explosive rounds sent deadly shards of steel hissing through the air and prevented men from leaving the cover of individual dugouts to escape the gassed areas. Each incoming round seemed to inflict casualties and soon the air filled with the agonized cries of wounded men.

Twenty-four-year-old Godfrey Warner Anderson took several fragmentation wounds to the chest.[44] Twenty-six-year-old Private Henry Kirchner died instantly when a large fragment pulverized the left side of his head so terribly he was nearly unrecognizable.[45] Corporal James Bennett Whipple of Wilton, Connecticut, braved the enemy fire to come to the aid of several wounded comrades. As the twenty-five-year-old raced from his dugout into the open, a thunderous explosion instantly killed him—shards of steel struck Whipple in the side of his head shattering the right half of his skull and face.[46]

Corporal James Bennett Whipple was killed instantly as he tried to rescue wounded comrades under heavy shellfire. Photo credit: Fred H. Whipple Sr.

After the bombardment dwindled down, corpsman raced to the beckoning cries for help. The shellfire inflicted numerous casualties. The risk of another barrage urged the able-bodied to hurry in evacuating their casualties and limit their own exposure away from the protection of their dugouts.

The bombardment necessitated the evacuation of four wounded and twelve victims of gas. Five 76th Company men lay dead.[47] Twenty-year-old Private Harold Alfred Brooks, a machinist from Rock Falls, Illinois, hovered near death. The blast concussion and shell fragments tore his stomach open and shattered his left femur bone.[48] As the smoke cleared and the dust settled back to the forest floor, a final breath gurgled from his lungs.[49]

The Germans continued the steady inundation of Bois de Champillon as the 76th Company evacuated their wounded comrades. The pandemonium along that portion of the woods prevented twenty-two-year-old Private Joseph Reed Whipple from noticing the mutilated body of his older brother, Corporal James Whipple, laying among the dead. From the moment the two boys enlisted in May of 1917, they had been inseparable. They underwent recruit training in the same company at Paris Island. Both brothers joined the 76th Company in Quantico and sailed for France together.

In a blinding flash, James's life ended with the explosion of an enemy shell in this remote patch of French woods. Joseph, already dealing with the terrifying and exhaustive experience of combat, now had to deal with the emotional trauma of losing his older brother.[50]

Along the eastern face of Bois de Champillon, Sergeant Gerald Thomas and the 3rd Platoon of the 75th Company dug into the field east of Bois de Champillon. The sounds of gunfire inside Belleau Woods hundreds of meters to the east rippled across the fields. "We still had only our individual packs and shovels," claimed Thomas, "but sounds emanating from the wood provided all the urging necessary for furious digging."[51] French soldiers of the 152nd Infantry Regiment, survivors of the failed counterattack, retreated through this sector of the American line throughout the day. According to Thomas they, "drifted back through our lines in ones and twos, sort of like stragglers."[52]

He convinced some of these exhausted members of the famed 'Les Diables Rouges,' to halt and reinforce the company as they labored under the weight of their Hotchkiss machine guns and tripods. "Our machine gun units had still not arrived," remembered Thomas. "We, therefore, prevailed upon one French Hotchkiss crew to stop with us and they set up their gun near my foxhole. We were as ready as we were going to be that day."[53]

Private Joseph Whipple. Photo credit: Fred H. Whipple Sr.

Much of the 75th Company's front had been under sporadic artillery throughout the day, but in the afternoon, German batteries drastically increased the volume of fire. "The enemy artillery had our range and the pounding became heavier every minute," remembered Private Gus Gulberg.[54] "Deeper and deeper we dug into mother earth."[55] Marines, caught in the open when the shelling began sprinted for the nearest hole. Privates Warren Findley Hoyle, George Whitefield Dodson Jr., Tony Louis Gandy, and Holden Edward Siegert, all crowded into the same shallow dugout. They tried to stay below ground during the bombardment. The threat of an enemy infantry attack following the barrage, however, prompted

June 3rd Chapter IV

twenty-two-year-old Private Hoyle, from Shelby, North Carolina, to peer over the edge of his hole.

Suddenly, a shell landed nearly on top of him. According to Gulberg, "He stuck his head out and as he did so a shell took his head off."[56] Fragments from the same round hit Private Dodson in the face—instantly killing him.

The explosion rendered both Privates Gandy and Siegert severely shell-shocked.[57] The shell exploded about three feet from Private Siegert of Newport, Minnesota, knocking him unconscious. When the barrage subsided, comrades pulled the critically

Private Warren Hoyle was killed instantly when a shell detonated nearly on top of his dugout. Photo credit: New York Times Mid-week pictorial.

wounded nineteen-year-old out of the gore-filled hole and summoned stretcher-bearers.

When Siegert eventually regained consciousness in the field hospital, he trembled uncontrollably, keeping his blue eyes wide-open and fixated on seemingly nothing. Even in the safety of the field hospital, he exhibited a profound shell-dodging twitch of the head, and for two days, he could not speak a word.[58]

German guns also targeted the woods northwest of La Voie du Chatel where the 84th Company served as the regimental reserve. Most of the company, lying on the ground, had not bothered to prepare dugouts, nor did they receive instructions to do so. According to Private James Hatcher, "A short time before that order reached us; we were laying quietly with our faces against the ground when a shell struck a tree only a short distance from where I lay, and exploded in the air."[59] In rapid succession, more rounds exploded in the treetops and wounded several men.

Private Holden Siegert was severely shell-shocked when a shell struck near the dugout he shared with Privates Warren Hoyle, George Dodson Jr., and Tony Louis Gandy. Hoyle and Dodson were killed. Gandy was also severely shell-shocked. Photo credit: NPRC.

One shell landed about twenty feet away from thirty-two-year-old Private Fred Bradley but miraculously did not explode. Private Joachin Sanchez, stunned by Bradley's divine fortune playfully yelled, "Bradley you'll never get shell-shocked!"[60] Within seconds, another round detonated overhead. Despite the ringing in eighteen-year-old Private Edward George Kahrs' ears, he heard the feeble cries of Sanchez screaming, "My God I'm hit."[61] Hatcher relived the shock of seeing Sanchez's terrible wound, "One fellow was struck in the body by a large fragment of steel and a ragged hole torn completely through him."[62] The massive piece of metal ripped into Sanchez's back and passed entirely through him—nearly disemboweling the twenty-three-year-old.[63]

"One man," according to Hatcher, "was thrashing about on the ground, apparently in mortal agony. I turned my head. I did not want to look at him."[64] The wounded man, twenty-nine-year-old Private Miller Jones, suffered a fragmentation wound below the left knee. According to Hatcher, "A few moments later we found that a piece of steel had laid open the skin across his shin.[65]

Stretcher teams snaked through the woods answering the cries of the wounded. They carried Sanchez through the still smoking forest. "I saw him being taken to the first aid station in pretty bad condition I thought," recalled twenty-four-year-old Corporal John Francis Pinson Jr. "He could talk but was very weak."[66] Hatcher witnessed Sanchez's departure as members of the company came to his side. They bid the dark-haired kid from New Orleans a final farewell, knowing they would never see him again. "As he was loaded onto a stretcher, he said feebly and in grim-faced agony, 'Goodbye boys, I won't see you anymore, but I know that you will win.'"[67]

During the late afternoon, German artillery fire once again hammered Marigny-en-Orxois. The rubble covering the streets revealed the volume of fire which had already destroyed much of the village. Shells continued to flatten structures, making any passage through the town's corridors and crossroads increasingly perilous.

Despite the incoming fire, thirty-five-year-old Corporal Louis Sharp Divine assisted a wounded comrade to the first aid station, and returned to the 5th Marines' Headquarters Company, just as the bombardment intensified. At 4:30 P.M., the explosion of an incoming shell riddled Divine with shrapnel. He lay mortally wounded in the streets as the fury of the barrage prevented stretcher-bearers from reaching him. When the shelling subsided, they finally recovered Divine and rushed him to an awaiting ambulance which sped away through the cobblestone streets. Before reaching the hospital, Divine succumbed to his wounds.[68]

Left: First Lieutenant Malcolm Johnstone. Photo credit: Alice Nelson. Right: First Sergeant Mack Byrd (seen here as a first lieutenant after the war). Photo credit: NARA.

Near Triangle Farm, elements of Company D, 2nd Battalion, 2nd Engineers, nearly the completed the construction of dugouts when, at 5:20 P.M., enemy shells inundated their position and killed twenty-five-year-old First Lieutenant Malcolm M. Johnstone of Arlington, Virginia. According to Private Hubert Snow, "We had just finished our dugout and piled up some cordwood for protection when the heavy firing began. Lieutenant Johnstone told us to go in, and he sat down by the side of a tree with a map when a shell fell, killing him instantly."[69]

Twenty-five-year-old First Sergeant Mack C. Byrd, of Elkin, North Carolina, recalled Johnstone dying instantly as result of, "A high explosive shell with almost a direct hit," which eviscerated him.[70] Byrd, the company's seemingly indomitable first sergeant, was wounded by shellfire shortly afterward while he was in charge of the company during the temporary absence of its company commander Captain Edwin N. Chisholm. Despite the agony caused by the shell fragment embedded into his knee, the square-jawed first sergeant masked the pain and refused to leave the company even after the captain returned.[71] In all Company D suffered seven casualties during the enemy's barrage that afternoon.[72]

June 3rd Chapter IV

[1] *Records of the Second Division (Regular)* Volume 5, N.P.
[2] Ibid., and U.S. Marine Corps Muster Rolls, 1893-1940, Record Group 127, NARA, Washington, D.C.,
and Daily Report of Casualties and Changes, June 3, 1918, Box 25, RG 127, NARA Washington D.C.Note: Nineteen-year-old Private Raphael Valerio, an Italian immigrant from Brooklyn, New York and twenty-two-year-old Earl Ellsworth Naud from Douglas County Washington were the two casualties who suffered wounds from shell fragments.
[3] Peter Wood Diary, N.P., Entry for June 3rd. Author's collection
[4] Letter July 20, 1918 Roland Fisher to his brother George C. Fisher Provided by Roland Fisher's nephew Howard George Fisher.
[5] Letter July 20, 1918, Roland Fisher to his brother George C. Fisher Provided by Roland Fisher's nephew, Howard George Fisher.
[6] *Diary of Peter Wood,* N.P., Entry for June 3rd, Author's collection.
[7] *Records of the Second Division (Regular)* Volume 5, N.P.
[8] "Controversy Over Legend Clarified By Marine Captain," *Quantico Sentry* (Quantico, VA), Volume 2 No. 3, June 12, 1936.
[9] Ibid., and Correspondence Joseph Hagan to Captain Lloyd W. Williams Post American Legion Berryville, VA 12 August 1963, copy of letter provided to author by Michael Miller.
[10] *Records of the Second Division (Regular)* Volume 5, N.P. Note: Williams was incorrect the 82nd, and the 83rd Companies were on the way to fill the gap, not the 84th Company.
[11] Official Military Personnel File for Private William Theodore Hayden, RG 127, NPRC St. Louis, MO.
[12] Official Military Personnel File for Private James Simpson Hodges, RG 127, NPRC St. Louis, MO.
[13] *Diary of Peter Wood,* N.P., Entry for June 3rd, Author's collection.
[14] Ibid.
[15] Ibid., and U.S. Marine Corps Muster Rolls, 1893-1940, Record Group 127, NARA, Washington, D.C.
[16] *Diary of Peter Wood,* N.P., Entry for June 3rd, Author's collection.
[17] Brigadier General Bleasdale interview by Benis Frank, Transcript, Marine Corps Historical Division Quantico, VA.

June 3rd Chapter IV

[18] Curtis Jr., *History of the Sixth Machine Gun Battalion*, 10.
[19] U.S. Marine Corps Muster Rolls, 1893-1940, Record Group 127, NARA, Washington, D.C.
[20] Ibid.
[21] Burial File of Private Charles H. Carey, Eye-witness statements by Private Maurice Jackman and Private Hood L. Haynie, Box 788, RG 92.9, Records of Graves Registration Services, NARA College Park, MD.
[22] Note: The mortally wounded man was Private Gabe Mansfield who died later that day.
[23] *Records of the Second Division (Regular)* Volume 5, N.P.
[24] Ibid.
[25] Collins, *The War Diary of Corporal Harry Collins*, Entry for June 3, 1918.
[26] *Records of the Second Division (Regular)* Volume 5, N.P.
[27] War Diary and Annexes, 237th Division, 3 June 1918, *Translation of War Diaries of German Units,* Vol. 4.
[28] History of the 74th Company, compiled by Sergeant Carl W. Smith, Box 35, RG 127, NARA College Park, M.D.
[29] Cowing and Cooper, *Dear Folks At Home,* 206.
[30] Ibid.
[31] Ibid.
[32] Ibid.
[33] Ibid.
[34] Jackson, *His Time in Hell, A Texas Marine in France,* 93.
[35] Ibid, 94.
[36] Ibid.
[37] U.S. Marine Corps Muster Rolls, 1893-1940, Record Group 127, NARA, Washington, D.C., and a newspaper clipping: "Wounded in Hard Fight," *The Austinite* (Austin, Chicago, IL), June 14, 1918, found in Box 300, RG 127 NARA, Washington D.C.
[38] Cowing and Cooper, *Dear Folks At Home,* 205-06.
[39] Jackson, *His Time in Hell, A Texas Marine in France,* 94.
[40] Ibid.
[41] Rexmond C. Cochrane, *Gas Warfare at Belleau Wood June 1918*, (Washington D.C.: U.S. Army Chemical Corps Historical Office Army Chemical Center 1957), 21.
[42] Ibid.
[43] Lieutenant Colonel Walter S. Gaspar, interview by Benis Frank 1975, Oral History Section Marine Corps Historical Division Quantico, VA, Marine Corps Oral History Collection, Gray Research Library, Quantico, VA.

[44] U.S. Marine Corps Muster Rolls, 1893-1940, Record Group 127, NARA, Washington, D.C.
[45] Burial File of Private Henry Kirchner, Box 2692, RG 92.9, Records of Graves Registration Services, NARA College Park, MD.
[46] Burial File of Corporal James Bennett Whipple, Box 5185, RG 92.9, Records of Graves Registration Services, NARA College Park, MD.
[47] U.S. Marine Corps Muster Rolls, 1893-1940, Record Group 127, NARA, Washington, D.C.
[48] Official Military Personnel File for Private Harold Alfred Brooks, RG 127, NPRC St. Louis, MO., and Burial File of Private Harold Alfred Brooks, Box 598, RG 92.9, Records of Graves Registration Services, NARA College Park, MD.
[49] Official Military Personnel File for Private Harold Alfred Brooks, RG 127, NPRC St. Louis, MO.
[50] Burial File of Corporal James Bennett Whipple, Box 5185, RG 92.9, Records of Graves Registration Services, NARA College Park, MD.
[51] General Gerald B. Thomas memoir, Alfred M. Gray Research Library, Quantico, VA.
[52] General Gerald B. Thomas, interview by Robert Asprey, Alfred M. Gray Research Library, Quantico, VA.
[53] General Gerald B. Thomas memoir, Alfred M. Gray Research Library, Quantico, VA.
[54] Gulberg, *A War Diary*, 24.
[55] Ibid.
[56] Ibid.
[57] U.S. Marine Corps Muster Rolls, 1893-1940, Record Group 127, NARA, Washington, D.C. Note: Private Tony L. Gandy returned to duty with the 75th Company September 7, 1918, and was severely wounded again September 14, 1918, near Thiacourt France by gunshot wounds to the left thigh face and left forearm. His left hand was also shattered. He died the next day.
[58] Official Military Personnel File for Private Holden Edward Siegert, RG 127, NPRC St. Louis, MO. Note: Private Siegert was diagnosed with psychoneurosis and concussion neurosis. He made a full recovery but did not return to duty. Before sailing to France, Private Siegert survived the wreckage of a troop train on July 18, 1917, near the town of Shamrock, Louisiana. The wreck killed Private William Stonebreaker of the 79th Company.
[59] Hatcher, *Citizen Soldier,* N.P.

[60] Burial File of Private Joachin Sanchez, Eye-witness statement by Private Edward G. Kahrs, Box 4271, RG 92.9, Records of Graves Registration Services, NARA College Park, MD.
[61] Ibid.
[62] Hatcher, *Citizen Soldier,* N.P.
[63] Burial File of Private Joachin Sanchez, Eye-witness statement by Sergeant John F. Pinson Jr., Box 4271, RG 92.9, Records of Graves Registration Services, NARA College Park, MD.
[64] Hatcher, *Citizen Soldier,* N.P.
[65] Ibid.
[66] Burial File of Private Joachin Sanchez, Eye-witness statement by Sergeant John F. Pinson Jr., Box 4271, RG 92.9, Records of Graves Registration Services, NARA College Park, MD.
[67] Hatcher, *Citizen Soldier,* N.P., and Burial File of Private Joachin Sanchez, Eye-witness statements by Private Edward G. Kahrs and Sergeant John F. Pinson Jr., Box 4271, RG 92.9, Records of Graves Registration Services, NARA College Park, MD. Note: Private Joachin Sanchez died June 12, 1918, from the wounds he received that afternoon.
[68] U.S. Marine Corps Muster Rolls, 1893-1940, Record Group 127, NARA, Washington, D.C., and Daily Report of Casualties, date of entry, Box 25, RG 127, NARA Washington D.C
[69] Burial File of First Lieutenant Malcolm Johnstone, Eye-witness statement by Private Herbert Snow, Box 2541, RG 92.9, Records of Graves Registration Services, NARA College Park, MD.
[70] Burial File of First Lieutenant Malcolm Johnstone, Eye-witness statements by Second Lieutenant Mack C. Byrd and Sergeant Frank F. Goodergis, Box 2541, RG 92.9, Records of Graves Registration Services, NARA College Park, MD.
[71] Mitchell, *The Official History of the Second Regiment of Engineers,* 147.
[72] *Records of the Second Division (Regular)* Volume 9, N.P.

June 3rd Chapter V

> *"My boy, the Marines are sitting on the only line they will occupy unless they advance. We are not going to fall back."*
> -Captain John Blanchfield 55th Company, 2nd Battalion, 5th Marines

On the extreme left of the division's front, near the town of Coulombs, the 23rd Infantry still held a position behind the French. The Germans remained active throughout the day, but the 23rd Infantry maintained a support role and did not engage the enemy. That afternoon, however, enemy artillery continuously targeted Company M, 3rd Battalion 23rd Infantry's position west of Premont. When the bombardment subsided, Cook Joseph Mertil encountered the body of twenty-five-year-old Private Adrien Desourdie of Essex, Massachusetts. Upon first glance, Mertil realized the explosion had instantly killed Desourdie who was struck in the back by a large shell fragment.[1]

In Coulombs, the 2nd Battalion, 23rd Infantry, pulled back to constitute the division reserve. Sergeant John Magoon, a former University of Boston student, kept vigilance throughout the afternoon as a battalion observer attached to Company F, 2nd Battalion 23rd Infantry. He stayed just behind the French front while the 2nd Battalion moved further back from the line. Magoon's advance position allowed him a complete view of the vast green pastures fronting the town of Germigny.[2] Despite German artillery fire, the day was relatively inactive.

During the afternoon, Magoon noticed distant figures along the horizon. They appeared to be an enemy troop formation. He watched through his binoculars from his observation post as groups of Germans deployed in a portion of the field defiladed from the French observation, which allowed the enemy to move undetected. Magoon immediately notified the French line and dispatched a courier before he telephoned regimental headquarters to explain the situation. After contacting regimental headquarters, he hung up the receiver of the field telephone, grabbed his binoculars, and watched intently as the Germans gained ground.[3]

Within minutes of Magoon sounding the alarm, the bark of French cannons surged through the air from the south, and quickly developed into a crescendo. Shells hissed in their low arching trajectory overhead. Within seconds, plumes of white smoke from rounds exploding along the horizon smothered the enemy formation.

Magoon watched through his field glasses as the bursting clouds of smoke appear hundreds of meters away just a second or two before the sound of the explosion became audible. The shells seemed to land in rapid succession. The barrage was short, violent and incredibly accurate. Through the dissipating haze covering the freshly pot-marked field, the enemy formation evaporated before reaching the French front line.[4]

June 3rd Chapter V

The German advance on the western portion of the division line was not limited to the 23rd Infantry's front. At 5:30 P.M. Lieutenant Colonel Wise received a message from Colonel Wendell Neville stating, "Information received that enemy are massing for attack on Bois de Veuilly. All French on your front will dribble back through your lines tonight whether attack is made or not. You must send me more information. Everything will be reported at once. Must have information to direct artillery."[5] With this information, Wise left his command post along the cemetery wall to inspect his battalion's front.[6] He immediately headed to the western portion of Bois de Veuilly to see Captain Wass.

From the wooded concealment of Bois de Veuilly, the Marines on Wise's left flank pinpointed individual German soldiers filtering into the woods several hundred meters across the field. These enemy troops closed in on the heels of the broken French counter-attack.

Since 11:30 A.M., the Germans made repeated attempts to advance on Bois de Veuilly, but they encountered withering fire from the machine gunners and rifleman dug in along ravines and woods before them.[7] Several Marines in the line carried scoped Springfield rifles and were eager to put them to use. Twenty-nine-year-old Private Walter Cook of the 43rd Company moved to an isolated and secluded position beyond the line with his rifle.

All morning and into the early afternoon, Cook waited for enemy soldiers to expose themselves carelessly. Steadily he made out occasional shadows lurking in the tree line several hundred meters across the pasture. Placing his sights on the distinguishable human figures moving in the distant woods, he slowly squeezed the trigger until the weapon recoiled. The crack of the rifle's report muffled in the open valley and blended with the distant sound of shots elsewhere along the line. As the shadowy adversary crumbled out of view, Cook reworked the bolt of his rifle and scanned the horizon for another target. Throughout the day, Cook hit anywhere from twelve to eighteen enemy soldiers skulking in the distant woods.[8]

The spectacle of the battalion's snipers attracted the curiosity of comrades. According to First Lieutenant Elliott Cooke of the 18th Company, "Word filtered down from the 43rd Company on our right that they were sniping at small parties of Germans trying to infiltrate around our flank."[9] Second Lieutenants Fred H. Becker and Chester H. Fraser, Army officers attached to the 18th Company, went to watch the display with excited curiosity and remained there for most of the day.[10]

In addition to the artillery fire frequently landing in Bois de Veuilly, occasional rounds from distant enemy machine guns snapped through the thickets and struck tree trunks with a hollow thud. Each passing bullet cautioned the men against any unnecessary exposure, but they braved the fire to watch the snipers do their handy work. Inevitably, an enemy slug found its mark. A round struck fifty-one-year-old Gunner James Gallivan of the 43rd Company in the right knee. The bullet, tumbling irregularly at the end of its long flight, entered on the outer lower third of Gallivan's right thigh but did not exit. The old veteran instantly buckled to the ground. The old man's face turned grey as several comrades treated the wound.

The stoic Irish-born Marine of twenty-four years did not fade in his rigid demeanor as stretcher-bearers hauled him out of the line. Second Lieutenant Fred Becker exclaimed, "I don't think he was hurt much although he used some real salty language as they carried him off."[11]

Gunner James Gallivan. Photo credit: NARA.

After leaving the 18th Company's front, Wise arrived at the 43rd Company and saw the litter bearers evacuating Gallivan. According to Wise, "I came up just as the stretcher bearers were taking him out. The old boy looked white; it was a bad wound. I thought if I could get him mad enough, he'd have a better fighting chance to recover. 'Gallivan,' I said, 'I never thought I'd see the day when an old soldier like you would shoot himself to get out of this mess.'"[12] The impetuous Gallivan, leaning on one elbow, sat up on the departing stretcher to look at Wise and hollered, "The only thing that saves ye from a batin' is me inability to rise!"[13]

Earlier in the morning, German high command directed the German 28th Ersatz Infantry to initiate a 10:00 A.M. assault on Bois de Veuilly, but this was postponed an hour to allow the artillery observation posts to move forward for better visibility.[14] With an improved view of the area, German spotters relayed better fire data to the batteries, and the effects were telling.

While Wise inspected the left half of his battalion's front, enemy guns bombarded the 43rd Company's sector of Bois de Veuilly with renewed ferocity. Shells tore through the timbered canopy and exploded as they hit tree trunks. Others blasted chunks of forest floor skyward and filled the woods with acrid smoke.

The barrage was short but concentrated and when it ended, the screams of wounded filtered through the woods. Dazed by the bombardment, twenty-eight-year-old John Marshall Russell became hysterical, experiencing a hindering of motor skills as comrades quickly assisted him to the rear.[15] Among the casualties, the body of thirty-six-year-old Sergeant

June 3rd Chapter V

John Wiley Rodgers of the 43rd Company lay scattered in the undergrowth. The sleeve of his tunic concealing the '9th Illinois, Company L, 30th U.S. Vol. H. Co.' ink inscribed in an eagle-draped shield tattooed on his left forearm—evidence of his twenty years of Army and Marine Corps service.[16] In a blinding flash, a single shell abruptly ended his distinguished military career.

Approximately a kilometer to the east, German batteries also targeted the sloping terrain in front of the 55th Company at Les Mares Farm. Wise, skirted the dangerously exposed ground between the northeastern corner of Bois de Veuilly and Les Mares Farm and arrived at the position of the 55th Company's 2nd Platoon. He discovered a handful of French Chasseurs dug in with his Marines. "They were still under a major commanding the 1st and 31st Battalions," remembered to Wise.[17] Conversing with the French officer, Wise recalled the somber demeanor of the major. "'It looks blue,' he told me. 'The whole German army has broken through. I don't think we will be able to stop them. What are you going to do?'" "'Our orders are to stick,' I told him.' He shrugged his shoulders."[18]

Looking back south from Les Mares farm over the ground he must cross to return to his command post; Wise noted the lack of cover. According to Wise, "The minute one left the group of buildings on Les Mares Farm there was not shelter at all. The moment I got out into the open the Germans in the woods started smoking me up. About a hundred yards ahead toward Marigny, the road dipped enough to give shelter. I sprinted that hundred yards in record time."[19]

The German barrage along the ground just in front of Les Mares preceded the efforts of the German 197th Division to push beyond the unimproved road south of the town of Bussiares and storm Hill 165. The German 28th Ersatz Infantry of the 197th Division was eventually able to swarm Hill 165 and envelope the southern tip of Bois Triangulairs positioned a kilometer north of Les Mares Farm.[20] The German 4th Reserve Corps directed the 197th Division to capture the line of Veuilly-Marigny-en-Orxois that day. Despite the failure of the French counterattack, their efforts disrupted and delayed the German efforts to seize Hill 165 and left the 197th Division two and a half kilometers shy of these objectives.[21]

Resuming the assault late in the afternoon forced the Germans to put the 26th Reserve Jäger Battalion in line between the 1st and 2nd Battalions, 273rd German Infantry. Efforts to advance during the late afternoon cost the 197th Division heavy casualties.[22] Delays hindered the continuation of the assault since the German guns nearly exhausted their ammunition during the daylong effort to break French counterattacks and wrestle away ground. Resupply was necessary to cover the continued advance of the 26th Jäger Battalion, but it caused a momentary delay in the scheduled assault. German soldiers, concealed behind the sloping terrain north of Hill 165, hugged the earth. German dead and wounded from the 1st and 2nd

Battalions, 273rd Infantry, littered the ground just behind them.[23] The bodies of French soldiers killed during the counterattacks earlier in the day dotted the northern face of Hill 165.

The resistance up to now was substantial enough to caution any unnecessary exposure, and the German infantry waited with anticipation. By 6:15 P.M., the distant thud of German guns signaled the pre-assault barrage. For fifteen minutes, their batteries north of the Clignon brook bombarded the French and American line with an increasing rate of fire.[24] Shells screaming overhead intensified the nerves of the already fatigued Germans. Two heavy German Minenwerfers of the 415th Trench Mortar Company, as well as the light Minenwerfers of the 273rd Infantry, fired from the southern edge of Bussiares.[25]

The barrage crept along the terrain raking the area fronting Les Mares Farm. German gunners also targeted the Bois Barons situated five hundred meters northwest of Les Mares Farm. They bombarded the woods south of Torcy, and the ravine running parallel to the Champillon-Bussiares road.[26]

As incoming rounds landed in the fields north of Les Mares Farm, First Lieutenant Lemuel Shepherd feared a German assault would follow the barrage. He raced along the 55th Company's front to steady the line and cautioned his men to stay vigilant for the possibility of an enemy attack. His thoughts quickly turned to the two squads holding the outpost he established earlier that morning on a summit dotted with a cluster of trees located west of the Champillon-Bussiares road. According to Shepherd, "I was very much concerned about this outpost. They were isolated out there. Since I had put them out there, I felt responsible that they all get back to our lines."[27] Shepherd grew increasingly concerned as shells exploded closer to his outpost every few seconds.

He left Les Mares Farm running the nearly 600 meters toward Captain John Blanchfield's command post situated in the apex of a patch of woods northwest of Champillon. Shepherd, winded from this trek, found Blanchfield, and recalled his conversation with the captain, "'Jim, I'm worried about that outpost. I sent them out there, and I think I ought to check on them.' I must say it was a foolish suggestion," Shepherd claimed, "because they had their orders to withdraw and probably would have done it at the proper time but I just wanted to go out there to ensure that they did. He said, 'yes I think it would be a good idea.'"[28]

Departing Blanchfield's command post, Shepherd ran back toward the farm where he summoned twenty-three-year-old Private Oscar Eugene Martin, a college student from Yadkin, North Carolina. Martin and his twenty-six-year-old brother, Private Augburn Dean Martin, joined the company only two months earlier.[29] According to Shepherd, "I had occasion to use Private Martin extensively both as company runner and my personal orderly."[30] Shepherd ordered Martin to accompany him. Never questioning the lieutenant, Martin kept pace just behind Shepherd as they

June 3rd Chapter V

left the confines of Les Mares Farm and raced into the center of the enemy's bombardment. "We started across the field," said Shepherd, "and I said to myself, 'we'll never make it—shells dropping all over the place."[31]

Exploding shells sent dirt flying over their heads. According to Shepherd, "I recall saying to my orderly, Pat Martin, 'if we get through this, we're really going to be lucky.'"[32]

As they ran half-crouched through the barrage, Shepherd suddenly stopped in his tracks when a German shell slammed into the ground right in front of him but did not explode. Shepherd remembered, "I paused for a moment to look at it. It was right there in front of me just ten feet away when it landed. I saw this shell land along with a lot of others. The dirt went up, and I just stood there waiting for the shell to go off. Thank God it was a dud."[33] Shepherd and Martin had no time to ponder the divinity of the moment and resumed their sprint for the outpost.

Lemuel Shepherd seen here after the war as a captain. Photo credit: VMI.

The bombardment passed further back toward the farm when Shepherd and Martin reached the forward outpost. Shepherd and Martin quickly joined the isolated group and watched the horizon along the sloping fields beyond the seclusion of their position as the Germans appeared hundreds of yards in the distance. They were scouts in the lead of the formation of the German 26th Jäger Battalion. They spread out across the open fields, swarming over the gentle crest of Hill 165.[34] According to Shepherd, "The outpost was on the forward side of this knoll where they had a good field of fire. I got behind the brow of the knoll."[35] The Marines watched the enemy formations advanced along Hill 165 by 7:55 P.M.[36]

According to Shepherd, "By now the Germans had worked their way around the hill, and it was just about dusk when they started closing in. We held our fire until they got within 300 or 400 yards. We had no machine gun, nor any arty."[37] Suddenly, the small outpost fired on the exposed Germans with well-aimed and disciplined shots, and the enemy formation scattered. According to Shepherd, "There were several trees on top of the knoll, and I leaned against one of them where I could look over the top of the little knoll and could direct the fire of the men on the outpost on the advancing Germans."[38]

Within seconds of the thunderous engagement, a German machine gun crew maneuvered into position and fired on Shepherd's men. Bullets cracked overhead, shredding the bark of the trees. According to Shepherd, "All of the sudden something hit me in the neck and swung me around, completely around."[39] The impact briefly stunned Shepherd who initially thought the slug might have passed through his neck. "My first reaction was to see if I could spit. I wanted to see if the bullet had punctured my throat and figured if I could spit I was alright."[40]

With the deafening melee of gunfire piercing his senses, Shepherd, gulping, tried to secrete saliva in his mouth, which dried out by the sudden adrenaline rush. "I spit into my hand to see if I was spitting blood, but I wasn't spitting blood, so I felt relieved," Shepherd recalled.[41] "I dropped back to behind the men, and we continued the firefight."[42] Assessing his injuries while his men engaged the enemy, Shepherd felt around his neck and noticed the wool of his tunic wet with blood. The bullet grazed the side of his neck. It tore a groove through the edge of the standing collar, breaking off the globe of his eagle, globe, and anchor collar emblem. Luckily, the slug missed his jugular vein.[43] "I was indeed a lucky beggar, as a half inch more would have finished me."[44]

Enemy machine gun fire took a toll on the outpost. A round struck twenty-nine-year-old Corporal Homer Watson Bonney in the right side of the jaw, fracturing the molar region of his mandible.[45] Twenty-year-old Private Charles Joseph Mooney suffered a gunshot wound to the right arm.[46] A bullet mortally wounded twenty-one-year-old Private Victor Joseph Roska in the abdomen.[47]

The violent exchange of gunfire gradually slowed, but the German machine positioned in a distant patch of woods kept Shepherd's men pinned down and enabled German soldiers to maneuver around them. Each time enemy soldiers came into view across the field, Shepherd's men tried to impede their efforts with well-aimed shots, but the Germans significantly outnumbered them. The exchange of fire continued, and several German soldiers passed through Bois Barons about 500 meters northwest of Les Mares Farm and continued to advance against increasingly heavy fire.[48]

Shepherd's forward detachment, already shorthanded, had to traverse hundreds of yards across the open field in clear view of the enemy to get back to the company's position. Evacuating their wounded made the task even more hazardous, so Shepherd decided to wait until after dark to pull back to the farm.

From the upstairs window of a house in La Voie du Chatel, Colonel Catlin watched the enemy's advance. "The Germans swept down an open slope in platoon waves, across wide wheat fields bright with poppies that gleamed like splashes of blood in the afternoon sun. The French met the attack and fell steadily back. First, I saw the French come back through the wheat, fighting as they came. Then the Germans, in two columns, steady as machines."[49]

In the face of the enemy advance from Bois Barons, several French Colonial troops fled in a mass exodus from the line, through Les Mares Farm, and eventually reached the outskirts of Marigny-en-Orxois. According to Captain Joseph Murray, "A battalion of French negro troops started past here saying they were going to Champillon, but returned about when half way past, saying they were going to the left."[50]

Wise watched from his command post along the cemetery wall north of Marigny-en-Orxois as these men fled. "Then suddenly, as though they had sprung up out of the ground, a battalion of Senegalese troops came rushing toward the rear through my extreme left. Only a few of them had kept their rifles. The bulk of them, weapons thrown away, were in a panic of retreat."[51]

The spectacle of the retreating colonial troops caught the attention of Captain Frank Whitehead, and members of the 5th Marine Regimental Headquarters Company dug in along the northwestern outskirts of Marigny-en-Orxois. From the over the summit between Bois de Veuilly and the road connecting the town of Marigny-en-Orxois to Les Mares Farm, Whitehead watched the French retreat from the front. According to Whitehead, "Noting that the company halted and fired several times during its progress over the sky-line, approximately 300 yards north of the position of the Headquarters Company, I directed a lieutenant to proceed to the crest of the hill and determine the position of the enemy."[52]

The fraught colonial troops to the left of the 5th Marines Headquarters Company continued their sporadic rifle fire against the approaching Germans. According to Captain Murray, "One of their officers reported enemy advancing slowly 1500 yards to front."[53] When the lieutenant sent by Whitehead returned, he reported the Senegalese troops were inadvertently firing at members of Lieutenant Colonel Wise's 2nd Battalion, 5th Marines along the line west of Les Mares Farm.[54]

From his command post, nearly three kilometers to the southeast, Catlin heard the distant crack of rifles and machine guns emanating from Les Mares Farm. Beyond the gently inclining fields north of Marigny-en-Orxois, the distant melee quickly developed into a thunderous exchange, a sign the Germans advanced within rifle range of the American line. "If the German advance looked beautiful to me, that metal curtain that our Marines rang down on the scene was even more so. The German lines did not break; they were broken," said Catlin, who viewed the exchange with a placid curiosity.[55] The intense engagement ended quickly when the Germans faltered in the face of blistering American fire. "They broke and ran for cover, though their first line hung on till dark, north of Champillon."[56]

June 3rd Chapter V

Shortly after the French colonials pulled back along the left flank of Les Mares Farm, one of Wise's runners summoned Whitehead to report immediately to the command post of the 2nd Battalion, 5th Marines. Whitehead raced towards the cemetery wall north of Marigny-en-Orxois. "I was directed to report to Captain Blanchfield on the firing line. The line was just forward of the crest and ran from the woods just east of the Ferme les Mares to and including the farm buildings," according to Whitehead.[57] Before he moved the sixty-two men from his Stokes mortar platoon, 37mm crews, and pioneer section to Les Mares Farm, Whitehead went alone to locate Blanchfield.[58]

Whitehead hurried toward Les Mares Farm. The deafening crack of rifle fire grew louder as he raced down the road from Marigny-en-Orxois. As a former enlisted man, Whitehead served in the Dominican Republic but was never exposed to the shelling and rifle fire he experienced on this day. As Whitehead approached the farm, he noticed several Marines out in front of the buildings still shooting at distant groups of retreating Germans, following their failed attack.

In a short time, the gunfire died out. Whitehead located Blanchfield who was desperately searching his command post for his misplaced signal pistol to call for a French artillery barrage. Blanchfield could not find his flare gun, but according to Whitehead, the captain improvised a new method. "Grasping a signal cartridge tightly in his fist he would pound the end on a rock until he succeeded in igniting the cartridge and then he would throw the cartridge into the air. The signal could not possibly be seen above the trees in the rear, but the captain persisted in his efforts until his burned hands could stand the pain no longer."[59] Fronting the farm, Whitehead made a note of the dense underbrush concealing potential enemy avenues of approach.

Aware of this potential threat, he approached Blanchfield and inquired about establishing a secondary position behind the line in case a sizable enemy attack forced the men to pull back. According to Whitehead, "This question did not please the old-timer at all, for he gave me the answer in no uncertain terms; saying 'My boy, the Marines are sitting on the only line they will occupy unless they advance. We are not going to fall back.'"[60] Whitehead remembered, "The captain instructed me to take over the defense of the farm buildings and to extend the line to the west as far as was possible with the sixty-two men under my command."[61]

The farm's buildings stood on both sides of the road connecting the property with Marigny-en-Orxois. Whitehead assumed the farm would undoubtedly be the focal point of an enemy assault. The bodies of French Colonial soldiers killed only hours earlier lay near the property and only served to heighten Whitehead's bleak premonition. He sent orders for his men to come forward, and, within minutes, the sixty-two-man detachment arrived at the farm.[62]

June 3rd Chapter V

Private Wayne French and the other Marines attached to the company's Stokes mortar section stripped all unnecessary gear to make room for additional rifle ammunition. The extra weight, however, slowed their pace, and speed was essential given the increased rate of German shellfire that day.[63]

Whitehead decided to establish a secure position among the buildings. His men maintained patrol contact to the west since the nearly half-kilometer stretch of open field between the farm and the edge of Bois de Veuilly remained unoccupied. Darkness would likely be the only concealment for anyone occupying this span of pasture. On the right flank, two squads of Whitehead's men also extended the property's defense east of the farm and soon dug fighting positions. Holding this eastern side of the farm's property enabled the Marines to enfilade any potential raid on the center of the line.

Thirty-six-year-old Second Lieutenant David Kipness, a Russian immigrant with nearly fourteen years in the Marine Corps, commanded the company's Stokes mortar section, and Whitehead put him in charge of the strongpoint among the farm's buildings.[64]

As Whitehead's men bolstered the defense of Les Mares Farm, Major Julius Turrill's 1st Battalion, 5th Marines, in reserve at Pyramide Farm, received orders to move north through the battered town of Marigny-aux-Lions. Instructions directed them to occupy a position along the northwestern outskirts of the village in a wooded coppice near the town's lavish chateau. Directives from division and brigade during the past forty-eight hours had already subjected the battalion to an endless period of movement from one sector of the front to another with virtually no rest. Incredulously, the exhausted men hoisted their packs and departed Pyramide Farm at dusk.[65]

From their new position at Marigny-aux-Lions, Turrill's Marines occupied a better position near the tenuous left half of the brigade's line to quickly respond to a potential German breakthrough between Bois de Veuilly and Champillon.

On the northern outskirts of Champillon, where the ground inclined west of the road to Bussiares, the 5th Section, 15th Company, 6th Machine Gun Battalion occupied a well-concealed position in the underbrush. They maintained an excellent field of fire covering this vital roadway. A gap in the brush fronting the machine gun's location was broad enough to give twenty-six-year-old Gunnery Sergeant Carl Harvie Horton good observation down the thoroughfare.

Earlier in the afternoon, infiltrating Germans fired a few shots at Horton's group, but they could not determine where the enemy shots emanated. Besides the artillery barrage along the road, which killed one, and wounded several members of the 15th Company hours earlier, things remained quiet during the late afternoon.

June 3rd Chapter V

Against the backdrop of distant gunfire, the six-foot-tall Horton, casually stood up in his dugout to sprinkle a pinch of tobacco into a Zig-Zag paper to roll a cigarette. Once he raised up just above the brush, a concealed enemy machine gun fired from down the causeway. A single round struck Horton in the left side of his torso near the shoulder, and he instantly wilted to the ground. The bullet passed through his spine, perforated his lungs, and exited the right side of his body. Paralyzed from the waist down, Horton wheezed and coughed up blood.

Marines from his gun crew struggled to drag their mortally wounded section leader out of the dugout and avoid the enemy machine gunner somewhere down the road. Their screams for help quickly attracted a litter team, and in minutes, comrades placed Horton on a stretcher and rushed him to a nearby dressing station.[66]

On the right flank of 2nd Battalion, 5th Marines, Private Roland Fisher remained at his advanced position concealed in a tree line well beyond the 51st Company's front. With his scoped Springfield rifle, he menaced German soldiers all day from distances as far as 1,400 yards away.[67] By the late afternoon, Fisher attracted the attention of several German machine gunners, "and if there is anything the Hun hates," said Fisher, "it's a sniper. The best of it was they thought I was shooting from another wood. They set up a couple of machine guns and started shooting into the woods, and I was picking the gun crew off all the time."[68]

Before the sun dipped below the western horizon, Fisher faded back to the 51st Company's line. His superior marksmanship accounted for six enemy soldiers during the day.[69]

To the right of Captain Lloyd Williams' 51st Company, Captain Dwight Smith's 82nd Company, 3rd Battalion, 6th Marines remained alert to possible enemy infiltration through the woods. Smith's Marines excavated individual dugouts following the barrage that claimed four men from the 2nd Platoon whose bodies lay unburied at the edge of the woods. During the evening, twenty-year-old Gunnery Sergeant Dana Clifton Lovejoy, in charge of a burial detail, chose several men to assist with the grizzly task. Lovejoy's group moved back to the edge of the woods where the bodies lay contorted in the same manner as they fell that afternoon amidst the shell craters dotting the ground. The gruesome task of committing the battered and torn bodies of their comrades, who were full of life only hours ago, infused each member of the burial team with a sense of their own mortality.

Teaming up, they pulled the four bodies to nearby shell holes. The limbs of the dead tumbling along the ground limply as the burial detail dragged them to the shallow graves. They rolled twenty-six-year-old Private Michael Zippay's body rolled down the side of a shallow crater.

At the bottom of the hole, one of the men positioned the remains so it would fit the rudimentary grave. Then they placed Private David Wisted's maimed corpse next to Zippay.[70] Lovejoy stood there emotionless over the

Private Harry Cochran was one of the four members of 2nd Platoon, 82nd Company killed June 3rd. Photo credit: New York Times Mid-week pictorial.

grave looking down at the two dead men lying side by side. Noticing the watch still fastened to Wisted's wrist, he impassively commented on how reprehensible it was to bury such a quality seventeen-jewel Elgin timepiece with the body.[71]

In another nearby hole, the shattered remains of twenty-one-year-old Private Harry King Cochran and twenty-two-year-old Private David Alfred Taggart lay abreast.[72] Once a member of the burial detail removed one of the identification tags from each body, they unceremoniously covered the dead men with dirt. They marked the graves and quickly returned to the company by crossing the open field as fast as they could to avoid enemy artillery.

The majority of the French troops who survived the morning's counterattack had retreated through the American line by evening. Several French soldiers passing through the 82nd Company's wooded front just to the south of Hill 142 encountered Captain Smith and urged the thirty-two-year-old Vermont native to move his company front further south. Smith did not yield and respectfully dismissed the Frenchman's request. When word of Smith's deed reached Brigadier General Harbord, he immediately sent his accolades to Colonel Catlin at La Voie du Chatel stating:

> ... Am very glad Captain 82nd Co, declined retire. Same order was given by French major to one of Wise's companies who also declined. It is not intended to confine the 82nd Co. to a poor position at a particular feature on the map. The Captain can move it forward or make his disposition to fit the tactical necessity of the case, the only limitations being that the American line as now constituted must not be passed by the Germans. It is not expected that the line held will necessarily be held by a continuous cordon.[73]

The dejected French continued their exodus through the 82nd Company and into La Voie du Chatel during the late afternoon. At a farmhouse in La

June 3rd Chapter V

Voie du Chatel, Corporal James Hatcher of the 84th Company was filling canteens for several comrades when he encountered several survivors of the ill-fated French counterattack. While passing through the edge of town, Hatcher gazed at the commotion inside the open doorway of the regimental dressing station. He noted the numerous casualties sprawled out on stretchers outside the facility waiting for treatment.

The buzzing activity in La Voie du Chatel made a prime target for German shells, so Hatcher rushed to fill the canteens and hurry back to the front. "On my way back to the company I met a small body of French troops filing toward the rear. I smiled and said 'Bonjour,' but they only stared at me," said Hatcher. "Those Frenchmen were thoroughly whipped. When we finally did succeed in getting some of them to talk they told us that the Germans would win anyway in the end in spite of anything the Americans could do and that we might just as well let them through to Paris then so the war would be over."[74]

The problematic gap between Wise's right flank and the left company of Shearer's battalion was partially filled by Smith's 82nd Company. The wooded terrain, however, required more men to hold the void. Colonel Catlin summoned Major Berton Sibley to his regimental headquarters in La Voie du Chatel, and explained that Smith, "found that their force was inadequate to properly fill the gap which existed."[75] Catlin instructed Sibley to assume command of the front from the 82nd Company all the way east for nearly a kilometer to Shearer's flank, which he believed was in Bois de Champillon. According to Sibley, "There was, I believe, a short written order governing this move but the instructions were for the most part given to me personally at the Regimental P.C."[76]

At Les Mares Farm, the newly arrived reinforcements from the 5th Regimental Headquarters Company bolstered the defense of the property. The beleaguered men of First Lieutenant Lemuel Shepherd's outpost, however, clung to their position hundreds of meters beyond the line in the face of a numerically superior German attack. Shepherd's men successfully held their position, but could not risk returning to the farm until sundown for fear of attracting enemy fire.

Dusk could not arrive soon enough for Shepherd's men. According to Shepherd, "By nightfall, the Germans were working around our position, within a couple hundred yards of us and we weren't strong enough to hold out there by ourselves all that night, so we withdrew and brought back a couple of the men who had been wounded."[77]

Once the men safely returned to the company lines, Shepherd applied a field dressing to his superficial yet bloody neck wound. The bullet had torn the side of the standing collar of his tunic and saturated the wool with blood, but he avoided death by a matter of inches. Once Shepherd stopped the bleeding, he walked to the dressing station. According to his recollections,

June 3rd Chapter V

"They wanted to evacuate me, but I said, 'hell no, it isn't bad.' It just cut a groove through my neck."[78]

On the right flank of Wise's battalion front, Captain Smith's 82nd Company held the line on the northern edge of the woods fronting Hill 142. They kept a very vigilant posture all day. At 8:20 P.M., he dispatched a message to Major Sibley stating:

> Have not been attacked yet. French major on our right says he expects attack tonight or early morning. Situation much better than I thought at first. Line was very difficult to reconnoiter and I was informed at first that all French was returning—this was not correct. I have filled up entire gap of French troops that did withdraw. Believe reinforcements should be in before dark if possible. Ammunition not yet received. Suggest that my support platoon be put up on front line and that Co. coming in be held in rear of our sector as support.[79]

Smith added, "Additional machine guns are urgently needed in our sector."[80] The support company Smith referred to was the 83rd Company of Sibley's battalion. Private James Scarbrough and elements of the 3rd Platoon, 83rd Company, had moved into the open field adjacent to the woods near La Voie du Chatel since enemy shellfire inundated the forest the previous day.

Orders for the 83rd Company to move forward disrupted their rest. According to Scarbrough, "They woke us up in the middle of the night to move again. It wasn't that hard because we were just sleeping under the stars, and with all the artillery fire around, you couldn't sleep anyway."[81]

A platoon of the 73rd Machine Gun Company commanded by twenty-five-year-old First Lieutenant Evans Spalding of Essex, Massachusetts, accompanied the 83rd Company.[82] According to Private Einar Wahl of the 73rd Machine Gun Company, "At dusk we fell into single file and started down a road toward the lines. Dead and wounded were liberally distributed along the road. Shell-shock victims acting like crazy men were being led to the rear by comrades. I will never forget that first trip through the darkness of tangled woods down to our first position."[83] According to Scarbrough, "We moved with a machine gun section to the south of a village named Torcy, and took up position along a long wood line."[84]

Once in the cover of the forest, Sibley, who assumed command of this sector of the line, made sure his men dug fighting positions as he surveyed the ground to the north. He recalled, "After arriving at the front on the night of June 3rd I made personal reconnaissance and learned that there was a battalion of French troops in front and to the right of the position we had taken."[85] His Marines labored in the dark to excavate individual dugouts.

For them, however, it was just another patch of woods and another hole to dig.

According to Scarbrough, "I remember we weren't in particularly good spirits, but there was a feeling of anticipation because we knew there was a large German force nearby and that meant we might get a shot at them."[86] Most of the 3rd Battalion's front had dug in along the edge of woods, and at some points they were only fifty yards away from German lines.[87]

The noise generated by Sibley's men attracted the attention of the 9th Company, 3rd Battalion, 460th German Infantry, who frequently swept the tree line with raking machine gun fire. The commotion also drew German artillery, which shook the forest.[88] According to Wahl, "Bullets whistling around us snipping off tree branches, big shells screaming and crashing in all directions, stumbling into shell-holes and over fallen trees, taking about three hours to reach our positions—it tested one's endurance to the limit."[89] Scarbrough recalled, "There was harassing machine gun and artillery fire all night, but we just kept our heads down and dug shallow holes to get out of the fire.[90]

The arrival of First Lieutenant Alfred Houston Noble's 83rd Company that night was memorable. According to Noble, a native of Federalsburg, Maryland, "My company got into a little-wooded area, as I remember, and properly got shelled that night. Two or three guns the Germans had brought up, and they apparently had seen we were in there, so they got a few shells in on us."[91] Wahl, arriving at his machine gun section's position in the woods, could overlook the moonlit terrain beyond the knoll of Hill 142. Once Wahl reached the edge of the woods, he collapsed. "Threw off my pack and ammunition boxes and fell right to sleep. Didn't even trouble to dig or find a hole."[92]

Captain Smith's concern over a possible enemy attack during the night remained a paramount concern since his earlier requests for badly needed ammunition went unfulfilled. 6th Marines' Headquarters Company eventually realized the predicament, and by 9:40 P.M., a supply wagon transported 956 bandoleers of 30.06 ammunition and 10,000 rounds of 8mm French Lebel cartridges for the Chauchats to the 82nd and 83rd Companies.[93]

Trying to pinpoint a rough layout of the enemy's position became a paramount issue—a task which fell members of the 3rd Battalion, 6th Marines' intelligence section. Beyond the tree line of the 82nd and 83rd Companies that night, First Lieutenant Ralph Marshall, as well as Privates Wilbur Moor and twenty-four-year-old Joseph Edward Rendinell, stealthily crept beyond the battalion's front. They moved by way of a shallow and narrow ravine to get closer to the suspected enemy front, which, based on the noise, was very close. The moonlight made Rendinell feel as if a great spotlight focused upon him. Marshall, flat on his stomach, peered back over his shoulder and motioned for Rendinell to crawl next to him. "My heart

June 3rd Chapter V

was going mighty fast," said Rendinell, who believed a large number of German troops stood on the other side of the ravine.

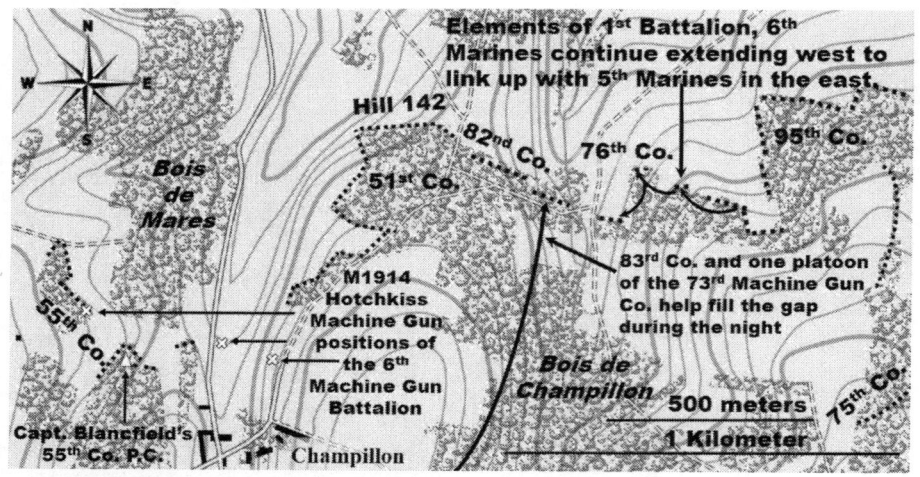

During the night of June 3rd, the 83rd Company moved into position in the Bois de Champillon to help further strengthen the loose liaison between the 5th and 6th Marines near Hill 142.

Feeling as if his heart ascended into his throat, Rendinell cautiously slithered forward. Despite his discreteness, his paranoid senses interpreted every crumple of grass a thousand times louder than it actuality sounded. The commotion he heard, and the movement he saw up ahead convinced Rendinell he was only a careless sound away from drawing the fire of a thousand German rifles. The patrol, satisfied with their findings, silently made their way back to the battalion lines.[94] Along portions of the front, only woods and pasture separated the Germans from the American lines.

---

[1] Burial File of Private Adrien Desourdie, Eye-witness statement by Cook Joesph, Box 1283, RG 92.9, Records of Graves Registration Services, NARA College Park, MD., and *Operations of 3rd Battalion, 23rd Infantry*, Box 57, RG 120.9.3, Records of the AEF, NARA College Park, MD.
[2] Headquarters Second Division AEF G.O. No. 40 July 5, 1918, Box 17, RG 120.9.3, Records of the AEF, NARA College Park, MD.
[3] Ibid.
[4] Ibid.
[5] *Records of the Second Division (Regular)* Volume 5, N.P.
[6] Ibid.
[7] War Diary and Annexes 197th Division 3 June 3 1918, *Translation of War Diaries of German Units,* Vol. 4.
[8] Official Military Personnel File for Private Walter Cook, RG 127, NPRC St. Louis, MO. Note: On December 10, 1918, Cook was recommended for the Medal of Honor by then Captain George F. Hill. Cook was reduced from the rank of Gunnery Sergeant to a Private only weeks earlier for reasons unknown.

[9] Cooke, "We Can Take It, We Attack," *Infantry Journal*, 6.
[10] Ibid.
[11] Ibid.
[12] Wise and Frost, *A Marine Tells it to You*, 201.
[13] Ibid.
[14] War Diary and Annexes 197th Division 3 June 3 1918, *Translation of War Diaries of German Units,* Vol. 4.
[15] Official Military Personnel File for Private John Russell Martin, RG 127, NPRC St. Louis, MO. Note: Private Russell was diagnosed as suffering from mental alienation on 11 June 1918. He was also diagnosed as having suffered from Dementia Praecox which was evidenced by attention disorders, negativism, mannerism, inaccessibility, emotional disharmony, auditory hallucinations, which he responded to, and disorientation seen through psychomotor retardation. He suffered from poor memory, difficulty in thinking, and he acted reclusively. At one point he commented that he believed he could stop the war by offering himself for crucifixion. A predisposition of these disorders was thought to exist before his enlistment.
[16] Official Military Personnel File for Sergeant John Wiley Rodgers, RG 127, NPRC St. Louis, MO. Note: While serving in the Panama Canal Zone with the U.S.S. Yorktown Marine detachment, Rodgers barely survived an abscessed liver as result of amoebic dysentery contracted while in the Philippine Islands in 1915.
[17] Wise and Frost, *A Marine Tells it to You*, 199.
[18] Ibid.
[19] Ibid, 200-201.
[20] War Diary and Annexes 197th Division 3 June 3 1918, *Translation of War Diaries of German Units,* Vol. 4.
[21] Ibid.
[22] Ibid.
[23] Ibid.
[24] Ibid.
[25] War Diary and Annexes 273rd Reserve Infantry 3 June 1918, *Translation of War Diaries of German Units,* Vol. 4.
[26] War Diary and Annexes 197th Division 3 June 3 1918, *Translation of War Diaries of German Units,* Vol. 4.
[27] General Lemuel C. Shepherd Jr., interview by Benis Frank, Alfred M. Gray Research Library, Quantico, VA.
[28] Ibid.
[29] U.S. Marine Corps Muster Rolls, 1893-1940, Record Group 127, NARA, Washington, D.C.

June 3rd **Chapter V**

[30] "Statement Regarding Bravery of Oscar E. Martin Former Private U.S. Marine Corps," by Lemuel Shepherd March 19, 1929, found in Official Military Personnel File for Private Oscar E. Martin, RG 127, NPRC St. Louis, MO.
[31] General Lemuel Shepherd, interview by Robert Asprey, Alfred M. Gray Research Library, Quantico, VA.
[32] General Lemuel C. Shepherd Jr., interview by Benis Frank, Alfred M. Gray Research Library, Quantico, VA.
[33] Ibid.
[34] Correspondence Shepherd to McClellan, 24 March 1919, *Operations of the 55th Company,* Box 29, RG 127 NARA Washington D.C., and War Diary and Annexes 197th Division 3 June 3 1918, *Translation of War Diaries of German Units,* Vol. 4.
[35] General Lemuel C. Shepherd Jr., interview by Benis Frank, Alfred M. Gray Research Library, Quantico, VA.
[36] War Diary and Annexes 197th Division 3 June 3 1918, *Translation of War Diaries of German Units,* Vol. 4.
[37] General Lemuel Shepherd, interview by Robert Asprey, Alfred M. Gray Research Library, Quantico, VA.
[38] General Lemuel C. Shepherd Jr., interview by Benis Frank, Alfred M. Gray Research Library, Quantico, VA.
[39] Ibid.
[40] General Lemuel Shepherd, interview by Robert Asprey, Alfred M. Gray Research Library, Quantico, VA.
[41] Ibid.
[42] Ibid.
[43] Ibid.
[44] Correspondence Lemuel C. Shepherd to his mother, 9 June 1918, Folder 29-30, Box 67, Virginia Military Institute Archives Preston Library, Lexington, VA.
[45] U.S. Marine Corps Muster Rolls, 1893-1940, Record Group 127, NARA, Washington, D.C.
[46] Ibid.
[47] Ibid.
[48] War Diary and Annexes 197th Division 3 June 3 1918, *Translation of War Diaries of German Units,* Vol. 4.
[49] Catlin, *With the Help of God and a Few Marines*, 92.
[50] *Records of the Second Division (Regular)* Volume 5, N.P.
[51] Wise and Frost, *A Marine Tells it to You*, 202.
[52] *The Aisne Defensive,* Whitehead to ABMC, Box 190, RG 117.4.2, NARA College Park, MD.
[53] *Records of the Second Division (Regular)* Volume 5, N.P.

June 3rd Chapter V

[54] *The Aisne Defensive,* Whitehead to ABMC, Box 190, RG 117.4.2, NARA College Park, MD.
[55] Catlin, *With the Help of God and a Few Marines*, 93.
[56] Ibid.
[57] *The Aisne Defensive,* Whitehead to ABMC, Box 190, RG 117.4.2, NARA College Park, MD.
[58] Ibid.
[59] Ibid.
[60] Ibid.
[61] Ibid.
[62] Ibid.
[63] Hamilton and Corbin, *Echoes From Over There,* 59.
[64] *The Aisne Defensive,* Whitehead to ABMC, Box 190, RG 117.4.2, NARA College Park, MD., and Official Military Personnel File for First Lieutenant David Kipness, RG 127, NPRC St. Louis, MO.
[65] Correspondence Rockey to ABMC, 16 December 1926, Box 190, RG 117.4.2, NARA College Park, MD.
[66] Burial File of Gunnery Sergeant Carl Horton, Eye-witness statement by Private Hood L. Haynie, Captain James P. Moriarty, Private Morris Jackman and Private Jason Thurston, Box 2354, RG 92.9, Records of Graves Registration Services, NARA College Park, MD., and Official Military Personnel File for Gunnery Sergeant Carl H. Horton, RG 127, NPRC St. Louis, MO. Note: Horton died June 30, 1918 at Base Hospital #6.
[67] Official Military Personnel File for Private Roland Fisher, Military Personnel File, NPRC.
[68] Correspondence Roland Fisher to his brother George C. Fisher, 20 July 1918, Provided to author by Roland Fisher's nephew, Howard George Fisher
[69] Official Military Personnel File for Private Roland Fisher, Military Personnel File, NPRC.
[70] Burial File of Private David Wisted, Eye-witness statement by Private Edward Smith Golden, Box 5299, RG 92.9, Records of Graves Registration Services, NARA College Park, MD.
[71] Burial File of Private David Wisted, Eye-witness statement by Private Robert Horton, Box 5299, RG 92.9, Records of Graves Registration Services, NARA College Park, MD.
[72] Ibid.
[73] *Records of the Second Division (Regular)* Volume 5, N.P.
[74] Hatcher, *Citizen Soldier,* N.P.
[75] Correspondence Sibley to the ABMC, 20 December 1926, Box 190, RG 117.4.2, NARA College Park, MD.

June 3rd Chapter V

[76] Ibid.
[77] General Lemuel C. Shepherd Jr., interview by Benis Frank, Alfred M. Gray Research Library, Quantico, VA.
[78] Ibid.
[79] *Records of the Second Division (Regular)* Volume 5, N.P.
[80] Ibid.
[81] Scarbrough *They Called us Devil Dogs,* N.P.
[82] *History of the Third battalion, Sixth regiment,* 13.
[83] Cowing and Cooper, *Dear Folks At Home,* 142-143.
[84] Scarbrough, *They Called us Devil Dogs,* N.P.
[85] Correspondence Sibley to the ABMC, 20 December 1926, Box 190, RG 117, NARA College Park, MD.
[86] Scarbrough, *They Called us Devil Dogs,* N.P.
[87] *History of the Third battalion, Sixth regiment,* 13.
[88] War Diary and Annexes 1st 2nd and 3rd Battalion 460th Infantry 4 June 1918, *Translation of War Diaries of German Units,* Vol. 4. Note: Sketch done by 460th Infantry puts the 9th Company of the 460th Infantry in position by 3:55 P.M. located in the 'L'-shaped woods.
[89] Cowing and Cooper, *Dear Folks At Home,* 143.
[90] Scarbrough, *They Called us Devil Dogs,* N.P.
[91] General Alfred H. Noble Interview, Alfred M. Gray Research Library, Quantico, VA.
[92] Cowing and Cooper, *Dear Folks At Home,* 143.
[93] *Records of the Second Division (Regular)* Volume 5, N.P.
[94] Rendinell and Pattullo, *One Man's War,* 94.

June 3rd Chapter VI

In the hole were the mangled bodies of three Frenchmen. Against the back of the hole on the side nearest me leaned one of the bodies, nearly bolt upright, with the head and neck almost gone.
  -Corporal Warren Jackson 95th Company, 1st Battalion, 6th Marines

During the night, artillerymen of the 2nd Field Artillery Brigade registered targets, established phone lines, formed battery observation points, and created liaison with the infantry units along the front. The arrival of the division's artillery earlier in the day considerably bolstered the American front.

The American artillery, along with several remaining French batteries, erupted along fields north and south of the Paris-Metz road. The night sky lit up with bright flickering muzzle flashes as the thunderous chorus of the cannonade echoed across the entire region for several kilometers. All night, French and American batteries of 75mm and 155mm guns pounded German positions. At a rate of twenty rounds per hour, each battery provided interdiction fire of their assigned sector of the enemy's front.[1]

Earlier in the evening, around 6:00 P.M., First Lieutenants Robert W. Kean and Roderick J. McIntosh, liaison officers with the 1st Battalion, 15th Field Artillery, accompanied Major Bailey, the battalion commander, in his Ford car. They traveled to inspect the area between Charly-sur-Marne and Mount de Bonneil along the northern banks of the Marne River. According to Kean, "We drove along the Marne. The empty town seemed ghostly. Not a soul in the streets. Not a dog barking. Only silence. All the bridges across the Marne on our right had been blown up and any communication across the river was impossible."[2]

In the east, they spotted American troops of the 30th Infantry Regiment, 3rd Division moving up the steep terrain to the left of the road near Mont de Bonneil. "The sun was low in the west and the well-kept fields all gave us a feeling of peace and security. It was hard to imagine that we were so close to the enemy. It was only the French observation balloon on the horizon far in the rear and the occasional boom of a gun in the neighboring sector that showed any sign of war."[3]

Once inside the town of Mont de Bonneil, the three American officers encountered French soldiers who directed them to the unit's command post. Kean remained outside the small building while McIntosh and Bailey entered to establish liaison with the French. The meeting with the French command staff was brief, and the two men departed the chateau headquarters with orders for their batteries to move forward after dark. This news compelled the three officers to conduct a hasty survey of the area before returning to the battalion.

June 3rd Chapter VI

During the evening, Captain George Wahl's Battery B, 1st Battalion, 12th Field Artillery worked to get their guns operation in the woods northwest of Paris Farm. Just behind them, Battery B, 1st Battalion, 17th Field Artillery initiated a barrage with their heavy 155mm guns. The thunderous blast from these cannons seemed to rattle the entire forest. The concussion from the muzzle blast swept the area like a windstorm as they fired over Wahl's battery. "Every time it fired it blew our blankets about and deluged us with dust. Everyone was firing constantly," remembered Wahl. "The battery's general field of fire was designated in the vicinity of Bouresches, so the sheaf was adjusted that evening over that town. Observation was very difficult to obtain."[4]

The immense firepower of these 155mm guns even attracted Major General Harbord's attention. He theorized, "I am strongly of the opinion that our 155's should be industriously employed all night in the back areas and crossroads of routes approaching our front from Bussiares to the Paris-Chateau Thierry road. The Germans are probably moving on all these important roads every night and the French artillery from motives of economy in ammunition are not registering on these points."[5]

The guns of Batteries D, E, and F, 2nd Battalion, 15th Field Artillery augmented the division's fire support by 7:00 P.M., once they moved into the line just north of the town of Coupru.[6] Immediately, the gun crews emplaced their cannons and shelled their designated targets. Throughout the evening, they fired on Hill 204 south of the Paris-Metz road and bombarded the village of Vaux.[7] Sometime during the night, forty-four-year-old Colonel Manus McCloskey, commanding the 12th Field Artillery, informed Colonel Catlin that the "Line fire of artillery is perfectly safe."[8]

Inside the village of Vaux, elements of the German 3rd Battalion, 47th Infantry Regiment endured incoming fire throughout the day, and according to the war diary, "The village was the target for surprise fires as soon as anything showed itself."[9] The thunderous explosions shook the village's centuries-old structures. The Germans detained several of the town's civilian occupants to their cellars. They remained under the guard of German soldiers from the 9th Company, 3rd Battalion 47th Infantry Regiment.[10] French and American artillery also devastated the town of Epaux, nearly five kilometers northeast of Belleau where the German 237th Infantry Division maintained their regimental command post. The barrage on Epaux continued through the night and disrupted all German wire communications inside the village by 11:30 P.M.[11]

When Major Bailey, as well as First Lieutenants Kean and McIntosh, returned to the battalion, the convoy of caissons, ammunition carts, supply wagons, and the 75mm guns of the batteries were ready to move into position. During the late evening, the 1st Battalion followed the same road along the northern banks of the Marne Bailey, McIntosh, and Kean had traveled in their reconnaissance toward Mont de Bonneil. Before reaching the village, the caravan turned off the road and went into positions. Bailey established his battalion headquarters in a small house at La Genetre Farm.[12] "The three batteries were ready for action by 8:30 P.M.," according to Kean.[13]

The battalion's location remained precarious, as there was no avenue of escape since the French destroyed all the bridges across the Marne. "If there had been a successful German attack we would have had no line of retreat," reasoned Kean.[14] "However, we were there to stop the German advance if possible. So we got into position for action as quickly as we could."[15] Despite the movement into position west of Mont de Bonneil, thirty-four-year-old Lieutenant Colonel Joseph Ray Davis, commanding the 15th Field Artillery, was uncertain of the exact location of his 1st Battalion. No liaison existed between Bailey's guns and the 9th Infantry, the unit his battalion was designated to support.[16]

During the night, while French and American batteries pounded German positions, the last survivors of the French counterattack filtered back through the 2nd Division line. Corporal Warren Jackson and the members of the 95th Company dug in along the northern fringe of Bois de Champillon. This night was especially dark due to the very limited moonlight. Jackson struggled to excavate his dugout in the sandy soil of an embankment. According to Jackson, "That night, a stillness reigned in marked contrast to the fearful fire of the afternoon before. The very quiet made me apprehensive of a coming storm as though the very jaws of hell were ready to swallow us up."[17]

The men were vigilant to possible German infiltration. Jackson was stunned to hear a voice in front of his position cry out, "'Camarade, je suis blesse. [Comrade, I am hurt]'"[18] The feeble plea for assistance emanated in front of a machine gun position and the unseen man claimed he had been wounded in the back or shoulder. Gunnery Sergeant James Ashwood, cognizant to potential enemy deceit, took no risk and immediately moved beyond the line and fumbled in the dark for the wounded man and grabbed hold of him. Feeling along his lumbar region, Ashwood ran his hand over a gaping wound in the man's back to verify his story. "The Frenchman stated that he had been wounded several days before when he was left by his retreating comrades. Only by the greatest effort had he been able to make his way back to our positions. The poor Frenchman—or was he lucky to get out of it?—was taken back to the hospital," remembered Jackson.[19]

For the 95th Company, the previous forty-eight hours of constant moving and digging in search of the right flank of the 5th Marines finally ended. Jackson recalled their extension of the line earlier that day. "As we walked down a slope, we came upon the bodies of Frenchman scattered about."[20] Jackson watched as twenty-three-year-old Sergeant Wilbur Summerlin, was "ransacking their packs, and I don't know what else, to get whatever suited his fancy."[21] Jackson remembered his initial shock over

June 3rd Chapter VI

Summerlin's indifference as he rummaged through dead men's gear. "I was amazed at his coolness and unconcern in doing what it took me weeks to learn to do, and then with a great sense of relief when I had finished the job."[22] As Jackson moved further down the line, he came upon yet another ghastly scene:

> Before I knew it I was at the edge of an opening in the bushes and trees, and at my feet was a large hole six or eight feet across. In the hole were the mangled bodies of three Frenchmen. Against the back of the hole on the side nearest me leaned one of the bodies, nearly bolt upright, with the head and neck almost gone. The body of one of the other men presented a sight scarcely less ghastly. The combined odor of the high explosive gas, which still lingered there, and the decaying bodies, sent me hurriedly away.[23]

Back at the company's position, Jackson informed Ashwood of the scene. "A few minutes later, when Buck [Ashwood] was summoning a work detail, I lay low—it was to bury the dead men, I knew."[24]

The withdrawal of the French troops along this sector created, yet again, a gap between the recently arrived 83rd Company and the two 95th Company platoons. During the night, panicked runners informed Major Sibley of the French withdrawal. Private Joseph Rendinell, serving under First Lieutenant Ralph Marshall's 3rd Battalion, 6th Marine Regiment's intelligence section, witnessed Sibley's reply when he learned of the French retreat, "Well, I can't help that. Let them go through. We have no orders to retreat," Sibley demanded.[25] He directed Marshall to take Rendinell to Lucy-le-Bocage and secure definitive information regarding this French retreat.

Inside Lucy-le-Bocage, Rendinell and Marshall looked for the 1st Battalion, 6th Marines' command post. The town was under artillery fire. Several shells had already exploded when the momentary scream of an incoming shell pierced the air. A sudden blinding flash and ear-splitting explosion scattered masonry fragments of a nearby wall. The concussion threw Rendinell into a nearby French soldier as he walked adjacent to the wall. The blast also knocked Marshall to the ground. As Rendinell regained his senses, everything around him came back into focus. "I got up and shook myself to see if I was all there and the lieutenant says, 'You don't need to worry no more. You wrote home and told your mother the Germans did not make the shell with your address on it, didn't you?'" Despite the narrow escape, Rendinell amusingly replied, "Yes, but they are sure knocking next door."[26]

The haggard soldiers of Company E, 2nd Battalion, 2nd Engineers, occupying Lucy-le-Bocage, had endured shellfire all day. They now braved another bombardment, which further pulverized the village's already crumbling buildings. The company suffered eighteen casualties from the enemy's continuous barrage of the town that day.[27] Darkness offered no respite for the engineers in Lucy-le-Bocage as German batteries continued bombarding the village.

Despite the extreme danger, the cooks assigned to E Company left their shelter and salvaged pots, pans, spoons and other utensils from the damaged homes abandoned by the town's residents. The mess crew established a galley inside one of the few houses still intact and cooked whatever food they found despite the incoming fire. The aroma of food and coffee filled the corridors of the broken village well into the night. During interludes in the shellfire, the mess crew carried food and hot coffee to their shell-weary comrades holding Lucy-le-Bocage.[28]

Around 10:00 P.M., the 55th Company and the 5th Marines' Headquarters Company holding the front at Les Mares Farm looked up in the sky to the north after a loud pop shattered the comparative quiet. Suddenly, a series of arching lights illuminated the entire area as they hissed in their descent in front of the farm. From the shelter of dugouts and haylofts in and around the property, the Marines watched the flickering light with a renewed curiosity.

Suddenly, more German signal rockets crashed to the ground and engulfed several haystacks in the field in front of the American line. The flames grew higher and danced along the horizon, putting everyone on alert. Private Wayne French and his comrades watched the burning piles of hay glow with a shimmering light several hundred meters out in front of their position.[29]

Against the backdrop of the fire, the silhouette of an enemy raiding party appeared. The Germans set the haystacks ablaze to illuminate the American's position. The tactic, however, backfired as the Marines easily spotted the German's movement and unleashed a blistering volume of gunfire. According to French, "A lively and almost good natured scrimmage began, but it was in dead earnest."[30] The crack of rifle fire developed into a roaring cacophony.

Just east of the farm's buildings, the two squads of Captain Frank Whitehead's 5th Marines' Headquarters Company poured enfilading fire into the flank of the German assault. The concentrated gunfire lasted only a few seconds. The shouts of sergeants ordering men to cease-fire once again restored tranquility along the line.[31] "We drove them back, keeping the ground before us clear and open," recalled French.[32] "When they came they would have to come in the face of the fire of hundreds of sharpshooters, trained to a hair, who had lived all their lives for that one moment and thought of no other."[33] The flames of the burning haystacks crackled in the distance throughout the night, and the farm's defenders remained on alert in anticipation of another attack.

For General Richard Von Conta's 4th Reserve Corps of German troops, the day's shortcomings reflected the waning nature of the drive. The

June 3rd Chapter VI

German 197th and 237th Division's attempts to reach Les Mares Farm and Bois de Veuilly failed. The elaborate consolidation of positions in Belleau Wood by the 461st Regiment suggested a slowing impetus, which altered the nature of the offensive. The ambition of the German 7th Army's drive in this region had changed, a fact reiterated by the German Crown Prince:

> In view of the situation, my Army Group Staff as early as June 3 opposed the continuation of the offensive in the form of open warfare. The attack must not be resumed except after systematic preparation and then only at a particularly favorable point, or in parts of the line where local straightening out was necessary. The resumption of the offensive in a south-westerly direction was to await the result of the attack on the southern front of the 18th Army.[34]

Early in the morning of June 4th, Von Conta tried to perpetuate an aggressive spirit among his ranks even as the advance stymied. He now realized the need for obtaining ground conducive for a defensive posture. His corps order predicated on the changing stance of the 7th Army's efforts:

> We are compelled to temporarily assume the defensive after positions most suitable for this purpose are captured. I insist that all commanders inform their troops, leaving no doubt in their minds, that our attack up to this time had passed far beyond the objectives that were first assigned, and had achieved far greater success than had been anticipated. The offensive spirit must be maintained even though a temporary lull in the attack seems to exist.[35]

Further proof that the momentum of the Blücher Offensive had vacillated was the lacked regiments and battalions categorized as first-class assault units present in Von Conta's 4th Reserve Corps. Fifty-seven-year-old General Major Otto Von Diepenbroick-Grüter's 10th Infantry Division was Von Conta's only first-class assault unit still occupying the front. The 10th Division, however, had suffered horrendous casualties since May 27th. The 47th Infantry, which was supposed to number approximately 2,550 riflemen, lost twenty-eight percent of its men in six days.[36] Five companies of the regiment were without a single officer. The regiment's 2nd Battalion could only muster a single company out of the remaining soldiers of what had once been four companies. The regimental commander reasoned, "I no longer consider the regiment able to attack."[37]

Worse yet, the rifle companies of the 398th Regiment averaged only forty men each, and they did not have enough troops to man the company's light machine guns.³⁸ The 398ᵗʰ Infantry's commander stated, "The troops are not fit for further attacks."³⁹ The commanding officer of the 6ᵗʰ Grenadier Regiment theorized, "It appears necessary that the troops be withdrawn out of range of the hostile fire and again refreshed thru the timely replacement of officers and men and given new training from the fundamentals up."⁴⁰ The 10ᵗʰ Division's artillery commander concluded his regiment needed at least three weeks rest to replenish their losses.⁴¹

Von Conta had two additional units of first class assault troops in reserve, but they too were exhausted and depleted since the initiation of the offensive on May 27ᵗʰ. The other three divisions along the 4ᵗʰ Reserve Corps' front were not categorized as attack units but merely designated as sector-holding divisions—further suggesting a reason for the temporary halt of offensive efforts in this area. At midnight, Von Conta delivered a corps order to his units, which made two crucial points:

1. The attack by the right flank of the 7ᵗʰ Army will be continued. Group Conta will be responsible for the flank protection of this attack. To accomplish this, the corps will fight for a position that is especially suited for defense. Such a position lies in the line: Veuilly – Marigny – La Voie du Chatel – Hill 201, about 1 kilometer west of Chateau Thierry.
2. The time for the attack will be ordered later. The attack will not occur before June 7ᵗʰ. Reconnaissance and preparations will be started at once.⁴²

Von Conta's directive was a significant development since it abruptly changed the scope of the offensive along this sector of the German 7ᵗʰ Army's drive. The immediate goal shifted from reaching Paris and instead focused on comparatively modest, local objectives which ultimately, albeit briefly, changed the posture of the German army that the Americans were about to face.

The battle, from this point, became a struggle for local control, and the momentum of the offensive adjusted accordingly along Von Conta's front. Americans, however, still occupied the objectives Von Conta's established for his troops.

---

[1] Operations of 2ⁿᵈ Field Artillery Brigade, Box 81, RG 120.9.3, NARA College Park, MD.
[2] Kean, *Dear Marraine,* 94.
[3] Ibid, 94-95.
[4] Wahl, Sector North-east of Chateau Thierry, Box 79, RG 120.9.3, NARA College Park, MD.
[5] *Records of the Second Division (Regular)* Volume 6, N.P.

June 3rd Chapter VI

---

[6] *Records of the Second Division (Regular)* Volume 8, N.P. and Summary of Events of Battery E, 15th Field Artillery, Box 84, RG 120.9.3, Second Division File, Records of the AEF, NARA College Park, MD.
[7] *Records of the Second Division (Regular)* Volume 8, N.P.
[8] *Records of the Second Division (Regular)* Volume 5, N.P.
[9] War Diary and Annexes 1st 2nd and 3rd Battalion, 47th Infantry 3 June 1918, *Translation of War Diaries of German Units,* Vol. 1.
[10] Ibid.
[11] War Diary and Annexes 237th Division 4 June 1918, *Translation of War Diaries of German Units,* Vol. 4.
[12] *Records of the Second Division (Regular)* Volume 8, N.P.
[13] Kean, *Dear Marraine,* 95.
[14] Ibid, 96.
[15] Ibid.
[16] Field Message from Lieutenant Colonel Davis to Major Bailey at 4:15 A.M., June 4, 1918, Box 82, RG 120.9.3, Records of the American Expeditionary Forces, NARA College Park, MD.
[17] Jackson, *His Time in Hell,* 95.
[18] Ibid.
[19] Ibid..
[20] Ibid.
[21] Ibid.
[22] Ibid.
[23] Ibid, 96.
[24] Ibid, 96.
[25] Rendinell and Pattullo, *One Man's War,* 95.
[26] Ibid, 95-96.
[27] Burton, *History of the Second Engineers 1916-1919,* 43.
[28] Ibid.
[29] Hamilton and Corbin, *Echoes From Over There,* 60.
[30] Ibid.
[31] *The Aisne Defensive,* Whitehead to ABMC, Box 190, RG 117.4.2, NARA College Park, MD.
[32] Hamilton and Corbin, *Echoes From Over There,* 60.
[33] Ibid.
[34] Wilhelm, Crown prince of Germany, *My War Experiences,* 323.
[35] War Diary and Annexes IV Corps 4 June 1918, *Translation of War Diaries of German Units,* Vol. 1.
[36] War Diary and Annexes 10th Division 4 June 1918, *Translation of War Diaries of German Units,* Vol. 1.
[37] Ibid.

[38] Thomason, *Second Division Northwest of Chateau Thierry,* Unpublished manuscript, Alfred M. Gray Research Library, Quantico, VA.
[39] War Diary and Annexes 10th Division 4 June 1918, *Translation of War Diaries of German Units,* Vol. 1.
[40] Ibid.
[41] Thomason, *Second Division Northwest of Chateau Thierry,* Unpublished manuscript, Alfred M. Gray Research Library, Quantico, VA.
[42] War Diary and Annexes IV Corps 4 June 1918, *Translation of War Diaries of German Units,* Vol. 1

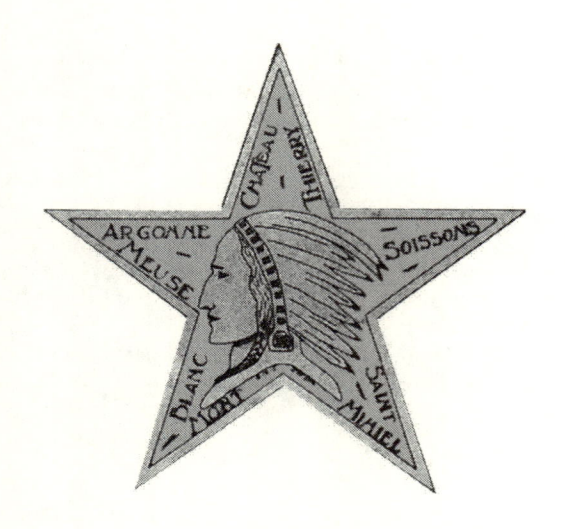

JUNE 4ᵀᴴ

June 4th Chapter I

Our artillery was making the most of the opportunity for unhampered firing and the night was illuminated so strongly by our own guns that it was possible to read fine print four out of every five seconds during the evening.
-First Lieutenant Wendell Westover Company A, 5th Machine Gun Battalion

By June 4th, The German 197th Division of General Von Conta's 4th Reserve Corps occupied a line from Veuilly la Poterie to Hill 165. From this position, the left flank of the 197th stood across the northern slopes of Hill 142 where it established liaison with the right flank of the Lieutenant General Albano Von Jacobi's 237th Division. Jacobi's line stretched to the southeast and encompassed Belleau Wood where the division's 461st Infantry consolidated its gains. From Belleau Wood, elements of General Otto von Diepenbroick-Grüter's German 10th Division extended the line east through the village of Bouresches which was held by Germann soldiers of the 3rd Battalion, 398th Infantry.

The German line, however, had strategic weaknesses. Fifty-seven-year-old Colonel Ernst Bernhard Victor Georg, commanding the German 210th Infantry Brigade of the 197th Division, summarized the situation on June 4th in the following memo sent to division headquarters:

> I have this morning inspected the positions and I reported to. . . . . That to remain in it any longer would mean at least the loss of hill 142, possibly also of the village of Champillon, the strips of woods east thereof as well as the village of Lucy-le-Bocage. Being positioned on hill 142, the enemy maintains a steady fire on the terrain south of Bussiares and Lucy-le-Bocage affords him a view into the rear area of our position. At the present time, individuals are able to move about only with the greatest possible caution.[1]

Georg further reasoned that as long as the Americans possess the Bois de Veuilly, the creek extending north from Marigny-en-Orxois, the Bois de Champillon, and other positions dubbed vital for Von Conta's 4th Reserve Corps to maintain a defense, the possibility of an unobserved counter-attack against the German line remained a real threat. These circumstances became a reality for General Von Conta's troops during the next forty-eight hours.[2]

During the night of June 3-4, the front held by Major General Bundy's 2nd Division shrunk to a more manageable line when Major Frank Whitley's 1st Battalion, 9th Infantry withdrew from the division's right. Initially, elements of the U.S. Army's 30th Infantry, 3rd Division operating near

June 4th Chapter I

Chateau Thierry was to relieve Whitley's men, but that did not occur. Colonel Preston Brown, the 2nd Division Chief of Staff, believed the presence of dismounted French Cavalry, still occupying Bois de la Morette, was a sufficient force to hold that position and did not require Whitley's battalion to await relief by the 30th Infantry.

Before the sun appeared above the eastern horizon, Whitley's tired and exhausted troops took to the road for yet another hike. They moved out of the line stretching from Le Thiolet to Bois la Morette and headed for La Longue Farm three kilometers southwest of Coupru to constitute part of the division's reserve.[3] Whitley's men spent the previous few days in constant movement. They endured long periods of sleeplessness, interrupted by moments of terror under enemy shellfire, and a general lack of food and water.

Since the enemy maintained an increasing rate of artillery fire throughout the night, nerves remained on high alert along the 4th Brigade front. Twenty-six-year-old First Lieutenant Lothar Reymond Long commanding the 6th Machine Gun Battalion's intelligence section at the battalion's headquarters in Montgrivault-la-Petit Farm, looked forward to the first real sleep allotted him to in days. The rest, however, did not last as the length of time he hoped. Long remembered:

> I was deliriously tired, and flopped for a couple of hours in an old farmhouse and like a darn fool took off not only all my equipment, but my shoes to sleep. Suddenly I felt someone grab and punch the hell out of me, and Major Cole was yelling 'Long, Long! Get up quick! A German patrol is headed right this-way' Say, you oughta seen Squib R. Long trying to put on his tin lid, pistol, dispatch case and shoes all at once. And lord almighty, when you get bounced out of a dead, dog-tired sleep that hour of night your morale is way down in the bottom of your shoes. We grabbed up what men of mine were around and beat it out of that farmyard like hell (it was right down in what was the front line at that particular moment—the line sort of see sawed around getting itself adjusted to topographical features those first few days) and ducked into the wheat. It was so darn dark our guns couldn't see where to fire on the patrol, and I guess the Germans didn't know how far ahead of their lines they were. There were a beaucoup bunch of 'em, though, and they prowled around the farm for a while, while we lay in the grain just a little ways off, with grenades and pistols ready. And then the first thing we knew they were gone—and the opportunity to wipe out a gang of Dutchmen lost.[4]

June 4th Chapter I

The arrival of Major Edmund Zane's 4th Machine Gun Battalion at approximately 6:20 A.M., gave the 2nd Division all of its machine gun assets. Zane's exhausted men eventually moved into Bois des Fonds Jars Ferme one kilometer east of Montreuil-aux-Lions. Inside those woods, the machine gunners along with 1st Battalion, 9th Infantry, constituted part of the division reserve. That status provided a well-deserved rest for Zane's men after an exhausting and frustrating three-day venture to the battlefront.

First Lieutenant Wendell Westover and Company A, 5th Machine Gun Battalion left Domptin before dawn where they stayed in reserve the day before, and traveled to Coupru just over a kilometer north. The previous afternoon, Captain Andrew Bruce ordered Westover, to scout the town of Coupru for the company's billeting arrangements.

First Lieutenant Lothar Long commanded the 6th Machine Gun Battalion's intelligence section. Photo credit: Madeleine Johnson.

When Westover returned during the night, the company prepared to depart Domptin. The darkness was alive with the thunder of the newly arrived American guns situated around Domptin. "Our artillery was making the most of the opportunity for unhampered firing and the night was illuminated so strongly by our own guns that it was possible to read fine print four out of every five seconds during the evening. The activity of the batteries near the village was bound to cause retaliation before long, yet Miller and I were too much impressed with the prospect of sleeping in good beds to worry."[5]

Once the company arrived in Coupru, Westover and another officer wasted no time in claiming their sleeping quarters, "We selected a corner room on the side of the house facing the Boche lines, laid our gas masks within reach, and were asleep almost at once."[6]

From their wooded positions just north and south of the Paris-Metz highway, guns of the 12th Field Artillery and part of the 17th Field Artillery Regiment bombarded the rear of the German line several kilometers to the north with interdiction fire. The 3rd Battalion, 17th Field Artillery remained

June 4th Chapter I

only a few hours away and eventually supplemented the division's firepower with their heavy 155mm guns.[7]

Battery C, 2nd Battalion, 17th Field Artillery moved into position during the night after being mistakenly led to a location within a kilometer of the front line by a disoriented guide. Somehow, they miraculously realized their predicament and pulled back without enemy observation. By morning, Battery C's guns occupied the correct designated positions and initiated bombardment of the enemy front.[8]

At 2:00 A.M., observers reported the presence of a large concentration of enemy troops near the town of Hautvesnes about four kilometers north of Les Mares Farm. Colonel Paul Malone, commanding the 23rd Infantry, relayed this information to the French and 2nd Division.[9] The available batteries of the 17th Field Artillery situated near La Loge Farm and in the woods northeast of Paris Farm, joined several 155mm batteries of the French Field Artillery, to place a thunderous barrage on this area. These guns also bombarded the area northwest of Bussiares.[10] The muzzle flashes from cannons tucked into the woods lit the southern horizon along the Paris-Metz up like a lightning storm.

The 75mm guns of the 12th Field Artillery also registered their fire during the night.[11] Sergeant Joseph J. Gleeson of Battery D, 2nd Battalion, 12th Field Artillery, claimed the American guns initiated a barrage at 3:00 A.M. and maintained their fire for the next six hours.[12] Once the artillery of the 2nd Division commenced fire, some of their rounds fell short. According to Corporal Warren Jackson of the 95th Company:

> Few of the shells went more than a hundred yards beyond our lines, and some hit in our positions. Knowing the experienced Germans outnumbered us, continually harassed by their artillery fire, and then to have our own guns threatening us with annihilation every moment—the anguish we suffered could not be described. What in the world could be the cause of this bombardment by our own guns? Why was the range not raised? We asked one another the questions in vain.[13]

During the day, Captain Oscar Cauldwell commanding the 95th Company was wounded by shell fragments. He turned command over to First Lieutenant Frederick Wheeler who had already suffered two wounds during the past two days. Wheeler held command until he was wounded a third time later that day.[14] Command then fell to twenty-three-year-old Second Lieutenant Morgan Reagan Mills Jr., a 1917 graduate of the Virginia Military Institute student from Richmond, Virginia.

Within twenty-five minutes German artillery batteries responded to the barrage on their lines. Incoming rounds crashed through the treetops in Bois

June 4th Chapter I

Left: First Lieutenant Frederick C. Wheeler of the 95th Company was wounded three times before he reluctantly agreed to be evacuated. Photo credit: Yale University. Right: Captain Oscar Cauldwell, seen here as a student at the U.S. Naval Academy, commanded the 95th Company. Photo credit: U.S. Naval Academy.

de Veuilly near the junction between the 5th Marines and 23rd Infantry.[15] The sporadic shelling was not concentrated and did little more than interrupt an already abbreviated rest for Lieutenant Colonel Wise's battalion.

The burnt haystacks, still smoldering in front of Les Mares farm following the enemy's failed raid hours earlier, permeated the night air with the strong scent of smoke. "A moon came up," remembered First Lieutenant Elliot Cooke, "and an occasional sentry whanged away at some shadow in the wheat, but otherwise nothing much happened."[16]

German shellfire also disturbed the sleeping troops of Company A, 5th Machine Gun Battalion in Coupru. The scream of incoming German 77mm rounds jostled First Lieutenant Wendell Westover and his comrades from a delightful rest. "One of the shells clipped a corner off the upper cornice of the house above our room, a second struck the house next door; the other two passed over into the fields beyond. The whine of their approach awoke us! Before the first one struck we were on our feet, gas masks in hand, and headed for the stairs leading into the wine cellar."[17]

The officers billeted in the house listened from the shelter of the basement for the approach of more shells. Convinced the barrage was complete, they headed back up to their room and went back to sleep. "Hardly had we begun to doze when another salvo woke us in the same manner," Westover remembered. "This time we were quicker and had

June 4th Chapter I

reached a position half way down stairs before the shells struck nearby buildings."[18]

During the night, Lieutenant Colonel Joseph Davis, commanding the 15th Field Artillery, grew increasingly frustrated over the whereabouts of Major Benjamin Bailey's 1st Battalion. Davis could not wait any longer and dispatched a heated message at 4:15 A.M. from regimental headquarters in Domptin. The courier sent to deliver the dispatch hunted in the darkness near 1st Battalion's reported location south of Mont de Bonneil. Upon finding Bailey, the runner presented him with Davis's fiery note stating:

> Coordinates just brought back by my adjutant. None received prior to that. No liaison agents from your headquarters have yet reported. No telephone line from your P.C. has yet been brought into this P.C. Adjutant 1st Battalion 9th Infantry informed me at 3:30 a.m. that they (Battalion Headquarters, 1st Battalion, 9th Infantry) were not in liaison with you. Please correct foregoing in so far as still requiring correction. 1st Battalion 9th Infantry has left its place in 2nd line and U.S. troops have relieved them, so they state. They state that 30th Infantry went in on right of position vacated by them. Get in liaison immediately with infantry in front of you. Send me to reach me before 10 am report as to location of your echelon. Report promptly when your batteries have finished adjustment fire on a base point.[19]

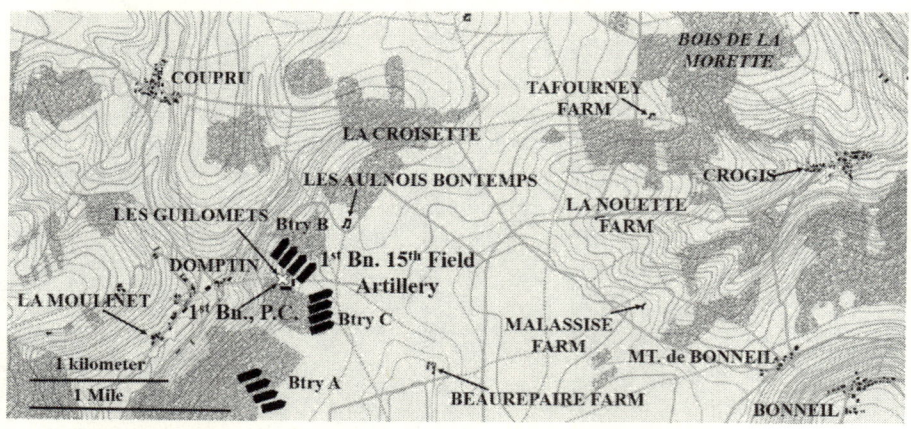

Battery positions of 1st Battalion, 15th Field Artillery on early June 4th.

Bailey immediately dispatched First Lieutenant Robert Kean to establish liaison with the infantry beyond their position. According to Kean, "Major Bailey asked me to go down to the French front and find out exactly where they were, as we had to know before we could protect them with artillery fire."[20] The young officer selected Corporal Oron L. Ladd and another man to accompany Kean to Mount de Bonneil. The sun, rising early in the northern French summer sky, gently illuminated the open fields dotted

June 4th Chapter I

with clumps of forest along the banks of the Marne. The three men had a significant distance to travel, but also had the difficult task of locating the French troops and then deciphering and relaying information to the battalion regarding their location.[21]

---

[1] 2nd Division summary of intelligence 210th Infantry Brigade to 197th Infantry Division 4 June 1918, Box 2-8, RG 120.9.3, Second Division File, Records of the AEF, NARA College Park, MD. Note: The reference to the Americans being on Hill 142 does not suggest the Americans occupied the entirety of the elongated hillock known as Hill 142, but rather occupied the southern portion of the hill at a point denoted on the map as '142.' From that particular point, the ground to the north declined towards the position occupied by the Germans. The attack on Hill 142, which occurred two days later, involved the Americans driving north from the point '142' denoted on the map toward the German-held woods.
[2] Ibid.
[3] *Records of the Second Division (Regular)* Volume 1, N.P.
[4] Correspondence from Lothar Long to his brother Albert Stoneman Long, 29 July 1918, Provided by Lothar Long's great-niece Madeleine Johnson.
[5] Westover, *Suicide Battalions*, 114-15.
[6] Ibid.
[7] History of the 17th Field Artillery, Box 85, RG 120.9.3, NARA College Park, MD., and History of the 3rd Battalion 17th Field Artillery, Box 85, RG 120.9.3, NARA College Park, MD.
[8] *Records of the Second Division (Regular)* Volume 8, N.P.
[9] *Records of the Second Division (Regular)* Volume 5, N.P.
[10] *Records of the Second Division (Regular)* Volume 6, N.P.
[11] Wahl, George D., Diary of a Battery Commander, Box 79, RG 120.9.3, NARA College Park, MD.
[12] Spaulding and Wright, *The Second Division American Expeditionary Force in France 1917-1919*, 253.
[13] Jackson, *His Time in Hell, A Texas Marine in France*, 97.
[14] U.S. Marine Corps Muster Rolls, 1893-1940, Record Group 127, NARA, Washington, D.C.
[15] *Records of the Second Division (Regular)* Volumes 6, N.P.
[16] Cooke, "We Can Take It, We Attack," *Infantry Journal*, 6.
[17] Westover, *Suicide Battalions*, 115.
[18] Ibid, 115-16.
[19] Field Message from Davis to Bailey at 4:15 A.M., June 4, 1918, Box 82, RG 120.9.3, NARA College Park, MD.
Also cited in Robert Winthrop Kean, *Dear Marraine 1917-1919*, (Washington D.C.: Library of Congress, 1969), 96.
[20] Kean, *Dear Marraine*, 93.
[21] Ibid, 93-94.

June 4th Chapter II

The next thing I remember, I was lying in a small depression perhaps 75 yards east of the house, canteens and all, getting my breath, making sure I had all my arms and legs and perhaps not quite sure whether I was in this world or the next.
    -Corporal Lloyd E. Pike 2nd Platoon, 79th Company, 2nd Battalion, 6th Marines

During the night, orders summoned the Marines of the 66th and 17th Companies of Major Julius Turrill's 1st Battalion, 5th Marines from their reserve position along the northern outskirts of Marigny-en-Orxois, and they departed before dawn.[1] They were to be used to extend Turrill's line to the west. As the distant sun broke the horizon, the exhausted troops of the 17th and 66th Company hiked toward the cover of trees spanning the terrain between Marigny-en-Orxois and Bois de Veuilly to avoid enemy observation.

They passed a group of French soldiers fleeing woods. Private Onnie Cordes of the 17th Company recalled, "On our way, we came in contact with many French soldiers who were running and shouting 'Alley! Alley! Boche! Beaucoup Boche! most!' But we did not go to France to run back, so we just kept on going. We moved into where the French had been and planted several Chauchat squads to stop old Fritz, which we did."[2]

The departure of the last French troops along the line by 4:00 A.M. put the Marines against General Von Conta's 4th Reserve Corps which made up the depleted and exhausted 7th German Army.[3] While half of Turrill's battalion moved to reinforce the line, the 49th and 67th Companies remained in place along the outskirts of Marigny-en-Orxois.[4]

When twenty-three-year-old First Lieutenant Robert Wallace Blake's platoon of the 17th Company entered the Bois de Veuilly, they passed along the back of the 43rd Company of Wise's 2nd Battalion with no knowledge of their destination nor the reason for the sudden movement. According to Blake:

> We knew very little about what was going on. I never saw any written orders nor had a map nor received anything but the sketchiest of oral orders. The situation was changing too fast. We just walked through a wood, over the crest of a ridge, down the far side to the edge of the wood where I ran into Gunnery Sergeant Sid Thayer who later was commissioned, who said the Germans were across the field to the front. We relieved no one. We saw only two French soldiers wandering to the rear. We were on the left flank of the 2nd Division with no one visible on our left.[5]

June 4th Chapter II

The density of the woods and the predawn darkness complicated the single-file movement of Turrill's two companies. Each man clung to the pack of the comrade walking ahead of him to keep from becoming separated in the dark. Due to the increased ferocity of the enemy's shellfire during the past twenty-four hours, the 17th and 66th Companies raced to conceal themselves from view before dawn broke. "There were no trenches," according to twenty-three-year-old Private George William Budde of the 17th Company. "We hid ourselves in the woods as best we could or dug rifle pits to protect us against the enemy snipers and to do a little sniping of our own."[6]

Thirty-five-year-old Captain John Francis Burnes's 74th Company still held a thin line due to the dispatch of the company's 1st and 2nd Platoons days earlier to try and extend the 1st Battalion, 6th Marines' left flank west towards the right of the 5th Marines. The other two platoons of the company stretched the line near Lucy-le-Bocage with one platoon north and one along the southern outskirts of town.[7]

During the night, the battalion's effort to once again shift west further extended the company's front between Lucy-le-Bocage the Bois de Champillon.[8] By 3:30 A.M., the 74th Company's position, supported by a handful of French machine guns still in and around Lucy-le-Bocage, welcomed the return of one of Burnes' dispatched platoons. The reassignment of the platoon greatly bolstered the company's front and allowed them to extend the line northwest and tie in with the 75th Company.[9]

On the southern outskirts of Lucy-le-Bocage, Private Asa Smith of the 74th Company pulled watch during the night of June 3-4. Smith walked back and forth along the bounds of the village in the comparatively quiet predawn darkness, but the distant sound of battle and rustling leaves kept Smith nervously alert. As he walked along the gently rising ground between the town and the southwestern edge of Bois de Belleau, he unwittingly silhouetted himself against the backdrop of the moonlit sky. A single gunshot immediately emanated from Bois de Belleau and echoed across the open terrain. Simultaneously, a bullet buzzed past Smith, followed immediately by a second round before he realized he was the target of this fire.[10]

Adjacent to the 74th Company, Marines of the 75th Company remained hunkered in their earthen abodes. They came under sporadic and at times heavy, artillery fire throughout the night. Private Gus Gulberg and his friend, twenty-two-year-old Private Albert Francis Brennan, occupied part of the company line extending into the Bois de Champillon, roughly the same area where the 76th Company suffered heavy casualties the day before. According to Gulberg:

> This particular position had been hit pretty hard by artillery fire and as we came in the German artillery was firing battery salvos. There

were a few French soldiers in this wood walking around with rosary beads in their hands saying prayers, while shrapnel rained all over the place. Brennan and myself dug in for dear life and in a remarkably short time, we were about four feet underground. We hugged the sides of our hole all night while the enemy gunners pounded us with everything they had. How could we ever hope to get out of this, thought we.[11]

By 3:30 A.M., the sun's faint appearance along the eastern horizon revealed that the haystacks in front of Les Mares Farm were still smoldering following the German's failed infiltration the previous night. Smoke hovered over the treetops and fields along the road to Bussiares. First Lieutenant Elliot Cooke watched from the northern fringe of Bois Veuilly as shells from one of the American or French batteries slammed into the distant field adding to the smoke covering the area. "Our own artillery moved in under the cover of darkness," remembered Cooke, "and at daylight began to register out in front. It was a dumb trick because their shells soon set the wheat on fire and smoke blotted out any observation beyond a couple of hundred yards. The Heinies were handed on a silver platter a perfect smoke screen behind which to form for an attack."[12]

Despite the low visibility that morning, Wise's battalion spotted a mass of Germans soldiers at 4:20 A.M. moving over the horizon near Hill 165 one and a half kilometers north of Les Mares Farm. This troop concentration was a renewed effort by the German 26th Jäger Battalion, 273rd Infantry, 197th Division, to capture Les Mares Farm.[13]

Other units of the German 28th Ersatz Infantry, 197th Division, succeeded in taking the village of Veuilly la Poterie the previous night, and by dawn June 4th, they filtered into patches of woods fronting the 43rd and 18th Companies in Bois de Veuilly.[14] Captain Charley Dunbeck, commanding the 43rd Company, immediately sent a runner with a message and a sketch of the area for an artillery barrage.[15] The Marines waited with anticipation for the fusillade of American shellfire to fall on the approaching Germans.

Across the 2nd Battalion, 5th Marines' front, men steadied themselves for the appearance of advancing enemy troops. At Les Mares Farm, snipers had been out since daybreak along the road fronting the farm's property.[16] Smoke from the burning haystacks continued to linger across the open pasture, but enough of the haze had cleared to give the Marines a clear field of fire. The batteries of the 2nd Division, responding to the German's movement, shelled the fields in front of Bois de Veuilly.

Marines at Les Mares Farm watched the projectiles inundate enemy positions throughout the early morning, and they were thrilled to witness revenge exacted upon on them. Before 8:00 A.M., Dunbeck relayed a message to Wise stating, "Barrage appeared to be about 200 yards in width, and between 700 and 800 yards to our front. It appeared to be an excellent barrage and was in the right place, although it could be much wider extending eastward. For a barrage against an attack it should be much lowered to about 300 yds in our front."[17]

Beyond the 18th Company's position, Captain Lester Wass's Marines spotted enemy soldiers infiltrating the distant woods. Wass's men identified gaps in the distant tree line where German troops moved about freely. When Wise visited the 18th Company during his inspection of the battalion front that morning, Wass pointed out the movement of the Germans in the distant woods. According to Wise:

> He reported that the clump of woods just out in front of him was full of Germans. It was only about seven hundred yards away. Some of his men had telescopic sights and had been sniping at those Germans since daybreak. They had knocked down nineteen he reported. He pointed out to me an opening the Germans had cut in the hedge on the edge of these woods—evidently for their guns to be hauled through when they advanced. From time to time as I stood there I could see individual German soldiers walking past.[18]

That morning, Wass instructed Private Alfred Schiani and his three-man automatic rifle team to move just beyond the company's position. The captain instructed them to crawl through the grain field in an isolated and concealed position and place a large volume of harassing fire on the woods through which German soldiers freely passed. As soon as Schiani and his crew moved a few hundred meters into the field, they attracted a blistering volley of German machine gun fire. Bullets hummed, cracked and hissed overhead and kicked up the dirt around the gun crew.

Schiani and his comrades sank to the ground as flat as possible. The screams of Wass and others back along the company's position, audible between pulsating bursts of enemy Maxims, urged the detachment to pull back.[19] The three men, lying as flat as possible against the dirt, slithered back toward the wood. Bullets passed through the stalks of grain less than a foot above their heads, but the returned to the tree line unscathed.

East of Bois de Veuilly, Second Lieutenant Lucius Lyle 2nd Platoon, 55th Company, and men of the 5th Marines' Headquarters Company spent the morning concealed in their foxholes along Les Mares Farm trying to avoid the attention of enemy artillery spotters. Lyle's tired, hungry, and sleep-deprived platoon grew agitated at their inactivity.[20]

During the morning, some of the men from the 5th Marines' Headquarters Company spotted Germans infiltrating into the northern-most point of Bois des Mares about 1400 meters north of their position. "These groups came down the road from Bussiares and dropped off into a sunken

June 4th Chapter II

path opposite the northern end of the woods," recalled Captain Frank Whitehead.[21]

The morning began with overcast skies, but after the sun cleared the horizon Marine snipers from the regimental headquarters company watched with steadied patients for enemy soldiers to appear in the distance. The men, lying prone in their foxholes, observed as sharpshooters carefully chose their unsuspecting victims. Those who had binoculars watched with curious excitement to see if their comrades were on target. This spectacle went on throughout the entire morning."[22]

French and American batteries, firing from positions several kilometers behind the front, maintained a steady bombardment of the Germans all day. In response to the American and French artillery, the Germans shelled the 2nd Division front with renewed intensity. The enemy guns created a deadly gauntlet along the ground between the front line companies and battalion and regimental headquarters of the 2nd Division. Rounds crashed around the command post of the 6th Machine Gun Battalion's left group positioned in a clump of woods southeast of Champillon.

Captain Frank Whitehead. Photo credit: NARA.

Delivering messages to the left group, Private William Fullington, a runner with the 77th Company, looked with envy upon his comrades who sought cover from the intense enemy artillery fire. "This running job is hell," Fullington confided. "They keep me carrying messages night and day while the other fellows are sheltered in their holes."[23] The 15th and 23rd Companies, 6th Machine Gun Battalion, comprising the left group, had suffered several casualties from enemy artillery over the past twenty-four hours. Because of the losses, several muleteers from the battalion's supply train moved up as replacements for gun crews.

Other members of the battalion's headquarters company patrolled the length of telephone lines, looking to fix sections of wire cut by enemy shellfire.[24] During the morning, Hotchkiss gun crews ran dangerously low on ammunition. Thirty-one-year-old Captain John Patrick Harvis, the battalion's quartermaster, braved the heavy incoming fire with several men to haul ammunition carts up a roadway within complete view of the enemy. Miraculously, Harvis and his Marines performed this feat unharmed.[25]

German artillery fire also fell near Captain Dwight Smith's 82nd Company, positioned in the woods south of Hill 142. The frequency of the enemy barrage dissuaded Smith's men from venturing too far from their dugouts. They passed the day with relative inactivity except for company sharpshooters who preyed upon German soldiers carelessly moving about in the open. At 9:30 A.M., enemy shells landed several hundred meters north of the 82nd Company's position.

The bombardment fell only thirty meters in front of the German soldiers of the 9th Company, 3rd Battalion, 460th German Infantry. The Germans of the 9th Company quickly realized that these were not French or American shells landing dangerously close, but short rounds from their own batteries. The proximity of the 9th Company's position to the American line prevented them from firing a signal into the air to notify their guns of the miscalculated range, so shell continued falling dangerously close to the German forward picket line.[26]

The Marines of the 83rd Company hardly took notice of the enemy's misdirected artillery fire. Several men slept through it. Others satisfied their hunger with hardtack rations which were nearly unpalatable without something to drink, but most of the men had long consumed all the water in their canteens. The arduous task of fetching refilling canteens for the company fell to some unfortunate individuals. "Water is very scarce," remembered Private Harry Collins, "and men going after water have to run the chance of being hit by German shells."[27] The only source of water was in the village of Champillon or La Voie du Chatel, which required the wretched souls acquiring the precious resource to cross between 500 meters and a kilometer of open fields under enemy observation.

From his command post at La Voie du Chatel, Colonel Catlin watched his men undertake this daring task. "In the midst of all this grim, tense seriousness there was something irresistibly ludicrous in the sight of our tireless runners hurrying back and forth all covered over with tin-ware, as they went for the precious water."[28]

Supplying water for members of the 2nd Platoon, 79th Company holding the line east of Triangle Farm fell inexplicably upon Corporal Lloyd Pike's shoulders. Enemy artillery made Pike's job especially hazardous. German batteries had inundated pre-registered targets from Lucy-le-Bocage to Triangle Farm since 8:00 A.M. that morning.[29]

Collecting the empty canteens and sliding them upon a wooden stick by the chains that connected the lid to the body of the container, Pike crawled through the undergrowth behind the platoon toward Triangle Farm. "The sun's rays glinting on these bright canteens may well have been visible to the enemy. However, I reached the house and found the well was in a

June 4th Chapter II

backyard enclosed in a high chicken wire fence some 12 or 14 feet high," remembered Pike.[30] With the back of the building facing the frontlines, the only way to gain access to the well was through the house. He used the bucket hanging on the well to draw water and painstakingly filled the canteens. According to Pike:

> I had filled the canteens and restrung them on the stick, preparing to go back through the house and return to my unit when an enemy artillery battery fired, followed immediately by the shrill rising whine of shells coming fast in my direction. There was only a split second between the sound of the incoming shells and their arrival. They slammed into the back of the house. Rocks and dust flew all over and the entire back of the house just collapsed.[31]

Exiting the house before it collapsed due to the extensive damage caused by repeated shellfire, Pike ran as fast as his adrenaline-induced legs, and water-filled cargo allowed him to move. "The next thing I remember, I was lying in a small depression perhaps 75 yards east of the house, canteens and all, getting my breath, making sure I had all my arms and legs and perhaps not quite sure whether I was in this world or the next. In due time I continued on my way back to my platoon, none the worse for wear and with full canteens for all hands," recalled Pike.[32]

Access to water also became a significant problem for the 78th Company who also utilized the well at the farmhouse in Triangle Farm. After dark proved to be the safest time for the men to secure water resupply, but even at night, the task remained perilous. According to Corporal Frank McClelland of the 78th Company, "One or two of us in our platoons would carry a bunch of canteens back each night and fill them at a well in the rear. We had to be very careful in carrying the metal canteens because just a tinkle of sound would likely bring a burst of machine gun fire."[33]

The previous night, members of the 78th Company, under cover of darkness, crept approximately 150 feet ahead of the line northwest of Triangle Farm to dig a sniper's post, which overlooked the village of Bouresches. The Marines of Captain Robert Messersmith's 78th Company manned this forward post in shifts and made reliefs only in the darkness.[34] According to McClelland, "Our position was well covered by enemy rifle, machine gun, and artillery fire, so we had to move cautiously even at night."[35]

The morning of June 4 was relatively quiet along the 78th Company's front. Members of Second Lieutenant Henry Leslie Eddy's 2nd Platoon spent much of the morning hidden from German artillery spotters and took advantage of the inactivity to nap. Around 9:30 A.M., Eddy arose from his command post on the south slope of the wooded ravine between Triangle

June 4th Chapter II

Farm and Bouresches to check on his men. He paid little attention to the risk of attracting machine gun fire from enemy positions in the distance.

Eddy returned safely a short time later and occupied the fighting hole he shared with thirty-six-year-old Gunnery Sergeant George William Hopke, a German immigrant and eight-year veteran of the Marine Corps. Twenty-year-old Private Joseph Elmer King, Eddy's orderly, took refuge in the same dugout.[36]

As the tranquility of the early morning persisted, Eddy removed his cumbersome helmet and the uncomfortable respirator hanging around his neck.[37] Eddy and King soon engaged in a casual conversation about the art of shooting at planes. Hopke, a steward of discipline, tactfully reminded Eddy about the necessity of wearing his helmet and gas mask at all times. Modestly, Eddy acknowledged the gunnery sergeant's inflexible, but necessary guidance, and satirically expounded that if he could rationalize the misery the same way that Hopke was able to deal with it, then he too would be happy.[38]

Second Lieutenant Henry Eddy commanded the 2nd Platoon of the 78th Company. Photo credit: Library of Congress.

At the tail end of Eddy's comment, the distant sound of an incoming shell left the men only a split second to react before it exploded. King recalled, "While we were talking a shell burst about 100 feet from us. I ducked low as I could, but the shell burst just overhead and to the right."[39]

Before the smoke and dust settled, the Marines petulantly cursed the enemy's interruption of their so-far peaceful morning, but Eddy remained silent. King discovered the motionless officer with a gaping hole above his eye where a shell fragment passed entirely through his head and instantly killed him. King noted the time on his watch at 10:04 A.M. before heading to the company command post to report the incident to Captain Messersmith. Moving Eddy's body back for burial would inevitably attract enemy artillery fire, so they left him where he lay in the dugout. Members of his platoon covered the fallen twenty-three-year-old with a blanket, and Hopke immediately assumed command of the 2nd Platoon.[40]

305

June 4th Chapter II

[1] Correspondence Rockey to ABMC, 16 December 1926, Box 190, RG 117.4.2, NARA College Park, MD.
[2] Cordes, *The Immortal Division*, 8.
[3] Operations of 2nd Field Artillery Brigade, Box 81, RG 120.9.3, NARA College Park, MD.
[4] Correspondence Rockey to ABMC, 16 December 1926, NARA College Park, MD.
[5] Robert Wallace Blake, *From Belleau Wood to Bougainville The Oral History of Major General Robert Blake USMC and The Travel Journal of Rosselet Wallace Blake* (Bloomington: Author House, 2004), 13-14.
[6] "On the Heels of the Hun," *Recruiters Bulletin*, November 1918, 34.
[7] Diary of Asa J. Smith 74th Company 6th Regiment U.S. Marines, Alfred M. Gray Research Library, Quantico, VA.
[8] History of the 74th Company, compiled by Sergeant Carl W. Smith, Box 35, RG 127, NARA College Park, M.D.
[9] *Records of the Second Division (Regular)* Volume 5, N.P.
[10] Diary of Asa J. Smith 74th Company 6th Regiment U.S. Marines, Gray Research Library, Quantico, VA. Note: The French, due to the fall of Bouresches that afternoon evacuated Bois de Belleau, and the Germans were quickly filling the vacancy.
[11] Gulberg, *A War Diary*, 25.
[12] Cooke, "We Can Take It, We Attack," *Infantry Journal*, 6.
[13] War Diary and Annexes 197th Division 4 June 1918, *Translation of War Diaries of German Units*, Vol. 4.
[14] War Diary and Annexes 197th Division 3 June 1918, *Translation of War Diaries of German Units*, Vol. 4.
[15] *Records of the Second Division (Regular)* Volume 5, N.P.
[16] *The Aisne Defensive*, Whitehead to ABMC, Box 190, RG 117.4.2, NARA College Park, MD.
[17] *Records of the Second Division (Regular)* Volume 5, N.P.
[18] Wise and Frost, *A Marine Tells it to You*, 199.
[19] Schiani, *A Former Marine tells it like it was and is*, 22
[20] *The Aisne Defensive*, Whitehead to ABMC, Box 190, RG 117.4.2, NARA College Park, MD.
[21] Ibid.
[22] Ibid.
[23] Diary of William W. Fullington, Pvt. USMC, Alfred M. Gray Research Library, Quantico, VA.
[24] Curtis Jr., *History of the Sixth Machine Gun Battalion*, 15.

June 4th Chapter II

[25] Official Military Personnel File for Captain John Patrick Harvis, RG 127, NPRC St. Louis, MO.
[26] War Diary and Annexes 460th Infantry 4 June 1918, *Translation of War Diaries of German Units,* Vol. 4., and War Diary and Annexes 1st, 2nd, and 3rd Battalion 460th Infantry 4 June 1918, *Translation of War Diaries of German Units,* Vol. 4.
[27] Collins, *The War Diary of Corporal Harry Collins,* Entry for June 4, 1918.
[28] Catlin, *With the Help of God and a Few Marines,* 98.
[29] War Diary and Annexes 20th Infantry Brigade, 4 June 1918, *Translation of War Diaries of German Units,* Vol. 1.
[30] Pike, *The Battle For Belleau Woods, As I Remember It About 60 Years Later,* 10.
[31] Ibid.
[32] Ibid, 11.
[33] Frank McClelland, Story of My Life, Personal Papers collection, Alfred M. Gray Research Library, Quantico, VA.
[34] Ibid.
[35] Ibid.
[36] Burial File of Second Lieutenant Henry Leslie Eddy, Eye-witness statement by Private Joseph E. King, Box 1475, RG 92.9, Records of Graves Registration Services, NARA College Park, MD.
[37] Burial File of Second Lieutenant Henry Leslie Eddy, Eye-witness statements by Major Robert E. Messersmith and Private Joseph E. King, Box 1475, RG 92.9, Records of Graves Registration Services, NARA College Park, MD.
[38] Ibid.
[39] Ibid.
[40] Ibid.

June 4th Chapter III

I knew I had to get up out of that hole and I didn't want to do it. Nothing about me wanted to. Every inch of my anatomy shrank from being exposed to so many different kinds of death. My arm muscles acted like wet dish rags and my feet were numb, but somehow I did pull out of that hole and wriggle down to the forward line of men.
-First Lieutenant Elliott Cooke 18th Company, 2nd Battalion, 5th Marines

As the sun grew warmer through the morning cloud cover, Major General Omar Bundy and his Division staff at Montreuil-aux-Lions prepared for the anticipated 8:00 A.M. transfer of control of the sector from the French to the 2nd Division. For Brigadier General James Harbord, this transfer of command returned Major Benjamin Berry's 3rd Battalion, 5th Marines to the brigade's control after they spent the previous days as corps reserve.

Harbord remained uncertain about the liaisons between his units, and therefore welcomed the return of Berry's men. At 8:50 A.M., however, Colonel Preston Brown urged Harbord to delay returning the battalion to the brigade until they confirmed Major Franklin Whitley's 1st Battalion, 9th Infantry had completed their movement to the rear as division reserve.[1]

The previous few days were relatively uneventful for the 3rd Battalion, 5th Marines while they remained the French 21st Corps' reserve battalion—a stark contrast to their exhaustive march to the front. Second Lieutenant George Gordon, an army officer attached to the 16th Company remembered:

> While we remained in the woods as reserve battalion, we had nothing to do but lay around and wait for a call to go to any part of the line that might need relief or help. For several days, things were quiet as far as we were concerned. An aerial engagement was the liveliest attraction as a French flier and a Boche Fokker went into action with the two being the only contenders. They flew around in a circle as each tried to maneuver so as to get in back of the other and then pump their machine guns until they got results. This continued for several minutes with all on the ground keenly watching, as both tried every trick at his command to get to the coveted position.[2]

During the late morning, Berry's men hiked to the cover of some woods just over a kilometer south of Marigny-en-Orxois to rejoin the brigade.[3] At 12:50 P.M., Berry dispatched a runner to inform Colonel Wendell Neville of the battalion's new location.[4]

June 4th Chapter III

As the 4th Brigade's line stabilized, the 3rd Brigade established liaison with the French units east of the 2nd Division's front. First Lieutenant Robert Kean, an adjutant with Headquarters 1st Battalion, 15th Field Artillery, and two enlisted men tried to locate the headquarters of French infantry units in front of them. Kean undertook this task at the impatient urging of the regimental commander.

By noon, they located the French. "Here I was greeted by much enthusiasm," said Kean, "and assigned a non-commissioned officer to take me down to the trenches. When I got there, it was noontime. We found the French soldiers on the downslope of the ravine at the edge of the Bois du Loup, a wood below Mont de Bonneil."[5] The steep timbered inclines south of the town of Crogis provided a backdrop to the French line. The dominant point of Hill 204, two kilometers northeast of Crogis, offered complete observation of the surrounding terrain for many kilometers. The thick forest covering the summit also gave good concealment to the Germans in possession of this high ground.

The elaborate French dugouts throughout the line thoroughly impressed Kean. "I was amazed to see what fine trenches these French had already built in their couple of days there. Our American soldiers would not have built such good trenches in a week, but the French from their long experience knew the value of deep trenches, and they had already something there which would protect them well if necessary."[6]

The presence of Kean and his two men caught the curious attention of French soldiers who rejoiced at the sight of the three Americans. "Everywhere I went, the French were having their noonday meal, and I was offered 'pinard' (the wine ration) by whatever officer was in charge. At the same time, my enlisted men were plied with it by the French enlisted men; they were so delighted to see the American soldiers—the first they had ever seen."[7] After establishing the crucial liaison, the men hurried back to their battalion headquarters at La Genette Farm.

Once the 2nd Division officially assumed command of the line from the French, Harbord relocated his brigade headquarters from Issonge Farm to La Loge Farm situated about two kilometers south. The new location had been the headquarters for the French division commander who had now abandoned the property upon transfer of command. "I left Issonge and promptly moved to La Loge," remembered Harbord. "It was a small farm house about three hundred yards north of the Paris-Metz highway, much less conspicuous than Issonge and equally convenient."[8]

The current headquarters at Issonge stayed in operation until the exact moment the new facilities at La Loge were established so as not to leave even a momentary lapse in maintaining an orderly command at every possible moment.[9]

June 4th Chapter III

Along the 6th Marines' front, Colonel Albertus Catlin braved enemy artillery fire to inspect his front. He wrote, "By the 4th the Germans seemed to have gained an inkling of what was in front of them, for their shell fire increased materially, and for two days the bombardment was terrific. There was the constant roar of heavy guns, punctuated by the explosion of bursting shells. They had evidently succeeded in bringing up some of their 150's, and they appeared to be preparing the ground for an advance."[10]

The German 10th Division noted the brazened nature of the French and Americans who seemed to move in the open with indifference or naivety. "The French are moving about without restraint in their lines west of Triangle."[11] Germans spotters were particularly astonished at the daring and inexperienced nature of one particular twenty-man detail seen moving casually along the road from Lucy-le-Bocage to Triangle Farm at 2:00 P.M.[12]

When Catlin reached Lucy-le-Bocage, he noticed the activity conducted in the open had quickly diminished compared to the previous few days due to the increase in the enemy's artillery fire. "The shells fell so thickly in the town that you could scoop up handfuls of shrapnel balls in the streets—round pellets about the size of marbles."[13]

The faint nauseating smell of gas hung in the air, a leftover aroma from the enemy's seven-hour concentration of gas, shrapnel, and high explosive projectiles dropped on that portion of the regiment's line the day before. The lingering gas remained so concentrated it necessitated the evacuation of two Marines from the 23rd Company, 6th Machine Gun Battalion who were overcome by the toxic fumes.[14]

When Catlin arrived along the 1st Battalion, 6th Marines' front, he found a seemingly continuous row of fighting holes occupied by his Marines. As he walked the line, greeting his men with a smile, he noted, "Each man had dug a hole six-feet long, two and a half feet wide, and three feet deep. Even the battalion commander had his hole. They looked shallow and open enough, but they did help; they offered good protection against flying splinters—against everything, in fact, except a direct hit."[15]

The regimental commander's presence exalted the men. Catlin took a few moments to visit with them. When nonchalantly discussing the nature of their subterranean living conditions, according to Catlin, "The men, in fact, jocosely referred to them as their graves."[16]

At Les Mares Farm, members of Captain Frank Whitehead's 5th Marines' Headquarters Company along with the 2nd Platoon, 55th Company continued their deadly harassment of enemy soldiers crossing the open space along the road out of Bussiares and into Bois des Mares. The Germans tried to gain access to these woods using the sunken path and moved in small groups.

June 4th Chapter III

Les Mares Farm. Photo credit: Marine Corps History Division.

By the afternoon, snipers from Headquarters Company killed and wounded several enemy soldiers attempting this short journey. Whitehead remarked, "This long-range shooting discouraged any further attempts to use this route in reaching the woods."[17] By the late afternoon, few Germans dared to cross this exposed lane.

In Bois de Veuilly, Captain Charley Dunbeck's 43rd Company noticed increased enemy activity just beyond a gentle rise along the ground which created a defilade approximately 800 meters away. The Marines watched individual enemy soldiers move over the crest of the field bisected by an east-west road. The sniper fire emanating from the American lines during the previous forty-eight hours as well as an increase in artillery forced the Germans to conceal their movement more effectively. The increased German activity compelled Wise to investigate.

By 11:00 A.M., he and Lieutenant Colonel Logan Feland, the regimental executive commander, reached Dunbeck's front in Bois de Veuilly. Feland notified regimental headquarters of the enemy's presence in a message stating, "Please put artillery fire on the east and west road near north line 263, halfway between Bois de Veuilly and Veuilly la Poterie. Germans in line along this road and hedge between Marigny-Veuilly road and ravine parallel to vertical line 171- Wise is with me."[18]

Tied into the left flank of Dunbeck's men, Captain Lester Wass's 18th Company remained alert that morning to enemy movement in the tree line hundreds of meters across the open field. Earlier that day, Wass's Marines noticed individual German soldiers passing freely across an open gap in the distant tree line. Heavy machine gun fire emanating from these woods thwarted Wass's efforts to establish a forward automatic rifle position.

However, by the afternoon enemy troops no longer crossed the open space through the trees since well-aimed Marine rifle fire killed and wounded several enemy soldiers who haphazardly traversed the gap in the woods. The effective shooting by Wass's Marines also attracted the attention of the Germans machine gunners, a factor Wass explained to the battalion commander. Luckily, the enemy's bombardment of Bois de Veuilly diminished significantly by the afternoon.[19]

The volume of incoming German shells, however, did not let up that afternoon for the 75th Company. From their position along the wooded slopes of Bois de Champillon, they noticed a lone German plane sailing over

June 4th Chapter III

the treetops at a low altitude. They gazed up from their dugouts out of curiosity as the aircraft approached from the rear and then circled. Instinctively the Marines raised their rifles steadying in on the low-flying plane.

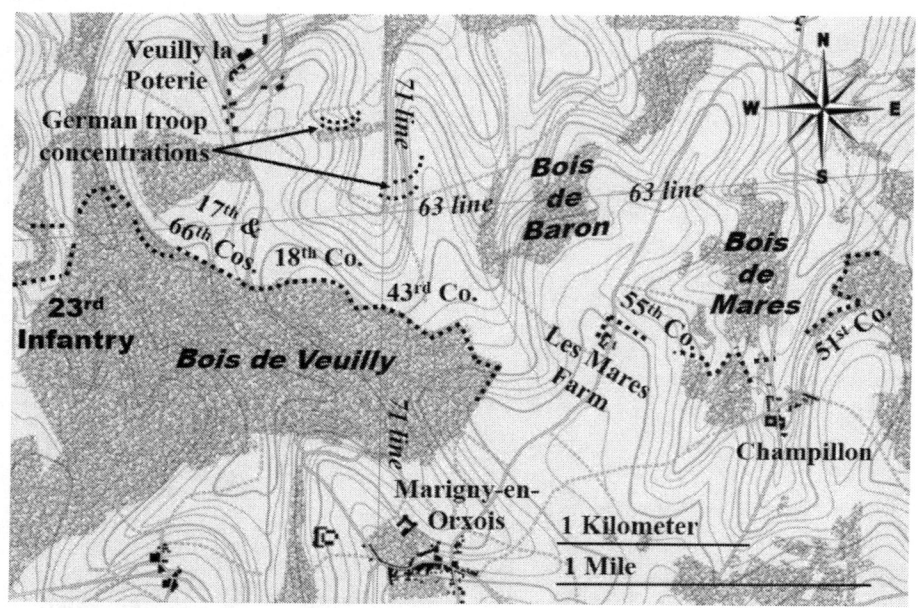

From the northern edge of Bois de Veuilly, Captain Dunbeck spotted German troops concentrations and called for a barrage on the German positions.

    Suddenly, twenty-four-year-old Captain Edward Canfield Fuller, commanding the company yelled, "Don't shoot, don't shoot. Stay down in your holes so he can't see you."[20] The buzz of the engine grew louder as the men crouched into their shallow dugouts looking up in hopes of catching a glimpse of the aircraft as it passed. Soon a crackling hiss emanated from the plane as it swooped overhead. The men recognized the smoke trail of a flare even before it descended to the earth in the field just in front of Sergeant Gerald Thomas's 3rd Platoon. They knew a barrage of enemy shells would soon follow, and for about five minutes, the men waited in paranoid anticipation.

    Within minutes, the distant thud of enemy guns reinforced their worst fears. In seconds, a gurgling roar followed instantly by a shattering explosion showered the men with dirt and debris. Each distant report of the enemy batteries caused the men of Thomas's platoon to bury their faces into the bottom of their shallow dugouts and pray for survival. Each shell shook the ground with immense force.

    The barrage kept the men helplessly pinned down. Several hundred meters across the field, a faintly visible line of enemy soldiers emerged from

June 4th Chapter III

the western tree line of Belleau Wood. "They came out of the wood opposite our position in close formation," remembered Private Gus Gulberg.[21] As the barrage subsided, the Marines steadied themselves to resist the approaching Germans, which broke formation and moved forward by rushes. "Word was passed to hold our fire until they were close enough to make good targets," exclaimed Thomas.[22]

French machine gunners, who dug in with the company the day before, adjusted the deflection wheels of their Hotchkiss guns and traversed the barrels of these menacing weapons. Each gun crew aimed down their pre-designated a lane of fire fronting the enemy advance. Cautiously and patiently, the 75th Company waited.

The Germans, barely a visible on the horizon at 800 meters, eventually grew into distinguishable human silhouettes at 500-600 meters distance. Suddenly, Fuller's Marines unleashed a wall of gunfire. According to Gulberg, "We opened up on them with a slashing barrage of rifles, automatics, and machine guns."[23] The rifle fire echoed across the fields between Bois de Champillon and the edge of Belleau Woods. The French machine gunners cut considerable gaps in the onrushing troops. At 500-600 yards, the enemy's advance collapsed.[24]

German survivors quickly dropped flat in the field. Gulberg

Gerald C. Thomas 75th Company seen here at the end of the war after receiving a commission. Photo credit: NARA.

stated, "They halted, withdrew a space and then came on again. They were brave men we had to grant them that."[25] Several enemy soldiers raced forward a few meters at a time. The number of Germans in each rush seemed to dwindle each time they reappeared above the tops of the waving fronds of wheat. The concentrated fire of the Marines and French devastated the Germans. Thomas said, "The attack came to about 400 yards and melted away."[26] According to Gulberg, "They fell by the scores, there among the poppies and wheat. Then they broke and ran for cover."[27] The Marines and French defenders showed no mercy upon Germans fleeing for the distant tree line and shot several as they retreated. As the echo of rifle fire along the battalion's line dissipated, the smell of gunpowder hung

June 4th Chapter III

heavy. Suddenly, the distant report of enemy trench mortars resonated across the pasture.

Marines of the 6th Regiment concealed in the trees somewhere along the line. Photo credit: Marius Eugene Vasse collection.

The enemy, now attuned to the American's position, registered their fire using a devastating weapon known as the Minenwerfer or trench mortar.[28] "Mortar shells are nasty things," Thomas opined, "as their very high trajectory permits them to drop right in your foxhole."[29] The men quickly retracted back into their shallow dugouts to withstand the barrage.

The increased activity in and around villages made them particular targets for German batteries. Near the town of La Voie du Chatel, an enemy barrage landed among elements of the 3rd Battalion, 6th Marines. One particular shell exploded on the other side of a massive tree behind which Private Rendinell of the battalion's intelligence section, tried to nap after several sleepless days. He recalled, ". . . I laid down in back of a tree and it seems like Fritz won't leave me rest. A shell bust close by and killed a mule and a piece of the shell tore a hole in my tree big enough to put my head in."[30] Although violently jostled awake, Rendinell remarkably escaped unharmed.

German shells also bombarded the extreme western edge of the 2nd Division's front. The 23rd Infantry, still in the town of Coulombs, endured heavy shelling throughout the day. The barrage regularly knocked the regiment's telephone lines out of service. Maintaining this critical means of communication fell to members of Company C, 1st Field Signal Battalion.

Even in the midst of incoming shellfire, these brave men worked in the open to locate and repair the broken lines.

At 4:00 P.M., Private First Class Romulus John Meehan, a twenty-five-year-old telegraph operator from Appleton, Wisconsin, tried to locate and repair the defective lines near the 23rd Regiment's command post. Twenty-six-year-old Sergeant Hasso Adolf Briese, also a telegraph operator from Terry, Montana, and Private Michael Dana Capsack worked with Meehan. The three men operated out in the open under heavy incoming fire. According to twenty-two-year-old First Sergeant Charles W. Stickney, a farmer from Clear Lake, Minnesota, a high explosive shell killed Meehan instantly. The blast concussion also knocked Capsack unconscious, and he died a half hour later having never regained consciousness. The explosion also killed Sergeant Briese.[31]

In addition to shelling the 2nd Division's front line positions, German batteries harrassed troop movements behind the front. First Lieutenant Wendell Westover of Company A, 5th Machine Gun Battalion looked to the north and east from Coupru and noticed five German observation balloons had surmounted the northern horizon. "On succeeding days the number grew to eight and nine, but the immediate result of their ability to see over our sector was a sad incident occurring that afternoon."[32]

A French anti-aircraft battery stopped along the road on the outskirts of the village and soon attracted the attention of enemy observation balloons. When the Germans lost sight of the French battery as it moved into the town, failing to appear on the other side, enemy guns quickly registered on Coupru. Westover claimed, "Three minutes later a salvo of two-hundred-and-tens tore into us."[33]

Projectiles which weighed nearly 250 pounds exploded with tremendous force. Westover remembered the devastating effect of these large shells, "Where there had been peaceful work a moment before, there was now a scattered mass of remnants. Fresh earth strewn about. Near-by windows were shattered, and walls chipped by the fragments."[34]

One of the shells soared over the red-tiled rooftops of the town's structures and exploded near a supply wagon where a team of pack mules parked. The shrapnel shredded one animal and critically wounded a soldier. "The mule lay torn and bleeding, and died within a few moments," remembered Westover.[35] "A man in the prime of condition was left a gasping, bloody bundle of torn flesh."[36]

Several other soldiers bravely left their shelter to pull the severely wounded man to safety. They carried him down the road to a dressing station. The men worked frantically trying to stop the bleeding. Comrades applied heavy-duty bandages from their first aid kits to the wounds. The thick white gauze dressings became saturated upon contact with the ghastly

June 4th Chapter III

wounds all over his body. "No need of drugs; the shock had eliminated all pain," claimed Westover.[37]

Captain Andrew Bruce, commanding the company, knelt beside the wounded soldier. Other men around the dying man calmly talked to him while they worked on his wounds. They tried to reassure him while silently trying to convince themselves he might live. Westover, shocked by the grizzly nature of the man's wounds, remained composed. "Difficult to speak with confidence," Westover divulged, "an open hand could have passed into the hole in his abdomen."[38]

Trying not to seem ingratiating, he asked the young soldier if there was anything he could do for him. The wounded boy remained alert enough to look Westover in the eye and, feigning a pleasant smile, asked for a cigarette. Unhesitating, Westover lit one and placed it delicately between the wounded kid's lips. The boy took a few long puffs as if he knew he was enjoying perhaps his last cigarette.[39]

As elements of the 3rd Brigade withstood the enemy's barrage of Coupru, plans were underway to shorten the 2nd Division's front. The 23rd Infantry which held an overextended line west of Bois de Veuilly received information that they would be relieved by the French that night.[40] The relief of Colonel Paul Malone's 23rd Infantry put Lieutenant Colonel Wise's Marines at the extreme eastern flank of the division.

On the left flank of Wise's battalion, Captain Wass needed to establish liaison with the French who were reportedly taking over the line. For this task, Wass approached First Lieutenant Elliott Cooke and directed him to take a few men to the left of the company's line to a French unit preparing to occupy the battalion's left. Cooke remembered the no-nonsense manner of Wass's instructions. "'Those Frogs want to see a couple of Marines,' he informed me. 'They've been told our uniform is the same color as the Germans' forest green and they don't want to shoot the wrong people. Take a couple of men over to their P.C. You're wearing O.D. so they probably won't make any mistakes on you.'"[41] Cooke simply acknowledged the order and took his small group along the wooded road toward the reported location of this French unit.

Cooke located a French major of the 167th Division and his staff several hundred meters west of the 2nd Battalion, 5th Marines' west flank. The French gazed upon these Americans before them with admiration and acknowledgment of the similarities between the dark green wool of the Marines' tunics and the gray color of the German uniforms. Cooke found the gentlemanly demeanor of the French officers quite charming as they gleefully welcomed their American counterparts and jovially discussed whatever the language barrier allowed.

One of the French officers culminated the short encounter by pouring each of Cooke and his men a shot of red wine. "The French major went even further," said Cooke, "and poured me out an extra big slug of cognac as a chaser."[42] The thick and pungent brandy exceeded the tolerance of his taste buds as it went down— warming his throat along the way. After the festive introduction, he realized they needed to return to the company. As Cooke walked back along the wooded road, he found that his feet were less agile than they were before the liquor.

While Cooke's group cordially interacted with their French liaison, enemy gunners, at 3:15 P.M., bombarded the already-shattered town of Marigny-en-Orxois with 150mm shells.[43] The large projectiles smashed huge craters into the crossroads and intersections and further complicated the passage of caissons through the village.

During the barrage, supply and communication assets traversing the town stopped, and troops ran for cover. Incoming rounds turned the already-damaged stone buildings of town into pulverized heaps of debris. The torrent of incoming fire was brief—only twenty rounds struck the village, but the shelling reminded the men of their immense vulnerability.[44]

By 4:00 P.M., enemy artillery fire landed approximately 500 meters in front of Les Mares Farm.[45] The fierce bombardment fell too far in advance of the line to bother the Marines holding the farm.[46] "The long-range rifle work had apparently deceived him as to our location," remembered Captain Frank Whitehead.[47]

From the battalion command post on the northern outskirts of the still-smoldering ruins of Marigny-en-Orxois, Wise also noted the sudden increase in artillery fire. "I got a hunch it would be a good thing to go out and look at the front line. I left my P.C. and went up to the ridge just in front of it. I reached the crest and stood still."[48] As he approached his battalion's front, Wise noticed, in the distance, a line of enemy troops. "I realized that I couldn't give an order that would be of any help."[49]

In an upstairs window of a house in La Voie du Chatel, Major Frank Evans, the 6th Marines' adjutant, observed the same thin wave of enemy troops with extreme anxiety:

> They were driving at Hill 165 from the north and northeast, and they came out, on a wonderfully clear day, in two columns across a wheat-field. From our distance, it looked flat and green as a baseball field, set between a row of woods on the farther side, and woods and a ravine on the near side. We could see the two thin brown columns advancing in perfect order until two thirds of the columns, we judged, were in view.[50]

From the very subtle high ground between Marigny-en-Orxois and Les Mares Farm, Wise stood and watched helplessly as the Germans advanced on his battalion front, I stood there and watched them come. It wasn't the

June 4th Chapter III

mass formation I had expected to see after what I had heard of German attacks. Those lines were well extended. At least six or seven paces of open space were between the men. There seemed to be four or five lines about twenty-five yards apart. They advanced slowly and steadily. I couldn't distinguish any leaders. I was frozen, but fascinated.[51]

From the property of Les Mares Farm, the Marines immediately spotted the approaching enemy and sounded the alert. Twenty-year-old Private Paul Bonner of New York City felt panic, excitement, and fear when a shrilled voice announced the presence of the approaching enemy.

Captain John Blanchfield, who was informed of the enemy advance hundreds of meters ahead, raced to reach his company's front and encouraged his men. Bonner remembered the captain's excitement, "'The devils are coming on,' he shouted. 'You have been waiting for them for a year; now go get them.' He was shouting in his Irish brogue and his blood was up."[52]

Bonner and several other men darted a short distance and formed a firing line along a dirt road in front of the farm. The men went prone. They peered intently over the top of the wheat to see if they could spot the enemy, but nothing was yet visible

As he watched in disbelief, Wise became concerned with the liaison on his battalion's flanks, which had been problematic for days. A 400-meter gap in the center of the 2nd Battalion, 5th Marines' front, however, added to Wise's anxiety. This weak spot between Les Mares Farm and the right of Captain Charley Dunbeck's 43rd Company in the Bois de Veuilly was tentatively-held by a group of French colonials the day before.[53] Several had retreated since taking over that position, and Whitehead could not determine if these French colonials remained in position west of the farm or not. From the property, the Marines could only see the corpses of the brave ones who died since taking over the line.[54]

Behind Wise's battalion, the report of the American guns resonated across the open. Within seconds, the horizon to the north erupted as shells exploded along the ground in the distance. Along the forward line at Les Mares Farm, Private Bonner recalled, "By the approach of our own breaking shell, we gauged the advance of the enemy and, sure enough, when the shells were breaking about a thousand yards away, we spotted the figures of the enemy marching on in single columns."[55]

South of the farm, Wise noted, "They came within close range. Not a shot had come from our lines. Not a man had tried any wild shooting at long range. Those ten months of drastic discipline and terrific training had done their work. From where I stood, I could see maybe five hundred yards down my line in either direction. In their fox holes, the marines lay motionless, watching over their rifle sights."[56]

June 4th Chapter III

Bonner eagerly watched as shellfire blanketed the field over which the enemy advanced. Now and then, a blossom of white smoke engulfed parts of the German column. More shells found their mark and tore gaps in the advancing enemy waves. "We all looked to see that our rifles were loaded. From somewhere along the road we got the command to fire. Sharpshooters only, I thought I heard them say but everyone fired," claimed Bonner.[57] "Up and down the line I could see my men working their rifle bolts," Wise remembered.[58] The rattle of automatic rifles caused the tall wheat in front of the gunners, to vibrate rapidly with each shot. The initial burst of gunfire devastated the first wave of Germans.

The second wave pushed forward firing on the move, but the relentless onslaught from the American line did not abate.

Private Paul Bonner 55th Company, 2nd Battalion, 5th Marines. Photo credit: "Echoes From Over There."

According to Bonner, "Those Germans just melted away. Whole columns went down and the others scattered to the right and left."[59] Survivors quickly dropped down into the concealment of the tall stalks of grain and desperately tried to avoid the withering gunfire.

Wise rushed back to his battalion command post, "to wait for the reports that would be coming in from the company commanders. I soon found that the attack had not extended beyond my flanks. The Germans hadn't even hit our line where we had machine guns. Rifles alone had stopped them."[60]

Within minutes, messages from his battalion front arrived. He learned the Germans ironically hit his line where it was comparatively stable and missed the points where liaison remained weak. "If ever there was a miracle in the war that was it. With a wide front, much of it open, to pick and choose, the German attack had smashed squarely into the center of those lone two and a half miles we held. Had that same force hit either of our flanks, they could have crumpled us and cleaned us up."[61]

June 4th Chapter III

Wise's concerns of his weakened flanks were largely unwarranted since several units reinforced his battalion's front that day. Wise, however, was unaware of these developments since the endless German shellfire that day cut telephone lines connecting Wise's command post to regimental headquarters. Therefore, information arrived by runners, which significantly delayed communications. Wise learned that his precarious right flank finally tied in with Major Maurice Shearer's 1st Battalion, 6th Marines earlier that day. The lack of contact with Shearer distressed Wise for days. Wise also learned that two companies from the 3rd Battalion, 6th Marines even moved in to help fill the gap the day before. He also discovered that the 17th and 66th Companies of Major Julius Turrill's 1st Battalion, 5th Marines moved up to extend his left flank through the Bois de Veuilly.[62]

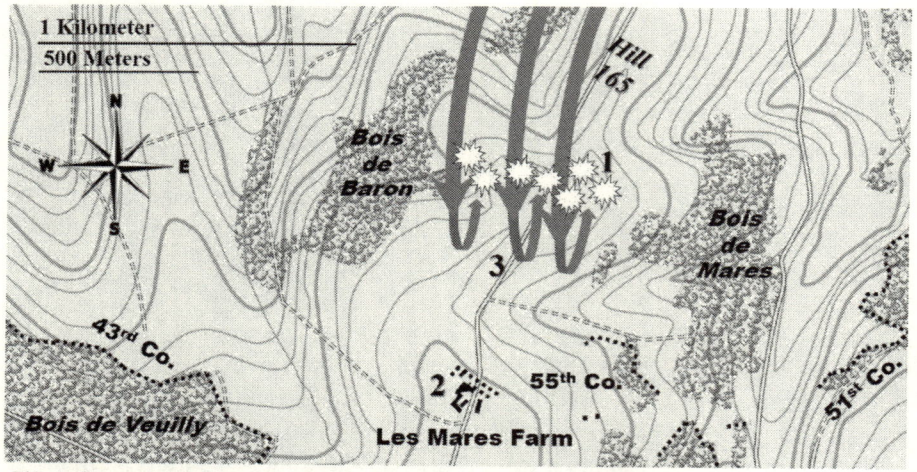

[1] A German probe towards Les Mares Farm was met with a concentrated artillery barrage that devastated the German advance. [2] The 2nd Platoon, 55th Company and a 62-man detachment from the 5th Marines' Headquarters Company defending Les Mares Farm unleash a withering volley of rifle fire. [3] The effects of Marine rifle fire from the defenders of Les Mares Farm as well as other platoons of the 55th Company repulsed the German advance.

The information put Wise's mind at ease over his battalion's delicate situation. The regular shelling of his battalion's front following the failed enemy attack suggested the Germans would not attempt another advance anytime soon.[63]

Wise personally wanted to inform Colonel Neville of the repulsed enemy attack, but his telephone lines were not operating.[64] Wise spotted an abandoned bicycle in the street and realized this was the most expeditious means of transportation to reach regimental headquarters on the northwestern outskirts of Marigny-en-Orxois. "I left Lieutenant Legendre,

June 4th Chapter III

my adjutant, at the P.C. to look after things, and rode that bicycle back to report in person to Colonel Neville at regimental P.C."[65]

Moving through the northern outskirts of Marigny-en-Orxois could not be done casually since the town seemed to be the constant target of enemy batteries. It resembled more of a debris field than a quaint rural French village. German shells reduced the town's once-beautiful chateaus and homes into half-crumbled masses of rubble. Thick wooden beams drooped from the ceilings of structures they once held up; their splintered ends jutted out from vast piles of shattered masonry. Weaving through the debris-covered streets on a bicycle, Wise reached regimental headquarters. Neville briefed him on the relief of his battalion scheduled for the next evening—a welcome relief after the last few days.[66]

Wise's journey back to his command post carried him mostly up inclining roads.[67] The pudgy forty-one-year-old decided to abandon the bicycle and walk the remainder of the distance back to his cemetery command post. He followed the route along the edge of Bois de Veuilly and encountered First Lieutenant Elliott Cooke of the 18th Company. Cooke and a few of his men were returning from the celebratory liaison with the French.

Against the backdrop of enemy shells breaking far in the distance, Wise was incredibly displeased to find one of his officers so far back from the battalion line. He unleashed a profanity-laced tirade as he approached Cooke who recalled:

First Lieutenant Elliott Cooke. Photo credit: Cybele Lane.

> He wanted to know what the this-and-that I was doing back there while the biggest battle of the war was going on down in the front lines. As I turned around to explain, he caught a whiff of my breath and went right up in flames. He denounced my ancestry, personal habits, and previous condition of servitude. His suggestion that I get the blankety-blank back where I belonged

was entirely superfluous on account of I was already going down the road as fast as my cognac-empowered feet would carry me.[68]

After his encounter with Cooke, Wise returned to his command post. "I found everything unchanged, except that Marigny was being shelled even more heavily than it had been since we arrived."[69] Cooke and his small group returned to the 18th Company's position in the northwest portion of Bois de Veuilly just as the distant report of enemy artillery fire from the north echoed across the open field. Cooke sprinted for cover, but then, trying to keep a brave and stoic bearing in front of his men, fought his instinct to run for the nearest hole. Cooke slowed his pace to a dignified walk. "I was positive the nose of the projectile was pointed directly at my belt buckle and my stomach cowered up against my backbone."[70]

Lieutenant Colonel Frederic M. Wise commanded the 2nd Battalion, 5th Marines. Photo credit: Marine Corps History Division.

The split-second scream of the incoming shell left no time to react. Cooke confessed, "Then with a final scream of rage the huge piece of ordnance tore itself into a thousand fragments. Even before the nasty buzz of jagged steel had passed, I heard another shell coming, then another, and still another. Well, too much was enough. To hell with dignity, songs or anything else. I took off, running, and whisked into a fox-hole like a scared gopher."[71]

The bombardment tore through the treetops of the 18th Company's position with renewed ferocity and soon smoke blanketed the woods and fronting field. Captain Wass's men hunkered down in their shallow dugouts hoping to survive the brief but intense barrage. Incoming rounds blasted dirt into the air which nearly filled the holes sheltering the cowering men. Leaves, detached from their branches by the force of the shell's detonation, gently meandered to the ground.

Suddenly, bullets clipped the bark of trees with a crack. The staccato of distant machine gun fire rippled across the field. Some rounds popped overhead, and others whined as they deflected off the ground and trees.

June 4th Chapter III

Believing that the barrage preceded another infantry probe, Cooke felt temporary paralysis by the visceral terror of it all. He explained:

> With the realization of that fact, every trace of cognac departed my system. My knees were still wobbly and my stomach upset, but it was from fright and not liquor. I knew I had to get up out of that hole and I didn't want to do it. Nothing about me wanted to. Every inch of my anatomy shrank from being exposed to so many different kinds of death. My arm muscles acted like wet dish rags and my feet were numb, but somehow I did pull out of that hole and wriggle down to the forward line of men.[72]

As Cooke crawled forward, one of the men screamed at him to move towards the refuge of his dugout. The smoke hanging over field obscured the Marines' view in front of the line. The crack of machine gun slugs prevented even the boldest of men from raising their heads to see if the enemy was advancing.

According to Cooke, "Machine gun bullets pelted at us with the crescending hiss of steam pouring from a hose. Yet the expected wave of charging, grey-clad figures did not appear. Somewhere out there they lurked behind that screen of smoke while we waited tensely for them to come on and fight."[73] The Marine lying next to Cooke managed to poke the barrel of his automatic rifle over the dirt parapet and fire. The cumbersome weapon recoiled in rapid succession as he blindly fired through the smoke at the unseen enemy.

On the left and right men straightened up enough from their prone position to peer above the top of their holes and shot into the distant smoke screen.[74] Above the thunder of the company's rifles, the rapid fire of two Hotchkiss guns of the 8th Machine Gun Company on the left added materially to the volume of steel the 18th Company delivered in response to the German's sweeping machine gun barrage. The exchange of gunfire gradually dissipated.

Up and down the line, voices of sergeants and corporals shouted 'cease-fire' to their squads. The men conversed excitedly following the intense exchange of fire. The bantered among each other. The fear-driven enthusiasm in their voices tried to mask the adrenaline still flowing immediately after the encounter.

After recovering his composure, Cooke noticed his close friend Second Lieutenant Fred H. Becker walking away with his sleeve torn away and an arm hung in a rudimentary sling tied against his body. Cooke darted over to him to assess the extent of his injury. He walked with Becker as the wounded second lieutenant meandered in the direction of the aid station. According to Cooke, "His eyebrows contracted in a grimace of pain, but he also managed to smile." Becker, the indomitable All-American football star from Iowa, downplayed his situation by exclaiming, "Nothing a good looking nurse and some honest to goodness chow won't fix up in a few days."[75]

As Beck staggered away, Second Lieutenant William Ashurst inquired whether Becker heard the shell that wounded him. Acknowledging Ashurst's sarcastic question, Becker hollered, "I heard about a thousand shells all around me, so I guess I heard the one that had my number."[76]

First Lieutenant Fred H. Becker. Photo credit: Robert Kaufman.

By 6:15 P.M., the American opposition encountered by the enemy near Champillon and Hill 142 throughout the day also attracted German artillery fire.[77] Along the southern portion of Hill 142, Marines of the 82nd and 83rd Companies, as well as a platoon of the 73rd Machine Gun Company ran for their dugouts when they heard the distant bark of enemy guns. Within seconds, high explosive German 105mm projectiles, falling at a rate of four rounds a minute, landed near the 82nd Company's position.[78] The lapse of time between each round allowed the men to judge the likely spot of the shell's impact from the safety of their foxholes and duck accordingly. Miraculously, Captain Dwight Smith's 82nd Company suffered few casualties.

Twenty-three-year-old Second Lieutenant Whitney Williams Stark, an Army officer from Rutland, Vermont, and former Amherst student assigned to the 83rd Company sustained a concussion from the blast. He exhibited signs of shell shock and comrades evacuated him off the line.[79] On the right of Smith's position, Captain Alfred Noble's 83rd Company escaped the bombardment unharmed. Twenty-one-year-old Private Lucius Harold

Smith, whose left knee was accidentally smashed by the careless swing of a pick while digging that afternoon, became the company's sole casualty that day.[80]

The forty-five-minute barrage south of Hill 142 also fell upon Captain Lloyd Williams's 51st Company. The distant rumble of German guns interrupted the company's activities.[81] The men, now twenty-four-hour veterans of the enemy's artillery fire, immediately sunk to the bottom of their dugouts anticipating the explosion of each incoming round. Shells landed in rapid succession and kept everyone pinned down. One round landed practically on top of twenty-two-year-old Private Isaac Neal Boone of Rockingham County, North Carolina, and killed him instantly. The explosion blew off his left arm, left foot and mangled the lower portion of his face.[82]

The bombardment took a severe toll on the nerves of twenty-one-year-old Gunnery Sergeant Richard Still Ross, an automobile mechanic from Topeka, Kansas. The day before, Ross braved incoming shellfire to dress the wounds of several Marines from his battalion despite showing subtle signs of shell shock. Ross vehemently dismissed any thought of evacuation and stayed with his platoon. As the barrage intensified that afternoon, a shell exploded near Ross. The concussion knocked him back and rendered him severely shell-shocked.[83] After the evacuation of Ross, twenty-seven-year-old Sergeant Jim Wilson Sutherland, of Camp, Arkansas, took command of the platoon during the barrage.[84]

By 7:00 P.M., the bombardment finally stopped, and momentary tranquility returned. Smoke and the smell of high explosives from the 200 shells that hit the company's front during the forty-five-minute barrage clung to the field and trees over the entire area.[85]

Across the Champillon-Bussiares road near Les Mares Farm, the forty-five-minute bombardment also fell upon the 55th Company's 3rd Platoon, wounding Second Lieutenant Arthur Tilghman. Several shell fragments perforated the

Second Lieutenant Arthur Tilghman commanded the 3rd Platoon, 55th Company. Photo credit: Fort Sheridan Association.

outer portion of the thirty-one-year-old platoon commander's left forearm, upper arm, and deltoid.[86] Despite the substantial blood loss, Tilghman's injuries were relatively superficial but extensive enough to necessitate his evacuation. His miseries, however, were not yet over. As the stretcher-bearers carried Tilghman from Les Mares Farm, pockets of lingering gas

June 4th Chapter III

overwhelmed him, and he suffered severe gas absorption and inhalation in addition to his wounded left arm.[87]

---

[1] *Records of the Second Division (Regular)* Volumes 4, N.P.
[2] Gordon, *Leathernecks and Doughboys*, 55-56.
[3] Field Message from Major Benjamin Berry to Colonel Wendell Neville at 12:50 P.M., June 4, 1918, Box 65, RG 120.9.3, Second Division File, Records of the AEF, NARA College Park, MD.
[4] *Records of the Second Division (Regular)* Volumes 5, N.P.
[5] Kean, *Dear Marraine*, 96-97.
[6] Ibid, 97.
[7] Ibid.
[8] Harbord, *The American Army in France*, 287.
[9] *Records of the Second Division (Regular)* Volumes 4, N.P.
[10] Catlin, *With the Help of God and a Few Marines*, 100.
[11] War Diary and Annexes 20th Infantry Brigade, June 4, 1918, *Translation of War Diaries of German Units*, Vol. 1.
[12] Ibid.
[13] Catlin, *With the Help of God and a Few Marines*, 100-101.
[14] U.S. Marine Corps Muster Rolls, 1893-1940, Record Group 127, NARA, Washington, D.C. Note: The two Marines from the 23rd Company were Nineteen-year-old Private Earl Frank Muren and twenty-one-year-old Private Clarence Wells Clark who were both gassed at 9:30 A.M.
[15] Catlin, *With the Help of God and a Few Marines*, 101.
[16] Ibid.
[17] *The Aisne Defensive*, Whitehead to ABMC, Box 190, RG 117.4.2, NARA College Park, MD.
[18] *Records of the Second Division (Regular)* Volumes 5, N.P.
[19] Wise and Frost, *A Marine Tells it to You*, 201.
[20] General Gerald B. Thomas memoir, Alfred M. Gray Research Library, Quantico, VA.
[21] Gulberg, *A War Diary*, 26.
[22] General Gerald B. Thomas memoir, Alfred M. Gray Research Library, Quantico, VA.
[23] Gulberg, *A War Diary*, 26.
[24] General Gerald B. Thomas memoir, Alfred M. Gray Research Library, Quantico, VA., and General Gerald B. Thomas, interview by Robert Asprey, Alfred M. Gray Research Library, Quantico, VA.
[25] Gulberg, *A War Diary*, 26.
[26] General Gerald B. Thomas, interview by Robert Asprey, Alfred M. Gray Research Library, Quantico, VA.
[27] Gulberg, *A War Diary*, 26.
[28] Note: The term Minenwerfer translates in German to 'mine thrower.'
[29] General Gerald B. Thomas memoir, Alfred M. Gray Research Library, Quantico, VA.
[30] Rendinell and Pattullo, *One Man's War*, 96.
[31] Burial Files of Private Michael Capsack, and Private First Class Romulus John Meehan, Eye-witness statements by Sergeant First Class Charles W. Stickney,

Boxes 784 and 3304, RG 92.9, Records of Graves Registration Services, NARA College Park, MD, and *World War I Selective Service System Draft Registration Cards, 1917-1918*, NARA, Washington, D.C.
[32] Westover, *Suicide Battalions*, 118.
[33] Ibid.
[34] Ibid.
[35] Ibid.
[36] Ibid.
[37] Ibid.
[38] Ibid, 119.
[39] Ibid.
[40] *Records of the Second Division (Regular)* Volumes 3, N.P.
[41] Cooke, "We Can Take It, We Attack," *Infantry Journal,* 6.
[42] Ibid.
[43] *Records of the Second Division (Regular)* Volumes 9, N.P.
[44] Ibid.
[45] *The Aisne Defensive,* Whitehead to ABMC, Box 190, RG 117.4.2, NARA College Park, MD.
[46] Ibid.
[47] Ibid.
[48] Wise and Frost, *A Marine Tells it to You*, 202-03.
[49] Ibid.
[50] Cowing and Cooper, *Dear Folks At Home,* 98.
[51] Wise and Frost, *A Marine Tells it to You*, 203.
[52] Hamilton and Corbin, *Echoes From Over There,* 70.
[53] *Records of the Second Division (Regular)* Volumes 5, N.P.
[54] *The Aisne Defensive,* Whitehead to ABMC, Box 190, RG 117.4.2, NARA College Park, MD.
[55] Hamilton and Corbin, *Echoes From Over There,* 70.
[56] Wise and Frost, *A Marine Tells it to You*, 203.
[57] Hamilton and Corbin, *Echoes From Over There,* 70.
[58] Wise and Frost, *A Marine Tells it to You*, 203.
[59] Hamilton and Corbin, *Echoes From Over There,* 70.
[60] Wise and Frost, *A Marine Tells it to You*, 203.
[61] Ibid, 204.
[62] Ibid.
[63] Ibid.
[64] Ibid, 205-06.
[65] Ibid, 204-05.
[66] Ibid, 205.
[67] Ibid.
[68] Cooke, "We Can Take It, We Attack," *Infantry Journal,* 6.

June 4th Chapter III

[69] Wise and Frost, *A Marine Tells it to You*, 205.
[70] Cooke, "We Can Take It, We Attack," *Infantry Journal*, 6.
[71] Ibid.
[72] Ibid, 7.
[73] Ibid.
[74] Ibid.
[75] Ibid.
[76] Ibid. Note: Becker returned to the Company just in time for the assault near Soissons where he was killed instantly during an artillery barrage.
[77] *Records of the Second Division (Regular)* Volumes 3, N.P.
[78] Ibid.
[79] U.S. Army Personnel—(including YMCA) attached to Marine Corps Organizations, Box 51, Record Group 127, NARA, Washington, D.C., and U.S. Marine Corps Muster Rolls, 1893-1940, Record Group 127, NARA, Washington, D.C.
[80] U.S. Marine Corps Muster Rolls, 1893-1940, Record Group 127, NARA, Washington, D.C.
[81] *Records of the Second Division (Regular)* Volumes 9, N.P
[82] Burial File of Private Isaac N. Boone Burial, Box 486, RG 92.9, Records of Graves Registration Services, NARA College Park, MD
[83] Official Military Personnel File for Gunnery Sergeant Richard Still Ross, RG 127, NPRC St. Louis, MO.
[84] Official Military Personnel File for Sergeant Jim Wilson Sutherland, RG 127, NPRC St. Louis, MO.
[85] *Records of the Second Division (Regular)* Volumes 9, N.P.
[86] U.S. Army Personnel attached to Marine Corps, Box 51, RG 127, NARA, Washington, D.C.
[87] Ibid., and Myron E. Adams, and Fred. Girton, *The Fort Sheridan Officers' Training Camps,* (Fort Sheridan: Fort Sheridan Association, 1920), 159. Note: Second Lieutenant Tilghman remained in the hospital for three months. He was assigned duty as commander of Central Prisoner of War Enclosure Number 1 located in Tours, France. On January 30, 1919, he became gravely ill with influenza which developed into spinal meningitis. He died February 12, 1919, in Tours, France.

June 4th Chapter IV

For a hundred yards on either side lay the wreckage of that need. Animals lined the ditches, dead by shellfire or merciful shooting; a few, blood spouting through punctured lungs as they breathed, were targets for our own pistols.
-First Lieutenant Wendell Westover Company A, 5th Machine Gun Battalion

With the successful emplacement 2nd Division's batteries, the 2nd Field Artillery Brigade Headquarters, located at La Loge Farm, assigned target information and firing data tables at 6:15 P.M. to each regiment.[1] The poor, unreliable, and often non-existent telephone communication with frontline units significantly inhibited the artillery's capacity to fire in support of the infantry brigades.[2]

Brigadier General William Chamberlaine, commanding the 2nd Field Artillery Brigade, avoided communication dilemmas by dividing his fire support into subsectors and assigned each infantry brigade an artillery regiment. Chamberlaine's logic rested on the idea that each brigade commander was an experienced artillery advisor and would be located nearby to direct and coordinate fire support and respond to immediate calls for artillery by front line units.[3]

Each artillery regiment's sector was echeloned in depth, and the battalion layout for each sector put two batteries in advance and one in the rear. This arrangement gave each infantry brigade the support of sixty 75mm cannons including the batteries of the French artillery regiments that remained in each subsector after the French 43rd Division turned command of the front to the 2nd Division.[4]

Lieutenant Colonel Joseph Davis, commanding the 15th Field Artillery, finally established contact with his 1st Battalion and learned that their position was south of Mont de Bonneil. He dispatched a message earlier that afternoon at 5:00 P.M. instructing Major Benjamin Bailey, commanding the 1st Battalion, to initiate immediate reconnaissance of the area around Ferme de Beaurepaire and the terrain east of Domptin and Les Aulnois Bontempts. Special instructions informed the battalion to occupy this region one battery at a time. Orders also specified that movement to this new position would occur no later than 8:00 A.M. June 6th.[5]

The battalion, still believing their orders directed them to support the French in front of them, had ventured too far to deliver effective supporting fire for the 3rd Brigade. According to First Lieutenant Kean, "It had been decided that our position, with no means of retreat, was too dangerous; and as the troops we were to support were the 9th Infantry, and not the French, it could be done better from a position further to the north; besides which from

June 4th Chapter IV

our present position we could not reach the Bois-de-Belleau and support the Marine Brigade, as this was beyond the range of our guns."[6]

Colonel Manus McClosky's 12th Field Artillery Regiment covered the 4th Brigade sector from the Paris-Metz road near Le Thiolet to the Bois de Veuilly. McCloskey established his headquarters at La Loge Farm where Brigadier General Harbord moved the 4th Brigade command post earlier that day.[7] From this location, McClosky could better facilitate the supporting fire of his batteries and those of the French 37th Regiment of Field Artillery.[8] Lieutenant Colonel Davis established his 15th Field Artillery Regiment's headquarters at Domptin. His batteries supported Brigadier General Edward Lewis's 3rd Brigade.

Lewis maintained his brigade headquarters in Ventelet a few kilometers northwest of Davis's command post. Control of all artillery in the division's sector fell to the commanding officer of the French 232 Regiment of Field Artillery.[9]

Colonel Albert J. Bowley, (right) and Colonel Preston A. Brown (left) seen here in the town of Montreuil-aux-Lions with French Colonel Aldebert de Chambrun in the center. Photo credit: NARA (acquired courtesy of Steve Girard and Mitch Ryder.)

Each subsector of artillery received the support of twenty-four 155mm Schneider guns of forty-two-year-old Colonel Albert Jesse Bowley's 17th Field Artillery Regiment.[10] Eighteen more 155mm cannons of the French 333rd Field Artillery augmented the division's firepower.[11] With the six batteries of his regiment split between the 3rd and 4th Brigades, Bowley established his headquarters at Montreuil-aux-Lions to keep in close contact with Chamberlaine at the artillery brigade's command post.[12] Each subsector received firing data to initiate interdiction fire of enemy-held towns and crossroads.[13]

Instructions directed the 1st and 2nd Battalions of both the 12th and 15th Field Artillery Regiments to begin an interdicting barrage on the vital causeways and villages behind the enemy's line at 9:30 P.M. that night.[14] The plan called for each battery to fire at pre-determined targets at specified times throughout the night. Individual bombardments, consisting of two phases, would begin at 9:30 P.M., 10:10 P.M., 10:40 P.M., 12:50 A.M., 2:15 A.M., and 2:40 A.M. In the first phase, set to begin at each of the designated times listed, each battery would provide concentrated fire for five minutes. Each gun had instructions to fire five shells a minute to disperse enemy troop concentrations.

The second phase of the night's operation required fire missions for all the batteries involved to deliver raking fire stretching for a kilometer in every direction from the concentrated targets of phase one. For the second phase, guns of each battery would fire at a rate of three rounds per minute for five minutes to catch any enemy supply caravans and personnel fleeing the initial concentration of fire during phase one.[15]

While messengers delivered the information about the night's preset fire mission to the various batteries of the 12th and 15th Field Artillery, German guns delivered an interdicting gas barrage on Lucy-le-Bocage at 6:30 P.M.[16] The bombardment saturated the landscape with the lingering fumes and accumulative pools of poison agents.[17] The concentration of gas made travel through the streets and the occupation of fume-riddled buildings in the village impossible without gas masks. The men of the 1st Battalion, 6th Marines, and the attached engineers wore their burdensome respirators for hours.

The intensity of the German's artillery fire along the 2nd Division front did not abate, and the movement of supplies to frontline positions became increasingly perilous. The 97th Company, which had reinforced Major Thomas Holcomb's 2nd Battalion 6th Marines near Triangle Farm days earlier, received orders to report back to La Cense Farm immediately.[18]

Upon the company's arrival, directions called for the men to form a work detail hauling ammunition three hundred meters back to Triangle Farm. As they prepared to depart La Cense Farm, additional orders told the 97th Company to wait until darkness to move due to the danger of moving such a large body of troops in the face of increasingly heavy shellfire.[19]

Corporal Havelock Nelson and the rest of the 97th Company used the delay to rest regardless of how abbreviated.[20] As the company remained at 2nd Battalion's headquarters in La Cense Farm, Nelson surveyed the devastation and damage of the property that was the result of a barrage the previous morning. The shattered and mutilated remains of 80th Company men killed in yesterday's bombardment lay in rows underneath a nearby tree awaiting burial.

June 4th Chapter IV

Incoming fire near the farm remained consistent enough the day before that sending burial parties to inter the dead was too hazardous. The sight of the dead caught the attention of Nelson and his comrades. "For several minutes we stood silently, staring at them under the grip of the strange fascination which the first sight of a person who has met violent death seems to hold for the average person. Most of them I had known by sight ever since the days of Quantico, but I cannot be certain of their names now."[21]

The burial of the 80th Company's casualties occurred later in the evening, and Sergeant Donald Paradis relived the somber moment when they interred their comrades killed the previous day. They carried the bodies to the corner of Bois de Clerembauts not far from the barn where they died. "They were laid side by side in a common trench. We were not allowed to witness the burial because of the danger of shellfire. Old Man Fear joined us that day and remained with us, as far as I'm concerned, every moment we were within range of German shellfire and rifle fire. We reacted to this emotion in various ways, over the next 32 harrowing days."[22]

While the 80th Company laid their comrades to rest in Bois de Clerembaus, three Marines from the 6th Marines' Headquarters Company departed Lucy-le-Bocage at 9:00 P.M. on a reconnaissance patrol to identify the exact location of the enemy's front. The sun faded enough beyond the western horizon to cover the three men's movement along the road between Lucy-le-Bocage and the village of Torcy.[23] The regimental intelligence officer, twenty-two-year-old Second Lieutenant William Alfred Eddy, a 1917 Princeton graduate, led the group. Thirty-year-old Private Willett Arthur Stair and twenty-two-year-old Private Mearl Colin Rockwell accompanied Eddy.[24] The three men waited until darkness before continuing north along the roadway.[25]

The distant rumble of French and American artillery fire echoed across the fields from the south, a signal that the division's batteries initiated the first phase of their bombardment for the night. Flashes along the southern horizon accompanied the dull roar of the American batteries going into action. The volume of fire in that first salvo seemed relentless.

Eddy's group remained tactical and calculated in their movements. The route north brought the men to a fork in the road where the dirt trail to the right led northeast toward Belleau Wood, but the men cautiously kept to the left side of the street and headed north toward a veer in the road where it skirted a small patch of forest. They encountered the broken and contorted bodies of two dead French soldiers in the undergrowth. The audible hum of numerous flies buzzing around the decomposing corpses accompanied the overpowering stench, and the three men eagerly continued north along the road away from the unbearable smell.[26]

Back at La Cense Farm, Corporal Havelock Nelson and other members of the 97th Company left under cover of darkness carrying ammunition to Triangle Farm. They started across the three hundred meters of open fields in a single-file column. Each man loaded himself with as many bandoleers of 30.06 ammunition as he could sling over his shoulders. Several men carried heavy wooden munition crates. According to Nelson, they "were warned repeatedly to move silently and to stop in our tracks without looking upward whenever flares were dropped from enemy planes cruising overhead. Scarcely had we emerged from the cover of the woods when the droning hum of a motor warned us of an approaching plane."[27]

The men, burdened under the weight of ammunition, moved forward as fast as they could. They tried to keep their head and eyes straightforward to follow their guide in the dark, but every few steps the men gazed up to determine the direction of the aircraft's approach. "The first flare was not long in coming," said Nelson.[28] "There was first the rapidly falling tiny spark whose descent was suddenly checked as the little parachute of the flare opened up, and then, the wheat field for seventy-five yards on all sides of use was as brilliantly illuminated as if it were noon."[29]

The men immediately stopped, and according to Nelson, ". . . eyes riveted to the ground, and nerves taut with the momentary expectation of hearing the whistle of falling bombs, or the crackling of machine gun bullets from the lazily cruising plane above."[30] To the relief and amazement of the men, the aircraft did nothing. As the flickering light of the enemy's flares faded, the ammunition detail continued forward until another fell from the sky. "Hardly would one flare burn out before another would take its place. So it was dash and 'freeze,' dash and 'freeze,' all the way across."[31]

When the carrying party reached Triangle Farm, they eagerly delivered the ammunition bandoleers and boxes and headed back across the open field toward La Cense. "This time our progress was facilitated rather than hindered by the flares as the plane or planes were operating a little further along the line, and the reflected light helped us to pick our way around the numerous shell-holes which already dotted the intervening field," Nelson claimed.[32]

Thirty minutes before the 2nd Field Artillery Brigade shelled their predetermined targets with concentrated and raking fire; German gunners once again bombarded Bois de Veuilly. 150mm shells tore through the treetops of the woods. Once again, the 18th and 43rd Companies of Lieutenant Colonel Wise's battalion buried their faces against the forest floor.[33]

Shells fell at a rate of three every minute for the next two and a half hours, just enough to keep everyone secluded in dugouts and unable to sleep.[34] One round exploded very close to the hole in which twenty-five-year-old Private Ira Hill Banister, a seaman from Boston, Massachusetts, sought cover. The blast uprooted a large tree which toppled over the onto Banister's hole. According to Gunnery Sergeant Marvin Scott, "The tree, having crushed him about the chest and shoulders, pinned him in his dugout."[35]

June 4th Chapter IV

Despite the incoming fire, several men rushed from their shelter to try and pull the tree off Banister. After a frantic effort, according to Scott, "He was extricated from his foxhole by comrades and carried to the rear on a stretcher."[36] Suffering from hideous wounds to the left shoulder and arm, Banister tried to stay calm as the litter team staggered in the darkness over the broken wooded entanglements of Bois de Veuilly. They carried their mortally wounded comrade hundreds of meters to the nearest dressing station.[37]

The muzzle flashes from the batteries of the 1st and 2nd Battalions of the 12th and 15th Field Artillery Regiments sheltered in the woods illuminated the night sky along the Paris-Metz road. Simultaneously, enemy gunners continued pounding Marigny-en-Orxois. Shells inundated the town all day, and now German batteries initiated a fifty-round barrage of 150mm projectiles.[38]

The town of Marigny-en-Orxois after the war. The buildings to the right show significant battle damage. Photo credit: Gilles Lagin.

Shells crushed already-damaged structures—sending chunks of shattered masonry through the air like shrapnel. Wise claimed, "The Germans kept up their shelling all night. Marigny was getting pretty badly battered. Fires kept springing up here and there."[39]

While the guns of the 12th and 15th Field Artillery finished the first phase barrage of their initial targets, Lieutenant Colonel Joseph Davis dispatched an urgent message to Major Bailey commanding the 1st Battalion, 15th Field Artillery warning him not to fire near Hill 204 or the tiny village of Courteau. This region, one kilometer west of Chateau Thierry, fell within the target area of the battalion's second phase raking fire designated by the 2nd Field Artillery Brigade.[40] Friendly patrols, however, operated in that area. Bailey's battalion received Davis's urgent message as they neared the end of their first phase fire mission. Davis's quick thinking likely prevented a disastrous bombardment of friendly troops.[41]

While American and French batteries bombarded distant German targets, soldiers from Captain Bruce's Company A, 5th Machine Gun Battalion reconnoitered the high ground south of Coupru to establish machine gun positions in case of an enemy breakthrough.

The area behind the village teemed with activity as supply wagons continuously passed to and from the main crossroads south of town. They were under enemy observation the entire time. Scattered debris from the enemy's constant bombardment littered the area. Westover recalled the devastation. "For a hundred yards on either side lay the wreckage of that need. Animals lined the ditches, dead by shellfire or merciful shooting; a few, blood spouting through punctured lungs as they breathed, were targets for our own pistols. Blasted wagons, a disabled truck or two, and a wide assortment of supplies were being removed by working parties before the coming of another day would make them an assistance to Boche observation of the locality."[42]

The horse-drawn caravans bringing loads of ammunition to the front increased their speed as they approached the dangerous crossroads, which were frequently shelled by the enemy. Captain Andrew Bruce noted the bold movement of these ammunition trains while ample daylight remained and in full view of enemy artillery spotters. "'That's one of the toughest jobs I know,' Bruce said. 'The infantry needs ammunition badly or they wouldn't be moving trains except at night.'"[43]

Westover and Bruce waited to observe the ammunition train's passage through the intersection before attempting to cross themselves. The rapid trot of the horse hooves suggested the lorry had accelerated its pace upon the approach of the intersection and the distant thud of enemy cannons echoed across the horizon. The sudden scream of an incoming shell pierced the air. "A leaping burst of flame," exclaimed Westover. "Black clouds of smoke. Hurtling fragments, earth and wood. A great concussion. Then the smoke spread out over the ground; the whirling fragments chunked into receptive earth; and the scene stood revealed. Three horses down; the other reared high in mortal agony. The caisson a pile of broken wreckage. Two men killed. One staggering aimlessly around another crawling slowly away from the horror."[44]

Despite the extreme danger of frequent incoming fire, Westover and Bruce continued to reconnoiter gun positions. They established fields of fire and select routes for ammunition resupply for Company A's reserve gun positions in the event of an enemy breakthrough.[45]

As the two men set up their reserve positions, American guns immediately initiated a bombardment. "A battery of 75's, answering a barrage call from the lines, had opened up behind us," recalled Westover. "Knowing the shells would clear horse and rider, they did not bother to give

June 4th Chapter IV

warning, though we were only twenty yards away. We didn't wait for the second salvo."[46]

While American and French batteries across the battlefront maintained a steady bombardment of German positions after dusk, Second Lieutenant William Eddy and his reconnaissance team crawled north along the edge of the Lucy-Torcy road with extreme caution. Privates Mearl Rockwell and Willett Stair accompanied Eddy along the path where it skirted the side of a patch of woods. Along the way, the men noted the body of an American laying in the open awaiting burial.[47]

After traveling more than a kilometer toward the enemy's lines, they left the road and disappeared into the adjacent field. The three men then crawled through the wheat to the northeast and stopped in the open to listen for activity. They lingered in the area for fifteen minutes and noted lots of enemy activity. The sudden sweeping beam of a German searchlight passed across the field and caused the men to cower with their faces to the ground to avoid detection.

They remained silent and listened to a distant voice emanating from the area of the searchlight. They also noted the distinct sound of a supply wagon moving along a path in Belleau Woods. The clap of horse hooves across the dirt trails echoed across the field. Eddy's group returned to the road carefully retracing their initial path trampled in the grain field. They continued further north by moving parallel to the road. Along the way, they discovered an enemy haversack. Rummaging through the pack, they took the material deemed vital for intelligence and continued even further north.[48]

Another reconnaissance mission unfolded that night when twenty-three-year-old Private Bert Belcher of Rochester, New York, a runner for Captain John Burnes of the 74th Company, was sent to scout the woods just to the northeast of Lucy-le-Bocage. Twenty-year-old Corporal Charles James Kapfer of Utica, New York, accompanied Belcher. Both men were armorers for 74th Company, but on this night, Burnes selected them to scout the terrain fronting the company's lines and maintain patrol contact on the company's right.

The two men waited until dark to move northeast of Lucy-le-Bocage and work their way along a ravine skirting the southern edge of Belleau Wood between the town and the village of Bouresches. The men cautiously moved across the open field disappearing into the night and completely unaware that they were heading into the German lines.[49]

As Belcher and Kapfer departed the lines in front of Lucy-le-Bocage, the 2nd Platoon, 55th Company at Les Mares Farm readied themselves for another potentially eventful night. Second Lieutenant David Kipness, commanding the 5th Marines' Headquarters Company's Stokes mortar section, augmented the 2nd Platoon's position in front of the farm's buildings.

June 4th Chapter IV

Because of the unsuccessful raid by German troops on the night before, Kipness and his men remained on a hair-triggered alert. Against the backdrop of distant artillery fire, Kipness heard the breaking and crunching of the stalks of wheat in front of his platoon's position. Captain Frank Whitehead commanding the sixty-two-man detachment from Headquarters Company at the farm recalled, "Lieutenant Kipness reported to me that he had heard the enemy working in the brush, and he believed that they were placing heavy machine guns preparatory to another raid. He was instructed to beat them to it and to stage a raid of his own."[50] Kipness summoned some of his men, and they cautiously crept away into the darkness.

While Kipness and his crew snaked their way through the fields to route a potential enemy attack, German gunners again bombarded Marigny-en-Orxois at 10:15 P.M. with yet another salvo of 150mm shells.[51] Just before the barrage began, twenty-nine-year-old Captain Charles Percy Holliday, a former enlisted Marine serving as the quartermaster for the 5th Marines, accompanied a horse-drawn wagon loaded with grenades towards the town.

Along the outskirts of Marigny-en-Orxois, Holliday encountered forty-six-year-old Captain James McCoy, the 5th Regiment's munitions officer from Fall River, Massachusetts. Holliday recognized McCoy's voice in the dark and stepped off the lorry to visit with him. McCoy instructed the driver where to deliver the grenades and then turned to greet his old friend. As the wagon pulled away, the two men stood along the roadside and casually conversed for a few minutes.

Just as they parted company, the distant report of enemy guns echoed through the night. Holliday remembered, "Captain McCoy then started for the town when a shell struck the road a few yards away, killing some of the mules hitched to the wagon. I ran forward to see what damage had been done, and I tripped over the body of Captain McCoy. After an examination I discovered he was dead; so I sent word to Captain DeCarre notifying him that Captain McCoy had been killed."[52] McCoy died instantly from the shell fragments that riddled him. His body lay along the road into the village of Marigny-en-Orxois for the remainder of the night.[53] The barrage continued for several minutes and dropped thirty 150mm shells into the town.[54] The concentrated shellfire started several fires throughout the village. The glow of burning structures silhouetted the broken structures against the dimly moonlit sky.

For the Marines at Les Mares Farm, the night also erupted into pandemonium as gunfire erupted hundreds of meters out in front of the property. Along the farm's right flank, the Marines of the 55th Company's 2nd platoon along with members of the regiment's headquarters company opened fire. Their well-directed rifle fire assailed enemy troops who were using the cover of night to set up a machine gun position fronting the farm. In a matter of seconds, the lively exchange ended. Soon after, members of

June 4th Chapter IV

Second Lieutenant Kipness' patrol snaked through the darkness and returned to the farm. They successfully aided in repulsing the enemy's efforts.

Kipness carried in hand several pairs of shoulder insignia he ripped from the tunics of dead Germans they just killed and brought them back to battalion headquarters.[55]

On the eastern portion of the 4th Brigade's front, soldiers of Company E, 2nd Battalion, 2nd Engineers carried out their orders at 11:00 P.M. to depart their current position in line with Major Holcomb's 2nd Battalion, 6th Marines near Triangle Farm. They moved nearly six kilometers east to occupy a reserve position in a patch of woods a kilometer south of the Marigny-en-Orxois.

Once in this new location, Company E was to receive a resupply of rations and a well-deserved rest.[56] For Corporal Lloyd Pike and the 2nd Platoon, 79th Company, the departure of the engineers came as a surprise. Pike had command of several automatic rifle teams that spent the previous days in support of the engineers. That night, he discovered Company E's section of the line occupied only by his Chauchat crews with no engineers in sight. According to Pike:

> I did not know exactly what I should do, but I felt I had some kind of command responsibility and should report the situation to my superior. I found Lieutenant Leonard and Captain Zane together in some building behind the line and reported the situation. I can still remember how this meeting hurt my feelings. Captain Zane told me he knew about the engineers leaving and that my group should remain in place. His attitude gave me the impression that he thought I was asking to withdraw. I had no such thoughts, and I left the conference as mad as a brand new corporal can get at a captain.[57]

Just behind Holcomb's battalion, Captain Bailey Coffenberg's 80th Company left La Cense Farm at approximately 10:00 P.M. They hiked nearly two kilometers northwest to Lucy-le-Bocage to relieve part of the over-stretched 75th Company of Major Maurice Shearer's 1st Battalion, 6th Marines. Trumpeter Hugo Meyer of the 80th Company described Lucy-le-Bocage as, "a wrecked village on the front line."[58]

By the end of June 4th, the dramatic increase in German artillery made life an endless hell for the men at the front. Near La Loge Farm, however, the experience for the 4th Brigade Headquarters staff was a stark contrast to the nerve-wracking existence along the frontlines. Brigadier General Harbord and his command spent the evening enjoying the comforts accessible only to rear echelon personnel.

Despite their location far behind the frontlines, Harbord's staff had to block all the light emanating from their building to avoid enemy artillery fire at night. "There was no embargo on noise, however," claimed

June 4th Chapter IV

Harbord.⁵⁹ With Colonel McClosky's 12th Field Artillery Regiment's headquarters staff also located at La Loge, the two groups listened to the performance of several of personnel who had instruments. McCloskey's group included several members of the famed Yale Banjo club.

According to Harbord, "To the ensemble talent, I contributed my aide Fielding S. Robinson, who played guitar and had brought one to war with him. Pell Foster, an army officer of one of the batteries, joined with a violin. Nearly every evening we had music."⁶⁰ To the backdrop of distant artillery, they enjoyed their impromptu concert.

In contrast to the brigade staff's recreational gathering, Second Lieutenant William Eddy, along with Privates Mearl Rockwell and Willett Stair continued their dangerous reconnaissance. Eddy's route took them several hundred meters southeast of Torcy just off the main road from Lucy-le-Bocage. They moved through the field to the east.

Near the enemy's front, they noted the sound of a man coughing four or five times just northwest of their position. They also listened to a faintly audible conversation between German soldiers in the distance that carried across the open. The specifics of the enemy soldiers' banter was indistinguishable at that distance, but the dialogue lasted on and off for half an hour.

At 12:00 A.M., they heard the clear and distinct sound of an enemy supply cart heading west along the Belleau-Torcy road. The speedy clap of horse hooves along the pavement suggested the caravan traversed the lane at a very rapid pace. The wagon slowed as it approached the turn north into the village of Torcy. A short time later another cart passed at the same speed followed by another going the opposite direction. By 1:15 A.M., Eddy was satisfied with the information he gathered. He led the group back to the Lucy-Torcy road. They moved two and a half kilometers back to Lucy-le-Bocage and arrived at 2:15 A.M.⁶¹

---

[1] *Records of the Second Division (Regular)* Volume 9, N.P.
[2] Operations of 2nd Field Artillery Brigade, Box 81, RG 120.9.3, NARA College Park, MD.
[3] Ibid.
[4] Ibid.
[5] Field Message from Lieutenant Colonel Davis to Major Bailey at 12:00 P.M., June 4, 1918, Box 82, RG 120.9.3, National Archives, College Park, MD.
[6] Kean, *Dear Marraine*, 97.
[7] Operations of 2nd Field Artillery Brigade, Box 81, RG 120.9.3, NARA College Park, MD.
[8] Ibid.
[9] Ibid.
[10] Ibid.
[11] Ibid.
[12] Ibid.

June 4th Chapter IV

[13] *Records of the Second Division (Regular)*, Volume 9, N.P.
[14] Ibid.
[15] Operations of 2nd Field Artillery Brigade, Box 81, RG 120.9.3, NARA College Park, MD., and *Records of the Second Division (Regular)*, Volume 9, N.P.
[16] *Records of the Second Division (Regular)*, Volume 9, N.P.
[17] Ibid.
[18] Nelson, "Paris-Metz Road," *Leatherneck*, 13.
[19] Ibid.
[20] Ibid.
[21] Ibid.
[22] Paradis, *The World War I Memoirs of Don V. Paradis* 43., and U.S. Marine Corps Muster Rolls, 1893-1940, Record Group 127, NARA, Washington, D.C.
[23] *Records of the Second Division (Regular)*, Volume 7, N.P.
[24] Official Military Personnel File for Private Mearl Colin Rockwell, RG 127, NPRC St. Louis, MO, and Official Military Personnel File for Private Willett Arthur Stair, RG 127, NPRC St. Louis, MO.
[25] *Records of the Second Division (Regular)*, Volume 7, N.P.
[26] Ibid.
[27] Nelson, "Paris-Metz Road," *Leatherneck,* 13.
[28] Ibid.
[29] Ibid.
[30] Ibid.
[31] Ibid.
[32] Ibid.
[33] *Records of the Second Division (Regular)*, Volume 6, N.P.
[34] Ibid.
[35] Burial File of Private Ira Banister, Eye-witness statement by First Lieutenant Marvin Scott, Box 231, RG 92.9, Records of Graves Registration Services, NARA College Park, MD.
[36] Ibid.
[37] Ibid. Note: Another Marine killed in this barrage was eighteen-year-old Drummer Charles Wesley Price who died at 10:30 P.M. in the Bois de Veuilly.
[38] *Records of the Second Division (Regular)*, Volume 9, N.P.
[39] Wise and Frost, *A Marine Tells it to You*, 205.
[40] Operations of 2nd Field Artillery Brigade, Box 81, RG 120.9.3, NARA College Park, MD.
[41] Field Message from Lieutenant Colonel Davis to Major Bailey at 9:40 P.M., June 4, 1918, Box 82, RG 120.9.3, Records of the American Expeditionary Forces, National Archives College Park,

MD., and *Records of the Second Division (Regular)*, Volume 6, N.P.
[42] Westover, *Suicide Battalions*, 120.
[43] Ibid, 121.
[44] Ibid.
[45] Ibid.
[46] Ibid.
[47] Note: This is most likely a deceased member of 1st Battalion 6th Marines who suffered many casualties that particular day from German artillery.
[48] *Records of the Second Division (Regular)*, Volume 7, N.P.
[49] Burial File of Private Bert Belcher, Eye-witness statements by Private Daniel Kelly, Private Percy B. Caley, and Private Irl W. Brown, Box 330, RG 92.9 Records of Graves Registration Services, NARA College Park, MD., and Diary of Asa J. Smith 74th Company 6th Regiment U.S. Marines, Alfred M. Gray Research Library, Quantico, VA.
[50] *The Aisne Defensive,* Whitehead to ABMC, Box 190, RG 117.4.2, NARA College Park, MD.
[51] *Records of the Second Division (Regular)*, Volume 9, N.P.
[52] Report on the death of officers of the 5th Marines, Box 25, RG 127, NARA Washington, D.C.
[53] Official Military Personnel File for Captain James McCoy, RG 127, NPRC St. Louis, MO., and U.S. Marine Corps Muster Rolls, 1893-1940, Record Group 127, NARA, Washington, D.C. Note: McCoy spent twenty years as a Marine and saw action in the Philippine campaign of 1901, Vera Cruz in 1914, and Haiti in 1915.
[54] *Records of the Second Division (Regular)*, Volume 9, N.P.
[55] *The Aisne Defensive,* Whitehead to ABMC, Box 190, RG 117.4.2, NARA College Park, MD.
[56] Burton, *History of the Second Engineers 1916-1919,* 43.
[57] Pike, *The Battle For Belleau Woods, As I Remember It About 60 Years Later*, 9.
[58] "Tales told by Overseas Marines," *Recruiters Bulletin*, August 1918, 30.
[59] Harbord, *The American Army in France*, 287.
[60] Ibid, 288. Note: Twenty-four-year-old Second Lieutenant Pell William Foster Jr. of New York City, was detached from 1st Battalion 12th Field Artillery to serve with Harbord's staff.
[61] *Records of the Second Division (Regular)*, Volume 7, N.P.

JUNE 5ᵀᴴ

June 5th Chapter I

The other fellow was completely soaked in the runner's blood by the time he was able to push the corpse aside and scramble out for fresh air.
  -Corporal James Hatcher 84th Company, 3rd Battalion, 6th Marines

Shortly after dark on June 4th, Colonel Paul Malone's 23rd Infantry Regiment moved out of their position stretching west of Bois de Veuilly. They hiked toward Montreuil-aux-Lions.[1] Malone's soldiers had held the front for days, and now the 167th French Division took over this part of the line. The field order displacing Malone's regiment reduced the width of the 2nd Division's sector significantly.

The brook running north out of Champillon nearly parallel with the road to Bussiares became the newly designated western limits for the 2nd Division. This new perimeter went into effect at 8:00 A.M. June 5th.[2] Despite this reduced front, Lieutenant Colonel Wise's battalion, along with the attached Hotchkiss crews of the 6th Machine Gun Battalion, as well as the 17th and 66th Companies still held the ground from the Champillon-Bussiares road all the way west through Bois de Veuilly. This position was well outside of the division's redesignated western limits. Wise's battalion, however, could not vacate until relieved by the French.

South of Hill 142, the 84th Company, 3rd Battalion, 6th Marines moved out of the forest just northeast of La Voie du Chatel during the night. They relocated to avoid enemy shells that seemed to target these woods frequently. The company moved north across the open pasture toward the tree line along the southern portion of Hill 142. Private James Hatcher claimed, "It was pitch black when we deployed at five pace intervals and lay down there at the edge of the trees. Some French troops had occupied that position a short time before and I was most obnoxiously impressed during the night with their lack of sanitary discipline."[3]

From this position, the 84th Company remained a kilometer behind the 82nd and 83rd Companies on the front lines near Hill 142. The 82nd and 83rd Companies moved into position days earlier to plug the vulnerable gap between the 5th and 6th Marines. Despite their position hundreds of meters behind the front, the precarious gap along this section of the line kept the Marines of the 84th Company alerted to possible enemy infiltration throughout the night.

Just southeast of Hill 142 the left flank of Major Maurice Shearer's 1st Battalion, 6th Marines positioned in Bois de Champillon, braced for another terrifying night along the front. Corporal Warren Jackson recalled the night "brought short and troubled snatches of sleep," as he took refuge in a five-foot dugout with twenty-four-year-old Private Theodore Carl Rosenow.[4] By dawn, the company shifted positions yet again, but much to the delight of Jackson who recalled, "There were more men than necessary to fill the front

June 5th Chapter I

line proper, and my hole, along with some other fellows', was some steps back. All I had to do while there was just sit and pick out the joys of life afforded."[5]

One misery visited upon the 95th Company line, however, came courtesy of a 37mm gun crew from the regimental headquarters company. The 37mm, a direct-fire weapon known as the one-pounder, fired its lethal volley at the distant German front. "I can hear it now as at intervals this little gun fired into the enemy lines. And the Germans replied with their big guns, so we wished our one-pounder would stop," Jackson recalled.[6]

Just over a kilometer east of the 95th Company, a lone French plane of the Escadrille [squadron] 252 buzzed over the American line around 8:25 A.M. and surveyed the layout of the battlefront. The aircraft ventured a kilometer east of the American lines. Just above the treetops of Belleau Wood, a staccato of German machine gun fire from within the woods sent a volley of bullets skyward toward the French aviator.[7]

Despite this brave reconnaissance, Germans planes quickly demonstrated their superiority of the skies. At 8:45 a.m., five German aviators flew unmolested over Hill 204 along the Paris-Metz Road.[8] Even Brigadier General Harbord, from his brigade headquarters at La Loge Farm, noted the enemy's domination of the skies that morning. The only friendly balloon observation that took place occurred twelve kilometers south of his brigade's front. "There are visible from these headquarters," noted Harbord, "four German balloons and no French balloons. The hum of German airplanes is almost constant over our front lines. It is recommended that the French authorities be called upon to show some of that superiority in the air which is referred to in almost every French and British paper recently."[9]

Later that morning, Harbord toured a section of the front via the Paris-Metz road over to the shattered village of Lucy-le-Bocage. The entire route, according to Harbord, had hardly a turn or curve in the road or even a sector of the line where an enemy balloon was not within view. According to Harbord, "Any activity or appearance of people along that line in sight of these balloons is followed within a very few minutes by shell fire."[10]

During the early morning, Sergeant Gerald Thomas and the 3rd Platoon of the 75th Company along the eastern edge of Bois de Champillon spent a seemingly quiet day compared to the intense activity the previous day. Earlier that morning, Second Lieutenant David Redford, commanding the 3rd Platoon, went to battalion headquarters in Lucy-le-Bocage. He returned with news that the battalion's original commander, thirty-seven-year-old Major John Arthur Hughes had returned from the Army Infantry Specialist School at Langres, France.

Hughes, absent since May 5th, took command of the battalion from Major Maurice Shearer. Hughes, however, knew nothing regarding the specific location of his companies. The battalion intelligence officer, Second Lieutenant Carleton Burr, suffered a slight wound earlier which necessitated temporary evacuation. Burr's absence left Thomas as the battalion's senior intelligence asset. According to Redford, Hughes wanted Thomas to report to battalion headquarters immediately. "I collected my gear, told my comrades goodbye and made my way back to the command post at Lucy," recalled Thomas.[11]

Once at Lucy-le-Bocage, Thomas found the seemingly invulnerable Hughes—a towering man whose giant frame fit his personality. Thomas, in his memories of Hughes, said, "He was a big, rugged type of fellow who fitted into everything."[12]

A Marine officer for seventeen years, Hughes' thunderous voice, hoarse from years of shouting parade-deck cadence and commands, catered to his harsh and often-despotic method of leadership, which affectionately earned him the nickname "Johnny the Hard." First Lieutenant William Mathews, the intelligence officer of the 2nd Battalion 5th Marines, remembered of Hughes, "Johnny, the Hard" Hughes was perhaps the best drillmaster of the Marine Corps . . . I can always remember him when he was drilling the battalion at Quantico before he took them overseas, and shouting the order, 'Heads up, goddamit, heads up!'"[13]

Marines throughout the corps knew of Hughes. During the battle for Vera Cruz in April of 1914, he earned the Medal of Honor for leading the 15th Company, 2nd Marine Regiment, which included then Sergeant Daniel Daly and a young Second Lieutenant Lester Wass, through two days of vicious nonstop street fighting.[14]

Hughes now had the responsibility of determining the battalion front from the chaos and confusion of the previous few days. Thomas recalled his conversation with Hughes just before they left to inspect the front, "He said, 'This thing's in a hell of a mess. And I've just got to know where my battalion is, and nobody can tell me where all my units are. I want you to go to the right of our line—find out where it is. Then work your way back along the line and plot the location of our units as well as you're able to do.' He didn't give me a map, but did give me some sketching papers."[15] Hughes added, "'I am going to start at the left, and we will meet some place within the battalion sector.'"[16]

Before carrying out this critical duty, Thomas sent for twenty-six-year-old Corporal George Frederick Kraus and his twenty-two-year-old younger brother, Private Carl Robert Kraus. These men, usually assigned to the 76th Company, served as battalion scouts and according to Thomas, "both of whom were talented sketchers."[17] Once the Kraus brothers reported to Thomas, the three men left Lucy-le-Bocage. They tried to locate what they believed to be the eastern-most flank of the battalion but instead discovered members of the 97th Company, which had been detached from the 3rd Battalion three days ago to fill a gap in the 2nd Battalion, 6th Marines' front near Triangle Farm. Thomas stopped for a moment to visit with Captain Robert Voeth commanding the 97th Company. "He [Voeth] pointed out the

June 5th Chapter I

lay of nearby units, including a gap of about a thousand yards that intervened between his left and the right of the 1st Battalion," recalled Thomas.[18] "The Kraus brothers and I worked our way along and accounted for everybody—we found that a good part of the 74th Company was down in front of the 75th and things were pretty well mixed up."[19]

Earlier that morning, inside the southwestern fringe of Belleau Wood, Private Bert Belcher and Corporal Charles James Kapfer of the 74th Company crept through the dense undergrowth trying to make as little noise as possible. The two men were detailed the night before to reconnoiter the woods and establish a liaison to the east. The slope of the wooded terrain and the density of the brush were unconducive to stealth.

The men became hopelessly disoriented and unknowingly filtered through a gap of the German 461st Infantry front situated along the southwestern edge of the woods. They meandered through the woods for hours completely unaware they had penetrated enemy lines.

Private Bert Belcher. Photo Credit: World War Service Record, Rochester and Monroe County, NY.

Suddenly, a German machine fired on them from somewhere to their right. Instinctively, both men dropped to the ground. In the same instant, several bullets from the initial volley struck Kapfer in the right arm and side. For a few seconds of terror and confusion, Kapfer flattened out with his face in the dirt to avoid the cascade of bullets striking the ground nearby. Several volleys hissed just over him and Belcher. The ear-splitting crack of the Maxim gun at such a close range was overwhelming. Kapfer noticed, at his side, the lifeless body of Belcher.

The same barrage of fire that struck Kapfer had killed Belcher instantly. The enemy gunner did not relent and continued shooting in short bursts. Despite the withering fire, Kapfer un-holstered his pistol and emptied an entire magazine of ammunition in the direction of the unseen enemy gunner. Realizing he had a quick moment to escape, Kapfer ran out of the kill zone despite his painful wounds.[20] German soldiers of the 461st Infantry later recovered Belcher's body.[21]

June 5th Chapter I

Kapfer stumbled over the irregular terrain and thick undergrowth as he fled. He staggered for several hundred meters before emerging out of the southern tree line in full view of the 74th Company's front. Private Asa Smith remembered seeing Kapfer in the distance crawling on his hands and knees toward the company's lines.[22] Twenty-year-old Private Edgar Pensinger Shrader also spotted Kapfer struggling back toward the company's position, "I was a runner too, and was in a machine gun outpost when the corporal came up."[23] Twenty-one-year-old Private Percy Burdelle Caley, a squad mate of Belcher's, recalled how the severely wounded and panic-stricken Kapfer was as he struggled to explain what happened. According to Caley, "The corporal came crawling back, his arm shot, he said Belcher, and he were waylaid and shot. Belcher was dead before he left him."[24] Comrades applied rudimentary dressing to Kapfer's wounds and immediately evacuated him to a dressing station.

Along the front of the 1st Battalion, 6th Marines, Sergeant Thomas and his battalion scouts, Corporal George Kraus and his brother Private Carl Kraus, continued surveying the line at the demand of Major Hughes. The major's instructions emphasized the need for haste in completing their mission, and according to Thomas, "Time had not afforded us much opportunity to conceal our movements."[25]

By mid-morning, the three men approached the position of the 3rd Platoon of the 75th Company. "In the edge of a wood just beyond the 3rd Platoon, a voice called to us, saying, 'You men get under cover, or you will draw fire.' It was our regimental commander, Colonel Catlin," Thomas remembered.[26] "In a minute Hughes came up by the side of Catlin and said, 'Thomas, go back to battalion headquarters. I know this part of the line, and you've got us on the other side so I'll meet you there in a few minutes.'"[27]

Corporal George F. Kraus 76th Company. Photo Credit: Marine Corps History Division.

On the far western flank of the 1st Battalion, 6th Marines, Corporal Warren Jackson, and his 95th Company comrades were falsely encouraged by the temporary lull in the artillery fire. They sat and bantered amongst each other about their hardship over the past few days. Jackson recalled his sense of complacency, "A part of the time we wandered along the lines, that is, until we learned better than to expose ourselves."[28] From Bois de Champillon, they could see across the open field toward the village of Torcy. The view allowed Jackson to watch enemy troops far in the distance. He remembered:

June 5th Chapter I

Some hundred yards out was a small ravine where the Germans were understood to be. Beyond was a gently rising swell, and near the crest of the hill some of the houses of the village could be seen. Over this hill, we saw a man leisurely walking one day. Undoubtedly, he was a German soldier, though he was too far away to know definitely. How strange it seemed—a German. Yes, there was actually one of them. One or two of the expert riflemen in the company had rifles equipped with telescopic sights, though no one fired.[29]

Just west of the 95th Company, Marines of the 83rd Company in position along the woods south of Hill 142, kept a careful watch on the distant tree line following a brief exchange of gunfire earlier that morning. At dawn, the Germans initiated a minor probe against the two platoons of Sibley's battalion, who easily repulsed the enemy without sustaining heavy losses.[30] When the late morning sun nearly peaked, the company returned to their mundane work inside the cover of the woods. They improved their dugouts, laid wire, and helped to better excavate and fortify machine gun positions for the platoon of 73rd Machine Gun Company holding the line with them.[31]

Despite the danger of shellfire, Colonel Catlin again visited his men along the front. Shortly after Catlin left the 1st Battalion's position, he walked over to visit the 82nd and 83rd Companies. For Private James Scarbrough and most of the other young Marines, the presence of any senior officer intimidated them, especially Catlin—a seemingly indomitable steward of the Marine Corps. The men all understood Catlin had survived the explosion of the USS Maine in 1898. They all knew he earned the Medal of Honor for actions at Vera Cruz.

The colonel's presence, however, did not stop Scarbrough's mischievous comrade, twenty-two-year-old Private Edward Joseph Steinmetz, a machinist from Hamilton, Ohio, from his usual frolics. Scarbrough watched as Catlin shook hands and greeted the men, "Steinmetz kept ribbing me saying, 'Go on and say hello to your old pal! Maybe he'll give you a drink from his canteen!' which mortified me that somebody was going to hear. I told him to knock it off, or we'd be spending the rest of the war in the stockade. Nobody else was in on the joke, so they didn't know what to think," claimed Scarbrough.[32]

As the 2nd Division prepared for another terrifying day, French officers of General Jean Degoutte's 21st French Corps assembled plans that morning to conduct an attack based on the idea that the Germans held advantageous terrain along the heights of the Clignon brook. The 2nd Division's line, as well as the 167th French Division, occupied less-than-ideal positions, and the 21st Corps wanted to seize the high ground south of and parallel to the

Clignon brook. Capturing that ground would ultimately straighten out the entire front.

The French 21st Corps' plan would not take long to orchestrate and could begin within the next twenty-four hours. Notifying and briefing the various battalions of the 2nd Division scheduled to conduct the attack, however, took nearly all of the intervening time. The 21st Corps' plan also required relocating some of the involved battalions several kilometers to designated jump-off points. Several units did not receive notification of the attack until the last minute. Given the less-than-perfect communication as well as the general ignorance of the terrain due to a lack of maps, the next forty-eight hours were almost guaranteed to be chaotic, confusing, and disastrous for the 2nd Division.

A readjust of the brigade's layout set to commence after dark was sent that morning to the 6th Regimental command post at Lucy-le-Bocage.[33] The 5th Marines' Regimental Headquarters at the rock quarry outside of Marigny-en-Orxois also received the command. This order directed Major Benjamin Berry's 3rd Battalion, 5th Marines to relieve Major Hughes's 1st Battalion, 6th Marines currently holding the front stretching from Lucy-le-Bocage northwest towards Bois de Champillon.[34] Hughes' battalion was to proceed nearly two kilometers south of Marigny-en-Orxois to serve as corps reserve.[35]

The same memorandum relieved Major Thomas Holcomb's 2nd Battalion, 6th Marines from their position stretching from Le Thiolet, north through Bois de Clerembauts, and all the way to Triangle Farm.[36] Once relieved by the 23rd Infantry, orders directed Holcomb's men to the northwest corner of Bois Clerembauts just behind the line near the 2nd Battalion headquarters at La Cense Farm.[37]

Compared with the previous forty-eight hours, things along the front remained comparatively quiet for Holcomb's Marines during the afternoon. Despite the relative calm, the threat of incoming artillery fire prompted the men to remain disciplined and avoid unnecessary movement which would undoubtedly attract fire. Corporal Frank McClelland of the 78th Company spent most of the day in the company's forward sniper post approximately 150 feet beyond the line—a position dug several nights earlier.

While at this location, McClelland noted the bright red tile rooftops of the village of Bouresches. "From this post, dug during the night, there was clear view of the town, possibly five hundred yards away. I occupied the post one day from before dawn to dusk. I cannot say that I scored any hits, although I fired a few rounds at brief appearances of ducking figures—they were alert to our sniping."[38]

At La Cense Farm, Sergeant Paradis, working as a battalion runner, recalled, "The Major spent considerable time at regimental headquarters. Runners came and went throughout the day. We knew action was planned. Late in the afternoon, Major Holcomb told me to take one runner to the

June 5th Chapter I

junction of the Paris-Metz and the Lucy-le-Bocage roads. Our orders were to intercept the ration carts and our field kitchens and guide them into Lucy-le-Bocage, a town north of the Paris-Metz road."[39]

As Paradis left La Cense Farm, Sergeant Gerald Thomas returned to Lucy-le-Bocage having completed his sketched layout of the right half of the 1st Battalion, 6th Marines' front. Inside the town, he awaited the arrival of Major Hughes as instructed. The major arrived about thirty minutes later, but before Thomas could confer with him about the battalion's line, Hughes exclaimed, "Well, as it turns out, we're not going to need this. Because this thing is such a mess that nobody can straighten it out and we're going to fall back to a ridge during the night about two miles from here, and we expect orders from regiment at any time to do that."[40]

With that information, Thomas could do nothing but wait and take refuge in one of the village's structures not too heavily damaged by shellfire. "Maybe a half hour or an hour later," remembered Thomas, "I heard a noise out in the street."[41] A courier vehicle carrying Major Benjamin Berry, commanding the 3rd Battalion, 5th Marines, arrived at Lucy-le-Bocage. Berry quickly leaped from the car and approached Hughes. "Dead-o," Berry yelled summoning Hughes as he rapidly walked toward him, "all orders are off. I'm going to relieve you during the night."[42] Berry gave very vague information about his battalion's orders to attack the following day, but Hughes did not receive this news very well.

According to Thomas, the major "indulged himself in some picturesque language regarding Berry and this new plan."[43] Berry welcomed this latest movement since his battalion remained out of the line as corps reserve for most of the engagement, and just returned to the brigade's command the day before. Hughes' men, desirous of rest, waited until the scheduled relief later that night.[44]

News of the planned movements due to the readjustment of the 2nd Division's front created a surge in foot and vehicle traffic behind the front. German artillery spotters were quick to observe the heightened activity. For men of the 84th Company, their relocation the previous night took them from the cover of the woods northeast of La Voie du Chatel and into the southern edge of the forest south of Hill 142.

This new location put the 84th Company even further northeast of the town of La Voie du Chatel, which made the hazardous job of a runner even more perilous since messengers had to traverse 500 additional meters of open field to deliver vital information to and from the village. The artillery-laced gauntlet between this new position and La Voie du Chatel caught up with one 84th Company runner that morning. According to Private James Hatcher:

> . . . A runner was just reaching company headquarters when he heard a shell approaching. He dived for a hole in which another

man lay, but the shell struck a tree and exploded in the air before the runner's body had reached the hole. A chunk of steel sliced off the top of his head and the body tumbled in upon the other man. Brains and blood gushed from the mutilated head. The other fellow was completely soaked in the runner's blood by the time he was able to push the corpse aside and scramble out for fresh air.[45]

At 10:00 A.M., shellfire inundated the woods northeast of La Voie du Chatel for approximately an hour, making passage along roads running out of the village virtually impossible.[46] By 11:00 A.M., German batteries targeted the small farm Maison Blanche, a property that hugged the north side of the Paris-Metz road where it curved to the east as it ascended a gentle wooded rise.[47]

Luckily, Colonel Catlin vacated the farm complex earlier that morning to relocate his regimental command post. He remembered, "It was on the 5th that, owing to the likelihood of early action, I moved my P.C. again, leaving Mont [Maison] Blanche and returning to the neighborhood of Lucy. By this move to an apparently more dangerous location it is probable that my life was saved, for a German shell reduced to a heap of ruins the room I had occupied at Blanche Farm very soon after I vacated it."[48]

Shells also inundated Lucy-le-Bocage. The constant bombardment reduced the town to a pile of shattered ruins, broken timbers, and crumbling masonry. During the late morning, incoming rounds exploded near an ammunition dump containing thousands of 30.06 and 8mm French Lebel rounds on the edge of the village. Within seconds, the munitions caught on fire. The flames grew and soon consumed entire crates of ammunition bandoliers. As the inferno engulfed the ammunition dump, German shells continued landing in and around the town.

Within seconds, bullets of all calibers cooked off in the blaze. Everyone in the village was forced to seek cover due to enemy shellfire. The ammunition fire intensified every second and soon developed into a blazing cauldron of exploding bullets and other munitions.

Despite the extreme danger of incoming shells, forty-four-year-old First Sergeant Daniel Daly of the 73rd Machine Gun Company left the shelter of a building and raced toward the burning ammunition dump. Rifle and machine gun rounds exploded like a string of firecrackers sending slugs and broken shell casings flying everywhere throughout the debris-riddled streets.

The exploding ammunition fueled the fire's intensity with each passing second, but none of this deterred Daly. He managed to extinguish the flames, which soon dwindled into a massive whirling plume of smoke that rose above the village. Rounds inside the burnt crates continued cooking off from the extreme heat for several minutes after Daly extinguished the flames, but his actions prevented further loss of vital ammunition and casualties.[49] The German shelling, however, did not end.

June 5th Chapter I

First Sergeant Dan Daly. Photo credit: Marine Corps History Division.

---

[1] ABMC, *2nd Division Summary of Operations*, 10.
[2] Ibid.
[3] Hatcher, *Citizen Soldier,* N.P.
[4] Jackson, *His Time in Hell, A Texas Marine in France,* 96.
[5] Ibid.
[6] Ibid, 97.
[7] *Records of the Second Division (Regular)* Volume 4, N.P.
[8] *Records of the Second Divisio (Regular)* Volume 9, N.P.
[9] *Records of the Second Division (Regular)* Volume 6, N.P.

June 5th Chapter I

[10] Ibid.
[11] General Gerald B. Thomas memoir, Alfred M. Gray Research Library, Quantico, VA.
[12] General Gerald B. Thomas, interview by Robert Asprey, Alfred M. Gray Research Library, Quantico, VA.
[13] Correspondence William R. Mathews to Robert Asprey, 21 February 1964, Box 8, Mathews, W.R. file 1962-1966, Robert Asprey Collection, Howard Gotlieb Archival Research Center, Boston University, Boston, MA.
[14] U.S. Marine Corps Muster Rolls, 1893-1940, Record Group 127, NARA, Washington, D.C.
[15] General Gerald B. Thomas, interview by Robert Asprey, Alfred M. Gray Research Library, Quantico, VA.
[16] General Gerald B. Thomas memoir, Alfred M. Gray Research Library, Quantico, VA.
[17] Ibid.
[18] General Gerald B. Thomas, interview by Robert Asprey, Alfred M. Gray Research Library, Quantico, VA.
[19] Ibid.
[20] Burial File of Private Bert Belcher, Eye-witness statements by Private Daniel Kelly, Private Percy B. Caley, and Private Edgar Shrader, Box 330, RG 92.9, Records of Graves Registration Services, NARA College Park, MD.
[21] War Diary and Annexes 237th Division 4 June 1918, *Translation of War Diaries of German Units,* Vol. 4. Note: The 237th Division made note that a corpse of a Marine from the 6th Marine Regiment was recovered. The report does not definitively identify the individual, but it is probable that the body was that of Private Belcher.
[22] Diary of Asa J. Smith 74th Company 6th Regiment U.S. Marines, Alfred M. Gray Research Library, Quantico, VA.
[23] Burial File of Private Bert Belcher, Eye-witness statement by Private Edgar Shrader, Box 330, RG 92.9, Records of Graves Registration Services, NARA College Park, MD.
[24] Burial File of Private Bert Belcher, Eye-witness statement by Private Percy B. Caley, Box 330, RG 92.9, Records of Graves Registration Services, NARA College Park, MD.
[25] General Gerald B. Thomas memoir, Alfred M. Gray Research Library, Quantico, VA.
[26] Ibid.
[27] General Gerald B. Thomas, interview by Robert Asprey, Alfred M. Gray Research Library, Quantico, VA.
[28] Jackson, *His Time in Hell, A Texas Marine in France,* 99.

June 5th Chapter I

---

[29] Ibid.
[30] *History of the Third battalion, Sixth regiment,* 14.
[31] Ibid, and Scarbrough *They Called us Devil Dogs,* N.P
[32] Scarbrough, *They Called us Devil Dogs,* N.P.
[33] *Records of the Second Division (Regular)* Volume 5, N.P.
[34] Ibid.
[35] Ibid.
[36] Ibid.
[37] Correspondence Captain Clifton B. Cates with Major X. H. Price ABMC, 22 November, 1926, Box 190 RG 117.4.2 ABMC Correspondence with former Division officers NARA College Park, MD.
[38] McClelland, Story of My Life, Alfred M. Gray Research Library, Quantico, VA.
[39] Paradis, *The World War I Memoirs of Don V. Paradis,* 43.
[40] General Gerald B. Thomas, interview by Robert Asprey, Alfred M. Gray Research Library, Quantico, VA.
[41] Ibid.
[42] Ibid.
[43] General Gerald B. Thomas memoir, Alfred M. Gray Research Library, Quantico, VA.
[44] *Records of the Second Division (Regular)* Volume 5, N.P.
[45] Hatcher, *Citizen Soldier,* N.P. Note: Private Hatcher does not identify the runner, but twenty-three-year-old Frank Shurtleff Carlson was killed by enemy artillery fire that day. He is the only member of the 84th Company killed June 5, 1918.
[46] *Records of the Second Division (Regular)* Volume 9, N.P.
[47] Ibid.
[48] Catlin, *With the Help of God and a Few Marines,* 103.
[49] Official Military Personnel File for First Sergeant Daniel Daly, RG 127, NPRC St. Louis, MO.

June 5th Chapter II

We did not dare stand up straight, as we would be exposed to enemy fire, and after several attempts to move the wounded men, we had to give it up, as he let out yells. He was badly wounded in the leg and thigh. One ankle was very badly broken.
-First Lieutenant William Mathews, Intelligence Officer 2nd Battalion, 5th Marines

Near the road running south of Champillon, machine gunners from the 15th Company, 6th Machine Gun Battalion withstood relentless shellfire throughout the morning. Despite the risk, several Marines ran critically needed boxes of 8mm Lebel ammunition to the gun crews positioned along the line. German 77mm rounds, known as whiz-bangs, which earned their nickname due to the split-second scream that occurred simultaneous to the shell's explosion, left virtually no time to react.

These projectiles slammed into the ground south of Champillon in rapid succession. One round landed among an ammunition detail instantly killing nineteen-year-old Private George Albert Gustafson, a clerk from the west side of Chicago.[1] Supplying machine gun ammunition remained a crucial necessity for the guns dug in along the front line where the precarious gap between the 5th and 6th Marines had existed for days. The ammunition detail continued their terrifying task day and night despite the incoming fire.

The German batteries also targeted troops of the newly arrived French 167th Division. These troops moved into the line on the left of the 2nd Division's re-designated western flank at the brook nearly parallel to the road between Bussiares and Champillon.

Despite the reduction of the American front, Lieutenant Colonel Wise's 2nd Battalion, 5th Marines, and the two detached companies of Turrill's battalion, as well as machine gun and engineer support remained in their old positions west of the newly established boundary.

In response to the increased enemy shelling, counterbattery fire, courtesy of the 155mm guns of the 17th Field Artillery, tormented the German's ability to shell the French and American line at will.[2] 17th Field Artillery spotters watched the distant horizon from forward observation posts situated in treetops and church steeples throughout the division's front.[3]

During the late morning and early afternoon, activity along the front of the 83rd and 82nd Companies remained calm except for occasional sniping. Long after Colonel Catlin departed following his visit, members of the 83rd Company resumed the deadly exchange of gunfire with enemy soldiers visible through the distant tree line of Hill 142. According to Private James

June 5th Chapter II

Scarbrough, "That afternoon we saw some German troops in the woods several hundred yards away, and we sniped at them a bit, but they were a long ways off. We had the feeling we were setting the stage for something big with all-out preparations that day."[4]

Private Harry Collins of the 82nd Company took a brief moment that afternoon to make an entry in his diary that precisely one year ago he stepped off the boat at Paris Island for his lively and memorable inception into the Marine Corps. Collins wrote, "One year ago today I was sworn into Marine Corps at Paris Island. My experiences have been varied and many and now I am opposite the Germans. Shells are screaming continually overhead."[5]

Since arriving in France the previous November, the realities of war compelled him to write a simple note on the inside cover of his journal—an entry that revealed the twenty-three-old Marine's awareness of uncertainty regarding his fate. The message simply requested, "In case of death send to Mrs. Cora Collins 830 Chestnut Street Nelsonville, Ohio."[6]

West of the 82nd and 83rd Companies, the men of the 55th Company at Les Mares Farm, remained vigilant throughout the day following the enemy's failed assault the previous afternoon. The company maintained an observation post in a haystack about thirty meters north of the farm.

At approximately 2:00 P.M., nineteen-year-old Corporal Francis Joseph Dockx of Boston, Massachusetts, occupying the observation post, heard what sounded like digging out in front of his position.[7] When he noted the suspicious movement in the wheat field, he immediately rushed back to the company front to notify them of the commotion. Dockx volunteered to return to the observation post accompanied by three other Marines. Departing the property, Dockx snaked through the tall wheat as inconspicuously as possible with his three comrades following. Just behind the group, twenty-one-year-old Gunnery Sergeant David Lambert Burford, a chisel-faced Marine of three years who spoke fluent Spanish, quickly selected two men to accompany him. Buford's group immediately followed Dockx's crew in case they ran into a perilous situation. Buford was a debonair specimen with dark brown-slicked back hair and a bronze-toned muscular complexion forged in the sun-drenched cotton fields of his family's Frankston, Texas homestead.[8]

Corporal Francis Dockx. Photo credit: New York Times Mid-week pictorial.

June 5th Chapter II

Buford scurried north of the farm to reach the edge of the grain field before Dockx, and his group advanced too far out of view.

Ahead of Buford's group, Dockx and his men crawled on their stomachs through the waist-high field. From their prone position, visibility was limited. Suddenly, through the dense wheat, the men spotted a group of Germans setting up a machine gun several dozen meters ahead. Dockx's group quickly moved toward the flank of the unsuspecting enemy. The Marines suddenly sprung forward from the concealment of the grain field and attacked. Firing the .45 caliber pistols, they took the Germans by surprise and killed several enemy soldiers before they could react.[9]

Despite the rapidity of the attack, an enemy machine gunner managed to traverse his weapon toward the onrushing Americans and unleashed a horrendous volume of fire. Within a split second, the attacking Marines dropped into the cover of the wheat. Several of the surviving Germans tossed grenades. Several enemy soldiers, surprised by the suddenness of the assault, ran back toward the cover of woods to the north. Racing toward the sounds of gunfire and explosions ahead, Buford and his two Marines joined the intense exchange as several of the escaping Germans came into view across a clearing in the field. Buford maneuvered toward the edge of the clearing and fired at the fleeing enemy troops as they raced across the open.

Gunnery Sergeant David Buford. Photo credit: NPRC.

Holding his .45 caliber pistol with match-like precision, Buford crouched to a knee and dropped seven Germans in rapid succession as they tried to run.[10] Enemy machine gunners continued firing through the tall wheat at incredibly close quarters. Dockx's group and Buford's men were all at different spots in the field, but they simultaneously crept toward the German position. With no other choice, Dockx's group initiated a desperate final rush that overwhelmed the enemy, who managed to fire a burst that instantly killed Dockx and twenty-year-old Corporal George Alex Mincey of Ogeechee, Georgia.[11] The encounter was brief but intense, and it occurred at an incredibly close range.

June 5th Chapter II

First Lieutenant William Mathews was with Lieutenant Colonel Wise when the encounter in front of the farm began. According to Mathews, "Just about noon, we heard machine gun firing out in the direction of Les Mars Farm."[12] Wise immediately instructed Mathews to investigate. When Mathews reached Les Mares Farm, he raced beyond the property as the gunfire dwindled.

By the time Mathews arrived on the scene, the engagement was over. He encountered Buford and the five survivors. Mathews quickly probed Buford for details. After Buford explained the situation, he pointed to Dockx's body which lay just beyond the haystacks.

Buford also directed Mathews' attention to the corpse of an enemy soldier they dragged back to the lines and left lying near a manure pile. He also claimed there were a few wounded Germans nearby. "Let me have a couple of your men, so I can go out and see what's left out there," demanded Mathews. Buford replied, "Oh, no, Mr. Mathews, We are all too unnerved now, we can't do it."[13]

Corporal George Alex Mincey
Photo credit: Walter Scott.

Convinced by Buford's sincerity, Mathews instructed the traumatized gunnery sergeant to make sure that twenty-five-year-old Sergeant Clarence Carleton Knepp and thirty-year-old Sergeant Paul Wood Britton of Rhode Island, go up into the haylofts of the barn to observe the fronting field with their rifles. Mathews felt comfortable searching the area where the firefight occurred if Knepp and Britton kept watch over the open pasture for any addition infiltration since both men were excellent shooters.[14] Twenty-two-year-old Sergeant James Henry Parsons of Barberton, Ohio, accompanied Mathews. Parsons belonged to the 51st Company, but he was now assigned to Mathews' battalion intelligence section.[15]

The two men crawled past the haystacks of Dockx's observation post. From there, they crept an additional fifteen meters where they came upon the scene of the initial encounter between Dockx and the Germans. The dead bodies of several enemy soldiers lay throughout the field. Mathews remembered:

> We crawled over them, and a few yards further came upon a body lying across one of the paths in the wheat. I stopped because I

could see the torso of the body rise and fall as it breathed. The upper part of the body was covered; head and all, with a German shelter half, while the lower part wore French sky blue britches and puttees. I called to him in a low voice to surrender several times before he pulled the shelter half off and turning his head murmured in French, 'Merci.' We did not dare stand up straight, as we would be exposed to enemy fire, and after several attempts to move the wounded men, we had to give it up, as he let out yells. He was badly wounded in the leg and thigh. One ankle was very badly broken. He kept murmuring, 'Feldwachen,' and kept pointing with one arm. We heard a groan a little farther off and got what he meant. We left him and crawled only a few feet when we came upon a young blond German lying on his back rolling back and forth groaning. He too was badly wounded in the thigh. He was barely conscious. I saw then that the only way to get them in would be by stretchers. I sent my sergeant in to get them. There were none at the farm, so Buford sent a couple of his men after some.[16]

Once Parsons returned to the farm to procure a litter for the wounded prisoners, he spotted a wire gate to a chicken coup and decided to make it an improvised stretcher. He tore it from the hinges and rushed back to Mathews.[17] They gently placed the wounded men on the gate and dragged them back through the tall wheat. Upon returning to the farm, the two prisoners received treatment and information about their capture was dispatched to 4th Brigade headquarters.[18] Patrols also dragged the bodies of a few dead Germans back to the farm. As members of the company got a close look at the enemy, First Lieutenant Lemuel Shepherd searched the pockets and remembered, "One of the dead Germans had a two mark silver coin in his pocket which I took for a souvenir of the occasion and still have it in my possession."[19]

Shortly after the vicious encounter in front of Les Mares Farm, members of the 43rd Company along the northern fringe of Bois de Veuilly kept a steady watch after hearing the short but violent exchange of fire just east of their position. Twenty-seven-year-old Sergeant Mike Wodarezyk, commanding the company's 4th Platoon, scanned the fronting field and soon noticed some obscure movement in the distance. He watched in disbelief as approximately 200 German soldiers deployed into a skirmish formation in a ravine beyond the platoon's front.

The ravine stood just north of the precarious 500-meter gap between Bois de Veuilly and Les Mares Farm. Wodarezyk jumped into action and moved the platoon forward into position along the northeastern edge of Bois de Veuilly to repulse any German assault on this vulnerable part of the line. Before the enemy could initiate the attack, Wodarezyk's Marines scattered them with accurate fire. The Germans responded, and a vicious firefight developed.[20]

A German push anywhere along the nearly 500 meter stretch of open space between Les Mares Farm and the edge of Bois de Veuilly loomed as a constant threat since this area remained undefended. Just before the firing erupted from Wodarezyk's 4th Platoon, Shepherd of the 55th Company also noticed the same cluster of enemy troops concentrating on this weak part of the battalion's front.

Shepherd believed that the French Senegalese troops he placed along this gap the day before still held this section of the line. Unbeknownst to Shepherd, the French colonial troops pulled back several hundred meters. Shepherd remained apprehensive whether the enemy advance justified an artillery barrage. "The cost of artillery had been so impressed upon us that you didn't just call on lightly—we knew the cost of each shell and the cost of an entire barrage."[21] Nonetheless, a signal flare fired into the air arched high into the sky over the farm, which signaled a barrage request. Within minutes, the distant bark of American and French guns sent shells into the advancing Germans. Simultaneously, Marines along the 2nd Battalion, 5th Marines' front tore into the enemy with deadly accurate rifle fire.

Shepherd felt satisfied that the artillery made short work of the enemy advance. He remembered, "I was with Blanchfield and decided to go up and check on the fight. I left the P.C. and started up the side of this hill between the woods and the P.C., and there was a vacant place in the line where I had put in a platoon of French colonials. They weren't there. So we had a couple hundred yards of line undefended."[22] Shepherd ran back toward the center of the farm's property to see where the Senegalese troops may have gone. "I got up to the farm and was told they had just pulled out; they're going back there now."[23] With twenty-year-old Private Edward Elvin Cabell, his orderly, Shepherd ran back over to the western edge of the farm and remembered:

> I remember going on the other side of the farmhouse to see what was going on over there—this was the far or west side—and all of the sudden with the Germans firing from the crest on this side and with me and my orderly, Cabell, behind some trees from this fire, the bullets started coming from the other direction from these Frenchmen who had fallen back 200 or 300 yards. They were firing in the direction of the enemy, but the Marines were between the Germans and the French.[24]

As bullets snapped all around, Shepherd and Cabell desperately tried to find the best cover available. "There I was, jumping from one side of this tree to the other, trying to keep from getting hit by German bullets on one side, and the bullets form the French platoon, which was fading into the distance, firing from the other. It was a real hot spot."²⁵ Before the two men escaped the blistering crossfire, a single round struck Cabell in the right knee, and he folded to the ground mortally wounded. Cabell tried to pull himself toward cover as machine gun slugs whistled and cracked around him.²⁶

As Shepherd struggled to get back to the cover of the farm's buildings, one of his other runners, Private Oscar Martin, braved the bypassing bullets to guide elements of a platoon from the 55th Company into position to cover this gap.²⁷ One by one, the reinforcements dropped into shallow fighting holes left behind days earlier by the French colonial troops. The Marines who formed the makeshift line delivered suppressive fire upon the enemy. Combined with the blistering rifle fire emanating from Sergeant Wodarezyk's 4th Platoon, 43rd Company in Bois de Veuilly several hundred meters to the west, the Germans soon scattered and the advance collapsed—their last attempt to seize Les Mares Farm.

Despite successfully thwarting the enemy assault, the Marines holding this gap remained in this isolated and highly exposed position throughout the day. They kept constant watch from their shallow dugouts but remained without food and water in the increasingly warm afternoon sun. Enemy snipers in the distance menaced their every movement as evidenced by the frequent crack of bypassing rounds or the dull thud as bullets glanced off the dirt.

Private Arvid Anderson (left) and his brother Albin Anderson who served with the 76th Company 1st Battalion, 6th Marines. Photo credit: Karen Anderson.

Despite the dangers of moving about in this open stretch of pasture, twenty-two-year-old Private Arvid Pike Anderson of the 17th Company braved the sniper fire to bring food and water to the men holding the gap. Anderson left the concealment of the eastern tree line of Bois de Veuilly and sprinted hundreds of meters across this part of the line loaded down with as many full canteens of water and rations as he could carry. The snap of occasional bullets screaming by or striking the ground at his feet did not deter his efforts. He made numerous exhaustive trips to bring even the slightest bit of relief to his comrades.[28]

As the Marines of Lieutenant Colonel Wise's battalion repulsed another German push on the line, the French 21st Corps headquarters informed the 2nd Division at 12:15 P.M. regarding the following day's attack.[29] The planned assault directed the French 167th Division's infantry regiments to seize the high ground south of the Clignon brook. This assault required the French 116th Infantry Regiment on the right and the 409th Infantry Regiment on the left to advance north.

The goal of the 116th Infantry Regiment's attack sought to deny the Germans access to the terrain west of Bussiares and south of the Clignon brook, which offered excellent defilade. These objectives lay between the village of Veuilly la Poterie and the north-south brook west of the town of Champillon.[30]

The French 21st Corps also instructed the 2nd Division to support the east flank of the French 116th Infantry Regiment's assault by capturing "the slopes of Champillon, up to and including the brook to the east of the slope and just west of Torcy."[31] This directive required the 2nd Division to attack and occupy the slopes of Hill 142 and gave the Americans a rather narrow 700 meter-wide front to advance on this particular objective.

The attack plan involved interdiction artillery fire around the objective to deny enemy reinforcements.[32] Instructions required the supporting batteries to register their designated targets and subject them to raking fire. Thirty minutes before the attack is to commence, a time not yet determined by General Degoutte, the supporting French and American artillery would initiate both preparatory and destructive fire on the objectives.[33]

The method of attack prescribed for the next day's offensive mentioned infiltration rather than an advance by waves while interdiction fire will bombard the area until the assault progresses.[34] The plan utilized all of the American and 167th French Division's artillery assets for the preparatory and counter-battery fire using high explosive shells.[35] The 4th Brigade would guide their advance on the progress of the 116th French Infantry Regiment on their left.[36]

For the attack, 4th Brigade Headquarters called upon Major Julius Turrill's 1st Battalion, 5th Marines to carry out the assault. The battalion's 17th and 66th Companies, however, still occupied a position reinforcing Lieutenant Colonel Wise's battalion in Bois de Veuilly. Turrill's 49th and 67th Companies, however, remained in place at his disposal along the northern outskirts of Marigny-en-Orxois.[37]

A conversation that afternoon between Brigadier General Harbord and the division chief of staff, Colonel Preston Brown, further addressed the Marines' role in the advance. "Respecting the relief of the Marine elements west of the brook of Champillon on the evening of June 5th, the commanding officer of Marines in that district will be instructed to assemble his command and march it to a point designated by General Harbord after the French have passed through and have satisfied themselves of their position. It is desirable that officers meet them and guide them in."[38]

Along the northern outskirts of Marigny-en-Orxois, artillery fire screeched over the 49th and 67th Companies all day as German batteries continued their destruction of the town. Smoke hovered above the town's crumbled structures. German guns also targeted the outskirts of the village where the 49th and 67th Companies dug in at the lower end of the sloping terrain north of the village's Chateau.

According to twenty-five-year-old Captain George Wallis Hamilton, commanding the 49th Company, "Old Jule Turrill, our battalion commander, got word that we were going to participate in an honest-to-god attack the next morning and selected my depleted company and the 67th to start things for his battalion."[39]

Rumors circulating among the men suggested that the battalion would play a role in tomorrow's planned assault. This information caused excitement among the Marines who sought retribution for the shelling they had endured over the previous few days. Twenty-one-year-old Second Lieutenant

Second Lieutenant Walter Frazier. Photo credit: Culver Academy.

Walter Dabney Frazier of Pittsburgh, Pennsylvania, commanding a platoon in the 49th Company, gathered his men around 3:00 P.M.

While Frazier briefed his platoon regarding the little information he possessed about the rumored attack the next day, the all-too-familiar thud of enemy guns echoed off in the distance. Before anyone could react, the momentary ear-splitting scream of an incoming shell erupted into a blinding flash amidst Frazier's gathered platoon. A large shell fragment killed Frazier instantly as it struck him in the middle back and passed entirely through his kidney.[40] Deadly shards of steel from the same round tore into several other members of the platoon including twenty-three-year-old Private James Sherman Schall, a carpenter from Armstrong, Pennsylvania. A fragment struck Schall in the face with such force it shattered most of his skull as well as facial bones and blew his lower jaw off killing him instantly.[41]

June 5th Chapter II

As other platoons of the company rushed toward the scene, they discovered twelve men of Frazier's platoon had been killed or wounded. Among the scattered carnage, lay the motionless body of nineteen-year-old Private Alfred Earl Weisbaker. Litter-bearers realized from the appearance of his twisted and broken remains that he was dead and moved on to aid others. Shards of steel also mortally wounded twenty-one-year-old Private George Edwin Williams of Detroit, Michigan. Marines dragged their casualties to cover in anticipation of more incoming shells. Stretcher-bearers rushed the most critically wounded to a nearby dressing station. During the evacuation, twenty-year-old Private James Bernard Kellum succumbed to his horrible wounds.[42]

The tragedy that befell Second Lieutenant Frazier's platoon quickly supplanted the momentary exhilaration exhibited by the 49th Company regarding news of tomorrow's attack. For Captain Hamilton, the loss of Frazier whom he considered, "my ideal of a kid lieutenant," and whom he affectionately referred to as 'Scotty,' weighed heavily on him.[43] The men huddled deeper into their dugouts and remained out of view. They spent the remainder of the afternoon awaiting definitive word regarding the rumored assault planned for the next day, but they were not sure they would live to see morning.

---

[1] Burial File of Private George A. Gustafson, Box 2024, RG 92.9, Records of Graves Registration Services, NARA College Park, MD.
and Official Military Personnel File for Private George Albert Gustafson, RG 127, NPRC St. Louis, MO.
[2] Operations of 2nd Field Artillery Brigade, Box 81, RG 120.9.3, NARA College Park, MD.
[3] *Records of the Second Division (Regular)* Volume 9, N.P.
[4] Scarbrough, *They Called us Devil Dogs,* N.P.
[5] Collins, *The War Diary of Corporal Harry Collins,* Entry for June 5, 1918.
[6] Ibid.
[7] William E. Moore, "The Bloody Angle of the A.E.F.," *The American Legion Weekly*, February 24, 1922, 17.
[8] Official Military Personnel File for Gunnery Sergeant David L. Buford, Military Personnel File, NPRC
[9] Moore, "The Bloody Angle of the A.E.F.," *The American Legion Weekly*,
[10] Ibid.
[11] Official Military Personnel File for Gunnery Sergeant David L. Buford, RG 127, NPRC St. Louis, MO.and Edwin N. McClellan, "The Nearest Point to Paris in 1918," *Sea Power*, June 1921, 258., and Moore, "The Bloody Angle of the A.E.F.," *The American Legion Weekly*, 17.
[12] Mathews, "Official Report to Headquarters, U.S. Marine Corps, September 28, 1921," Box 8, Asprey Collection, Howard Gotlieb Archival Research Center, Boston University, Boston, MA.
[13] Ibid.
[14] Ibid.

[15] Official Military Personnel File for Sergeant James Henry Parsons, RG 127, NPRC St. Louis, MO.

[16] Mathews, "Official Report to Headquarters, U.S. Marine Corps, September 28, 1921," Box 8, Asprey Collection, Howard Gotlieb Archival Research Center, Boston University, Boston, MA.

[17] Ibid.

[18] *Records of the Second Division (Regular)* Volume 4, N.P.

[19] Shepherd, Jr. Memoirs, boyhood-1920, Folder 29-30, Box 67, Virginia Military Institute, Lexington, VA.

[20] Official Military Personnel File for Sergeant Mike Wodarezyk, RG 127, NPRC St. Louis, MO.

[21] General Lemuel Shepherd, interview by Robert Asprey, Alfred M. Gray Research Library, Quantico, VA.

[22] Ibid.

[23] Ibid.

[24] Ibid.

[25] General Lemuel C. Shepherd Jr., interview by Benis Frank, Alfred M. Gray Research Library, Quantico, VA.

[26] Ibid.

[27] "Statement Regarding Bravery of Oscar E. Martin Former Private U.S. Marine Corps," by Lemeul Shepherd March 19, 1929, Official Military Personnel File for Private Oscar Martin, RG 127, NPRC St. Louis, MO.

[28] Official Military Personnel File for Private Arvid Pike Anderson, RG 127, NPRC St. Louis, MO. Note: The 17th and 66th Companies reinforced the 43rd and 18th Companies' thinly-stretched line in Bois de Veuilly.

[29] *Records of the Second Division (Regular)* Volume 4, N.P.

[30] ABMC, *2nd Division Summary of Operations*, 11.

[31] *Records of the Second Division (Regular)* Volume 4, N.P.

[32] Operations of 2nd Field Artillery Brigade, Box 81, RG 120.9.3, NARA College Park, MD.

[33] Ibid.

[34] Ibid. Note: Interdiction fire refers to bombardment placed on an area or point to deny the enemy access to the area.

[35] Operations of 2nd Field Artillery Brigade, Box 81, RG 120.9.3, NARA College Park, MD.

[36] *Records of the Second Division (Regular)* Volume 4, N.P.

[37] Lieutenant Colonel Julius H. Turrill interview with by Joel D. Thacker Muster Roll Section Headquarters U.S.M.C. December 11, 1918, Box 17, RG 127, NARA, Washington, D.C.

[38] *Records of the Second Division (Regular)* Volume 4, N.P.

June 5th Chapter II

---

[39] Correspondence from George W. Hamilton to a friend 'V', 25 June, 1918, Box 300, RG 127 NARA, Washington D.C.

[40] Burial Files of Privates George E. Williams, James B. Kellum and Alfred E. Weisbaker, Boxes 5231, 2622, and 5145, RG 92.9, Records of Graves Registration Services, NARA College Park, MD.

[41] Burial File of Private James B. Schall, Eye-witness statement by First Sergeant William A. Van Train, Box 4313, RG 92.9, Records of Graves Registration Services, NARA College Park, MD.

[42] Burial File of Second Lieutenant Walter Dabney Frazier, Eye-witness statement by Private Clarence Jenni, Box 1733, RG 92.9, Records of Graves Registration Services, NARA College Park, MD., and U.S. Marine Corps Muster Rolls, 1893-1940, Record Group 127, NARA, Washington, D.C. Note: The 49th Company suffered nine wounded, and three killed in action or died of wounds.

[43] Correspondence from Hamilton to a friend 'V', 25 June, 1918, Box 300, RG 127 NARA, Washington D.C.

June 5th Chapter III

Some of us may not live to see the end of this war, but the world will be the better for it. I just hope I do not get machine-gun bullets through the stomach, linger on, and die.
-First Lieutenant Charles Boyd Maynard 1st Platoon, 84th Company, 3rd Battalion, 6th Marines

At 4:35 P.M., 2nd Division headquarters at Montreuil-aux-Lions telephoned Brigadier General Harbord's brigade command post at La Loge to inform him that the French 21st Corps would attack at 3:45 A.M. the next morning.[1] Major Julius Turrill's 1st Battalion, 5th Marines, ordered to support the advance of the 167th French Division the next morning, retained only half of their men. Two companies, the 17th, and 66th remained in position with the 2nd Battalion, 5th Marines west of the Champillon-Bussiares road, well beyond the division's newly established western limits.[2] They had to remain in this critical section of the front until relieved by the French who still had not arrived by late that afternoon.

Just outside the battered town of Marigny-en-Orxois that afternoon, Lieutenant Colonel Wise waited at his command post along the cemetery wall in anticipation of another enemy assault on his battalion's front. He remembered, "All that day the shelling continued, though we never caught a sight of a German anywhere. My telephone line had been shot out the day before. During the afternoon a runner came up calling me back to regimental headquarters"[3] Wise left to meet with Colonel Neville at the regimental command post at the rock quarry just northwest of Marigny-en-Orxois.

In his brief discussion with Neville, Wise recalled, "My battalion was to be relieved by the French that night. Pulling out of our line, we were to go to a piece of woods northeast of La Voie du Chatel and act as supports for the First and Third Battalions of the Fifth Marines."[4] Neville relayed scant detail about the objectives for the next day's attack, including an assault on Belleau Woods. "The French, Colonel Neville said, were placing heavy stress on the capture on that piece of woods which they viewed as the key to the whole line."[5] Wise returned to his battalion command post, and immediately summoned his company commanders to inform them of the planned relief.[6]

Along the 3rd Brigade's sector, soldiers of the Major Arthur Edward Bouton's 2nd Battalion, 9th Infantry held the left portion of the regiment's line. Earlier that the day, Bouton ordered a patrol of one officer and twenty men to venture beyond the woods of La Croisette, located just over a kilometer south of Le Thiolet. From there, the plan required them to proceed by trail over three kilometers east toward the village of Crogis.

June 5th Chapter III

The patrol was set to depart at 6:00 P.M., and move to a designated point and wait until 9:30 P.M. after dark. The patrol would continue up the slopes of Hill 204 to take a direct route into the village of Vaux. From there, the patrol was to follow the Paris-Metz road back west and arrive at Le Thiolet no later than 1:00 A.M. From Le Thiolet instructions called for them to take a direct route back to La Croisette.[7]

By 6:30 P.M., the patrol, led by twenty-five-year-old First Lieutenant Victor August Hoersch of Davenport, Iowa, departed the woods of La Croisette. They used the defilade of the terrain to avoid drawing the attention of enemy artillery spotters as they moved east.

By 6:25 P.M., the 4th Brigade headquarters notified 2nd Division that the two German prisoners brought in to Les Mares Farm earlier that afternoon by First Lieutenant Mathews and Sergeant James Parsons were on their way to them in Montreuil-aux-Lions. The two enemy soldiers were captured following the intense engagement with Gunnery Sergeant David Buford and several Marines from the 55th Company. Due to the very critical condition of one of the prisoners, brigade suggested that an interpreter should be on hand as soon as the two men arrive.[8]

First Lieutenant Victor August Hoersch seen here in 1915 as a student at the University of Iowa. Photo credit: University of Iowa.

When the two German captives reached Montreuil-aux-Lions, interrogators immediately questioned them despite their condition, and they divulged vital information. The two prisoners belonged to the 1st Company, 26th Jäger Battalion, 7th Saxon Jäger Regiment, 197th German Division.[9]

The critically wounded prisoner generated enough strength to talk. He was an Oberjager (Corporal) and explained that his small detachment received orders for the reconnaissance and ambush patrol of the American line the night before. The group, he claimed, consisted of thirty-five soldiers and one Feldwebel (Sergeant Major) and a machine gun.

While this group infiltrated the line, according to the prisoner, one of his comrades said that they were opposed to American troops. Up to that point, they did not know they opposed any other army besides the French along this front. Regarding his unit's disposition, the prisoner also stated, "in the advance line there was no complete lines of trenches, but points of resistance and occasional shelters had been dug. Very little work had been done as the men were very tired and only small working parties were available from units in the rear."[10]

When officials at division headquarters interrogated the other wounded prisoner captured by Mathews and Parsons, they immediately asked him where he obtained his sky blue French artillery breeches he wore. The injured man claimed that his supply depot issued the trousers to him back in April.[11] He became very nervous and apprehensive during the interrogation. He also suffered terrible pain from his wound. He went on to say he was the only man in his unit that had these trousers.

The two prisoners appeared to corroborate each other's stories. The man wearing the blue trousers said he belonged to a patrol unit, which had been off by itself for all he knew. He noted that the volume of fire they endured during the past two days was much more substantial than before. He claimed to be unaware of any specific plans regarding an attack by his unit. His battalion had advanced continuously since May 27th. His unit's current position in front of some village that he could not identify consisted of partially constructed trenches.[12]

The men spent most of the daytime under cover of some woods and made little improvement of positions since they anticipated resuming their movement along the adjusting lines. The battalion's casualties had been light. They were well equipped and received a consistent supply of ammunition and food. The company, according to the prisoner, consisted of between eighty to one hundred men, and four light machine guns commanded by a Lieutenant named Aurzner.[13]

While Bundy's headquarters interrogated the two prisoners captured by the 4th Brigade, First Lieutenant Hoersch and twenty men from 2nd Battalion, 9th Infantry continued their patrol along the division's east flank after dark. At approximately 7:30 P.M., as Hoersch's men moved east along the trail between La Croisette and Crogis, enemy batteries bombarded positions in the rear of the American line.

The first volley of incoming shells was the start of a 2,000-round barrage consisting mostly of shrapnel and high explosive projectiles.[14] The bombardment hammered the Bois la Morette just south of the Paris-Metz road.[15] The movement of Hoersch's patrol near the village of Crogis evidently caught the attention of artillery spotters from the German 10th Division.[16] South of Bois La Marette, 150mm rounds also fell upon the property of Tafournay Farm.[17]

During the entire barrage, Hoersch skillfully kept his patrol concealed and under cover until they could veer south toward La Nouette Farm. Once there, Hoersch noticed that the terrain sloping down toward Chateau Thierry offered optimal surveillance to the east.[18]

June 5th Chapter III

While Hoersch's patrol secured information regarding the layout of the area, 2nd Division Headquarters received word from the French units on their right stating that "We sent reconnaissance patrols into the woods of Hill 204 during last night and today. This woods is not occupied and we are about to carry our line forward to it. The village of Vaux was also visited by our patrols. Enemy patrols also pass through but the village is not permanently occupied by the enemy."[19] Despite the perilous movement under heavy incoming fire, Hoersch successfully led his men back to the line unscathed.[20]

Captain Robert F. Hyatt, (holding megaphone) commander of F Battery, 2nd Battalion, 15th Field Artillery Regiment, seen here on June 5, 1918. Photo credit: NARA.

While German guns pounded the right half of the 2nd Division's line, the 1st Battalion, 15th Field Artillery Regiment moved from positions east of Domptin to better support the 9th Infantry who extended their front to cover regions near Triangle Farm when the dismounted French Cavalry unit in the area vacated their position.[21]

The extension of the 9th Infantry's line required the 1st Battalion, 15th Field Artillery to prepare their guns, caissons, and supply caravans for the three-kilometer movement northeast to Bois de la Morette.[22] Battery commanders established firing positions in the woods south of the Paris-Metz road by the town of Bourbelin. First Lieutenant Robert Kean, one of

June 5th Chapter III

F Battery, 2nd Battalion, 15th Field Artillery in support of the 9th Infantry on the afternoon of June 5th. Photo credit: NARA (Acquired courtesy of Steve Girard.)

the 1st Battalion's liaison officers, recalled, "The necessary telephone lines were strung and on the next day I set up my observation posts in the front American lines of the 9th Infantry. These were situated at the edge of the Bois-de-la-Morette overlooking a valley and the German lines."[23]

Another observation post along the front of the 9th Infantry allowed twenty-six-year-old Captain Jerome Jackson Waters Jr., from Eagle Pass, Texas to adjust fire of his battery's fire to destroy German machine gun emplacements.

On the western sector of the division's line, Colonel Catlin received information that the 82nd and 83rd Companies of Major Sibley's 3rd

Captain Jerome J. Waters Jr. pictured as a student at Texas A&M. Photo credit: Texas A&M.

Battalion, 6th Marines would be relieved from the woods just south of Hill 142 by Turrill's men after dark. At 9:00 P.M., Major Frank Evans, the 6th Marines adjutant, relayed instructions for the night's relief to Sibley, who was with his two companies along the tree line just south of Hill 142. Evans's message explained:

June 5th Chapter III

> Your battalion will be relieved sometime tonight by Turrill's battalion, when the 82nd and 83rd are relieved proceed via Champillon via present regimental headquarters to Ferme Blanche where your battalion will go into reserve. Orders will be given to the C.O. 84th Company and C.O. 97th Company to report to you at Ferme Blanche. The platoon of the 73rd Company will remain in place. Guide will be found at regimental headquarters, Colonels office to conduct you to Ferme Blanche.[24]

As Sibley received these orders, a patrol consisting of one officer and three men departed the 83rd Company's line south of Hill 142. They believed the enemy occupied positions on Hill 142 situated roughly 350 yards west of a narrow ravine running north to south along the eastern slope of the hill. The patrol sought to venture north, bypass the flank of the suspected German line, and approach the enemy from their rear.[25] By 9:00 P.M., enough daylight remained to make their movements visible to the enemy lines, so upon clearing their company's wooded position, they slithered through the fields on their bellies and waited until dark to proceed toward the distant ravine.[26]

On the outskirts of Marigny-en-Orxois, Major Turrill, having learned of his battalion's involvement in the next day's advance, still lacked specific details about his Marines' role in the assault. Two of his companies, the 17th, and 66th, were detached from his command to reinforce the western half of Wise's battalion in Bois de Veuilly. They awaited relief from the French throughout the evening.

While news of tomorrow's planned attack spread among the men of the 49th and 67th Companies just behind the front at Marigny-en-Orxois, the 17th and 66th Companies endured the steady bombardment of their frontline position throughout the night. Along the 17th Company's line, twenty-four-year-old Private Paul William Durr, a former grocery store manager from Raritan, New Jersey, maintained constant vigilance as the company's gas sentry in addition to his duties as a runner.[27]

As incoming rounds exploded through the woods, a large fragment slammed into Durr's upper right leg—penetrating deep into the fleshy region of the thigh. Despite the pain, he remained at his post without pause. Durr continued calling for the Marine who was scheduled to relieve him, but his summons went unanswered. Despite the pain, Durr stayed at his position to warn the rest of the company to don respirators if gas shells should land in the area.[28]

The 66th Company, holding a section of the front next to the 17th Company in Bois de Veuilly, awaited the arrival of the French scheduled to relieve them later that night. Incoming German shellfire kept the men hunkered in their hastily excavated dugouts. Shards of lethal steel rained down from rounds exploding in the treetops. One fragment struck Nineteen-year-old Private Walter Brotherton of West Somerset, Kentucky, in the hip and arm. Twenty-year-old Private Lester Leroy Feriend suffered fragmentation wounds to the hip and leg. Steel from another shell ripped into twenty-year-old Private Walter Aloysius Crane's right arm.

Another round exploded near Private Joseph Charles McLaughlin and knocked the twenty-six-year-old nearly unconscious and rendering him completely shell-shocked.[29] The cries from wounded men calling for a corpsman obliged some to leave the shelter of their dugouts and race into the open to help their fellow Marines. This courageous commitment went against every instinct of survival, yet they answered the desperate pleas of their comrades.[30]

Behind the lines of the 66th Company, twenty-two-year-old Second Lieutenant Daniel William Bender, was in charge of a work detail counting ammunition bandoliers in anticipation of the relief that night. Working with Bender, twenty-four-year-old Sergeant Cleo Baxter Davis sat resting against a tree sorting through the bandoliers.[31]

Twenty-year-old Private Stanley Diem Carpenter, a former clerk from Pittsburgh, Pennsylvania, served as a company runner and stayed behind the lines near Bender's working party waiting for messages to deliver. Carpenter spent most of the day racing through Bois de Veuilly, avoiding occasional incoming shells to deliver information.

Just as he prepared to depart Bender's working party with another message, the sudden scream of an incoming round pierced the air. Bender, who was casually conversing with Sergeant Davis when the round smashed through the treetops, remembered, "We were talking when a shell came over and burst not five yards from us."[32] A large fragment struck Davis in the side of the face and killed him instantly.[33] Several shards of steel perforated Carpenter's back as the force of the explosion threw him to the ground. The blast also threw Bender backwards. He recalled how suddenly the shell's detonation killed Davis, and vividly recalled, "I was blown some few yards, and when I got to my feet, he [Davis] was dead."[34]

Nearby Carpenter struggled to move as the pain of his injuries set in. Fragments from the high explosive shell shattered his ribs as they ripped through his back. As the dust and smoke cleared, Carpenter moaned for help. Twenty-three-year-old Private Glenn B Ranney recognized Carpenter's tormented screams. With shells crashing into the 66th Company's front, Ranney and several others left their dugouts and rushed to help their mortally wounded comrade.[35]

Laying on his stomach, Carpenter struggled for air—each gasping breath gurgled louder as his lungs filled with blood.[36] Ranney summoned litter bearers nearby who braved the incoming fire to reach Carpenter.[37] Gently they hoisted the dying twenty-year-old onto the stretcher and carried him back to a dressing station in Marigny-en-Orxois. Carpenter remained

June 5th Chapter III

there until an ambulance could take him back to Field Hospital number 1 in the town of Bezu-le-Guery nearly three kilometers south away.[38]

When the shellfire subsided, thirty-two-year-old Corporal Albert Ernest Herzog of the 66th Company walked back through the woods to the spot where the incoming shell killed and wounded both Carpenter and Davis. Herzog discovered Carpenter's Springfield rifle laying on the ground. He picked it up to examine it for any signs of damage. He discovered it to be in perfect working order as he pulled the bolt back. According to Herzog, "My rifle was broken, and I used his the next day."[39] He rushed back to his dugout with his newly acquired weapon.

Private Stanley Diem Carpenter.
Photo credit: author's collection.

Since the division's arrival in the line four days earlier, the casualty rates reached levels that necessitated replacement troops. The division also sought the immediate return of any personnel previously detached from the division. The 6th Marines alone sent twelve of its officers and eleven enlisted men to attend a variety of 1st Army Corps schools in Gondrecourt, France, in the weeks and months before the battle began. Since most of these men completed their class or were near the end of their courses, the 1st Army Corps arranged for their rapid return to the respective units given the developing situation near Chateau Thierry.

Trucks appropriated for their hasty return eventually arrived to carry them nearly 233 kilometers back to the battlefront. The sluggish voyage along highways, still packed with civilian and military traffic, took three exhausting days.[40] Among the men aboard one of the vehicles was twenty-one-year-old Second Lieutenant Paul Schuster Taylor of the 78th Company, 2nd Battalion, 6th Marines. During the trip, Taylor and other officers pondered and conversed tirelessly about the situation awaiting them at the front since they had only the flimsiest information regarding the battle.

Earlier that day, while riding in the back of the same vehicle as Taylor, twenty-six-year-old First Lieutenant Charles Boyd Maynard of Pullman, Washington, eagerly engaged in the conversation and speculation regarding what awaited them when they returned to their units. Maynard, who had commanded the 1st Platoon, 84th Company, 3rd Battalion, 6th Marines, shouted above the loud rumble of the vehicle's engine, and prophetically claimed, "Some of us may not live to see the end of this war, but the world will be the better for it. I just hope I do not get machine-gun bullets through the stomach, linger on, and die."[41]

Also returning to the division was twenty-one-year-old Second Lieutenant Louis Felix Timmerman Jr. of Leonia, New Jersey. Timmerman, a former Princeton student, came from a very wealthy family. He had been detached from the 83rd Company, 3rd Battalion, 6th Marines since May 3rd to attend the 1st Army Corps' Infantry course at Gondrecourt, France. While undergoing instruction, Timmerman reunited with twenty-two-year-old Second Lieutenant John "Jack" Ralph Hardin Jr., an old college friend from Princeton who attended the same course. All of these officers were at school when the crisis developed in the vicinity of Chateau Thierry. Timmerman claimed, "At this time the (school) authorities didn't even know where the 2nd Division was. They thought it was up in the north somewhere near Montdidier. In any event, our orders were to proceed to Paris to get further orders to report to the division."[42]

First Lieutenant Charles B. Maynard.
Photo credit: Author's collection.

After an exhausting three-day journey, they finally arrived the evening of June 5th. Timmerman reported to 6th Regiment Headquarters at La Voie du Chatel and said, "Major Evans told us to report to our companies the next day and have some food at regimental headquarters which we did. Then Jack [Hardin] and I went out in the adjoining field and laid down to spend the night there."[43]

Second Lieutenant Taylor also cheerfully reunited with his 1st Platoon comrades of the 78th Company holding the line just north of Triangle Farm. The joyful reunion turned somber when Gunnery Sergeant George William Hopke relayed the tragic news about Taylor's friend Second Lieutenant Henry Leslie Eddy, the Army officer commanding the company's 2nd Platoon who was killed the previous day. Only a few hours before Taylor's return, members of the company brought Eddy's body back to Montreuil-aux-Lions for burial in the southwest corner of the village cemetery—a more dignified burial than most men would receive.[44] According to Taylor, "Lieutenant Eddy was one of the most popular officers we ever had with us. Everybody liked him very much."[45]

At the crossroads leading from the Paris-Metz road just south of Lucy-le-Bocage, Sergeant Donald Paradis, a battalion runner for 2nd Battalion, 6th Marines, and another man spent hours waiting for the arrival of the field kitchens and ration carts. They intended to intercept and redirect the mess crew into the village of Lucy-le-Bocage. Paradis stated:

> We were in position in a ditch besides the crossroads by four o'clock. It was about three quarters of a mile from headquarters up a rising grade. So when we were in position we had a wonderful view of our entire lines, at least where they were supposed to be. We could see shells bursting, none near us, about a half a mile away in Lucy-le-Bocage. We could see shells bursting there and all around the town. That sort of changed our outlook; naturally, our orders remained valid, we simply regarded ourselves lucky for having reached the crossroads without the harassing shellfire catching up with us.[46]

Several hours later, the field kitchens arrived in plain view along the road. According to Paradis, "About an hour before dark we were horrified to see our field kitchen rolling over the hill toward us in broad daylight and a perfect target."[47] Paradis ran to head off the mess crew. He quickly pleaded and eventually coaxed the mess men to hurry along and get out of view as soon as possible. Once they noted the numerous fresh shell holes all around the area, the mess crew drastically accelerated their movement into Lucy-le-Bocage.

Paradis remained with the crew to guide them. "I stayed with the field kitchen until we had it parked under the roof of a shed at the edge of town."[48] Knowing that his own company already relocated to the eastern outskirts of Lucy-le-Bocage, Paradis darted through the debris-littered streets in search of them. "There seemed to be no one in the town so I tried moving forward down to the dry creek bed trying to find our outfit."[49] He crept for hundreds of meters along the gulley that stretched east outside of the village.

The ravine deepened along the extreme southwestern portion of Belleau Wood. Paradis recalled, "The creek bed was four to six-foot deep, good cover, I thought and just as I rounded a bend in the creek a German soldier came skulking around the next bend."[50] Momentarily paralyzed in disbelief, Paradis remembered, "He was as surprised as I and ducked out of sight before I could shoot. I watched the bend for a while for movement and decided, 'This is no place for me.'"[51]

---

[1] *Records of the Second Division (Regular)* Volume 1, N.P.
[2] Ibid.
[3] Wise and Frost, *A Marine Tells it to You*, 206.
[4] Ibid.
[5] Ibid.

[6] Ibid.
[7] Patrol Order, 9th Infantry Operations Report, Box 84, RG 120.9.3, Second Division File, Records of the AEF, NARA College Park, MD. Note: Accompanying sketch in the file verified in detail the patrol route.
[8] *Records of the Second Division (Regular)* Volume 4, N.P.
[9] *Preliminary Interrogation of Two Prisoners Captured June 5, 1918, North of Champillon,* 2nd Division summary of intelligence, Box 35-3, RG 120.9.3, Second Division File, Records of the AEF, NARA College Park, MD.
[10] Ibid.
[11] Ibid.
[12] Ibid.
[13] Ibid.
[14] *Records of the Second Division (Regular)* Volume 9, N.P.
[15] Ibid.
[16] War Diary and Annexes 10th th Division 5 June 4 1918, *Translation of War Diaries of German Units,* Vol. 1.
[17] *Records of the Second Division (Regular)* Volume 9, N.P.
[18] *Records of the Second Division (Regular)* Volume 7, N.P.
[19] *Records of the Second Division (Regular)* Volume 4, N.P.
[20] Headquarters Second Division AEF G.O. No. 40 July 5, 1918, Box 17, RG 120.9.3, Records of the AEF, NARA College Park, MD.
[21] Kean, *Dear Marraine*, 97.
[22] Ibid.
[23] Ibid, 97-98.
[24] *Records of the Second Division (Regular)* Volume 7, N.P.
[25] Patrol Report Colonel Catlin to Brigadier General Harbord, 6 June 1918, Box 300, RG 127, NARA, Washington D.C.
[26] Ibid.
[27] Note: A gas sentry was to alert the rest of the company to the presence of gas during a barrage.
[28] Official Military Personnel File for Private Paul William Durr, RG 127, NPRC St. Louis, MO.
[29] U.S. Marine Corps Muster Rolls, 1893-1940, Record Group 127, NARA, Washington, D.C.
[30] Note: The 66th Company suffered six casualties that night 2 of whom were mortally wounded.
[31] Correspondence Lieutenant Daniel W. Bender to Mattie Davis (mother of Sergeant Cleo Davis) 25 September 1918, found in Official Military Personnel File for Sergeant Cleo Baxter Davis, RG 127, NPRC St. Louis, MO.

June 5th Chapter III

³² Ibid.
³³ Ibid.
³⁴ Ibid.
³⁵ Burial File of Private Stanley Carpenter, Eye-witness statement by Private Glenn B. Ranney, Box 803, RG 92.9, Records of Graves Registration Services, NARA College Park, MD., and Official Military Personnel File for Private Stanley Carpenter, RG 127, NPRC St. Louis, MO.
³⁶ Official Military Personnel File for Private Stanley Carpenter, RG 127, NPRC St. Louis, MO. Note: His lung was reported to have been pierced by the blast.
³⁷ Burial File of Private Stanley Carpenter, Eye-witness statement by Private Glenn B. Ranney, Box 803, RG 92.9, Records of Graves Registration Services, NARA College Park, MD.
³⁸ Official Military Personnel File for Private Stanley Carpenter, RG 127, NPRC St. Louis, MO. Note: Private Stanley Carpenter died at Field Hospital 16 in the town of Juilly at 3:00 A.M. June 6, 1918.
³⁹ Burial File of Private Stanley Carpenter, Eye-witness statement by Private Albert E. Herzog, Box 803, RG 92.9, Records of Graves Registration Services, NARA College Park, MD.
⁴⁰ Louis Felix Timmerman, interview by Robert Asprey, April 23-24, 1964, Transcript, Personal Papers Collection, Alfred M. Gray Research Library, Quantico, VA.
⁴¹ *Paul Schuster Taylor* interview by Suzanne B. Riessin May 26, 1970, Earl Warren Oral History Project, *California Social Scientist. Volume I: Education, Field Research, and Family*, Bancroft Library, University of California, Berkeley, CA.
⁴² Louis Felix Timmerman, interview by Robert Asprey, Alfred M. Gray Research Library, Quantico, VA.
⁴³ Ibid.
⁴⁴ Burial File of Second Lieutenant Henry Leslie Eddy, Box 1476, RG 92.9, Records of Graves Registration Services, NARA College Park, MD.
⁴⁵ Burial File of Second Lieutenant Henry Leslie Eddy, Eye-witness statements by Captain Paul S. Taylor, Box 1476, RG 92.9, Records of Graves Registration Services, NARA College Park, MD.
⁴⁶ Paradis, *The World War I Memoirs of Don V. Paradis,* 43.
⁴⁷ Ibid.
⁴⁸ Ibid.
⁴⁹ Ibid, 44.
⁵⁰ Ibid.
⁵¹ Ibid.

June 5th Chapter IV

The hike back out of the valley was not made in column of squads, but in single file. The men slipped silently through the dark woods, always keeping a tree between themselves and the Germans. An occasional crude wooden cross marked the filled-in fox holes where several of the lads stayed on.
-First Lieutenant Elliott Cooke 18th Company, 2nd Battalion, 5th Marines

During the evening of June 5th, thirty-two-year-old First Lieutenant Jonas Henry Platt of New York City arrived at the devastated village of Marigny-en-Orxois and soon joined Captain Hamilton's 49th Company. Platt, a replacement from the 137th Company, 2nd Replacement Battalion, recalled, "Captain Hamilton's company had holes in it that must be corked before it could go over the top the next morning, and I was to be one of the corks."[1]

When Platt joined the company, instructions directed him to his new platoon's location where he found the men taking advantage of the idleness to get some much-needed slumber under the soft comfort of liberated linens, blankets, and other creature comforts from some of the village's abandoned homes. "I'll never forget the first sight of my command. Here and there, the men lay on the ground, with their muddy feet sticking out from beneath salmon-pink coverlets, baby-blue satin quilts, even lace curtains that they had taken from the ruined Chateau. In one spot three of them, like innocent little cherubs, their tin hats slanted over their eyes, rested on an uncovered pair of box springs with a bolster shared between them."[2]

The indifferent demeanor Platt's men exhibited in the face of incoming shellfire, which fell near enough to shake the ground, surprised Platt who had never been on an active front since arriving in France. "The boche were dropping plenty of iron things around us," he said. "He was sending over just enough whiz-bangs to make things uncomfortable."[3]

The men had grown accustomed to the sound of incoming artillery fire, and several managed to find a degree of morbid humor in the enemy's routine harassment. One Marine, according to Platt, "raised himself pettishly from his incongruous bed, staring in the direction of Germany, and exclaiming: 'Aw Fritz, pipe down! Cut it out! Can't you let a fellow rest?' Whereupon, he would flop to the ground again, jerk the covers up about his neck, wiggle his dogs, a Marine never calls a foot anything but a dog—and resume his snoring."[4]

Despite the steady bombardment, other members of the 49th Company used the opportunity to make a meal of the local livestock injured by shellfire. According to Platt:

June 5th Chapter IV

Over in the woods somewhere I heard a cow, that had wandered into the range of fire, bawling. And almost immediately, I noticed that where there had been lumps of humanity under various silken coverlets, there was now only nothingness. Instinctively I felt that something was about to happen to the regulation which provided that accidental death from shrapnel or shell fire must be the only means of procuring animal food. I was hungry. The boys were hungry, fearfully hungry. But there were regulations!⁵

Almost immediately, the unmistakable crack of a rifle shot echoed through the woods, followed by the audible agonized groan of the cow. Then the sound of a second shot resonated through the trees. Platt started for the woods to investigate the commotion. "Then, before I had moved ten feet, four wild-eyed mess sergeants, one with his baby-blue coverlet dragging behind him where it had caught on a belt hook, galloped past, dragging out their bayonets as they dived into the woods."⁶

Before the young first lieutenant reached the tree line and exerted his new authority as the new platoon commander, a young Marine appeared before him snapped to attention and saluted. In a passive, child-like voice, the timid young man explained that shrapnel had struck the cow and that the mess sergeants were in the midst of butchering it with intentions of hauling large sections of the animal to the basement of the chateau where the galley crew can barbeque the meat. The boy then followed up with, "I have been sent to ask would the lieutenant like some cow stew, sir?"⁷ Before Platt could answer the young Marine's question, a few of the mess sergeants emerged out of the tree line rapidly headed for the chateau with large chunks of freshly butchered meat in hand.

Platt, as the new platoon commander, did not want to break up an opportunity for the men to enjoy their first real meal in quite some time. He recalled, "I grinned and nodded, and the bland-like, innocent Marine hurried away to assist at the barbeque."⁸

Jonas Platt seen here after the war as a Captain. Photo credit: NARA.

June 5th Chapter IV

In a short time, the aroma of stew emerged from the chateau and soon attracted the attention of the rest of the company. Platt remembered, "Marines were coming to life everywhere. Mess kits that had not been really used in days were beginning to clatter, and the men gathered in groups, their eyes bulging, and a longing expression on their faces that would have melted the heart of the Hindenburg Statue."[9] Nothing could stop the men from partaking in the feast, not even the constant incoming of German shells that succeeded in dropping a round on the grounds of the chateau. "It knocked Marines, stones, furniture, everything about. It half buried one sergeant and sent another through a window. But in five minutes they were back on the job, and the pot boiled on," Platt remembered.[10]

As members of the 49th Company salivated over the preparation of their first hot meal in days, French troops of the 167th Division on their way to relieve elements of the 2nd Battalion, 5th Marines along the northern fringes of Bois de Veuilly marched past the Chateau. "A French machine gun crew passed us going to the front line."[11]

Upon seeing the Americans standing outside the chateau where they prepared the stew, one of them hollered, "Bon Chance [Good luck]."[12] One Marine mockingly replied, "And say frogs, old chaps, you hold that line till we stow away this chow, will yer?" The expressionless French soldiers responded, "Ah, oui, M'sieurs. Dejeuner, n'c'est pas? [Ah yes gents, Breakfast is it not?]" Obviously unable to understand them, the Marine continued in his sarcastic patronage of the French soldiers and replied, "Surest thing you know. You said a mouthful!"[13]

As the Marines gathered outside the Chateau to investigate the source of such a pleasant and appetizing aroma, Platt spotted his close friend forty-three-year-old First Lieutenant Clarence "Seaweed" Ball, who joined the 66th Company the day before as a replacement. Ball had served with Platt at Quantico the previous February when both men belonged to the 2nd Replacement Battalion.

Ball was distracted that evening by the smell of beef stew emanating from inside the chateau as he departed regimental headquarters to return to his company in the northern edge of Bois de Veuilly. "One sniff and he made a dive for two pails lying nearby," said Platt. Ball quickly filled the two containers to bring to his platoon. He steadily tried to balance the heavy stew-filled buckets before crossing the open span between Marigny-en-Orxois and Bois de Veuilly. "In reply, the boche began sending over everything he had-whiz bangs, 'sea bags,' high explosives, 'G.I. cans,' and what not."[14]

According to Platt, "'Seaweed' took one look and squinted an eye. 'It's going to be a good trick if I do it,' he announced, and started off through the barrage to his boys ahead, balancing his pails of cow stew like a performer on a tight rope as he dodged the shells."[15] Platt watched his friend painstakingly walk down the gentle slope toward Bois de Veuilly. He

June 5th Chapter IV

hollered to Ball to be careful. "In the dim light I saw him look over his shoulder. 'You said it,'" Ball replied.[16]

Inside Bois de Veuilly, company runners for twenty-five-year-old First Lieutenant Walter Thomas Hyssop Galliford's 66th Company braved the continuous shellfire to travel the distance between the front lines and battalion command post. The shelling made an already difficult job exceedingly problematic. Projectiles of all caliber frequently tore through the treetops. The detonation of these large rounds shook the forest floor and illuminated the night sky with a split-second flash. French and American artillery also unleashed their barrage as the batteries registered targets to soften up objectives for the attack scheduled to begin at dawn.[17] Despite the intense bombardment, Ball passed unscathed through Bois de Veuilly with the two large buckets of beef stew for his platoon. Platt learned of Ball's success when "Two hours later, a dispatch rider, with the mud gear shot off his motorcycle, roared up to me, jumped off, saluted and handed me a message. It read: 'Never spilled a drop.-Ball.' Nor had we. The cow stew had been devoured—to its last atom."[18] For too many 49th Company Marines, they unknowingly ate the final meal of their lives.

First Lieutenant Clarence Ball seen here after the war as a captain. Photo credit: Duward Massey.

For the remainder of the evening, Platt's men lingered on a hair-trigger alert when rumors circulated that someone spotted two suspected German spies dressed as French soldiers wandering the front line. One of the reported adversaries somehow evidently escaped. The increased intensity of incoming enemy shellfire generated paranoia and wild rumors of enemy combatants disguised as French or American troops. The reports of suspicious looking figures lurking around the area triggered a search in the immediate vicinity.

Platt formed two patrols to scour the woods for the suspected enemy agents. The only evidence they found was a white cloth believed, by the patrol who recovered it, to be some signal flag, perhaps to the enemy artillery. The company First Sergeant, thirty-eight-year-old Robert Eugene Conner, a salty veteran of the corps with eighteen years' service, inspected the fabric. "A momentary flash of a night light; then an exclamation of deepest disgust," recalled Platt as he witnessed the old first sergeant resentfully growl, "Aw, you idiot! Signal flag nothing. Don't y' know a woman's nighty when y' see one?"[19]

Nothing came of Platt's hunt for the suspected enemy spies, but in only a few moments, Captain George Hamilton, "stumbled toward me with orders to put the company into combat formation."[20] The instructions to assemble came from Major Julius Turrill who remembered, "Then about one or two o'clock on the morning of the 6th we got orders to go up and make an attack on Hill 142, which is about two kilometers southwest of Torcy."[21]

As the 49th and 67th Companies of Turrill's battalion assembled to move toward their designated jump-off point for the morning's assault, the 17th and 66th Companies remained in position along the northern edge of Bois de Veuilly with Lieutenant Colonel Wise's battalion awaiting relief by the French who still had not appeared.

Despite having half of his battalion at his disposal, Turrill summoned both commanding officers of the 17th and 66th Companies to report to him immediately. First Lieutenant Robert Blake, a platoon commander with the 17th Company remembered, "Captain [Roswell] Winans had been called to Battalion Headquarters and left me with instructions to follow with the company as soon as we were relieved by the French."[22] The instructions given to Turrill by regiment were vague, and in turn, the information Turrill had relayed to his company commanders remained ambiguous.

As Turrill's battalion prepared for the pre-dawn movement to the jump-off point, four Marines from the 83rd Company prepared to finish the final phase of their patrol of Hill 142. Secluded in the wooded ravine east of the hill, they spent much of the night trying to bypass the eastern end of the German line to try and flank them and identify their position. The abbreviated darkness of summer nights in northern France created a hazy moonlit sky, so the four Marines took every measurement to concealment themselves. Every movement that rustled the foliage along the shallow gulley seemed to resonate loudly in the calm of the night.

Suddenly, from the east, the muffled crack of a distant rifle shot broke the calm. The four men briefly froze before looking around and at each other in the murky darkness as they tried to figure out the source of the gunfire. It appeared to emanate hundreds of meters to the east in the direction of American positions along the northern fringe of Bois de Champillon and the Lucy-Torcy road.

The shot also alerted a group of Germans, who quickly noticed the commotion in the ravine as the patrol foolishly silhouetted themselves against the moonlight. More gunfire from the east scattered the small patrol. At that point, with their position compromised, they retraced their steps back toward the company lines. Passing along the trampled path over which they first crawled, they reentered the lines at 1:15 A.M. The last two men in the column noted the movement of what they believed to be a three-man

German patrol nearby crawling through the grain field.[23] The Marines returned unscathed.

Across the 4th Brigade front, guns of the 12th Field Artillery initiated their bombardment of the approaches to Hill 142 in preparation for the 3:45 A.M. attack.[24] The muzzle flashes of cannons flickering between the distant tree lines lit up the horizon as other batteries of the regiment joined in the thunderous chorus.

Battery D, 2nd Battalion, 12th Field Artillery situated in the woods northwest of Paris Farm started registering their targets. Gun crews traversed and elevated barrels to the appropriate quadrant and deflection. The soldiers on the gun line spent their previous days catching sleep whenever possible since they had continuously manned the guns after dark the past two nights, and this one would be no different.

Sergeant Joseph J. Gleeson took a brief moment to records in his diary, "Fired all night. Hundreds of guns were firing and such a war! Undesirable!"[25] Each gun crew blasted away throughout the night leaving hardly a moment without the deep cavernous roar of artillery fire.

On the northern outskirts of Marigny-en-Orxois, Lieutenant Colonel Wise left his command post with orders for his companies to move since the relief troops of the French 116th Infantry finally trickled into the line in isolated groups after midnight.[26] The concussion of their fire resonated across the fields as they pummeled the German line along the Clignon brook. Against the backdrop of this deafening display of firepower, elements of the 116th French filed into Bois de Veuilly. The French soldiers briefly conversed with members of Lieutenant Elliott Cooke's platoon of the 18th Company who learned of the morning's scheduled assault.

After four miserable days along the front, Cooke's men eagerly left their position to the relieving French troops and departed the frontline. According to Cook, "The hike back out of the valley was not made in column of squads, but in single file. The men slipped silently through the dark woods, always keeping a tree between themselves and the Germans. An occasional crude wooden cross marked the filled-in fox holes where several of the lads stayed on."[27] The battalion moved to a patch of woods located a few hundred meters northeast of La Voie du Chatel per regimental instructions.[28]

The rest of the 18th Company, as well as rest of the battalion, followed Cooke's platoon as they departed Bois de Veuilly. Exiting the woods, Cooke's men skirted the northern portion of Marigny-en-Orxois and found the village's structures merely crumbled remnants of what they had been days earlier. The wreckage of buildings obstructed and narrowed the town's roadways where piles of broken masonry, splintered wood, and shattered glass crunched under the procession of hobnailed boots of the Marines passing by in the dark.

June 5th Chapter IV

Burning structures provided partial illumination for the men to survey the damage as they marched past. Cooke Remembered, "While passing the brick-walled cemetery of Marigny we saw that shells had uprooted the ancient dead and destroyed their last abode. The air was laden with the sweetish stench of death."[29] Wise's men continued their hike along the road between Marigny-en-Orxois and La Voie du Chatel. Each Marine maintained sufficient distance from the man in front so they would not get lost in the dark. They finally entered the woods north of La Voie du Chatel only to find a battery of American artillery preparing to fire a barrage.[30]

When the procession of 18th Company men entered the woods, Captain Lester Wass halted the column and ordered them to dig. The forest held very little underbrush, which made excavating dugouts much easier. "The men were tired of digging, and anyway, there were not enough entrenching tools to go 'round. But the holes could be dug without picks and shovels as we soon found out," recalled Cooke.[31]

As his men excavated dugouts, Wise ventured north through the woods a few hundred meters and established his battalion command post under a thicket of saplings on the northern tree line along the side of the roadway that bisected the woods and stretched a kilometer north to Champillon.[32] Between periods of digging and smoking cigarettes, the men took a moment to eat whatever cold rations they still had. They soon learned, however, that this new position a few hundred meters back from the frontlines offered them no better safety. According to Cooke:

> Following the first salvo from the American guns, Fritz set out to silence the battery that shared the woods with us. And he didn't show much discrimination in placing his shells. We caught as many as the artillery and in no time at all everyone was scratching dirt. The more fortunate had something to work with, but tables of equipment do not contemplate officers digging holes. Just the same we needed holes, and deep ones too. Tables or no tables, I burrowed three feet underground with a mess-kit cover, knife, fork, and fingernails. It didn't take me long to do it, either. We dug while our artillery banged away all night and the Boche banged right back at them. Fritz steam-rolled that woods again and again and we had to lie there and take it.[33]

As Wise's battalion settled into the woods near La Voie du Chatel, the exhausted soldiers of Company D, 2nd Battalion, 2nd Engineers also reached the same forest following a nearly six-kilometer hike from Le Thiolet.[34] Twenty-four-year-old Private First Class Frank J. Michael, a railroad worker from St. Louis, Missouri, and Private First Class Thomas J. Powers, worked together to excavated a dugout large enough to fit both of them. When they finished, the two men stretched out a blanket roll and slept.[35] The distant rumble of artillery compelled them to pull blankets further up over their heads as if to somehow mentally distance themselves, if but for a few hours, from the proximity of war.[36]

Within hours of Company D's arrival, the rest of the 2nd Battalion, 2nd Engineers joined them in the woods.[37] Soldiers of thirty-six-year-old Captain Jesse Lowen's Company F left their reserve position south of Marigny-en-Orxois and entered the woods northeast of La Voie du Chatel around 2:00 A.M.

Once in place, they alleviated themselves of heavy packs and engineering equipment.[38] Company E joined the other two companies of the battalion shortly afterward. Both E and F Companies had enjoyed a rest over much of the previous twenty-four hours and were able to replenish their rations.[39]

On the eastern sector of the 4th Brigade's front, the Marines of Captain Randolph Zane's 79th Company were relieved by elements of the 23rd Infantry during the night. Zane's men moved about a kilometer northwest into the Bois de Triangle. Corporal Glen Hill of the company's 2nd Platoon recalled, "The night of June 5th our company moved over to a spot about a half mile from Bouresches. It was long after midnight before we got bedded down in fox holes of the men we relieved."[40] The exhausted men had been without any prolonged rest for nearly six days.

Corporal Lloyd Pike also with the company's 2nd Platoon, stated, "I remember little of this relief except that we left the front line and took up a support position in a patch of woods."[41] Despite the thunder of artillery throughout the night, the men slept soundly. Hill recalled, "I had a chance to find a hole under a huge boulder. It had a nice layer of grass and leaves, and I didn't wake up until about 20 minutes to five on June sixth. What a sleep I had!"[42]

Once relieved by the 23rd Infantry, the 96th Company moved back from the eastern edge of Bois de Clerembauts towards the battalion headquarters at La Cense Farm. According to Second Lieutenant Clifton Cates commanding the company's 4th Platoon, "We were relieved on 5 June and fell back in a position in the woods—we thought we were going back for a rest."[43] Nineteen-year-old Private Harold Ivan Turney of Detroit, Michigan, remembered the movement through the nearly 200 acres of forest in Bois de Clerembauts took most the night and once again deprived the men of sleep. "The reserve was in a thick woods, and it was about daybreak when we reached there."[44]

The men, realizing they would stay in that position for a while, spent much of the night digging in and did not sleep until after dawn.[45] The 80th Company remained in position along the eastern outskirts of Lucy-le-Bocage. With the span of his 2nd Battalion, 6th Marines' line drastically reduced, Major Thomas Holcomb recalled, "Our front was then held by the 78th and 79th Companies in line and the 80th and 96th in support."[46]

With the ebb of artillery fire rippling across the night sky, the 2nd Division would assume the offensive within hours, yet the division front, which was drastically reduced in width, remained far from organized. Several units scheduled to be involved in the attack had not been notified, much less moved into their designated positions from which they were to initiate the assault. Officers at the company and even battalion level remained supremely ignorant to the terrain before them due to inaccurate and generally unavailable maps.

No one from the 2nd Division or even the French 21st Corps appears to have coordinated whatever intelligence may have been gathered regarding potential enemy strong points. Several rudimentary patrols at battalion and even regimental level were conducted and should have provided a general understanding of the enemy's positions.

Second Lieutenant Clifton B. Cates commanded the 4th Platoon of the 96th Company. Photo credit: Marine Corps History Division.

The incredibly small window of time between the French 21st Corps' planning and scheduled implementation of the offensive, however, left no time to coordinate whatever vital information might have been obtained.

Regardless of the short timetables, several obstacles faced the division's attack. The small-scale hachured maps were not only inaccurate, but many of the company commanders did not have copies of them. The lack of protocol for coordinating intelligence left attacking units oblivious to what resistance they might face.

Critically slow and inefficient communication created uncertainty regarding the attainment of objectives or the status of troops involved in the attack. One thing, however, remained absolute—the scheduled advance for June 6th would commence regardless of circumstances. Irrespective of ignorance regarding objectives, or whether they reached the jump-off point in time, the men were going to attack.

For too many young Americans, the sunset of June 5, 1918, would be the last they would ever see. For several men, hastily drafted letters to loved ones would be the last their family would ever hear from them. Conversations among the men that night often became the final memory of a

June 5th Chapter IV

beloved comrade who would not live to see the end of another day. For many of the Americans in the 2nd Division, the next twenty-four hours would be the worst day of their young lives.

---

[1] Captain Jonas Platt, "Holding Back the Marines," *The Ladies Home Journal*, Sept. 1919, 27. Note: Platt identifies the town as La Voie du Chatel, but it's likely he meant Marigny-en-Orxois as the company was still on the northern outskirts of the Chateau at Marigny-en-Orxois until the predawn of June 6th just before the attack when they moved north of Champillon.
[2] Ibid.
[3] Ibid.
[4] Ibid.
[5] Ibid.
[6] Ibid.
[7] Ibid.
[8] Ibid.
[9] Ibid.
[10] Ibid.
[11] Ibid.
[12] Ibid.
[13] Ibid.
[14] Ibid.
[15] Ibid.
[16] Ibid.
[17] Wahl, Sector North-east of Chateau Thierry, Box 79, RG 120.9.3, NARA College Park, MD.
[18] Platt, "Holding Back the Marines," *The Ladies Home Journal*, 114.
[19] Ibid.
[20] Ibid.
[21] Ibid.
[22] Blake, *From Belleau Wood to Bougainville*, 14.
[23] Patrol Report Catlin to Harbord, 6 June 1918, Box 300, RG 127, NARA, Washington D.C.
[24] Wahl, George D., Diary of a Battery Commander, Box 79, RG 120.9.3, NARA College Park, MD.
[25] Spaulding and Wright, *The Second Division American Expeditionary Force in France 1917-1919*, 253.
[26] Wise and Frost, *A Marine Tells it to You*, 206.
[27] Elliot Cooke, "We Can Take It, We Attack," *Infantry Journal*, July-August (1937), 7.
[28] Wise and Frost, *A Marine Tells it to You*, 206.
[29] Cooke, "We Can Take It, We Attack," *Infantry Journal*, 7.
[30] Ibid.
[31] Ibid.
[32] Wise and Frost, *A Marine Tells it to You*, 207.
[33] Cooke, "We Can Take It, We Attack," *Infantry Journal*, 7.
[34] *History of the Second Engineers 1916-1919*, 41.

June 5th Chapter IV

---

[35] Burial File of Private First Class Frank J. Michael, Eye-witness statement by First Sergeant Frank P. Stanley, Box 3340, RG 92.9, Records of Graves Registration Services, NARA College Park, MD.
[36] Ibid.
[37] Burton, *History of the Second Engineers 1916-1919*, 41.
[38] Ibid, 45.
[39] Ibid, 43-45.
[40] Correspondence from Hill to Neufeld, 17 January 1979, Alfred M. Gray Research Library, Quantico, VA.
[41] Pike, *The Battle For Belleau Woods, As I Remember It About 60 Years Later*, 11-12.
[42] Correspondence from Hill to Neufeld, 17 January 1979, Alfred M. Gray Research Library, Quantico, VA.
[43] General Clifton B. Cates, interview by Robert Asprey, Alfred M. Gray Research Library, Quantico, VA.
[44] Harold I. Turney, "Says he Likes Parris Island Better than he does Paris, France," *Recruiters Bulletin*, July 1918, 6.
[45] Newspaper clippings sent to headquarters Marine Corps by F.M. Stites, Box 300, RG 127 NARA, Washington D.C.
[46] Correspondence Lieutenant Colonel Thomas Holcomb to Joel D. Thacker headquarters Marine Corps, 12 December 1918, Box 70, Records of the American Expeditionary Forces, NARA College Park, MD.

CONCLUSION

Conclusion

While the final hours of June 5th faded away, a chapter in the annals of the American Expeditionary Forces' battle experience also closed—the official conclusion of what formally became known as the ten-day Aisne defensive campaign.[1]

The nearly 27,000 men of the 2nd Division, however, remained oblivious to this historical distinction. Their only recognition of it came almost a year after the war in the form of a one-eighth-inch by inch and a half bronze clasp bearing the word 'Aisne' affixed to the rainbow-colored ribbons of their victory medals. For ninety-two men of the 2nd Division who died during the past several days, this meager little accouterment went to their next of kin. For those who endured and survived the previous seven days, no medal or award could adequately epitomize the terrifying experience of life at the front.

Over the course of the previous six days, the 2nd Division withstood a variety of hellacious experiences. The men had spent hours packed in trucks that took them to the active sector only to hike dozens of kilometers over dust-choked roads to reach the front lines.

Once they arrived, the troops spent consecutive days without sleep and food. They dug fighting holes at every stop only to relocate to a new position as the division's battle lines stabilized. They helplessly watched wounded comrades gasp away their final moments of life. They saw men blown to pieces by the enemy's unrelenting shellfire.

They engaged German soldiers with rifle and machine gun fire at great distances. Some men spent nights burying the mutilated, dismembered and decomposing bodies of fellow Marines, soldiers and corpsmen—a memory that would linger in their minds forever. The division had suffered 554 casualties, including 462 wounded or gassed, and ninety-two killed in action or died of wounds.[2] American casualty, however, would get exponentially worse in the coming weeks.

Following the unsuccessful German efforts to seize the bridges over the Marne River in Chateau Thierry and establish a crossing on June 1st and 2nd, Von Conta's 4th Reserve Corps shifted their efforts west. His troops wheeled their advance along a nearly ten-kilometer front just west of Chateau Thierry. This development required the French 21st Corps to place arriving units of the American 2nd Division along the front in a patchwork manner wherever the latest German push seemed most perilous.

Days after reaching the front, American troops of the 2nd Division occasionally encountered Von Conta's men, in brief, sporadic and distant exchanges of rifle and machine gun fire. German batteries also subjected the 2nd Division's line to ever-increasing artillery bombardment. By June 3rd, Von Conta's units occupied Bouresches, Belleau, Torcy, and Bussiares. They also seized the heights along the southern banks of the Clignon brook. The Clignon Valley was critical to the Germans as a protected position running parallel to the Paris-Metz Road, and only about six and a half

Conclusion

kilometers north of this vital causeway.[3] Von Conta's troops also captured the 200-acre span of Belleau Wood, which served as the strategic nucleus for the entire ten-kilometer battlefront.

Before the last remnants of the exhausted and broken French Army withdrew behind the Americans, they made gallant attempts to hold and even counterattack the Germans, which provided Major General Bundy's 2nd Division a crucial window of time to strengthen and organize their front.

On June 4th, the same day the 2nd Division officially assumed command of the line, Von Conta's troops, per Corps order, assumed a temporary defensive posture. His directive specifically instructed the units of his 4th Reserve Corps to push beyond their present position and capture ground beneficial for the defense.[4]

After Von Conta's directive, all ensuing attempts by his men to seize terrain more suitable for the defense occurred with a posture entirely different from the offensive nature exhibited in first days of Operation Blücher. These subtle German efforts, however, continued putting German troops within range of American rifle and machine gun fire.

Changes in German posture along the ten kilometers west of Chateau Thierry gave a general impression that the 2nd Division's solidification of the line was a significant variable to obstructing Operation Blücher's success in propelling the center of the 7th German Army towards Paris. Other than the noticeable change in the enemy's posture since June 4th, American and French high command had every reason to believe that Germans intended to continue towards Paris.

Only days into the offensive, German goals regarding Operation Blücher quickly went from its original diversionary intent to exploiting the early success and making it the main advance in the early—a fateful decision that compelled the 7th Army to try and attain too much with insufficiently allocated men and resources to attain such grandiose objectives. The fluctuating emphasis in pushing specific sectors of the 7th Army forward, the increasingly narrow front, and the ensuing supply dilemmas all affected the disposition of Von Conta's 4th Reserve Corps at the center of the 7th Army's drive by June 5th.

While 2nd Division firepower did not solely cause the cessation of Von Conta's offensive efforts, the American presence would ultimately deprive the Germans of the opportunity to resume their advance by providing Degoutte's 21st Corps the troops needed to conduct a hastily-planned attack of their own scheduled for June 6th. Degoutte's decision would ultimately put many of the soldiers and Marines of the 2nd Division on the offensive for the first time since their arrival in France—a reality that would subject many of them to one of the most defining days of their young lives.

Volume II discusses the 2nd Division's attack on June 6th in meticulous detail. The assault focused on three primary objectives which included Hill 142, Bois de Belleau, and the town of Bouresches. The attack set a new

Conclusion

precedence in casualties for the American Expeditionary Forces, one that would be surpassed by later engagements. However, June 6, 1918, for the first time, saw American troops conduct offensive operations against the enemy on what was perceived to be one of the most contested and strategically significant sectors of the Western Front in late spring 1918.

---

[1] The Aisne Campaign, also referred to as the Third battle of the Aisne, lasted from May 27th to June 5th.
[2] ABMC, *2nd Division Summary of Operations*, 23.
[3] Spaulding and Wright, *The Second Division American Expeditionary Force in France 1917-1919*, 50.
[4] War Diary and Annexes 4th Reserve Corps 4 June 1918, *Translation of War Diaries of German Units*, Vol. 1.

Bibliography

Archival Material

National Archives College Park, Maryland

Record Group 120.9.3, Records of combat divisions, 2nd Division Files boxes 1-90, Record Group 120 Records of the AEF.

Record Group 92.9, Burial Files, Records of Graves Registration Organizations, 1917-54, Record Group 92 Records of the Quartermaster General's Office. Burial files were obtained for the following individuals:

Banister, Ira	Beaty, Shelton B.
Belcher, Bert	Glick, Frank L.
Boone, Isaac N.	Gustafson, George
Brock, Joe M.	Hackney, Charles
Brooks, Harold	Harris, Homer G.
Brown, Charles F.	Horton, Carl
Capsack, Michael	Jenkins, John O.
Carey, Charles H.	Johanningmeier, O.
Carpenter, Stanley	Johnstone, Malcolm
Debacker, Albert	Joy, Charles L.
Desourdie, Adrien	Kellum, James B.
Eddy, Henry L.	Kirchner, Henry
Frazier, Walter	Kolinsky, Victor
Lomax, Fred E.	Stine, George C.
Maggoine, Charles	Stubbs, Wesley J.
Mart Gentry	Thompson, John
Meehan, Romulus	Watson, Marvin
Michael, Frank J.	Weisbaker, Alfred
Mortorff, Earl M.	Whipple, James
Parker, Charles A.	Williams, George
Sanchez, Joachin	Wisted, David
Schall, James B.	Zaico, Paoset
Snow, Frank	

Record Group 117.4.2, Correspondence with officers of the 2nd Division AEF. Records relating to

World War I frontline maps and accompanying "Summaries of Operations," Record Group 117, Records of the American Battlefield Monuments Commission.

National Archives Washington D.C.

Record Group 127, Records relating to Marine Participation in World War I, Entry 240.

Record Group 163, Records of the Selective Service System (World War I), 1917 – 1939. Microfilm publication M1509. (Also accessed on ancestry.com)

National Personnel Records Center in St. Louis, Missouri

Official Military Personnel Files, 1905 – 1998, Record Group 127, NPRC St. Louis, MO. Personnel files were obtained for the following individuals:

Anderson, Arvid
Broderick, Joseph
Brooks, Harold
Buford, David L.
Carpenter, Stanley
Cook, Walter
Croka, William
Daly, Daniel
Davis, Cleo
DeRoode, Louis R.
Durr, Paul
Elwood, Joseph P.
Fisher, Roland
Freund, Warren
Glick, Frank L.
Gustafson, George
Hall, David
Harvis, John
Hayden, William
Hodges, James
Horton, Carl

Kelly, Thomas J.
Kipness, David
Kishler, Edwin P.
Long, Eugene H.
Madden, Simon J.
Martin, John
Martin, Oscar E.
Mathews, William
McCoy, James
Morgan, Peter
Parsons, James
Rockwell, Merl C.
Rodgers, John
Ross, Richard
Siegert, Holden
Stair, Willett
Sutherland, Jim
Tester, Albert O.
Voeth, Robert
Wass, Lester
Wodarezyk, Mike

Alfred Gray Research Library in Quantico, Virginia

Records of the Second Division (Regular) Volumes 1-9. Washington: The Army War College, 1927. (Only volume 5 was examined at this location)

Personal Papers collection:

Diary of Asa J. Smith 74th Company 6th Regiment U.S. Marines, American Expeditionary Force Second Division.

Diary of William W. Fullington, Pvt. USMC June 12, 1917-August 13, 1919.

Frank McClelland, Story of My Life.

Correspondence from Glen Hill to G.M. Neufeld, 17 January 1979.

Arthur Clifford letters.

Correspondence Chester Lancaster to Bob Queen, 4 June 1976.

Clifton B. Cates papers.

General Clifton B. Cates, interview by Robert Asprey, June 25, 1963, Transcript.

General Gerald B. Thomas, interview by Robert Asprey, June 11, 1963, Transcript.

General Lemuel Shepherd, interview by Robert Asprey June 20, 1963, Transcript.

Louis Felix Timmerman, interview by Robert Asprey, April 23-24, 1964, Transcript.

General Alfred H. Noble interview, 1968, Transcript.

General Gerald B. Thomas memoir.

Captain John West, "Belleau Wood."

John W. Thomason, *Second Division Northwest of Chateau Thierry, 1 June-10 July 1918,* unpublished manuscript.

Oral History collection:
Brigadier General Victor F. Bleasdale interview by Benis Frank, Transcript.

Lieutenant Colonel Walter S. Gaspar, interview by Benis Frank 1975.

General Lemuel C. Shepherd Jr., interview by Benis Frank, Quantico, VA, 1967.

University of Oklahoma Bizzell Memorial Library

Records of the Second Division (Regular) Volumes 1-9. Washington: The Army War College, 1927. (Volume 5 missing)

Penn State University Library

Translations of War Diaries of German Units Opposed to the Second Division (Regular) *1918, Chateau Thierry,* Volumes 1-4. Washington: The Army War College, 1930-32.

Maneuver Center of Excellence Donovan Research Library at Ft. Benning, Georgia

Major Robert E. Messersmith, "Operations of 78th Company Sixth Regiment Marines at Belleau Wood, June 1 to June 13, 1918. Personal Experience." Advanced Infantry Course 1928-1929 Fort Benning Georgia.

Major John R. Mendenhall, "Operations of the 7th Machine Gun Battalion (Third Division) in the Vicinity of Chateau Thierry, France, May 31-June 4, 1918. Personal Experience." Advanced Infantry Course 1929-1930 Fort Benning, Georgia.

Library of Congress, Washington D.C.

> Veterans History Project, American Folklife Center
> Leo Joseph Bailey collection
> (AFC/2001/001/76979)

Virginia Military Institute Archives Preston Library, Lexington, Virginia

> General Lemuel C. Shepherd, Jr. papers.

Bancroft Archival Library, University of California, Berkeley, California

> Paul Schuster Taylor interview by Suzanne B. Riessin May 26, 1970, Earl Warren Oral History Project, California Social Scientist. Volume I: Education, Field Research, and Family.

Minnesota Historical Society in St. Paul, Minnesota

> LaRoy S. Upton papers, 1887-1927.

Howard Gotlieb Archival Research Center, Boston University, Boston, Massachusetts

> Mathews, W.R. file 1962-1966, Robert Asprey Collection, Howard Gotlieb Archival Research Center, Boston University, Boston, MA.

Herbert Hoover Presidential Library and Museum, West Branch, Iowa

> Hanford MacNider Papers 1902-1967, Manuscript Collections.

Pocumtuck Valley Memorial Association (PVMA) Library, Deerfield, Massachusetts

> Ashley Family Papers.

Unpublished Material

Unit Histories

Curtis Jr., T. J. Captain USMC. *History of the Sixth Machine Gun Battalion, Fourth Brigade, U.S. Marines, Second Division and Its Participation in the Great War*. Neuweid on the Rhine: N.P, 1919.

Burton, Allan. *History of the Second Engineers 1916-1919*. N.P, N.D.

History of the 96th Company 6th Regiment in World War I. Washington D.C., N.P., 1967.

Harry B. Field and Henry G. James. *Over the Top with the 18th Company 5th Regiment U.S. Marines, A History*. Rodenbach: N.P., 1919.

History of the Third Division United States Army in the World War for the Period December 1, 1917, to January 1, 1919. Andernach: N.P., 1919.

Memoirs

Gordon, George V. *Leathernecks and Doughboys*. Chicago: N.P.: 1927.

Pike, Colonel Lloyd E. *The Battle For Belleau Woods, As I Remember It About 60 Years Later*. N.P., 1977.

Diary of Peter Preston Wood 81st Company 6th Machine Gun Battalion. N.P., Author's collection.

Diary of Jerry Davin 55th Company, 5th Marines, N.P., Author's collection.

Cordes, Onnie. *The Immortal Division*. Palm Beach: Merriman Press, 1990. Note: Despite the press information printed in the manuscript, this memoir was never published and made available.

Hubert, John "Chick" *Memories of C Company 2nd Engineers*. N.P., 1979.

Unpublished works obtained through author's correspondence

Marie Silverthorn provided massive quantities of material regarding her grandfather, First Lieutenant General Merwin Silverthorn. This included several scrapbooks, letters ranging from 1917-1919, and several newspaper clippings.

Correspondence Joseph Hagan to Captain Lloyd W. Williams Post American Legion Berryville, VA 12 August 1963, a copy of a letter provided to author by Michael Miller.

Joe Fischer provided material including letters, newspaper clippings on his great uncle, Corporal Robert Fischer 20th Company.

Cathy Lewis provided material including letters, newspaper clippings and images of her grandfather Private Joyce Lewis 20th Company.

Madeleine Johnson provided the letters of her great uncle, Captain Lothar Long 6th Machine Gun Battalion.

Howard George Fisher provided the letters of his uncle, Private Roland Fisher 51st Company.

Peter Ward, *"Join The Marines," the sign said By Peter Christian Ward* drafted verbatim by his daughter Marjorie May Ward in 1965. Copy furnished to Lenny Moore by Peter Ward's granddaughter Mary Kathyrn Sagedal. A Copy furnished in an email to the author by Lenny Moore May 6, 2012.

John R. Canfield III provided the author interviews, images and articles about his grandfather, Sergeant Roger Canfield 43rd Company.

Robert Chardon, "Lemuel Cornick Shepherd Jr., A Marine's Marine 1896-1990", (N.P., N.D.), 1. This is an unpublished paper written by the great-grandson of Lemuel Shepherd.

Published Material

Books

Asprey, Robert B. *The German High Command at War, Hindenburg and Ludendorff Conduct World War I.* New York, NY; William Morrow and Company, Inc., 1991.

Blake, Robert Wallace. *From Belleau Wood to Bougainville The Oral History of Major General Robert Blake USMC and The Travel Journal of Rosselet Wallace Blake.* Bloomington: Author House, 2004.

Boyd, Thomas. *Through the Wheat.* New York: Scribner's Sons, 1923.

Catlin, Albertus W. *With the Help of God and a Few Marines.* Garden City: Doubleday, Page and Co., 1919.

Cochrane, Rexmond C. *Gas Warfare at Belleau Wood June 1918.* Washington D.C.: U.S. Army Chemical Corps Historical Office Army Chemical Center 1957.

Derby, Richard. *Wade in Sanitary, The Story of a Division Surgeon in France.* New York: G.P. Putnam and Sons, 1919.

Gulberg, Gus. *A War Diary.* Chicago: Drake Press, 1927.

Harbord, James G. *Leaves from a War Diary.* New York: Dodd, Mead & Company, 1925.

Harbord, James G. *American Army in France 1917-1919.* Boston: Little, Brown, and Company, 1936.

Hemrick, Levi E. *Once a Marine.* New York: Carlton Press, Inc., 1968.

Kean, Robert Winthrop. *Dear Marraine 1917-1919.* Washington D.C.: Library of Congress, 1969.

Ludendorff, Eric. *My War Memories.* Volume 2. London: Hutchinson and Co., 1919.

Mitchell, W.A. *The Official History of the Second Regiment of Engineers and Second Engineer Train United States Army in the World War.* San Antonio: San Antonio Printing Co, 1938.

Morgan, Daniel E. *When the World Went Mad, A Thrilling Story of the Late War, Told in the Language of the Trenches.* Boston: Christopher Publishing House, 1931.

Rogerson, Sidney. *The Last of the Ebb.* London: Greenhill Books 1937.

Scanlon, William T. *God Have Mercy On Us.* New York: Houghton Mifflin Company, 1929.

Scarbrough, Byron. *They Called us Devil Dogs. Morrisville:* Lulu, 2005.

Schiani, Alfred. *A Former Marine tells it like it was and is.* New York: Carlton Press Inc., 1988.

Westover, Wendell. *Suicide Battalions.* New York: G.P. Putnam's sons, 1929.

Wilhelm, Kaiser Crown prince of Germany. *My War Experiences.* London: Hurst and Blackett, 1922.

History of the Third battalion, Sixth regiment, U.S. Marines. Hillsdale, Akers, Macritchie & Hurlbut, 1919.

Multiple authors:

American Battle Monuments Commission. *2nd Division Summary of Operations in the World War.* Washington: U.S. Government Printing Office, 1944.

Craig Hamilton and Louise Corbin. *Echoes From Over There, Stories Written by Soldiers Who Fought Over There.* New York: The Soldiers' Publishing Company, 1919.

Frederick M. Wise and Meigs O. Frost. *A Marine Tells it to You.* New York: J.H. Sears and Company, Inc., 1929.

General Robert Lee Bullard and Earl Reeves. *American Soldiers Also Fought.* New York: Longmans, Green and Co., 1936.

Joseph E. Rendinell and George Pattullo. *One Man's War: The Diary of a Leatherneck.* New York: J.H. Sears and Company, 1928.

Kemper F. Cowing and Courtney Ryley Cooper. *Dear Folks At Home.* Boston: Houghton Mifflin Company, 1919.

Myron E. Adams, and Fred. Girton. *The Fort Sheridan Officers' Training Camps.* Fort Sheridan: Fort Sheridan Association, 1920.

Oliver Spauling and John Wright. *The Second Division American Expeditionary Force in France 1917-1919.* New York: Hillman Press, 1937.

Edited Works:

Collins, Harry. *The War Diary of Corporal Harry Collins. Edited* by David Fisher and George Clark, Pike: Brass Hat, 1996.

Hatcher, James E. *Citizen Soldier I: World War I Recollections of Pvt. James E. Hatcher, USMC.* Edited by Gilbert Hart, published Kindle Edition only, Dec. 13, 2013.

Jackson, Warren R. *His Time in Hell, A Texas Marine in France: The World War I Memoir of Warren R. Jackson.* Edited by George Clark, Novato, CA: 2001.

Linn, Louis C. *At Belleau Wood with a Rifle and a Sketchpad: Memoir of a United States Marine in World War I*. Edited by Laura Jane Linn Wright and B.J. Omanson, Jefferson: McFarland and Company, Inc., 2012.

Paradis, Donald V. *The World War I Memoirs of Don V. Paradis, Gunnery Sergeant USMC*. Edited by Lt. Col. Peter Owen. Morrisville: Lulu, 2010.

Sellers, James McBrayer. *World War I Memoirs*. Edited by William W. Sellers and George Clark, Pike: Brass Hat, 1997.

Magazines, Journals and Newspapers

"Controversy Over Legend Clarified By Marine Captain." *Quantico Sentry* (Quantico, VA), Volume 2 No. 3, June 12, 1936.

"Heroes of Belleau Wood Come Back Smiling." *Recruiters Bulletin*, September 1918.

"On the Heels of the Hun." *Recruiters Bulletin*, November 1918.

"Tales told by Overseas Marines." *Recruiters Bulletin*, August 1918.

Cooke, Elliot. "We Can Take It, We Attack." *Infantry Journal,* July-August (1937).

Dunton, Orley. "Mussing Up the Prussian Guard, The Idea that Reversed the German War Machine," *Hearst's,* December 1918.

McClellan, Edwin N. "The Nearest Point to Paris in 1918." *Sea Power*, June 1921.

Moore, William E. "The Bloody Angle of the A.E.F." *The American Legion Weekly*, February 24, 1922.

Nelson, Havelock D. "Paris-Metz Road." *Leatherneck*, January 1940.

Platt, Jonas Captain. "Holding Back the Marines." *The Ladies Home Journal*, Sept. 1919, 27.

Powis, Albert. "A Leatherneck in France 1917-1919." *Military Images Magazine*, September-October, 1981.

Turney, Harold I. "Says he Likes Parris Island Better than he does Paris, France." *Recruiters Bulletin*, July 1918.

Wertheim, L. Jon "Unsinkable." *Sports Illustrated*, April 2, 2012.

Online Material

Memoirs of 2nd Lieutenant William B. Jackson, 77th Company, 6th Machine Gun Battalion, http://www.monongahelabooks.com/jackmem10.html.

Leeke, Jim, "Hughie Miller," Society for American Baseball, 2011, http://sabr.org/bioproj/person/e32e4445

Ancestry.com provided lots of help filling in details on the biographical detail of individuals.

INDEX

American Expeditionary Forces: ii, 37, 42, 90,
1st Army Corps School: 53, 374-75
1st Division: 45, 50, 53-54.
16th Infatnry: 53-54.
2nd Division: i, ii, 47-48, *48*, 56-57, 61, 66, 68, 69, *69*, 73, 79, *80*, 93, 138, 140-41, 146, *147*, 148, 181, 187, 189-91, 201, 206, 208, 211, 213, 227, 282, 290-93, 297, 299, 301, 307-08, 313-15, 328, 330, 342, 347-49, 354, 361,366-67, 369, 374, 386-87, 390-91.
4th Brigade: ii-iii, v, 45, 49, 72, 94, 158, 167, 185, 191, 212-13, 228, 292, 309, 330, 338, 359, 362, 368-69, 384, 386.
5th Marines: ii, v, 51-53, 55, 62, 64-65, 73-74, 76, 79, 89, 94, 127-28, 132, 145, *147*, 149, 156-59, 162, *167*, 167-68, 186, 194, 197-99, 205, 215, 227-28, *231*, 241, 243, 247, 254, 260, 267-70, 282, 284, 294, 297-98, 299-300, 307, 309, 315, 317, *318-319*, 321, 337, 345, 349-50, 355, 360, 362 367, 379, 381.
Headquarters Company: 162, 234, 255, 268, 273, 285, 301-02, 310-11, *320*, 336-37.
Stokes Mortar section: 269-70, 336.
Pioneer sections: 268.
37mm section: 269.
8th Machine Gun Company: 212, *213*, 323.

1st Battalion: ii, iv, 55, 62, 73, 94, 145, *147*, 156, 194, 270, 298, 320, 362, 367,
17th Company: ii, 55, 62, 73, 94-95, 145, 298-99, 361, 372, 383,
49th Company: 195, 363-64, 379, 381-82.
2nd Platoon: 195.
66th Company: 62, 298, 372-74, 381-82.
67th Company: 298, 362-63, 372, 383.
2nd Battalion: v, 52-53, 64, 73, 76, 94, 127-28, 149, 157, 159, *167*, 167, 186, 198-99, 206, 216, 229, 242, 244, 261, 268-69, 271, 300, 308, 316, 318, *319*, *322*, 355, 360, 367, 379, 381.
18th Company: v, 52, 64-65, 73-74, 77, 127-30, 160-61, 165-66, *167*, 229, 262-63, 301, 308, 311, 321-23, 367, 379, 384-85.
4th Platoon: 161.
43rd Company: 74, 160, 165, 262-64, 298, 300, 311, 318, 359, 361.
4th Platoon: 359-61.
51st Company: 162, 165-66, 216, 229, 231, 242-44, *245*, 246-47, 271, 325, 358.
55th Company: v, 53, 65, 73, 94, 128-29, 131, 149, 158-60, 162-66, *167*, 227, 261, 264-65, 285, 301, 310, 325, 336-37, 256, *318-19*, *320*, *324*, 356, 360-61, 368.
2nd Platoon: 301, 310, 356, *320*.
3rd Platoon: 325.

INDEX

3rd Battalion: 51, 65, 132, 308, 349-50.
16th Company: 51, 66, 132, 308.
20th Company: iv, v.
45th Company: v, vi.
47th Company: v, 74.
6th Marines: ii, v, 45, 47, 50, *50*, 61, *63*, 63, 66-68, 79, 83-85, *86*, 87, 89, 91, 96-97, *101*, 103, *104*, 106-07, *107*, 110, *112-13*, 113, 135-36, *137*, 148, 151, 166, 168-69, 175, 185-87, 194-96, 198-99, 212, 214, 216, 218, 223, 227, 229-31, *231*, 248, 271, 275, *275*, 281, 284, 299, 310, 314, 317, 320, 331-32, 338, 343, 345, 347, 349-50, 355, 367, 371, 373-74, 386.
Headquarters Company: 186, 234, 275, 332, 344.
37mm section also see *one-pounder section*: 344.
73rd Machine Gun Company: 212, 227, 233, 274, 324, 348, 351, 372.
1st Battalion: 67-68, 87, 103, *104*, *112-13*, 113, 136, *137*, 166, 169, 186, 196, 198-99, 216-17, 227, *232*, 249, 281, 284, 299, 310, 320, 331, 338, 343, 347, 349-50, *361*.
74th Company: 105, 136-37, 168, 198, *199*, 249, 299, 336, 346-47.
1st Platoon: 198, *199*, 249, 299.
2nd Platoon: 198, *199*, 249, 299.
75th Company: 45-46, 68, 87, 96-97, 103-05, 111-12, 136, 169, 198, 217, 230, 253, 299, 311, *313*, 313, 338, 344, 347.
3rd Platoon: 111, 137, 169, 217, 252, 312, 344, 347.
76th Company: vi, 169, 198, 251-52, 299, 345, *347*, *361*.
95th Company: 67, 87, 96, 102, 105, 112-13, 136, 149, 170, 197-201, *199*, 216, 242-43, 249-50, 281, 283-84, 294, *295*, 344, 347-48.
2nd Battalion: v, 45, 47, 63, *63*, 66, 85, *86*, 97, *101*, 148, 150-51, 175, 187, 196, 218, 223, 338, 345, 349, 374-75, 386.
78th Company: 45, 47, 87, 98-99, 102, 120, 176, 178-79, 304, *305*, 349, 374-75.
1st Platoon: 98, 102, 176, 374.
2nd Platoon: 102, 120, 176, 304, 305.
3rd Platoon: 102.
4th Platoon: 102.
79th Company: v, 47, 66, 85-86, 97, 99-100, 102, 119-20, 175-77, 180-81, *181*, 185, 224, 231, 298, 303, 338, 386.
2nd Platoon: 47, 86, 100, 120, 175-77, 179, 224, 231, 298, 303, 338, 386.
3rd Platoon: 85, 97, 101, 175.
4th Platoon: *181*, 181-82.
80th Company: *63*, 64, 67, *86*, 97, 162, 217, *220*, 221, 330-31, 337, 385.

INDEX

96th Company: iv, 98-100, *152*, 175, 179, 218, *222*, 223, 386, *387*.
4th Platoon: 98, 386, *386*.
3rd Battalion: ii, 50, 66, 83, 87, 96, 106-07, *107*, 110, 135, 185, 195, 214, 229, 231, 248, 271, 275, 314, 320, 343 367, 371, 374-75.
82nd Company: ii, 229, 231, 233, 242-43, 249, 271-74, *272*, 303, 324.
2nd Platoon: 231-32, 271 *272*.
83rd Company: iv, 66, 106, 109, 187, 274-75, *275*, 284, 303, 324, 344, 348, 355, 356, 372, 375, 383.
3rd Platoon: 187-88, 274.
84th Company: v, 83, 87, 106-07, 189, 214, 229, 254, 273, 343, 350, 367, 372, 374.
97th Company: vi, 46, 50, 88, 96, 106-09, 135-36, 185, 189, 195, 224-25, 229, 331-32, 345, 372.
1st Platoon: 106, 109, 189, 196.
1st Squad: 196.
2nd Squad: 196.
3rd Squad: 196.
4th Squad: 196.
6th Machine Gun Battalion: iv, 51, 63, 75, 88-89, 118, *119*, 120, *121-22*, 124, 137, 141, 150, *152*, 153, 164, 167-68, 189, 224, 247, 270, 292, *293*, 302, 310, 343, 355.
Headquarters Company: 302.

15th Company: 120-21, *121-22*, 124, 164, 168, 199, 247, 270, 345, 355.
5th Section: 270.
23rd Company: 75, 120, 310.
77th Company: 63, 75, 89, 118-20, *119*, 124, 137, 151-53, *152*, 189, 224, 302.
81st Company: 51, 63, 88, 118, 120, 124, 150-53, 168, 199, 229, 242-43, 246.
2nd Replacement Battalion: 379, 381.
137th Company: 378.
3rd Brigade: v, 95, *95*, 157, 191, 203, 214, 228, 309, 315, 329-30, 367.
9th Infantry: 53-54, *54*, 61, 72, 75-76, 84, 89, *92*, 91-93, 98, 100, 180-82, 203, 212, 214, 283, 291, 293, 296, 308, 329, 367, 369-71.
Regimental Machine Gun Company: 212.
1st Battalion: 92, 100, 182, 291, 293, 296, 308.
D Company: 182.
2nd Battalion: 367, 369.
3rd Battalion: 72, 75, 180.
K Company: 180.
L Company: 180.
M Company: 72, 75, 180.
23rd Infantry: 62, *78*, 78-79, 93-95, 127, 145-46, 156-57, *147*, 165, 194, 212, 261-62, 294-95, 314, 316, 343, 349, 386.
2nd Battalion: 194, 261.
F Company: 260.
3rd Battalion: 62, 78-79, 127, 145, 156.
I Company: 156.

408

INDEX

M Company: 62, 79, 93-94, 127, 145, 261.
4th Machine Gun Battalion: 157, 293.
5th Machine Gun Battalion: 54-55, 62, 67, 83, 138-39, 146, 157, 194, 202-03, 214, 291, 293, 295, 315, 329, 335.
A Company: 54-55, 62, 67, 83, 139, 146, 157, 194, 203, 214, 291, 293, 295, 315, 329, 335.
B Company: 83, 202.
C Company: 203
D Company: 203
2nd Engineers: 67, 110-11, *111*, 141, 146-48, 168, 175, 179, 199, 224-25, 230, 256, 284, 338, 385-86.
1st Battalion: 110, *111*, 146.
B Company: 146
1st Platoon: 146.
C Company: 146
1st Platoon: 146.
2nd Platoon: 146.
3rd Platoon: 146.
4th Platoon: 146.
D Company: 148, 223, 254-55, 385-86.
2nd Battalion: 111, 147-48, 168, 175, 179, 224, 230, 256, 284, 338, 385-86.
E Company: 148, 175, 178, 230-31, 284, 338, 386.
F Company: 148, 168, 175, 199-200, 386.
2nd Field Artillery Brigade: 190-91, 235, 281, 329, 333-34.
12th Field Artillery Regiment: 191, 228, 236-38, *237*, 282, 293-94, 330, 339, 384.
1st Battalion: *236-37*, 237-38, 282.
Battery A: 238.
Battery B: 237-38, *238*, 282.
2nd Battalion: 191, 294, 384.
Battery D: 191, 294, 384.
15th Field Artillery Regiment: 139, 191, 212, 215, 228, 236, 281-83, 296, *296*, 309, 329-31, 334, 370, *370*.
1st Battalion: 139, 211, 214, 235, 280, *295*, 308, 333, 369.
Battery C: 235.
2nd Battalion: 235, 281, *369-70*.
Battery D: 236, 282.
Battery E: 236, 282.
Battery F: 236, 282, *370-71*.
17th Field Artillery Regiment: 191, 228, 235-36, 238, *238*, 282, 293-94, 330, 355.
1st Battalion: 235, 238, *238*, 282.
Battery B: *238*, 238, 282.
2nd Battalion: 294.
Battery C: 294.
3rd Battalion: 293.
2nd Military Police Company: 138.
1st Field Signal Battalion: 157, 314.
Company C: 314.
15th Ambulance Company: 162.

INDEX

3rd Division: 42, 57, 209, 281, 291.
7th Mobile Machine Gun Battalion: 57-58, 209.
30th Infantry: 53, 281, 291-92, 296.
1st Corps School: 54, 374.
33rd Infantry *canal zone*: 27.
French Army: 42, 75, 123, 207, 209, 392.
5th Army: 42.
6th Army: 40-41, 47-48, 56-57, 61, 68-69, 72, 76, 79.
10th Army: 41.
7th Corps: 69.
21st Corps: 79, 84, 91, 202, 308, 348-50, 362, 367, 387, 391-92.
22nd Division: 39.
43rd Division: 110, 145, 202, 209, 213, 216, 228, 234, 244, 329.
152nd Infantry Regiment also see *'Les Diables Rouges' (Red Devils)*: 152, 197, 201, 249, 253.
214th Infantry Regiment: 152.
356th Infantry Regiment: 152, *152*, 175, 206.
1st Battalion: 175.
5th Battalion: 206.
164th Division: 93, 202.
37th Artillery Regiment: 149, 330.
232nd Artillery Regiment: 149.
333rd Artillery Regiment: 330.
167th Division: 316, 343, 348, 355, 362, 367, 381.
116th Infantry: 362, 384.

409th Infantry: 362.
192nd Division: 93.
2nd Hussars: 93.
4th Hussars: 93.
Escadrille [squadron] 252: 344.
German Army: 1, 35, 37, 123, 206, 264, 287, 298, 392.
1st Army: 57, 207.
6th Army: 37.
7th Army: 39, 41, *56*, 56-57, 206-07, 209, 286-87, 392.
18th Army: 206-08, 286.
4th Reserve Corps (Von Conta): 40-41, *56*, 56-57, 206-09, 264, 285-87, 291, 298, 391-92.
231st Division: 57, 209.
17th Foot Artillery: 57.
501st Field Artillery: 57.
10th German Division: 194, 286-87, 291, 310, 369.
6th Grenadier Regiment: 287.
47th German Infantry: 282, 286.
2nd Battalion: 286.
3rd Battalion: 282.
9th Company: 282.
398th German Infantry: 150, 194, 206, 286-87, 291.
2nd Battalion: 150, 206.
3rd Battalion: 150, 291.
9th Company: 150.
10th Company: 150.
11th Company: 150.
12th Company: 150.
197th Division: 40, 206, 214, 264, 286, 291, 300, 368.
210th Infantry Brigade: 291.

INDEX

415th Trench Mortar Company: 265.
7th Saxon Jäger Regiment: 40, 368.
26th Jäger Battalion: 264, 266, 300, 368.
1st Company: 368.
273rd Infantry Regiment: 264-65, 300.
1st Battalion: 264.
2nd Battalion: 264.
28th Ersatz Infantry: 263-64, 300.
237th Division: 206, 214, 230, 282, 286, 291.
460th Infantry Regiment: 275, 303.
3rd Battalion: 275, 303.
9th Company: 275, 303.
461st Infantry Regiment: 206, 249, 286, 291, 346.
462nd Infantry Regiment: 206.
British Expeditionary Forces: 35, 158.
1st Army: 37.
2nd Army: 37.
3rd Army: 36.
5th Army: 36.
8th Division: 40.
62nd British Division: 158.
150mm Cannon *German*: 230, 317, 333-34, 337, 369.
155mm Cannon *French also see Schneider*: 108, 190-91, 235, 238, 281-82, 294, 330, 355.
75mm Cannon *French*: 98, 107, 159, 167, 191, 202, *238*, 281-82, 294, 329.
77mm Cannon *German*: 251, 295, 355.

8mm Lebel: 58, 275, 351, 355.
Acy-en-Multien, France: 138.
Adams, James P. 2nd Lt.: 102.
Aisne River: 38.
Akers, Herbert H. Sgt.Maj.: 234.
Allen, Thaddeus S. Pvt.: 99, *99*, 102, 170, 178, 180.
Anderson, Arvid P. Pvt.: *361*, 361.
Anderson, Frank W. Cpl.: 62, 79, 93-94, 127, 145.
Annamites *Annamese*: 65.
Ashurst, William W. 2nd Lt.: 130, 324.
Ashwood, Forest J. "Buck" GySgt.: 250, 283-84.
Bailey, Benjamin Maj.:
Bailey, Leo J. Pvt.: 72, 75.
Ball, Albert M. Pvt.: 112.
Ball, Clarence "Seaweed" 1st Lt.: 381, *382*.
Banister, Ira H. Pvt.: 333-34.
Barnett, George Maj.Gen.: 21.
Bass, William A. Pvt.: 169.
Baston, Albert P.: 14.
Bathlémont, France: 54.
Beaty, Shelton B. Pvt.: 168, 200.
Beaugrenier-Diepp-Paris road: 51, 63.
Beauvais: 45, 47-48.
Becker, Fred H. 2nd Lt.: 64, 74, 130, 262-63, 323-24.

INDEX

Belcher, Bert Pvt.: 336, *346*, 346-47.
Belleau village of: 391.
Belleau Wood: i, ii, iii, 11, 61, 64, 152, 188, 206, 209, 214, 217, 222, 230, 253, 286, 291, 313, 332, 336, 344, 346, 367, 376, 392.
Belleau-Torcy road: 197, 339.
Bender, Daniel W. 2nd Lt.: 373.
Berg, Albert H. Pvt.: 219.
Berry, Benjamin S. Maj.: 51, 74, 132, 308, 349-50.
Bezu-le-Guery: 148, 374.
Bixler, Harvey Pvt.: 247.
Blake, Robert W. 1st Lt.: 298, 383, 401.
Blanchfield, John Capt.: 65, 162-63, 165-66, 227, 261, 265, 269, 318, 360.
Bleasdale, Victor F. 2nd Lt.: *122*, 121-23, 247.
Bois Barons: 265, 267-68.
Bois de Belleau See Belleau Wood: i, 198, 202, 299.
Bois de Champillon: 112-13, 136, 149-50, 169-70, 197, 249, 251-53, 273, 283, 291, 299, 311, 313, 343-44, 347, 349, 383.
Bois de Clerembauts: 100-02, 113, 118-20, 124, 148, 152, *152*, 175, 179, 182, 196, *223*, 222, 224, 332, 349, 386,
Bois de la Morette: 92-93, 292, 370.
Bois de Triangle: 152, 386.

Bois de Veuilly *also see Veuilly Woods*: 145, 162, 166, 262-64, 268, 270, 286, 294, 298, 311, 316, 318, 321-22, 330, 333-34, 343, 359-62, 372-73, 381-84.
Bois des Fonds Jars Ferme: 293.
Bois des Mares: 301, 310.
Bois du Loup: 309.
Bois Triangulairs: 264.
Bonneil, France: 92.
Bonner, Paul Pvt.: 318-19.
Bonney, Homer W. Cpl.: 267.
Bonilla, Manuel: 28.
Boone, Isaac N. Pvt.: 325.
Bourbelin: 370.
Bouresches: 4, 101, 120, 124, 150-51, 168, 175, 189, 206, 209, 282, 291, 304-05, 336, 349, 386, 391-92.
Boury, France: 62.
Bouton, Arthur E. Maj.: 93, 367.
Bowley, Albert J. Col.: 330.
Boyd, Thomas A. Pvt.: 46.
Boyle, William H. Pvt.: 169.
Bradley, Fred Pvt.: 255.
Brailsford, Thomas R.: 30.
Brancalasso, Foster Trmptr.: 189.
Brannen, Carl A.: 30.
Bregy, France: 212.
Brennan, Albert F. Pvt.: 299-300.
Briese, Hasso A. Sgt.: 315.
Britton, Paul W. Sgt.: 358.
Brock, Joseph M. Pvt.: 161-62.

INDEX

Brotherton, Walter Pvt.: 373.
Brown, Charles F. Pvt.: *190*, 190.
Brown, Preston Col.: 48-49, 91, 95, 127, 148, 292, 308, 362.
Brown, Stephen Sgt.: 53.
Brown, Thomas W.: 17.
Bruce, Andrew D. Capt.: 54-55, 138-39, 146, 157, 293, 316, 335.
Budde, George W. Pvt.: 299.
Buford, David L. GySgt.: *357*, 356-59, 368.
Bullard, Robert L. Lt.Gen.: 206.
Bundy, Omar Maj.Gen.: *48*, 47-48, 68, 91, 95, 110, 129, 141, 209, 228, 291, 308, 369, 392.
Burnes, John F. Capt.: 299, 336.
Burr, Carleton 2nd Lt.: 344-45.
Bussiares, France: 122-23, 163-66, 170, 199, 202, 206, 213, 227, 233, 242, 247, 264-65, 270, 282, 291, 294, 300-01, 310, 325, 343, 355, 362, 367, 391.
Cabell, Edward E. Pvt.: 360-61.
Caley, Percy B. Pvt.: 347.
Camp Baker: 20, 26.
Canal Zone *Panama*: 27, 29.
Canfield, John: 13.
Canfield, Roger I.: 13.
Cantigny: 45, 50, 54.
Capsack, Michael D. Pvt.: 315.
Case, Gerald F.: 17.
Carey, Charles H. Pvt.: *248*, 248.
Carleton College *Northfield, Minnesota*: 19-20, 179.
Carpenter, Stanley D. Pvt.: 373-74.
Carter, Daniel B. Pvt.: 161.
Cates, Clifton B. 2nd Lt.: 98, 100, 386, *387*.
Catlin, Albertus Col.: 49-50, *50*, 80, 85, 96, 98-99, 107, 109, 113, 145, 147-48, 153, 168, 185-87, 195, 197, 202, 224, 227, 229, 248, 267, 268, 272-73, 282, 303, 310, 347-48, 351, 355, 371, 401.
Cauldwell, Oscar R. Capt.: 199, 294, *295*.
Chamberlaine, William BGen.: 228, 236, 329-30.
Chamigny, France: 215, 236.
Champillon: 120-23, 136, 162-66, 168, 170, 199, 216, 229, 231, 233, 242, 244, 247-48, 265, 268, 270, 291, 302-03, 324-25, 343, 355, 362, 367, 372, 385.
Champillon-Bussiares road: 122, 164-66, 170, 199, 223, 244, 247, 265, 325, 343, 367.
Charly-sur-Marne, France: 281.
Chars, France: 62

INDEX

Chateau Thierry: 48, 56-58, 79, 84, 207, 209, 282, 292, 334, 369, 374-75, 391-92.
Chaton, France: 191.
Chauchat: 8-9, 167, 231, 275, 298, 338.
Chaumont, France: 57.
Chaumont-en-Vexin: 45, 47, 49, 57, 61, 67, 79, 109.
Chemin des Dames: 38-40, 45, 47, 56, 68, 208.
Chisholm, Edward N. Capt.: 148, 256.
Christmas, Lee: 28.
Clark, Eugene O. Pvt.: 66.
Clemenceau, Georges PM.: 41.
Clifford, Arthur Sgt.: 75.
Clignon brook: 265, 348-50, 362, 384, 391.
Clignon heights: 213.
Cocherel, France: 95, 228, 236.
Cochran, Harry K. Pvt.: 232, 272.
Coffenberg, Bailey M. Capt.: *63*, 64, 218, 338.
Cogne, Erving H. Pvt.: 195.
Cole, Edward B. Maj.: 51, 120, 124, 153, 167-68, 185, 292.
Collins, Harry F. Pvt.: 231-32, 249, 303, 356.
Collins, John W. Pvt.: 188.
Colorado School of Mines: 29.
Compans-la-Ville, France: 157.
Conde-en-Brie, France: 58.

Conner, Robert E. 1st Sgt.: 382.
Cooke, Elliott D. 1st Lt.: iv, 27-29, 52, 64-65, 73, 76-77, 86, 96, 127-31, 135, 160-62, 262, 285, 295, 300, 308, 316-17, 321-24, 351, 379, 384-85.
Corbin, William O. Capt.: 244.
Cordes, Onnie J. Pvt.: 73, 94, 145, 298.
Coulombs, France: 146, *147*, 156-57, 194, 202-03, 212, 214, 261, 314.
Coupru, France: 84, 89, 91-92, 127, 214, 282, 292-93, 295, 315-16, 335.
Courcelles, France: 52.
Courchamps-Licy-Clignon road: 165.
Crane, Walter A. Pvt.: 373.
Craonne, France: 38.
Crogis, France: 309, 367, 369.
Croka, William B. 1st Lt.: 190, *190*.
Cuba: 53.
Curtis, Thomas J. Capt.: 141.
Daly, Daniel 1st Sgt.: 345, 351, *352*.
Darche, Harris A. Chaplain: 45-46, *46*.
Dartmouth: 52.
Davin, Jerry M. Pvt.: 73.
Davis, Cleo Sgt.: 373-74.
Davis, Joseph R. Lt. Col.: 283, 296, 329, 330, 334-35.

INDEX

Debacker, Albert Pvt.: 231.
DeCarre, Alphonse Capt.: 337.
Deckro, Floyd H. Pvt.: 246.
Degenhardt, John O. Pvt.: 161.
Degoutte, Jean M.J. Gen.: 95-96, 132, 141, 348, 362, 392.
Derby, Richard Lt. Col.: 48-49, *49*, 148.
DeRoode, Louis R. Capt.: 118-19.
Desourdie, Adrien Pvt.: 261.
Diaz, Porfirio: 29.
Dickman, Joseph T. BGen.: 57.
Dingle, William Pvt.: 175.
Diphenylchlorarsine: 251-52.
Divine, Louis S. Cpl.: 255.
Dockx, Francis J. Cpl.: *356*, 356-58.
Dodson Jr., George W. Pvt.: 253-54, *254*.
Domptin, France: 214, 228, 293, 296, 329-30, 370.
Donnelly, Ed B. Pvt.: 243.
Duchêne, Denis A. Gen.: 47, 68-69.
Dunbeck, Charley Capt.: 160, 300, 311, *312*, 318.
Duncan, Walter W. Cpl.: 222.
Dunn, Harold H. Sgt.: 178.
Dunton, Orley M. Pvt.: 175, 179.
Durr, Paul W. Pvt.: 372.

Eddy, Henry Leslie 2nd Lt.: 102, 304-05, *305*, 375.
Eddy, William A. 2nd Lt.: 230, 332, 336, 339.
Eiffel Tower: 67.
Elliott, Charles B. Maj.: 127, 145, 156.
Eloup, France: 209.
Epaux, France: 282.
Epernay, France: 207.
Esckilsen, Lawrence W. Cpl.: 232.
Evans, Frank E. Maj.: 49-50, 105, 317, 371, 375.
Fechet, D'Alary Capt.: 203.
Feland, Logan Lt. Col.: 228-29, 311.
Feriend, Lester L. Pvt.: 373.
Ferme de Beaurepaire: 329.
Ferris, William C. Cpl.: 136,
Field Hospital number 1: 148, 374.
Fischer, Robert M.: 16-17, 19.
Fisher, Roland H. Pvt.: 165, 242-43, 271.
Flanagan, Joseph M. Pvt.: 188.
Flanders, *French Flanders*: 41, 207.
Foch, Ferdinand J.M. Marshal: 37-38, *41*, 41-42.
Fokker, *German Plane*: 308.
Forêt de Retz: 206, 208.
Fox, Milo P. Maj.: 110, *110*.

INDEX

Fraser, Chester H. 2nd Lt.: 130, 262.
Frazier, Walter D. 2nd Lt.: *363*, 363-64.
Frederickson, Michael Cpl.: 200.
French Colonial troops also see *Senegalese troops*: 268, 360-61.
French, Wayne Pvt.: 270, 285.
Freund, Warren Cpl.: 196.
Fuller, Edward C. Capt.: 312-13.
Fullington, William W. Pvt.: 118, 302, 396.
Galliford, Walter T.H. 1st Lt.: 382.
Gallivan, James Gun.: *263*, 263.
Gandelu, France: 76-77, 145, *147*, 209.
Gandy, Tony L. Pvt.: 253-54, *254*.
Généralissime *Foch, Ferdinand*: 37.
Gentry, Mart Cpl.: *169*, 169, 200.
Geores, Carl H. Pvt.: 53.
Georg, Ernst B. Col.: 291.
Germans *See specific units*
Germigny, France: 261.
Gisors, France: 51.
Gleeson, Joseph J. Sgt.: 191, 294, 384.
Glick, Frank L. 1st Sgt.: *220*, 220.
Goldfield Consolidated Mining Co.: 28.

Gondrecourt, France *1st Army Corps School*: 374-75.
Gordon, George V. 2nd Lt.: 51, 66, 132, 308.
Gordon, Paul W. Pvt.: 232.
Green Jr., James O. Capt.: 62, 79, 94.
Grice, Benjamin Pvt.: 180.
Group, Arthur K. Cpl.: 182.
Gulberg, Martin "Gus" Pvt.: 45, 87, 97, 104, 112, 136-37, 253, 254, 299, 313.
Gustafson, George A. Pvt.: 355.
Hackney, Charles B. Cpl.: 180.
Hagan, Joseph A. 1st Lt.: 244, *245*.
Haig, Douglas F.M.: 37.
Hall, David W. Pvt.: 189.
Hamilton, George W. Capt.: 363-64, 379, 383.
Harbord, James G. BGen.: 45, 72, 83-85, 89, 91, 95-97, 109-11, 124, 147, 154, 168, 185-87, 197, 202, 230, 248, 272, 282, 308-09, 330, 338-39, 344, 362-63, 367.
Hardin Jr., John R. 2nd Lt.: 375.
Harris, Homer G. Pvt.: 180.
Harvard: 27, 39, 72, 237.
Harvis, John Patrick Capt.: 302-03.
Hatcher, James E. Pvt.: 83, 87-88, 106-07, 189, 214, 229, 254-55, 273, 343, 350.
Hautvesnes, France: 294.

INDEX

Hayden, William T. Pvt.: 245.
Hayes, James H. Lt. Col.: 48.
Hebner, William J. Cpl.: 231.
Heinz, Edward L. Pvt.: 169.
Heizer, Robert S.: 26.
Hemrick, Levi Pvt.: 64, 97, 102, *219*, 218-20, 223.
Hensley, Willard E. Cpl.: 196.
Herzog, Albert E. Cpl.: 374.
Hess, Elmer 1st Lt.: 139, 212, 215.
Hill 126: 206.
Hill 142: 120-21, 124, 158, 162-63, 165, 170, 186, 197-99, 216-17, 227-29, 232, 242, 249, 272, 274-75, *276*, 291, 303, 324-25, 343, 348, 350, 355, 362, 371-72, 383-84, 392.
Hill 165: 164, 234, 264-66, 291, 300, 317.
Hill 182: 224.
Hill 201: 180, 287.
Hill 204: 282, 309, 334, 344, 368, 370.
Hill, Fred W. Cpl.: 234.
Hill, Glen Cpl.: v, 86, 99-100, 175-77, 179-80, 224, 373, 386.
Hill, Sidney Cpl.: v, 86, 170, 176.
Hirschfield, Leo M.: 16.
Hodges, James S. Pvt.: 246.

Hoersch, Victor A. 1st Lt.: *368*, 368-70.
Holcomb, Thomas Maj.: 85-86, 97-98, 100, 102-03, 148, 177, 185, *187*, 187, 195-96, 218-22, 223, 331, 338, 349, 387.
Holliday, Charles P. Capt.: 337.
Holt, Jefferson L.: 199, *200*.
Honduras: 28.
Hopke, George W. GySgt.: 305, 375.
Horton, Carl H. GySgt.: 270-71.
Hotchkiss, M1914 8mm Lebel Machine Gun: 58, 63, 118, 124, *152*, 152-53, 165, 168, 189, 199, 213, 247, 253, 302, 313, 323, 343.
Hotel de Ville in Montreuil-aux-Lions: 139, 148.
Hoyle, Warren F. Pvt.: *254*, 253-54.
Hubbard, Samuel T. Capt.: 39.
Hubert, John "Chick" Pvt.: 25-26, 146.
Hughes, John A. Maj.: 344-45, 347, 349-50.
Hughes, John A. Pvt.: 236.
Hunt, Leon W. Pvt.: 169.
Hurlburt, Melvin H. Pfc.: 168.
Indo-Chinese: 66.
Ingram, Charles A. Sgt. Maj.: 220.
Issonge Farm: 111, 147, 185, 309.

INDEX

Jackson, Gilder D. 1st Lt.: 76, 130.
Jackson, Warren R. Cpl.: 67, 87, 96, 103, 105, 112-13, 136, 149-50, 170, 197-98, 200-01, 216, 250-51, 281, 283-84, 294, 343-44, 347.
Jackson, William B. Cpl.: 89, 119.
Jacob, Frank M. Pvt.: 74.
Jenkins, John O. Cpl.: 231.
Johanningmeier, Ollie H. Cpl.: 223.
Johnson, Louis W. Cpl.: 233.
Jones, Miller Pvt.: 255.
Joy, Charles L. Cpl.: 19, 178-79, *179*.
Judd, Roy A. Pvt.: 234.
Kahl, William F. Cpl.: 46.
Kahrs, Edward G. Pvt.: 255.
Kapfer, Charles J. Cpl.: 336, 346-47.
Kean, Robert W. 1st Lt.: 236, 281-83, 296, 309, 329, 370.
Kellum, James B. Pvt.: 364.
Kelly, Thomas J. Sgt.: 186-87.
Kennedy, Edward A. 1st Lt.: 50.
King, Joseph E. Pvt.: 305.
Kingman, Matthew H. Capt.: 120-21, *121*, 123-24, 168, 199.
Kipness, David 2nd Lt.: 270, 336-38.

Knepp, Clarence C. Sgt.: 358.
Kolinsky, Victor Pvt.: 180-81.
Kraus, George F. Cpl.: 345-47, *347*.
Kraus, Carl R. Pvt.: 345-47.
Krause, Max GySgt.: 222, *222*.
La Croisette: 367-69.
La Genetre Farm: 283.
La Loge Farm: 228, 237, 294, 309, 329-30, 338, 344, 367.
La Longue Farm: 292.
La Nouette Farm: 92, 369.
La Voie du Chatel: 107-09, 120-21, 135-36, 185, 187, 189, 195, 197, 209, 212, 227, 229, 231-34, *232*, 238, 254, 267, 272-74, 287, 303, 314, 317, 343, 350-51, 367, 375, 384-86.
Ladd, Oron L. Cpl.: 296.
Ladd, Shaler 1st Lt.: 124, 150, 246.
Lancaster, Chester F. Pvt.: 87.
Landers, Keneston P. Pvt.: 232.
Langres, France: 344.
Larget Farm: 203.
Larsen, Henry Capt.: 51.
Lay, Harry Maj.: 72.
La Cense Farm: 102, 119-20, 153, 187, 195-96, 218, *220*, *221*, *222*, 222, 224, 331-32, 338, 349-50, 386.
Le Thiolet, France: 92, 98, 100, 110, 118, 146, 189,

INDEX

190, 224, 292, 330, 349, 367-68, 385.
Lee, William E.: 13.
Legasse, Martin *French Interpreter*: 72, *84*.
Legendre, James H. 2nd Lt.: *52*, 52, 64-65, 320.
Leonard, Wallace 1st Lt.: 175-76, 338.
Les Aulnois Bontemps: 93, 180, 212.
Les Glandons: 194.
Les Mares Farm: 158-60, 162-64, 166, *167*, 197, 209, 227, 264-70, 273, 285-86, 294-95, 300-01, 310, *311*, 317-18, *320*, 325, 336-37, 356, 358-61, 368.
Lewis, Edward M. BGen.: 95, 330.
Lewis, Harry T. Maj.: 54-55.
Lewis, Joyce S.: 18-19.
Lewis, William: 18-19.
Linn, Louis C. Pvt.: 137-38, 140.
Linnell, Howard T.: 16.
Liptac, Leo L. Sgt.: 218.
Lizy-sur-Ourcq, France: 95, 128, 236.
Locke, Karl W. Cpl.: *246*, 246.
Loconville, France: 61.
Lomax, Fred E. Pvt.: 220-22.
Long, Lothar R. 1st Lt.: iv, 124, 292, *293*.
Loughborough, Robert H.R. 2nd Lt.: 165
Lovejoy, Dana C. GySgt.: 271.

Lowen, Jesse Capt.: 386.
Lucy-Bouresches Road: 124.
Lucy-le-Bocage: 98-99, 101-03, *104*, 105, 109-13, *112*, *113*, 120-21, 124, 136-37, 148, 151, 153, 168-69, 197-99, *199*, 209, 214, 217, 228-30, 249, 251, 284-85, 291, 299, 303, 310, 331-32, 336, 338-39, 344-45, 349-51, 375-76, 386.
Ludendorff, Erich F.W. Gen.: 35-38, 40-41, 206-09.
Lufkin, Nathaniel H.: 16.
Lyle, Lucius Q.C.L. 2nd Lt.: 164, 166, *167*, 301.
M1911 also see *Colt .45 caliber*: 177, 357.
MacNider, Hanford 1st Lt.: 91-92.
Madden, Simon J. Cpl.: 230.
Maggoine, Charles Pvt.: 156.
Magonistas: 29.
Magoon, John Sgt.: 261.
Maison Blanche *also Ferme Blanche* : 351, 372.
Malone, Paul B. Col.: *78*, 78, 93, 95, 127, 145, 156, 194, 294, 316, 343.
Mansfield, Gabe Pvt.: 247, *248*.
Mare Island, California: *15*, 16, 19, 178,
Marigny-en-Orxois: 108, 129, 137, 140, 158-62, *160*, 165, *167*, 167, 202, 209, 215-16, 227, 229, 233-35, *235*, 255, 264, 268-69, 291,

INDEX

298, 308, 317, 320-21, *334*, 334, 337-38, 349, 362-63, 367, 372-73, 379, 381, 384-86.
Marne River: 40-42, 56-58, 128, 206-09, 215, 236, 281-83, 297, 391.
Marshall, Ralph W. 1st Lt.: 50, 275, 284.
Martin, Augburn D. Pvt.: 265.
Martin, Oscar E. Pvt.: 166, 265-66, 361.
Matheny, Frank S. Cpl.: 55, 73, 95.
Mathews, William R. 1st Lt.: v, 158-60, 162-63, 165-66, 244, 345, 355, 358-59, 368-69.
Mattfeldt, Clyburn O. Maj.: 91.
Mattingly, Barak: 24-25.
Maxim Machine Gun: 9, 301, 346.
May-en-Multien, France: 69, 72-73, 76-77, 79, 83, 88, 93-95, 118, 157.
Maynard, Charles B. 1st Lt.: v, 367, 374, *375*.
McCarthy, William J. Pvt.: 190.
McClelland, Frank Cpl.: 304, 349.
McCloskey, Manus Col.: 282, 330, 339.
McCoy, James Capt.: 337.
McEvoy, Thomas T. 1st Lt.: 109, 135, 196.
McIntosh, Roderick J. 1st Lt.: 281-82.

McKeown, John W. Pvt.: 64.
McLaughlin, Joseph C. Pvt.: 373.
McNulty, John 1st Sgt.: 119-20, *119*, *152*.
Meaux, France: 47-49, 61, 65, 68-69, 72-76, 78-79, 89, 132, 139, 157.
Medal of Honor: 345, 348.
Meehan, Romulus J. Pfc: 315.
Mendenhall, John R. Capt.: 57.
Mertil, Joseph Cook: 261.
Messersmith, Robert E. Capt.: 45, 47, 87, 98-99, 101-02, 176, 179, 304-05.
Mexican Border Campaign: 14, 53.
Meyer, Hugo A. Trmptr: 218, 223, 338.
Michael, Frank J. Pfc.: 385.
Miller, Hugh S.: 24.
Mincey, George A. Cpl.: 357, *358*.
Minenwerfers *or* Trench Mortars: 265, 314.
Monro, William L. 2nd Lt.: 237.
Montgrivault-la-Petit Farm: 124, 141, 247, 292.
Montreuil-aux-Lions: 79, *80*, 84-85, 87-89, 95-97, 102, 105, 110, 118, 127-29, 132, 138-39, 141, 145-48, 156-57, 185, 190-91, 202, 212, 215, 228, 235-37, 293, 308, *330*, 330, 343, 367-68, 375.

INDEX

Mooney, Charles J Pvt.: 267.
Moore Jr., Lucius L. 2nd Lt.: 190.
Morgan, Daniel E. Cpl.: 75, 89, 118-19.
Morgan, Peter GySgt.: *201*, 201.
Mortorff, Earl Pvt.: 231.
Mount de Bonneil: 281, 296.
Murray, Charles I. 1st Lt.: *181*, 181-82.
Murray, Joseph D. Capt.: 74, 229, 268.
Nagel, Clarence Pvt.: 109.
Napoleon: 38.
Naval Academy *U.S.*: 118, *295*.
Nelligan, Willard C. Pvt.: *249*, 249-51.
Nelson, Havelock D. Cpl.: 46, 50, 88, 96, 106-09, 185, 189, 196, 223-24, 331-33.
Neufchâteau, France: 68.
Neuilly, France: 52.
Neusse, Miles Cpl.: 230-31.
Neville, Wendell Col.: *132*, 132, 156-59, 194, 202, 216, 227, 229, 262, 308, 320-21, 367.
Nicaragua: 25, 29.
Noble, Alfred H. 1st Lt.: 106, 107, 275, 324.
Norwich University: 229.
Noyon-Montdidier: 45, 53.
oberste heeresleitung *German General Headquarters:* 206.
Olivet College: 19.
Olson, Oscar E. Cpl.: 168-69.

Omnibus tripods *For the M1914 Hotchkiss 8mm Lebel Machine Gun*: 63-190.
Operation Blücher: 38, 56-57, 206, 286, 392.
Operation Georgette: 36-38.
Operation Michael: 36-37.
Oppy Woods: 158.
Ormoy-Villiers: 157.
Osborne, Weedon E. Lt.J.G.: 86.
Ourcq River: 72.
Paradis Don V. Sgt.: 23-24, 61, 64, 67, 85-86, 98, 218-22, 332, 349-50, 375-76.
Paris Farm *Ferme Paris*: 98-110, 103, 107, 110-11, 118, 120, 138, 237-38, 282, 294, 384.
Paris Island, South Carolina: 23-25, 30, 112, 252, 356.
Paris, France: 27, 37-38, 40, 45, 51, 53, 61, 63, 66-68, 72, 91, 105, 135, 138, 196, 273, 287, 375.
Paris-Metz highway: 84, 91-93, 98-100, 103, 105, 108, 110-11, 118, 120, 124, 127, 129, 138-39, 146, 175, 180, 182, 189-91, 202-03, 214, 218, 220, 237, 281-82, 293-94, 309, 330, 334, 344, 350-51, 368-70, 375, 391.
Parker, Charles A. Cpl.: 182.
Parsons, James H. Sgt.: 358-59, 368-69.

INDEX

Pearce, Robert R. Pvt.: 246.
Peoples, John D. Cpl.: 189.
Pershing, John Gen.: 35, 37, 39, 42, 57.
Petain, Philippe Gen.: 42, 57.
Philadelphia Naval Yard: 13-14.
Philippine Insurrection: 53.
Pigott, Raymond Pvt.: 200.
Pike, Lloyd E. Cpl.: iv, 47, 97, 99, 177, 179, 231, 298, 303-04, 338, 386.
Pinson Jr., John F. Cpl.: 255.
Plan Hagen: 207.
Platt, Jonas H. 1st Lt.: 379-83.
Pol, France: 158.
Pontoise, France: 66.
Porcupine, Ontario: 29.
Powers, Thomas J. Pfc.: 385.
Powis, Albert Pvt.: 62, 94.
Puerto Cortes, Honduras: 28.
Pugh, Jack J. Pvt.: 46-47.
Pyramide Farm: 129-30, 132, 147, 149, 157-59, *167*, 194-95, 270.
Quantico, Virginia: 252, 332, 345, 381.
Raffington, Charles S.: 199.
Raleigh, Cecil 2nd Lt.: 102.
Randolph, John A. Father: 200.
Ranney, Glenn B. Pvt.: 373.

Redford, David A. 2nd Lt.: 96, 103, 137, 344-45.
Reisner, Edmund L.: 30.
Rendinell, Joseph Cpl.: 275-76, 284, 314.
Rheims, France: 38, 40-42, 206-07.
Richardson, Bert A.: 15.
Richardson, Morris C. GySgt.: 88.
Ringer, Stanley A.: 13-14.
Robinson, Fielding S. 1st Lt.: 21, *84*, 339,
Rockey, Keller E. Capt.: 94.
Rockwell, Mearl C. Pvt.: 332, 336, 339.
Roosevelt, Ethel: *49*.
Roosevelt, Kermit Capt.: *49*.
Roosevelt, Quentin 2nd Lt.:*49*.
Roosevelt, Theodore: 28, *49*, 49.
Rosenow, Theodore C. Pvt.: 343.
Roska, Victor Joseph Pvt.: 267.
Ross, Richard S. GySgt.: 325.
Sampson, Ralph O. Pvt.: 222.
Sanchez, Joachin Pvt.: 255.
Santo Domingo, Dominican Republic *Occupation 1916*: 52, 132.
Sanders, Joseph: 225.
Scanlon, William T. Cpl.: v, 106, 109, 135, 189, 195-96.

INDEX

Scarbrough, James R. Pvt.: iv, 25, 66, 109, 188, 274-75, 348, 356.
Schall, James S. Pvt.: 363.
Schiani, Alfred Pvt.: 21, 66, 77-78, 301.
Schneider, John G. 1st Lt.: *221*, 220-21.
Scott, Marvin GySgt.: 333-34.
Sellers, James M. 2nd Lt.: 98, 102.
Senegalese troops: 268, 360.
Sens, John Pvt.: 177,
Serans, France: 50.
Shearer, Maurice E. Maj.: 103, *104*, 106, 113, 136, *137*, 166-67, 169, 186, 196-201, 216-17, 227-29, 231, 233, 249, 273, 320, 338, 343-44.
Shepherd, Lemuel C. 1st Lt.: *20*, 20-21, 53, 94, 129, 131, 162-64, 166, 227, *265*, 265-67, 273, 359-61.
Sherman, Stephen G.: 14-15.
Shrader, Edgar P. Pvt.: 347.
Sibley, Berton W. Maj.: 87-88, 105, 107-08, 121, 135, 195, 229, 234, 273-75, 284, 348, 371-72.
Silverthorn, Merwin: 14-15.
Siegert, Holden E. Pvt.: 253-54, *254*.
Smith, Archelaus Cpl.: 220.

Smith, Asa J. Pvt.: 105, 136-37, 168, 299, 347.
Smith, Dwight F. Capt.: 231-33, 243, 271-75, 303, 324.
Smith, Holland M. Maj.: *84*.
Smith, Lucius H. Pvt.: 324-25.
Smith, Mark A. 1st Lt.: 88
Snow, Frank H. Pvt.: *188*, 188.
Snow, William A. Maj.: 110.
Soissons, France: 38, 40-42, 48, 68, 206-08.
Somme region: 65.
Spanish American War: 53.
Spencer, Arthur G. 1st Lt. 146.
Spotsylvania battle: 53.
Springfield M1903 rifle: 8, 9, 100, 137, 151, 176, 178, 262, 271, 374.
St. John's College *Annapolis, Maryland*: 106, *107*.
Stair, Willett A. Pvt.: 332, 336, 339.
Steinmetz, Edward J. Pvt.: 348.
Stearns, Stanley: 15.
Stine, George C. Sgt.: 181-82.
Stites, Joseph G. Cpl.: 223.
Stockham, Fred Sgt.: 25.
Stowell, George A. Capt.: 198-99, 251.
Strumtruppen: 36.

423

INDEX

Stubbs, Wesley J. Pvt.: 180.
Sulzbach, Herbert Lt.: 36.
Summerlin, Wilbur Sgt.: 283-84.
Sumner, Allen M. Capt.: 51, 168, 199, 246.
Sundberg, Harry M. Pvt.: 200.
Swanson, Clarence V.: 15.
Swensen, Sigurd M.: 15.
Tafournay Farm: 92, 369.
Taggart, David A. Pvt.: 232, 272.
Tannenberg *1914 Battle*: 56.
Taylor, Paul S. 2nd Lt.: 374-75.
Tegucigalpa, Honduras: 28.
Tesoro, John J.: iv, 30.
Texas A&M University: 30, 223, 371.
Texas National Naval Volunteers: 30.
Thayer, Sid GySgt.: 298.
Thomas, Gerald C. Sgt.: 68, 87, 96-97, 103, 105, 111-12, 169, 217, 253, *313*, 312-14, 344-47, 350.
Thompson, John P.S. Pvt.: *223*, 223.
Tijuana, Mexico *The battle of*: 29.
Tibbetts Jr., Frederick E. 1st Lt.: 238.
Tilghman, Arthur 2nd Lt.: 164, 325.
Timmer, Peter Cpl.: 113.
Timmerman Jr., Louis F. 2nd Lt.: 375.

Torcy, France: 166, 197, 201-02, 206, 228, 249, 265, 274, 332, 336, 339, 347, 362, 383, 391.
Triangle Farm: 98-99, 101-02, *103*, 119-20, 124, 148, *152*, *153*, 175-76, 178, 180-81, 185, 187, 209, 225, 231, 256, 303-04, 310, 331-33, 338, 345, 349, 370, 375.
Trilport, France: 68.
Tupa, Frank J.: 15.
Turney, Harold I. Pvt.: 386, 405.
Turrill, Julius S. Maj.: 94, 145, 156, 194, 270, 298-99, 320, 355, 362-63, 367, 371-72, 383.
United Fruit Company: 28.
University of Boston: 261.
University of Denver: 89.
University of Illinois: 109, 158.
University of Iowa: 64.
University of Kansas: 26.
University of Michigan: 26.
University of Minnesota: 14-17, *15*, *16*, 19.
University of Tennessee: 98.
Upton, Emory Gen.: 53.
Upton, LaRoy S. Col.: 53-54, 61, 75-76, 91, 93.
USS Maine: 348.
Vanek, Charles J. Pvt.: 176.
Vaudancourt, France: 51.
Vaux: 209, 282, 368, 370.

INDEX

Ventelet, France: 127, 129, 145-46, 203, 330.
Vera Cruz, Mexico *battle 1914*: 52, 132, 345, 348.
Verdun *1916 Battle*: 56.
Verdun sector: 45.
Vesle, River: 40, 208.
Veuilly la Poterie: 291, 300, 311, 362.
Veuilly Woods: 165.
Villers-Cotterêts: 206.
Vincy-Manœuvre, France: 148.
Virginia Military Institute: 20-21, 120, 294.
Voeth, Robert William Capt.: 50, *108*, 107-08, 189, 195, 345.
Von Boehn, Max Gen.: 39, 206-07.
Von Conta, Richard Heinrich Karl Gen.: 41, *56*, 56-57, 206-09, 285-87, 291, 298, 391-92.
Von der Schulenburg, Count Col.: 207.
Von Blücherwho, FM.: 38.
Von Diepenbroick-Grüter, Otto Gen. Lt.: 286, 291.
Von Hindenburg, Paul Field Marshall: 35.
Von Hülsen, Bernhard Lt.Gen.: 209.
Von Hutier, Oskar Gen.: 206.
Von Jacobi, Albano Lt.Gen.: 206, 291.
Von Mudra, Bruno Gen.: 206.
Von Thaer, Albrecht Col.: 38.

Von Unruh, Walter Maj. Gen.: 206, 208-09.
Waddill, Edmund C. Maj.: *156*, 156.
Wahl, Einar A. Pvt.: 212-13, 227, 233, 274-75.
Wahl, George Douglas Capt.: 237-38, 282.
Wallace, Carleton: 14.
Wass, Lester S. Capt.: 52, 130, 160-62, 165, 262, 301, 311, 316, 322, 345, 385.
Waters, Jerome J. Capt.: *371*, 371.
Watson, Edwin M. Maj.: *237*, 237.
Watson, Marvin Pvt.: 195.
Weisbaker, Alfred E. Pvt.: 364.
Wertz, James C. GySgt.: 188.
West Point (United States Military Academy): 53, 57, 79, 92, 110, *111*, 203, 237.
West, John Albert 2nd Lt.: 85-86, 97, 101.
Weston, Albert Pvt.: 180-81.
Westover, William 1st Lt.: 54-55, 62, 68, 83, 138-39, 146, 157, 194, 202-03, 214, 291, 293, 295, 315-16, 329, 335.
Wheeler, Frederic C. 1st Lt.: 150, 200, 251, 294, *295*.
Whitehead, Frank Capt.: 162, 234, 268-70, 285, *302*, 302, 310-11, 317-18, 337.
Whiting, Deshler Maj. 194.

INDEX

Whiting, Thomas S. 1st Lt.: 218, 222.
Whitley, Franklin L. Maj.: 92, 100, 291-92, 308.
Wiedemann, Fritz Capt.: 39.
Wilhelm, Friedrich Kaiser: 56-57, 209, 402.
Williams, Floyd G. Cpl.: 247.
Williams, George E. Pvt.: 364.
Williams, Lloyd W. Capt.: 162, 165-66, 216, 227, 229, 231, 242-44, 271, 325.
Williams, Marshall B.: 15.
Williams, Richard N. 1st Lt.: 27, 72, 84.
Wilmer, Pere Capt.: 220-21.
Winans, Roswell Capt.: 383.
Winter, Edwin H.: 17, 19.
Wise, Ethel: 52.
Wise, Frederic M. Lt. Col.: 128-30, 149, 157-60, 162, 165-68, 186, 197-01, 206, 212, 216, 227-31, 233, 234-35, 242-44, 248-50, 262-64, 268-69, 272-74, 295, 298, 300-01, 311, 316-22, 333-34, 343, 355, 358, 362, 367, 372, 383-85.
Wisted, David G. Pvt.: 232, 271-72.
Wodarezyk, Mike Sgt.: 359-61.
Wood, Peter P. Sgt.: 51, 63, 88-89, 120, 124, 150, 168, 242-43, 246-47, *247*.

Wood, Thurston E. 1st Lt.: *237*, 237.
Ypres: 36.
Zaico, Paoset Pvt.: 156.
Zane, Edmund L. Maj.: 157, 293.
Zane, Randolph T. Capt.: 66, 100, 338, 386.
Zebrowski, Frank Pvt.: 180.
Zippay, Michael Pvt.: 232, 271.

Made in the USA
Middletown, DE
01 December 2020